T0140345

Linking Sensitive Data

Peter Christen • Thilina Ranbaduge • Rainer Schnell

Linking Sensitive Data

Methods and Techniques for Practical
Privacy-Preserving Information Sharing

 Springer

Peter Christen
Research School of Computer Science
The Australian National University
Canberra, ACT, Australia

Thilina Ranbaduge
Research School of Computer Science
The Australian National University
Canberra, ACT, Australia

Rainer Schnell
Institut für Soziologie
Universität Duisburg-Essen
Duisburg, Germany

ISBN 978-3-030-59708-5   ISBN 978-3-030-59706-1 (eBook)
https://doi.org/10.1007/978-3-030-59706-1

This Springer imprint is published by the registered company Springer Nature Switzerland AG
The registered company address is: Gewerbestrasse 11, 6330 Cham, Switzerland

To Gail, with all my love.
P. C.

To my loving family.
T. R.

To Katrin, my perfect match.
R. S.

Foreword

By now, the potential that data science has for benefitting society must be obvious to everyone. As more and more large data sets describing people and their behaviour accumulate, so the opportunities for improving public policy, for enhancing the efficiency of service industries, for increasing the efficiency of healthcare systems, and for a host of other ways of bettering the human condition are becoming apparent. Many of these possibilities arise as a consequence of linking data sets. Research programs in many countries have been established with the specific aim of combining data from disparate sources to enable opportunities that none of the data sets alone could do.

But all advanced technologies must be handled with care. And this is as true for data science, and in particular for data-linkage technology, as it is for nuclear or bio-technology. To achieve the gains which can be made by linking data sets, we need more than the physical and mathematical advances enabling us to do it. We must also have buy-in from those described by the data. We must handle their data with discretion, preserve their privacy when they want us to, treat their confidential data as sacrosanct, and only disclose what they want us to disclose. And, indeed, more than all this, we must often manage to do it in the face of malicious actors, keen to break into the databases to identify individuals and their characteristics.

Clearly this is a very challenging problem, so I am delighted that the authors of this book, leading experts in the domain of linking sensitive data, have provided us with the answers.

In an extraordinarily comprehensive discussion of linkage technology the book runs over regulatory frameworks, technical details, and practical application. It describes how matching methods work and how to evaluate their performance — something which is in my view under-rated and yet critically important. It covers all the major concepts and methods, including such things as Bloom filters and differential privacy, and also lesser known ideas likely to become more important in the future. But it is not simply an abstract technical manual — it also discusses practical matters such as computational efficiency, which are critical if the methods are to be used in practice. And it does all this in a highly accessible way, telling a fascinating story, ranging from the women who sorted through piles of London Underground tickets in the 1930s linking journeys so they could understand travel patterns, to modern cutting-edge technology involving possibly billions of data points.

This timely book will become a key text for a wide variety of data scientists, whether they are concerned with enhancing the human condition in the public domain, or with launching the latest start-up using data from a variety of sources.

London, UK   *David J Hand*
                                                                        Imperial College, London

Preface

Sensitive personal data are created in many application domains, and there is now an increasing demand to share, integrate, and link such data within and across organisations in the public and private sectors. The ultimate aim of such linkage is to enable detailed data analysis that is not possible on individual data sets. The strong emphasis given to pseudo anonymisation (pseudonymisation) in recent privacy legislation, such as the Health Insurance Portability and Accountability Act (HIPAA) in the US and the EU's General Data Protection Regulation (GDPR), calls for novel solutions to allow secure sharing of sensitive information. Furthermore, the difficulty of obtaining individual consent for population covering databases requires the use of privacy-preserving record linkage methods.

Most scientists would consider as the aim of their profession the increase of knowledge by systematically testing theories to explain observed data. Since research also involves generating ideas, the amount of data needed for research cannot, in all cases, be minimised. Therefore, it makes sense to exempt scientific research from general data protection principles such as data minimisation. For example, the GDPR excludes scientific research and official statistics from many general data protection principles. This book is written from the perspective that linking data is a useful tool for scientific research. As other tools, linkage techniques can be used for malicious purposes as well. Therefore, a societal agreement for the use of such techniques is required. The techniques described in this book are designed to minimise the potential misuse of linking data.

A key message of this book is that any database that contains sensitive information about individuals in plaintext can be vulnerable to data breaches and attacks by adversaries, both external and internal to an organisation, as well as unintentional revealing or publication due to human or technical mishaps. Encoding personal sensitive information using the techniques and methods we discuss in this book can significantly reduce the risks of sensitive data being breached or revealed. This is because significant efforts would be required by an adversary to reidentify individuals in an encoded database.

This book covers modern technical answers to the legal requirements of pseudonymisation as recommended by privacy legislation. We describe advanced techniques and concepts for linking sensitive databases using privacy-preserving methods. Using such techniques there is no need to exchange or share private or confidential data that could be used to identify individuals. The book covers topics such as modern regulatory frameworks for sharing and linking sensitive information, concepts and algorithms for privacy-preserving record linkage and their computational aspects, practical considerations such as dealing with dirty and missing data, as well as privacy, risk, and performance assessment measures. Existing techniques for privacy-preserving record linkage are evaluated empirically and real-world application examples that scale to population sizes are described. The book also includes pointers to freely available software tools, benchmark data sets, and tools to generate synthetic data that can be used to test and evaluate linkage techniques.

Intended Audience

The intended audiences of this book include applied scientists, researchers, and practitioners in governments, industry, and universities who are concerned with developing, implementing, and deploying systems and tools to share sensitive information in administrative, commercial, or medical databases. Examples include researchers in public health, road injury research, demography, criminology, history, education, and urban planning, as well as IT managers in hospitals and in government agencies, lawyers in official statistics, data custodians in administration, and public health researchers.

Furthermore, we believe this book to be of high value to graduates from computer science and related fields coming out of university who are starting to work in an organisation that is tasked with linking sensitive data. The non-technical parts of the book will also be of value to decision makers in organisations that are linking sensitive databases as these corresponding chapters will provide high level descriptions of the main concepts of how modern computer based methods can be used to link sensitive data while at the same time the privacy of the individuals whose records are stored in these databases is being protected.

Organisation

This book consists of fourteen chapters grouped into four parts, and two appendices. The first part introduces the reader to the topic of linking sensitive data, the second part covers methods and techniques to link such data, the third part discusses aspects of practical importance, and the fourth part provides an outlook of future challenges and open (research) problems relevant to linking sensitive databases.

The first part consists of three chapters, where the first introduces the topic and motivates why linking databases is an important topic to consider in today's data driven society, and why linking sensitive data can lead to benefits in a variety of application areas as illustrated by several case studies. The second chapter then covers current regulatory frameworks and how they make novel techniques that allow anonymous linking of sensitive data necessary. This chapter also touches on statistical disclosure control (SDC) and how linking sensitive data relates to SDC. We end the first part of the book with Chapter 3 which covers the general aspects of how data can and have been linked, how data quality affects the linking of data, how to evaluate various aspects of the linkage process, and the general challenges of linking databases. We end this chapter with an introduction and formal definition of privacy-preserving record linkage.

We begin the second part of the book with Chapter 4 where we discuss the different conceptual protocols of how sensitive data can be shared and linked between organisations, as well as different models of privacy assumed in these protocols. This is followed by Chapter 5 where we discuss how risk, privacy, and utility can be measured and assessed, and how encoded sensitive data can be attacked by adversaries. We also provide an overview of the related important topic of statistical disclosure control methods. In Chapter 6 we then describe the various building blocks required to link sensitive data, ranging from encoding and encryption techniques to methods that allow names and addresses to be compared, as well as approaches to securely calculate functions across two or more parties. Based on these building blocks, in Chapter 7 we then cover the different techniques that have been proposed over the past two decades to allow the privacy-preserving linkage of sensitive data. In Chapter 8 we describe in detail Bloom filter encoding, the currently most widely used approach to linking sensitive data in a privacy-preserving way, and we discuss advantages and problems with this technique. Chapter 9 continues to cover Bloom filter encoding by describing several recently proposed cryptanalysis attack methods that have been developed with the aim to reidentify sensitive values encoded in Bloom filters, and hardening techniques that aim to overcome these attacks. We conclude the second part of the book with Chapter 10 discussing computational aspects that are becoming increasingly important as the databases to be linked are becoming ever larger. We describe blocking and indexing techniques, approaches that make use of modern parallel and distributed computing platforms, and how to link multiple (more than two) or even many (dozens to thousands) of sensitive databases.

The third part of the book in Chapter 11 discusses various practical aspects of linking sensitive databases, including how to deal with low quality data or incomplete or even missing data, and how to link heterogeneous, temporal, and dynamic data that are becoming more widespread in today's Big data applications, where data are collected in an ongoing basis and therefore often need to be processed, linked, and analysed in (near) real time. We also discuss practical implementation aspects, how to set and tune parameters for the algorithms and techniques described in the third part of the book, and what computational requirements to consider for practical use of these techniques. In Chapter 12 we then present a comparative evaluation of selected privacy-preserving record linkage techniques on example data sets, and how these techniques perform with regard to linkage quality, scalability, and the privacy protection they provide. Chapter 13 concludes the third part of the book with descriptions of selected real-world applications where sensitive databases are being linked in practice.

The fourth part of the book consists of Chapter 14 where we discuss future research challenges and directions, both practical problems as well as open conceptual challenges. We also describe new challenges posed by Big data applications, as well as the linking of other types of data such as biometric and genetic information about individuals, which opens up not only technical challenges but also new legal and ethical questions.

Finally, in Appendix A we provide pointers and describe currently existing software systems that allow the linkage of sensitive data. We limit ourselves to freely available, open-source software rather than commercial systems. In Appendix B we then provide further details about the evaluation presented in Chapter 12 to allow the interested reader install the software used for this evaluation and rerun the presented experiments.

We provide an extensive glossary, on page 397, covering many terms relevant to linking databases, sensitive data, and privacy aspects related to record linkage. Further notations used in this book are described on page xxi.

A companion Web site at https://dmm.anu.edu.au/lsdbook2020 provides additional material, such as the Python programs we used for the empirical evaluation described in Chapter 12 and Appendix B, any errata of the book, as well as electronic versions of the table of contents, glossary, and references.

Keywords: Data linkage, record linkage, data matching, entity resolution, administrative data, personal data, microdata, privacy, privacy-preserving, anonymisation, pseudonymisation, encoding, encryption, hashing, Bloom filter, GDPR, HIPAA.

Acknowledgements

The idea of this book started when the three of us were participating at the *Data Linkage and Anonymisation* programme held in 2016 at the *Isaac Newton Institute* (INI) for Mathematical Sciences at the University of Cambridge, UK. We therefore like to thank the INI for their fantastic support during this programme, which was funded by EPSRC grant EP/K032208/1.

We also like to thank David J. Hand, OBE, Imperial College London, for writing an inspiring foreword highlighting the importance of the topics covered in our book. A special thanks goes to our editor Ralf Gerstner from Springer, who supported this book project right from the start, and the anonymous reviewer who provided valuable detailed feedback and helpful suggestions. We like to thank Christian Borgs, Anushka Vidanage, and Sirintra Vaiwsri for co-authoring parts of certain chapters, Abel Kho and Brad Malin for advise and providing pointers to US resources on linking sensitive data, and Frauke Kreuter for commenting on the first part of the book. A big "thank you" goes also to Asara Senaratne, Anushka Vidanage, Charini Nanayakkara, Nishadi Kirielle, Sirintra Vaiwsri, Yanling Chen, and Youzhe Heng, for providing valuable feedback and proof-reading drafts of this book. All remaining errors are of course ours.

Peter Christen likes to acknowledge the Simons Foundation which supported his stay in Cambridge in 2016. He also likes to acknowledge the *Administrative Data Research Centre Scotland* (ADRC-S) and the *Digitising Scotland* project which funded his stays in Edinburgh, as well as Tash Vest in Greenwich, and Divers Lodge Lembeh and Liberty Dive Resort, both in Indonesia, where parts of this book were written. Peter furthermore likes to acknowledge the funding he received from the Australian Research Council (ARC) for conducting research on how to link sensitive databases under the two Discovery Projects DP130101801 and DP160101934.

Thilina Ranbaduge is sincerely thankful for the funding provided by the Australian Research Council (ARC Discovery Project DP160101934) for his research, without which it would not have been possible. He also thanks the

Research School of Computer Science and the Australian National University for offering him an opportunity to conduct his research studies. The school and university are well supportive of early career researchers.

Rainer Schnell thanks the University of London, City, to kindly relieve him from some of the duties in London to spend several months at the Isaac Newton Institute in Cambridge in 2016. He was supported by the German Research Foundation (DFG) by six different research grants on record linkage since 2005 (DFG-Grants 5369360, 200001560, 161924790, 407023611, 258933986, 87664861). Without these fundings, the development of many techniques described in this book would have been impossible. As part of these grants, DFG funded the setup of the German Record Linkage Center for its first years.

Canberra,   *Peter Christen*
Canberra,   *Thilina Ranbaduge*
Lechtingen,   *Rainer Schnell*
10 August 2020

Contents

Part III Practical Aspects, Evaluation, and Applications 287

Notations

In the following we describe the style and mathematical notations used throughout this book. Additional notations will be introduced in specific chapters and sections as required. Furthermore, the glossary starting on page 397 describes many terms relevant to the topics covered in this book.

Throughout the book we show example textual values with single quotes, such as 'John Smith'; while we show example attribute (or field) names in small caps font, for example FIRSTNAME or POSTCODE.

With regard to mathematical symbols and equations, we denote simple variables such as numbers or text strings using lowercase italics font (such as a, b, c); lists, sets, and vectors using lowercase bold font (for example $\mathbf{a}$, $\mathbf{b}$, $\mathbf{c}$); while for matrices, lists, and sets of lists, vectors, or sets we use uppercase bold font (such as $\mathbf{A}$, $\mathbf{B}$, $\mathbf{C}$). Sets in the mathematical sense do not have an order, while lists and vectors (both one-dimensional) and matrices (two-dimensional) are ordered collections of elements. We denote sets with curly brackets, for example the set $\mathbf{s}$ of numbers from 1 to 9 (unordered) could be $\mathbf{s} = \{5, 9, 1, 3, 8, 2, 7, 6, 4\}$. Lists and vectors are shown with square brackets and their elements are indexed from 0 onwards. For example, the ordered list $\mathbf{l}$ of numbers from 100 to 106 is denoted by $\mathbf{l} = [100, 101, 102, 103, 104, 105, 106]$, where the first element in $\mathbf{l}$ is $\mathbf{l}[0] = 100$ and the fifth element is $\mathbf{l}[4] = 104$. Similarly, elements in a matrix are denoted by their row and column indices, both starting from 0. For example, $\mathbf{M}[1, 3]$ will be the element in the second row and fourth column in matrix $\mathbf{M}$.

We denote the number of elements in a set (its size) and the length of a text string (number of characters), list, or vector (number of elements) with two vertical bars: $l = |\mathbf{s}|$. For the example set $\mathbf{s}$ given above, this would give $l = 9$, while for the string $s = $ 'hello' its length $l = |s|$ is $l = 5$. We use $||$ to symbolise the concatenation of strings, for example 'hello' $||$ 'World' results in the concatenated string 'helloWorld'.

For operations on bit vectors, such as Bloom filters as described in Chapters 8 and 9, we use $\wedge$ for the bitwise AND, $\vee$ for the bitwise OR, and $\oplus$

for the bitwise XOR (exclusive OR) operations, where the outcomes of these operations are shown in the following three tables.

Bitwise AND

x	y	$x \wedge y$
0	0	0
0	1	0
1	0	0
1	1	1

Bitwise OR

x	y	$x \vee y$
0	0	0
0	1	1
1	0	1
1	1	1

Bitwise XOR

x	y	$x \oplus y$
0	0	0
0	1	1
1	0	1
1	1	0

For example, for the two bit vectors $\mathbf{b}_1 = [1, 0, 0, 1]$ and $\mathbf{b}_2 = [1, 1, 0, 0]$, we obtain $\mathbf{b}_1 \wedge \mathbf{b}_2 = [1, 0, 0, 0]$, $\mathbf{b}_1 \vee \mathbf{b}_2 = [1, 1, 0, 1]$, and $\mathbf{b}_1 \oplus \mathbf{b}_2 = [0, 1, 0, 1]$.

Part I
Introduction

This first part of the book introduces the topic of linking sensitive databases. In Chapter 1 we motivate the need for linking databases that contain sensitive personal or confidential information, discuss what kinds of data can be linked, provide examples of where linking sensitive data is required and/or can be beneficial, and describe current impediments that prevent the linkage of sensitive databases.

In Chapter 2 we then describe the non-technical requirements of linking sensitive data with regard to existing regulatory frameworks across the world, with a focus on relevant privacy frameworks such as the GDPR and HIPAA in the European Union, the UK and the US, but also discussing key aspects of how other countries deal with privacy issues around sensitive data.

In Chapter 3 we then provide a high level overview of the general concepts and techniques for information sharing, data integration, record linkage, the key steps involved in linking sensitive data, as well as data quality aspects and how to evaluate the linkage of data. We also introduce the ideas behind privacy-preserving record linkage which will build the basis for the chapters of the second part of the book.

Chapter 1
Introduction

Abstract In this chapter, we show that linking individual records from different databases is indispensable for many research purposes and data usage in practical applications. Almost all analyses of Big data sources require linking several databases containing information about the same or similar populations. We discuss examples of applications from medicine, economics, and official statistics. Since the GDPR and other legal restrictions usually require pseudonymisation, the use of error tolerant pseudonymisation methods becomes necessary. Based on the increasing number of research published in diverse areas we show that the need for the techniques presented in this book is becoming more important.

1.1 The Increase in Linking Data

The digital transformation of health, administrative, and commercial processes has led to vast amounts of data being collected. These data can be used for research purposes, for example, in the medical and social sciences. In particular, the ability to combine multiple databases with traditional research data such as surveys has created new opportunities for data analysis. Methods for combining information from different databases about the same entities are called record linkage methods [109, 274]. Record linkage is an increasingly popular research technique in many academic and applied fields of study, as can be seen by the steady increase in the number of publications that can be found about this topic, as shown in Figure 1.1.

The rate of adoption is different between academic subjects. The main literature database in medicine (PubMed) since 2011 lists on average more than one publication per day on record linkage[1]. By comparison, record linkage has been used rarely in sociology, which is still widely based on surveys.

---

[1] See: https://www.ncbi.nlm.nih.gov/pubmed

© Springer Nature Switzerland AG 2020

P. Christen et al., *Linking Sensitive Data*, https://doi.org/10.1007/978-3-030-59706-1_1

Fig. 1.1 The number of publications per year with the queries *'record linkage'* (for all fields) and *'record linkage + sociology'* (for sociology only) retrieved from Google Scholar.

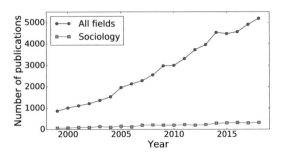

However, other academic fields in the social sciences show changes in the kind of data mostly used. For example, in economics, an increase in the use of administrative data compared to the use of survey data since the 1980s can be observed. In the four leading economic journals, the proportion of publications based on administrative data increased by an average of more than 30% between 1980 and 2010[2] [101].

These differences in adopting record linkage techniques between the academic subjects might be because different types of data are available in surveys and in databases. Administrative data about persons contain information on facts and observables; while survey data contain mostly self-reported data, including subjective states of mind such as attitudes or traits. As characterised by Hand (with emphasised text according to Hand) [258]:

> In a real sense, administrative data often tell us what people *are* and what they *do*, not what they *say* they are and what they *claim* to do.

Many research questions in economics don't need this kind of information. However, increasingly surveys now use linked administrative data to reduce response errors or respondent burden. For example, in social surveys, the request for record linkage is sometimes framed by mentioning that linking would allow for using information already known, thereby shortening the interview.

In general, using administrative data to substitute a respondent's answers in surveys might be useful for difficult questions such as the year of when the house where the respondent lives was built [427]. Furthermore, sensitive questions such as about details on social security benefits, might be substituted by administrative data. However, the proportion of studies based on record linkage will most likely remain different between fields of study.

---

[2] The journals are: American Economic Review, Econometrica, Journal of Political Economy, and Quarterly Journal of Economics.

1.2 Why Should Data be Linked at All?

The main reason for linking databases is that different attributes about the same entity may be stored in different databases, potentially held by different organisations. In medical research, the obvious example is treatment data in one or more hospital databases and the outcome (date of death) in a mortality database. By linking these separate pieces of information, the benefits or potential harm of treatment can be evaluated with objective facts. In medical research, literally 'data save lives' (which has been the motto of several initiatives to promote the linkage of medical data sets).

In fields other than medicine, the advantages of linking data are often more of a methodological nature. Many databases, such as censuses, birth records, or social security files, may contain data on a complete population, and therefore studies using such data seldom lack statistical power. Furthermore, subgroups rare in a population can be found in these data sets.

In addition, traditional data collection methods based on surveys and censuses increasingly fail to obtain an interview from a designated respondent. In survey methodology, this rise of non-response has been observed in all modern societies during the last decades, but most clearly in the US [259, 413]. A small proportion of the increase is due to higher levels of mobility and less time spent at home. However, the larger share of non-response is due to the refusal of respondents [86]. Most likely, this is the consequence of the ever-rising number of surveys, an increase in mistrust of government and science, fear of crime, and in some cases of disguising political campaigning as social research. Using other data, especially administrative data instead or in conjunction with surveys, is widely regarded as one of the few options to reduce bias from non-response during the design of a study.

Finally, many administrative databases are official records, indicating real-world events such as births, deaths, diagnoses, imprisonments, unemployment spells, examination results, and so on. By contrast, most research data sets in the social sciences contain self-reported information, such as reports of behaviour, intentions, or attitudes. Such accounts are prone to memory errors, misreporting, or non-response for specific questions (item non-response). Therefore, survey methodology uses linked data to identify, control, and eliminate the statistical effects of such errors. Examples are given in Section 1.6.5. Similar arguments can be made for other sources of data.

Experimental Data:	Survey Data:	Administrative Data:
• Examples: Clinical studies, psychological experiments • Data collection to test a specific hypothesis • Mostly small samples • Simple data structures • Systematic data collection • Known population	• Examples: National household panel surveys • Data collection for scientific purposes • Usually more than one research topic • May yield large data sets • Might require complex data structures • Systematic data collection • Known population	• Examples: Pension insurance, driving license register, unemployment insurance • Data collection not for scientific purposes • Usually huge data sets • Might require complex data structures • Mostly uncontrolled data collection • Often considerable data editing effort required • Known population

Sensor Data:	Social Media Data:	Transactional Data:
• Examples: GPS data, sports watches, road sensors • Data collection not for scientific purposes • Often commercially owned • Usually huge data sets • Usually only very few variables • Usually no covariates^a • Usually unknown population	• Examples: Twitter, Facebook, Instagram • Data collection not for scientific purposes • Mostly commercially owned • Usually huge data sets • Usually requires complex coding • Usually only very few variables • Usually no covariates^a • Usually unknown population	• Examples: call records, billings, shopping baskets • Data collection not for scientific purposes • Often commercially owned • Usually very large data sets • Might require complex data structures • Usually no covariates^a • Usually unknown population

Fig. 1.2 Traditional (top row) and Big data (bottom row) data sources, adopted from [539]. ^{a} Covariates are variables (attributes) used for the explanation (or prediction) of other variables.

1.3 Sources of Data and their Linkage

In the social sciences and related fields, most traditional research is based either on experimental or survey data. However, digitisation made a variety of different sources of data available for research, as shown in Figure 1.2[3].

Many of the new forms of data could be subsumed under the buzzword Big data. Especially administrative data could be considered as Big data relevant to the medical and social sciences [135]. In general, it is hardly clear what Big data are and how these data could be used for research [300]. A closer look at the data sources in Figure 1.2 reveals that different kinds of Big data need to be distinguished, since they differ in size, type of measurements, and population coverage.

---

[3] The top row of this figure is based on a figure from [135]. The figure is adopted from [539].

However, some common characteristics of the new kinds of data are apparent. Already in 1999, Angrist and Krueger [22] distinguished such data sources from the traditional data sources by the fact that these data were not collected for research or scientific purposes.

These non-traditional data sources have one common disadvantage: Although they may have many records, they often contain only a few attributes. Therefore, information from multiple separate data sets often has to be integrated, linked, or shared in some way to allow meaningful data analysis.

Most medical and social scientists prefer to use data sets containing information on individual units of study, most often information on persons. Such data are denoted as microdata. Record linkage is used to identify information on the same entity in different databases and merge this information into microdata that contain information on the same entity from multiple databases. Record linkage is, therefore, a core technology for Big data analytics in the social and medical sciences.

Technically ideal is linking with a universally available unique national identification number (NID), also known as an entity identifier [109]. Such NIDs are available in Europe, for example for Denmark, Finland, Norway, and Sweden[4]. If such NIDs are available, linking databases is technically trivial: either the NID is used directly for linking, or encoding with a secret key (a hash) is used as an identifier, as we discuss in Chapters 6 and 7. Records with the same NID value across two or more databases are assumed to refer to the same individual.

However, in many applications NIDs are not available or their usage is forbidden by law or due to privacy or confidentiality concerns [619]. Under these circumstances, indirect identifiers, such as names or dates of birth, have to be used for linking.

1.4 Direct and Indirect Identifiers

Databases may contain information that may be specific to individuals. Such information is usually referred to as Personally Identifiable Information (PII). If a database contains an attribute, which has a unique value for each entity of a population that directly establishes the identity of the entity, then this attribute is a unique identifier. Examples are national identification numbers, social security numbers, driver's licenses, or patient identifiers. In databases that cover large populations, certain names, dates of birth, and addresses are generally not unique by themselves. For example, it is likely that several individuals have the common surname 'Smith' (in English speaking countries) or 'Meier' (in German speaking countries) in such large databases. However, when joining such quasi-identifiers with other information, the combination

---

[4] For a comprehensive review of NIDs, see: https://en.wikipedia.org/wiki/National_identification_number

Table 1.1 Proportion of false links (false matches) by available quasi-identifying attribute combination using a data set of 78,881,936 records based on the US Social Security Death Master file, as reported by Hillestad et al. [276].

Quasi-identifying attribute combination	False match rate
Surname	0.980
Surname and date of birth	0.286
Surname, date of birth, and first name	0.009
Surname, date of birth, and zipcode	< 0.001
Surname, first name, and year of birth	0.294
Surname, first name, and zipcode	0.028
Surname, first name, year of birth, and zipcode	< 0.001
Surname and year of birth	0.833
Surname, year of birth, and zipcode	0.075

may allow identification. Such quasi-identifiers are therefore indirect identifiers[5].

The effect of combining indirect identifiers on the probability of correct identification can be demonstrated with data taken from Hillestad et al. [276]. As can be seen in Table 1.1, just a few indirect identifiers combined may be sufficient to uniquely identify a specific person in a database containing 78,881,936 records (in this case, deaths registered in the US Social Security Death Master File).

In principle, all attributes in a database could be considered as indirect identifiers. For example, if the construction date of a house at the address of a mother at birth, the postcode, and the birthday of the mother are available in two different databases, then the combination of these attributes can be used for linking (for an example, see the Swedish Metropolitan project in Section 1.6.4.2). However, most databases do contain only a few common attributes for linking, and these are the indirect quasi-identifiers used for most administrative purposes. These common attributes generally include names, gender, dates of birth, places of birth, and addresses. Therefore, indirect identifiers are mostly understood as such attributes and widely used for the identification of entities.

Most indirect identifiers are not stable over time, and they can be recorded with errors. For example, Winkler [643] reported that 25% of true matches in a US census operation would have been missed by exact matching (where two values or two strings, such as two dates of birth or two names, need to the be same character by character). The UK survey 'Understanding society' tried to link children to their school records (National Pupil Database). With exact matching on names, date of birth, gender, and postcode, only about 63% of the children could be matched [294].

---

[5] The terminology in the field is ambiguous. For example, names and phone numbers have been denoted as direct identifiers by Garfinkel [224].

Record linkage tries to link databases containing error-prone indirect quasi-identifying identifiers [109, 274]. This generally requires error-tolerant comparison functions, also known as approximate matching functions, which we describe in detail in Section 6.8. Since such indirect identifiers may reveal the identity of a person, these identifiers have to be protected against unauthorised access. This might be desirable in general, but for sensitive data, the protection against identification might be required by law or be a necessary condition for research.

1.5 What are Sensitive Data?

The existence of personal information in databases is unavoidable in modern societies. Laws regulate access to this information. Unauthorised access to personal information for its misuse is usually named a data breach, as we discuss in Section 5.3. Technical measures to minimise the likelihood of data breaches are the subject of computer security studies [567]. Even in the absence of misuse of information, the fact that personal information is known publicly, or at least known to other people, might make a subject feeling embarrassed, humiliated, or exposed. Therefore, what exactly is considered as sensitive data highly depends on cultural norms and the legal history of a local jurisdiction. To give an example, for the most part, web browsing history seems not to be covered by privacy regulations in the US [452].

Following the classification of sensitive topics of survey questions by Tourangeau and Yan [597], it might be useful to distinguish three different types of sensitive data:

- Information might be considered as out of bounds for the government or anyone else to know. The knowledge of information can be seen as an invasion of privacy, regardless of the content of the information. Examples given include religion or income [597]. Subjects may think that no one should know this.
- Information might increase the likelihood of negative consequences for the subject. For example, a previous conviction might – if known – imply the loss of a job.
- Information might reveal socially undesirable traits. Examples might be sexual preferences or extreme political opinions.

Most discussions of the concept of sensitive data remain vague [452]. A minimum definition would cover data whose unauthorised access would violate law or regulations. Given the classification described above, we consider a more extensive meaning of sensitive data as more appropriate:

Sensitive data are data whose unauthorised access would make the subject of the data feel uncomfortable or could imply negative consequences for the subject.

1.6 Example Case Studies

To illustrate the wide range of applications of record linkage on data which might be considered as sensitive, we now present several case studies of the use of linking in different fields. These case studies should make it clear why privacy-preserving record linkage techniques [619] (as described later in this book) are often necessary, although – currently – the linkage in many applications is done without employing such techniques.

1.6.1 Financial Fraud

An obvious field for the application of record linkage is financial fraud, which can take many different forms. A typical variant is identity theft [20, 473]. Here, the stolen identifiers of a victim are used to illegally obtain goods, services, or money. For the detection of this kind of fraud, credit risk companies are collecting information on consumers from many different sources. Other companies use this aggregated information for evaluating if they should do business with a specific customer, for example provide a loan to the customer. The number of requests on the credit history of a specific customer is also stored. If, for example, the number of these requests for a specific customer within a short period of time exceeds a certain threshold, this might indicate a case of identity fraud [640].

To build a central registry of credit histories, record linkage across many different data sources of financial transactions of customers is needed. Since many countries do not have unique personal identification numbers, the process has to use quasi-identifiers such as names and dates of birth. Therefore, the process is error-prone. Credit risk companies mostly use very conservative strategies in record linkage: They usually try to avoid at all costs to link records not belonging to the same person (false positive links, as we discuss in Section 3.4). However, the process is usually based on cleartext linkage. At least the employees of the credit risk companies know the identifiers of a very large subset of a population and (most likely) their financial details. Hence, the privacy of the population covered by a credit registry has been subject of fierce debates [302].

To solve a specific problem of this kind of fraud, Arp et al. [27] suggested a privacy-preserving strategy to share data between different merchants to detect customer fraud without revealing sensitive information about their customers. They suggested to map identifiers (for example, addresses, grouped product prices, and transaction details such as changes to baskets while ordering) into binary vectors (known as Bloom filters, a technique we describe in detail in Chapters 8 and 9) and compare only these binary vectors. The information about customers is thereby protected, and companies do not have to exchange information which might be used by other companies to their advantage (for example, making better offers to these customers).

1.6.2 Law Enforcement and Counter Terrorism

Given the vast amount of information available in passenger lists, car rentals, visa or passport applications, student permits, phone and Internet records, online orders, arrest records, and so on, it seems evident that law enforcement and intelligence agencies are using and linking data from multiple sources [377]. Examples of such governmental data sharing and mining programs are given in [209] and [431].

Linking records for counter terrorism offers further challenges in addition to those common to all record linkage projects. Gomatam and Larson [235] list four specific challenges:

1. the databases involved tend to be very large,
2. the number of true matches is expected to be extremely small,
3. standardisation methods for foreign names and addresses might not be available,
4. and finally, both false matches and false non-matches can be costly.

Furthermore, these are dynamic databases with records about existing entities being modified and records about new entities being added on a constant basis. Linking dynamic databases adds a layer of complexity [116, 137, 493]. Finally, as Larson [377] notes, it is reasonable to expect that terrorists (and other criminals) want to avoid detection and take steps to do so. In the absence of excellent ground truth data (examples of known true matching and non-matching record pairs, also known as training data or gold standard data), calibrating a record linkage procedure for counter terrorism will be difficult. The linkage might generate either too many false positives (suspecting many innocent people) or false negatives (missing true suspects).

For example, after 9/11, the State Criminal Police Offices in Germany linked data from universities, citizens' registration offices, and the Central Register of Foreigners and filtered all male persons aged 18 to 40 which are or have been students, are Muslims, and were born in Islamic countries. The resulting 31,988 records were linked with other data sets, for example, pilot licences or jobs requiring security clearances. In total, more than 200,000 records were checked. The operation resulted in not a single prosecution. All files were deleted in 2003. Afterwards, in 2006, the linkage operation was declared illegal by the highest court in Germany [93]. The court considered a preventive police dragnet to be compatible with personal rights only if there is a concrete danger, not as a prevention strategy.

The general problems of computational counter terrorism have been summarised by Jonas and Harper [309]: There seem to be very few patterns clearly indicating likely terrorist activity, and there is a lack of suitable training data sets. In many practical settings, this combination will generate too many false links to be useful. Finally, the public knowledge of the use of databases collected or compiled for research or administration will cause unintended consequences by the public, for example, a decline in response rate for surveys or consent rate for the use of medical data for research [377].

1.6.3 Health Service Research

Health Service Research (HSR) is a multidisciplinary field of inquiry that examines access to, and the use, costs, quality, delivery, organisation, financing, and outcomes of health care services [295]. For this purpose, linking of patient records between hospitals, insurance companies, and other database owners in the health care sector is a widely used research strategy. Far more frequently than in other fields of medicine, records of the entire population are linked in HSR.

The availability of population covering databases which needed to be linked has triggered the foundation of an organisation to foster communication between research centres specialised in health record linkage: the International Population Data Linkage Network (IPDLN)[6]. This network organises a biannual conference, and publishes the International Journal of Population Data Science (IJPDS)[7] which has linking population data as one of its focus areas. We give two examples for health service research using population covering databases.

1.6.3.1 Linking Data on Newborns

Different measurements on newborns (birth weight, survival of the first week, and so on) are internationally considered as important indicators for the quality of a health system [659]. Therefore, databases containing comparable information on medical details of newborns are of considerable interest for medical research (for an example, see [67]). In Europe, 18 countries are routinely linking birth and death certificates for newborns [150]. However, researchers are interested in more details than just survival. Therefore, in some countries medical data of all newborns are merged (and linked) across hospitals involved in handling newborns[8].

---

[6] See: https://www.ipdln.org

[7] See: https://ijpds.org

[8] Further examples are the publications of the European Peri-Stat project, see: https://www.europeristat.com

This implies that in some countries data from more than 1,000 hospitals have to be linked. If the linkage can use unique personal identifiers, the process is much easier than in countries without such identifiers. It is therefore not surprising to see that linkage studies on newborns are concentrated in the Nordic countries that have such unique personal identifiers. Almost half of the 516 studies published in the period from 2001 to 2011, as identified in a review [150], originated in these countries.

If no unique person identifiers are available, linkage has to rely on medical variables such as birthweight, estimated duration of pregnancy (gestation age), circumflex of the head, and event characteristics such as date and time of delivery and mode of delivery (caesarean or not). Furthermore, the names of the mothers are helpful for linkage, if they are available. In practice, they are often missing for more than 10% of records [550].

A medical data set on newborns might include hundreds of medical, social, and financial attributes in addition to names and addresses. This results in a data set that contains detailed and highly sensitive personal information about mothers and their babies. If linkage of this kind of data across many different institutions is necessary, stringent safeguards against misuse are required. For example, medical information needs to be separated from all other data [340], and names need to be encoded or encrypted using appropriate techniques [619]. This, however, is currently not the standard procedure in Europe [150].

1.6.3.2 National Health Insurance Data in Germany

On the 7th of November 2019, the German parliament passed the E-Health 2 law[9]. Among many other technical details, the law established a research institute which will link medical data of all 73 million people in Germany insured by compulsory health insurance provided by 109 different health insurance companies. Technically, linking should be simple, since every person should have a unique health insurance identifier (which was introduced in 2012). Based on experience with similar identifiers [249, 278], it is safe to assume that in practice, some persons will have more than one identifier value, and that the identifier will be missing for some emergencies, newborns and foreigners. Therefore, linkage using standard quasi-identifiers (encrypted or unencrypted) seems to be unavoidable for a subset of the population.

However, the law requires a pseudonymisation of all identifiers. The method to be used is not described in the law. Instead, the technical requirements of the actual encryption method will be specified by the German Federal Office for Information Security (BSI). The law was not particularly noted by the public, but comments in the newspapers were mostly negative. The leading cause of resentment was the fact that a person cannot object

---

[9] Parliament Protocol 19/124, see page 15374 in: http://dip21.bundestag.de/dip21/btp/19/19124.pdf

to having their data linked. Furthermore, during the public hearings, the
security of pseudonymisation, in general, was doubted [554].

1.6.4 Longitudinal Studies

Medical researchers, as well as social scientists, use longitudinal data to study
attribute changes of persons over time. If measurements of the same group
of individuals are taken at different points in time, these types of study are
named panel studies. A subset of panel studies are cohort studies, where a
cohort is defined as a group experiencing the same event, such as a marriage, birth, or diagnosis of a specific type or group of illnesses at the same
time [411]. Panel studies require that data of the same person is identified
in different databases and linked after identification. Therefore, panel studies
are examples of where record linkage is required.

The linking is usually done either by a stable identifier such as a national
identification number, or by using quasi-identifiers. What kind of identifier
is used depends on the design of the study. Notable is the difference between
a prospective and a retrospective panel. A prospective panel starts with a
sample and follows the members of the sample over time. A retrospective
panel begins with a sample and tries to find previous records of the sample
members in a larger population database. We will give two strikingly different
research applications of prospective panels.

1.6.4.1 Prospective Panel Studies based on Self-generated
Identification Codes

In prospective panel studies based on surveys, respondents are usually identified by name, gender, and date of birth. In rare cases, such as for twins,
additional identifiers may be needed. However, when the topic of the survey
is highly sensitive, identifiers which might be used to identify respondents
outside the research contexts, such as names and dates of birth, are not applicable. Examples are panel studies of students or school children who are
known drug users or showed criminal behaviour. In such settings, biometric identifiers, such as fingerprints or iris scans, would generate even more
concern by the research subjects.

In such settings, self-generated identification codes are widely used. The
most common variants of these codes are based on asking respondents for
personal attributes, which should be stable and highly salient, such as subsets
of date of birth, gender, initials of parents, name of pets, or previous schools,
and so on. Most of these codes use between three and nine code elements.

Although the time between data collections using these codes rarely exceeds one year, the match rates are generally disappointing: A recent review

reports exact match rates of 65.3% as an average of 25 such studies, where many applications use a one-off match rule, but the resulting average match rate can still be low (80.9%) [31]. Since the number of records is small in most studies using such codes, in general the actual matching is done manually or semi-manually. To improve the use of self-generated identification codes, Schnell et al. [544] suggested codes consisting of more attributes and the application of record linkage procedures based on the Levenshtein edit distance (which we discuss in Section 6.8) to deal with variations in codes.

Self-generated identification codes have been used in different research fields since the 1970s. For example, Leyland et al. [387] applied the capture-recapture technique to estimate the number of HIV positive street prostitutes in Glasgow, Scotland. Over a sample of 53 nights during seven months, in total 206 streetworking prostitutes were contacted. On each occasion she was seen working, the initials of her name and her date of birth were asked. This string was used as an identifier. 197 women were asked for saliva samples, 159 provided samples of which four were HIV positive. Based on the reoccurrence of the codes and a mathematical model of birth-death processes commonly used in biology [69], the total number of women active in twelve months was estimated at 1,150. The estimated number of HIV positive women among them was 29 [409].

1.6.4.2 Linking Different Registries over the Lifespan: The Swedish Metropolitan Project

In 1964, the Swedish Metropolitan project started to study the long-term effects of social stratification with special regards to education and deviance. The cohort was defined as all boys and girls born in 1953 and living in the Stockholm area on 1 November 1963, regardless of where they were born [576]. Starting with a school survey in 1966, a large number of different registries, ranging from school data to criminal records, were linked to the survey data during the next 20 years.

The resulting database contained (just for the parents) nationality, social assistance received, father's prison record, marital status, occupations, employment, housing conditions, education, and income. In addition, for the cohort members, the files contained details on delivery conditions, decisions of Child Welfare Committees, school grades, hours of absence and truancy, offences known by the police, psychological and physical tests, examinations of conscripts for military service, occupation, social class, employment, marital status, housing, courses taken at universities, days and periods of sick leave, social assistance received, births and deliveries, diagnoses and dates of admission and discharge from hospitals, presence of injection scars, offences committed and criminal sanctions received [281].

As linkage key the Swedish national identification number was used. The resulting data set contained information on 15,117 cohort members. Although in accordance with Swedish law, the project received unfavourable public international media attention in February 1986 [575]. Shortly after that, the Data Protection Authority demanded the deidentification of all existing data sets of this project. The data sets were still analysed, but not linked to any new data.

Nearly 20 years later, researchers became interested in updating the Metropolitan data and applied for a reactivation of the study. After data controllers and ethical review boards agreed, in 2004/2005 a database containing information on work, income, health, and mortality for the years 1991 to 2002 for all persons born before 31 December 1985 and living in Sweden was matched to the Metropolitan data. Although no more direct identifiers were available in the Metropolitan and the new data set, matching the files were quite successful. Of the original cohort, 167 have died by 1981. Of the remaining 14,950 records, 96% could be matched [576].

A common cause of unmatched persons seems to be due to emigration. The linking was based on gender, number of flats in a given building and its year of construction, marital status and occupation of the parents, and so on. Although denoted by the researchers as a probabilistic matching approach [575], the linkage was based on deterministic rules and clerical review. The resulting data set was renamed as the Stockholm Birth Cohort (SBC) study. In 2018, a new data set with updated data was matched to the SBC data set using the same matching process as in the previous update. In total, 14,608 of the initial cohort (96.6%) could be matched [17]. This data set is available for analysis only onsite in a secure, controlled environment in Stockholm.

1.6.5 Survey Methodology

In the social sciences, the vast majority of empirical studies is based on sample surveys [531]. The academic field dedicated to the effects of sampling, design features, respondents, data collection modes, and data processing on survey results is called survey methodology [64, 242, 541].

1.6.5.1 Record Linkage for the Study of Non-sampling Errors

An important source of errors in surveys are non-sampling errors such as nonresponse, human memory errors, or social desirability response bias (giving socially acceptable answers to intimate questions) [638]. To minimise nonsampling errors, survey methodologists need access to ground truth data. Increasingly, administrative data is used for the comparison and validation of survey respondent answers in surveys. Although administrative data have their own sources of errors, the causes of these errors are different from non-sampling errors in surveys [61].

Two different designs for using administrative data for validation of surveys are used: forward record check and reverse record check. In forward checks, the sample is drawn at first and independently of the validation data, surveyed, and the answers checked in a database containing the validation data. In a reverse record check study, the database containing the validation data is used as the sampling frame, and the answers in the survey are validated with the already known data [241]. The second variant is usually easier to implement, However, both types have been used.

A standard example for survey errors is over-reporting of voting in elections. There are many different explanations for this consistent bias, for example question effects, memory bias, social desirability, and so on [149]. Important in the context of this book are two facts:

1. Administrative data of individual participation in a public vote or election is available in some countries, for example, the US or, occasionally, in Switzerland.
2. The matching of official records of voting to survey respondents is not trivial if no national identification number is available.

Depending on the criteria used, a forward check study has reported that between 45.6% and 77.4% of the survey respondents could be matched to official records [55]. The failure to match respondents to their government records might be the cause of research artefacts in voting turnout studies.

Reverse check studies use a register as the sampling frame. Therefore, no record linkage beyond deduplication and address updates are necessary. Therefore, these kinds of studies might be easier to implement, but access to registers of interest might be difficult in practice. For example, Preisendörfer and Wolter [481] report on two surveys in which 456 respondents answered a questionnaire which seemed to them as a standard survey. However, the sample was selected using a registry of persons convicted by a court before the survey (2005 to 2008). Most of the offences were minor, such as shoplifting, fare dodging, or drink-driving. The survey asked – among many other things – for previous conviction (about 2/3 gave true answers). Getting permission to access this data has taken about two years[10].

It should be noted that in practical applications of record linkage outside of medicine, the matching is often done without dedicated linkage software or tested algorithms. For example, Averdijk and Elffers [35] matched 8,887 respondents of a victimisation survey in Amsterdam to police records in a semi-manual process. They used initials, surname, postal code, street name, house number, age, phone number, and gender for linking. In the absence of ground truth, the authors used both strict and more lenient criteria for matching and reported no substantial differences in the final linked data

---

[10] Personal communication, Peter Preisendörfer and Rainer Schnell, 25 November 2019.

set when using different match decision rules. Due to the lack of standard
software implemented in the base versions of statistical packages such as SAS,
SPSS or Stata, the use of formal record linkage procedures is only slowly
increasing.

1.6.5.2 Implementing Surveys

Record linkage is used in different stages of implementing surveys, for example [537]: (1) constructing frames, (2) finding rare populations, (3) validating
responses, and (4) checking the privacy of a data set before release. We give
some examples for such applications.

- **Constructing sampling frames**: Scientific surveys are based on random samples, which are defined as samples where each element of the
  population has a known probability of getting sampled. For the computation of this inclusion probability, a list of elements of the population
  (or at least a list of clusters of elements of the population, such as spatial
  areas or buildings) is needed. Such lists are denoted as sampling frames.
  Record linkage is essential for the deduplication of sampling frames.

- **Using set intersection to find rare populations**: Linking subjects
  between independently collected data sets allows the computation of set
  intersections. An example is a US study to determine the proportion of
  physicians changing their medical speciality depending on age. Less than
  0.4% of the employed Americans are physicians; and only very few will
  change their profession. To find them, Jacobs et al. [298] used record linkage. All physicians working in the US have a record in the AMA Physician
  Masterfile. Around one third of these records are updated yearly with a
  survey. By linking the files of 1994 and 1998 containing more than 500,000
  physicians, the proportion of doctors with changing speciality was estimated as less than 1.1%. Interestingly, the probability of a professional
  change seems to be nearly independent of age [298].

- **Validating survey responses**: In the practice of survey research, it is
  widely assumed that socially undesirable traits or behaviours are under-
  reported. This assumption is rarely tested. An exception is a record linkage study by Maxfield et al. [406], who compared the responses of 1,196
  young adults (mean age 28.7 years) with administrative records on imprisonments. They conclude that 21% of all subjects with no history of
  arrest reported at least one arrest to the interviewers.

- **Linking over time and across different databases**: The Scottish
  Health Surveys of the adult population of Scotland have been linked
  to administrative death data. Katikireddi et al. [337] have used respondent reported demographics and alcohol consumption (units per week and
  binge drinking) from surveys done in 1995, 1998, 2003, and 2008 to 2012,
  to predict alcohol-attributable admission to hospitals or death. Although

alcohol consumption did not differ substantially with socioeconomic status, the risk of harm due to alcohol was strongly increased among people of lower socioeconomic status.

- **Checking anonymity for scientific use files**: The demand for social research microdata has increased the number of available Scientific Use Files (SUF). The release of such files depends on the degree of anonymity, which can be assured to the respondents. Therefore methods for an empirical disclosure risk assessment are needed, as we discuss in Sections 2.6 and 5.5. An obvious candidate is record linkage. The percentage of correctly linked record pairs between a SUF and available public data can be used as a measure for disclosure risk. Domingo-Ferrer and Torra [164] demonstrated that record linkage for the reidentification by cluster analysis of highly correlated variables does not necessarily require shared variables between the publicly available data set and a SUF. A similar approach has been published slightly earlier by Bacher et al. [37]. Recently, Domingo-Ferrer et al. [161] generalised and formalised this idea of attacking a SUF using record linkage.

1.6.6 Official Statistics

Another important field for record linkage is official statistics. Official statistics are compiled by National Statistical Institutes (NSIs) such as Statistics Netherlands (CBS), the US Census Bureau, the Australian Bureau of Statistics (ABS), the Office for National Statistics (ONS) in the UK, or Statistics Norway. A central task for all NSIs are censuses. In Europe, according to the EU regulation 763/2008 of the European Parliament, all member states are obliged to conduct a census every ten years. Census data are used for many different purposes, for example to allocating seats in democratic representations or federal funds according to population size, population estimates, projections for health care and educational planning, determining the need for traffic infrastructure, and providing the margins for the computation of survey weights [450].

1.6.6.1 Conducting a Census

As the goal of a census is a complete enumeration of a population, the costs of traditional censuses are becoming prohibitive. As a rule of thumb, a traditional census based on questionnaires is usually calculated at roughly around € 10 to 15 per person. A United Nations report [601] gives a range for 23 countries between 4.9 US Dollars per person in Malta to 48.9 Dollars in the US. For example, in the UK the 2011 Census costs over the 12-year planning and operational period were £ 478 million [448], while the estimate for the German Census 2021 is € 994 million [153]. However, despite these considerable costs, attempts to quantify the net gain by producing accurate census estimates showed that a census delivers benefits clearly in excess of its costs [39, 449]. A recent independent evaluation of the Australian census has found that a value of 6 Australian Dollars was created to the Australian economy for every Dollar invested in the Australian census [378].

To avoid the high costs of traditional censuses, most European countries are therefore in the transition process to register-based censuses [602]. In those countries which have central registers and a unique national identification (NID) number, a register-based census is much easier than in countries without central registers and no NID numbers. Countries without NID numbers have to use indirect quasi-identifiers for a register-based census. An example in Europe is Germany, where the censuses after 2021 will be based on registers. This will require the linkage of data from about 10,000 town registers, tax registers, social security databases, pension databases, a special register for migrants, driver licence databases, and so on.

1.6.6.2 Removing Multiple Responders from a Census

In traditional census operations based on enumerations, some individuals are counted more than once. For example, they have multiple residences, belong to more than one household, or they simply answer twice, for example by answering online and per mail. In the UK, the identification of such duplicates in census processing is named the Resolve Multiple Responses (RMR) process. RMR is essentially a deduplication process based on name, date of birth, and address. However, in addition very specific decision rules (for example, based on household compositions, language used for answers, missing names, and so on) have been developed and are used in the UK census. Concerning the 2011 census, about 237,200 duplicates were detected and removed [448].

1.6.6.3 Estimation of Census Undercounts

Since census results are used for determining the number of seats in a parliament and the allocation of state funds for regional development programmes, the accuracy of a census is of political importance. Although most modern censuses generally achieve high accuracy, the precision differs between subgroups of the population. This problem is denoted as differential undercount [450].

The most widely used method for estimating the coverage of a census is a Post Enumeration Survey (PES). A PES is an independent random sample of the same population as the census tries to enumerate, followed by a comparison of each person found in the PES with the census. A statistical estimation of under- and overcoverage with a PES requires independence of all procedural steps of the PES from the census [603].

The British PES is the Census Coverage Survey (CSS). The results of a record linkage of all persons in the CSS with the persons enumerated in the census are used to estimate the coverage of the census. The official report for the 2011 census estimated that about 3.79 million people were missed in the census and subsequently included in the census outputs through statistical adjustment [448].

Harper and Mayhew [263] tried to estimate the UK census undercoverage for a densely populated inner London borough independently of any census operations. By linking locally available administrative data (GP register, school census, electoral register, council tax register, council tax and housing benefits, births, deaths, housing waiting list, local land, and property gazetteer), they estimated a census undercoverage of 1.7%, with the undercoverage rate varying between different age groups, as described in detail by Harper [262].

1.6.6.4 Linking Historical Censuses

In the US, the Census Bureau keeps a census closed to the public for 72 years [604]. Accordingly, the 1940 US census has been made available for research in 2012. A project led by Warren[11] aims to link records from the 1940 Census to records for respondents to a series of longitudinal surveys, such as the Panel Study of Income Dynamics and the Health and Retirement Study [522]. Although these panels contain detailed information about the respondents themselves, they have much less information about the social and economic conditions of their families and neighbourhoods during childhood. To study the outcomes of these early living circumstances, the linkage of census data will provide researchers in demography, the social sciences, and public health with large, national databases hardly available anywhere else.

1.6.6.5 Correcting for Under-reporting by Linking Administrative Data, Sensors, and Surveys

Increasingly, official statistics is using register information and other data sources in combination with survey data. As an example for the combined use of surveys, register data, and sensors, we describe an application of the National Statistical Institute of the Netherlands (CBS). The CBS is required to estimate transported shipment weight of all trucks at quarterly and annual intervals. The main data are collected by a survey, the Dutch Road Freight Transport Survey (RFTS). As most surveys, the RFTS suffers from

---

[11] See: http://grantome.com/grant/NIH/R01-AG050300-02

non-response. In addition, transportation surveys impose burden on the respondents, since they have to report all trips of a truck for a certain time episode. Therefore, transportation surveys are prone to under-reporting and as a consequence to underestimation.

To correct the estimated shipment weight, Klingwort et al. [354] recently linked the RTFS with data from a sensor network on Dutch roads (the weigh-in-motion road sensor data), the Dutch vehicle register, and the Dutch enterprise register, on a microlevel. The sensor network is coupled with a number plate registration system, so the measured weight of a truck is associated with the licence plate and information about date and time when a measurement was taken. This data was linked by using the licence number with the vehicle register and the enterprise register to obtain information about trucks. Finally, the reported trips in the survey were linked with the data observed in the sensor network. By using a capture-recapture technique, a correction factor for the shipment weight estimated by the survey was calculated.

1.6.6.6 Linking Large Surveys to Administrative Data

The American Community Survey (ACS) is the largest survey of the US Census Bureau, covering topics from employment and commuting to housing [428]. About 3.5 million people are surveyed each year. Participation is mandatory. The ACS is linked to administrative data such as different social security and federally funded benefits program databases. Although the Social Security Number (SSN) is widely available in US administrative data, the ACS does not ask for the SSN. Instead, a person is given a unique protected identification key (PIK). For assigning the PIK, a record linkage system called PVS is used [632]. PVS uses names, date of birth, geographical information, and household composition, to link records [404]. About 90% to 94% of ACS records are linked, but the match rate is lower for some age, race, and groups of Hispanic origin [427].

1.6.6.7 Labour Force Surveys

For estimation of unemployment with high precision, in official statistics, Labour Force Surveys (LFS) based on panel surveys are often designed in a special way. This kind of panels partitions the sample into subgroups and keeps the respondents of a subgroup for a limited number of data collections (waves) in the sample. After that, the respondents of a subgroup are replaced by a fresh random sample of the population. This survey design is called rotating panel, and the subgroups are called rotation groups [317].

For example, each year the German Mikrozensus (covering 1% of all households) replaces 25% of the households surveyed in a previous year. Therefore, a household remains in the sample for four years. The US Current Population

Survey (CPS) is designed similarly. The CPS is a monthly survey of about 60,000 households. Since 1953, the survey uses one rotation group per month. There are eight rotation groups. Each group is interviewed for four consecutive months, then paused for eight months, and again reinterviewed in the following four months. The group is then dropped and replaced by a new sample. For many analyses of rotational panels, the longitudinal character of the sample design is ignored. To fully use the longitudinal information, linkage taking care of rotation groups, available characteristics, and identifiers for households and persons, might be challenging. For example, the composition of households might change due to migration and mortality, non-response at household- and personlevel might reduce the available data and, of course, there might be recording errors. The problems and solutions for longitudinal record linkage of the CPS are described by Rivera et al. [517].

1.7 Ethical Challenges

The previous case studies should have made it clear that record linkage has ethical implications. At first, linking increases the amount of information available about a person. The resulting ethical considerations are the topic of research on consenting to record linkage, statistical disclosure control, and data privacy. These will be discussed in some detail in Chapter 2.

But there are further ethical challenges related to the use of linked databases. For example, some populations are excluded from databases and therefore cannot be linked. In survey methodology, this is denoted as the undercoverage problem [241]. If the probability of inclusion in a resulting linked database is correlated with social characteristics, that database will contain a smaller proportion of records of this group. Algorithms acting on that database and decisions based on it will show biased estimates.

These kinds of problems have been discussed in an emerging academic field dedicated to the construction and use of Big data from a societal perspective called critical data studies [516]. For example, the use of machine learning methods for the classification of people for insurance policies, job applications, or criminal profiling has been subject of such studies. An example is an experiment reported by Datta et al. [146], where the setting of gender in Google's advertisement settings impacts the kind of job advertisements that are shown to a user: simulated males were shown advertisements for jobs with large salaries more frequently. Although no one intended this, the application of machine learning using biased training data or unequal class sizes might perpetuate inequality. These kinds of effects are often referred to as algorithmic bias [250]. As machine learning based techniques are increasingly being used in the context of linking (sensitive) databases [109, 360], the issue of bias in linked data sets needs to be considered. We discuss this topic in more detail in Section 11.2.4.

This book discusses the technical problems of linking sensitive databases using privacy-preserving techniques from a computer science point of view, not the legal constraints or social consequences of record linkage. These problems have the attention of academic specialists in those fields. However, we hope that the techniques discussed in this book are applied only after a relevant institutional ethics board has permitted to do so. Since the focus of this book is on privacy-preserving record linkage techniques, their application will reduce the privacy risks for research subjects. Therefore, we are confident that the techniques discussed will help increase the amount of data available for research and, at the same time, improve the privacy of members of the populations covered by the databases involved.

1.8 What this Book Covers

This book presents state-of-the-art methods for protecting person identifiers containing variations and errors, but still allowing record linkage, for producing microdata for data analysis. We assume microdata are collected by either government service providers such as health, social security, transport, and so on, or by commercial companies such as telecommunication or financial service providers, or resulting from survey operations. In most cases, such microdata will refer to a natural person, but – depending on the context of research – data on businesses will also be covered by the topics discussed in this book.

The first part of the book gives an introduction to record linkage in general. In the following chapter, exemplary privacy regulations will be discussed, and the basic concepts of record linkage will be introduced in Chapter 3.

The second part discusses the core privacy aspects and technical building blocks for record linkage of sensitive data. Protocols, privacy metrics, and technical tools such as random number generators and hash functions are described. These techniques are used for different encoding and encryption techniques, of which one popular method uses binary vectors (known as Bloom filters [68]). Construction, attacking, and hardening Bloom filter based encodings are described in detail. Since the sizes of the databases to be linked could be substantial, efficiency in computing is of concern and is discussed in a separate chapter.

The third part of the book is dedicated to practical applications of the techniques described here. Institutional settings constrain the implementation of methods, real-world data contains missing data, and computational issues may require modifications of methods not thought of before their actual use in practice. We also include an example empirical evaluation of a set of privacy-preserving linkage techniques, and describe several recent applications where such techniques have been used in practical real-world linkage settings.

The final part of the book gives a summary of future research directions we are expecting. The book concludes with descriptions of available software, as well as test data collections and data generators which can be used for the evaluation of new algorithms or implementations of record linkage techniques.

The glossary starting on page 397 describes many relevant terms used throughout the book to help the reader who is unfamiliar with certain topics.

1.9 Summary and Further Reading

Linking records from different databases containing information about the same entities is a task required in many application domains, ranging from medical research to counter terrorism. Since the databases to be linked may be very large and cover a whole population under study, special techniques for reducing the amount of computation are required. Furthermore, since the identification of the same entity is most often based on imperfect data, the linkage has to consider variations and errors in quasi-identifiers such as names and addresses. An introduction to the general problems of record linkage is provided in several recent books [109, 266, 274, 432].

A systematic discussion of issues in the use of administrative data and Big data for the estimation of statistical parameters for a population can be found in a chapter by Biemer [61], while privacy problems resulting from the use of databases on populations are discussed by Elliot et al. [187] and Torra [595]. Hand discusses the topic of data ethics in a rapidly changing world where data are underpinning many aspects of today's economy and society [258].

Chapter 2
Regulatory Frameworks

Abstract In this chapter, we review ethical and legal regulatory frameworks as relevant to the topic of linking sensitive databases that contain personal information. With reference to the declarations of Helsinki and Taipei, the resulting importance of research ethics committees is explained. Thereafter, we describe formal regulations for linking databases in selected countries. The European Data Protection Regulation (GDPR) and its implementation in different European countries are outlined first (Austria, Germany, UK). We discuss the Caldicott principles, important in the UK but not well known in Europe. We then describe the basic principles of the Common Rule and the Health Insurance Portability and Accountability Act (HIPAA) in the US. For comparison, the legal regulations in Australia and Switzerland are outlined. We then introduce best practice approaches, such as separating microdata and identifiers, using technical and organisational measures to restrict data access, and implementing organisational structures and procedures such as the Five Safes. Finally, we highlight the importance of the embedding of research involving sensitive databases within organisational and societal settings, both for the evaluation of privacy as well as preconditions for research.

2.1 Privacy Norms: The Privacy Paradox and Contextual Integrity

Although large parts of the general population are aware of digital privacy issues in principle[1], in their daily life most citizens seem to be willing to accept the terms of service of digital services or software without noticing [444].

This contradiction has given rise to the scholarly literature regarding the privacy paradox: The divergence between declared intentions to disclose personal information and actual behaviour [443]. This contradiction is still ap-

---

[1] A comparative survey on attitudes to privacy in Europe is described in [194].

© Springer Nature Switzerland AG 2020
P. Christen et al., *Linking Sensitive Data*, https://doi.org/10.1007/978-3-030-59706-1_2

parent more than a decade after it was first raised. For example, in 2019 the New York Times reported on the availability of 12 million longitudinal tracks of smartphones (including security officers of the US president) [593]. The practice of collecting such potentially sensitive data is according to US laws.

At the same time, access to current (non-historical) anonymised census microdata for research is restricted in most Western countries to high-security computing environments. Research access to health data is even more restricted than access to census data. This apparent discrepancy of data governance is hard to explain at first.

Health data are widely considered as the most sensitive type of data. However, collecting this kind of data is nearly inevitable. The same argument could be made for many types of administrative data. Since these data are already there, the concept of privacy as intrusion is hardly applicable to these kinds of data. The former director of the US Census Bureau, Kenneth Prewitt, distinguishes between privacy and confidentiality as the difference between "don't ask" and "don't tell" [482]. Health data, official statistical data, and other population covering administrative databases might be seen more in the realm of confidentiality. Furthermore, these data are collected for specific purposes, and their use for research might be perceived by subsets of the population as a violation of privacy principles, denoted by Helen Nissenbaum as the concept of contextual integrity [440].

In this concept, privacy norms are seen as prescribing information flows according to five variables: sender, recipient, subject, information type, and transmission principle [441]. The latter, transmission principle, are constraints on information sharing. An example is the need for informed consent before information is shared. These privacy norms depend on the context they are applied in. Therefore this conceptual framework is often referred to as privacy in context. Any change of the variables in an information flow might be seen by humans as a breach of contextual integrity.

However, many ethical guidelines for research permit the use of data for other purposes than initially intended and beyond the requirement of consent. For example, the World Health Organisation (WHO) guidelines for health surveillance [650] emphasise that the recording of names and other identifiers might be legitimate for health surveillance in certain circumstances (with an explicit mentioning of record linkage). Furthermore, individuals have an obligation to contribute to surveillance when complete databases are required, and proper protection is in place. Under these circumstances, the WHO guidelines state that informed consent is not ethically required. Jurisdictions usually allow some exceptions of data privacy regulations for specific research purposes (including official statistics). Since data privacy is no fundamental right irrespective of any circumstances, to better understand the base for research exemptions, we have to review the fundamental ethical principles of research.

2.2 Basic Ethical Principles of Research

After the second World War, during the Nuremberg trials of German physicians, the need for criteria to differentiate between ethical and non-ethical experiments on humans became clear. The Nuremberg verdict on 22 August 1947 contains a set of ten basic principles for experiments on humans [577]. This first description of medical ethics became known as the Nuremberg code. Building on these principles, in 1964, the Declaration of Helsinki was adopted by the World Medical Association (WMA). Since then it has been extended and modified repeatedly[2]. A notable extension is the WMA Declaration of Taipei on Ethical Considerations regarding Health Databases and Biobanks. This extension was adopted by the WMA in 2002 and revised in 2016[3].

Furthermore, the Council for International Organizations of Medical Sciences (CIOMS), an international organisation established by the WHO and the United Nations Educational, Scientific and Cultural Organisation (UNESCO) in 1949, also published a revision of the Ethical Guidelines for Biomedical Research involving human beings in 2016[4]. A comparative discussion of data sharing in these guidelines is given by Ballantyne [40].

Although intended for medical research, the declaration states a set of ethical principles that are widely considered as essential for all research on humans. Some principles especially relevant to the topics covered in this book are:

7. Medical research is subject to ethical standards that promote and ensure respect for all human subjects and protect their health and rights.
8. While the primary purpose of medical research is to generate new knowledge, this goal can never take precedence over the rights and interests of individual research subjects. (. . .)
17. All medical research involving human subjects must be preceded by careful assessment of predictable risks and burdens to the individuals and groups involved in the research in comparison with foreseeable benefits to them and to other individuals or groups affected by the condition under investigation. Measures to minimise the risks must be implemented. (. . .)
22. The design and performance of each research study involving human subjects must be clearly described and justified in a research protocol. (. . .)
23. The research protocol must be submitted for consideration, comment, guidance and approval to the concerned research ethics committee before the study begins. (. . .)

---

[2] See: https://www.wma.net

[3] See: https://www.wma.net/policies-post/wma-declaration-of-taipei-on-ethical-considerations-regarding-health-databases-and-biobanks

[4] See: https://cioms.ch/wp-content/uploads/2017/01/WEB-CIOMS-Ethical-Guidelines.pdf

24. Every precaution must be taken to protect the privacy of research subjects and the confidentiality of their personal information. (...)

The requirement that a research protocol has to be approved by a research ethics committee is now nearly universal in most democratic societies. In the US, such institutions are mostly denoted as Institutional Review Boards (IRBs). In addition to these basic principles, depending on the jurisdiction, further regulative frameworks and laws apply.

In this book we concentrate on linking sensitive data from different database owners (or data custodians or data holders). In the literature, the distinction between linking and sharing data is not always clear. For data sharing in general, the same or other regulations might be relevant [316].

In the remainder of this chapter we will discuss some details of the regulations we consider as required background knowledge for applied researchers. We include the European Union, the UK, and the US because some essential aspects of their specific jurisdictions are largely unknown abroad. We added Austria and Switzerland because they recently introduced legal frameworks and technical solutions which might be of interest for researchers in other countries. Germany and Australia are included because they are federal states, don't have a unique identifier in their databases, and have vastly different solutions for the problem of linking sensitive databases. However, for specific research proposals under one or more jurisdictions, legal advice by specialists is required in any case.

2.3 Regulations in the European Union and the United Kingdom

Data protection in Europe is characterised by the existence of many different regulations at the national and European level. A general overview of such regulations is given in a handbook by the European Agency of Human Rights [197]. The most important legal framework is the European General Data Protection Regulation (GDPR), which became active in May 2018 [195]. Containing 99 articles and 173 interpretative explanations (recitals), the GDPR is a complicated and often vague text [621]. However, the main principles are [419]:

1. lawfulness (processing personal data requires a legal basis),
2. transparency (data subjects must be informed about the purpose of processing of their personal data),
3. purpose limitation (processing only for a specific purpose),
4. data minimisation,
5. accuracy of processed data,
6. limitation of the duration of data storage,
7. integrity and confidentiality of data processing.

The GDPR regulates the processing of personal data, and it distinguishes between different kinds of data:

1. personal data (information relating to an identifiable person),
2. special categories of personal data (sensitive data, including information on ethnic origins, political opinions, religion, trade union membership, genetic or biometric features, health and sexual orientation),
3. pseudonymous data (identifiable only with additional information, which is stored separately),
4. anonymous data (a person is not identifiable).

The GDPR does not contain an explicit definition of anonymous data [419]. Furthermore, the interpretation of pseudonymous data is subject of debate among lawyers [570, 572]. Since the GDPR mentions pseudonymisation fourteen times, this class of techniques seem to be important for data protection legislation. Pseudonymisation is considered by the GDPR as an appropriate technical and organisational measure "... designed to implement data-protection principles ..." (Article 25 of the GDPR). Recital 26 of the GDPR contains the following sentence:

> To ascertain whether means are reasonably likely to be used to identify the natural person, account should be taken of all objective factors, such as the costs of and the amount of time required for identification, taking into consideration the available technology at the time of the processing and technological developments.

This sentence seems to set commonsense limits of efforts to a reidentification attack (as we discuss further in Chapters 5 and 9), but since recitals are not legally binding, it is not clear how the recital will be adopted to binding law in European jurisdictions or legal practice. A short discussion of the legal aspects of pseudonymisation in the context of the GDPR is given in a report for the Royal Society and British Academy [521].

For research using sensitive personal data, the GDPR contains many exemptions [412]. Article 89 mentions "derogations relating to processing for archiving purposes in the public interest, scientific or historical research purposes or statistical purposes". The details of these exemptions are not clear, especially the mode of consent required for different forms of research [419, 621]. For example, in population covering research, obtaining consent from a population will be impossible in practice. It should be noted that recent medical guidelines, such as CIOMSs or the WMA Declaration of Taipei discussed before, concentrate on individual consent for interventional or observational research [40], but not research using existing population covering databases. However, there is a discussion among experts on medical ethics of a potential "duty to participate in digital epidemiology" [41, 416]. Most of the criteria for the existence of such a duty apply to population covering research in general.

The GDPR requires additional local laws for the application within a European jurisdiction. That could result in stricter regulations than before the GDPR was enacted. An example is Ireland, where the Department of Health has decided for a restrictive interpretation of the GDPR. Here, very detailed explanations need to be provided to patients before consent can be given. As a result, explicit consent is required for nearly all research data usages in Ireland [128].

Furthermore, the potential differences between jurisdictions may create additional problems for cross-national research. Although the GDPR can be seen as an important step towards privacy legislation with special exemptions for research, working out the implications of the GDPR for research in all European countries will require considerable time and efforts. Foremost, clear interpretations for consent for research based on population covering databases, and the handling of pseudonymised data for research are needed. A study for the European Parliament [457] on the implications of the GDPR for research states:

> ... the GDPR permits the processing of pseudonymised data for uses beyond the purpose for which the data was originally collected. However, it remains uncertain what technical degree of pseudonymisation is required under the GDPR's provisions. In particular, both the CJEU [Court of Justice of the European Union] and UK courts appear to have adopted the more pragmatic approach of classifying pseudonymised data as anonymised data when transferred without a key. Reducing uncertainty in this domain is highly important to clarify the conditions for sharing deidentified data ...

The same report stresses the need to clarify the exceptions subject to Article 89(1) with respect to permitted processing for statistical and scientific purposes, establish guidelines for the use and monitoring of anonymisation and pseudonymisation technology, develop institutional guidelines that assist researchers involved in transnational transfers of personal data outside the EU, and further details [457]. Currently, the GDPR seems to be perceived by many European researchers neither as an enabler nor as a hindrance for current research practice [523].

2.3.1 Austria

Since 2018, the European GDPR enhanced by the Austrian Data Protection Law (DSG) regulates data processing in Austria, where the full text of all data protection laws in Austria is available at the homepage of the Austrian Data Protection Agency[5]. Of general interest is the Austrian solution for record linkage in administrative contexts.

Austria operates a central register of residents (ZMR). All individuals living in Austria have a number in this register. This ZMR number is used to compute domain-specific personal identifiers, denoted as bPK. This number is a SHA-1 hash (see Section 6.2 for a discussion of hashing techniques) of a

---

[5] See: https://www.dsb.gv.at/gesetze-in-osterreich

ZMR and a domain identifier (for example BBA-STA is the domain identifier for Statistics Austria). These hash values are transformed into a string of 28 human-readable ASCII (text) characters, which is used as the bPK. Details of how the bPK identifiers are generated is described on the homepage of the Austrian Federal Ministry for Digital and Economic Affairs[6]. While the domain identifiers are public, the ZMR numbers are not. Some applications require the active involvement of a person (with an electronic ID-card) while others do not.

Official statistics in Austria uses the bPK for census operations and other statistical purposes. Recently, other national statistical institutes are considering to adopt this model of the use of a national identification number [362]. A similar scheme is described by Quantin et al. [485] for the linking of administrative data in France.

2.3.2 Germany

Germany is subdivided into 16 constituent states which have separate data protection agencies. In addition, there is a federal data protection agency. Official statistics are produced by 14 state agencies[7] and a federal coordinating agency. Currently, no unique national identification number is available in Germany. There is a universal tax identification number, but its use is limited to tax purposes by law. Since a unique identification number has been prohibited by the Federal Constitutional Court (Bundesverfassungsgericht), the introduction of identification numbers is the subject of debates [403]. Record linkage of databases held by different organisations is usually done on social security numbers (available for employees only) and mainly on quasi-identifiers such as names and dates of birth. In some applications, specific identifiers such as health insurance numbers can be used.

Besides the GDPR, separate federal laws regulating the access and use of official statistics, social security databases, and medical databases have to be obeyed. An overview of the German jurisdiction for research data is given in [513]. In 2019, the Federal Constitutional Court decided that German privacy laws have to be considered if they provide a higher protection level than the European law [284]. Therefore, legal advice by specialists is nearly unavoidable for all research proposals that involve population databases.

The constraints described so far make record linkage on population databases across organisations challenging in Germany. In general, individual con-

---

[6] See: https://www.bmdw.gv.at/Ministerium/DasBMDW/ Stammzahlenregisterbehoerde/Bereichsspezifische_ Personenkennzeichen/Beschreibung-von-bereichsspezifischen- Personenkennzeichen.html

[7] Berlin / Brandenburg and Hamburg / Schleswig-Holstein have only one common statistical office each.

sent is considered by most data protection officers as required. In a few areas, such as medical quality control or data on newborns (as we discussed in Section 1.6.3), special laws permit the linkage on population databases without consent and notifications. In rare exceptions, a limited linkage of social security databases to surveys or other databases have been permitted [23]. Furthermore, at least one state (Hamburg) has linked data on individual pupils longitudinally without personal consent [207]. If such linkages are allowed in general is a topic of debate in the juridical literature [402].

Overall, linking sensitive databases without consent is possible in Germany, but usually requires special laws or permissions of many agencies. Which permits are needed depends on the databases involved. Since no standard operating procedure for handling linkage requests exists in Germany, linking sensitive databases across different organisations is always a tedious process [540]. With the exception of social security databases, compared to Australia, the UK, or New Zealand, record linkage of national databases is rarely attempted in Germany.

2.3.3 United Kingdom

The core of the data protection legislation in the UK has been the Data Protection Act 1998 (DPA)[8]. Processing of personal data is allowed if either a person has given consent, or for medical purposes. For the interested reader, a review of UK data legislation relevant for research is given in a report for the Royal Society and British Academy [521]. Data protection in the UK in general is described by [97]. In the DPA, medical purposes include medical research and the management of healthcare services. Personal data may be used if:

1. the data are not used to support decisions with respect to particular individuals,
2. no substantial damage or distress is likely to be caused to any individual, and
3. no research results are made available in a form which identifies an individual.

Given these principles, the Data Protection Order 2000 allows the processing of sensitive data, when the processing is in the substantial public interest and necessary for research purposes[9]. When the GDPR came into effect in 2018, it has been incorporated into the Data Protection Act (2018). This act leaves much of the original DPA unchanged, but some new principles (such as the "right to be forgotten") have been incorporated[10].

---

[8] See: https://www.legislation.gov.uk/ukpga/1998/29
[9] See: https://www.legislation.gov.uk/uksi/2000/417/schedule/made
[10] See: https://www.ukcgc.uk/gdpr

This general legal framework has been extended with concern to medical data by two import reviews. In 1997, a commission (named after the chair of the panel, Dame Fiona Caldicott) published a report on data confidentiality within the National Health Service (NHS) [95]. Since 1998, every NHS organisation needs to have a person safeguarding the confidentiality of patient information. These persons are referred to as Caldicott Guardians. A useful manual concerning their duties and further reports are available on the homepage of the UK Caldicott Guardian Council (UKCGC)[11]. Most important in the context of this book has been the 2013 publication of a second report [94]. In this second report, a new principle was introduced:

> The duty to share information can be as important as the duty to protect patient confidentiality.

The report emphasises that health and social care professionals should have the confidence to share information in the best interests of their patients within the confidentiality framework described by the report. These professionals should be supported by the policies of their employers, regulators, and professional bodies.

This additional principle is a quite distinctive advantage for the use of medical research data in the UK compared to other European countries. Together with a set of guidelines by the Information Commissioner, the legal and organisational frameworks for conducting record linkage studies are favourable for research in the UK. Details for the use of anonymisation are given in a guideline by the Information Commissioner [293], and data sharing is described in another report by the Information Commissioner [292] and the second Caldicott report [94], while consent options are discussed in a report by the National Data Guardians [429]. A guideline for deciding if disclosure of confidential patient information without consent is justified in the public interest is given by the UK Department of Health and Social Care [154]. However, extending the strategy of linking population covering databases to administrative data in general seems to be challenging even under this circumstances [313].

In 2013, a five year funding period for a nationwide linkage partnership named Administrative Data Research Network (ADRN) started. The ADRN has been replaced in 2018 by the Administrative Data Research UK (ADR-UK), which is initially funded for three years with an investment of £ 44 million[12]. The aims of the ADRN and ADR-UK are to provide researchers with access to linked and deidentified administrative data to enable them to conduct economic and social research, thereby maximising the potential of administrative data as a resource for high-quality research in the UK.

---

[11] See: https://www.gov.uk/government/groups/uk-caldicott-guardian-council

[12] See: https://www.adruk.org

2.4 Regulations in the United States

For sharing and linking data, many different laws and regulations apply in the US, for example, the Privacy Act (1974), the Health Insurance Portability and Accountability Act of 1996 (HIPAA), the Family Educational Rights and Privacy Act of 1974 (FERPA), the Children's Online Privacy Protection Act (COPPA), and the Computer Matching and Privacy Protection Act. The legal complexities of linking data in the US are described by Petrila [471], while more details on privacy laws in the US, in general, are discussed by Grama [238].

A central regulation in the US is Federal Policy for the Protection of Human Subjects, better known as the Common Rule. This ethical standard is adopted by twenty federal agencies in the US for research on humans. First published in 1981 and revised in 2018, the Common Rule is nearly universally accepted by academic institutions for conducting research. The revised version of the common rule came into force in January 2019[13]. Among other things, the Common Rule governs the details of Institutional Review Boards (IRB) overseeing research proposals in the US.

The Health Insurance Portability and Accountability Act (HIPAA) is the primary law regulating healthcare information in the US since 1996. In the context of data sharing, HIPAA is of central importance, since legal frameworks rarely provide detailed guidance on data deidentification (anonymisation), but HIPAA is an exception [445]. HIPAA Section 164.514(a) describes two different methods for data deidentification:

1. An expert with appropriate knowledge and experience determines that the risk is very small.
2. 18 attributes have to be deleted: Names, geographic subdivisions smaller than a state, details of dates (except year) for dates directly related to an individual (including birth date, admission date, discharge date, date of death), telephone and fax numbers, email addresses, social security numbers, medical record numbers, health plan beneficiary numbers; account numbers, certificate/license numbers, vehicle identifiers and serial numbers, including license plate numbers, device identifiers and serial numbers, URLs, IP addresses, biometric identifiers (such as finger and voice prints), photographs and any other unique identifying number, characteristic, or code.

The second option seems to be easier to verify. For compliance guidelines concerning HIPAA we refer the interested reader to El-Emam [185] and Trinckes [600]. However, a HIPAA compliant database might still allow the identification of some records as was investigated by Benitez and Malin [51].

Petrila [471] summarises the complex data sharing jurisdiction by emphasising that "...none of these laws create a categorical prohibition against us-

---

[13] See: https://www.federalregister.gov/documents/2017/01/19/2017-01058/federal-policy-for-the-protection-of-human-subjects

ing sensitive identifying information for research purposes (...). Information *can* be retrieved and retained, but it must be done so securely". In practice, the efforts to implement a record linkage project will include intricate legal negotiations, since no standard procedures seem to exist in the US.

2.5 Regulations in other Countries

We now briefly describe regulations in two countries outside the EU and the US to illustrate different approaches to regulate access to and linkage of sensitive databases.

2.5.1 Australia

The Australian Parliament passed the Privacy Act in 1988 to regulate the processing of personal information by Australian Government agencies and other organisations. Handling of health data is given special considerations in Sections 95 and 95A of the Privacy Act. Guidelines for Sections 95 and 95A are available on the homepage of the National Health and Medical Research Council (NHMRC)[14]. In addition to the Privacy Act there is a National Statement for Ethical Conduct in Human Research [430] which was updated in 2018.

A comprehensive review on the availability of data for research and other purposes in Australia, including the legal framework and suggestions for improving, is given in a report by the Productivity Commission of the Australian government [483], while further details on privacy regulations for health research in Australia are discussed by Paterson and McDonagh [466].

In 2019, there were more than 200 Human Research Ethics Committees (HRECs) in Australia[15]. HRECs review all research proposals involving human participants. To assist these HRECs, Section 95A of the Privacy Act gives a framework to assess proposals for data processing for health research without individuals' consent. HRECs have to ensure that the public interest in the research activities substantially outweighs the public interest in the protection of privacy.

Although access to administrative data for research without consent is possible in principle, a large number of governance requirements have to be met [213]. Each linkage proposal has to be assessed by a HREC and the data custodians of each database. In practice, the approval process seems to be intricate due to overlapping regulations and unclear responsibilities [213].

---

[14] See: https://www.nhmrc.gov.au.

[15] See: https://www.nhmrc.gov.au/research-policy/ethics/

Therefore, health and medical databases seem to be underutilised for research since the obstacles for linking data seem to be too high [144]. However, infrastructure and examples of protocols for establishing standard procedures for linkage projects are increasingly available in Australia [82, 214, 414, 422].

2.5.2 Switzerland

The national statistical institute in Switzerland is the Federal Statistical Office (in German: Bundesamt für Statistik, BFS). In 2010, Switzerland adopted a register-based census [92]. Due to the changing jurisdiction, a unique social security number was included in all statistical databases of the BFS. Further details on the unique identifier in Switzerland (AHVN13) are discussed by Winterleitner and Spichiger [646]. This inclusion of a unique identifier significantly increases the opportunities for record linkage. If the legal requirements are fulfilled, official data on persons can be linked. The appendix of the technical guidelines for linkage in Switzerland contains references to all laws relevant for this purpose, for example, the Bundesstatistikgesetz, the Registerharmonisierungsgesetz, and the Bundesgesetz über den Datenschutz [622]. Therefore, the BFS has established a routine procedure for a linkage request. This includes a standardised application form for a linkage project. In 2015 in total 22 applications were received, 21 a year later[16]. Due to this infrastructure, record linkage in Switzerland has become easier.

For example, the Swiss national cohort is a large medical linkage study in Switzerland. Before 2010, linkage was based on quasi-identifiers such as date of birth, gender, and geographical identifiers [76]. After the 2010 census, linkage could be based on the social security number. Although the Swiss national cohort is not allowed to use social security number directly, the members of the study received a unique pseudo identifier based on their social security number. Therefore, linkage of the cohort with annual census data and register data (such as mortality, marriage and divorce registries, and annual surveys) is greatly facilitated by such a unique identifier[17].

2.6 Statistical Disclosure Control

Reidentification of a person or other entity in a database or data set can be done by direct identifiers (such as names and dates of birth) or indirect identifiers (such as combining information on characteristics such as age,

---

[16]   See: https://www.bfs.admin.ch/bfs/de/home/dienstleistungen/
datenverknuepfungen/allgemein.html

[17] See: https://www.swissnationalcohort.ch/record-linkage

occupation, region, and so on). Privacy-preserving record linkage [253, 619, 620] is mainly concerned with privacy protection of direct identifiers.

Protection of indirect identifiers is a traditional application field in statistics and mostly denoted as statistical disclosure control (SDC) [173]. Especially in official statistics, statistical disclosure control methods are essential tools for the privacy assessment of databases. Therefore, regulative frameworks for statistics contain definitions and criteria for the evaluation if information can be used to identify statistical units in a database by disclosing individual information. The previous sentence is, for example, the definition of confidential data in the EU Regulation 223/2009 on European statistics in Article 3, Paragraph 7[18].

Statistical disclosure control is used, for example, in the publication of statistical tables, where rare combinations of attribute values could be used to identify individuals. Therefore, tables are modified by aggregating, rounding, or suppression of counts or other statistics. To prevent the use of carefully selected queries to identify individuals, special measures must be taken (this is also the primary purpose of the concept of differential privacy, as we describe in Section 6.3.3).

Statistical disclosure control for microdata is challenging. The data has to be modified, but in a way which should not reduce its utility for data analysis. New techniques to achieve this balance between risk and utility are under constant development. The list of available methods includes adding noise, data swapping, sampling, recoding, and top-coding. Sometimes even synthetic data sets are used, where the records are not representing actual units, but are samples from estimated distributions. We discuss methods for statistical disclosure control in more detail in Section 5.5, and the interested reader is referred to Duncan et al. [173] for an extensive coverage of this topic.

In this book, we consider the application of statistical disclosure control methods for the data intended for analysis as one element of best practice approaches as we describe next.

2.7 Best Practice Approaches

The security and privacy of the identifiers and the databases used in a record linkage project depend on many factors, not on a specific technique alone. This idea is the core of the concept of functional anonymity [188]. Among the factors to be considered are the motivation of an adversary (an organisation or individual who aims to gain access to sensitive or confidential data through illegal means), the potential consequences of disclosure, the governance structures, data security and other infrastructural properties, and the amount, quality, and overlap (with the sensitive data to be attacked) of the

---

[18] See: https://eur-lex.europa.eu/LexUriServ/LexUriServ.do?uri=OJ: L:2009:087:0164:0173:en:PDF

auxiliary data available to an adversary. Therefore, a privacy assessment has to include not only the data but also its environment. The data environment [187] includes other data, data users, data governance processes, and infrastructures [188].

A crucial aspect of infrastructure are the organisational measures taken to control data access, which we discuss next. After that, human data processors and their ethical guidelines are mentioned. Finally, we will summarise recent recommendations on data governance and the social embedding of research.

2.7.1 Organisational Measures

Many national statistical institutes, institutional review boards and research ethics committees, have adopted the Five Safes approach to evaluate a research proposal, including record linkage projects [152]:

1. Safe projects: Is this use of the data appropriate?
2. Safe people: Can the researchers be trusted to use the data in an appropriate manner?
3. Safe data: Is there a disclosure risk in the data itself?
4. Safe settings: Does the access facility limit unauthorised use?
5. Safe outputs: Are the statistical results non-disclosive?

Two of the Five Safes (numbers 3 and 5) in this list refer to statistical disclosure control, as discussed previously and in Section 5.5. The other three safes restrict the kind of access to the data. In practice, different methods for regulating data access can be distinguished: User agreements for offsite use, remote analysis systems, virtual data centres, and secure onsite centres [454]. All but the first of these options are variations of safe havens as secure environments for population-based research and statistical analysis [592]. Such secure environments or research data centres have been established under different names in, for example, Canada, the UK, the US, and Germany.

Of course, reidentification attempts within a research data centre are prohibited. For example, the German Federal Statistics Act (BStatG) forbids linking official statistics data with other data for the purpose of re-establishing a link to individuals or other entities such as businesses. Some jurisdictions seem to forbid reidentification of research data in general. However, if no exemptions are granted, such regulations might discourage investigation and research into information security [466]. The organisational and legal measures applying within a research data centre should make attacks or misuse of microdata by researchers difficult.

However, the actual linking of databases is usually not done by a research data centre or data repository. Although different organisational models for sharing and linking population covering databases are in use [310], most often, a trusted third party is used for linking population covering databases.

An example is the health domain, where databases are sometimes provided by hundreds of hospitals. Usually, identifiers and data are separated in such settings [340], as we discuss in detail in Section 4.2. Under these circumstances, the remaining risk in a linkage project depends on the processes within the linkage unit.

General data protection regulations such as the GDPR require that data processing of personal data has to be secure, such that unauthorised access is impossible. For a trusted third party, this principle usually requires that the file containing the list of corresponding units (entities) of a record linkage project has to be deleted immediately after the project is completed, and no backups are retained. The GDPR refers to "appropriate technical and organisational measures" (TOM) to ensure proper processing of such information [630]. Examples for TOMs are physical and electronic access controls including passwords and the secure disposal of memory systems [347]. Given appropriate TOMs, an outside attack should be unsuccessful. Leakage due to human error (lost computers, DVDs, USB flash drives, or hard drives) or misconfigured systems seems to be much more likely. These kind of problems are not specific to systems and organisations that are tasked with linking sensitive databases, but to IT systems in general, as we discuss further in Section 5.3. Proper IT management should prevent such mishaps.

This line of reasoning results in one remaining attack scenario: An insider attack within a linkage unit. If the linkage is done on plaintext (cleartext), a potential privacy breach is just the misuse of already accessible information. This is clearly a crime, but not an attack. If a potential privacy breach within a linkage unit requires technical effort for a reidentification, because identifiers are encoded or encrypted, we have a reidentification attack by an insider, as we discuss in more detail in Section 5.4. Preventing this kind of attack is the aim of privacy-preserving record linkage techniques, the topic of this book.

2.7.2 Professional Guidelines

In addition to the general ethical guidelines of research and the limits set by a given jurisdiction, professions usually have their own ethical guidelines. Most data scientists would agree to a general ethical guideline such as the motto of IPUMS, the Integrated Public Use Microdata Series project at the Institute for Social Research and Data Innovation, University of Minnesota[19]:

> Use it for good – never for evil.

However, as a practical guideline, something more specific is needed. Therefore, many professional guidelines of data-centric professions are in existence. For example, the revised European Statistics Code of Practice

---

[19] IPUMS has created the largest accessible database of census microdata, see: https://ipums.org

consisting of sixteen principles was adopted by the European Statistical System Committee (ESSC) in 2017. Principle 5 emphasises that statistical confidentiality is guaranteed by law, penalties are prescribed for any wilful breaches of statistical confidentiality, and administrative, technical and organisational measures are taken to protect the security and integrity of statistical data [196]. Principle 9 demands the use of administrative and other data to avoid duplicating requests for data. While adhering to confidentiality and data protection requirements, data sharing and data integration are promoted to minimise response burden.

Another example is the American Statistical Association. It operates on ethical guidelines which contain details on privacy [134]. Section D of the Guidelines demands protection of:

> (...) the privacy and confidentiality of research subjects and data concerning them, whether obtained from the subjects directly, other persons, or existing records.

Furthermore, an ethical statistician:

> (...) anticipates and solicits approval for secondary and indirect uses of the data, including linkage to other data sets, when obtaining approvals from research subjects and obtains approvals appropriate to allow for peer review and independent replication of analyses.

And finally:

> In contemplating whether to participate in an analysis of data from a particular source, refuses to do so if participating in the analysis could reasonably be interpreted by individuals who provided information as sanctioning a violation of their rights.

2.7.3 Social Embeddings of Research: Ethical, Legal, and Societal Implications of Research

Research is always embedded in a social setting and might have consequences for some or all members of a society. These aspects are often denoted as ethical, legal, and societal implications of research. In a review of such implications for population data science, Jones and Ford [310] give the following recommendations for researchers:

1. understand and comply with all relevant data protection legislation and regulations,
2. select and operate a suitable framework to enable the safe use of data to be enacted and evaluated,
3. develop a suite of transparent policies and procedures with clear responsibilities and accountabilities,
4. provide clear and accessible information on how population data will be used,

5. work closely with data providers and respect their due diligence processes,
6. take public views into account, beyond the strict requirements of legislation, to promote inclusivity and social licence,
7. support researchers in understanding and complying with their responsibilities for good conduct with data,
8. enable the best-quality, most granular data to be used for research, without compromising privacy and security,
9. acknowledge problems as soon as they arise and correct them as soon as possible, and
10. learn from other initiatives and share good practices as an ongoing process to avoid ethical pitfalls.

We consider Point 6 as particular important. Just acting within limits given by the jurisdiction is not sufficient to prevent unfavourable media coverage of a project. Therefore, a clear public description of the procedures, usages, and advantages are essential for conducting a record linkage project. As the history of the Swedish Metropolitan project (see Section 1.6.4) has demonstrated, academic publications alone might not be sufficient to gain and maintain public support for a record linkage project that is based on sensitive databases.

If people decide rationally on their consent to share and link data, they will weigh the perceived benefits and risks resulting from consent. This idea of a privacy calculus is due to Laufer and Wolfe [379] (for early resulting research see Smith et al. [565]). Since the perception of scientific research as beneficial in general is not universal [19, 439], the main driver for public support of record linkage projects will be perceived risk.

Since the probability of privacy risks are difficult to estimate, trust in the institutions conducting research is a necessary condition for public support of data use [634]. Trust is the result of repeated demonstration of successful interactions causing no harm. Therefore, always acting according to the principles in guidelines for best practices and clearly demonstrating the lack of any harm and hopefully yielding common benefits from research will be the best policy to gain and maintain public support for linkage projects.

Getting individual consent or at least a social licence for research involving sensitive databases is essential, but not sufficient for a research project. Formal approval is needed. As mentioned before, the required processes are not clearly spelled out in many countries. To foster national record linkage projects covering multiple jurisdictions and organisations, the development of standard operating procedures for applying for a linkage, getting permissions and conducting the linkage is required [340]. The issues to be resolved are given by Moore et al. [422] as:

1. establishing the collaboration across national and state based linkage infrastructures,
2. standardising ethical application forms across multiple jurisdictions,

3. establishing a process for approval of the use of a database by a data custodian,
4. standardising application forms and nomenclature across record linkage centres, and
5. preparing comprehensive metadata on the databases available for linkage.

However, for a nationwide linkage project, two different approval documents are usually needed: A document stating that the record linkage project is of public interest and this interest will outweigh individual privacy concerns, and a second document stating that the use of the generated linked data set for a specific project is according to law. Currently, the process for applying for both kind of documents is not clearly spelt out and standardised in many jurisdictions. A recent report by the Organisation for Economic Cooperation and Development (OECD) on health governance concluded that, among other issues, international collaboration is needed to [445]:

• support countries in developing the norms necessary for governments to accredit data processors,
• develop guidance for the implementation of project approval bodies,
• support countries to evaluate which national legal frameworks for the protection of health information privacy provide adequate protections to facilitate multicountry statistical and research projects,
• review current practices in patient consent and in waivers to consent to reach a common understanding about mechanisms that are privacy protective, and
• review developments in data security risks and threats and mechanisms to address them.

This book aims to contribute to the last mentioned topic. The other topics will require international collaboration and interdisciplinary attempts to initiate legal processes for clear jurisdictions for research involving sensitive databases.

2.8 Summary and Further Reading

In this chapter we have discussed and reviewed regulatory frameworks in various countries as relevant to the topic of linking sensitive databases. As we have shown, different jurisdictions have vastly different approaches to regulate access, usage, and linking of sensitive databases. This has resulted in a variety of technical and organisational solutions for research on population covering databases.

The conceptual framework of privacy as control of information flow was introduced by Nissenbaum [440], while privacy problems resulting from the use of databases on populations are discussed by Elliot et al. [187]. Introductions to traditional techniques of statistical disclosure control are given by

O'Keefe and Rubin [454], Duncan et al. [173], and Templ [590]. Technical details on privacy engineering, including US privacy regulations and standards by the International Organization for Standardization (ISO), are described by Stallings [573]. Reviews of regulative frameworks for privacy problems of research data are given by the European Union Agency for Fundamental Rights [197], and by Dove and Phillips [169]. A comparative review of health data governance is given by the OECD [445].

Chapter 3
Linking Sensitive Data Background

Abstract This chapter covers background topics relevant to linking databases, with a focus on linking sensitive data. We first provide a short history of linking data, and then give an overview of the record linkage process with a flow chart and descriptions of the major steps involved when linking databases. We discuss aspects of data quality that can influence the outcomes of a linking process, and we highlight the importance of data preprocessing in any linkage application. Next, we present measures that can be used to evaluate the linkage process with regard to linkage quality and completeness, as well as complexity and scalability when linking large databases. Linking sensitive databases can involve a variety of challenges, which we discuss in this chapter. We then introduce the topic of privacy-preserving record linkage (PPRL), and provide a formal definition. We also contrast the general record linkage process with the PPRL process and describe the additional requirements of PPRL over traditional record linkage.

3.1 A Short History of Linking Data

The requirement in various domains to link databases is nothing new. This task has been considered by researchers and practitioners in a variety of domains for many decades. Even before electronic computers became ubiquitous in governments and businesses, there were applications where bringing individual pieces of data together would allow new insights that were not possible on individual sets of data. Early examples include census collections, where linking records by the same individuals or households over successive censuses, often collected ten years apart, would allow deeper understanding of changes in populations over time. Another illustrative example is shown in Figure 3.1, where employees of Transport for London were tasked on an annual basis to sort tickets to identify the patterns of travels by commuters,

© Springer Nature Switzerland AG 2020
P. Christen et al., *Linking Sensitive Data*, https://doi.org/10.1007/978-3-030-59706-1_3

Fig. 3.1 Women working for the London Underground (now Transport for London, TfL) in 1936 sorting through piles of tickets with the aim to conduct traffic analysis. This task can be seen as an early 'data science' project where information from disparate sources (underground stations) needed to be sorted and linked before traffic patterns could be analysed. © TfL from the London Transport Museum collection.

which would allow to better predict the expected number of passengers and thus improve train timetables and services.

In the context of the public health system, Percy Stocks in 1944 described the idea of record linkage to measure morbidity [579]:

> The ultimate aim is to keep for every individual a record of every event of health significance from the time of conception to death, and to establish a system by means of which a person does not cease to exist statistically when he removes to another administrative area.

Similarly, Halbert Dunn in 1946 described the idea of a 'book of life' for every individual in a population [175]. He also used the term record linkage to describe his idea of creating such books by linking records from birth, marriage, and death certificates, as well as records about individuals collected by the health and social security systems. Each such book would start with a birth and end with a death record. Because these diverse databases unlikely would have common unique identifiers for each person, the linkage would have to be based on comparing names, addresses, dates of birth, and other partially identifying information which are known as quasi-identifiers. As we discuss later in this chapter, this aspect of linking databases is still one of the biggest challenges today.

Dunn realised that having such books for a whole population can provide a wealth of information that is not available otherwise, and allow governments to improve the public health system, national statistics, and better plan services and allocation of funding. Dunn also realised that such books would help to identify individuals, and thus raise privacy concerns. Furthermore, Dunn acknowledged the challenges of dealing with very large volumes of data, as well as the various data quality issues posed by the characteristics and the changing nature of personal data, as well as variations and errors in the way personal data are recorded.

From the late 1950s onwards, Howard Newcombe and his team pioneered the use of electronic computers to automate the process of linking vital records to realise Dunn's idea [435, 436]. They also proposed the basic ideas of probabilistic record linkage, where larger numerical weights are given to those attributes that contain information that is more useful to distinguish and link records of individuals, as we describe in more detail below.

In 1969 the two statisticians Ivan Fellegi and Alan Sunter published their seminal paper on probabilistic record linkage [204] which formalised the ideas proposed by Newcombe and his colleagues. They proved that, under certain assumption, an optimal probabilistic decision rule can be found that minimises linkage errors. Their approach required to compare the values in the attributes available in common across the two databases to be linked, and it calculates for each such attribute a match weight based on the assumption that the attribute contains a certain amount of errors, as we describe in more detail in the side box on page 54. This probabilistic approach to linking databases as proposed by Fellegi and Sunter over fifty years ago is still widely used in application areas such as national statistics and the health domain.

Various extensions and improvements to the basic probabilistic record linkage approach have been developed in the past decades [274]. Among them, the perhaps most important was to incorporate approximate string comparison functions, which we discuss in detail in Section 6.8. A second improvement was to calculate frequency-based match weights, because it is more likely that two records with a rare surname refer to the same person versus two records with a common surname like 'Miller' or 'Smith' [478, 645]. Improved parameter estimation using a statistical technique known as expectation-maximisation (EM) has also led to improvements in linkage quality [642].

Since the mid nineties, with the advent of more mature database and storage technologies and the resulting increase in data being collected by businesses and governments, computer science researchers have investigated the topic of linking databases where there are no unique entity identifiers available. One first application was the detection and removal of duplicate records about the same customer in business databases. Such duplicates can lead to increased costs, for example advertisement mailouts, as well as reduced data quality [272, 491]. In contrast to the approaches developed by statisticians, computer scientists focused on the scalability of deduplicating or linking very large databases, as well as on using sophisticated string comparison functions to identify records about the same person even if these records contain (typographical) errors and variations [273, 420, 421].

The past twenty or so years have seen a massive increase in interest in methods and techniques to link databases in areas ranging from national security and crime and fraud detection, all the way to linking administrative databases for health and social science research. Much work has been conducted in the domain of computer science, where advancements in artificial intelligence (AI), and especially in statistical machine learning, have led to new types of linkage algorithms [107, 186]. While the majority of these

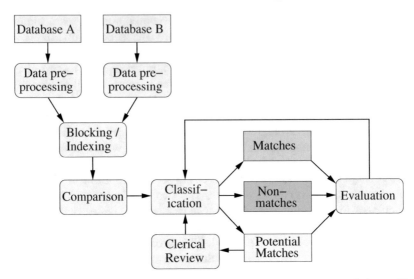

Fig. 3.2 The general process of linking two databases, as adapted from Christen [109]. The steps are described in Section 3.2.

novel approaches are still mainly based on calculating similarities between the attributes of records, such as the names, addresses, and dates of birth of individuals, more recent approaches have started to incorporate relationships between entities (such as the same address shared by several people who live in the same household), resulting in potentially much improved linkage quality at the costs of increased computational requirements [58, 167, 220, 315].

The increasingly large databases to be linked in today's Big data era have also led to novel techniques that make use of parallel and distributed computing systems [348, 353]. With the massive increase in storage of sensitive personal information by both businesses and governments in the past few decades, linking such sensitive or confidential databases has opened new challenges posed by privacy and confidentiality concerns and corresponding policies and regulations. Novel techniques have been developed, commonly known as privacy-preserving record linkage [253, 619] (to be introduced later in this chapter), that facilitate linking sensitive databases across organisations while protecting any sensitive or confidential data during the linkage process. We properly introduce this topic in Section 3.6 and cover many aspects of it in more detail in the remainder of this book.

3.2 The Process of Linking Records across Databases

The general process of linking records from two databases is shown Figure 3.2. Here we assume, without loss of generality, that we aim to identify which record in the first database (A) refers to the same real-world entity as a record in the second database (B). The same steps as we describe below are also applicable when a single database is to be deduplicated, i.e. where we aim to identify and link all records that refer to the same entity in a single database [432].

Data preprocessing: The first step in the linkage process is to preprocess the databases used for linkage. This step is also known as data cleaning, data cleansing, or data standardisation [109]. This is an important step to ensure the attribute values used to compare records in the following steps follow the same conventions, codes, formats, and have the same structure. The linking of records across databases is often based on the personal information available in quasi-identifying attributes, such as name and address details. Data quality issues when such information is being entered or recorded can therefore significantly affect the outcomes of a linkage project. We discuss data quality aspects in more detail in the following section.

Tasks involved in the data preprocessing step range from simple conversion of all letters into either all upper- or lowercase and removal of unwanted characters and white spaces, to complex data segmentation and parsing techniques where multivariate attribute values such as full addresses are split into their individual components. For example the full address '42 Miller Rd, 2000 Sydeny' would be parsed, split, and standardised such that the street number would be set to '42', the street name to 'miller', the street type to 'road' (based on a lookup table that converts street type abbreviations to full words), postcode to '2000', and where the city name would be corrected to 'sydney' [109, 126].

The output of the data preprocessing step are cleaned and standardised databases where each attribute contains a well-defined, cleaned and standardised piece of information about the entities in the databases to be linked.

Blocking and indexing: The second step of the linkage process deals with the quadratic comparison space when each record from one database would be compared with all records in the other database [110]. For example, assume we aim to link two databases containing 1,000,000 and 5,000,000 records, respectively. If each of the 1,000,000 records in the first database is compared with all records in the second database then a total of 5,000,000,000,000 (five trillion!) record pairs would have to be compared. At the same time, if we assume the input databases are deduplicated (each contains only one record per unique person), then a maximum of 1,000,000 record pairs can correspond to true matches (refer to the same person).

Blocking and indexing techniques aim to reduce this generally huge number of possible record pair comparisons through the use of algorithms and data structures that efficiently and with low computational costs generate sets of candidate record pairs that likely correspond to true matches. We note that the terminology for this step of the record linkage process differs across disciplines. Blocking is the term commonly used in disciplines where record linkage is applied, while it also refers to a very specific technique to reduce the number of record pairs that are to be compared [109, 274]. On the other hand, indexing in the context of record linkage is the more general term used by computer scientists to describe any technique that aims to make the record linkage process more scalable to large databases [110].

A large number of blocking and indexing techniques for linking databases have been developed over the past few decades [110, 461]. A most basic one, known as standard blocking, is to split the databases according to the values in a set of attributes, known as a blocking key or blocking criteria [110], and to insert all records that have the same blocking key value into one block. For example, if a postcode attribute is used as blocking key then all records that have the same postcode value will be inserted into one block, and thus only records with the same postcode value will be compared with each other in the next step of the linkage process.

Because of data quality issues, such as wrongly recorded attribute values, often several such blocking steps (or iterations) are conducted using different blocking keys to ensure true matches are inserted into the same block in at least one of these iterations.

We will discuss blocking and indexing in the context of linking sensitive databases in more detail in Chapter 10.

Comparison: In the third step of the linkage process, candidate record pairs are formed from all records that are in the same block, and these record pairs are then compared in more detail to find how similar their attribute values are. Given the majority of attributes used to compare records contain textual information, such as names and addresses, and the data quality issues already mentioned for such personal information, the exact comparison of such values in many situations is not sufficient to obtain high linkage quality. For example, 'christine' and 'christina' are highly similar names, however an exact (character by character) comparison would result in these two strings being seen as different. Therefore, so called string comparison functions need to be applied [109]. These functions generally return a numerical value of similarity, where 0 means the two compared strings are totally different, such as 'peter' and 'david', a similarity of 1 means they are the same, and a value between 0 and 1 means they are somewhat different, such as 'gail' and 'gayle'. Figure 3.3 shows some examples of such approximate comparisons.

Many such string comparison functions have been developed [109, 252, 308, 369, 433, 568, 654], some of those specifically aimed at personal (English) names [301, 642], while others are generic and can be applied on any type of strings [109]. For other types of data, such as dates or numbers, specific comparison functions that return similarities between 0 and 1 are also available [109]. We discuss comparison functions used as building blocks for linking sensitive databases in detail in Section 6.8.

In general, several attributes are compared for every candidate record pair that is generated from the blocking step. Each comparison of two attribute values of a record pair results in a similarity value between 0 and 1, thus forming a comparison vector for each compared record pair, as illustrated

RECID	FIRSTNAME	SURNAME	STRNUM	STRNAME	CITY	BIRTHYEAR
a1	kristine	smithers		main rd	brisbane	1968
b4	christina	smith	21	miller st	brisbane	1970
	0.82	0.91	0.0	0.67	1.0	0.5

RECID	FIRSTNAME	SURNAME	STRNUM	STRNAME	CITY	BIRTHYEAR
a6	joanne	fawkner	42	john st	dickson	1981
b2	john	faulker	42	st john st	dixon	1982
	0.82	0.87	1.0	0.8	0.85	0.75

Fig. 3.3 Two example comparison vectors calculated when different approximate string comparison functions are applied. For string attributes containing names and addresses, the shown similarities were calculated using the Jaro-Winkler [478] function, while edit distance [143] was employed for the birth year comparison.

in Figure 3.3. These vectors of similarities are then used in the next step to decide the match status of these record pairs.

Classification: In this step of the linkage process a decision model is used to decide if a pair of compared records is a match (the two records are assumed to correspond to the same real-world entity), a non-match (the two records are assumed to refer to two different entities), or (depending upon the decision model used [243]) a potential match (where the model cannot make a clear decision). The latter class can include, for example, a pair of records where the names and dates of birth are the same but the address values are different, and it is therefore unclear if these two records refer to the same person or not. Pairs of records in this class of potential matches therefore need to be manually classified in the clerical review step as we describe below.

Different types of classification techniques have been developed over the past few decades. The most simple type are classifiers based on a similarity threshold, where for each compared record pair the similarities in its comparison vector are summed, and if this sum is above a certain threshold then the pair is classified as a match, otherwise as a non-match. The traditional probabilistic record linkage technique developed by Fellegi and Sunter [127, 204, 274, 532] is a variation of this threshold-based approach, where match weights are calculated for different attributes as we describe in more detail in the side box on page 54.

While statisticians have focused on classification techniques that assume a certain underlying distribution of matches and corresponding probability models [216, 274, 525], computer scientists have either employed clustering or supervised classification techniques. Clustering techniques solve the record linkage problem by grouping (clustering) all records that correspond to the same entity into one cluster, such that ideally each entity is represented by one such cluster [269]. Clustering techniques are generally unsupervised methods that do not require ground truth or training data in the form of true matches

Probabilistic record linkage weight calculation

When linking databases, the lack of entity identifiers requires records to be compared based on their commonly available attributes. These attributes are often personal details such as names, addresses, and dates of birth. Such values can however be recorded wrongly, contain variations, be out of date, or even be missing. Because the number of unique values and their distributions can vary across attributes, different weights should be assigned to different attributes. These weights should reflect the importance of an attribute when deciding if two records refer to the same person or not. For example, two records with the same postcode value are less likely to refer to the same person compared to two records that both have the same rare surname, such as 'Ranbaduge'.

Fellegi and Sunter [204] formalised this idea by calculating such match weights. They proved that under certain assumptions their approach leads to an optimal decision function when record pairs are classified into matches, non-matches, and potential matches based on the sum of the calculated attribute match weights and two thresholds. Their basic idea was to calculate a match (also known as agreement) and a non-match (also known as disagreement) weight, w_a and w_d, for each attribute based on the likelihood that two agreeing attribute values do refer to the same or to different entities, and similarly the likelihood that two disagreeing attribute values do refer to the same or to different entities [643].

For example, assume two databases contain a MONTHOFBIRTH attribute [109], with twelve values 'Jan' to 'Dec' equally common. Assume we also know that 5% of all records in these two databases have a wrong month of birth value. Now assume we have two randomly picked records, one from each database, where we know they are a true match and refer to the same person. The likelihood that both records have the same month of birth value is 0.95 because of the 5% error. We call this the m-probability, with $m = 0.95$. Conversely, with a 0.05 likelihood the two records have different months of birth values, where $1 - m = 0.05$. Now assume we have again two randomly picked records, one from each database, where we know they refer to two different people. The likelihood these two records have the same month of birth value is $1/12$ if we do not consider the 5% error rate. We call this the u probability, with $u = 1/12 = 0.083$. The likelihood that these two records have a different month of birth value is $11/12$, with $1 - u = 0.917$.

Using these probabilities, we can calculate the match weight for this attribute as $w_a = log_2(m/u) = log_2(0.95/0.083) = 3.511$, while the non-match weight is calculated as $w_d = log_2((1-m)/(1-u)) = log_2(0.05/0.917) = -4.196$. As a result, a candidate pair to be compared where both records have the same month of birth value will be assigned the weight 3.511, while a pair with different months of birth values will be assigned the weight -4.196.

and true non-matches. Rather they use the similarities calculated between records to group similar records together.

Supervised techniques, on the other hand, do require ground truth data (also known as training data or gold standard data) of known true matches and true non-matches which allow a classification model to be learned from the characteristics of these examples. Many well known machine learning based supervised classification techniques, such as decision trees [130, 186] or support vector machines [62, 107], have been employed in the context of linking databases for classifying record pairs. Generally supervised techniques are able to outperform unsupervised techniques with regard to the linkage quality they achieve [361].

To overcome the problem of lack of ground truth data in many applications where databases are to be linked, the topic of active learning [557] has attracted significant interest in the domain of linking sensitive databases for many years [530, 589]. The idea of active learning is to include human domain expertise into the classification process, by providing selected examples (of difficult to classify record pairs) that are most useful for improving the quality of a ground truth data set used to train a supervised classifier. Over several iterations, a sequence of classifiers is built, each better than the previous one, and a larger and more representative ground truth data set is created in this process [25, 48]. In experimental evaluations it has been shown that with even a few hundred manual evaluations of difficult to classify record pairs such techniques are able to achieve linkage quality comparable to fully supervised methods [122, 124].

The majority of classification techniques classifies each compared record pair as a match or a non-match independently from all other compared pairs. This can result in a violation of the transitive closure (or transitivity) property [109], as we discuss in more detail in the side box on page 56. Clustering techniques deal with this challenge of transitivity directly by solving the transitive closure through grouping all records that are assumed to refer to the same entity into one cluster.

The last decade has seen the development of a novel type of classification technique for record linkage known as collective entity resolution [58]. These techniques not only take attribute similarities into account when making decisions about which record pairs (or groups) should be classified as matches, but they also consider relationships between entities. For example, in bibliographic databases where the aim is to find all publications by the same author, one can take co-author relationships as well as common publication venues into account [167, 315]. While such novel classification techniques have shown promising results in certain application domains, their more expensive computational requirements [511] and the possible lack of relationship information in the databases to be linked have so far limited their use in practical real-world linkage applications.

Clerical Review: For the record pairs classified as potential matches, as illustrated in Figure 3.2, a manual clerical review process is often used to decide their final match status (match or non-match). In this process, record pairs are individually assessed by human experts who might have access to additional data (such as previous linked databases or external resources) to support their manual decision making.

For large databases that lead to many potential matches this process can become time consuming and expensive because ideally domain experts, that

---

Link constraints and transitive closure

The classification of individual record pairs into matches and non-matches is often not the final outcome of a record linkage project. Depending upon the application and characteristics of the databases being linked (if they are known to contain duplicates – more than one record per entity – or not), the final linkage outcome might only allow one-to-one links, where a record from one input database can be linked to a maximum of one record from the other database. One-to-many and many-to-one link constraints allow a record from the first database to be linked to multiple records of the second input database, or vice versa. Many-to-many linkages, finally, have no such link constraints. To obtain one-to-one and one-to-many (or many-to-one) links, either a greedy approach (taking the best links with highest similarities first) or optimisation algorithms that find an overall optimal one-to-one assignment solution that maximises the number and quality of matches that can be obtained, need to be applied [109].

In the case of one-to-many (many-to-one) link constraints, and for many-to-many linkages, if a classifier was used where each record pair is classified as a match or a non-match individually from all other pairs, then the transitive closure might be violated. Using the example in the above figure, if the record pair (r1,r2) was classified as a match (assumed to refer to the same entity), and the pair (r2,r3) was also classified a match, then the pair (r1,r3) must also be a match, even if it was classified as a non-match or never compared because r1 and r3 were never included in the same block. Similar problems hold for the pairs (r1,r4) and (r2,r4).

As can also be seen from this figure, the classification of individual record pairs can also lead to chains of matches, and such chains need to be processed (broken) in some way to obtain a linkage result that fulfils any link constraints and that does not violate transitivity [170, 432].

---

are familiar with the characteristics of the data and their possible quality issues, need to be employed to make accurate decisions.

Evaluation: In this final step of the linkage process, the obtained linkage results, pairs of compared records classified as matches or non-matches, are assessed with regard to their quality as well as completeness. Ideally, the set of linked record pairs (classified matches) should be highly accurate and include as many true matches as possible. Furthermore, the complexity of the linkage process can also be evaluated with regard to how many candidate record pairs as generated in the blocking step were compared, as well as how much time and resources (memory and disk space) were required to conduct a linkage project. We discuss this topic in more detail and present commonly used evaluation measures in Section 3.4.

3.3 Data Quality Aspects Relevant to Linking Databases

One commonly occurring challenge when linking databases is the lack of common unique identifiers across the databases to be linked. Therefore, records need to be compared based on the attributes that are available in all these databases. If these records are about people, then personal details such as their names, addresses, telephone numbers, dates of birth, and so on, can be compared. However, the values in such attributes are not always of high quality for a variety of reasons, including misspellings of names, out of date addresses, or missing values [109]. Such data quality aspects can make linking databases a challenging endeavour [643].

Many real-world databases in diverse application domains contain noisy, inconsistent, and missing data [45, 484]. It is generally accepted that 'dirty data' of poor quality costs governments and businesses billions in lost revenue, extra required efforts, or wrong decision making [384]. The 'garbage-in garbage-out' principle holds for most types of data processing and analysis, because low input data quality will unlikely lead to high quality outcomes.

There are various approaches to formalise and assess data quality. A first approach is to recognise there are different dimensions to data quality that can be measured. We now briefly review those data quality dimensions relevant to linking databases [45, 109, 384]:

- **Accuracy**: How accurate are the attribute values used for linking? Is it known how data was entered or recorded? Were checks and validation performed on the data?

- **Validity**: Do the attribute values conform to constraints, rules, and limits of their domain? For example, are (human) age values between 0 and say 120 years, or do all date of birth values in a database have a valid month value (January to December). Note that validity is different from accuracy, as an attribute value can be valid but not accurate with regard to the true real-world value it reflects.

- **Completeness**: How complete are the attribute values used for linking? How many records have missing data values? Which quasi-identifying attributes used for a linkage do have missing data values?

- **Consistency**: How consistent are the values within a single database in the attributes used for linking, for example with regard to formats and structure; and how consistent are these values across the two or more databases to be linked?

- **Timeliness**: When were the attribute values used for linking collected or last updated? Were they updated at the same time in all databases? If not then aspects such as people changing their addresses or names can become problematic and result in lower linkage quality [287, 392, 496].

- **Accessibility**: Are the attributes required for linking available in all the databases to be linked? Are there enough attributes to allow detailed comparisons (to distinguish entities from each other) and accurate classification?

- **Believability**: Can the attribute values in the databases to be linked be regarded as credible and true? Or is it possible that values are wrong or impossible? Have they been faked or do inappropriate values occur?

An assessment of these data quality dimensions will allow a better understanding of potential challenges when linking databases, improved selection of the attributes used for linking (especially in the blocking and comparison steps described above), and a corresponding suitable selection of appropriate techniques for each step of the linkage process.

There are many different causes that can lead to poor data quality [384], where some of them can be specific to certain applications and/or types of data. The causes relevant to linking databases include that [109]:

- the databases to be linked come from different organisations;
- different formats and encodings are used across these databases, a problem especially prevalent if different software systems have been used for the collection and storage of data;
- input rules and constraints used during data entry have been bypassed;
- the databases have been recorded at different points in time;
- due to some subjective judgement not enough detailed information has been stored to allow accurate linking;
- security or confidentiality restrictions might mean not all relevant and required data will be available for a linkage;
- data are stored in complex representations which make it difficult to extract the information required for linking;
- the volume of data makes it impractical, given operational and time constraints, to employ certain linkage techniques which would be best suited to achieve high linkage quality; and
- data needs and thus what was stored in a database have changed over time.

Given many linkage projects rely upon personal identifying information for linking data, such as the names and addresses of people, data quality aspects specific to personal data are highly crucial for good quality linkage results. However, personal identifying information has some unique characteristics that are different from most other types of data, and these can lead to challenges in the linkage process [643].

- Unlike for normal words in many languages (where there is only one correct spelling for a word), there are often several variations for what is commonly seen as the same personal name. For example, 'Gail', 'Gayle', and 'Gael' are all valid first names that are pronounced very similarly, and Table 3.1 shows twenty variations of 'Abigail', the full version of this name.

Table 3.1 Twenty name variations of 'Abigail' (the most commonly occurring version), as reported by the Oxford Record Linkage Study in 1999 [226].

Abagayle	Abbeygale	Abbigale	Abbygel	Abiaguil
Abaigeal	Abbiegale	Abbygail	Abbygieal	Abiegail
Abbegail	Abbie-Gayle	Abbygale	Abegail	Abigael
Abbeygail	Abbigail	Abbygayle	Abegale	Abigail

- In daily life, individuals often use or are given nicknames, such as a shortened version of their proper first name (for example 'Bob' for 'Robert' or 'Tash' for 'Natasha').
- Names are language and culture specific [467], with different name formats and structures used across the world. Examples are name pre- or suffixes, like 'Jr' or 'Snr', or compound names such as 'Taylor-Thomas'.
- Individuals can change their names over time, which most commonly occurs when somebody gets married or divorced. In some countries it is also possible to legally change ones own name.
- Name transliterations from one language into another often do not have a single correct translated version but rather multiple transliterations are possible [467].
- In many countries and languages, some names, both given and surnames, occur very common while many others are very rare and might occur only once even in a large database covering a full population. As a result, linkage methods need to consider these frequencies, as discussed in the previous section, because common names make it less likely than rare names that two records with the same name refer to the same individual.

These issues make linking data based on personal information highly challenging, because the name values for the same person might differ across two databases. In our increasingly multicultural world where people are more mobile than ever before, where international travels, global businesses and living abroad are common, suitable standardisation of personal identifying information becomes crucial [109].

The way data are being entered or recorded can also influence data quality. When data are manually entered (typed), then typographical errors are not uncommon, especially in name and address values, because a spell check is potentially not of much use. Various studies have been conducted to analyse the types and distributions of errors and variations introduced by manual data entry processes [143, 252, 369, 477]. Some of these studies found that errors in names often occur around the middle and second half of longer names, while other studies identified that shortened or abbreviated values are the most common errors. An early study on spelling errors in general words found that over 80% of errors were single character errors [143], such as an insert or a delete of a character (like 'accross' into 'across' and vice versa), or a character substitution (like 'vest' into 'best').

Different types of errors or variations are introduced when data are being entered based on somebody listening to a spoken name or address (for
example over the telephone or from a recording) [109]. This will, besides possible typing errors, also lead to phonetic mistakes from mishearing a name
or simply assuming a certain name spelling (as in the above example, a person might assume the potentially more common name 'Gail' rather than
'Gayle'). A third type of common mistakes comes from digitising (scanning)
and automatic character recognition techniques, commonly known as optical
character recognition (OCR). The types of mistakes most commonly to occur
when handwritten words are processed using OCR are substitutions of similar looking characters such as 'g' and 'q' or 'S' and '5', or the replacement
of a single with two characters such as 'm' with 'r n' or 'b' with 'l i', or the
other way round [252, 477].

While personal identifying details are crucial pieces of information for
many record linkage applications, their specific data quality characteristics
can make them challenging to use. We discuss the practical considerations
related to data issues in more detail in Chapter 11.

Furthermore, such data are commonly seen as sensitive personal data and
protected by privacy or confidentiality regulations. This might mean such
data are not accessible for a linkage application, and instead anonymised
data need to be used for linking, as we discuss in Section 3.6.

3.4 Evaluation Measures

The linkage process and its outcomes can be evaluated along three main
aspects: (1) linkage quality and completeness, (2) linkage complexity and
scalability, and (3) privacy protection (only for those techniques that provide
privacy-preserving linkages, as we discuss in Section 3.6). In the following
we only consider the first two aspects, while the third, privacy evaluation
measures, will be covered in detail in Section 5.2.

3.4.1 Linkage Quality Measures

In order to be able to evaluate the quality of a linkage outcome, ground
truth data in the form of true matching and true non-matching record pairs
are required [109]. The requirement of such ground truth data is similar to
the evaluation of supervised classifiers in many other domains, ranging from
machine learning and fraud detection to medical studies [257].

In the context of linking data, if we assume the final classification of the
compared record pairs into the class of matches (two records are assumed
to refer to the same entity) and non-matches (two records are assumed to

Fig. 3.4 Example illustration of the classification outcomes for record linkage [109]. As discussed in Section 3.4, TP refers to true positives, FP to false positives, TN to true negatives, and FN to false negatives. © Springer-Verlag Berlin Heidelberg 2012, reprinted with permission.

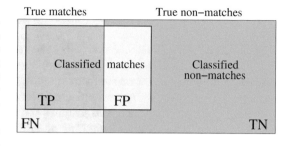

		Classified classes	
		Matches	Non-matches
True	Matches	True Positives (true matches)	False Negatives (false non-matches)
classes	Non-Matches	False Positives (false matches)	True Negatives (true non-matches)

Fig. 3.5 Error or confusion matrix illustrating the outcomes of a record linkage classification [109], as discussed in Section 3.4. © Springer-Verlag Berlin Heidelberg 2012, reprinted with permission.

refer to different entities), and assuming we have a set of ground truth record pairs in the form of true matches and true non-matches available, then the following four classification outcomes are possible [109, 260]:

- **True Positives** (TP): These are the compared record pairs that have been classified as matches and that are true matches.
- **False Positives** (FP): These are the compared record pairs that have been classified as matches, but they are not true matches. For these pairs the classifier has made a wrong decision. These pairs are also known as false matches.
- **True Negatives** (TN): These are the compared record pairs that have been classified as non-matches, and they are true non-matches.
- **False Negatives** (FN): These are the compared record pairs that have been classified as non-matches, but they are actually true matches. For these pairs the classifier has made a wrong decision. These pairs are also known as false non-matches or missed matches.

It is important to note that we are evaluating links between records. While this is valid in situations where individual records are linked across databases, once we are interested in linking groups of records (for example all individuals living in a household, all births of children by the same parents, or all publications by the same author), then evaluating links can become ambiguous in some situations [426]. Rather, assessing the quality of the linked groups (clusters) becomes more meaningful. We discuss this issue in more detail in Section 3.4.2.

In Figure 3.4 we illustrate how this space of compared record pairs is split into these four outcomes, and in Figure 3.5 we show the four outcomes using the commonly used error or confusion matrix [109, 260]. The overall objective of any classification for record linkage is to correctly classify as many true matches (TP) as possible while keeping the number of false matches (FP) and missed matches (FN) as small as possible.

Based on the four counts of TP, TN, FP, and FN, it is now possible to calculate a variety of single number measures. The ones most commonly used for evaluating record linkage are [109]:

- **Accuracy**: This linkage quality measure considers both true matches as well as true non-matches and is calculated as $A = \frac{TP+TN}{TP+FP+TN+FN}$. While this measure is widely used for classification problems in machine learning and data mining [254], when linking databases the class imbalance of having many more true non-matches versus true matches (due to the quadratic comparison space we described in Section 3.2) makes this measure unsuitable for evaluating the linking of databases. It is easy to obtain very high accuracy results by simply classifying all compared record pairs as non-matches, however this would not be a good outcome for most linkage projects [109].

- **Precision**: This is a quality measure commonly used in information retrieval to assess the quality of (Web) search results [647], and increasingly also in the context of linking databases. It is calculated as $P = \frac{TP}{TP+FP}$. Precision measures how many of the classified matches are in fact true matches. Because it does not consider the number of true non-matches (TN), it does not suffer from the class imbalance problem in the way accuracy does. In the medical domain precision is known as the positive predictive value (PPV) [65].

  Note that precision measures only one aspect of the quality of classified matches. It is possible to get a very high precision by for example setting a classification threshold very high. This means only record pairs with very high similarities are classified as matches. While high precision is achieved with such a setting, recall (discussed next) will likely be very low with this setting.

- **Recall**: This is a second quality measure commonly used in information retrieval, often in combination with precision [647]. It is calculated as $R = \frac{TP}{TP+FN}$. Recall measures how many of the true matches are correctly classified as matches. It also does not include the number of true non-matches. In the medical domain recall is known as the true positive rate, hit rate, or as sensitivity [663], and it is commonly used to assess the results of epidemiological studies.

  As with precision, it is possible to achieve a very high recall value by for example setting a classification threshold very low. This means almost all compared record pairs, even those with low similarities, are classified as matches. While high recall is obtained with such a setting, precision will likely be very low with this setting.

It is important to note that there is a trade-off between precision and recall. Many classifier techniques, as discussed in Section 3.2 above, allow parameters to be set that influence the classification outcomes. For example, a similarity threshold can be lowered or increased resulting in different numbers of record pairs being classified as matches or non-matches, respectively. When the threshold is lowered, then more record pairs are classified as matches, and the number of true matches (TP) normally increases but so does the number of false matches (FP), while at the same time the number of true non-matches (TN) and false non-matches (FN) decreases. Increasing a similarity threshold leads to opposite changes.

From a practical perspective, it is therefore often possible to either obtain a linkage result with higher precision but lower recall, or the other way round. However, it is often not possible to obtain a very high value for both precision and recall [109]. Depending upon the objective of a linkage project, and what follow-up analysis or processing will be done on the linked data set, a user has to decide on suitable classifier parameter settings to obtain the desired linkage results.

- **F-measure**: This quality measure combines precision and recall into one single number using their harmonic mean, calculated as $F = \frac{2 \cdot P \cdot R}{P+R} = \frac{2TP}{FP+FN+2TP}$. It is a type of averaging that is only high if both precision and recall are high, and is therefore often used to obtain a compromise linkage solution in those cases where precision and recall are both seen to be of equal importance.

  While the F-measure is commonly used in research studies to compare different linkage methods and techniques (for example in comparative evaluations of novel linkage algorithms [361]), recent research has identified a fundamental problem with the F-measure when used in such situations [260]. A simple mathematical transformation shows that the harmonic mean of precision, P, and recall, R, can be reformulated as an arithmetic mean:

$$F = \frac{2TP}{FP + FN + 2TP} = wR + (1-w)P, \quad \text{where } w = \frac{FN + TP}{FP + FN + 2TP}. \quad (3.1)$$

The weight w given to recall (and weight $1 - w$ given to precision) can however not be selected by a user based on their desire to assign different importance to recall and precision. Rather, as the above equation shows, the weights given to recall and precision depend upon the numbers of classified matches. As a result, when comparing two record linkage classification algorithms on the same databases (and therefore the same number of true matches), where one of these has classified, for example,

50, 000 record pairs as matches while the other has classified 80, 000 pairs as matches, then the comparison of their corresponding F-measure values is not valid because precision and recall will be weighted differently [260].

All of the above presented measures assume that the costs for a linked record pair and a non-linked record pair, both either true or false, are the same. In many practical applications this is however not the case. False matches (FP) and false non-matches (FN), especially, will have different costs associated with them depending upon how the linked data will be used. Imagine, for example, that two health databases are to be linked with the objective to identify potential cancer patients based on their medical history and to invite them for early cancer screening. A true match would in this case be a patient invited to take a cancer test (which might be costly) who actually is developing cancer, while a false match is a patient invited for screening who is not developing cancer (and thus the costs for the test for this patient could be seen as wasted). A missed match, on the other hand, would mean a person who is developing cancer is not invited for screening and therefore might develop cancer and ultimately die from this disease. Incorporating costs into the linkage classification step can therefore help to obtain cost optimal linkage results [625].

In this section we have discussed numerical quality measures that are based on the numbers of true and false matches, false non-matches, and potentially true non-matches, as shown in the error matrix in Figure 3.5. These measures do not take the actual application into account where a linked data set is being used, such as for further analysis in a research study.

Recent work by Doidge and Harron [159] has investigated linkage quality in the context of how false matches and false non-matches can bias and influence the outcomes of research studies that are based on a linked data set. The authors present eleven linkage structures of how a linked data set relates to the two source databases being linked (for example as the intersection or overlap of the two source databases). Each of these structures can introduce different types of bias and thus lead to various implications that an analyst who works with a linked data set needs to be aware of.

3.4.2 Group Linkage Quality Measures

Randall et al. [504] explored how graph measures can be used to identify the quality of linked groups of records in cases where one-to-many, many-to-one, and many-to-many links are possible (as we discussed in the side box on page 56). Three graph measures were explored: (1) completeness, calculated as the number of edges in a graph out of the total number of possible edges that connect each pair of nodes in the graph; (2) the diameter of a graph calculated as the largest distance between two nodes in the graph (where the distance between two nodes is the smallest number of edges that have to be traversed to reach one node from the other); and (3) bridges, which are edges that if removed would split a graph in two not connected subgraphs.

The hypothesis explored by Randall et al. [504] is that the more densely connected a graph that represents a group of records is (the more classified matches – edges – there are between the records in a group), the less likely the group contains wrongly matched records. Similarly, in such a graph the diameter and if the graph contains a bridge can be used as measures to assess the quality of groups of linked records. Experiments on large real health databases showed that such graph measures are highly precise in identifying wrongly matched records in groups [504]. However, in these experiments many groups only contained two records or they were fully connected graphs, and graph measures were not able to identify wrong matches in such groups.

While the discussion so far has considered a link-based evaluation of linkage quality of individual classified record pairs (classified links), in the context of linking groups of records traditional measures such as precision and recall can become ambiguous. Recent work by Nanayakkara et al. [426] has shown that it is possible to get different linkage outcomes in the form of different groupings (or clustering) of records that have exactly the same precision and recall result. However, some of these groupings might have larger clusters of linked records while others have smaller clusters, where the quality of these clusters will be different. Depending upon the final usage of a linked data set, it can be more important to understand the quality of the obtained clusters rather than the quality of individual linked record pairs.

For example, assume a group of five records where four of these are members of the same household and linked correctly, while the fifth record is wrongly included in the group. There are ten linked record pairs in such a group of five records, $(5 \cdot 4)/2$, and in this example four of these links are false matches and only six are correct matches, $(4 \cdot 3)/2$. This results in a precision of 0.6 for this group of records, and if we assume no other true matching record was missed then the group has a recall of 1.0. This low precision however does hide the fact that four out of five records in this group were linked correctly, potentially providing useful information about this household.

Instead of using precision and recall to measure the quality of group record linkage outcomes, Nanayakkara et al. [426] developed an approach where groups of linked records are classified into seven categories based on their true link / group status and their classified / predicted link status:

1. **Correct singletons**: Records that are singletons (not linked to any other record) in both the ground truth data and the predicted groups.
2. **Wrongly grouped singletons**: Records which appear as singletons in the ground truth data but that were wrongly assigned to a group of records in the prediction.
3. **Missed group members**: Records which are part of a group in the ground truth data but that were wrongly classified as a singleton (have no link to any other records) in the prediction.

4. **Exact group matches**: Groups of more than one record that are exactly the same in the ground truth data and in the prediction.

5. **Majority group matches**: Predicted groups (more than one record) where at least half of their records come from the same group in the ground truth data.

6. **Minority group matches**: Predicted groups (more than one record) where less than half of their records come from the same group in the ground truth data.

7. **Wrongly assigned members**: Records in a predicted group (more than one record) that are in a different group in the ground truth data.

Assigning records to these seven categories is a more complex process than simply counting the quality of individual links for the error or confusion matrix shown in Figure 3.5, because each record in a predicted group can only be assigned to one ground truth group. Specifically, for groups consisting of more than one record that are not exact group matches, one needs to map between ground truth and predicted groups such that the best prediction for a ground truth group is identified. While calculating these group based linkage quality measures, therefore, requires more effort, in a set of experiments on real data, Nanayakkara et al. [426] showed that the proposed seven categories can provide more detailed and unambiguous results compared to link-based measures such as precision and recall.

3.4.3 Linkage Complexity Measures

While linkage quality is arguable the most important aspect of a linkage project with regard to the obtained linked data set, being able to assess the complexity of a linkage process is also important. Especially as the databases to be linked are becoming larger, certain linkage techniques, such as specific blocking, comparison, or classification methods, might not be applicable given the operational requirements of an organisation, such as their available computing equipment or the available time to conduct a linkage.

One way to evaluate the complexity and scalability of a linkage process is to measure the resources required, such as time, memory, and disk space (storage) use, when linking two databases. Such an evaluation is however dependent upon the computing platform used, and therefore not easily comparable with other linkage applications.

The opposite of such a practical approach to evaluate linkage complexity is to theoretically assess the computational (and potentially communication) complexity [356] of the algorithms employed to link databases. In the domain of computer science, such a theoretical complexity analysis is commonly done using the Big-O notation, as we describe in the side box on page 68. Such an analysis however only provides information about general behaviour of an algorithm, for example if its runtime scales linearly or quadratic as the sizes of the databases to be linked increase.

A better way to evaluate linkage complexity is based on the number of candidate record pairs generated in the blocking / indexing step as described in Section 3.2 above, as well as their quality. In order to do so, let us define the total number of matched and non-matched record pairs that can be generated from two databases as n_M and n_N, respectively, where $n_M + n_N = m \cdot n$, and where m and n are the numbers of records in the two databases to be linked [109]. For the deduplication of a single database containing m records, $n_M + n_N = m(m-1)/2$. Now assuming some form or blocking or indexing has been applied, where s_M and s_N are the numbers of true matching and true non-matching candidate record pairs generated by the blocking or indexing technique. Generally, it holds that $(s_M + s_N) \ll (n_M + n_N)$, which means the total number of candidate record pairs is much smaller than the number of all possible record pairs. We can now define three linkage complexity measures [109]:

- **Reduction ratio**: This complexity measure corresponds to the ratio of candidate record pairs from blocking / indexing versus all possible record pairs and is calculated as $RR = 1 - \left(\frac{s_M + s_N}{n_M + n_N} \right)$. A high reduction ratio means a blocking or indexing technique has removed many record pairs. It is important to understand that reduction ratio does not take the quality of these candidate record pairs into account.

- **Pairs completeness**: This complexity measure also considers the true match status of candidate record pairs and is calculated as $PC = \frac{s_M}{n_M}$. Pairs completeness corresponds to recall as discussed before, and it measures the number of true matching candidate record pairs generated by blocking or indexing over all true matching pairs across the two databases being linked. A lower pairs completeness value means more true matching record pairs have been removed by an indexing or blocking technique, leading to lower linkage quality [109].

- **Pairs quality**: This third complexity measure also considers the true match status of candidate record pairs and is calculated as $PQ = \frac{s_M}{s_M + s_N}$. Pairs quality corresponds to precision as discussed before, and it measures the number of true matching candidate record pairs generated in blocking or indexing over the total number of candidate record pairs generated.

As with the trade-off between precision and recall discussed above, there is a similar trade-off between pairs completeness and pairs quality. However, ideally an indexing or blocking technique should result in a high pairs completeness value rather than a high pairs quality value. A low pairs quality value means the candidate record pairs generated in indexing / blocking contain potentially many false matches. These are however compared in detail and then classified in the comparison and classification steps of the linkage process. A low pairs completeness value, on the other hand, means potentially many true matching record pairs are already removed in the indexing

Computational complexity analysis using Big-O notation

In computer science, the complexity of algorithms, with regard to how much runtime or memory space they require, is commonly assessed using the Big-O notation [356][a]. The basic idea is to consider the behaviour (the asymptotic upper bound) of an algorithm as the input size grows.

For example, an algorithm which as input has a list of numbers and it always returns the first element of that list has a runtime complexity that is independent of the size of the input list. Taking the first element in the list can be performed in one computational step that does not depend upon the length (number of elements) of the list. On the other hand, finding and returning the maximum element of a list has a linear complexity in the length of the list, if we assume the list is not sorted. This is because the second algorithm needs to check every element in the list, and compare it with the so far found maximum value.

When using the Big-O notation, we would say that the first algorithm, returning the first element in a list, is of $O(1)$ (constant) time complexity because its runtime is independent of the size of the input, while the second algorithm has a $O(n)$ (linear) time complexity which means its runtime grows no faster than linearly with the increase of the input size.

A formal mathematical definition of the Big-O notation can be given as follows [36]. Assuming f and g are two functions and x their input, then $f(x) = O(g(x))$ means that $\exists c \ \forall x \ |f(x)| \leq c \cdot |g(x)|$, where c is a constant positive value and $x \to \infty$. In words, the growth rate of $f(x)$ is always smaller than the growth rate of $g(x)$. The $O()$ is therefore a worst-case upper limit, as it provides an upper bound on the growth rate of the function f.

An important aspect is that constant values are not considered when calculating the computational complexity. For example, the three functions $f_1(x) = x^2 + 10x$, $f_2(x) = 5x^2 + 999,999$, and $f_3(x) = 100x^2$ all have a quadratic complexity of $O(n^2)$ because as x gets larger and larger the results of these three functions are dominated by the x^2 factor.

The most common classes of complexities according to the Big-O notation form a hierarchy which is: $O(1)$ for constant, $O(log(n))$ for logarithmic, $O(n)$ for linear, $O(n \, log(n))$ for log-linear, $O(n^2)$ for quadratic, $O(n^3)$ for cubic, $O(n^c)$ for polynomial, $O(c^n)$ for exponential, with $c > 1$, and $O(n!)$ for factorial. In practice, any algorithm that has a higher than linear complexity, i.e. has a complexity of $O(n \, log(n))$ or more, can potentially become problematic if the input sizes, such as the numbers of records in the databases to be linked, become larger.

---

[a] For an easy accessible introduction see: https://rob-bell.net/2009/06/a-beginners-guide-to-big-o-notation/

/ blocking step and therefore they cannot be compared in the comparison step. These pairs are implicitly classified as non-matches, thereby resulting in a lower final linkage quality.

3.5 Major Challenges to Linking Data

Even though linking databases has a long history, this topic is far from being solved with new challenges posed by the Big data era we are now living in, as well as new privacy and confidentiality regulations and policies [112]. The following list describes the main issues that have been and still are making linking databases a challenging undertaking for many real-world applications. Research is being conducted to address many of these challenges.

- **Scalability to linking large databases**: With the increase in automated data collection and online services in both the private and public sectors, many organisations now hold databases that potentially cover a large portion of a population in a country or even worldwide. Therefore, databases with records about many millions or even billions of individuals are now not unusual. Novel indexing and blocking techniques, as well as parallel and distributed algorithms, are therefore required to make the linkage of such large databases possible.

- **Linking data from many sources**: While in the past a linkage was often conducted on only two databases, today applications increasingly require that information from multiple, potentially many, sources need to be integrated. For example, imagine a research project that aims to identify all patients who have visited hospitals in several regions in a country over the past ten years in order to find temporal and spatial patterns of diseases. Such a project would have to identify records for the same patient that match across subsets of a large number of hospital databases.

- **Linking heterogeneous data**: Automated data collection means that records about entities not just contain traditional information such as textual and numerical details for example of the health or financial affairs of individuals, but increasingly also social network data, multimedia files such as images and videos, as well as geotagged information (for example locations attached to images) or even location traces from smartphones. Traditional techniques that assume mainly textual data are being used for linkage (such as names and addresses) are not suitable for such new types of data, and novel methods and algorithms that can deal with new types of data need to be developed for all steps of the linkage process.

- **Linking data of low quality and with missing values**: While automated data collection and online services will allow improved quality checks when data are being entered or recorded, they might also lead to intentionally misleading or missing information. In a Web form, for example, individuals might decide to enter false or faked values if they do not want to reveal personal information but a field is set as mandatory. Invalid telephone numbers in the form of '01-2345-6789' or '99-9999-9999' might occur in a database but these should not be used for linking. Similarly, missing values might occur if people choose not to provide details, or if databases with different schemas (different sets of attributes) are being compared, resulting in a limited set of useful common quasi-identifying attributes that can be compared. Furthermore, if historical data are to be linked then data quality issues such as typing errors, OCR mistakes, or phonetic errors might occur as we discussed in Section 3.3. All these different data quality issues require specific methods and techniques in order to achieve high linkage quality. We discuss this challenge further in Section 11.2 within the context of linking sensitive data.

- **Linking dynamic and temporal data**: Many organisations today are collecting, processing and analysing data in (near) real time as services and transactions are increasingly being conducted online (for example finance, shopping, and government services such as social security and taxation). As a result, instead of linking static databases, the problem becomes one of linking individual records to databases that contain records about many individuals, potentially about a large population, that are continually updated and where new records are added in an ongoing fashion. An example would be real-time linking to verify identities in the context of consumer credit applications [115].

  Related to linking dynamic data is the challenge of linking temporal data, where for each record a timestamp indicates when the record was created or last updated. If two records to be compared have timestamps several years apart, for example, then giving a high match weight to address attributes might not be advisable given it is common for a significant proportion of a population to change their address over a period of several years [287, 392]. We discuss this aspect of temporal and dynamic data in more detail in Section 11.2.3.

- **Considering linkage quality in follow-up analysis and processing**: In many organisations, the area which is concerned with linking databases is often different from the area that is tasked with the analysis or further use of linked data. Similarly, if the linkage of data is conducted by a different organisation to the one which uses the linked data, for example for a research study, then often no information about the linkage method, linkage quality and completeness, nor the input data quality, are provided to the consumers of the linked data sets. As a result, it is commonly assumed that linked data are perfect, complete, and do not have any bias. In reality this is often not the case because a linkage conducted on real-world data will likely lead to false matches and false non-matches.

  Often certain subpopulations are under-represented in linked data. Migrants or homeless people might be missing due to their unusual names or lack of address details, respectively. The potential errors and biases introduced during the linkage process, while highly important for any accurate follow-up use of linked data, have only been considered recently, with the majority of this work conducted by the health research community [159, 225, 267, 509].

- **Evaluating linkage quality and privacy protection**: As we discussed in the previous section, to properly evaluate linkage quality ground truth data in the form of true matches and true non-matches are required. However, such ground truth data are often not available in practical linkage applications. Obtaining or (manually) generating true matches can be very time consuming and expensive, and in some cases (such as when linking historical data) might not be possible at all with absolute certainty [514]. The outcomes of a manual clerical review process, as described in Section 3.2, can potentially be used as ground truth data. However, given the potential matches manually classified in clerical review are generally the most difficult ones, their classification might not always be correct. Some studies have shown that even domain experts can make mistakes when manually classifying difficult cases [563]. Manually generated ground truth data might also not be complete (if for example there are not enough resources or time available to identify all true matches) or they might be biased for example to matches that are more easily to classify. Completely accurate evaluation of linkage quality, and similarly completeness, might therefore not be possible in certain situations.

  The evaluation of linkage quality and completeness becomes even more challenging when the linkage of sensitive data is based on encoded or encrypted data, as we discuss in the next section. In this situation, the organisation conducting the linkage does unlikely have access to un-encoded (plaintext) attribute values, such as names and addresses, that allow manual evaluation. Therefore, it might not be possible to generate ground truth data at all. Some initial work has investigated how partial masking (hiding) of sensitive information could still allow manual clerical review [370].

  How to evaluate the privacy protection provided by a privacy-preserving record linkage approach (as we discuss in the following section) is also an open challenge. As we cover in Chapter 5, a variety of privacy measures have been proposed so far [178, 325, 615], however none of these has shown to be adequate for an appropriate and accepted evaluation of privacy in the context of linking sensitive databases.

- **Evaluation frameworks and benchmark data collections**: Related to the challenge of evaluating linkage quality and completeness is the issue of publicly available frameworks that allow different linkage methods and techniques to be comparatively assessed, as well as the lack of available real-world data collections that can be used for such evaluations. Privacy and confidentiality concerns limit or even restrict what kind of data can be made publicly available. Because personal details are generally covered by privacy legislation, only few databases are available that can be used for the evaluation of linkage methods and techniques [111, 361].

  An alternative to using real-world data is to generate synthetic data that have similar characteristics as real data [107], such as distributions of values, dependencies between values, correlations between attributes,

as well as error characteristics [118, 121, 598]. Synthetic data have the
advantages that they can be generated with well-defined error characteristics, they have known match status which allows linkage quality and
completeness to be calculated, and they are publishable (as is the generator software). We discuss this topic of synthetic data in more detail in
Section A.3.

Evaluation frameworks and test data collections are crucial to better understand the advantages as well as weaknesses of different linkage methods and techniques with regard to different types of data to be
linked, different data quality aspects, as well as the performance of these
techniques with regard to linkage quality, scalability to large databases,
and privacy protection a linkage technique provides. Without such frameworks it will be difficult for practitioners to make an informed decision
about what type of linkage technique(s) to employ within their organisation. As we discuss further in Section 14.1 and Appendix A, while various
software systems (open-source as well as commercial) are available that
implement a variety of record linkage techniques, no comprehensive overall evaluation framework does exist at the time of writing.

- **Linking sensitive data across organisations**: This final challenge
  is the topic of the remainder of this book. Given the data used to link
  records across databases in many applications are about people, personal
  details such as names, addresses, gender, dates of birth, and so on, are
  required during the linkage process. While this is generally not a problem if a linkage is conducted on databases held by the same organisation,
  once databases with such sensitive information are to be linked across
  organisations, then privacy and confidentiality are of paramount concern. In certain cases privacy regulations might prohibit the linkage of
  certain sensitive databases. Example domains include health, biomedical
  and social science research, crime and fraud detection, as well as collaborations between public and private sector organisations. There are many
  applications where linked data in these domains could be used to answer
  questions and open new opportunities for research and policy development that are not possible on individual databases. As we discuss next,
  linking sensitive databases without the need for revealing any private or
  confidential information can open up such new opportunities.

3.6 Introduction to Privacy-Preserving Record Linkage

Now that we have described the general process of sharing and linking data,
discussed issues related to data quality, how to evaluate the outcomes of a
linkage, and highlighted the major challenges to linking databases, we can
formally define the problem of how to link sensitive databases across organisations without the need to reveal any private or confidential information.

This process is most commonly known as privacy-preserving record linkage (PPRL) [253, 619], the term we use throughout this book; but it has also been given other names including blindfolded record linkage or private record linkage [125, 178, 371].

Given all the general challenges for linking data we described in the previous section also hold in the context of PPRL (with the additional challenge of privacy preservation added), any PPRL technique that is to be of practical use in real-world linkage applications needs to be capable of (1) efficiently and effectively link large numbers of records from two or more databases; (2) correctly identify the true matching record pairs or sets with high accuracy to achieve high linkage quality; and (3) preserve the privacy of sensitive attribute values of all records (and thus entities) in the source databases. We now formally define PPRL as follows [619]:

Definition 3.1. Privacy-preserving record linkage (PPRL)
Assume DO_1, DO_2, ..., DO_n, with $n \geq 2$, are the n database owners with their respective databases $\mathbf{D}_1, \mathbf{D}_2, ..., \mathbf{D}_n$. The linkage across all these databases determines which of their records $r_1^i \in \mathbf{D}_1$, $r_2^j \in \mathbf{D}_2$, ..., $r_n^k \in \mathbf{D}_n$ match according to a decision model $\mathcal{C}(r_1^i, r_2^j, ..., r_n^k)$ that classifies each record pair (r_a^i, r_b^j), with $1 \leq a, b \leq n$ and $a \neq b$, into the two sets $\mathbf{M}$ of matches (where records r_a^i and r_b^j are assumed to refer to the same entity) and $\mathbf{U}$ of non-matches (where the records are assumed to refer to different entities). The objective of PPRL is that at the end of the linkage process the database owners only learn which records they have in common (in $\mathbf{M}$) according to $\mathcal{C}$ without the actual values of any other records being revealed to any other database owner or any party external to the database owners.

The outcomes of a PPRL project will be that only information about the set of record pairs (or record sets, if more than two databases have been linked) in $\mathbf{M}$ will be known to the database owners. This can mean that only the record identifiers of matched pairs or sets in $\mathbf{M}$ are revealed to the database owners, or that selected attribute values of these records are shared among them. Alternatively, the outcomes of a privacy-preserving linkage can mean that each database owner sends the values of some selected attributes for each of their matched records to another party, such as a researcher, who will then combine these records received from the different databases in order to conduct a study on the linked records.

We illustrate the general PPRL process for linking two sensitive databases in Figure 3.6, where this process is based on the general record linkage process shown in Figure 3.2. As can be seen, the PPRL process mostly follows the general linkage process with the exception of the additional data encoding / encryption step which is applied after the databases have been cleaned and standardised. The assumption is that the databases to be linked are held by different organisations, and that only encoded or encrypted data are exchanged between any of the parties involved in a linkage project, including the

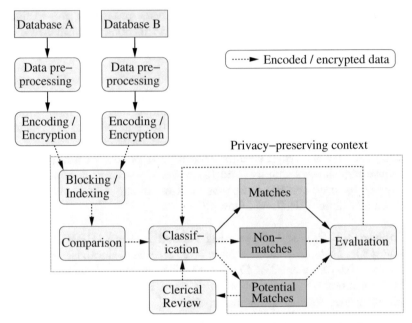

Fig. 3.6 The general process of privacy-preserving linking two databases, as described in Section 3.6. The highlighted box includes all steps of the linkage process that are conducted on encoded or encrypted data. Adapted from [109].

organisation that will conduct the linkage. In Section 4.3 we discuss different protocols of how such a privacy-preserving linkage between organisations can be conducted, and in Chapter 6 we then describe a diverse range of encoding and encryption techniques that can be used in such protocols.

The purpose of the encoding / encryption step is to modify the attribute values required for linkage (specifically for blocking and comparison) in such a way that the sensitive values of the input database of a specific database owner are secured from any reidentification attempt by any other party involved in a linkage, or from any external adversary that might get access to the encoded data. Equally important, given our discussion about data quality and the crucial aspect of allowing for approximate matching of attribute values, is however also that the encoded or encrypted values do allow for suitable blocking or indexing of the databases, and enable approximate matching of encodings in order to obtain approximate similarities between records. These two requirements are important for any record linkage to obtain high linkage quality.

The remainder of the book will cover all aspects of PPRL in detail, ranging from the methods and techniques that have been developed for PPRL to various practical aspects as well as future challenges and directions for research and development.

3.7 Summary and Further Reading

In this chapter we have discussed the necessary background topics that are of relevance for better understanding of the content of the second part of this book, Methods and Techniques. We have provided a short history of linking data, discussed the linkage process and its major steps, highlighted the important aspect of data quality and the way it can affect how data can be linked, showed how linkage quality and complexity can be evaluated, and have given an overview of the major challenges involved when linking databases. In the previous section we then introduced the topic of how to link sensitive databases in a privacy-preserving way, and we formally defined privacy-preserving record linkage (PPRL). In the following chapters we discuss the various methods and techniques involved in PPRL in detail.

A variety of books have been published in recent years that cover the topic of linking, or more generally integrating, databases. The traditional approaches based on Fellegi and Sunter's probabilistic record linkage methods are covered in the books by Newcombe [437] and more recently by Herzog, Scheuren, and Winkler [274]. The edited book by Harron, Goldstein, and Dibben [266] discusses various methodological aspects of linking databases across several domains and topics. The three recent books by Talburt [587], Naumann and Weiss [432], and Christen [109] provide overviews of linkage methodologies and techniques from the computer science perspective. Data quality is covered in detail by Batini and Scannapieco [45], while Doan, Halevy, and Ives [158] provide a comprehensive overview of the larger area of data integration. A variety of statistical issues related to the analysis of linked (or more general integrated) data are discussed by the recent edited book by Zhang and Chambers [661].

Introductions to the probabilistic record linkage approach by Fellegi and Sunter in the context of epidemiological research, official statistics, and injury prevention research are provided by Sayers et al. [532], Winkler [643], and Clarke [127], respectively. Winkler [643] also discussed data preparation in detail and provided name and address standardisation examples.

We are not aware of any other books that specifically cover the linking of sensitive data. There are, however, two extensive survey and overview articles by Vatsalan et al. [619, 620], where the first provides a detailed taxonomy (which we summarise in Section 7.1) of many dimensions related to PPRL while the second focuses on linking sensitive databases in the context of Big data. Bonomi et al. [73] also review techniques that can be used to link sensitive databases, and they discuss open research questions and challenges. A short overview article by Christen also highlights the general challenges involved when linking databases [112].

Part II
Methods and Techniques

This second part of the book provides a detailed description of methods and techniques that have been developed over the past two decades to enable the linkage of sensitive databases.

In Chapter 4 we provide a high level overview of different protocols that have been developed to link sensitive databases across organisations, their requirements and limitations, as well as additional aspects such as access control and secure key exchange that are important when employing these protocols in real-world applications. We also present the privacy models that are commonly assumed within these protocols, and the assumptions of these models with regard to how parties involved in a protocol are expected to behave.

In Chapter 5 we then discuss issues related to risk assessment when linking sensitive databases, including how to measure privacy, risk, and utility. Various attack methods have been proposed aimed at reidentifying encoded sensitive values, and we provide a description of these techniques. Related to risk are anonymisation and statistical disclosure control methods, which we also discuss in this chapter.

In Chapter 6 we then describe the technical building blocks that are commonly used in techniques to link sensitive databases, such as random number generators; hashing, anonymisation, encryption, and encoding methods; as well as phonetic encoding techniques and functions to calculate similarities between textual (string) and numerical values. We also discuss the main ideas behind secure multiparty computation methods and how these have been used for linking sensitive databases. We conclude this chapter with a discussion about how to choose suitable techniques for certain scenarios and applications.

In Chapter 7 we provide an overview of the actual techniques that have been developed to encode sensitive values, and to compare and link such encoded values. We cover a diverse range of techniques as proposed in different research domains in the past two decades. We end this chapter with a discussion of which encoding and comparison techniques are suitable for what applications and linkage scenarios, and we discuss the advantages and weaknesses of techniques with regard to their usage in real-world linkage applications.

In Chapter 8 we then cover in detail Bloom filter encoding, currently one of the most popular techniques used to link sensitive databases. Bloom filter encoding has been implemented in several real-world linkage applications in different countries. We describe in detail the different hashing and encoding techniques used for Bloom filter based linking of sensitive databases that contain textual as well as other types of data, and we discuss suitable parameter settings for Bloom filter encoding.

Recent research has identified various vulnerabilities of Bloom filter encoding when used for linking sensitive data. In Chapter 9 we describe several sophisticated cryptanalysis attacks that aim to reidentify sensitive values in Bloom filter encoded databases. Hardening techniques that aim to make Bloom filter encoding more resilient with regard to such attack methods have been developed, and we cover these techniques in this chapter and discuss their advantages and weaknesses. We also discuss – based on current attack and hardening methods – best practice approaches when using Bloom filter encoding in the context of linking sensitive data.

We conclude the second part of the book in Chapter 10 where we cover the important topic of computational scalability which is required to make the linking of large sensitive databases practical for real-world applications. We also discuss how modern parallel and distributed computing platforms can be used to enable the linking of large databases, and issues and challenges that occur when more than two databases are to be linked.

Chapter 4
Private Information Sharing Protocols

Abstract In this chapter we describe different aspects of information sharing protocols aimed at linking sensitive databases. We first discuss the different roles of the parties that can participate in these protocols. Next we describe the general principle of separating identifying data from sensitive microdata in a linkage process, and provide the details of the basic two-party, three-party, and multiparty protocols that can be used for different linkage scenarios. We then describe the different adversarial models that are being used to model the privacy risks and protection provided by these protocols, such as the honest-but-curious and malicious models. Finally, we cover additional aspects that need to be considered when private information sharing protocols are employed in practice, such as frameworks for key exchange as well as access control.

4.1 Roles of Different Linkage Participants

In the context of linking sensitive databases, depending on the linkage protocol to be used (as we describe in Section 4.3), different types of parties can participate in the linkage process. In general, we assume that sensitive databases are linked across organisations, and therefore the privacy and confidentiality of these databases need to be considered through the use of privacy-preserving record linkage methods and techniques. The roles of these parties can be categorised as follows.

- **Database owner**: The database owners are the providers of the databases to be linked [109]. According to the linkage protocol employed, the database owners may participate in the record comparison and classification steps (as we discussed in Section 3.2), or alternatively only encode their databases (as we cover in Chapters 6 to 8) before sending them to a linkage unit (as we discuss next). Financial institutions, medical service

© Springer Nature Switzerland AG 2020
P. Christen et al., *Linking Sensitive Data*, https://doi.org/10.1007/978-3-030-59706-1_4

providers, or government agencies are some examples of database owners. While a database owner can also be seen as a data custodian, a data
custodian is not necessarily the owner of the data they take care of.

- **Linkage unit**: A linkage unit is a special party that participates in the
  linkage process such that it may or may not be external to the database
  owners [84, 503, 507]. In general, a linkage unit does not have any data to
  be linked by itself, but it conducts the linkage of the databases sent to it
  by the database owners. While most linkage protocols and actual linkage
  techniques do require a linkage unit, some do not [619]. We describe these
  different protocols in Section 4.3.

- **Global facilitator**: A global facilitator is a party which helps a group
  of database owners to negotiate their common objective of linking their
  sensitive databases, and assists them to plan on how to achieve this objective [399]. Aspects to be facilitated can include the exchange of parameters and the selection of quasi-identifying attributes to be used for
  the linkage among the database owners, as well as the communication of
  secret passwords and other information about the linkage process that
  is required by all database owners and potentially also the linkage unit.
  A global facilitator can also create a global summary (or view) about
  the databases to be linked at the beginning of a protocol which can be
  used by the database owners to make decisions about the next steps in
  the protocol. For example, a global facilitator can be used to identify the
  common attributes across all databases to be linked. In situations where
  these attributes and/or the schema of the databases to be linked are sensitive or confidential, then a privacy-preserving schema matching protocol
  can be employed [533], which can be based on a private set intersection
  protocol as we describe in Section 6.5.

- **Global Authority**: A global authority is another special party which
  plays the role of a central, possibly public, semi-trusted regulatory agency
  in a linkage protocol [331, 334]. As we describe in Section 4.5, some
  global authorities, called key or certification authorities, can be used to
  generate the necessary secret keys (public and private) as required by
  cryptographic functions (encryption and decryption) used in the linkage
  process [333].

- **Data Consumers**: Data consumers are the data users in the linkage
  process [63]. After the linkage of sensitive databases has been conducted
  and a linked data set has been produced, the identifiers, and values from
  selected attributes (of the record pairs or sets classified to be matches)
  are sent to a data consumer to allow further processing or analysis of the
  linked data set. Database owners, data analysts, and external researchers
  can be considered as data consumers.

An additional party relevant to the linking of sensitive data is a data controller, an organisation not directly involved in a linkage but providing rules,
policies, and permissions to the parties involved in actual linkage projects.

A variety of actual linkage techniques have been developed to link sensitive databases across organisations using some or all of these types of roles. As we describe in detail in Chapter 6, different methods have been developed to protect the privacy of the individuals in these databases and to maintain the security of the encoded data that are communicated between the parties that participate in a protocol [84, 624].

In Section 4.3 we will describe how these different types of roles can collaborate in a variety of ways to link sensitive databases across organisations. First, we describe the general principle of separating the identifying data required to conduct the linkage from the (often highly sensitive) microdata, which is to be used for further processing or analysis by a data consumer.

4.2 Separation Principle

The separation principle [340] is a mechanism that can be used to link data in a way that protects the identities of individuals in the databases used in the linkage process, as well as in the merging process that is used to create the final linked data set that consists of linked and merged records. As we discuss in Chapter 13, the separation principle is being applied across the world in many practical applications that link sensitive databases.

The crucial aspect of the separation principle is that each participant (or party) in a linkage protocol does only have access to the data it requires in order to perform its role in the protocol. In such an approach, those involved in the actual linkage of records can only see the quasi-identifying attributes required to generate the links between records (such as names, addresses, and dates of birth). On the other hand, those involved in the analysis of a linked data set only obtain deidentified microdata (also known as content or payload data) that are specific to the requirements of their planned (and generally approved) analysis of the data. These microdata are the attributes that are needed to conduct the planned study. They can include clinical information, welfare payments, or service utilisation, which potentially can be highly sensitive. In a database context, such a separation of the quasi-identifying attributes from the sensitive microdata, and splitting the set of attributes of records into two accordingly, is known as vertical partitioning of a database. The side box on page 84 shows an example application of the separation principle.

By separating these two types of data, anybody involved in the preparation of a linked data set and its analysis can either only see quasi-identifying data of individuals, or only microdata. Quasi-identifying information by itself might not be highly sensitive, while deidentified sensitive microdata can often not be assigned to a specific individual, especially after statistical disclosure control techniques have been applied, as we discuss in Section 5.5.

Example application of the separation principle

The separation principle assumes that the database owners separate the quasi-identifying attributes used for the linkage from the microdata (content or payload data) used for the analysis before sending the quasi-identifying attributes to a linkage unit. Let us assume that two database owners want to link and merge the records in their sensitive databases, and provide the merged records to a data consumer, such as a researcher. Following the separation principle, the linkage of these two databases would consist of the following steps, as illustrated below:

1. The database owners separate the quasi-identifying attributes from the content attributes, as shown in different colours in the figure.
2. The database owners send the quasi-identifying attribute values (first names and surnames) together with the record identifiers to the linkage unit, which will compare record pairs to identify the pairs that are matches and need to be merged.
3. The linkage unit sends the identifiers of the linked record pairs back to the database owners, together with a merge identifier, r_M.
4. The database owners send their microdata together with the merge identifiers to the data consumer who can merge records with the same merge identifier. Once the microdata of the linked record pairs are merged they can be used for different analysis purposes.

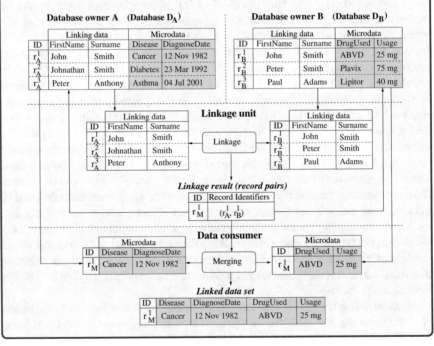

For example, let us assume a linkage unit that is creating the links between two health databases. If there exist two records, one in each database to be linked, of a person named Peter Miller, then the linkage unit will only see the name and address of this person, and limited other demographic information common across the databases to be linked that is required to identify the linked record pairs. No health, financial, or any other personal information about Peter Miller is however accessible by the linkage unit. On the other hand, the researcher who will be using the linked data set to conduct a study will only see a record with a random identifier that contains the medical details of a person together with other attributes needed for the analysis, such as a broad age group, the gender, and the region (such as the postcode area) where the person lives (without any information that allows the reidentification of this specific Peter Miller).

The separation principle is one way to provide protection of the identities of individuals in databases during the linking process [340]. This principle assures database owners that their sensitive data will be used appropriately and that security obligations will be met. However, it is important to note that analysing the deidentified linked data set might still provide enough information to allow the reidentification of an individual even after personal quasi-identifiers (such as names and addresses) have been removed. A unique combination of medical details, age group, gender, and geographic location might be enough to uniquely identify an individual, as has been shown in practical scenarios [140]. We discuss this topic in more detail in Chapter 5.

However, the drawback of the separation principle is that it still requires that plaintext quasi-identifying information has to be sent from the database owners to the organisation that is undertaking the linkage. This can make such information vulnerable to be disclosed (accidentally or willingly). Metadata, such as the names of a database or file (for example 'HIV-patients-2017.csv') can potentially lead to the disclosure of sensitive personal information about the individuals whose names and addresses are stored in such a database or file (even after medical details have been removed). Ideally, to prevent such possible disclosure, no plaintext (unencoded) quasi-identifying or other sensitive data should ever have to be exchanged between parties. This is what the privacy-preserving record linkage techniques we present in the following sections and chapters aim to achieve.

It is the responsibility of all parties involved in a linkage project, both the database owners and the linkage unit, to appropriately anonymise the data before they are made available to data consumers. This needs to be done in accordance with the requirements of any relevant privacy and confidentiality regulations, as well as other specific requirements by the database owners about access and use of any generated linked data set that is based on their contributed input database(s). The separation principle can make this a difficult undertaking, because the linkage unit does not see any sensitive microdata of the linked records, and each database owner only sees its own attributes that are part of the linked sensitive microdata.

In general, how the separation principal is applied depends on the requirements of the parties that are participating in a linkage protocol. If a linkage unit is employed then the database owners need to prepare their respective databases before sending them to the linkage unit. As discussed above, common practice is to separate any personal quasi-identifiers from the microdata after which a database with only the quasi-identifying attributes is transferred to the linkage unit. Each database record is assigned with a unique random identifier which is used to link microdata across records from the two database owners to generate the linked data set. Note that this merging of linked records cannot be done by the linkage unit because in such a case it would get in possession of both identifying and microdata, which would allow the linkage unit to assign sensitive microdata to individuals.

In the presence of a trusted linkage unit (a secure and trusted institution), the database owners can send their entire database to this linkage unit. In this situation the linkage unit will be responsible to conduct a linkage project following its policies, regulations and guidelines, and provide researchers with safe and secure access to the linked data set in line with the requirements of the database owners as well as government laws and regulations. In this scenario, the linkage unit may apply the separation principle through role separation. This is achieved by allowing the people who link records to only access the identifying data (the information used for linking, quasi-identifiers such as dates of birth, names, and addresses) that are needed to facilitate the linkage, but no other information contained in individual records. The identifiers of the linked records are then provided to other people (within the linkage unit) who are merging records, and who are given access to the sensitive microdata, but not the identifying data of individual records. The linked data set without any identifying information is then given to a researcher for analysis purposes. This approach provides separation based on access limitations that ensure no individual has access to more than one role (linking or merging) for a given project or database, and no role has access to both the input databases and the linked data set generated from these databases.

The first approach described above requires the database owners to apply the separation principle, while in the latter case the linkage unit is required to apply the separation principle if access to data is approved and permitted by both the linkage project and legislation.

An important aspect of the separation principle is therefore that no attribute should be used both for the linkage as well as provided to the data consumer of the linked microdata, especially if a privacy-preserving linkage protocol (as we discuss below) is employed where attributes are encoded or encrypted individually. Anybody who gets access to both the plaintext and encoded (or encrypted) attribute values could use this information combined to try to break the encoding or encryption process using one of the attack methods we describe in Section 5.4. For example, if a linkage is conducted that includes a postcode attribute to link records, and postcode is also included in the microdata, then this would allow an adversary to see if she can find a mapping between the encoded postcode values (as used for linkage) and the plaintext postcode values (as used by the data consumer).

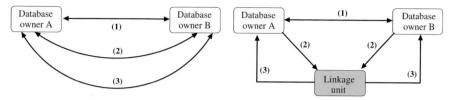

(a) Two–party protocol, linking without a linkage unit   **(b)** Three–party protocol, linking with a linkage unit

Fig. 4.1 The general protocols for linking sensitive databases between two organisations (or parties) [620]: (a) two-party protocol without a linkage unit, and (b) three-party protocol involving a linkage unit, as we describe in Section 4.3. In both types of protocols the basic communication steps between the participating parties can be given as: (1) agreement of settings, parameter values, and secret keys (this can potentially involve a global facilitator as we discussed in Section 4.1); (2) communication of the (somehow) encoded or encrypted quasi-identifier attribute values required for the linkage; and (3) exchanging or returning the linkage result. Adapted from [620]. © Springer International Publishing AG 2017, reprinted with permission.

4.3 Linkage Protocols

Over the past two decades a variety of linkage protocols, and actual techniques for linking sensitive databases, have been proposed. The protocols outlined here are designed to provide protection of sensitive private and confidential information and to ensure the database owners that the data they provide in a linkage protocol will be appropriately protected and managed. These protocols are additional to the separation principle described in the previous section, in that they provide significantly improved privacy protection of the identifying data used for linking using encoding and/or encryption of the identifying data before they are being exchanged between parties.

By assuming each database to be linked is owned by a different database owner, different types of linkage protocols can be categorised based on the types and numbers of parties that participate in a protocol[1].

- **Two-party protocols**: In two-party protocols only two database owners are participating in the linkage process [290, 392, 611, 618, 651]. In this type of protocol, the two database owners communicate directly with each other to perform the linkage of their records. This will make such a protocol more secure since no records are shared with any external party. Generally, as illustrated in Figure 4.1, two-party protocols start by the two database owners agreeing upon and exchanging any required information such as parameter settings, preprocessing methods, encoding or encryption methods, and any secret keys that are needed. This first

---

[1] Note that the terminology we use here follows what is generally used by the privacy-preserving record linkage community [619, 620], and is somewhat different to the terminology used in the context of secure multiparty computation [394].

step of a protocol can potentially be conducted with the help of a global facilitator, as we discussed in Section 4.1.

The second general step of two-party protocols consist of the secure exchange of encoded or encrypted attribute values to conduct the linkage, followed by the third step which is the exchange of the identified matched records. A major challenge with any two-party protocol is that they can become more complex and expensive than three-party protocols (as we discuss next) in terms of computation and communication. More sophisticated encoding or encryption mechanisms, and often iterative linkage approaches [611], are required in two-party protocols because both database owners need to know the full details of any encoding or encryption technique used (as we describe in Chapter 6), and therefore they can potentially try to identify any sensitive information contained in any messages they receive from the other database owner.

- **Three-party protocols**: In three-party linkage protocols two database owners are performing the linkage of their sensitive databases using a third party, commonly known as the linkage unit [84, 323, 507, 639]. As with two-party protocols, the first step in three-party protocols consists of the database owners exchanging any required information such as parameter settings, preprocessing methods, encoding or encryption methods, and any secret key(s). Again a global facilitator can potentially be involved in this process. After the database owners have preprocessed and encoded or encrypted their databases (as we discuss in Chapter 6), they send these encoded or encrypted databases to the linkage unit to perform the linkage by calculating the similarities between the encoded or encrypted values, and classifying compared record pairs into matches or non-matches [619]. The results of this process, specifically the record identifiers of the pairs or sets of records classified as matches, are then sent back to the database owners who can then either exchange the details of the matched records with each other, or send the values of a selected set of attributes of the matched records to a data consumer. The general setting of a three-party protocol is shown in Figure 4.1.

The advantage of three-party protocols over two-party protocols is that three-party protocols do not require complex linkage techniques to ensure that the two database owners cannot learn any sensitive information from each other during the linkage process (assuming the parties involved in a protocol do not collude with each other, as we discuss in the following section). Many three-party protocols are therefore more efficient because they require less complex encoding or encryption of the databases to be linked. On the other hand, the linkage unit is often considered to be semi-trusted (as we discuss in the following section). Therefore, it might aim to learn the sensitive values in the encoded records that are sent to it by the database owners. Furthermore, given the linkage unit will have access to the encoded or encrypted databases from both database owners, there is a risk that these databases can be attacked in a variety of scenarios and using various methods which we discuss in Sections 5.4 and 9.1.

- **Multiparty protocols**: A further characterisation of linkage protocols is if they can be extended to the linking of sensitive databases from more than two parties or not [620]. Similar to two-party and three-party protocols, multiparty linkage protocols can be performed with or without a linkage unit, where again the linkage unit would conduct the linkage between the encoded or encrypted databases sent to it by the database owners.

  Similar to two-party protocols, the security of multiparty protocols can be increased by removing the linkage unit in the linkage process [374, 418, 498, 613]. However, with an increase in the number of parties (and thus databases) involved in the linkage process more sophisticated techniques are required, both for computation and communication, to enable the efficient, secure, and scalable linking of multiple databases [494].

  In multiparty protocols with a linkage unit, all database owners have to agree on the set of parameters, quasi-identifying attributes, secret keys, and data preprocessing methods to be used in the linkage process [318, 359, 453]. However, the linkage process needs to be conducted using scalable and efficient techniques due to the exponential growth of the comparison space with the number of records from multiple databases that need to be compared. We discuss these computational aspects in more detail in Chapter 10.

  In general, multiparty protocols are more susceptible to collusion, a topic we describe in Section 5.4, where some database owners work together with the aim of identifying sensitive information from the database of another, non-colluding, party [615]. Therefore, more secure as well as more efficient linkage techniques are required for multiparty linkage protocols, and this topic is still an active area of research.

Now that we have defined the different conceptual types of linkage protocols, in the following sections we discuss a variety of aspects that need to be considered when such a protocol is considered for the linkage of sensitive databases in a real-world application.

4.4 Adversarial Models

In general, the parties taking part in a linkage protocol can be assumed to be either fully trusted (also known as honest), semi-trusted (also known as honest-but-curious), and untrusted (also known as malicious) [394]. A fully trusted party in a linkage protocol follows the steps of the protocol and does not try to learn any sensitive information from any data it receives from any other party, or combine its own data with data from another party (possibly external to the protocol) to learn sensitive information from another party. A semi-trusted party, on the other hand, while following the steps of a linkage protocol, can be curious and try to learn or infer sensitive information from the data it receives from the other parties, potentially combined with its own data or data obtained from an external party. Finally, untrusted parties can perform certain undesirable actions that cannot be prevented while they participate in a linkage protocol. Specifically, an untrusted party can refuse to participate in the protocol at any time, can send different, invalid, or arbitrary (wrong or faked) input instead of its own (correct and valid) input, and it may abort the protocol prematurely.

Realistically, since the parties involved in a linkage protocol cannot always be fully trusted, linkage protocols must be able to guarantee the privacy of the sensitive data of each database owner when performing computations and communications between the parties involved in a protocol. Therefore, depending upon the actions that a semi-trusted or untrusted party is allowed to take, a protocol that is used to link sensitive databases is assumed to follow one of several conceptual adversarial models, as we describe next. These models are commonly used in the field of cryptography, and especially in the area of secure multiparty computation (SMC) [394]. We discuss SMC techniques in more detail in Section 6.5.

For linking sensitive databases across organisations, the following adversarial models can be considered:

- **Honest-but-curious**: Most of the protocols proposed in the context of linking sensitive databases follow the honest-but-curious (HBC) adversarial model [11, 178, 499, 611, 619]. This model is also known as the semi-honest or passive adversary model [251, 394]. In this model, all parties that participate in a protocol are seen as semi-trusted, as discussed before. They follow the steps of the linkage protocol, but they are curious to learn about the sensitive information in the databases owned by the other parties. For example, in a three-party linkage protocol, while following the protocol steps, a database owner or the linkage unit, assuming they follow the HBC assumption, can store the data they receive from any other party. This includes the final linkage results [229]. These data can be used by a party to potentially infer sensitive attribute values contained in another party's database by applying a frequency analysis or cryptanalysis attack method [120, 372], as we describe in detail in Section 5.4 and Chapter 9. For example, a database owner can perform a frequency analysis of the data it has received from another party to obtain a frequency distribution of sensitive attribute values.

  A linkage protocol can be considered as secure under the HBC adversary model only if all parties that participate in the protocol cannot infer any sensitive information other than the records classified as matches at the end of the protocol. However, under the HBC model collusion between parties is possible, where a subset of parties can work together using the data they have received to learn about the sensitive information of another, non-colluding, party [394]. We describe collusion in more detail in Section 5.4.

- **Malicious**: The malicious adversarial model assumes that the parties involved in a linkage protocol are untrusted parties (as discussed above) that may not follow the steps of the protocol. Rather, they can behave arbitrarily or maliciously [251, 394]. In the protocol steps, a malicious database owner can send invalid or faked data to learn about any sensitive information of another database owner. For example, a malicious database owner can add a faked record to its database for a Boris Johnson living in London (even though it does not have a real individual with these characteristics in its database) in order to learn if the other database being linked contains an individual with these details (if the linked data set ends up containing a linked record pair for a Boris Johnson).

  Linkage protocols developed under the malicious privacy model mainly use SMC techniques [656], which employ advanced encryption and encoding techniques to ensure no malicious party can learn any sensitive information from any other party [388, 418]. The use of SMC techniques makes linkage protocols under the malicious adversary model to generally have higher communication and computation complexities compared to linkage protocols which follow the HBC model. Malicious adversaries are also called active [394].

  In general, for any protocol that aims to link sensitive databases, providing security in the presence of malicious adversaries would clearly be preferred because this would ensure that no adversarial attack can succeed. However, the evaluation of security under this model is difficult due to the unpredictable ways malicious (untrusted) parties can deviate from the protocol steps. Such unpredictable behaviour might not be identified for a party in the linkage protocol because the party might try to mask its malicious behaviour [229, 392, 418]. So far, limited work has been done in the context of linking sensitive databases using the malicious adversarial model.

- **Covert model**: Typically, in most protocols to link sensitive databases the participating parties are assumed to be following either the HBC or malicious adversarial models. However, in many real-world settings, the assumption regarding the HBC behaviour might not be secure enough, while security in the presence of malicious adversaries might be excessive and expensive to achieve.

  The covert adversarial model lies between the HBC (semi-honest) and malicious models, where it might better align with many real-world settings where adversaries are willing to actively cheat (and therefore are not semi-honest) but only if they are not caught doing so [32]. The covert model assumes the parties participating in a linkage protocol may deviate arbitrarily from the steps of the protocol in an attempt to cheat, and learn sensitive information from another party, until they are being caught. The model assumes that a database owner who is cheating in a linkage protocol can be caught by an honest party with a given probability (although not with a probability close to 1).

This probability is known as the deterrence factor [394]. For example, let us assume the deterrence factor is equal to 0.6. Then, any attempt to cheat by an adversary (for example a misbehaving database owner) can be detected by the honest parties with a likelihood of 60%. The greater the probability that the adversary is caught the greater the deterrent is for this party to cheat.

The covert adversarial model matches the case for many business, financial, political, and diplomatic contexts where the honest behaviour of the participating parties in a linkage protocol cannot be assumed, but where companies, institutions, or individuals cannot afford the embarrassment, loss of reputation, and negative press associated with being caught cheating. However, the linkage protocols developed for this privacy model generally require computationally expensive techniques (such as oblivious transfers and homomorphic encryption, as we discuss in Chapter 6) to perform the communication between parties while providing mechanisms to detect cheating parties [32, 237].

- **Accountable computing**: Accountable computing, also called accountability computing, is a framework which is applicable for many real-world applications that require privacy or security without the complexity and computational costs required for a linkage protocol that uses SMC techniques under the malicious adversarial model [303, 304]. The idea behind accountable computing is that a database owner that correctly follows the protocol can be proven to have done so and consequently it can be proven if some other database owner has disclosed data or has deviated from the protocol (this is different from the covert model where a misbehaving party can only be detected with a certain probability). Accountable computing enables practical utility over HBC protocols while providing detection capability over the malicious model. At the time of writing, this adversarial model has not been used in any protocol aimed at linking sensitive databases.

  Although a malicious party in an accountable computing protocol may learn information that they should not know and that can potentially damage the result of the protocol, such behaviour could be detected under the accountable computing framework using a SMC protocol that incorporates a verification phase [304]. Such a verification phase is designed in a way that it can reveal whether or not any malicious behaviour has been performed by a participating party during the execution of the protocol without revealing any information regarding the private input of each participating party. In general, the verification phase of a SMC protocol under the accountable computing framework requires the participating parties to commit their private inputs so that any subsequent change to their input values can be detected. A third-party verifier is then used in the protocol to detect if the participating parties followed the required computational steps of the protocol. Randomisation can be introduced to the private inputs of the participating parties to prevent the verifier from learning anything regarding the private input of the participating parties.

Because the verification phase under the accountable computing framework does not leak any additional information about the private inputs of the participating parties, and because this phase can be repeated as many times as needed with different verifiers, the degree of trust for a verifier is lower than for most third-party HBC protocols. In particular, much of the computational costs of a SMC protocol would be required in the verification phase which only needs to be run to expose a malicious party when a disclosure is detected, or auditing is performed to verify honest behaviour among all collaborating parties. This enables accountable computing protocols to approach the efficiency of HBC protocols. Furthermore, the accountable computing framework does not need to resist a malicious party which allows any SMC protocol under the accountable computing framework to be less complex than a SMC protocol under the malicious adversary model.

4.5 Additional Aspects of Private Information Sharing Protocols

How to conduct the linkage of sensitive databases across organisations in practice, using encoded or encrypted versions of these databases, is not straightforward and requires a variety of aspects to be considered. Many of these aspects have not been established and considered enough in the often simplified conceptual environments used by most research projects that are only considering the algorithmic and security aspects of linking sensitive databases [619, 620].

In general, the practical requirements of a linkage project vary due to the characteristics of the data and the participating organisations that are involved, and the linkage environment that is used for a project. In this section we discuss two major aspects that are common to all projects that aim to link sensitive databases across organisations: secure key exchange algorithms and access control. In Chapter 11 we then cover a wide variety of practical issues that also need to be considered when linking sensitive databases in practice, ranging from data to implementation and organisational aspects.

4.5.1 Secure Key Exchange Algorithms

As we will discuss in Section 6.4, encryption is a privacy technique that has been used in various protocols that are aimed at linking sensitive databases. Under encryption based linkage techniques, the participating parties use one or more cryptographic algorithms to encrypt the values in their databases to be used for linking, and a linkage technique is then applied on these encrypted values to identify matching records [318, 328, 506].

When such encryption algorithms are used in a linkage protocol, encrypted messages need to be communicated between the parties involved in the protocol, for example from database owners to the linkage unit. The sender and receiver who wish to process these encrypted messages must be equipped with a mechanism to securely encrypt their data into messages, and then decrypt the messages received from another party.

It is common to use a secure key for encryption and decryption algorithms used in the linkage process. If a symmetric key algorithm is being employed [535], then the same key is used for both encryption and decryption algorithms, where the key needs to be shared (or each party will need a copy of the same key) [230]. In an asymmetric key algorithm (also known as public key algorithms) [535], two keys, known as the public and private keys, are generated by each party, where a party only needs to know the public key of another party to encrypt a message aimed for this other party, while the private key is kept secret and used by its owner to decrypt messages that were encrypted with its public key [229, 230].

In applications where cryptographic algorithms based on symmetric keys are used, secure communication channels are required to exchange secret keys between participating parties such that no unauthorised party can obtain a copy of the keys used in a protocol. The key exchange problem describes ways to exchange whatever keys or other information that are needed before any encryption or decryption can be performed by a party [125].

In contrast to symmetric key algorithms, public key cryptography protocols only require that the public keys can be sent over non-secure channels or shared in public. Since a private key is only available to its owner and kept secret, only the owner can decrypt a message encrypted with its corresponding public key [230]. However, in terms of computing requirements, public key cryptography is more demanding and therefore its use might be limited for general purpose encryption. Due to its strong privacy guarantees, many applications employ public key cryptography exclusively to share secret keys, where these keys are then used for the generally much faster standard symmetric key algorithms [72, 222, 609].

Over the years many public key protocols have been proposed with a special focus on performance for key exchange, including RSA [72], Diffie-Hellman [230], or Elliptic Curve Diffie-Hellman [18]. However, some protocols face problems with identity spoofing, that requires a sender of a public key to guarantee its true ownership of the public key such that the receiving party

---

Public key infrastructure

In many applications, public key cryptography is used to provide security characteristics such as confidentiality, integrity, and authentication [1]. A public key infrastructure (PKI) can be used that serves as a foundation upon which applications, systems, and security components can be built [581]. In situations where large amounts of data need to be encrypted, a PKI can be established for the distribution of secret keys to facilitate efficient encryption and decryption processes where public key cryptography may not be suitable. The aim of PKI is to enable secure communication channels for the exchange of data, credentials, and values in environments that are not secure, such as the Internet [470].

PKI consists of policies, services, and protocols that provide security and interoperability for implementing the use of public key cryptography for the management of keys and certificates. In PKI, trust can be established through different roles [192, 470], including certification authorities (CA), registration authorities (RA), and directory services (DS). The generation, distribution, and management of public keys and their associated certificates are allowed through these roles, where the implemented digital certificates can then be used to identify different entities [581].

A CA helps to establish trust between entities that are unknown to each another through registration and providing key certificates. Once a key certificate is signed by a CA, it vouches for the identity of the entities and allows unknown entities to establish trust between them. A RA accepts requests for certificates and authenticates the entity making the request that ensures the validity and correctness of the registration. A DS usually provides entity information on behalf of a CA to ensure unique identification of an entity within the CA's domain [192].

The following example shows how PKI can be used in the context of linking sensitive databases across the two parties Alice and Bob:

1. Alice and Bob each first generate a public and private key pair.
2. Alice and Bob each send their public keys, their names, and descriptive information to a RA.
3. The RA validates Alice and Bob's credentials and forwards their certificate requests to the CA.
4. The CA generates a certificate for Alice and Bob's public keys by formatting their public keys and other information, signs the certificate with its private key, and then sends it to Alice and Bob.
5. Alice and Bob each authenticate the other party's public key using the certificate received from the CA, and then generate a common secret symmetric key using each other's authenticated public keys.

Alice and Bob can now encrypt their databases using the secret symmetric key and send it to the linkage unit to perform the linkage.

---

can be sure (or at least confident) that a public key it received actually does belong to its supposed owner. Public key infrastructures (PKIs) have been proposed as a solution for the problem of identity authentication, where a PKI helps to authenticate or verify the identity of parties when they are communicating with each other [1]. As we describe in more detail in the side box on page 95, PKI can be used in the context of linking sensitive databases between different parties to securely exchange the secret keys to be used for encryption and decryption and encoding of sensitive data.

4.5.2 Access Control Mechanisms

Access control is a common fundamental security technique that is used to regulate the authorisation of who or what can view or use resources in a computing environment. This concept is generally employed to minimise the risks of unauthorised access to physical and logical systems or data held at an organisation [211, 464].

Unlike cryptographic techniques, access control mechanisms limit who can see data records and their corresponding data sources, and how different parties can manipulate these resources [14]. One aspect of access control mechanisms is identity management, systems or frameworks that support the creation and management of identities that have certain access rights to a given information technology system. Access control can be combined with cryptographic techniques such as PKI, as discussed before, to allow confidential information to be transmitted safely via an insecure communication channel such as the Internet.

Access control mechanisms have seen much development over the past decades. Some access control mechanisms are being designed to satisfy the security needs in a controlled environment, such as an electronic health records database maintained within a hospital. Others have been proposed to meet the security requirements of a federated environment that is connected to unsecure public networks such as the Internet [14, 211].

Organisations use different access control models depending on their privacy policy requirements and the security levels of the information technology and data they are trying to protect. Out of the many different models proposed, Discretionary Access Control (DAC), Mandatory Access Control (MAC), and Role-Based Access Control (RBAC) are commonly used access control principles that have been recognised as official standards for any sensitive data environment [528]. DAC was the first standard introduced that controls each user's access to information on the basis of the user's identity and authorisation. The second principle, MAC, governs access on the basis of the security classification of users and the data stored in a system. MAC is often used in government environments where classifications are assigned to system resources and the operating system or security kernel that grants or denies access to those resource objects based on the security clearance of a user or device. RBAC is a widely used access control mechanism that regulates user access to information on the basis of the activities particular types of users may or may not execute on a system [211, 464].

Access control systems can be complex and challenging to manage in dynamic information technology environments that involve on-premise and/or cloud systems. Since access control must be integrated into an organisation's information technology environment, it is important to decide which access management systems are applicable and required based on the organisation's privacy and computer security policies, as well as any relevant government regulations [14].

4.6 Summary and Further Reading

In this chapter we have discussed different aspects related to information sharing protocols in the context of linking sensitive databases. We described the different types of roles the organisations that participate in a linkage protocol can have, and then provided detailed descriptions of different linkage protocols such as two-party, three-party, as well as multiparty protocols. We also discussed the fundamental principle of separating quasi-identifying attributes from sensitive microdata (content or payload data), where no party in a protocol should ever have access to both these types of sensitive personal information about individuals. We then described the different privacy models that have been proposed to characterise adversaries, as well as two additional aspects of relevance when linking sensitive databases; how to securely exchange secret keys and access control mechanisms. In the following chapter we discuss aspects related to assessing risks, before covering in detail the different building blocks, and the actual methods and techniques that have been developed to link sensitive databases in Chapters 6 to 8.

Recent surveys by Verykios et al. [626], Treptin [599], Durham et al. [177], and Vatsalan et al. [619], and the book chapters by Schnell [538] and Vatsalan et al. [620] provide more details about the various privacy aspects that are related to linking sensitive databases. The book by Adams and Lloyd [5] discusses public key infrastructure in detail, while the book chapter by Samarati et al. [527] is a good starting point to learn more about various aspects related to access control.

Furthermore, we refer readers interested in more detail about the separation principle to Kelman et al. [340] and Jones et al. [312], while Holman et al. [282] provide technical details on how to implement the separation principle in a real-world linkage system. A recent review of privacy models by Domingo-Ferrer et al. [162] provides more insight into the adversarial models that are applicable when sensitive databases are being linked.

As we discuss in the following chapters, most of the existing private information sharing protocols follow the honest-but-curious or malicious adversarial models, and therefore more research needs to be conducted to develop novel information sharing protocols that are applicable in more realistic privacy models such as the covert or accountable computing models.

Chapter 5
Assessing Privacy and Risks

Abstract An important aspect of any applications that facilitate the linking of sensitive data is their evaluation with regard to the privacy protection they provide, as well as the risks of a potential successful reidentification of sensitive information in any encoded or encrypted database used by such an application. In this chapter we discuss how to measure privacy and risks in the context of conducting privacy-preserving linking of sensitive databases, and we present the different types of attacks that potentially can be applied on encoded or encrypted databases where the aim of an adversary is to learn about the sensitive information contained in such databases. We also discuss the related topic of statistical disclosure control methods, which have been used by many national statistical institutes in the context of publishing sensitive microdata while at the same time ensuring that the release of such data protects the identity of all subjects in the released data.

5.1 Measuring Privacy and Risks when Linking Sensitive Data

In Section 3.4 we discussed how traditional linkage applications, that are not considering privacy during the linkage process, can be evaluated with regard to the quality of an obtained linked data set as well as the complexity of the linkage process. When sensitive databases are linked using a privacy-preserving record linkage method as defined in Section 3.6, then evaluating the privacy protection achieved by such a method is of equal importance.

Linkage quality and complexity can be evaluated using, for example, precision, recall and reduction ratio [109]. Each of these measures has an actual meaning and can be interpreted as a ratio or a probability. For example, precision (see page 62) is the proportion of compared record pairs classified as matches that are true matches, or equivalently it is the probability of a true match given a predicted match [260]. As such, these measures are similar

© Springer Nature Switzerland AG 2020
P. Christen et al., *Linking Sensitive Data*, https://doi.org/10.1007/978-3-030-59706-1_5

Table 5.1 Privacy spectrum as proposed by Reiter and Rubin [515] in the context of anonymised Web transactions, where a value between 0 and 1 can be seen as the probability that the sender of an anonymous message can be identified.

Absolute privacy	Beyond suspicion	Probable innocence	Possible innocence	Exposed	Provably exposed
0					1

to temperature or wind speed, in that they do have a direct interpretable meaning (which is not necessarily grounded in the physical world). Privacy, on the other hand, is a concept that is much more difficult to measure and evaluate, or even to conceptualise [363]. It can have different meaning in different contexts and situations, and for different organisations that participate in the linkage of sensitive databases. No single accepted mathematical framework, such as the ones used to measure linkage quality and complexity, does currently exist for measuring privacy.

Not having an interpretable meaning for privacy does not mean no attempt should be made to measure it. Being able to calculate a numerical value for privacy is highly important, because it will allow experimental evaluations and empirical tests of different methods and techniques to be conducted and results to be compared. This will provide knowledge about which methods and techniques perform better or worse in certain situations or applications, or on data sets of certain types or with certain characteristics.

Besides privacy there are other important concepts that are difficult to measure. One example is justice, which is not easy to measure as a numerical value because it is highly contextual [133]. On the other hand, there are useful numerical measures that do not have an interpretable meaning. One example is Grade Point Average (GPA), which is used across the world to assess the performance of university students and rank or group them. However, unlike a precision of 0.85, there is no direct meaning to a GPA of 3.86.

While no standard numerical measure for privacy has so far been developed, as we discuss in this chapter, several measures for privacy have been proposed that can be used to evaluate different methods and techniques for linking sensitive databases. As with the linkage quality and complexity measures described in Section 3.4, a numerical value, ideally in the range of 0 to 1, should be calculated to measure privacy.

One method to calculate such a numerical value for privacy has been proposed by Reiter and Rubin in the context of anonymising Web transactions, called the privacy spectrum [515]. As shown in Table 5.1, in this approach a numerical value measures the degree of privacy obtained against an adversary on a scale ranging from 0 to 1. These values can be seen as the probability that the identity of the sender of a transaction is exposed. Ideally, such a simple numerical privacy measure could also be used in applications where sensitive databases are being linked.

However, defining meaningful privacy measures in the context of linking sensitive databases is more complex than calculating a single number. Overall, the aim when linking sensitive databases, as we defined in Section 3.6 on page 73, is to prevent the reidentification of sensitive attribute values in an encoded or encrypted database used for linkage. Being able to identify sensitive attribute values can potentially, but not necessarily, lead to the reidentification of an individual person in such a database (known as identity disclosure [174]). Disclosure of different sensitive attributes can potentially also lead to different levels of harm. Furthermore, even the disclosure of a wrong sensitive attribute can potentially cause damage [376]. For example, wrongly disclosing the illness of a patient in a hospital database as HIV instead of cancer might lead to significant reputational damage to that patient.

If an adversary learns through an attack (as described later in this and also in Chapter 9) that a certain record in an encoded sensitive database must contain, for example, the value 'Smith', then this, by itself, will not lead to the reidentification of a certain individual if we assume there are many people named 'Smith' in the population from where the records in the database are likely coming from. Additional attributes need to be disclosed (such as first name, address, and so on) in order for the adversary to learn enough details to be able to identify an individual with certain details without doubt. On the other hand, assuming only one individual in a population has the name 'Nanayakkara', then even learning that an encoded record contains the character sequence 'ayakkar' (so not a full attribute value) could mean an identity disclosure can occur if no other individual in that population contains the string 'ayakkar'.

Ideally, it should be possible that for each record in an encoded or encrypted database, and for each person in a population who is represented by a record in such a database, a specific risk of disclosure for their attribute values and their actual identity can be calculated. It should furthermore be possible to aggregate these risks over all records in a database in a variety of ways. We discuss measures to achieve this in the following section.

As the above examples (of 'Smith' and 'Nanayakkara') show, there are different aspects of how privacy can be measured when sensitive databases are being linked using privacy-preserving record linkage techniques [615]. This makes it difficult to define single number measures in the same way as is possible for evaluating linkage quality and complexity. In the following section we describe several measures that have been developed to assess the privacy protection provided by privacy-preserving linkage techniques. Some of these privacy measures are highly related to the risk measures used in statistical disclosure control, as we discuss in Section 5.5. Note that calculating a risk of disclosing sensitive private information is also relevant in areas such as social networks, where knowing some public information about a user in one network can potentially lead to identity or attribute disclosure for the same individual in another social network [21].

5.2 Privacy Measures for Linking Sensitive Databases

Two different approaches have been proposed to measure privacy when linking sensitive databases. The first set of measures are based on information theory concepts, such as information entropy and information gain [559], to measure how much information can be gained after a database of sensitive values has been encoded or encrypted compared to the corresponding plaintext database. The second set of privacy measures are based on the risk measures used in statistical disclosure control (as we discuss in Section 5.5), where these measures calculate the risk of reidentification, as we discussed above.

Both types of measures assume an adversary has access to a global database, $\mathbf{G}$, which contains unencoded plaintext records consisting of quasi-identifying attributes about individuals (like their names, addresses, dates of birth, and so on), and an encoded or encrypted sensitive database, $\mathbf{D}^E$, where the quasi-identifying attribute values are anonymised (for example replaced with some type of code) but some sensitive attributes are available as microdata in plaintext form (such as medical or financial details). We assume that all individuals in $\mathbf{D}^E$ also occur in $\mathbf{G}$. If we define the set of all individuals in $\mathbf{G}$ as $\mathbf{I}_G$, and the set of all individuals in $\mathbf{D}^E$ as $\mathbf{I}_{D^E}$, respectively, then it holds $\mathbf{I}_G \supseteq \mathbf{I}_{D^E}$ (often a worst-case of $\mathbf{I}_G = \mathbf{I}_{D^E}$ is assumed for a privacy analysis).

The aim of the adversary is to learn which record in $\mathbf{D}^E$ corresponds to the same entity as a record in $\mathbf{G}$, allowing the adversary to learn the sensitive personal information of an individual in $\mathbf{G}$.

5.2.1 Information Entropy based Privacy Measures

Several standard information theory measures, such as entropy, information gain (IG), and relative information gain (RIG) have been used to assess the possibility of inferring a value in the global plaintext database, $\mathbf{G}$, given the encoded database $\mathbf{D}^E$ of the sensitive plaintext database $\mathbf{D}$ [178, 322]. These measures assume the worst-case scenario of where $\mathbf{G} \equiv \mathbf{D}$, because otherwise the calculated entropy values are not comparable. We provide a very short introduction to information entropy in the side box on page 103.

In the context of linking sensitive databases, and following the notation used by Durham [178], Karaksidis et al. [322], and Vatsalan et al. [615], the entropy $H(\mathbf{D})$ of a database $\mathbf{D}$ is defined as:

$$H(\mathbf{D}) = -\sum_{a \in \mathbf{D}} (n/|\mathbf{G}|) \cdot log_2 (n/|\mathbf{G}|), \qquad (5.1)$$

Information entropy

In information theory, entropy measures the average amount of information or uncertainty inherent in the possible outcomes of a random variable [559]. Entropy is a function of the probability distribution over the set of all possible values of a random variable. The entropy, H, of a random variable X with possible outcomes x, each with probability $p(x)$, is defined as:

$$H(X) = -\sum_{x} p(x) \cdot log_2\ p(x).$$

Information entropy can be seen as a measure of unpredictability. For example, if all possible messages in a system are always 'yes', then the entropy of this system will be lowest, namely 0.0 (because the next message will again be 'yes'). On the other hand, if messages either have a value of 'yes' or 'no' at random with a probability of 0.5 each then entropy is maximum, 1.0, because it is difficult to predict if the next message is a 'yes' or a 'no'.

---

where n denotes the number of attribute values a in $\mathbf{D}$ that match with a value in the global database $\mathbf{G}$, and $|\mathbf{G}|$ is the total number of records in $\mathbf{G}$.

Information Gain (IG) is closely related to the entropy measure. IG is a metric that can be used to assess the difficulty of inferring information about values in the original database, $\mathbf{D}$, assuming an adversary has access only to its encoded version, $\mathbf{D}^E$, or alternatively, how having knowledge of $\mathbf{D}^E$ can reduce the uncertainty of inferring $\mathbf{D}$ [178, 322]. The IG between $\mathbf{D}$ and $\mathbf{D}^E$ is defined as:

$$IG(\mathbf{D}|\mathbf{D}^E) = H(\mathbf{D}) - H(\mathbf{D}|\mathbf{D}^E),$$

where $H(\mathbf{D}|\mathbf{D}^E)$ is the conditional entropy between $\mathbf{D}$ and $\mathbf{D}^E$ [322]. Lower values for IG mean that it is more difficult to infer information about $\mathbf{D}$ from $\mathbf{D}^E$. The measure of relative information gain (RIG) finally provides a normalised scale (ranging from 0 to 1) with regard to the entropy of $\mathbf{D}$ and is defined as:

$$RIG(\mathbf{D}|\mathbf{D}^E) = \frac{IG(\mathbf{D}|\mathbf{D}^E)}{H(\mathbf{D})}. \qquad (5.2)$$

Again, the lower the value of RIG the more difficult it is for an adversary to learn information about the original database $\mathbf{D}$ assuming they have access to only the encoded database $\mathbf{D}^E$.

A main drawback of information entropy based privacy measures such as IG or RIG is that they require the global database $\mathbf{G}$ to be the same as the original plaintext database, $\mathbf{D}$, that was encoded into $\mathbf{D}^E$ to make the calculated entropy values comparable. Furthermore, these measures can only calculate a single overall numerical measure that characterises the privacy protection provided by the encoded database $\mathbf{D}^E$. In reality, however, different records in $\mathbf{D}^E$ will have different privacy risks [615]. The disclosure risk based measures we discuss next overcome both these limitations.

5.2.2 Disclosure Risk based Privacy Measures

Vatsalan et al. [615] introduced a set of disclosure risk [588] based measures that can be used to evaluate and compare different techniques used when linking sensitive databases. Measuring disclosure risk for each individual record in an encoded database $\mathbf{D}^E$, again assuming an adversary has access to a global database $\mathbf{G}$ (where for the corresponding sets of individuals it holds $\mathbf{I}_G \supseteq \mathbf{I}_{D^E}$ as we discussed before), allows different aggregated measures to be calculated.

In the following we describe the four aggregated measures proposed by Vatsalan et al. [619] in detail. A reader who wishes to skip this technical description is referred to the side box on page 106 which shows example calculations for these four aggregated measures.

Disclosure risk is assessed based on the likelihood of reidentifiability of a record in $\mathbf{D}^E$ by using the global database $\mathbf{G}$ to which records in $\mathbf{D}^E$ are matched to. For each record in $\mathbf{D}^E$ a probability of suspicion, PS, is calculated as the number of records in $\mathbf{G}$ that can be matched with the given record in $\mathbf{D}^E$. As shown in Equation 5.3, the values of PS are normalised into 0 and 1, where $PS = 1$ indicates that a certain record in $\mathbf{D}^E$ can be exactly reidentified with one record in $\mathbf{G}$ based on one-to-one matching, while $PS = 0$ means a record in $\mathbf{D}^E$ could correspond to any record in $\mathbf{G}$ and therefore no useful reidentification is achieved.

As with the information entropy based privacy measure shown in Equation 5.1, if we assume that n is the number of records in the global database $\mathbf{G}$ that match to a record r in the encoded database $\mathbf{D}^E$, then the normalised probability of suspicion of record r is calculated as:

$$PS(r) = \frac{1/n - 1/|\mathbf{G}|}{1 - 1/|\mathbf{G}|}, \tag{5.3}$$

where $|\mathbf{G}|$ is the total number of records in $\mathbf{G}$. Using the normalised PS values for all records in $\mathbf{D}^E$, four aggregated privacy measures based on disclosure risk can now be defined [615].

1. **Maximum disclosure risk** (DR_{Max})
   This measure is the maximum value of PS for any record in the encoded sensitive database $\mathbf{D}^E$, and therefore shows the maximum risk of reidentification (highest disclosure risk) for any record in that database. It is calculated as:
   $$DR_{Max} = \max_{r \in \mathbf{D}^E}(PS(r)).$$

2. **Mean disclosure risk** (DR_{Mean})
   This measure is the average of the PS values of all records in $\mathbf{D}^E$. It can be used to evaluate the average disclosure risk for a record in that database. If the number of records in the encoded database is $|\mathbf{D}^E|$, this measure is calculated as:

   $$DR_{Mean} = \frac{\sum_{r \in \mathbf{D}^E} PS(r)}{|\mathbf{D}^E|}.$$

3. **Median disclosure risk** (DR_{Med})
   The median disclosure risk gives the centre of the distribution of disclosure risk values by taking into account the distribution of the PS values of all records in the encoded database $\mathbf{D}^E$. By assuming the list of PS values of all records in $\mathbf{D}^E$ is sorted from the lowest to the highest, and PS_m is the probability of suspicion of the middle of this list (if $\mathbf{D}^E$ contains an odd number of records) or PS_m and PS_{m+1} are the probabilities of suspicion of the two middle records (if $\mathbf{D}^E$ contains an even number of records), then the median disclosure risk can be calculated as:

   $$DR_{Med} = \begin{cases} (PS_m + PS_{m+1})/2 & \text{if } |\mathbf{D}^E| \text{ is even,} \\ PS_m & \text{if } |\mathbf{D}^E| \text{ is odd.} \end{cases}$$

4. **Marketer disclosure risk** (DR_{Mkt})
   This measure defines how many values in the encoded database can be exactly reidentified with a probability of suspicion of $PS = 1$, calculated as the fraction of records in $\mathbf{D}^E$ that have a $PS = 1$:

   $$DR_{Mkt} = \frac{|\{r : PS(r) = 1 \ and \ r \in \mathbf{D}^E\}|}{|\mathbf{D}^E|}.$$

Together, these four measures allow a much better evaluation of the privacy risk of an encoded database, and depending upon the sensitivity of the encoded values or the application scenario of how the encoded database is being used (for example only internal to one organisation or shared with other organisations), a different aggregated risk measure might be most useful. The marketer risk, DR_{Mkt}, is potentially one of the most useful measures because it clearly highlights the proportion of records in $\mathbf{D}^E$ that have the highest possible risk (of $PS = 1$) being identified. An example of how to calculate these four disclosure risk based measures is provided in the side box on page 106.

Besides the advantage of being able to calculate a variety of aggregated privacy measures, because one probability of suspicion value is calculated per record in the encoded database $\mathbf{D}^E$, this approach also allows the visualisation of these PS values, as is illustrated in Figure 5.1.

Furthermore, the above measures can be modified by taking a user acceptance risk into account [615]. This is based on the idea of k-anonymity (which

---

Example disclosure risk calculation

Assume we have a small data set of fifteen records, and for each of these records the risk of reidentification was calculated using Equation 5.3 [615], resulting in the following (sorted) list of probability of suspicion, $PS(r)$, values:

$$[1.0, 1.0, 1.0, 1.0, 0.5, 0.5, 0.5, \mathit{0.2}, 0.2, 0.1, 0.1, 0.1, 0.1, 0.1, 0.1]$$

The four disclosure risk measures described before are calculated as:

1. The maximum disclosure risk, DR_{Max}, is 1.0 because the maximum value in the list is 1.0.
2. The mean (average) disclosure risk, DR_{Mean}, is 0.433 given the sum of these fifteen $PS(r)$ values is 6.5, resulting in an average of $6.5/15 = 0.433$.
3. The median disclosure risk, DR_{Med}, is 0.2 given the element in the middle of this list (the eighth element, shown in italics) is 0.2.
4. Finally, the marketer disclosure risk, DR_{Mkt}, is 0.266 because four of the fifteen $PS(r)$ values are 1.0, leading to the calculation of $4/15 = 0.266$ for this disclosure risk measure.

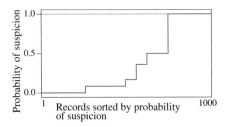
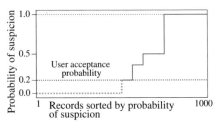

Fig. 5.1 Examples of probability of suspicion, PS, values for a database of 1,000 records, sorted from lowest to highest. The left hand side plot shows the case without a user acceptable risk while on the right hand side the probability of suspicion is set to 0 for all records with a risk below the user acceptance risk of $k = 5$ ($1/5 = 0.2$), shown as the dashed line below the dotted lower horizontal line at 0.2.

we cover in Section 6.3.2), where the user is willing to accept a probability of suspicion of up to $PS < 1/k$, where k is the number of records in $\mathbf{G}$ that match to one record in $\mathbf{D}^E$ according to Equation 5.3. For all records in $\mathbf{D}^E$ where their value of PS is less than $1/k$ we set their $PS = 0$, as is illustrated in the right hand side of Figure 5.1.

5.3 Data Breaches and Mishaps when Dealing with Sensitive Data

Now that we have discussed how to measure privacy and risk in the context of linking sensitive databases, the question arises how can an adversary actually get access to an encoded database and learn about the sensitive personal or otherwise confidential information stored in such a database. This process of an adversary trying to infer sensitive information from encoded data is commonly known as an attack. A successful attack leads to a data breach where the adversary gains unauthorised and illegitimate access to confidential or sensitive data [34].

A deliberate attack by an adversary is different from the unintentional loss or publication of sensitive or confidential data due to technical or human mistakes [567]. Such mishaps when dealing with sensitive data can for example occur when a trusted employee sends an email containing sensitive data to the wrong recipient, copies a sensitive file to the wrong folder making it publicly available on a Web site, or loses a DVD, USB flash drive, or even a laptop with highly sensitive data on a train or plane.

Data breaches, on the other hand, are the results of deliberate attempts by adversaries to gain access to specific sensitive or confidential data they are interested in. There have been many stories in the news about data breaches, mostly involving data about customers as held by commercial businesses, but also at non profit organisations, and even government agencies and universities [34]. Recent work has reported that the majority of losses of sensitive data were due to errors, such as loss resulting from device theft or because of system malfunctions [567].

Many data breaches involve external adversaries, commonly labelled hackers in the press, which aim to gain access to sensitive personal information for financial or other gain. Direct financial gain can be obtained if the breached data contain complete details of credit cards and their owners (including names, full sixteen digit numbers, expiry dates, and the card verification number on the back of cards) as this allows the adversary to immediately use a card for fraudulent activities such as online purchases. Indirect financial gain is obtained via identity fraud [20] where the adversary uses the identified personal details from the breached database to obtain services and benefits they are not entitled to.

Besides financial gain, databases containing sensitive information have been attacked and breached with the aim to obtain confidential material such as information related to the national security of countries, elections of governments, military secrets, or commercial in confidence information such as commercial research and development or patent applications. In many reported data breaches it is unclear who the actual adversaries were, and tracing them can be challenging [34].

There are also cases where sensitive personal information has been breached and disclosed for pure personal reasons. A recent such case was reported in Singapore in 2018[1], where the personal details of several thousand HIV patients were made publicly available by the partner of a senior employee of Singapore's National Public Health Unit who had access to this data.

---

[1] See: https://www.moh.gov.sg/news-highlights/details/unauthorised-possession-and-disclosure-of-information-from-hiv-registry

While such cases are rare, they highlight that any database that contains unencoded sensitive information about individuals (such as their contact details, plus financial or medical information) can be vulnerable to attacks by adversaries, both external and internal. Encoding personal sensitive information, as we discuss in detail in the next four chapters, can significantly reduce the risks of sensitive data about individuals to be revealed because no quasi-identifying information is contained in plaintext in such encoded databases. An adversary would require significant efforts to reidentify individuals in an encoded database. However, as the different attacks we describe below show, even encoded data can potentially be vulnerable to certain types of attacks.

One aspect of attacks on databases that are aimed for medical or social science research and contain sensitive encoded personal information together with plaintext sensitive microdata (such as medical details), is the question what the motivation would be of an adversary to attack such databases. Unlike direct financial benefits, the only profitable way to gain financially from successfully disclosed personal details would be to blackmail those individuals who have certain compromising medical conditions or other characteristics that would damage their reputation. Such blackmailing on a large scale would however incur significant costs for the adversary. The other motivations, such as attacking a medical database for pure personal reasons or for the purpose of revenge on an individual or organisation (as with the example from Singapore described above), are likely to be a very rare events.

To summarise, a key aspect, not just of linking sensitive data but also of handling sensitive data more generally, is that storing, processing, and exchanging such data in plaintext form does make them significantly more vulnerable to attacks and mishaps. If sensitive data are encoded or encrypted, on the other hand, then even if breached or revealed unintentionally, an adversary still needs to apply further efforts to try to reidentify the actual sensitive values in such encoded or encrypted data. If appropriate encoding and encryption methods are used then any such reidentification is either provably impossible or will require significant computational efforts as well as expert knowledge in cryptography.

A major message of this book is therefore to encourage the use of encoding and encryption techniques to better protect sensitive databases while still enabling the linking of such data across organisations. We discuss such techniques in the following four chapters. First we describe different types of attacks on sensitive data in more detail.

5.4 Attacks on Sensitive Data

Attacking encrypted or encoded data has a long history going back hundreds if not thousands of years [562]. For example, the use of frequency analysis to identify encoded values was first described in the 9th century by the Arab scientist Al-Kindi who compared the relative frequency of each symbol in an encoded text with the relative frequencies of equivalent symbols derived from text which he believed had a similar frequency distribution of values as the secret encoded text [562].

The study of analysing codes with the aim to identify their hidden information is known as cryptanalysis [562], and attacks that aim to conduct such identifications are known as cryptanalysis attacks. Many different cryptanalysis attacks have been proposed. While some are specific to certain encoding or encryption algorithms, others are more general and independent of the encoding method used, and are applicable to several types of encoded data. Most attacks assume an adversary has access to a database that likely contains values from a similar domain, and potentially with similar frequencies, of what is assumed to be in the encoded database that is being attacked and analysed by the adversary.

In the context of linking sensitive databases, as we describe in more detail in Chapters 8 and 9, techniques based on encoding sensitive values into bit vectors (lists of 0s and 1s) have shown to be popular. These bit vectors can, however, contain patterns of frequently co-occurring 1-bits, which can be analysed and correlated to frequent values in a plaintext database, such as common first names or surnames. Several sophisticated cryptanalysis attacks that exploit such frequent patterns within and across bit vectors have been developed [119, 120, 123, 367, 371, 372, 438, 629]. Given the popularity of such bit vector based encodings in the context of linking sensitive databases, we cover these attacks in detail in Chapter 9.

In the following we describe the general types of attacks that can potentially been used to reidentify sensitive values in an encoded or encrypted database. We start with attacks on the likely least secure and most unpredictable component of any application that deals with sensitive data: humans.

5.4.1 Insider Attacks and Social Engineering

Attacks on encoded sensitive databases can be both technical (described in the following subsections) and non-technical. One non-technical type of attack is an insider attack (such as the example from Singapore described above), while another type is social engineering.

The most famous and most publicised insider attack so far has been by Edward Snowden who, working as a system administrator for the US National Security Agency with almost unlimited system access rights, was able to access highly classified US national security information. Through a lack of oversight, Snowden was able to extract and later publish such classified information.

More generally, an insider attack is when a trusted employee of an organisation is able to get access to sensitive data and furthermore can copy such data in some form and later disclose it to the public or sell it to another organisation (in which case such an attack might never be discovered). Common mechanisms to prevent insider attacks include access control mechanisms (as we discussed in Section 4.5), confidentiality agreements (with possible prosecution and even jail terms if sensitive information is being disclosed), stringent monitoring procedures of employees (including that nobody is allowed to be in a room with access to sensitive data by herself or himself), and technical limitations (such as physically preventing any portable storage devices or cameras to be accessed by employees). A recent example is the development of the SafePod[2] environment in the UK to enable secure access to sensitive data for researchers.

Social engineering is another non-technical type of attack, where an adversary aims to gain knowledge of crucial pieces of information such as secret passwords through so called phishing or other methods of deceit. Phishing is the process of sending faked emails asking, for example, for password updates where an unsuspected individual is redirected to a faked (made-up) Web site (which looks like an organisation's real Web site) to update their password, thereby providing their existing login credentials. Similarly, phishing attacks can be conducted over the telephone, where an adversary for example claims to be an IT administrator of a company who requires a password to upgrade the IT equipment of an employee. Once in possession of login credentials, the adversary can then try to identify further crucial information such as the program codes and secret keys used to encode or encrypt sensitive databases.

To prevent such insider and social engineering attacks, proper screening and training of all personnel who will be able to access sensitive information is of utmost importance. These should not be one-off initial training modules, but ongoing confirmation that employees understand their duties with regard to protecting the sensitive data they are trusted with.

5.4.2 Dictionary Attacks

In a dictionary attack, the assumption is that the adversary has gained access to an encoded database, and also knows the encoding method and all required secret keys (passwords) used in the encoding process. What the adversary does not know is the actual values encoded in the encoded database they have gained access to.

Using publicly available data, ideally a large database covering a full population, the adversary can use their knowledge of the encoding method and secret key(s) and simply apply this encoding method on all values in the public database to see if any encoding that is generated does match exactly with a value in the encoded sensitive database. If such a match occurs then

---

[2]   See: https://esrc.ukri.org/files/funding/funding-opportunities/
safepod-brochure/

the adversary has learned that the corresponding value from the plaintext database occurs in the matching record in the encoded database.

A dictionary attack can be made more difficult if each value that is encoded (using one of the methods we discuss in the following chapters) is combined with a secret key (or password) that is only known to the organisation(s) that encode their sensitive values. For example, assume first names are encoded into hash values using a one-way hash function such as SHA-1 or SHA-2 [535], as we describe in Section 6.2. If no secret key is used in this encoding process, then the adversary, who we assume knows the encoding method, simply needs to encode all first names from a public database (such as a telephone book or a list of popular baby names) to identify all matching encodings which provide the adversary with all encoded first names in the database.

On the other hand, assume each first name is concatenated with a secret key. For example, a first name 'tom' is concatenated with the secret key 'XwU7xQ!' into 'tomXwU7xQ!' before being encoded. Then, assuming the adversary does not know this secret key, it will be nearly impossible for the adversary to successfully conduct a dictionary attack because he would have to try all possible secret keys concatenated with all possible first names, leading to a very large number of possible encodings to try. If a secret key can be any string for any length, the number of possible secret keys will be very large. This approach is generally known as keyed cryptographic hashing (functions such as HMAC [364]), as we describe in more detail in Section 6.2.2.

5.4.3 Frequency Attacks

If an adversary does not have knowledge of the encoding method and its parameters used, but only has access to an encoded database, they can still mount an attack on the frequency distribution of the encodings in the encoded database. For this attack we assume the adversary has some knowledge about the type of values encoded in a database, for example they know that the records contain the names and addresses of patients living in a certain country or region.

A frequency attack is based on the frequency distribution of a set of encoded values which are compared to the frequency distribution of a set of plaintext values. Even without knowing the encoding method and its parameters used during the encoding process, it is possible that some encoded values can be reidentified by matching their frequencies with the frequency distribution of plaintext values in a public database [397, 438, 620]. If, for example, the most common surname is 'smith' followed by 'miller' in a plaintext database, then the two most common encodings with similar frequencies (or frequency percentages) in an encoded database will likely correspond to these two surnames.

Fig. 5.2 The frequency distribution (for the thirty most common values) of hash encoded CITY values compared with the distributions of plaintext values for the FIRST-NAME, SURNAME, and CITY attributes from a North Carolina Voter Registration database [111]. These distributions highlight that the frequencies of encoded city values closely match those of plaintext city values, allowing an adversary to reidentify some frequent city values.

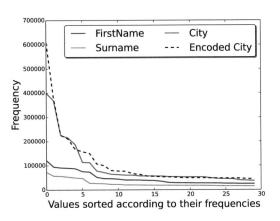

We illustrate this idea in Figure 5.2 where we show the frequency distribution of hash encoded city values (using HMAC [364], a technique we discuss in Section 6.2.2) compared with the distributions of plaintext values for the FIRSTNAME, SURNAME, and CITY attributes from a North Carolina Voter Registration database [111], where the encoded database was from April 2019 while the plaintext database was from April 2014. These distributions highlight that the frequencies of encoded city values closely match those of plaintext city values in the public voter database, allowing an adversary to reidentify some frequent city values.

Once an adversary has gained knowledge of at least one encoded frequent value, they can then try to identify the encoding method and its parameter settings by conducting a type of dictionary attack where the encoding and assumed encoded plaintext value are known for a few frequent values, but not all details of the encoding method. The actual encoded values, such as bit strings or character strings and their length, provide the adversary with knowledge of the type of encoding method that was used. In the following chapters we discuss such encoding methods in detail.

5.4.4 Composition Attacks

In composition attacks, an adversary needs to have background knowledge (auxiliary information) about the individual databases that are to be linked, specifically the inclusion of certain records in these databases. Using such auxiliary information from the different databases that have been linked, the adversary can for example learn the distances or similarities between sensitive attribute values of a given record [223, 389].

As an example of such an attack, assume two hospitals in the same city release encoded patient-discharge information. Because they are in the same city, some patients have likely visited both hospitals with similar illnesses. By using the overlapping patient population in these encoded databases, an adversary can try to identify the illness of a person he knows and who lives in this city.

A specific type of composition attack is the known scheme attack [165], where an adversary knows the details of the encoding method that has been used by the database owners, but not the secret key(s). The adversary can, for example, analyse the frequency distribution of encodings generated in a blocking process (as we discussed in Section 3.2) and compare them with the block sizes obtained when applying the same blocking method on a related plaintext database. Similar block sizes will likely be generated by the same blocking method independent of any secret keys being used during the block encoding process [165].

5.4.5 Collusion Attacks

In applications where several organisations or parties (such as database owners, as we described in Section 4.1) collaborate with the aim to link their sensitive databases, potentially with the support of other parties, collusion can occur between some of these parties [129, 453, 615]. Recently, in different domains ranging from online rating, auctioning, and mobile computing, many data related applications that involve multiple parties have experienced behaviour of collusion as some participating parties were trying to gain access to unauthorised data, or otherwise gain benefits [16, 80]. In the context of linking sensitive databases, the aim of collusion is to learn the sensitive data of another not colluding party by the colluding parties sharing their own data and parameter settings [11, 624].

A collusion attack can be seen as a variation of an insider or social engineering attack, because it requires collaboration between parties and their agreement to share their own sensitive data as well as details of the encoding process with other parties. One can for example imagine a collusion attack where an employee is blackmailed to provide the encoding parameters or even an encoded database to another party to allow that party to conduct the attack.

Different types of collusion scenarios might occur with regard to the protocol employed to link sensitive databases between organisations, as well as the types and numbers of parties in the different roles involved in the protocol, as we described in Section 4.1. Generally, collusion can happen by a subgroup of parties working together, with or without the involvement of the linkage unit who is tasked with linking the encoded data. Based on the different link-

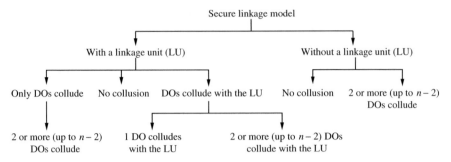

Fig. 5.3 Collusion scenarios that are possible in different linkage models with and without a linkage unit (LU), and assuming n database owners (DOs), where $n \geq 2$, as we discuss in Section 4.3. © T. Ranbaduge 2018, reprinted with permission.

age models discussed in Section 4.3, we can categorise the different possible collusion scenarios as illustrated in Figure 5.3 [502].

As can be seen from this figure, let us assume n database owners participate in the process of linking their sensitive database with or without the use of a linkage unit. For the model without a linkage unit, a group of database owners can collude with each other to identify the private input of one or more other database owner(s). The possible collusion scenarios can be categorised into two: no collusion, and collusion between two or more database owners (at most $n - 2$) where they aim to identify the sensitive data of one or more other non-colluding database owner(s) they communicate with.

In the no collusion scenario all the participating parties can be trusted and no actions are carried out by any database owner to learn the sensitive data of any other database owner. However, such a scenario might be impractical in some real applications, especially in commercial environments, as we discussed in Section 4.4. The second scenario (where two or more database owners collude) is more realistic in real-world situations where multiple database owners (at most $n - 2$) might be colluding with each other to learn the sensitive data of another database owner [394, 502].

For the scenarios with a linkage unit, collusion can occur either between the database owners only, or between the linkage unit and one or more database owner(s). Apart from the two collusion scenarios described above, database owners can collude with the linkage unit in two different ways: (1) one database owner colludes with the linkage unit trying to identify the sensitive data of another database owner that it communicates with, and (2) two or more (at most $n - 2$) database owners collude with the linkage unit to learn the sensitive data of one or more non-colluding other database owner(s). Since the linkage unit is often assumed to follow the honest-but-curious adversarial model (as we discussed in Section 4.4), both of these collusion scenarios can be realistic in practical linkage applications. This requires any linkage application that is used in a semi-honest or malicious context to be collusion resistant [394].

For both the linkage scenarios with or without the linkage unit the risk of collusion between $n-1$ database owners is not solvable if all database owners obtain the final linkage result. For example, in a four-party linkage protocol if three of the database owners collude with each other then they can potentially learn the sensitive data of the remaining database owners by matching their own input data with the final linkage result. Because multiparty linkage applications are increasingly being considered both in the private and the public sectors (as well as across these sectors), the challenges discussed here about collusion need to be carefully evaluated for any real-world application where sensitive databases are being linked across multiple organisations.

5.4.6 Linkage Attacks

Unlike the previously described attacks, a linkage attack is not aimed at sensitive data that contain encoded quasi-identifying attributes that are to be used for linking with other sensitive databases. Rather, it is an attack on an anonymised data set that contains (potentially sensitive) microdata in plaintext, such as medical, educational, or financial details, or occupation or shopping information, about individuals, as well as certain demographic details about these individuals, for example their gender, age, or the postcode where they live. In a linkage attack, the adversary aims to match anonymised records to records in an external, not deidentified, data set she has access to [162, 583]. Such an external data set must contain some demographic attributes (such as the ones described above), as well as further identifying details such as names, addresses, or telephone numbers, that allow the adversary to uniquely identify individuals. External data sets that can be used for a linkage attack might include, for example, public telephone books or online directories (Whitepages), or public voter databases that are accessible to an adversary with no or little effort [111], or that can be purchased by anybody.

For a linkage attack to be successful, the adversary requires an external data set that has a set of attributes in common with the plaintext microdata in the anonymised data set (for example the demographic attributes described above). If a unique combination of values in these attributes occurs in exactly one record in both the micodata of the anonymised data set and the external data set, then the adversary can link these two records. This will lead to the reidentification of sensitive microdata about the person who is represented by the linked anonymised record [162]. Besides demographic attributes (such as gender, age, birth year, or postcode) described above, other attributes that potentially allow to link records are medical details (episodes of care, or rare diseases, procedures, or treatments), education details such as degrees obtained when and from which university, or even patterns of shopping transactions or consumer preferences.

Matches between more than one record in each data set, or partial matches of some but not all attributes, will make a reidentification less certain but might still provide the adversary with enough information to learn the sensitive personal information of certain individuals. In Section 5.5 we describe how the risk of such linkage based disclosure can be measured.

A famous successful linkage attack was presented by Latanya Sweeney [583] who successfully linked public hospital records from the US state of Massachusetts with a voter list from the same state. She was able to successfully reidentify the medical record of the then governor of Massachusetts, and found that 12% of over 50,000 voters had a unique date of birth. Furthermore, combining dates of birth with gender increased uniqueness to 29%. Dates of birth and 9-digit zipcodes were unique for 97% of all voters in this data set. As a result, Sweeney showed that an adversary who has enough detailed information in (otherwise) anonymised microdata can successfully reidentify the records of individuals using suitable external data that contain a set of attributes that is also available in the anonymised microdata.

The success of a linkage attack crucially depends upon the availability of relevant information to the adversary. Considering or modelling what information is available to an adversary can be difficult [161], especially in today's networked world where many individuals have a presence online in several social media platforms. It is likely that an adversary can collect or infer certain details about many individuals in a population from their online behaviour or directly from the information they post online (such as calculating a possible age of a person based on the years of their high school or university graduations, or gender from their photos).

While the linkage attack scenario discussed so far assumes an adversary uses an external data set for the attack, a somewhat different scenario is for a linkage attack to be conducted by a member of a data owning organisation involved in a legally permitted linkage. For example, a curious employee of an organisation (database owner) DO_A might have access to a data set $\mathbf{D}_A$ containing quasi-identifying attributes of individuals and additional information such as medical data. This data set $\mathbf{D}_A$ is legally used for a linkage with a second data set $\mathbf{D}_B$ of another organisation, DO_B, also containing quasi-identifying attributes of individuals and additional information. One or more independent linkage units produce a linked data set $\mathbf{D}_L = \mathbf{D}_A \cap \mathbf{D}_B$. As usual, $\mathbf{D}_L$ does not contain any quasi-identifying attributes. However, if the curious employee of DO_A can get access to the data set $\mathbf{D}_L$, she can compute the intersection $\mathbf{D}_{B*} = \mathbf{D_L} \cap \mathbf{D}_A$. Due to linkage errors, the intersection $\mathbf{D}_{B*}$ is only an approximation to the intersection $\mathbf{D}_A \cap \mathbf{D}_B$. However, either the size of the intersection or the identity of the individuals in the intersection might be the sensitive information the curious employee is interested in. Examples are databases of people with incompatible professions (in Germany, a lawyer can for instance not be the CEO of a real estate agency) or databases of rare diseases whose co-occurrence make a sensitive diagnosis likely.

This kind of attack could be considered as a linkage attack by an insider. As such, it can be made harder by limiting access to the data set $\mathbf{D}_L$. If this data set is to be used for scientific research (known as a scientific use file), then technical or organisational measures such as the Five Safes (as we discussed in Section 2.7.1) are necessary to prevent this kind of attack.

This latter form of a linkage attack can also be used by an organisation as a method to assess the disclosure risk of microdata. To evaluate how sensitive the content of their anonymised microdata are with regard to disclosure risk (as we discuss further in Section 5.5), organisations such as national statistical agencies that are releasing scientific use files usually conduct linkage attacks on such microdata for testing before releasing the data.

5.4.7 Motivation, Costs, and Gains of Attacks

An important aspect of attacks on sensitive databases are the questions what the motivation is for an attack, what an adversary can gain from the attack, and if an attack is worth the efforts and costs for the adversary. As we discussed in Section 5.3, besides financial gains for the adversary, the motivation can also be to learn national or military secrets, or confidential commercial or political information. The willingness of the adversary and the amount of efforts put into an attack will depend upon what the adversary can potentially gain from the attack. The ability of an adversary to mount an attack is also crucial, as are the risks and repercussions if the adversary is detected and identified. There is a large difference between the willingness and ability, and potential gain of knowledge, of a state sponsored adversary trying to obtain highly sensitive national security information versus a teenager trying to unlock the secret diary of his sibling.

The potential financial or other gains of an adversary when attacking medical, census, survey, or research databases that contain sensitive personal information is likely much less than what an adversary can potentially gain when attacking a commercial database that contains personal financial information such as credit card details. As a result, as at the time of writing, we are not aware of any published specific attack on medical, census, survey, or research databases. However, given the potential reputational loss to an organisation if such an attack on their sensitive data would occur, it is crucial for organisations not to be complacent and rather follow best practice approaches to encoding and encryption of the sensitive personal information in their databases.

While low financial gain will not prevent attacks on medical or research databases, better understanding what would motivate an adversary and the costs and benefits involved in attacking databases that contain sensitive personal details (but no financial information) is therefore important. Thus far limited work has explored this topic. Wan et al. [635] have recently developed a game theoretic framework to analyse the costs and benefits of attacks that aim to reidentify health databases such as those used in medical information sharing systems. The assumption of this work is that an adversary will only attack a database if they can gain some benefit from the attack, where their gain outweighs their costs. Wan et al. in their work showed that it is possible to share significant amount of data in such ways that there is no overall gain for an adversary [635].

5.5 Statistical Disclosure Control Methods

In many jurisdictions, organisations wishing to publish statistical results or microdata are required to ensure that the release of data protects the identity of entities in such data. Traditionally, this task was an obvious problem faced by national statistical institutes. In this context, the problem was named statistical disclosure control (SDC) [173]. The aim of SDC is the development and application of techniques applied to data to minimise the risk of disclosing information about individuals while maintaining the usefulness (utility) of the modified data for the intended purpose.

In the context of linking sensitive data, depending upon if a linked data set is to be made public rather than being used within a secure environment, SDC techniques might need to be applied in order to minimise disclosure risk. Note also that SDC techniques have been developed by a variety of research communities, where Torra [595] provides a unified perspective.

5.5.1 Statistical Disclosure Control Techniques

Given this initial application described above, many SDC techniques have been developed for the protection of tabular data to be published (for a review of these techniques, see Hundepool et al. [288]). More relevant for this book are procedures applied before releasing microdata. SDC techniques are most often classified as either non-perturbative or perturbative. Non-perturbative methods reduce data details by recoding, rounding, sampling, or suppression of attribute values. Generalisation techniques such as k-anonymity, as we will discuss in Section 6.3.2, are examples of non-perturbative methods. In contrast, perturbative methods modify attribute values, for example, by adding noise, as we will cover in Section 6.3.1. Here we describe some of the most widely cited SDC techniques for microdata. For details we refer the interested reader to the technical literature [162, 173, 288].

Attacking population covering data sets is simpler than attacking a data set which includes only a subset of a population. This is because a subset will likely have a less diverse range of quasi-identifying attribute values, and it is not clear if a record about a certain individual is included in the subset or not. Therefore, sampling records for publishing data sets is a widely used non-perturbative SDC technique. For example, many national statistical institutes do not allow access to the census or other large data sets in total, but they permit access to scientific use files consisting of randomly selected subsets such as a 70% sample of a 1% population sample.

One of the oldest and most widely used SDC techniques consists of coarsening the categories of attributes. In the context of SDC, this is mostly denoted as recoding. Here, different categories of an attribute are coded as one category. For example, if some categories of marital status are rare in a database (such as 'widowed' and 'divorced'), then these categories might be recoded as 'single'. For continuous distributions, forming intervals (binning) can be considered as recoding for SDC purposes. A simple variant is called bottom- or top-coding, where attribute values beyond a threshold are coded as one category. An obvious example for top-coding is monthly income, where all values exceeding a certain limit are coded as the value at the limit. To prevent exact matching of a database record with other databases potentially containing information of the same record, rounding of continuous values to values with less precision might also be applied as a SDC measure.

By combining multiple (categorical) attribute values, a record might become uniquely identifiable. To prevent this, a technique denoted as local suppression is widely used. Local suppression replaces certain existing attribute values by missing data in a way that the number of records with the same combination of attribute values is increased. The simplest implementation identifies records with an individual disclosure risk above a threshold and then replaces all values of the attributes under consideration by missing values [591].

Perturbation techniques replace actually observed data by noise, summary statistics, estimated data, or swapped data. Therefore, adding noise to observed data might be considered as the simplest perturbative SDC method. Simply adding random noise will reduce the correlation between perturbed attributes, and adding correlated noise to preserve correlations might be regarded as a superior SDC method [85].

Microaggregation for numerical data consists in forming homogeneous groups of records and replacing the critical numerical attribute values by a summary statistic such as the mean of this group. Such homogeneous groups can be created by sorting on stratification attributes, principle components, or by cluster membership after clustering [591]. Widely used is MDAV (Maximum Distance to Average Vector), a technique where the groups are formed by the multivariate Euclidean distance of records [160].

Another microdata perturbation technique is denoted as Post-Randomisation Method or PRAM [236, 286]. Basically, in PRAM the attribute values of a record are replaced with other values (or noise) according to a prespecified transition probability matrix. However, specifying such a transition matrix is not straightforward.

As a building block for more elaborate techniques, swapping deserves mentioning. For a given record, swapping exchanges a set of attribute values with the same set of attribute values from a different record. All kinds of restrictions on the allowable set of attribute values (for example, conditioning on certain attributes as income or gender) can be imposed. As a stand-alone technique, swapping is rarely used. More common is rank-swapping. Ordinal or numerical attribute values are ranked and swapped with other ranked values, where certain restrictions on the allowable range of ranks are applied.

Over-imputation consists of deleting potential disclosing attribute values in a given record and estimating the then missing values by a statistical model. Since the imputation result might violate edit rules (for example, predicting a widowhood for children), additional consistency checks are required for over-imputation. Over-imputation is conceptually simple but rarely used in practice.

A final perturbative SDC technique is shuffling [424]. Sensitive attribute values are ranked, the ranks are predicted by a regression model, and then the sensitive values are replaced by predictions of the same rank as the actual sensitive value. Therefore, the information loss resulting from shuffling depends on the goodness of fit of the prediction model.

5.5.2 Evaluating Statistical Disclosure Control Techniques

All SDC techniques imply the degrading of data quality and data utility. Data scientists, statisticians, and subject matter specialists are rarely enthusiastic concerning the use of SDC techniques. However, the risks of publishing data are obvious when sensitive attributes are concerned. For the evaluation of the success of SDC techniques, metrics for data utility and disclosure risk are required.

Measures of disclosure risk have to consider the kind of attacks plausible in a given context and the auxiliary information available for the adversary [187, 188]. Many different kinds of attacks have been described in the literature. A privacy attack on a microdata set can be successful if, for example [405]:

- the majority of the records in a group of records have the same sensitive attribute value,
- background knowledge allows eliminating most or all but one sensitive value in a group of records,
- the distribution of the values in an attribute is skewed,
- the values of an attribute in a group of records are different but semantically similar (for example, belong to the same known income interval),
- a close numerical value of an attribute can be inferred, and

- in-depth knowledge on the used SDC method allows the partial reversal of the technique by an adversary.

Detailed examples of these attacks are given by Matwin et al. [405].

Measures of disclosure risk are mostly based on key attributes (such as age and marital status), which are determined according to hypothetical disclosure scenarios [591]. For discrete (categorical) attribute values, records with unique combinations of key attribute values have a high risk of reidentification. A record with a unique combination of key attribute values is denoted in the SDC literature as sample unique. If a combination is unique in the population, the record is a population unique. Basic risk measures are based on counts of population and sample unique records. For example, Taylor et al. [588] discuss five different measures of disclosure risk for records, where the assumption is that the adversary has access to an external data set that covers a whole population and contains both quasi-identifying attributes as well as key attributes which overlap with the sensitive microdata. The five measures discussed by Taylor et al. [588] are:

1. the expected number of population uniques,
2. the expected number of sample uniques that are population unique,
3. the expected number of correct matches among sample uniques,
4. the probability of a correct match given a unique match, and
5. the probability of a correct match,

where for the last three measures a match is defined between a record in the microdata and a record in the population that have the same values in a set of key attributes.

Further details of disclosure risk measures, for example for numerical attributes, risk measures at file-level, or global risk measures, are beyond the scope of this book. For such measures we refer the interested reader to the book by Templ [590].

Measures of information loss (or loss of utility) due to SDC methods are generally based on computations of divergence between estimated parameters based on the original and modified data. For example, differences in means, variances, correlations, eigenvalues, and so on, are used to evaluate the impact of the data modifications applied [54].

However, these kind of measures are specific for certain attributes and certain data analysis results. Two global measures for information loss have been suggested by Woo et al. [649]. In this work, the modified and unmodified data sets are merged (stacked), and either logistic regression or cluster analysis is performed on the merged data set. Indices based on the estimated propensity score to belong to the unmodified data set or based on the cluster membership are used to quantify the ability to discriminate between the modified and unmodified data sets. A detailed example of the computation is given by Templ [590].

The application of more elaborate SDC techniques and the computation of measures of disclosure risk have been cumbersome until two programs became available as open-source software: μ-Argus[3] and sdcMicro[4]. μ-Argus is widely used by national statistical institutes in Europe. The more recent version of sdcMicro may seem more user-friendly. An excellent introduction to applied SDC techniques is given by Benschopp et al. [54], while a detailed description for sdcMicro is provided in the book by Templ [590] (one of the developers of sdcMicro).

5.6 Summary and Further Reading

In this chapter we have covered the topic of how to assess privacy and risks in the context of linking sensitive databases. We have shown that measuring privacy is not as straightforward as measuring for example linkage quality. One reason for this is that currently there are no accepted measures for privacy. A single numerical privacy measure might also not be adequate for assessing and comparing different privacy-preserving record linkage techniques. We have then covered existing measures that have been proposed to assess privacy, either based on information entropy or the risk of disclosure.

In the second part of this chapter we have described data breaches and the different types of attacks that can be attempted by an adversary who aims to learn information from a sensitive, potentially encoded or encrypted, database. These attacks range from social engineering to the collusion between a group of parties involved in a protocol to link sensitive databases between organisations. We also discussed the motivation an adversary might have when attacking a sensitive database, and the costs and gains of such an attack. We finally discussed the related topic of statistical disclosure control as commonly employed by national statistical institutes that aim to release useful data. At the same time these institutes are required to ensure any released data does not allow any identification of sensitive values nor of identities.

We refer readers interested in privacy evaluation measure for linking sensitive databases to the article by Vatsalan et al. [615]. The book by Singh [562] provides a history of techniques developed to encode and encrypt information, and how these codes have been broken. Statistical disclosure control is covered in detail in the books by Domingo-Ferrer et al. [162], Duncan et al. [173], and Hundepool et al. [288], while Torra [595] discusses a wide range of data privacy issues in the context of Big data.

---

[3] The source code of μ-Argus is available at: `https://github.com/sdcTools`

[4] The R program sdcMicro is available via CRAN at: `https://cran.r-project.org/web/packages/sdcMicro/index.html`, and the most recent version is located at: `https://github.com/sdcTools/sdcMicro`

Chapter 6
Building Blocks for Linking Sensitive Data

Abstract This chapter covers in detail the various techniques that are employed as building blocks in protocols used to link sensitive databases. These include techniques to generate random values, as well as various hashing, anonymisation, and encryption techniques. We also cover the basic building blocks used in secure multiparty computation approaches such as secure summation and secure set intersection, and discuss differential privacy. We then describe methods for phonetic encoding, statistical linkage keys, and measures that can be used to calculate similarities between two values. We conclude the chapter with a discussion about the applicability of such building blocks when they are used in the context of linking sensitive databases.

6.1 Random Number Generation

Many algorithms used to encode or encrypt data require random numbers to be generated, for example to perturb or modify data in unpredictable ways. For a sequence of truly random numbers it would be impossible to predict the next number generated in the sequence given all previously generated random numbers in the sequence are known [307, 355]. Generating random numbers, and testing for randomness in sequences of numbers, have a long history with systematic research on these topics going back at least to the early twentieth century [569].

Given a computer is a deterministic machine, however, it is not trivial to generate sequences of truly random numbers without any external source of randomness. As a result, there are different classes of random number generators [307]. The first class are so called pseudo-random number generators (PRNG) while the second class are true random number generators.

A PRNG, also known as a deterministic random bit generator [43], overcomes the problem for a computer to gain access to (external) sources of true randomness through the use of computer algorithms that use cryptographic

© Springer Nature Switzerland AG 2020

P. Christen et al., *Linking Sensitive Data*, https://doi.org/10.1007/978-3-030-59706-1_6

Seeded pseudo-random number generation

Standard functions or modules implementing a PRNG are available in most programming languages, spreadsheet programs, and database systems. The following example shows four lists of the first ten random numbers in the range of 1 to 100 generated using ten calls to the `randint(start,end)` function (with `start=1` and `end=100`) of the standard Python `random` module[a] where different seed values have been set using the `random.seed(s)` function:

- Seed s=0:　50, 98, 54,　6, 34, 66, 63, 52, 39, 62
- Seed s=1:　18, 73, 98,　9, 33, 16, 64, 98, 58, 61
- Seed s=42: 82, 15,　4, 95, 36, 32, 29, 18, 95, 14
- Seed s=0:　50, 98, 54,　6, 34, 66, 63, 52, 39, 62

As can be seen, when using the seed s=0 for the second time (last line above), the same sequence of numbers is being generated as when this same seed was used previously (first line above).

---

[a] See: https://docs.python.org/3/library/random.html

---

functions to generate a sequence of bits where the properties of such a sequence approximate the properties of a truly random sequence of bits. These sequences are determined by an initial *seed* value given to the PRNG, where using the same seed value will always generate the same sequence of pseudo-random numbers for this PRNG. The above side box provides an example of such a seeded pseudo-random number generation.

The advantage of a PRNG is therefore that when using a specific seed it is possible to generate the same sequence of pseudo-random numbers over and over again. This is used in some encoding techniques employed in the context of linking sensitive databases. One example is random hashing for Bloom filter encoding as we discuss in Section 8.2.4, where values extracted from attributes are used as the seeds to generate sequences of random numbers, and therefore the same attribute value (same seed) will result in the same sequence of random numbers.

However, while the overall behaviour of pseudo-random numbers is approximately random, given they are based on computer algorithms it is possible to potentially predict the next number in such a sequence [307]. Therefore, in general a PRNG is not suitable for cryptographic applications that do require randomness where there must be a guarantee about how difficult it is to predict the next number in a sequence. A subclass of PRNG algorithms, known as cryptographically secure PRNG [307], do provide such a guarantee, and these algorithms are usable for cryptographic applications. Statistical tests can be applied to check if a sequence of numbers is random enough to be used for cryptographic applications [307].

A true random number generator (TRNG), also known as a non-deterministic random bit generator [43], on the other hand, produces truly random sequences of bits that depend upon some external unpredictable factor such as a physical source of randomness. This source gathers noise (also known as entropy), generally from outside a computer system. This noise is then used to generate a sequence of truly random numbers. Personal computers can provide various sources of randomness that potentially can be used, including keyboard typing and mouse movement activities, disk operations, and system interrupts. However, such sources might not provide enough randomness on an ongoing basis. They can also be user dependent because individuals are known to have their own characteristic of typing (key strokes per minute and intervals between typing) which possibly results in not fully random patterns.

Alternative sources of randomness include analogue circuits such as ring oscillators, or the measurement of physical phenomenon such as thermal or atmospheric noise, or even the properties of quantum mechanics at atomic levels[1]. As one example, cosmic background radiation or radioactive decay as measured over short timescales represent sources of randomness [307]. Another example is to use hundreds of lava lamps photographed many times per second where the unpredictable movement of different coloured wax provides a source of true randomness [465].

6.2 Hashing Techniques

The use of hashing techniques in the domain of computer science has a long history. The concept of hashing was first mentioned in the context of information retrieval and storage by the German researcher Hans Peter Luhn in 1953 [102]. He suggested the allocation of information into buckets in order to speed up searching for information in storage systems. Today, hashing is a core technique used in a diverse range of computer programs and algorithms, ranging from databases to Web search. Hashing is also of high relevance for techniques that aim to link sensitive databases in privacy-preserving ways, where hashing techniques are commonly used to encode sensitive personal information.

The general idea of hashing, or more specifically a hash function, is to map values that are of arbitrary sizes, such as textual strings that can have different lengths, to fixed sized values such as integer numbers that are in a specific range. A hash function therefore converts input values into hash values or hash codes. These hash values are then used as indexes or pointers into a hash table of fixed size. An example hashing approach and hash table are shown in Figure 6.1.

A good hash function should have the following properties [102]:

- Uniformity, which means that the values that are expected to be hashed should be mapped as uniformly as possible across the space of possible hash values.

---

[1] For an online quantum random server see: https://qrng.anu.edu.au/

Fig. 6.1 Example illustration of hashing name strings to integer numbers. As can be seen, there is a hash collision where both 'jen' and 'kim' are hashed to the same number 28.

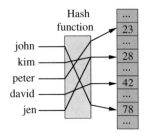

- Deterministic, which means that hashing the same input value will always result in the same hash value.
- Efficiency, which means the hashing of inputs from a potentially very large space (think of text strings of various lengths such as names and addresses) should take a small amount of time (computing steps in the hash function used), where the time used to calculate a hash value (and access the corresponding element in a hash table or insert a new element into the table) is independent of the number of elements that have previously been hashed into that table, and also independent of the size of the hash table used.
- Defined range, which means it is desirable that one can specify the size of the generated hash table by for example setting the range of integer hash values to the $[0, m-1]$ interval, allowing for m different hash values.

The motivation behind using hashing techniques for linking sensitive databases is their ability to transform sensitive quasi-identifying attribute values, such as names, addresses, or dates of birth, into a representation that is smaller, usually of fixed length, and that does not directly allow the reidentification of the individual represented by a set of hash values (assuming that the hash table that maps sensitive values into hash values is not accessible to an adversary) [488]. Hash values can significantly reduce runtime, memory usage, and disk storage requirements [102].

Although hashing is generally fast and efficient, there are several limitations that can cause problems when hashing is used in the context of linking sensitive databases. First, hashing in general is not similarity preserving (we will discuss one type of hashing technique, known as locality sensitive hashing, that does preserve similarities in Section 6.2.3 and in the side box on page 133). This is a major problem because comparing hash values will only allow the identification of exactly matching attribute values. Even a single character difference between two attribute values being hashed ('christine' versus 'christina') will lead to a completely different hash value (as per the properties of hash functions described above). As a result, the important aspect of allowing for approximate comparisons of strings, as we discussed in Section 3.2, is generally not possible when hashed values are being compared.

Furthermore, when mapping input values to hash values, as the example in Figure 6.1 shows, it is possible that the same hash value is calculated for more than one input value (in the example both 'jen' and 'kim' are hashed to the integer number 28). Such mapping of several input values to one hash value is known as a hash collision [102]. Collisions usually occur because of the limited range, m, of the output space of the hash function used. If more than m different input values are to be hashed then collisions are inevitable. When hashing is used in the context of linking sensitive databases, then matching records based on their hashed quasi-identifying attribute values can lead to false matches if there are hash collisions. In our example, 'jen' and 'kim' would be seen as the same first name if the matching is based on the hashed integer values shown in Figure 6.1.

On the other hand, while hash collisions can lead to false matches (and thus reduced linkage quality), from a privacy perspective, hash collisions can actually improve the privacy of sensitive data. For example, let us assume an adversary gains access to a hash encoded database. As we described in Section 5.4.2 and below, the adversary can perform a dictionary based attack on the hash values in the encoded database to try to identify the corresponding hashed sensitive input values. Here we assume the adversary knows the hash function used and also has access to a large database of known plaintext values such as first names or surnames, or town and city names. If several values in the adversary's database are mapped to the same hash value (a collision), then the adversary cannot directly identify the corresponding hashed input values because it could be any of the values mapped to this hash value. Therefore, the more collisions there are the less certain an adversary can be about the hashed input values. This results in better privacy protection against such dictionary based attacks, however, at the cost of reduced linkage quality as we discussed above.

While hash collisions can improve the privacy protection of certain hashed sensitive input values (those involved in collisions), the majority of input values being hashed are unlikely involved in collisions (as otherwise linkage quality will suffer substantially) and therefore there are no privacy guarantees when hashed values are used in the context of linking sensitive databases. In Chapters 7 and 8 we will cover more advanced techniques that have been developed to allow the privacy-preserving linking of sensitive databases, where many of these techniques are based on hashing techniques. In the following three subsections we describe three specific categories of hash functions that are commonly used as building blocks for techniques that aim to link sensitive databases: one-way hashing, keyed cryptographic hashing, and locality sensitive hashing.

6.2.1 One-way Hashing

One-way hash functions convert an input value into a hash value or hash code (for example 'john' into '61409aa1fd47d4a5332de23cbf59a36f') in such a way that having access to only a hash value will make it nearly impossible with current computing technology to learn the hashed input value [535, 578]. This means it is practically infeasible to invert the hash function to generate the input value if one has access only to a certain hash value.

The most well known types of one-way hash functions are the Message Digest (MD) and Secure Hash Algorithms (SHA) which include MD5, SHA-1, and SHA-2 [535]. These algorithms are used widely in applications such as secure network protocols (for example TSL, SSL, and IPSec), and for verification and validation purposes such as to verify that a message has not been tampered with during communication. For example, after downloading a file containing some piece of software, a user can calculate the MD5 hash of this file, where the full file is given as input to the MD5 hash algorithm. By comparing the resulting MD5 hash value with the hash value that is published by the software owner for this file one can check if there have been any changes or corruptions to the downloaded file. If the file has been changed or corrupted during transmission, even by only a single bit, then the resulting MD5 hash values would be different.

The likelihood of collisions, as we discussed before, for most of the commonly used one-way hash functions is very low given their very large range [535]. MD5 hashes have a length of 128 bits, SHA-1 hashes are 160 bits long, and SHA-2 hashes are between 224 and 512 bits long. The resulting ranges of these hash functions are therefore from 0 to $2^{128} - 1$ all the way to 0 to $2^{512} - 1$, where 2^{128} is a decimal number with 39 digits and 2^{512} a decimal number with 155 digits. For SHA-2 with a hash length of 256 bits, an upper bound of the probability of a hash collision between two input values is approximately $1/2^{128}$ as calculated using the birthday paradox [417] (assuming the input values are drawn uniformly at random). This is a probability of around 0.000000000000000000000000000000000000003.

One-way hashing of quasi-identifying values can be used to link databases across organisations when it is not possible to exchange or share the sensitive plaintext values [180, 486]. To conduct such a hashing-based linkage, each database owner first encodes their quasi-identifying values using a one-way hash function. This can be done either on an attribute by attribute basis, resulting in one hash value per attribute, or by concatenating a set of quasi-identifying attribute values of a record into one long string, resulting in one single hash value per record [505]. Employing a three-party protocol, as we discussed in Section 4.3, these hash values can then be sent to a third party, such as a linkage unit, to conduct the comparison and matching of records using these hash values. If the compared hash values are the same then the corresponding attribute or record pair is considered as a match. However, as we described above, due to data quality issues that can occur in quasi-identifying attribute values, such as spelling variations or mistakes in names, records that do not have exactly the same value in the hashed quasi-identifying attributes will be encoded into different hash values and therefore classified as non-matches. We discuss hashing-based techniques to link sensitive databases in more detail in Section 7.4.

Because a one-way hash function is easy to compute on any input value but very difficult to invert (with regard to the required computational efforts) [535, 578], the identification of the input value from a hash value is said to be impossible. The only feasible attack on one-way hashed values would be a dictionary attack (as we discussed in Section 5.4.2) where an adversary (such as a curious employee at the linkage unit) needs to know the one-way hash function used, and can then hash a large number of input values (such as all first names and surnames from a public telephone directory) until the hash function generates a hash value that is the same as a hash value in the hashed sensitive database. In the case where an adversary does not know which one-way hash function has been used, he can try a set of existing hash functions until he successfully finds a pair of matching plaintext and hash values. A successful dictionary attack would seriously jeopardise the confidentiality of one-way hash encoded sensitive values when they are used in the context of linking sensitive databases [486].

A possible solution to overcome the risk of dictionary attacks is to concatenate the input values with a secret key or password before applying the one-way hash function [487]. This secret value must only be known to the database owners but not the linkage unit which conducts the matching of records based on the comparison of hash values (sent to it by the database owners) [538]. Any organisation that does not know the secret key value would find it very difficult to successfully mount a dictionary attack because it would not only have to hash all possible input values in its plaintext database (such as all first names and surnames from a telephone directory), but try all possible secret key values [245] in combination with all possible input values, as we have described in Section 5.4.2.

6.2.2 Keyed Cryptographic Hashing and Message Authentication

Another possible way to prevent dictionary attacks in hashing is to use a keyed hash encoding approach during the data encoding process. In keyed cryptographic hashing, a secret key is used to enhance the security of encodings, as is illustrated in Figure 6.2. Such a secret key, only known to the organisation who conducts the encoding, will substantially improve the privacy of the encoded data [245].

In the context of linking sensitive databases, such a secret key used for encoding values is generally shared between the database owners who are encoding the sensitive quasi-identifying attribute values in their databases. Therefore, an encoding approach based on keyed cryptographic hashing can only avoid a dictionary attack by an external adversary, but not a collusion

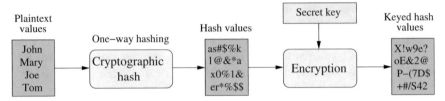

Fig. 6.2 An example keyed cryptographic hashing scheme. A one-way cryptographic hash function first converts the input message into a fixed-length hash value, which is then combined with a secret key to generate a keyed hash value.

attack (as described in Section 5.4.5), where the secret key would be shared by one of the database owners with the adversary. However, without having knowledge of the secret key, it is very difficult to retrieve the corresponding input values even though the hash function is known by the adversary. Due to the security guarantees provided by using a secret key, keyed cryptographic hashing schemes are used in applications which require message authentication or password checking [578].

In order to protect the information authenticity in keyed cryptographic hashing schemes, most commonly a form of message authentication code (MAC) is employed by the hashing mechanism [535, 578]. A MAC generates a value, called authentication tag, that protects both the integrity of the data in the message as well as its authenticity. The Hash-based Message Authentication Code (HMAC) [364] function (also known as keyed hashing for message authentication) is one such approach which uses a secret cryptographic key and a one-way hash function. HMAC can simultaneously verify both the data integrity and the authentication of a hashed value. When an HMAC value is generated for a given input value, a one-way hash function such as SHA described in the previous section, can be used. The security of an HMAC code depends on the underlying one-way hash function, the key size, and its quality [535]. HMAC first extends or shortens the secret key, k, to make its length conform to a certain block size (which is generally set to 64 bits [364]), and then generates an inner and outer padded key, k_i and k_o, respectively, from this length adjusted secret key. The message, s, to be hashed and the two padded keys are combined into an HMAC value as $hmac(k, s) = h(k_o||h(k_i||s))$, where h is the hash function used (such as SHA-1 or SHA-2), and $||$ symbolises the concatenation of strings.

Because they use a secret key and a one-way hash function, keyed cryptographic hashing schemes are secure against dictionary attacks by an external adversary. Without knowing the secret key, a dictionary attack will not be successful in identifying the encoded sensitive value for a given hash value. However, as we discussed in Section 5.4, frequency attacks are still possible on keyed cryptographic hash values. An adversary can use the frequency distribution of a set of hash values and match it with the frequency distribution of a set of known plaintext values, such as postcodes or surnames, as extracted from a public database, as illustrated in Figure 5.2. This frequency alignment allows the adversary to identify corresponding hash values for the most frequent values in the database without requiring any knowledge about the hashing approach used to encode the sensitive values.

To overcome such frequency attacks on keyed cryptographic hash values, a record specific salt value can be added to the encoding process. Before the encryption is applied in the encoding process, as shown in Figure 6.2, each one-way hash value is concatenated with a record specific value [637], additional to a single secret key for the whole database. Since the salt value will be different for individual records, the same sensitive value from different records being hashed will result in different hash values. Therefore, the frequency distribution of hash values will not follow the frequency distribution of the original sensitive values being encoded. This makes the frequency alignment by an adversary to identify the corresponding sensitive input value for a given keyed hash value extremely difficult.

Attributes that are suitable for use as salt values need to be accurate, complete, and not contain values that can change over time [538]. Example attributes include places, dates, or years of birth, if available for all records in a database to be encoded, because the true values in these attributes cannot change over time. Wrong recording of dates of birth and other data quality issues can of course still mean these values differ for the same person across the databases to be linked. There are, however, situations where no attributes are available that are accurate, stable over time, and complete, to be suitable as salt values in keyed hash encoding. Census databases that only contain age values (instead of dates or even years of birth) are one example where the use of salting in the encoding process might not be possible [469].

6.2.3 Locality Sensitive Hashing

Locality sensitive hashing (LSH) [291] is a well known type of hashing method that is aimed at identifying similar high dimensional data objects in very large databases or document collections. LSH is a core technique used by many Internet search engines where the data objects to be compared are Web pages, or in applications where textual documents, such as PDFs, need to be compared to for example identify similar essays or assignments submitted by students that might indicate plagiarism [385].

In general, LSH uses several hash functions, chosen uniformly and independently from a certain type (or family) of hash functions, to generate several hash values for each data object, where these hash values can then be compared and similarities between them can be calculated. An important aspect of LSH is that two data objects with a small distance (or high similarity) in the original comparison space will also have more hash values in common compared to data objects that have a larger distance (lower similarity) in the

original comparison space. LSH provides theoretical probability guarantees
with regard to similarities, as we describe below [291, 385].

LSH involves the use of a family of hash functions (known as LSH families) to map data objects into partitions (buckets) in such a way that similar
data objects are mapped to the same partition with high probability, while
guaranteeing that dissimilar data objects are not mapped into the same partition with high probability. LSH not only preserves data characteristics in
the hashing space, it also guarantees the collision probability between similar
data objects [291].

Formally, a LSH hash family is defined for a specific metric distance function, d (see the side box on page 158 for the requirements of such a function),
a threshold $t > 0$, an approximation factor $c > 0$, and a hash function h
from this LSH family which maps data objects from the metric space to hash
values. For any two data objects, x and y, it then holds [385]:

- if $d(x, y) \leq t$ then $h(x) = h(y)$ with probability at least p_1 (which means
  x and y are hashed to the same hash value).
- if $d(x, y) > c \cdot t$ then $h(x) = h(y)$ with probability at most p_2.

A LSH family is of interest if $p_1 > p_2$, which means data objects that are
more similar to each other are more likely hashed to the same hash value
than data objects that are less similar to each other.

Each family of hash functions used in LSH is sensitive to a specific distance function and should be selected based on the type of objects between
which distances are to be calculated [385]. Euclidean LSH (ELSH) is locality
sensitive to the Euclidean distance metric which maps data objects in the
Euclidean space by grouping nearby projections calculated based on the values of these data objects [145]. Hamming LSH (HLSH) is locality sensitive
to the Hamming distance which is commonly used for bit vectors (binary arrays) that represent a Hamming space. Min-wise independent permutations
LSH, also known as MinHash [87], is another LSH based hashing technique
that is commonly used in applications that require approximated similarity
computations between sets, such as in text mining [291]. MinHash allows the
efficient estimation of the Jaccard similarity (see Section 6.8.1) between two
sets by only comparing the minimum hash values. We provide an example of
MinHash in the side box on page 133.

While LSH is a commonly used technique for indexing and searching nearest neighbours in high dimensional data, it has also been used in the context
of linking databases as a blocking technique to efficiently generate candidate
record pairs [178, 328, 494]. In this context, each database owner first generates a MinHash or HLSH representation for each record in their database,
and then sends these hash representations to a linkage unit to apply LSH
based similarity calculations. Records with the same LSH hash value(s) are
considered to be candidates that need to be compared in more detail using
a suitable comparison method. Given the popularity of bit vectors to encode
sensitive values in the context of linking sensitive databases (as we discuss

MinHash signature generation

MinHash is a locality sensitive hashing (LSH) approach that approximate the Jaccard similarity [385]. The idea of MinHash is that the probability of two sets to generate the same MinHash values (known as a MinHash signature) is equal to the Jaccard similarity (sim_J) of those two sets if a sufficiently large number of suitable hash functions are used. This allows MinHash to efficiently estimate the similarity between two sets each containing a number of elements. Formally, the probability, p, that two sets $\mathbf{s}_1$ and $\mathbf{s}_2$ will generate the same MinHash value for a hash function h can be defined as follows:

$$p[h(\mathbf{s}_1) = h(\mathbf{s}_2)] = \frac{|\mathbf{s}_1 \cap \mathbf{s}_2|}{|\mathbf{s}_1 \cup \mathbf{s}_2|} = sim_J(\mathbf{s}_1, \mathbf{s}_2).$$

Assuming we employ k hash functions, $\{h_1, h_2, \ldots, h_k\}$, we can compute an estimated Jaccard similarity (sim_{J_e}) between $\mathbf{s}_1$ and $\mathbf{s}_2$ as:

$$sim_{J_e}(\mathbf{s}_1, \mathbf{s}_2) = \frac{\sum_{i=1}^{k}[h_i(\mathbf{s}_1) = h_i(\mathbf{s}_2)]}{k} \approx sim_J(\mathbf{s}_1, \mathbf{s}_2),$$

where $[h_i(\mathbf{s}_1) = h_i(\mathbf{s}_2)]$ returns 1 and $[h_i(\mathbf{s}_1) \neq h_i(\mathbf{s}_2)]$ returns 0. To generate MinHash signatures, let us assume two sets $\mathbf{s}_1 = \{B, C, D\}$ and $\mathbf{s}_2 = \{A, B, C\}$ that have a Jaccard similarity of $sim_J(\mathbf{s}_1, \mathbf{s}_2) = 1/2$. Suppose we select two random permutations $RP_1 = (2, 3, 0, 1)$ and $RP_2 = (0, 3, 1, 2)$ to represent the two hash functions h_1 and h_2, respectively. For each hash function we can select the index of the element of the first row that is 1 (the set contains the element) as the MinHash value of this hash function. Below we illustrate this process on $\mathbf{s}_1$ and $\mathbf{s}_2$.

To generate a MinHash signature for each set, we concatenate these MinHash values into a list. Following the example above, we generate the MinHash signatures $Sig_1 = [2, 3]$ and $Sig_2 = [2, 0]$ for sets $\mathbf{s}_1$ and $\mathbf{s}_2$, respectively. Based on the similarity (fraction of MinHash values in common) between the two MinHash signatures we can estimate the Jaccard similarity between the original sets as $sim_{J_e}(\mathbf{s}_1, \mathbf{s}_2) = 1/2$.

in detail in Chapters 8 and 9), Hamming LSH especially has attracted interest as an efficient blocking technique to facilitate scalable linkage of large encoded sensitive databases [178, 334].

Even though LSH has many advantages in computing similarities between high dimensional objects in large databases [385], it cannot always guarantee the correct estimation of similarities. Furthermore, because LSH estimates the similarity between data objects based on their low dimensional representations, it often requires a large number of hash values to ensure accurate enough similarity estimations. If not enough hash functions are used, then similar data objects might not have enough common LSH hash values to be classified as similar. As a result, in the context of blocking of records when databases are to be linked, LSH has been shown to be highly sensitive with regard to the setting of its parameters [9]. While certain settings might result in good linkage quality, even small changes in parameter values can lead to a substantial reduction in the number of true linked record pairs.

6.3 Anonymisation and Pseudonymisation Techniques

Over the past few decades the challenge of protecting the privacy of sensitive personal information, such as names, addresses and dates of birth, has gained significant attention in many application domains. Often privacy and confidentiality regulations prevent the owners of sensitive databases from sharing any details of the records in these databases with any other organisation, or from making such data publicly available for example for research studies. Data privacy can be challenging in terms of ensuring the utility of data while simultaneously protecting the privacy of all individuals and their sensitive identifiable information. In this section we discuss how data anonymisation and pseudonymisation can be used to ensure data privacy and security, and in the following Section 6.4 we then describe how encryption techniques can be employed as building blocks when sensitive databases are to be linked.

Data anonymisation is the process of either encrypting, modifying, masking, or removing personally identifiable information from databases, such that the entities or individuals who are represented by records in such databases remain anonymous. Data can be considered anonymised when they do not allow any reidentification of the individuals to whom they relate, and it is not possible that any individual can be identified from the anonymised data by any further processing, or by linking such data with other (public) information that is available or likely will become available in the future [191].

The Beyond 2011 Programme established by the Office for National Statistics (ONS) in the UK for the production of population and socio-demographic statistics has indicated the importance of anonymisation of data to ensure privacy. According to their report Matching Anonymous Data [446], personal identifiers can apply to any person, living or dead, direct or through interaction, including their dependants, ascendants, and descendants. Examples of sensitive data that need to be considered for anonymisation are names (including family name or surname, first name, middle name, or patronyms), contact details (including postal addresses and telephone numbers), dates (such as dates of birth), unique identification numbers (including social security numbers in the US, fiscal codes in Italy, national insurance numbers in the UK, and Medicare and patient identifiers in many countries), and bank account details (including international bank account numbers and credit card numbers). Each of those, by itself or in combination with others, might allow the unique identification of an individual.

Pseudonymisation enhances data privacy by replacing most identifying attributes within a data record by one or more artificial identifiers, called pseudonyms [277]. In general, a single pseudonym can replace a collection of attribute values, or an individual pseudonym can replace an individual attribute value. The main advantage of using pseudonyms is that they make records less identifiable while remaining suitable for a variety of data analysis and data processing tasks [434].

The recently proposed concept of functional anonymisation [188] considers the whole of the data situation, which means both the actual sensitive data and their data environment. When we apply any form of data confidentiality we are in essence hoping to ensure that anonymised data remains anonymous, even after it has been shared or released within an existing or into a new data environment. Importantly, any data environment also includes the people who are present in that environment and have access to data, and their skills, knowledge, and motivation, the governance framework that covers the data environment, as well as any technical infrastructure that is used to store, access, process, analyse, and protect sensitive data.

Recently, the European Council has made pseudonymisation of record linkage identifiers factually mandatory [277]. Specifically, the General Data Protection Regulation (GDPR) defines pseudonymisation in Article 4 as[2]:

> ...the processing of personal data in such a way that the data can no longer be attributed to a specific data subject without the use of additional information, provided that such additional information is kept separately and is subject to technical and organisational measures to ensure that personal data are not attributed to an identified or identifiable natural person.

Therefore, according to this definition, to pseudonymise a sensitive database, any additional information, such as the secret keys (passwords) used to pseudonymise the database, need to be kept separately and securely in order to prevent an adversary to be able to undo the pseudonymisation process or otherwise be able to learn which pseudonyms do refer to individual persons.

In contrast to data anonymisation, data pseudonymisation substitutes or replaces any identifying characteristics of sensitive data of an individual with a pseudonym in such a way that the individual cannot be directly identified by using such pseudonymised data, but rather additional information is required to facilitate any reidentification. The legal distinction between anonymised and pseudonymised data is its categorisation as personal

---

[2] See: https://gdpr-info.eu/art-4-gdpr/

data [277]. Pseudonymous data still allows for some form of reidentification (even indirect and remote), while anonymous data cannot be reidentified [594].

In any project aimed at linking sensitive databases, it is of advantage to use a combination of techniques to ensure that private or confidential values are sufficiently deidentified. There are inherent limitations in some anonymisation and pseudonymisation techniques, such as directory replacement (for example, making changes to the names of individuals within the data while maintaining consistent relations between other attribute values) and data scrambling (such as swapping of letters or digits in personal data) techniques, that involve a partial mixing or obfuscation of values in records but that can still lead to a reidentification of individuals in an anonymised databases [451, 582].

Furthermore, as data localisation laws (laws that enforce how data can be processed inside a certain country, and how sensitive data can be transferred to other countries) are becoming more common, the consideration of how data can be transferred across different countries is of increasing importance [91]. The rules for cross-border transfers of sensitive data commonly mention that any form of data protection based upon encryption techniques alone (that guarantee the security of data based on mathematical formulas) is not permitted [423]. This is specified clearly in some data protection regulations, such as in GDPR Article 44[3]. This article states that before transfer of personal data to an organisation in another country one or more security mechanisms designed to ensure an adequate level of data protection needs to be employed, such that the processing of personal data must not allow identification of a specific individual without the use of additional information. Furthermore, such additional information that is required to identify a person should always be kept separate and should not be shared with the recipient organisation. Data anonymisation can therefore be used as an effective method for cross-border data transfer because there is a guarantee that it is not possible to reidentify individuals whose sensitive personal information are stored in such anonymised data.

Careful consideration is required when selecting appropriate techniques that can guarantee data privacy. Further consideration should also be given to additional databases that an organisation such as the linkage unit (as described in Section 4.4) may obtain to conduct the linkage, and which could allow it to try to reidentify individuals. It is important to note that the effectiveness of any anonymisation or encryption technique should be evaluated regularly to ensure that it is sufficiently robust to prevent the reidentification of individuals. Such evaluations can be carried out by using existing privacy attacks or statistical disclosure risk measures.

We next describe two main forms of anonymisation, namely randomisation and generalisation, followed by a discussion of differential privacy [181], a

---

[3] See: https://gdpr.eu/article-44-transfer-of-personal-data/

more recently developed privacy concept that limits the disclosure of sensitive information of records in a database when microdata or aggregated data are to be published.

6.3.1 Randomisation

The aim of randomisation techniques is to alter sensitive personal or confidential data in order to remove any links between sensitive values and the individuals that have these values in order to prevent an adversary from reidentifying or associating sensitive values to individuals [162]. Various randomisation techniques have been developed, including noise addition [85, 163, 221, 350] and swapping or permutation [142, 210, 655]. Note that randomisation techniques are also employed in the context of statistical disclosure control, as we discussed in Section 5.5.

Noise addition (or noise injection) involves the addition of random values to sensitive personal data in order to reduce the risk that an individual can be identified or associated with a certain sensitive value [85, 561]. For example, in a database that contains the salaries of individuals, each individual's salary could be increased or decreased by a small random amount to obfuscate their actual salary. This addition or subtraction of values should only be done within a certain range as otherwise any analysis based on the randomised salary values will become less accurate. However, any noise addition will mean the randomised data will suffer some loss of its statistical properties even while privacy is satisfied, thus potentially making the data less useful for a user. Therefore, when adding noise into a database a balance between privacy and utility is always sought [512].

Basic statistics, such as average, median, and standard deviation, for a whole database of randomised values should ideally be kept as close to the original average, median, and standard deviation as possible. Furthermore, noise addition needs to be conducted such that these basic statistics also hold for important (depending upon the final use of the data) subgroups of individuals in a database. For example, male and female individuals will likely have different average salaries, and therefore any noise addition should consider the basic statistics for these groups of individuals separately and noise addition should be adapted accordingly.

Permutation, on the other hand, involves the swapping or shuffling of values between the records of individuals, making it harder to identify a particular individual [163, 529, 655]. Following the same example as above, the salaries of individuals could be randomised by swapping the salary values across records such that they are no longer connected to other information about each individual. Because such swapping or shuffling of values does not change any individual value, the original basic statistics are not modified at all. However, as discussed above, if certain subgroups are of interest, then swapping needs to be conducted only within these subgroups. Swapping salary values irrespective of the gender of individuals will likely increase the average salary of females and lower it for males, thereby reducing the accuracy of any gender based analysis that involves salary distributions.

Compared to randomisation, permutation is a useful technique to reduce the risk of inference and the linking of records between databases based on certain attribute values. While noise addition might prevent an adversary from learning the actual sensitive values of individuals, a person with a very high salary will still, even after noise addition, be an individual with a high salary (possibly even higher if a random value was added to his salary). The individual is therefore still identifiable as a high income earner, and possible linkable to one or a few records in another database based on her high salary value. On the other hand, if salary values are swapped then such a sensitive association between records is not possible any more.

6.3.2 Generalisation

The idea behind data generalisation techniques is to overcome the problem of reidentification of individual records by generalising the values in certain attributes in a database in such a way that reidentification from the generalised database is not possible. This can be done by modifying the scale or details of values in quasi-identifying attributes. For example, a database containing the full dates of birth of individuals could be generalised to only the year of birth. As opposed to each individuals' exact date of birth (which might be unique for many individuals, especially in smaller databases), many individuals will likely share the same year of birth value.

Masking of full attribute values can be seen as a special case of generalisation. In masking, values in a sensitive attribute will be replaced with a wildcard character such as '*', or simply removed, for certain records that do have a sensitive value in that attribute. For example, in a medical database all records that have the sensitive value 'HIV' in a disease attribute will have this value replaced with '*'. Such a masking approach will obviously substantially reduce the utility of a database, and therefore generalisation techniques that aim to keep as much original values as possible in sensitive attributes, while still providing privacy, are preferable.

A variety of such generalisation techniques aimed at anonymising sensitive data have been developed, including k-anonymity, l-diversity, and t-closeness [6, 390, 526]. k-anonymity [584] is a popular privacy model that has been used to generalise sensitive values in such a way that reidentification of individuals from the generalised data is not feasible. A k-anonymised database is said to have the k-anonymity property if an individual that is represented by a record in the database cannot be distinguished from at least $k - 1$ other individuals whose information also appears in the database. In the context of linking sensitive databases, k-anonymity can be achieved by making sure a group of k records in a database have the same values in their quasi-identifying attributes. As a result, groups of size k will be formed where these groups can for example be used as the blocks from where records are to be compared [110]. We illustrate this idea in the side box on page 140.

In general, k-anonymity provides privacy protection against identity disclosure of individuals. However, in some cases k-anonymity does not prevent attribute disclosure, which can occur when all records in a group of k records have the same sensitive value. For example, k records might have the same gender, age range, and state where these people live in (preventing specific identification of individuals). However, if for all of them their medical records say they have a certain sensitive illness, such as HIV or cancer, then one can learn that any patient with the given gender, age group, and living in that state in the given database has this illness.

To overcome this weakness of k-anonymity with regard to attribute disclosure, Machanavajjhala et al. [400] introduced a new generalisation method known as l-diversity. The main idea of l-diversity is to provide a minimum level of diversity for the sensitive attribute in each group of k-anonymous records. For each group of k records there need to be $l > 1$ different (sensitive) values, making it not possible to associate a certain record in the group with a certain sensitive value. For example, with $l = 3$, a group of records might be assigned one of the three sensitive values 'HIV', 'Cancer', and 'Flu'. We show an example of generalisation of a small data table using k-anonymisation and l-diversity in the side box on page 140.

Even though l-diversity can be used to mitigate the risk of attribute disclosure by ensuring there are at least l well represented values of a sensitive attribute for each k-anonymous group of records, the formulation of l-diversity is not completely satisfactory as it is vulnerable to skewness and similarity attacks [6, 390].

In a skewness attack the adversary explores the attribute disclosure in records when the overall distribution is skewed and even when it satisfies l-diversity within a group of k records. To illustrate this, let us consider the following example. Assume we have a database with an attribute that for each individual contains information if the person has an illness categorised as positive (less severe) or negative (a severe illness), and we apply l-diversity where each group of records needs to have $l = 2$ diversity. Now let us assume a given group of records has an equal number of positive and negative illness values. Even though this group satisfies 2-diversity, it increases the privacy risk for the identification of an individual having a negative illness with a 50% likelihood, which can be significantly higher than the real distribution in the full population (or full database) of a severe illness. On the other hand, a group of records where 99% have a positive and only 1% have a negative illness has a lower privacy risk for an individual being identified to have a negative illness. This example illustrates that with l-diversity, if we assume that an adversary does not have access to the global distribution of the values

Example of k-anonymity and l-diversity data generalisation

Generalisation aims to limit the risk of an individual being reidentified (known as disclosure risk). In this example, we illustrate the generalisation of a small data table using k-anonymity and l-diversity, where suppression (values represented by an asterisk '*') has been applied. AGE, GENDER, and POSTCODE are the quasi-identifiers, and DISEASE the sensitive attribute.

Original data table

AGE	GENDER	POSTCODE	DISEASE
21	m	2602	Gastric ulcer
22	m	2604	Gastritis
25	f	2611	Stomach cancer
27	f	2612	Obesity
32	f	2602	HIV
33	f	2603	HIV
34	m	2604	Heart disease
35	m	2601	Chest pain
36	m	2604	Cancer

($k = 2$)-anonymised data table

In k-anonymisation, a record in a database needs to be identical to at least $k - 1$ other records with respect to its quasi-identifying attributes. Below we show the data table after ($k = 2$)-anonimisation has been applied.

AGE	GENDER	POSTCODE	DISEASE
2*	m	260*	Gastric ulcer
2*	m	260*	Gastritis
2*	f	261*	Stomach cancer
2*	f	261*	Obesity
3*	f	260*	HIV
3*	f	260*	HIV
3*	m	260*	Heart disease
3*	m	260*	Chest pain
3*	m	260*	Cancer

($l = 4$)-diverse data table

While k-anonymity provides privacy against identity disclosure, it does not provide enough privacy against attribute disclosure. See the third group of records in the above table with disease 'HIV'. To overcome this limitation, l-diversity can be applied to ensures each group of records has at least l distinct values in the sensitive attribute.

AGE	GENDER	POSTCODE	DISEASE
2*	*	26**	Gastric ulcer
2*	*	26**	Gastritis
2*	*	26**	Stomach cancer
2*	*	26**	Obesity
3*	*	260*	HIV
3*	*	260*	HIV
3*	*	260*	Heart disease
3*	*	260*	Chest pain
3*	*	260*	Cancer

in the sensitive attribute, he can still learn the distribution of such values by just looking at the l-diverse table to infer information about the original distribution of the sensitive attribute values [6].

In a similarity attack an adversary can learn information about a sensitive attribute when a l-diverse group of records has semantically similar sensitive attribute values. For example, let us assume a database with two attributes age and disease, and a group of records that has age values in the range [20-30] and diseases related to stomach problems. If an adversary has knowledge of an individual with an age of 25 and that this individual has a record in this database, then he can infer this individual has a stomach related disease, because all diseases in the group of records with ages in the range [20-29] are stomach related. Such a similarity attack is possible on a l-diversified database because l-diversity only takes into account the diversity of sensitive values in the group, but does not consider the semantic closeness of these values.

The t-closeness generalisation model [390] introduces further refinements to the group based l-diversity anonymisation method by reducing the granularity of a data representation. The requirement of t-closeness is that the distribution of values in a sensitive attribute in any k-anonymous group is close to the distribution of this sensitive attribute in the overall database.

According to Aggarwal and Yu [6], for numeric attributes it is more effective to use t-closeness anonymisation than other privacy-preserving anonymisation methods. This is because in the t-closeness generalisation model the values of a sensitive attribute are treated differently with respect to their distribution in a database while in other anonymisation methods all values are considered in a similar way irrespective of their distributions in the database.

6.3.3 Differential Privacy

The concept of differential privacy [181, 391, 442] has emerged as an alternative to randomisation as discussed in Section 6.3.1. In randomisation, noise in the form of random values is added to or subtracted from sensitive values to remove the link between individuals and their sensitive values. This often does provide no or only limited privacy protection. One example is a person with a very high salary who even after randomisation is the only person in a database with a very high salary. Differential privacy, on the other hand, provides a strong mathematical foundation of the loss of privacy of individuals whose records are stored in a database when sensitive values from that database are being published [442].

Differential privacy was initially designed to support interactive querying of sensitive databases and to aggregate results by adding noise to each result of a statistical query, such as Count (number of records in a database that fulfil a certain criteria) or Sum (the summation of values of a certain attribute in a subset of records in a database). This is needed because such queries can result in a small number of values being returned that can identify individuals. For the above example of the person with a very high salary, differential privacy can be guaranteed by ensuring a certain amount of random noise is added into the database such that any query to count how many people with a very high salary are available in that database will not return a count of 1.

Differential privacy is a general model of privacy, where different privacy techniques can be employed. In this context of interactive querying of a sensitive database, the basic idea of differential privacy is to add noise to the result of a statistical query in such a way that this result does not compromise the privacy of any individual in that database. In other words, the result of the query does not reveal if a certain individual is represented by a record in this database or not. The result of any statistical query run on the database should therefore not depend on the data of a single individual [181].

The magnitude of noise added in differential privacy depends on a privacy parameter, ϵ, and the sensitivity of a given query set [183]. The formal definition of ϵ-differential privacy is that for a given anonymisation algorithm, $\mathcal{A}$, that randomises statistical query results, and two databases, $\mathbf{D}_1$ and $\mathbf{D}_2$, that differ in a single record that represents one individual, the following probability calculation holds:

$$p(\mathcal{A}(\mathbf{D}_1) \in S) \leq e^\epsilon \cdot p(\mathcal{A}(\mathbf{D}_2) \in S), \qquad (6.1)$$

where $\epsilon > 0$ is a positive real number, and S is the set of all possible subsets of the output generated by $\mathcal{A}$. A commonly used form of randomisation for numerical values in differential privacy is to add noise from a Laplace distribution [182], an exponential distribution that is symmetric around 0.

Differential privacy has recently attracted significant interest in various application domains, ranging from publishing census data in anonymised ways [2], all the way to anonymising sensitive user statistics collected in Web browsers [190].

In the context of linking sensitive databases, differential privacy has been used to first anonymise the input databases to generate differentially private blocks before they are being used in a linkage protocol [290], to generate private synopsis (subsets of records) that are used to identify possibly matching record pairs in such synopsis, and to harden Bloom filters by randomly flipping bits in a differential private manner, as we discuss in Section 9.5.6.

6.4 Encryption Techniques

Encryption is a major tool used in data security where sensitive data need to be protected from unwanted actions of unauthorised users, such as cyber attacks or data breaches. In general, encryption is used as a privacy technique to encrypt sensitive data in such a way that only authorised parties can access that data while preventing unauthorised or malicious parties from accessing the encrypted data. Unlike the hashing-based encoding techniques, such as one-way hashing, discussed in the previous section, encryption techniques allow sensitive data to be encrypted by one party and then decrypted back into their original form by an authorised party. As we discuss in this section, encryption techniques prevent unauthorised access to sensitive data either during communication of such data between different parties, or while sensitive data are being stored by one party (which can be viewed as communication of sensitive data through time).

In encryption processes it is common that a secret key, also known as a password, is used for the encryption and decryption algorithms. The use of such a key ensures that any decryption of sensitive data can only be performed by a user with the correct decryption key. Furthermore, encryption is commonly based on a mathematical function or algorithm that encrypts data in such a way that without having access to the correct decryption key it is impossible to decrypt any corresponding encrypted data.

The idea of encrypting data to hide sensitive information has been used for thousands of years. A simple early encryption scheme is commonly known as Caesar cipher [562]. This approach is part of a family known as substitution ciphers, where each character in a given alphabet is replaced with another character from the same alphabet. In the Caesar cipher, each character is replaced (shifted) with the character a fixed number of places up from the character. For example, with a shift of four, 'a' will be replaced with 'e', 'h' with 'l', while 'x' will be shifted wrapped around to 'b':

```
abcdefghijklmnopqrstuvwxyz
efghijklmnopqrstuvwxyzabcd
```

With this shift of four the word 'hello' will be encrypted into 'lipps'.

For this encryption scheme, the secret encryption key is the number of positions that characters are shifted, four in our example. To decrypt a word that was encrypted with the Caesar cipher one simply shifts characters the same number of positions in the opposite direction down the alphabet. An obvious weakness of the Caesar cipher, besides its limitation of providing only 25 possibilities for encrypting a message, is that an adversary can mount a frequency attack (as we described in Section 5.4.3) and count how often each character occurs in an encrypted string. Aligning the resulting frequency distribution with the frequency distribution of characters in a large plaintext string (with text from the same language) will likely provide the information required to identify which most common encoded character corresponds to which most common plaintext character, thus allowing an adversary to calculate the number of positions that characters were shifted in the encoding step. Over the last two thousand years encryption algorithms have improved significantly from such simple substitution ciphers [562].

In any security architecture, encryption cannot by itself prevent any interference by an adversary, however encryption can make it as difficult as possible for the adversary to be able to learn anything about the encrypted sensitive data. Encryption is therefore applied in diverse areas of applications ranging from encrypting sensitive government databases to encrypting online credit card transactions. Modern data encryption software, also known as a cryptosystem [562], generally consist of three components: key generation, encryption, and decryption. Combined they provide a security scheme which theoretically can only be broken with large amounts of computing power [535].

The Dutch cryptographer Auguste Kerckhoff first proposed the requirements of a good cryptosystem in 1883 [342]. He proposed six principles to design a practical cryptosystem, where his second principle is now best known as Kerckhoffs's principle. This principle states that:

> ... the design of a system should not require secrecy, and compromise of the system should not inconvenience the correspondents.

This means that a good cryptosystem should only depend upon the secrecy of the key used to encrypt and decrypt messages, but not on the secrecy of any other components [535]. Specifically, this principle states that the algorithms used to generate a secret key, and to encrypt and decrypt messages, should be made publicly available. This principle has become the essential guideline for designing algorithms in modern cryptography where key generation, and the encryption and decryption algorithms, are generally announced publicly, and where their encryption strength depends only on the security of the secret encryption key.

In the following we describe different encryption schemes that can and have been used as building blocks in the context of linking sensitive databases.

6.4.1 Symmetric Key Encryption

In symmetric encryption, the same secret key is used for both the encryption and decryption processes. Before symmetric encryption can be used, the secret key must be exchanged between the participating parties. This ensures that only parties that have access to the secret key can decrypt any data that was encrypted with this key. Figure 6.3 shows an example of a symmetric encryption process between two parties.

In the encryption and decryption processes, the sender and recipient can use a specific password as the secret key, or a random string of letters and numbers can be used that has been generated by a cryptographically secure pseudo-random number generator (PRNG) [307], as we discussed in Section 6.1. A symmetric key encryption scheme is secure enough if and only if the secret key is kept secure and only intended parties can access it. Furthermore, the security of symmetric encryption systems is based on the difficulty of guessing or identifying the corresponding secret key used. The security

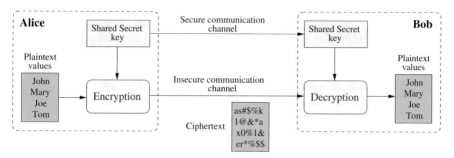

Fig. 6.3 An example of symmetric key encryption between two parties, Alice and Bob. As illustrated, before any communication of encrypted data can take place, both Alice and Bob need to agree on a secret symmetric key which requires them to communicate through a secure communication channel. Once the secret key is shared, sensitive data encrypted using this key (ciphertext) can be sent through an unsecured communication channel. Both parties can encrypt and decrypt data.

provided by symmetric encryption can be scaled by increasing the entropy of the secret key used. For every bit added to the length of a symmetric key that is randomly generated, the difficulty of cracking the encryption through a brute force attack essentially doubles [535].

In general, there are two types of symmetric encryption algorithms, block and stream ciphers [535]. In block cipher algorithms, a sequence of bits is encrypted as a block using a specific secret key. As data are being encrypted, the previously encrypted data need to be saved in a memory system as they wait for a complete block to be encrypted. On the other hand, in a stream cipher algorithm data are encrypted as a stream of bits instead of being saved in the encryption system's memory. Some popular symmetric encryption algorithms include the Advanced Encryption Standard (AES), the Data Encryption Standard (DES), the International Data Encryption Algorithm (IDEA), and the Rivest Cipher 4 (RC4) [535]. AES, DES, and IDEA are block cipher algorithms while RC4 is a stream cipher.

Compared to other techniques, such as public key encryption discussed next, symmetric key encryption systems are generally faster and more efficient because they use a single secret key. Therefore, because of their efficiency, symmetric algorithms are commonly used for encrypting large amounts of data, such as database or file system encryption. Furthermore, because of the relative simplicity of symmetric systems they require less computing power than asymmetric encryption algorithms such as public key encryption.

While symmetric encryption provides efficient algorithms for data encryption, one major disadvantage associated with this type of encryption is the inherent problem of transmitting the secret key used to encrypt and decrypt data. If such a key is shared over an unsecured connection (an unsecured communication channel), it is vulnerable to being intercepted by a malicious or unauthorised party. If an unauthorised user gains access to a particular secret key, the security of any data encrypted using that key is compromised.

Furthermore, the use of a specific key multiple times can also reveal some information to an adversary that can potentially be used to reconstruct the key. The use of the same key multiple time is known as key exhaustion in cryptography [138]. If the same key is used many times this can eventually leak information about the plaintext that has been encrypted or the information of the key itself. This is especially happening in block ciphers such as AES where a plaintext or the key that has been used for encryption can be attacked after 2^{32} blocks have been encrypted [42].

To overcome such problems, many practical applications that require high security use a combination of symmetric and asymmetric encryption (as we discuss next) to establish a secure connection between parties while a key hierarchy is used to ensure that master keys are not overused, as well as the appropriate rotation of keys that are used to encrypt large volumes of data. However, as we discussed in Section 4.5.1, in any case proper key management strategies must be employed to prevent that encrypted data are becoming not usable due to a lost encryption key.

6.4.2 Public Key Encryption

Public key encryption, also known as asymmetric key encryption, uses two separate keys to encrypt and decrypt sensitive data [535]. In general, the key used for encryption is known as the public or encryption key, while the key used for decryption is known as the private key, secret key, or decryption key. Public and private keys are generated as large numbers based on a mathematical algorithm. The algorithms used in a public key cryptosystem must also ensure that the generation of the private key based on its corresponding public key is computationally infeasible [535].

Each party involved in a public key cryptosystem generates their own public and private keys. The public keys of all parties are then shared among the parties, or even made publicly visible to anybody in a key repository. However, the private key of each party is kept secret from any other party. Figure 6.4 shows how public key encryption can be used by two parties.

For example, let us assume Alice wants to send some sensitive data to Bob. To do so using public key encryption, Alice must obtain Bob's public key. Alice takes Bob's public key and, together with the corresponding encryption algorithm, encrypts her data and sends the encrypted data (the ciphertext) to Bob. Because of the nature of the public-private key pair and the fact that Alice and Bob have agreed on using a public, standard encryption algorithm, Bob can use his private key to decrypt Alice's data. Most importantly, only Bob, because no one else knows his private key, can decrypt Alice's data. Anyone who intercepts their communication or receives the encrypted data will not be able to decrypt this data because they don't have Bob's private key. Public key encryption therefore overcomes the major drawback of sym-

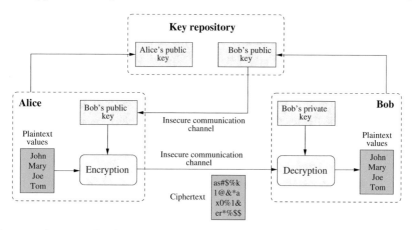

Fig. 6.4 An example of public key encryption between two parties, Alice and Bob. As illustrated, each user initially generates a pair of keys, known as the public and private keys, where the public keys are given to a key repository while the private keys are kept secret by each party. The public keys are used to encrypt sensitive data while the private keys are used to decrypt data encrypted with the corresponding public key, as we describe in Section 6.4.2.

metric encryption of requiring a secure communication channel to exchange the shared secret key [562].

Whitfield Diffie and Martin Hellman first publicly proposed asymmetric, public key encryption in 1976 [155]. The concept had been independently and covertly proposed by James Ellis, Clifford Cocks, and Malcolm Williamson several years before while working for the British Intelligence and Security organisation (now the UK's Government Communications Headquarters, GCHQ) [344]. The method by Diffie and Hellman uses numerical modulo operations on very large prime numbers to produce encryption (public) and decryption (private) keys. The most popular public key encryption system is the RSA algorithm that was developed by Ron Rivest, Adi Shamir, and Len Adleman in the late 1970s [519].

Many popular modern communication protocols, such as OpenPGP and SSL, and software programs such as Internet browsers, rely upon asymmetric cryptography for encryption and digital signature functions which are required to establish a secure connection over an insecure network such as the Internet, or to validate a digital signature. Because public keys that need to be shared are generally too large to be easily remembered, they are stored on digital certificates for secure transport and sharing. Similar to symmetric key encryption, the strength of a public key encryption system depends upon the size of the public and private keys used [535]. Doubling the key length delivers an exponential increase in security but a corresponding decrease in the performance of the encryption and decryption processes.

Public key encryption does, however, not provide authentication of the communicating parties and it is thus vulnerable to a man-in-the-middle attack [535], where an adversary can intercept and delete messages, and even generate new messages if encryption (public) keys are available to him. As we described in Section 4.5.1, a public key infrastructure (PKI) can be used for asymmetric encryption to deliver confidentiality, integrity, and authenticity. This requires that a user can verify that a public key is authentic, that it belongs to the person or entity claimed, and that it has not been tampered with or replaced by a malicious third party. In a PKI, digital certificates are issued by entities known as Certificate Authorities (CAs). As the example in the side box on page 95 illustrates, a PKI can be used in a context where sensitive databases need to be linked between organisations.

6.4.3 Homomorphic Encryption

Homomorphic encryption schemes allow calculations to be conducted between data in an encrypted form (ciphertext) to generate a result of these calculations that is also encrypted [3]. The decrypted result of a calculation conducted on homomorphically encrypted values will be the same as the results of the same calculation performed on the unencrypted data.

For example, assume two given numbers, n_1 and n_2, that belong to the two database owners Alice and Bob, respectively. First, Alice and Bob encrypt their numbers into an encrypted form, ϵ_1 and ϵ_2, respectively, using a homomorphic encryption function $E()$, where $\epsilon_1 \leftarrow E(n_1)$ and $\epsilon_2 \leftarrow E(n_2)$. Based on a homomorphic addition scheme [3], Alice and Bob can compute the summation of n_1 and n_2 using the corresponding encrypted values, denoted as $(\epsilon_1 + \epsilon_2)$. The decryption of $(\epsilon_1 + \epsilon_2)$ is then equal to the addition of the original, unencrypted, values n_1 and n_2, denoted as $n_1 + n_2 = D(\epsilon_1 + \epsilon_2)$, where $D()$ is a homomorphic decryption function.

More generally, an encryption scheme is called homomorphic over a certain operation $\star$ if the following equation holds [3]:

$$E(m_1) \star E(m_2) = E(m_1 \star m_2); \quad \forall m_1, m_2 \in M, \tag{6.2}$$

where $E()$ is the homomorphic encryption function and M is the set of all possible messages.

Homomorphic encryption schemes can be categorised into partially (somewhat) and fully homomorphic schemes [3, 380]. Fully homomorphic schemes can perform addition and multiplication [456] or any arbitrary calculation [394]. However, current fully homomorphic schemes are computationally not efficient due to their complex encryption and decryption operations. Partially homomorphic encryption schemes only support a limited number of operations on encrypted data, however, they are much faster and thus more practical [456].

As we discussed in the previous section, in most homomorphic encryption schemes a key pair, known as public and private (secret) key, is used to encrypt and decrypt the sensitive input values [394]. The public key is kept publicly available to any party that participates in a protocol while the private key is not shared with any other party and kept secret by the party who generates the key pair. Some homomorphic encryption systems provide probabilistic encryption [234], where successive encryptions of the same input value using the same public key will generate different encrypted values with high probability [657], while decrypting an encrypted value using a private key returns the correct original input value. These techniques can potentially be useful to hide information about frequent values being encrypted.

In the context of linking sensitive databases, homomorphic encryption has been used to calculate the similarities (of numerical, categorical, and string data types) between sensitive values held by different database owners [318, 333, 506, 616].

6.5 Secure Multiparty Computation

Secure multiparty computation has been introduced as a solution to overcome the problem of performing computations on sensitive data across parties [394]. Secure multiparty computation enables several parties to be involved in a computation with their sensitive input data, where at the end of the computation no party learns anything about any other party's sensitive input but all parties learn the final result of the computation. Secure multiparty computation techniques have been employed as building blocks not just in the context of linking sensitive databases, but also for privacy-preserving data mining [394] and other application areas.

The idea of conducting secure computations between two databases was introduced by Yao in 1986 [656], and later extended by Goldreich et al. [231] for multiple databases owned by different parties. Under a secure multiparty computation protocol, a variety of encryption schemes, such as homomorphic encryption as described in the previous section, and techniques such as secure summation, secure set union, secure set intersection, and secure scalar product, have been proposed [394]. In the following we describe some of these techniques that have been used in protocols that aim to link sensitive databases for accurate computation while preserving the privacy of sensitive input values [166, 333, 507, 616].

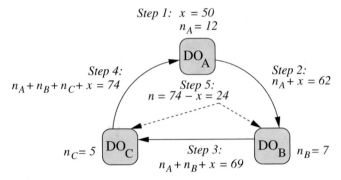

Fig. 6.5 An example secure summation protocol between three database owners DO_A, DO_B, and DO_C, who wish to calculate the sum of their sensitive input values n_A, n_B, and n_C, respectively. In this example, DO_A starts the protocol by generating a random number $x = 50$ (step 1) and adding x to its sensitive input n_A. DO_A then sends this partial sum to DO_B (step 2). In steps 3 and 4, DO_B and DO_C, respectively, update the partial sum they receive from the previous database owner by adding their own sensitive input value to the partial sum, and sending it to the next database owner. Finally, in step 5, after it has received the total sum from DO_C, DO_A subtracts x from $n = n_A + n_B + n_C$. DO_A finally distributes this sum n to the other database owners that participate in the protocol. © T. Ranbaduge 2018, reprinted with permission.

6.5.1 Secure Summation

Secure summation is a type of secure multiparty computation protocol that has been used in a variety of approaches to link sensitive databases [129, 498, 616]. This protocol allows multiple (more than two) cooperating database owners to calculate the sum of their individual sensitive input values (assumed to be numbers) without having to reveal their input to any other parties that participate in the protocol, while all parties learn the final summed result. Note that such protocols do not work for only two parties, because from the sum of two numbers each party can easily calculate the input value of the other party by simply subtracting its own value from the sum.

An example of the idea behind a basic secure summation protocol [129], is illustrated in Figure 6.5. Let us assume three database owners, DO_A, DO_B, and DO_C, and their sensitive input values, n_A, n_B, and n_C, respectively. The database owners want to compute the summation of their numbers as $n = n_A + n_B + n_C$. The secure summation protocol starts by DO_A choosing a large random number x (which it does not share with any other party), and adding x to its input n_A. Then DO_A sends this partially summed value, $x + n_A$, to DO_B. Since x is random and kept secret by DO_A, DO_B cannot learn anything about the sensitive input n_A of DO_A.

DO_B adds its private input value, n_B, to $x + n_A$, and sends the partial sum $x + n_A + n_B$ to DO_C. Following the same steps as DO_B, DO_C adds its input value n_C to the partial sum it received from DO_B, and then sends the updated calculated partial sum $x + n_A + n_B + n_C$ back to the first database owner, DO_A. As the final step, DO_A subtracts x from the final sum and the resulting value $n = n_A + n_B + n_C$ is distributed to DO_B and DO_C. At the end of this calculation each database owner only knows the total sum, from which they are unable to learn the sensitive input values of the other database owners.

This basic secure summation protocol assumes the participating database owners are not colluding. If some of them do, they might be able to identify the secure input of another party. For example, assuming five database owners, DO_1 to DO_5, participate in such a secure summation protocol. If DO_2 and DO_4 are willing to share their private inputs, n_2 and n_4, then they can calculate the sensitive value n_3 of DO_3, because the partial sum of DO_2 subtracted from the partial sum of DO_4 is equal to $(x + n_1 + n_2 + n_3 + n_4) - (x + n_1 + n_2) = n_3 + n_4$, from which DO_4 can subtract it own value n_4 to learn the sensitive input n_3 of DO_3.

Several variations of secure summation protocols have been developed to provide improved privacy guarantees even for scenarios where some database owners are colluding with the aim to learn the sensitive input values of another, non-colluding, party. A survey by Ranbaduge et al. [502] describes eight secure summation protocols and discusses their privacy under a variety of collusion scenarios.

6.5.2 Secure Set Intersection

Secure set intersection protocols have been used in techniques to link sensitive databases to obtain the intersection of sets of values or records held in different databases without any participating database owner having to reveal its full set of values [11, 166, 639]. The intersection of multiple input sets are the elements that occur in all these sets.

For example, assume three database owners who like to identify the postcode values that occur in common in their three databases. Assume the first database contains the set of postcodes $s_1 = \{2000, 2001, 2618, 3200, 4177\}$, the second database the set $s_2 = \{2001, 2190, 2618, 3790, 4177, 7630\}$, and the third database the set $s_3 = \{1204, 2001, 2618, 3009, 4177, 6320\}$. The postcodes in common to all three databases is the set $s_c = \{2001, 2618, 4177\}$. At the end of a secure set intersection protocol, the three database owners therefore only learn that they have these three postcodes in the set s_c in common but nothing about the not common postcodes in the individual sensitive databases.

Secure set intersection protocols generally use either commutative [7] or homomorphic [456] encryption schemes. Several efficient secure set intersection protocols have been introduced with a linear communication complexity in the sizes of the input sets [639]. However, these protocols are computationally still expensive because they are based on complex encryption algorithms. Some protocols can be parallelised to improve their performance and scalability [166]. A variation of a secure set intersection protocol is a protocol where the participating parties only learn the cardinality of the resulting set intersection as the number of elements that are common to all databases (such as $|s_c| = 3$ in the above example), but not the actual common elements [605]. Furthermore, some secure set intersection protocols can also be used in scenarios where no third party, such as a linkage unit, is available to carry out the intersection of the encoded sets sent to it by the individual database owners [605, 606].

6.5.3 Oblivious Transfer Protocols

Oblivious transfer protocols [489] have been used in several protocols to link sensitive databases [453, 639] due to their capability of exchanging sensitive values among the parties that participate in a protocol while preserving the privacy of these values. Specifically, an oblivious transfer protocol allows one party to send several of its sensitive input values to a receiver in a way that protects these sensitive values from both the sender and receiver by ensuring that the sender does not learn which of its input values is selected by the receiver, and the receiver does not learn any information about the other input values sent by the sender besides the value it has selected. In general, oblivious transfer protocols are expensive in terms of computation and communication requirements, and they can become the efficiency bottleneck in protocol design.

6.5.4 Secret Sharing

Secret sharing [49] (also known as secret splitting [535]) refers to methods for distributing a secret amongst a group of parties, each of whom is allocated with a share of the secret. The general idea of a secret sharing scheme is that the secret value of a participating party can be reconstructed only when a sufficient number of shares are combined together. In such a setting each individual share is of no use as it cannot be used to construct the private input of a party.

Threshold secret sharing schemes, where a secret shared between n parties can only be recovered if $1 < t \leq n$ parties cooperate to recover the secret, were first introduced by Shamir [558] and Blakley [66] in 1979. Different other secret sharing schemes were proposed over the years [336] and their properties studied [49, 105]. Secret sharing has been used as a building block in protocols that aim to link sensitive databases to determine links between records without revealing the identities of the individuals in these records [382].

6.6 Phonetic Encoding

Phonetic encoding is the process of converting a string, usually assumed to be a name, into some form of code depending upon how the string is being pronounced (spoken) [109]. The idea of using such phonetic codes is that they group names together that are written differently but sound similarly when spoken [109, 375]. Phonetic encoding techniques are used in a variety of applications, including spell checkers (finding similar sounding word alternatives) and person search (finding alternative name spellings).

In the context of linking databases, as we described in Section 3.2, phonetic encoding techniques are commonly used in the blocking step to group records with similar sounding quasi-identifying attribute values into the same block to allow their detailed comparison [109]. It is possible to also use phonetic encoding techniques in the comparison step when linking databases, in which case quasi-identifying attribute values are first converted into their phonetic codes using a suitable phonetic encoding algorithm. Then these codes are compared, where the same code means the corresponding attribute values would be considered a match, while if the codes are different the corresponding attribute values would be considered a non-match. There are also privacy-preserving record linkage techniques that use phonetic encoding either as a data preprocessing step before further anonymisation [487], or even as the main anonymisation approach [321], as we describe in Section 7.3.

One aspect which can limit the use of phonetic encoding functions is that they are often language specific, because names (or words in general) are spoken differently in different languages which would result in different phonetic encodings. While most phonetic encoding algorithms assume the strings to be encoded are names or words from the English language, there are various modifications and variations of phonetic encoding algorithms in other languages [375, 542]. Some phonetic encoding algorithms, such as Double-Metaphone [472] even generate two encodings for one input string if there are spelling variations of this string.

In Table 6.1 we provide example encodings using several popular phonetic encoding algorithms, where we refer the reader to Christen [109] for detailed descriptions of these algorithms. In the side box on page 154 we describe in detail how the popular Soundex [524] algorithm works.

The Soundex phonetic encoding algorithm

The Soundex phonetic encoding algorithm is one of the oldest methods to convert names into codes according to how they are pronounced [283, 375, 664]. The developer of Soundex, Russell, patented his idea in 1918 [524]. Despite its drawbacks, as we discuss below, Soundex is still widely used and implemented in many database systems as well as applications and tools to link databases [109]. The algorithm assumes American-English language pronunciation, and converts an input string (assumed to be a name) into a code that consists of one letter and three digits using the following steps:

1. Keep the first letter of the input string.
2. Convert all following letters (all except the first letter of the input string) into digits according to the following transformation table:

a, e, h, i, o, u, w, y → 0	l → 4
b, f, p, v → 1	m, n → 5
c, g, j, k, q, s, x, z → 2	r → 6
d, t → 3	

3. Remove all zeros.
4. Replace all adjacent repetitions of the same digit with a single digit.
5. If the resulting code contains less than three digits then pad the code at the end with zeros until there are three digits.
6. If the code contains more than three digits only keep the first three and remove all following digits.

At the end of this process, an input string is converted into a code made of one letter followed by three digits. As an example of how repetitions are handled, the name 'abbiegale' is first converted in 'a11002040' (steps 1 and 2 above), then 'a1124' (step 3), and finally 'a124' (step 4). The short name 'pete' is first converted into 'p030' (steps 1 and 2), then 'p3' (step 3), and finally 'p300' (step 5), while the long name 'christine' is first converted into 'c06023050' (steps 1 and 2), then 'c6235' (step 3), and then truncated to 'c623' (step 6). These three examples are also shown in Table 6.1.

While a main advantage of Soundex is its simplicity compared to modern techniques that use more complex phonetic rules [109], a major disadvantage is that Soundex keeps the first letter of the input string. As can be seen from Table 6.1, similar sounding names such as 'christine' and 'kristine' are therefore encoded into different Soundex codes ('c623' and 'k623', respectively). A second disadvantage is that for longer input strings, that lead to Soundex codes that need to be truncated, the letters at their end will not be considered. One simple way to overcome both of these drawbacks is to not only encode a string, but also its reversed version. For example, 'christine' is reversed to 'enitsirhc' and 'kristine' to 'enitsirk', and both will be converted into the Soundex code 'a532'.

6.7 Statistical Linkage Keys

A special method to encode values in quasi-identifying attributes is to generate a combination of selected character sequences extracted from such at-

Table 6.1 Examples of different phonetic encodings for selected names, where variations of the same name are grouped together. Adapted from Christen [109].

Name	Soundex	NYSIIS	Double-Metaphone	Phonex	Phonix
peter	p360	pata	ptr	b360	p300
pete	p300	pat	pt	b300	p300
pedro	p360	padr	ptr	b360	p360
petra	p360	patr	ptr	b360	p360
smith	s530	snat	sm0 / xmt	s530	s530
smythe	s530	snat	sm0 / xmt	s530	s530
smithers	s536	snat	sm0r / xmtr	s536	s538
abigail	a124	abag	apkl	a124	V124
abigayle	a124	abag	apkl	a124	V124
abbigale	a124	abag	apkl	a124	V124
christina	c623	chra	krst	c623	k683
christine	c623	chra	krst	c623	k683
kristina	k623	cras	krst	c623	k683
krystina	k623	cras	krst	c623	k683

tributes. Concatenated, these are known as a statistical linkage key [335]. A specific version of such a statistical linkage key was developed and has been successfully used by the Australian Institute of Health and Welfare (AIHW).

Known as the SLK-581 [335][4], this method generates a statistical linkage key using the following steps:

- Take the second, third and fifth letters of the surname. If a surname has less than five characters then pad it with the digit '2'. For example, 'Tan' is encoded as 'an2'.
- Take the second and third letters of the first name. If a first name has less than three letters again pad it with '2'. For example, 'Li' is encoded as 'i2'.
- Take the full date of birth using the format 'DDMMYYYY', and pad it with a leading 0 if the day and/or month number is/are below 10. For example, 8 August 1957 is encoded as '08081957'. If a full date is known only approximately or not at all then special codes are used [335].
- The gender is encoded as '1' for male, '2' for female, and '9' if unknown.

For example, a record for 'Charlotte Nanayari' born on the 23 November 1991 would be encoded into the SLK-581 value 'anyha231119912', while 'Sissie Kirbe' (with unknown gender) born on the 19 August 1992 will have an SLK-581 value 'ireis190819929'.

The SLK-581 method has been used extensively in the health domain in Australia [335], and because it does provide some privacy protection it has

---

[4] See: https://meteor.aihw.gov.au/content/index.phtml/itemId/349510

also been applied for the linkage of sensitive databases [508]. This is because having access to an SLK-581 value might not always allow the reconstruction of the exact quasi-identifying values of the input record that was used to generate this SLK-581 value. However some recent work has shown more modern encoding techniques, such as those we discuss in the following chapters, do provide improved privacy protection compared to SLK-581 while still resulting in high linkage quality [508].

6.8 Similarity Measures

A crucial aspect when linking sensitive databases is that the quasi-identifying attributes used to compare records can contain values where variations and errors can occur, and where values can be missing or out of date [109]. As we discussed in Section 3.3, such data quality issues make it necessary to not simply compare attribute values in an exact way only, where a single character difference would mean two values are different. Rather, techniques are required that allow the comparison of values in approximate ways such that variations and errors are taken into account.

In the context of linking sensitive databases, the majority of quasi-identifying attribute values to be compared are generally string values such as names and address details. Other types of attributes are dates (such as dates of birth), or numerical values such as ages. One important aspect is that some attributes that consist of digits only, such as postcodes or dates (if they are recorded in ISO 8601 standard format 'YYYYMMDD' [296]) should not be treated as numerical data. Instead they can be considered as strings, or in the case of dates be compared using specific date comparison functions [109], as we discuss in Section 6.8.4.

Many different comparison functions have been developed, most of them aimed at calculating similarities between string values [252, 301, 308, 369, 433, 568, 642, 654]. A detailed discussion of many of these functions is provided by Christen [109]. It is important to note that different such similarity functions will calculate different numerical similarity values for the same pair of input values, as for example can be seen in Table 6.2 on page 163. This does not mean that some of these are correct similarities and others are wrong. Rather, different similarity functions consider different characteristics of variations between strings. The user needs to decide which technique is most suitable for their types of data and linkage application [109].

The result of a comparison of values is generally a numerical similarity value (or score), where a higher similarity value means the compared attribute values are more similar to each other than compared values that obtain a lower similarity value. These similarity values are commonly normalised into the 0 to 1 interval, where a similarity of 1 means the two compared values are the same, a similarity of 0 means they are completely different (for example do not share a single character, such as 'david' and 'peter'), and a similarity between 0 and 1 means the two compared values do have some commonalities (such as 'peter' and 'petra').

There is a relationship between similarities and distances [109], as we discuss in detail in the side box on page 158, where it is often possible to convert distances into similarities and the other way round. As we will describe below, a common type of function used to compare approximate similarities between strings is based on the number of edit operations required to convert one string into another, leading to what is known as an edit distance [109].

In the following we discuss in more detail the most important types of similarity functions that are being used as building blocks when values from sensitive databases are being compared. Table 6.2 provides similarity values as calculated for a set of example string value pairs.

6.8.1 Set-based Similarities between Strings

One commonly used approach to calculate a similarity between string (textual) values is to convert the strings into sets of shorter substrings, known as character q-grams (or n-grams) [109], and to then count the number of such q-grams two strings have in common. The idea is that the more similar two strings are the more character q-grams they will share.

The generation of these q-grams is based on a sliding window approach, where overlapping substrings of $q \geq 1$ characters are extracted from a string. For example, when using $q = 2$ (known as bigrams or digrams [343]) the string 'peter' is converted into the list of q-grams [pe, et, te, er], while 'petra' is converted into [pe, et, tr, ra]. These two strings have the same beginning 'pet' and thus the same two bigrams 'pe' and 'et'.

Rather than using lists of q-grams, where the same q-gram might occur multiple times, it is common practice to convert these lists into sets of q-grams, where a set only contains unique q-grams. For example, the string 'aniana' is first converted into the bigram list [an, ni, ia, an, na], and then into the set {an, ni, ia, na} where the bigram 'an' only occurs once.

There are different approaches of how the similarity between two sets of q-grams can be calculated [109]. Assume two strings, s_1 and s_2, have been converted into their corresponding sets of q-grams, $\mathbf{q_1}$ and $\mathbf{q_2}$. We can obtain the number of common q-grams, c, as the size of the intersection of the two q-gram sets, $c = |\mathbf{q_1} \cap \mathbf{q_2}|$, where $|\cdot|$ denotes the size of a set (the number of its elements). If we denote the sizes of the two individual q-gram sets with $l_1 = |\mathbf{q_1}|$ and $l_2 = |\mathbf{q_2}|$, then the following three approaches are most commonly used to calculate similarities between strings based on their q-gram sets, where each calculates a similarity between 0 and 1:

Similarities and distance metrics

We define with $s = sim(v_i, v_j)$ a similarity function that calculates a numerical value s between two values v_i and v_j that can be strings, numbers, dates, and so on, where it holds that $0 \leq s \leq 1$. The general requirement of such a similarity function are [109]:

- $sim(v_i, v_i) = 1$: Comparing a value with itself results in an exact similarity.
- $sim(v_i, v_j) = 0$: The similarity of values that are completely different from each other is 0. What accounts for 'completely different' depends upon the type of data that are being compared.
- $0 < sim(v_i, v_j) < 1$: An approximate similarity between exact similarity and total dissimilarity is calculated if the two compared values are somewhat similar to each other. What 'somewhat similar' means again depends upon the type of data that are being compared.

The relationship between the mathematical concept of a metric distance function [254] and a similarity function is that a metric distance $dist(o_i, o_j)$ between two objects (or points), o_i and o_j, must fulfil the following four requirements:

1. $dist(o_i, o_i) = 0$: The distance from an object to itself is zero.
2. $dist(o_i, o_j) \geq 0$: The distance between two objects is always a non-negative number.
3. $dist(o_i, o_j) = d(o_j, o_i)$: The distance between two objects is symmetric.
4. $dist(o_i, o_j) \leq dist(o_i, o_k) + dist(o_k, o_j)$: The triangular inequality between any three objects must always hold. This inequality states that the direct distance between two objects is never larger than the summed distances between the two objects via a third object o_k.

The triangular inequality is a powerful concept used in many areas of computer science because it allows to reduce the number of distance calculations that need to be conducted between sets of objects [136, 660].

There are different approaches to convert a distance value d into a similarity value s. One is to calculate $s = 1/d$, where it is assumed the distance $d > 0$, while a second approach is to calculate $s = 1 - d$, where it is assumed that the distance value is normalised between $0 \leq d \leq 1$.

$$\text{Overlap coefficient: } sim_O(s_1, s_2) = \frac{c}{min(l_1, l_2)} \tag{6.3}$$

$$\text{Jaccard coefficient: } sim_J(s_1, s_2) = \frac{c}{l_1 + l_2 - c} \tag{6.4}$$

$$\text{Dice coefficient: } sim_D(s_1, s_2) = \frac{2 \cdot c}{l_1 + l_2} \tag{6.5}$$

All three functions return a similarity of 1 if the two q-gram sets, $\mathbf{q}_1$ and $\mathbf{q}_2$, are the same, and a similarity of 0 if they have no q-grams in common (which means $c = 0$). Note that the Dice and Jaccard similarities can easily be converted from one to the other: $sim_J(s_1, s_2) = sim_D(s_1, s_2)/(2 - sim_D(s_1, s_2))$, while $sim_D(s_1, s_2) = 2 \cdot sim_J(s_1, s_2)/(1 + sim_J(s_1, s_2))$, which means they are monotonic in one another. Both the Jaccard and Dice coefficient similarity functions are used in the context of linking sensitive databases, for example to compare quasi-identifying attribute values that have been encoded into bit vectors [543, 564, 619], as we discuss in detail in Chapter 8.

There are some variations of the basic approach of using a sliding window over a string to extract its list of q-grams. One is to first pad a string at the beginning and end with special characters (which should be different from all the characters that occur in any of the attribute values to be encoded). Padding provides information about what q-grams occur at the beginning and end of strings, and this can potentially help to improve the quality of linked databases [109]. The idea is to pad a string both at the beginning and end with $q - 1$ special characters, if q is the length of the q-grams to be generated, before the string is converted into its q-grams. If, for example, $q = 3$ (trigram) is used, and if we use an underscore '_' as the padding character, then 'peter' will be padded into '__peter__' resulting in the list of trigrams [__p, _pe, pet, ete, ter, er_, r__].

A second variation of the basic approach is to use positional q-grams, where each q-gram extracted from a string value is also given its position within the string. For example, 'peter' would be converted into the list of positional bigrams ($q = 2$) as [(pe,1), (et,2), (te,3), (er,4)]. Having positions of where q-grams do occur within strings allows a modification of how the number of common q-grams, c in the above equations, is being counted. It is now possible to only consider q-grams as common if they occur within a certain maximum distance from each other. So a positional q-gram (pe,1) from one q-gram set might be counted as common with a positional q-gram (pe,3) in another q-gram set, but not with (pe,12) because these two occurrences of 'pe' are too far apart (eleven positions) from each other.

6.8.2 Edit-based Similarities between Strings

Compared to counting common q-grams between the strings to be compared, edit-based similarity functions count how many edits in the form of insertions, deletions, substitutions, or transpositions of characters are required to transform one of the two strings being compared into the other. This number of edits is commonly known as the edit distance [109, 433].

The most basic edit distance function, known as the Levenshtein edit distance [386], is defined as the smallest number of single character insertions, deletions, and substitutions that are needed to convert one string into another string. Each of these edit operations is generally assumed to have a cost of one. For example, to convert the name 'gail' to 'gayle', we can substitute 'i' with 'y' and then insert (add) 'e', resulting in an edit distance of two (two edit operations).

The edit distance between two strings is generally calculated using a dynamic programming algorithm [308], as we illustrate in the side box on page 161. This algorithm has the drawback of requiring a number of computational steps that is quadratic in the lengths of the two strings being compared. If the first string contains l_1 characters and the second string l_2 characters, then the dynamic programming algorithm requires $l_1 \cdot l_2$ steps to calculate the final smallest number of edit operations that is needed to convert the first string into the second string. This means this algorithm has a quadratic, or $O(n^2)$, complexity following the Big-O notation we discussed in the side box on page 68. As a result of this rather expensive algorithm, calculating the edit distance between long strings (such as street addresses, or product or company names) can become slow compared to the set-based similarity functions discussed above (which generally have a number of computational steps that is linear in the lengths of the strings being compared).

While Levenshtein edit distance only considers the three operations insert, delete, and substitute, a modification known as the Damerau-Levenshtein edit distance additionally also considers transpositions between adjacent characters [143]. For example, while the Levenshtein edit distance between 'sydney' and 'sydeny' is two (either two substitutions or one insert and one delete), the corresponding Damerau-Levenshtein edit distance is one because only one transposition of 'n' with 'e' is required.

The edit distance calculated between two strings is a non-negative number, where a distance of 0 means the two strings are the same, and the larger the distance is the more different the two strings are (because more edit operations are required to convert one string into another). If we assume all basic edit costs are 1, then the maximum number of edit operations between two strings is the length of the longer of the two strings, $max(l_1, l_2)$. This is because we can first substitute all characters of the shorter string with the corresponding characters at the same positions of the longer string (l_1 substitutions if we assume $l_1 \leq l_2$), followed by $l_2 - l_1$ inserts (given $l_2 \geq l_1$), resulting in a total of $l_1 + (l_2 - l_1) = l_2$ edit operations (with l_2 being the length of the longer of the two strings). It is now possible to convert a Levenshtein edit distance into a normalised similarity between 0 and 1 as:

$$sim_{ED}(s_1, s_2) = 1.0 - \frac{ed(s_1, s_2)}{max(l_1, l_2)}, \qquad (6.7)$$

where the function $ed(s_1, s_2)$ calculates the Levenshtein edit distance between the two strings s_1 and s_2, and where $l_1 = |s_1|$ and $l_2 = |s_2|$ are the lengths of the two strings.

While generally the costs assigned to each type of edit are fixed, there are methods that can learn the costs of edits using machine learning techniques based on training data in the form of pairs of strings and the edit operations between them [62]. Given enough suitable training data, such techniques can even learn character specific edit costs. For example, if quasi-identifying

---

Edit distance calculation

The most common approach to calculate the edit distance between two strings, s_1 and s_2, is to use a dynamic programming algorithm [308] which finds the minimum number of edit operations required to convert s_1 into s_2. This algorithm is based on an edit matrix, where s_1 is assigned along the left side and s_2 along the top row of the matrix, as can be seen in the two examples below (adapted from Christen [109]).

If we denote such an edit matrix with $\mathbf{M}$, then the cell $\mathbf{M}[i,j]$ in row i ($0 \leq i \leq l_1$) and column j ($0 \leq j \leq l_2$), with $l_1 = |s_1|$ and $l_2 = |s_2|$ being the lengths of the two strings to be compared, corresponds to the number of edits required to convert the first i characters of s_1 into the string made of the first j characters of s_2. For example, cell $\mathbf{M}[4,2]$ in the left matrix (with value 2) corresponds to the number of edits required to convert 'giea' into 'ga' (two character deletions). The empty cells at the top left of the matrices indicate the empty string.

		0	1	2	3	4
			g	a	i	l
0		0	1	2	3	4
1	g	1	0	1	2	3
2	i	2	1	1	1	2
3	e	3	2	2	2	2
4	a	4	3	2	3	3
5	l	5	4	3	3	3

		0	1	2	3	4	5
			p	e	t	e	r
0		0	1	2	3	4	5
1	p	1	0	1	2	3	4
2	e	2	1	0	1	2	3
3	t	3	2	1	0	1	2
4	r	4	3	2	1	1	1
5	a	5	4	3	2	2	2

The dynamic programming algorithm begins by filling in the first row and first column of $\mathbf{M}$ with the corresponding column or row values: $\mathbf{M}[0,j] = j$ in row 0 and column j (with $0 \leq j \leq l_1$), and $\mathbf{M}[i,0] = i$ in row i and column 0 (with $0 \leq i \leq l_2$). The remaining cells of the matrix $\mathbf{M}$, with $i > 0$ and $j > 0$ are then filled row by row using the following iterative approach:

- If $s_1[i] = s_2[j]$, then $\mathbf{M}[i,j] = \mathbf{M}[i-1,j-1]$
  (the same character in s_1 at position i and in s_2 at position j).
- If $s_1[i] \neq s_2[j]$, then

$$\mathbf{M}[i,j] = min \begin{cases} \mathbf{M}[i-1,j] + 1 & \text{a deletion,} \\ \mathbf{M}[i,j-1] + 1 & \text{an insertion, or} \\ \mathbf{M}[i-1,j-1] + 1 & \text{a substitution.} \end{cases} \quad (6.6)$$

The final Levenshtein edit distance between s_1 and s_2 is then the value in the lower right corner cell of the matrix, $ed(s_1, s_2) = \mathbf{M}[l_1, l_2]$.

As Equation 6.6 shows, the row-wise completion of the edit matrix $\mathbf{M}$ only requires two rows of $\mathbf{M}$ to be stored at any time [433]. Therefore, while there are $l_1 \cdot l_2$ computational steps required to complete the edit distance matrix $\mathbf{M}$, only $2 \cdot min(l_1, l_2)$ memory is required.

---

attribute values have been scanned and converted into text strings using optical character recognition (OCR) techniques [252, 477], then an OCR error substituting 'S' with '5' is much more likely than a replacement of 'M' with 'Z', and so a smaller edit cost should be assigned to the operation substituting

'S' with '5' than the one substituting 'M' with 'Z'. It has been shown that learning character specific edit costs can substantially improve the quality of linked databases [62].

6.8.3 Calculating Similarities between Numerical Values

While the majority of quasi-identifying attributes used to compare records in the context of linking sensitive databases contain textual string values, in some applications there might be numerical values that need to be compared.

One example application is to identify similar patients across different hospital databases, where numerical values such as the age of patients, or health indicators such as their weight, height, or blood pressure, can be used to find records about similar patients [614].

Similar as with string data, only allowing for exact matching numerical values will not be of much use due to data quality issues as well as actual variations (such as in the weight of a person). Some tolerance range should be allowed, where pairs of values within that range are still considered to be somewhat similar, while pairs of values outside of that tolerance range are considered to be different [109].

Assume we have two numerical values, n_1 and n_2, which we want to compare in order to calculate a similarity in the range 0 to 1 between these two numbers. As we did with strings, if $n_1 = n_2$ then we set the similarity to 1. To allow for some tolerance and calculate a similarity between n_1 and n_2 if they are not the same, we define a maximum absolute difference value, d_{max}, which we are prepared to tolerate. As illustrated in Figure 6.6, if the absolute difference between n_1 and n_2 is less than d_{max}, $|n_1 - n_2| < d_{max}$, then we calculate an approximate similarity using the following equation:

$$sim_N(n_1, n_2) = \begin{cases} 1.0 - \left(\frac{|n_1 - n_2|}{d_{max}}\right) & \text{if } |n_1 - n_2| < d_{max}, \\ 0.0 & \text{otherwise.} \end{cases} \quad (6.8)$$

Values that have an absolute difference equal to or larger than d_{max} will result in a similarity of 0. For example, assume we have two age values, $n_1 = 42$ years and $n_2 = 45$ years, and we set $d_{max} = 5$ years. Following Equation 6.8, the absolute difference between n_1 and n_2 is 3, leading to a similarity $sim_N(42, 45) = 1.0 - 3/5 = 1.0 - 0.6 = 0.4$.

For some attributes, especially those with large value ranges and skewed distributions, such as salary, having an absolute maximum difference might not be suitable. For example, while the absolute difference between the two salaries $10,000 and $20,000 is the same as between $210,000 and $220,000, clearly one would see the latter pair of salaries to be more similar with each other than the first pair. The alternative to using absolute difference is there-

Table 6.2 Examples of different string similarities for selected name pairs. Adapted from Christen [109].

String 1	String 2	Jaccard q=2	Dice q=2	Overlap q=2	Edit-Dist	Jaro	Jaro-Winkler	Soundex
nichleson	nichulson	0.78	0.88	0.88	0.78	0.93	0.96	1.00
jones	johnson	0.67	0.80	0.80	0.43	0.79	0.83	0.00
massey	massie	0.67	0.80	0.80	0.67	0.89	0.93	1.00
abroms	abrams	0.83	0.91	1.00	0.83	0.89	0.92	1.00
hardin	martinez	0.40	0.57	0.67	0.50	0.72	0.72	0.00
itman	smith	0.43	0.60	0.60	0.00	0.47	0.47	0.00
jeraldine	geraldine	0.78	0.88	0.88	0.89	0.93	0.93	0.00
marhta	martha	1.00	1.00	1.00	0.67	0.94	0.96	1.00
michelle	michael	0.86	0.92	1.00	0.62	0.87	0.92	1.00
michelle	michele	1.00	1.00	1.00	0.88	0.96	0.97	1.00
julies	julius	0.83	0.91	1.00	0.83	0.89	0.93	1.00
tanya	tonya	0.80	0.89	1.00	0.80	0.87	0.88	1.00
dwayne	duane	0.57	0.73	0.80	0.67	0.82	0.84	1.00
sean	susan	0.60	0.75	0.75	0.60	0.78	0.80	0.00
jon	john	0.75	0.86	1.00	0.75	0.92	0.93	1.00
jon	jan	0.50	0.67	0.67	0.67	0.78	0.80	1.00
decatur	decatir	0.75	0.86	0.86	0.86	0.90	0.94	1.00
higbee	highee	0.80	0.89	1.00	0.83	0.89	0.92	0.00
higbee	higvee	0.67	0.80	0.80	0.83	0.89	0.92	1.00
lacura	locura	0.83	0.91	1.00	0.83	0.89	0.90	1.00
iowa	iona	0.60	0.75	0.75	0.75	0.83	0.87	0.00
lst	ist	0.50	0.67	0.67	0.67	0.78	0.78	0.00
campell	campbell	0.86	0.92	1.00	0.88	0.96	0.97	1.00
galloway	calloway	0.71	0.83	0.83	0.88	0.92	0.92	0.00
frederick	fredrick	1.00	1.00	1.00	0.89	0.96	0.98	1.00
jesse	jessie	0.75	0.86	1.00	0.83	0.94	0.97	1.00
jonathon	jonathan	1.00	1.00	1.00	0.88	0.92	0.95	1.00
julies	juluis	0.83	0.91	1.00	0.67	0.89	0.92	1.00
yvette	yevett	1.00	1.00	1.00	0.67	0.89	0.90	1.00
dixon	dickson	0.50	0.67	0.80	0.57	0.79	0.83	1.00
peter	ole	0.17	0.29	0.33	0.20	0.51	0.51	0.00
delfinni	delfini	1.00	1.00	1.00	0.88	0.96	0.97	1.00
ein	eni	1.00	1.00	1.00	0.33	0.56	0.60	1.00
do	od	1.00	1.00	1.00	0.00	0.00	0.00	0.00
doe	deo	1.00	1.00	1.00	0.33	0.56	0.60	1.00
prap	papr	1.00	1.00	1.00	0.50	0.83	0.85	0.00
papr	prap	1.00	1.00	1.00	0.50	0.83	0.85	0.00
gail	gayle	0.50	0.67	0.75	0.60	0.78	0.83	1.00
vest	west	0.60	0.75	0.75	0.75	0.83	0.83	0.00
sydney	sydeny	1.00	1.00	1.00	0.67	0.94	0.96	1.00
tsetung	zedong	0.33	0.50	0.50	0.43	0.64	0.64	0.00
ishara	asara	0.60	0.75	1.00	0.67	0.82	0.82	0.00
charini	nishadi	0.50	0.67	0.67	0.14	0.62	0.62	0.00
anushka	dinusha	0.62	0.77	0.83	0.57	0.81	0.81	0.00
sirintra	siri	0.50	0.67	1.00	0.50	0.83	0.88	0.00

Fig. 6.6 Illustration of the linear extrapolation using the numerical absolute difference similarity between two values n_1 and n_2 as given in Equation 6.8 [109]. © Springer-Verlag Berlin Heidelberg 2012, reprinted with permission.

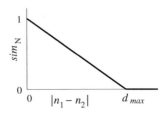

fore to use percentage difference, where instead of the absolute value difference in Equation 6.8 a percentage difference between two numerical values is calculated [109].

6.8.4 Calculating Similarities between Date Values

Date attributes, such as date of birth, occur commonly in databases to be linked. They can be very powerful quasi-identifiers because (assuming they are recorded accurately) they should not change over time for the same individual. Two records that have the same date of birth are more likely to correspond to the same person compared to two records with the same gender or the same city value [274].

Dates can be written in a variety of formats, ranging from long textual descriptions like 'Sunday 27th October 2019' to formats made of digits only, like '27-10-2019' or '20191027' where the latter is the ISO 8601 standard date format in the form of 'YYYMMDD' [296]. One important and sometimes confusing aspect is that dates in the US are written in the format 'MM-DD-YYYY' while in most other countries they are written as 'DD-MM-YYYY'. For some dates it will be clear from the day and month values which component is the month and which is the day ('27-10-2019' is clearly in the 'DD-MM-YYYY' format), while for other dates this is not clear ('12-10-2018' is a valid date in both the 'MM-DD-YYYY' and 'DD-MM-YYYY' format).

One way to compare dates is to split them into their corresponding day, month and year components, and then to compare these components individually. This however will not consider the cyclic nature of dates [614]. The day '01-01-2000' is only one day after day '31-12-1999', they however only share three '1' digits with each other. Considering these two dates as string values and calculating their Levenshtein edit distance would result in a similarity of $1/8$ (if we first remove the '-' characters) because with the exception of the first '1' all other digits require some edit operation.

An alternative approach to compare dates is to convert them into the number of days that have passed since a given fix date, known as an epoch date, and then to compare these day numbers as numerical values using either the absolute or percentage difference methods described previously.

The epoch date used should be set to a date long ago in the past to ensure all date values in a database become positive day numbers.

The nature of dates, consisting of day, month, and year components, however leads to some other specific aspects that need to be considered.

- In applications where a day or even a month value is not known, users commonly enter '01' as default value. As a result, many databases for example in the health domain have a much increased percentage of people born on the 1st of January of each year (think of an emergency department database where the exact dates of birth of many accident victims might be unknown).

- In some applications day and month values can be swapped without these mistakes being recognised (for example, due to the different ways of recording dates in the US and the rest of the world as we discussed above). In such a case, a special kind of comparison function might be appropriate where the year values are compared normally, while the month and day values are flipped in one of the two dates (month from the first date is compared with day of the second date, and day of the first date with month of the second date). If this results in an exact match of day and month value then this can indicate that the day and month values have been swapped in one of the two dates.

- If the difference between two dates is only in the month value, while both year and day values are the same, then using the numerical absolute difference approach (described above) might lead to similarities of 0 if the maximum difference tolerated is set to a small value of only a few days or weeks. However, if the dates are considered as strings then only one out of eight digits might differ. For example, the two dates '24-01-2017' and '24-09-2017' are 243 days apart (likely larger than the d_{max} value), but they have only one digit difference (and thus have an edit distance similarity of 7/8 if the '-' are disregarded).

An important aspect of date attributes is therefore that, for a given application, a user needs to carefully evaluate the format, accuracy, and error characteristics of the values in such attributes before selecting a similarity function that is suitable to compare date values.

6.9 Choosing Suitable Building Blocks

In this chapter we have discussed a variety of techniques that have been used as building blocks in protocols and algorithms that are aimed at linking sensitive databases. These techniques include random number generators, different hashing, anonymisation, and encryption techniques, approaches to phonetically encode string, statistical linkage keys, and techniques to compare string, numerical, and date values in order to calculate similarities between them.

When tasked with the practical linking of records across sensitive databases held by different organisations, the three main dimensions to be considered are (1) linkage quality, (2) scalability (linkage time and resource usage), and (3) the privacy protection provided by the building blocks used by a certain linkage protocol.

There is generally a trade-off between these three dimensions [615], in that optimising one or two of these dimensions comes at the cost of the third dimension not being optimal. For example, linkage techniques that are fast and scale to the linkage of very large databases might not be able to provide strong privacy protection, while techniques that do provide strong privacy guarantees might not scale to the linking of very large databases. Some key questions that need to be considered when tasked with linking sensitive databases include:

- What is the quality of the databases to be linked, specifically the quality of the values in the quasi-identifying attributes used for linking? Are these values likely to be missing or contain variations or errors (as we discussed in Section 3.3)? If data quality is high and quasi-identifying attribute values are correct and accurate, and there are no missing data, then exact matching techniques using some form of hashing or encryption can be applied. On the other hand, if data quality is low then approximate matching techniques are required, which likely involves a more complex encoding of values to facilitate similarity calculations.

- How many records do the databases to be linked contain, and how many databases are to be linked (two or more)? Can all possible record pairs between the two databases be compared, or does some form of blocking, indexing, filtering or parallelisation (as we discussed in Section 3.2 and Chapter 10) need to be applied? Any application of blocking, indexing, or filtering will potentially limit the application of certain encoding or encryption technique, while any parallelisation will require appropriate computing hardware as well as specialised knowledge.

- What is the expected threat scenario of the environment in which the sensitive databases are being linked? Can the organisations involved be fully trusted (including all the individuals working on a linkage project), or are some of the organisations semi-trusted or not trusted at all (as we discussed in Section 4.4)? Depending upon the expected threat scenario and corresponding adversary model, different privacy techniques will be required which will influence how sensitive databases are being linked, and the time and resources needed for conducting such linkages.

It is important to understand that currently no existing technique or protocol to link sensitive databases in a privacy-preserving way does provide the best solution across all three dimensions discussed above. In any practical application, the relative importance of each of these three dimensions needs to be carefully assessed to allow suitable building blocks, algorithms, and protocols to be selected [615]. In Chapter 11 we will cover additional aspects that are of importance in practice, such as data related issues and technical expertise required to implement or deploy certain linkage techniques, legal and ethical aspects, as well as IT requirements.

In the following chapters we describe different actual techniques that are using the building blocks discussed in this chapter to link sensitive databases in such ways that no identifying personal data about individuals need to be shared between organisations that aim to link their sensitive database, nor with any other organisation, and where all sensitive data are protected from external adversaries.

6.10 Summary and Further Reading

The topics covered in this chapter span a wide area of core computer science topics that range from data mining to cryptography. Many different techniques have been developed for hashing, anonymisation, encryption, phonetic encoding, and similarity calculations.

For readers interested in random number generation we recommend the recent book by Johnston [307]. An extensive summary and taxonomy on hashing techniques was recently provided by Chi and Zhu [102], while the theoretical and practical aspects of locality sensitive hashing are covered in the book by Lekovec et al. [385].

Various aspects of data anonymisation are covered by the introductory work by Domingo-Ferrer et al. [162], Traditional statistical techniques for anonymiation, such as masking and generalisation, are also covered in the book by Duncan et al. [173]. A framework covering a wide variety of aspects of anonymisation, including technical, legal, social, and ethical, is described in the book by Elliot et al. [187]. For a non-technical introduction to differential privacy we refer the reader to Nissim et al. [442].

Encryption techniques and the related topic of computer security are topics covered in many books. Readers interested in the history of codes and encryption will find the book by Singh [562] an interesting read, while for more technical descriptions of cryptographic algorithms and protocols the seminal work by Schneier is recommended [535].

Finally, phonetic encoding and similarity functions have a long history in the context of linking databases, and the interested reader is referred to extensive surveys on these topics such as the one by Navarro [433] on string matching, while Christen [109] also covers these topics specifically in the context of linking databases.

Chapter 7
Encoding and Comparing Sensitive Values

Abstract Over the past nearly two decades researchers from different domains, including statistics, the social and health sciences, and computer science, have developed a variety of techniques to link sensitive databases in a privacy-preserving way. Many of these techniques have so far not been used in practical applications for a variety of reasons that range from security weaknesses or limitations in linkage capabilities to prohibitive computational requirements. We begin this chapter with a taxonomy that has been developed to categorise techniques for encoding and comparing sensitive databases based on different dimensions ranging from privacy and technical to practical aspects, and we provide a general discussion of the different generations of techniques that have been developed. We then give brief overviews of specific techniques, including those based on phonetic encoding, hashing, public reference values, embedding into multidimensional spaces, and secure multiparty computation. We end the chapter with a discussion on the suitability of these types of techniques for different linkage scenarios.

7.1 A Taxonomy of Techniques for Linking Sensitive Values

An extensive taxonomy to categorise techniques for encoding and linking sensitive databases based on five major dimensions and a total of fifteen criteria has been developed by Vatsalan et al. [619]. This taxonomy can help to group similar techniques together, and it facilitates their comparative evaluation. In the following we briefly discuss these five dimensions, and for each outline the individual criteria. All of these criteria are described or discussed in more detail in other sections of this book, to which we refer to.

- **Privacy aspects**: This dimension considers three criteria that characterise the privacy aspects of a given technique: (1) The number of parties involved in a protocol used to link sensitive databases, as we discussed in Section 4.3. (2) The adversarial model the parties in a protocol are assumed to follow, such as the honest-but-curious or malicious models we described in Section 4.4. (3) The actual privacy techniques employed to encode and compare sensitive values across databases. These techniques are the main topic of the remainder of this chapter, as well as the following two chapters.

- **Linkage techniques**: This dimension covers the different aspects that are relevant to the general topic of linking databases (not just sensitive databases that require privacy-preserving techniques). The three specific criteria of this dimension correspond to the three main steps of the general record linkage process we discussed in Section 3.2: (1) Blocking / indexing, the techniques used to facilitate the linking of large databases. (2) Comparison, the techniques employed to compare quasi-identifying attribute values that can contain variations and errors, as we discussed in Section 6.8. (3) Classification, where the compared records are classified into matches (the compared pairs of records are assumed to refer to the same entity) or non-matches (the compared pairs of records are assumed to refer to different entities).

- **Theoretical analysis**: This dimension covers three types of theoretical aspects that are of importance when linking sensitive databases: (1) Scalability, which can be assessed conceptually using the Big-O notation we covered in the side box on page 68. (2) Linkage quality, which can be assessed conceptually with regard to if a technique supports exact matching or approximate matching, and what types of data (strings, numbers, and so on) can be encoded and compared by a given technique. (3) Privacy vulnerabilities of a technique with regard to the different attacks we covered in Section 5.4.

- **Evaluation**: This fourth dimension covers the same three criteria of the previous dimension, theoretical analysis, but now from a practical and experimental point of view: (1) Scalability, and (2) linkage quality, where the evaluation measures we described in Section 3.4 can be used to empirically measure how actual implementations of certain encoding and linkage techniques behave in experiments on real-world or synthetic data (a criterion of the next dimension). (3) Privacy, which can be evaluated in actual practical linkage applications using the different privacy measures we discussed in Section 5.2.

- **Practical aspects**: This final dimension also consists of three criteria: (1) Implementation, which is basically how a technique, assumed to be described in a publication or as an actual software product, has been implemented (such as the programming language used). (2) Data sets, which is about what types of data, real-world or synthetic, have been used in a published experimental evaluation of a privacy-preserving record linkage technique; and if these data sets are publicly available for others to use or if they are confidential. (3) Finally, application area, which describes if a technique is specifically aimed at the linkage of sensitive databases from a certain application area or domain, such as health, e-commerce, or finance, or if the technique is usable across different application areas.

The taxonomy developed by Vatsalan et al. [619] describes these different dimensions in much greater detail, and then also provides an extensive review and categorisation of techniques to link sensitive databases based on this taxonomy.

7.2 Generations of Privacy-Preserving Linkage Techniques

In the following sections we will describe in detail the different types of actual techniques that have been developed to encode and link sensitive databases. On a conceptual level these techniques can be categorised into different generations.

The idea of encoding sensitive values to allow their comparison without having to exchange or share these values across organisations was first proposed by French health researchers in the mid 1990s [180, 488]. Since then a diverse range of techniques have been developed, as we discuss in the remainder of this and the following two chapters.

We can define the first generation of privacy-preserving linkage techniques as those that only facilitate exact matching of values (possibly with phonetic encoding applied as a data preprocessing step to overcome some variations in quasi-identifying values). Most of these first generation techniques are based on some type of hashing, as we describe in Section 7.4.

The second generation of techniques then tackled the challenge of how to allow approximate matching of sensitive values without these values having to be shared across organisations. Notable first such techniques were proposed by Du and Atallah in 2000 [172] who developed a protocol for secure access to remote databases where approximate matching is possible, and by Atallah et al. [30] in 2003 who presented a protocol that facilitates secure edit distance calculations (as we discussed in Section 6.8.2) across two parties where both parties only learn the final edit distance between the two sensitive input strings. Churches and Christen [125] then showed how hash encoded q-grams can be used to securely calculate the Dice coefficient similarity (Equation 6.5) between sensitive values, as we illustrate with an example in the side box on page 176. While all these approaches are able to calculate approximate similarities between values in a privacy-preserving way, scalability to link large sensitive databases was not a focus and the techniques of this generation mostly have high computational and communication complexities.

This crucial practical aspect of computational efficiency which is important in many real-world applications that aim to link large sensitive databases was then addressed by techniques which we categorise as the third generation. Blocking techniques that are applicable on encoded sensitive values, as well as efficient scalable encoding and linkage techniques, have been developed since the mid 2000s, with a first approach for privacy-aware blocking published by Al-Lawati et al. in 2005 [11]. The majority of work on the topic of linking sensitive databases that has been published in the past fifteen years can be categorised into this third generation of techniques [619].

We are currently in a phase where a fourth generation of techniques to encode and link sensitive values is being developed. Such techniques include methods to link new types of sensitive data (such as hierarchical codes [551], numerical, date and time values [614], or geographical locations [200]), as well as databases that contain missing values [103], or temporal databases where the quasi-identifying attribute values of entities are known to change over time and therefore similarity calculations need to be adjusted [495, 496]. Techniques are also being developed to make existing encoding techniques more resilient to the attacks we described in Section 5.4 (we cover this topic in detail in Section 9.5).

7.3 Phonetic Encoding based Techniques

Phonetic encoding algorithms are mainly used in linkage protocols to group attribute values together that have a similar pronunciation, as we described in Section 6.6. The use of phonetic encoding can provide privacy because similar attribute values are encoded into the same phonetic code, resulting in a many-to-one encoding (several sensitive values are represented by the same phonetic code, as we illustrated in Table 6.1).

Furthermore, phonetic encoding can lead to a reduction in the number of record pairs that need to be compared (if only pairs with the same phonetic code are compared), thereby increasing the scalability while also supporting approximate matching of those values that have the same phonetic encoding. However, phonetic encoding can also result in a reduction of linkage quality because false matches are generated when records with attribute values that are different but generate the same phonetic encoding (or encodings across several quasi-identifying attributes) are classified as matches.

Karakasidis et al. [325] proposed a three-party protocol where the sensitive values of all quasi-identifying attributes used for linking are individually encoded using the Soundex approach we described in Section 6.6 and illustrated in the side box on page 154. Once each database owner has converted the sensitive values of its own database into Soundex encodings, these encodings are encrypted using a secure hash function (as discussed in Section 6.2) where all database owners use the same encryption method and the same

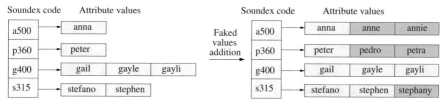

Fig. 7.1 An example of the phonetic encoding approach with faked values added, as proposed by Karakasidis et al. [325] (adapted from [619]). In this example, each phonetic code represents three attribute values, some of which are faked added values as shown on the right hand side of the figure.

encryption key. The encrypted values are then sent to a linkage unit that will conduct the matching of records, and classify those compared record pairs as matches that have a certain number of encrypted Soundex encodings in common.

However, significant privacy leakage can occur with this approach due to the frequency distribution of encrypted phonetic encodings. The linkage unit can mount a frequency attack, as we discussed in Section 5.4.3, to identify for example which frequent encrypted encoding corresponds to which frequent Soundex encoded plaintext value. To overcome this weakness of their approach, Karakasidis et al. [325] proposed to inject fake values into the encoded databases before they are encrypted and sent to the linkage unit, as illustrated in Figure 7.1. Three different injection strategies were discussed with the aim to reduce the relative information gain privacy measure we described in Section 5.2.1 (the information the linkage unit can learn from the encoded databases it receives). An experimental evaluation showed that reasonable privacy can be obtained with such a phonetic encoding based matching approach at the costs of potentially requiring a quite large number of faked records to be added to a sensitive database [325].

In follow-up work, Karakasidis and Verykios [322] then used such a phonetic encoding approach (together with injection of fake records) only for the blocking step of a privacy-preserving record linkage framework, where counting Bloom filters [199] (instead of simple bits, lists of integer counters are used that can hold the number of times an element has been hashed into a certain Bloom filter bit position) were used to facilitate edit distance calculations (as we discussed in Section 6.8.2) between encoded quasi-identifying attribute values. The values in each attribute used for blocking were encoded using several phonetic encoding approaches, and fake records were added to distort the frequency distributions of the resulting blocks to ensure the linkage unit or any external adversary cannot conduct a frequency attack on these blocks.

More recently, Etienne et al. [193] evaluated the use of phonetic encoding in the context of private blocking techniques. Their evaluation showed how

errors and modifications in quasi-identifying attribute values can affect the
quality of blocking in different ways.

7.4 Hashing-based Techniques

Hashing is a set of techniques used widely in the context of linking sensitive
databases, with a long history going back to the mid 1990s [180]. However,
hashing techniques have a variety of weaknesses that can be exploited by an
adversary via privacy attacks. As we introduced in Section 6.2, techniques
such as one-way hashing typically generate a unique hash value for each individual plaintext value thus allowing an adversary to mount a dictionary
attack to identify possible encoded plaintext values, as we described in Section 5.4.2. Though dictionary attacks can be mitigated using a secret key or
password, hashed values can also be attacked using frequency analysis where
the frequency distribution of hash values is compared with the frequency
distribution of plaintext values in a public database, as we discussed in Section 5.4.3. Even though such weaknesses can potentially allow an adversary
to reidentify sensitive hash encoded values, simple direct methods such as
one-way hashing are still being used today due to their simplicity and ease
of implementation [245].

We have discussed the different hashing techniques that are used as building blocks in protocols and techniques employed to link sensitive databases
in Section 6.2. In the following we now describe actual such linkage protocols
and techniques.

Dusserre et al. [180] and Quantin et al. [486] were the first to propose a
privacy-preserving approach for linking sensitive records from multiple databases using a linkage unit as a third party to conduct the linkage. The proposed approach utilised a salted hash algorithm which combines a one-way
secure hash function, such as SHA [535], with two additional pads to avoid
dictionary attacks. The proposed approach uses a deterministic salt generation algorithm which ensures that the same input value is always hashed to
the same hash encoding. Because of the usage of such a deterministic salt the
approach significantly reduces randomness in the generated hash encoding,
which means this approach can be susceptible to frequency attacks where
frequent sensitive values result in frequent hash encodings. This approach
has however been successfully used in France for nearly two decades to link
sensitive health databases between statistical institutes and health research
centres [485].

Following a similar construction to Quantin et al. [486], Weber et al. [637]
proposed a simple heuristic approach for privately linking medical data in a
three-party protocol. The proposed approach aims to generate a single linkage key for each record taking the first two characters of the first names and
surnames, and combining them with the date of birth, to produce a highly

	FirstName	Surname	BirthDate	Linkage key	Hash code
Alice's record	Anne	Jones	11/05/1895	anjo11051895–xx	cd2e3fe8d0b
Bob's record	Annie	Jonson	11/05/1895	anjo11051895–xx	cd2e3fe8d0b

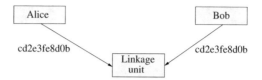

Fig. 7.2 An example of the hashing-based exact matching approach (adapted from [619]), where Alice and Bob are the names given to the two parties that aim to link their sensitive data. Variations of which were proposed by Bian et al. [59], Dusserre et al. [180], Quantin et al. [486], Van Eycken et al. [608], and Weber et al. [637]. Each of these used somewhat different methods of how the linkage keys are generated and hashed. The string '-xx' appended to the linkage key is the secret key (password) value added to prevent a dictionary attack [486].

unique statistical linkage key (similar to SLK-581 as we discussed in Section 6.7) which is then hashed using the MD5 secure hash algorithm [535]. Figure 7.2 illustrates the basic idea behind this approach. The authors experimentally validated the use of such a linkage key and showed that it can provide better linkage results compared to the usage of full names and dates of birth. Furthermore, because this approach does generate unique linkage keys for each person with high likelihood, it can mitigate the vulnerability of the encoding with regard to a frequency attack. However, this approach does not allow approximate similarity calculation, and if there are errors or variations in the first two characters in names then a true link will be missed.

A similar approach for a deterministic linkage method was proposed by Bian et al. [59]. The method hashes two variations of the concatenation of first name, surname, date of birth, and either gender or race, using a salted secure hash algorithm, and then matches records that have been encoded into the same hash value. The method was evaluated on large real-world health databases where it achieved a precision of over 97%, however the recall achieved was reported at only 75%. An open-source software tool was developed (which we describe in more detail in Section A.1), which allowed the deduplication of 3.5 million records down to 1.7 million unique patient records across six health databases from Florida.

Churches and Christen [125] proposed one of the first techniques that allowed approximate matching of encoded quasi-identifying values in a three-party protocol. Their approach, named blindfolded record linkage, first converts values into q-grams. Multiple subsets of q-gram sets are then encoded into hash values by converting a q-gram set into a string and hashing the string using a secure hash algorithm such as SHA [535]. The same encoded hash value across two records means the same encoded q-gram subset. Using

Blindfolded record linkage example [109, 125]

Let us assume two database owners, named Alice and Bob, where Alice has the value 'abbie' in her record a1 and Bob has the value 'abbi' in his record b2. Using bigrams ($q = 2$), Alice generates the set {ab,bb,bi,ie} and Bob generates the set {ab,bb,bi}. Alice next generates all subsets of her bigram set with one bigram removed, and Bob does the same with his bigram set, resulting in the following bigram subsets (with the original bigram sets included at the beginning):

Alice: {ab,bb,bi,ie}, {bb,bi,ie}, {ab,bi,ie}, {ab,bb,ie}, **{ab,bb,bi}**
Bob: **{ab,bb,bi}**, {bb,bi}, {ab,bi}, {ab,bb}

The bigram subset in common to Alice and Bob is highlighted in bold font. Both database owners now hash each of their q-gram subsets into hash encodings by converting each set into a string (and concatenating the string with a secret key known only to the database owners) and applying a secure one-way hash function that was agreed upon by the database owners. They then send these hash encodings together with the number of bigrams in the corresponding subset, the record identifier, and the total number of bigrams in the string value, to the linkage unit. For the above example, and assuming simplified hash encodings, the two database owners will send the following tuples to the linkage unit:

Alice: ('772xu7f6f3b4v8r', 4, a1, 4)
('b2dc1et7d4u1w0', 3, a1, 4)
('49e3e4c457a1qx1', 3, a1, 4)
('61d3472b3d1bd2', 3, a1, 4)
('3180795ad08u', 3, a1, 4)

Bob: **('3180795ad08u'**, 3, b2, 3)
('bd2802v3c7x1z2', 2, b2, 3)
('a95bx427a3p4s4', 2, b2, 3)
('34b6d8m05t1t51', 2, b2, 3)

The linkage unit can now identify hash encodings that appear in both Alice's and Bob's tuples, and for such common encodings calculate the Dice similarity coefficient [109]. For the given example, only the hash encoding '3180795ad08u' (shown in bold font) occurs in common (indicating a common bigram subset). From this tuple we know that it is based on a subset containing three q-grams. The Dice coefficient of these two tuples is calculated as $\frac{2 \cdot 3}{3+4} = \frac{6}{7}$, because the tuples provide the total number of bigrams in the corresponding sensitive values, 3 and 4, respectively. This similarity is the same as the similarity between 'abbie' and 'abbi' when calculated using the unencoded bigram sets.

additional information such as the length of the encoded q-gram sets allows the calculation of the Dice similarity (which we discussed in Section 6.8.1). We provide an example calculation of this method in the side box above.

Besides allowing similarity calculations between sensitive values, this approach will provide much less frequency information that an adversary can exploit compared to the basic hash encoding based approaches discussed above. Furthermore, the authors of [125] also discussed different linkage scenarios where multiple parties can be used to separately compare sensitive values from one quasi-identifying attribute, followed by the combination of these similarities by another party. The main drawback of this approach is that the required construction of many q-gram subsets is not feasible for many real-world applications because of its high computational requirements and communication overhead. This overhead was calculated at between five hundred and over five thousand times more than communicating only the q-gram sets for surnames and Australian town names, respectively [125].

An alternative way to encode q-grams into hashed values to allow for approximate similarity calculations is the Bloom filter encoding technique proposed by Schnell et al. [543]. Given its popularity both with regard to research and development of novel varieties and improvements of Bloom filter encoding, as well as its increasingly widespread application in real-world linkage applications [24, 84, 475, 480, 507], we dedicate the following chapter to describe this popular technique in detail. We then discuss its vulnerabilities with regard to cryptanalysis attacks, and hardening methods to overcome such attacks, in Chapter 9.

Related to Bloom filter encoding is another hashing-based encoding method proposed by Smith [564] which, similar to Bloom filters, encodes sensitive values into bit vectors (lists or arrays of 0 and 1 values). This method uses the locality sensitive hashing (LSH) method of MinHash, which we discussed in Section 6.2.3 and illustrated in the side box on page 133, where hash values are used to look up randomly generated bit strings in a list of tables, an approach known as tabulation hashing [468]. This method showed both more accurate similarity calculations and improved privacy protection. The method generates one bit vector of length l for the sensitive quasi-identifying attribute value (or values) of each record in a sensitive database, as we now describe in more detail.

Let us assume values from a single quasi-identifying attribute are to be encoded. First, l hash tables each containing random 64-bit strings are generated. The sensitive attribute value of a record is then converted into a q-gram set, and for each of the l bit positions, a random bit string is selected (from the corresponding previously generated hash table for that bit position) based on the MinHash values generated from the q-gram set. Only the least significant bit is then used from each of the selected l random bit strings, and these bits are concatenated to generate the final bit vector of length l bits that encodes a given sensitive value. The concatenation of only the least significant bits prevents the direct mapping of the 1-bits in a bit vector to q-grams. Privacy attacks which have shown to be successful on Bloom filter encodings, as we discuss in Chapter 9, will therefore not be successful on this novel encoding method. However, a major drawback of this method is that it requires significant computational resources to generate the hash tables and MinHash values compared to the more efficient Bloom filter encoding. Exper-

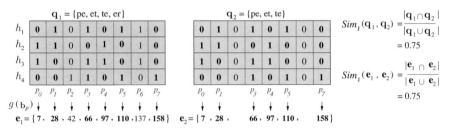

Fig. 7.3 An example of two-step hash encoding as proposed by Ranbaduge et al. [497]. The two values 'peter' and 'pete' are first converted into q-gram (bigram) sets, q_1 and q_2, and hashed into bit vectors (rows) of length $l = 8$ using the $k = 4$ hash functions $h_1()$ to $h_4()$. This results in the two shown bit matrices. Every bit position p (column) that contains at least one 1-bit, is then hashed again using a second hash function, $g()$, which maps bit patterns to integers that are unique per position (for example, the bit pattern '0110' in positions p_0 and p_4 is hashed into 7 and 97, respectively). The sets of integers, e_1 and e_2, are then the encodings of the sensitive input values ('peter' and 'pete'), and are used to privately calculate the Jaccard similarity. © Springer Nature Switzerland AG 2020, reprinted with permission.

iments conducted were only on small data sets [564], and for encoding very large databases the practical use of this tabulation hash encoding method needs to be evaluated further.

To overcome the privacy weaknesses of Bloom filters (as we discuss in Chapter 9) and the high computational requirements of the tabulation hash encoding by Smith [564], Ranbaduge et al. [497] proposed a novel two-step hash encoding method that combines bit vectors with integer encodings. As illustrated in Figure 7.3, similar to Bloom filter encoding, k hash functions are used first to encode the q-gram sets extracted from quasi-identifying attribute values. However, instead of using a single Bloom filter for all k hash functions, in this approach each hash function maps q-grams into a separate bit vector of length l. This generates a bit matrix with k rows (one per hash function) and l columns. In the second encoding step, a different hash function is then used for each position (column) in such a bit matrix to hash any non-zero bit pattern into an integer, where the hashing of the same bit pattern at different positions results in different integer values. This is required because otherwise the resulting integer encodings could match integers from other positions, leading to increased Jaccard similarities and therefore false matches [497].

The generated sets of integer values are then the encodings that represent q-gram sets, and the Jaccard similarity (see Equation 6.4) between such encoded integer sets can be calculated with high accuracy. Experiments on real-world databases showed that this approach is nearly as fast as Bloom filter encoding and only requires between 10% to 20% more memory compared to Bloom filters. The approach is able to obtain higher linkage quality than both the Bloom filter and tabulation hashing based encoding methods. It also exhibits higher privacy protection due to the two hashing steps that prevent

Plaintext database

RECORD ID	FIRSTNAME (F)	SURNAME (S)	GENDER (G)	BIRTHYEAR (B)
r_1	Peter	Smith	M	1986
r_2	John	Miller		1982

Encoded database

RECORD ID	Match-key 1 (F‖S‖G‖B)	Match-key 2 (F‖S‖B)	Match-key 3 (F‖B)
r_1	$hmac(PeterSmithM1986)$	$hmac(PeterSmith1986)$	$hmac(Peter1986)$
r_2		$hmac(JohnMiller1982)$	$hmac(John1982)$

Fig. 7.4 An example of the match-key encoding method proposed by Randall et al. [505] using different attribute combinations. The top table shows the plaintext database attributes for two records and the bottom table shows the generated example match-keys using the $hmac()$ hashing function [364] described in Section 6.2.2. Note that no match-key (hash code) is generated if an attribute combination has a missing value. ‖ symbolises the concatenation of strings.

an adversary from learning anything about the bit matrices generated in the first hashing step and thus the q-gram sets that were encoded into these bit matrices.

A different hashing-based approach to link sensitive databases was proposed by Randall et al. [505]. This approach combines hash encoding with the Fellegi and Sunter match weight calculation method [204] we described in the side box on page 54. The idea is to first calculate match and non-match weights for all quasi-identifying attributes to be used in a linkage, and then to assess each possible combination of attributes, their match (same values in an attribute) and non-match (different values in an attribute) patterns, and their combined weights. For example, assuming four attributes, FIRST-NAME, SURNAME, CITY, and POSTCODE, there are $2^4 = 16$ combinations of attribute matches and non-matches. These range from all four attribute values to match, to no match in all four attributes.

Based on a set of ground truth data in the form of known true matches, only those attribute combinations are then selected that achieve a high linkage quality (based on the F-measure [260], as we discussed in Section 3.4). Each of the selected attribute combinations of matches then becomes a so called match-key [505], where for each record a match-key value is generated by concatenating the values of those attributes that are in the match-key, and hashing this concatenated string value. A match-key can for example be (FIRSTNAME, SURNAME, BIRTHYEAR), resulting in concatenated string values such as 'JohnMiller1982' that are hash encoded. This approach can result in overall high linkage quality because only attribute combinations that are known to achieve high F-measure results are being used. An example of how match-keys are generated is shown in Figure 7.4.

However, as with other hashing-based linkage techniques, this match-key based approach can be susceptible to frequency attacks if there are encoded match-key values that occur multiple times because their frequencies can be exploited by an adversary. Vidanage et al. [628] proposed such a frequency-based attack on this match-key encoding approach and showed that the vulnerability of the approach can be substantially reduced when all frequent match-keys are being removed from the encoded database.

A few other protocols have used hashing in combination with cryptographic schemes to improve the privacy of the linkage process. However, such protocols generally result in a significant increase in the complexity of a linkage due to the complex computations in most existing encryption schemes.

Van Eycken et al. [608] proposed a secure three-party protocol that uses an exact matching technique to classify sensitive health records across different databases. This approach is based on exact matching of hash encodings, which are generated using a secure one-way hash function and a public key encryption algorithm in order to prevent dictionary attacks. The two database owners first merge the values of the quasi-identifying attributes used for a linkage into a single string per record. These strings are then hashed and sent to a linkage unit which compares these hash encodings and classifies record pairs using a deterministic rule based classifier [109]. Experiments conducted on Belgian health databases showed that the accuracy of the classification increased if the concatenated strings included complete date of birth values. While this approach is cost effective, it is likely not suitable for many real-world applications because it can only perform exact matching of the hash encoded quasi-identifying attribute values.

A linkage protocol that combines multiple keyed hashes with public key encryption was recently proposed by Guesdon et al. [245]. The protocol employs a linkage unit to conduct the comparison and classification of the encrypted databases received from the database owners. The protocol uses two rounds of keyed hashing, where public key encryption is only used for the transmission of the hash encodings to the linkage unit. The linkage unit can decrypt the encrypted hash encodings it receives and conduct a matching on the decrypted hash encodings. However, as with other linkage protocols based on hashed quasi-identifying attribute values, this protocol remains susceptible to frequency attacks because commonly occurring sensitive values will result in common hash encodings that potentially can be reidentified, as we discussed in Section 5.4.3.

7.5 Reference Values based Techniques

Several approaches to linking sensitive values are based on the idea of using reference values that are available in public databases, such as telephone directories or voter lists, or values that are generated randomly. Based on

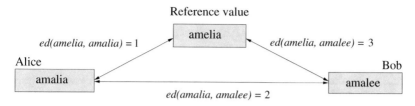

Fig. 7.5 An example of the reference values based approach proposed by Pang et al. [458] (adapted from [619]), where $ed()$ refers to the edit distance function described in Section 6.8.2. The triangular inequality holds as: $ed(amalia, amalee) \leq ed(amalia, amelia) + ed(amelia, amalee)$.

such a list of reference values, that need to be known to all database owners, the database owners can calculate the similarities (or distances) between their sensitive quasi-identifying attribute values and such reference values. They can then either share these similarities with other database owners, or send them to a linkage unit which can calculate the similarity (or distance) between two sensitive values via a public reference value using the triangular inequality (see the side box on page 158 for a description of the triangular inequality).

As illustrated in Figure 7.5, Pang et al. [458] were the first to investigate this idea in a three-party protocol with the aim to achieve a scalable protocol for linking sensitive databases. A common set of public reference values is assumed to be available to all database owners, and the calculated distances between sensitive and reference values, such as the edit distances between strings [109, 386, 433], are calculated and sent to a linkage unit. Based on the triangular inequality, the linkage unit can then identify the pairs of sensitive values that must be closest to each other (if they have small distances to the same reference value). To make the approach more robust, the distances between sensitive values and several reference values were calculated and averaged. The experimental evaluation performed by Pang et al. [458], however, showed that the linkage quality obtainable by this approach depends on the characteristics of the reference values used.

Vatsalan [610] then used the reverse triangular inequality in a two-party protocol, combined with binning of the similarities between sensitive and reference values, to hide the actual similarities between sensitive values from both database owners. Binning is required because learning the exact similarity between one of its own sensitive values and the sensitive value of another database owner will allow a certain database owner to potentially reidentify the other sensitive value. While this approach can achieve good linkage quality in a two-party setting, there is a trade-off between privacy protection and linkage quality based on the number of generated bins. While more bins result in better linkage quality, because less values (and their similarities) are allocated in each bin, the protocol becomes more vulnerable to revealing sensitive information between the database owners given each bin might only contain a small number of values. Furthermore, with a larger number of smaller bins the number of false non-matches (missed matches) also increases, resulting in lower recall but higher precision, while a smaller number of larger bins will lead to an increase of recall but decrease of precision [610].

Public reference values have most recently been used by Vaiwsri et al. [607] in the context of hardening Bloom filter encoding, as we cover in more detail in Chapters 8 and 9. Specifically, a public set of reference values was used to improve the differential private based hardening method of BLoom and fLIP (known as BLIP) [13], where random bits in Bloom filters (that represent encoded sensitive values) were flipped based on how similar a sensitive value is to a reference value. We refer the reader to Section 9.5.6 for a more detailed description of this hardening method.

A common challenge for all reference values based approaches to linking sensitive databases is the question of how to select suitable reference values, both their numbers and their diversity. Randomly selecting values from a real-world database to use as reference values might lead to a skewed set of values, while randomly generating values (such as random character strings) could potentially provide a larger variety. However, randomly generated values might not be representative of the distribution of the quasi-identifying values in the sensitive databases to be linked.

Vaiwsri et al. [607] tackled this challenge by ensuring all selected reference values are different from each other, by only including a value into the set of reference values that is not similar to any other value already in that set using an approximate string comparison function and a suitable low similarity threshold. Bonomi et al. [74], on the other hand, applied frequent pattern mining [98] to identify substrings of varying lengths that occur frequently in a given set of reference values, and then only used these identified frequent substrings as the actual reference values. The larger a set of reference values is the more accurate the similarities between two sensitive values (via one or more references values) can be calculated. While this generally leads to improved linkage quality, it can also reduce the privacy protection provided by a reference values based linkage technique [610].

7.6 Embedding-based Techniques

Another way to achieve the privacy-preserving linking of sensitive data is by embedding sensitive values into a multidimensional space in such a way that values that are similar to each other are close to each other in the mapped space, for example based on one of the string similarity or distance functions we discussed in Section 6.8.

Mapping values into multidimensional spaces is a common technique used in various applications of computer science, such as in information retrieval [647] where words are represented by high dimensional vectors. In the general context of linking databases, Jin et al. [305] developed an indexing (blocking) technique named StringMap which first embeds textual strings into a multidimensional similarity-preserving Euclidean space, from where blocks are then generated using an overlapping clustering technique which finds groups of points (representing strings) that lie close to each other [132, 407].

In an early work, Scannapieco et al. [533] addressed both the problem of privacy-preserving schema matching and privacy-preserving linking of sensitive values. Schema matching is the task of identifying which attributes or fields in two database tables contain the same type of information [47]. The schema matching component of this approach works by a linkage unit sending a global schema as well as a secure hash function to the two database owners. Each database owner can map the schema of its own sensitive database onto this global schema and then hash encode the mapped global attributes. A mapped attribute that occurs in both sensitive databases will result in the same hash encoding. The database owners therefore only need to find the common hash encodings to identify the attributes they share. This approach will not reveal the names of the actual sensitive attributes in each of the databases to the other database owner, and it also does not reveal the names of any attributes that are not common to both database owners.

For the actual linking of sensitive values, the approach by Scannapieco et al. [533] then embeds sensitive quasi-identifying values into a multidimensional metric space using a mapping algorithm similar to StringMap as developed by Jin et al. [305] for blocking. Similar to the approaches discussed in the previous section, this multidimensional space is generated using a set of reference strings that are only known to the two database owners. Only the distances between sensitive and reference values are sent to the linkage unit, which then classifies pairs of values as matches that have a distance between each other below a maximum distance threshold.

As a follow-up work, the component for linking sensitive values of the three-party protocol by Scannapieco et al. [533] was converted into a two-party protocol (that does not require a linkage unit) by Yakout et al. [653]. Their approach also embeds sensitive values into a multidimensional metric space using a set of reference values known to the two database owners. Each sensitive value is converted from its multidimensional vector (representing the embedded sensitive value) into a complex number. These complex numbers are then exchanged between the two database owners, such that each can generate the pairs of complex numbers that are within a maximum distance from each other. These pairs correspond to pairs of similar sensitive values that likely correspond to matches. In a final step, the database owners then calculate the actual distances between the multidimensional vector representations of all likely matched pairs using a secure scalar product protocol, and those pairs that are very similar are classified as matches.

Bonomi et al. [74] further improve the embedding step by Scannapieco et al. [533] and Yakout et al. [653] by investigating how to best select the reference strings used to generate the multidimensional space. Rather than randomly selecting such strings, or using a farthest first approach which selects strings as different from each other as possible [279], the authors use a frequent pattern mining algorithm to identify, in a large set of reference strings, those substrings of different lengths that occur more than a user determined number of times in this set of reference strings. To improve privacy, a differential privacy mechanism with Laplace noise [391] is employed to randomly perturb the frequencies of such frequent substrings. This ensures an adversary would not be able to identify the exact set of reference strings selected even if she knows the frequency threshold used. Experimental results conducted showed that this improved approach to select reference values achieved both better linkage quality as well as better scalability compared to the original embedding method proposed by Scannapieco et al. [533].

Karapiperis et al. [327, 328] proposed an embedding approach to encode numerical values into binary vectors to allow distance calculations between such encoded values. The embedding generates random intervals that lie within the range $[b_1, b_2]$ of where the numerical values to be encoded are expected to occur. For example, for human age values one can set $b_1 = 0$ and $b_2 = 125$. For a user specified acceptable distance threshold, t, similar to the threshold we discussed in Section 6.8.3 for comparing numerical values, a binary vector is then generated for each numerical value to be embedded. Given this embedding approach is closely related to Bloom filter encoding, we describe it in more detail and provide an example illustration in Section 8.4.2.

7.7 Differential Privacy based Techniques

As we discussed in Section 6.3.3, differential privacy has been used in the context of linking sensitive databases where the records in such databases are first anonymised to generate differentially private blocks, or to generate private synopsis (subsets of records) to identify possibly matching record pairs in such synopsis [290, 373]. However, He et al. [270] showed that these differential privacy based sensitive linkage approaches do not ensure an end-to-end privacy guarantee for non-matching records in the databases that are being linked. More specifically, such an end-to-end privacy guarantee assures that no participating database owner would be able to calculate any statistics of the records in the other database(s) that are not matching with any record in its own database.

To overcome this information leakage on non-matching records, He et al. [270] proposed a novel privacy model based on differential privacy, named output constrained differential privacy, to construct efficient linkage protocols for sensitive databases that offer an end-to-end privacy guarantee for any non-matching record after the matching record pairs have been identified. Following this privacy model, the authors proposed a two-party protocol where two database owners collaborate to identify matching records in their databases. The protocol hides non-matching records by adding Laplace noise to the blocking strategy. The database owners first hash their records into a set of blocking according to an agreed blocking protocol.

The generated blocks are then perturbed by inserting a carefully chosen number of dummy records into each block from a truncated and discretised Laplace distribution, such that this final noise added set of blocks guarantees the end-to-end privacy of non-matching records. In the noise addition process, the protocol selects these dummy records from an expanded domain, such that they do not match with any records in the true domain. Finally, the database owners perform a secure two-party matching protocol to classify the compared candidate record pairs into matches. Such a protocol can be based on secure multiparty computation techniques such as garbled circuits [656] or homomorphic encryption [456].

However, the protocol proposed by He et al. [270] has two limitations. First, due to the agreed blocking protocol each database owner still learns the number of non-matching records of the other database owner in each block. This information can potentially lead to the identification of the amount of noise added in each block which may be undesirable. The second limitation is that the predefined blocking scheme does not allow each database owner to generate set of blocks in an optimal setting, where records are simply assigned to blocks based on an agreed set of blocking rules that can lead to some blocks becoming too large.

Following the same privacy model proposed by He et al. [270], Rao et al. [510] proposed a three-party protocol that uses a third party to conduct the linkage of two sensitive databases in a honest-but-curious privacy setting [394]. In contrast to the protocol proposed by He et al. [270], the database owners first block their databases independently into a set of blocks, where they again add a certain amount of dummy records as noise into these blocks. Each database owner then encrypts the records (including the dummy records) in each block using its own public key and sends those encrypted records to the third party. Each database owner also computes a set of differentially private synopses for its blocks where each synopsis includes the extent of the block and the amount of noise added to each block.

The set of synopses is then also sent to the third party, the linkage unit. Using these synopses, the linkage unit prunes unnecessary comparisons between records in blocks that do not occur in both databases, and informs the database owners which of their blocks need to be compared, and the number of secure comparisons that is required for each pair of blocks. Further, the linkage unit applies a randomisation process to the encrypted records that are to be compared, and then sends these randomised candidate record pairs back to the database owners. Finally, the database owners use a secure cryptographic matching protocol to jointly compute the matching records. While the protocol provides an end-to-end privacy guarantee that allows a database owner to further hide the statistics of non-matching records from the other database owner after the linkage process is completed, this protocol

M

		p	e	t	e	r
		0	1	2	3	4	5
p	1	0	1	2	3	4
e	2	1	0	1	2	3
d	3	2	1	1	2	3
r	4	3	2	2	2	2
o	5	4	3	3	3	3

=

Alice holds:

		*	*	*	*	*
		0	0	0	0	0	0
p	1	0.4	0.4	0.3	1.2	2.7
e	2	0.2	-0.3	0.4	2.1	1.6
d	3	1.3	0.9	1.5	0.8	1.5
r	4	2.1	1.5	1.2	0.5	1.1
o	5	2.4	1.7	1.7	1.5	**1.2**

+

Bob holds:

		p	e	t	e	r
		0	1	2	3	4	5
*	0	-0.4	0.6	1.7	1.8	1.3
*	0	0.8	0.3	0.6	-0.1	1.4
*	0	0.7	0.1	-0.5	1.2	1.5
*	0	0.9	0.5	0.8	1.5	0.9
*	0	1.6	1.3	1.3	1.5	**1.8**

Fig. 7.6 An example of the two-party edit distance calculation approach proposed by Atallah et al. [30] (adapted from [619]), where '*' refer to characters unknown to a party. The edit distance matrix **M** is shared between the two database owners such that neither knows the actual value in any cell of the matrix. Only the final edit distance, the value shown in bold in the lower right corner of the matrix, will be shared between the two database owners.

still requires additional computation due to the extra randomisation process performed by the linkage unit compared to the two-party protocol proposed by He et al. [270].

7.8 Secure Multiparty Computation based Techniques

As we discussed in Section 6.5, secure multiparty computation (SMC) has been introduced as a solution to overcome the problem of performing secure computations on sensitive data across different organisations [394]. SMC enables several parties to collaborate in a computation protocol with their private sensitive input values, where at the end of the protocol no party learns anything about any other party's private input but all parties learn the final result of the computation. In the context of comparing sensitive values, SMC techniques have been used in a variety of ways.

A two-party protocol to calculate the edit distance (as we discussed in Section 6.8.2) between two sensitive strings or sequences was proposed by Atallah et al. [30]. The idea of the approach is to split the edit matrix, as for example shown in the side box on page 161, between the two parties, as is shown in Figure 7.6. The actual value in each cell is shared between the two database owners. For example, if a matrix cell contains the value 2 then one database owner might have the value 0.5 and the other the value 1.5. To make the iterative calculation of this matrix privacy-preserving, homomorphic encryption together with a secure minimum finding protocol for shared data was employed. To describe this protocol, assume a vector $\mathbf{c} = \mathbf{a} + \mathbf{b}$ of numerical values, where one database owner has $\mathbf{a} = [a_1, \ldots, a_n]$ and the second database owner has $\mathbf{b} = [b_1, \ldots, b_n]$. To identify if $c_i \geq c_j$ or not, the two database owners can compare $a_i - a_j$ (known only to the first database owner) and $b_j - b_i$ (known only to the second database owner) which follows from $c_i \geq c_j \Leftrightarrow (a_i - a_j) \geq (b_j - b_i)$ without revealing their actual values.

This approach can be used to calculate the minimum value required in the edit matrix calculations in Equation 6.6. However, using this approach will reveal the index of the minimum value in a vector to the other party, thereby indicating if the value in a matrix cell is based on an insertion, deletion, or substitution operation. To overcome this drawback the authors applied a random permutation to these vectors before they are compared [30]. At the end of the protocol, the two database owners exchange the final edit distance (the value in the lower right corner of the edit matrix, $\mathbf{M}$, illustrated in Figure 7.6). While this protocol allows the secure calculation of edit distances between sensitive string values held by two parties, it requires a quadratic number of communication steps per string pair, making it not scalable to the linking of large sensitive databases.

A three-party protocol for scalable linking of sensitive databases based on generalisation (such as k-anonymity, as discussed in Section 6.3.1) combined with a SMC protocol was proposed by Inan et al. [289]. In the first step, k-anonymity [584] is applied by the two database owners on the sensitive quasi-identifying attributes, resulting in generalised databases. The generalised values are then hash encoded and sent to a linkage unit, which can classify record pairs into non-matches and potential matches depending upon how many hash encoded generalised attribute values a record pair has in common. Non-matches are those pairs that have no or only a few (below a certain threshold) hash values in common. All potential matches are then processed further using a more expensive SMC step (which is based on homomorphic or commutative encryption) to calculate the actual similarity or distance between record pairs, for example using a homomorphic Euclidean distance calculation [290]. One advantage of this method is that the threshold setting allows a user to trade-off between precision and recall of the resulting linked record pairs. Kantarcioglu et al. [318] provided extensive security and privacy proofs of the steps of this approach, as well as a more detailed experimental evaluation which showed its effectiveness with different databases and also when linking sensitive data from more than two organisations.

Kuzu et al. [373] proposed a similar approach to Inan et al. [289] where in a three-party protocol a global facilitator (as we discussed in Section 4.1) first generates clusters of similar quasi-identifying values from a set of public reference values (such as the first names from a public telephone directory) using hierarchical clustering. These clusters are then sent to the database owners to conduct local blocking on their sensitive databases. Records are assigned to the most similar cluster based on their quasi-identifying attribute values. Before blocks are sent from one database owner to the other to conduct matching, they are encrypted using a homomorphic encryption scheme (as we described in Section 6.4.3). In order to obfuscate the sizes of blocks, faked records are added using a differential privacy mechanism. Due to this mechanism, a database owner cannot infer if a particular record is included in an encrypted block or not. For those record pairs in the same block, SMC techniques then need to be employed to calculate the actual similarities between encrypted quasi-identifying attribute values.

Acknowledging that such SMC techniques generally have high computational and communication costs, the authors proposed to use a third party as a linkage unit [373]. The database owners use a homomorphic encryption scheme (as we discussed in Section 6.4.3) and an encoding of q-grams into encrypted binary vectors to calculate the Jaccard similarity between string values, while numerical values are homomorphically encrypted to allow the calculation of Euclidean distances. Even though the use of blocking improves the efficiency of this approach, the SMC techniques employed mean there are still significant compuational and communication requirements. For example, to link two databases with 10,000 records each required to transfer 1.1 GBytes of data [373]. This means this approach is unlikely to be practical for the linkage of large sensitive databases.

A three-party protocol based on a homomorphic encryption scheme was recently proposed by Lazrig et al. [382]. It uses properties of homomorphic encryption where pairs of database owners collaborate to first generate key converters (a method to convert the encryption such that similar values will be encrypted with the same key without requiring any decryption to be conducted along the way [382]). Next each database owner encrypts its own sensitive values using its own private key, and a third party, known as the honest broker, can then combine the encrypted sensitive values with the corresponding key converter to convert encrypted values into another encrypted form. Similar values will be encrypted using the same key, thereby allowing the identification of exact matching sensitive encrypted values. While provably secure, the practical applicability of this method is not clear because no experimental evaluation has been presented.

Wen and Dong [639] proposed two secure protocols for linking sensitive values, where one is limited to only exact matching of values, while the other allows approximate matching. The exact matching approach uses a SMC based secure set intersection protocol named oblivious Bloom intersection, while the approximate matching approach additionally incorporates locality sensitive hashing. Oblivious Bloom intersection is a SMC protocol that uses hash functions to efficiently and securely find the intersection of two sets [166]. The protocol uses garbled Bloom filters, where instead of a bit vector a vector of λ-bit strings is used, and each element being hashed is split into k λ-bit shares using an XOR-based secret sharing scheme [166]. Garbled Bloom filters allow probable set membership testing.

In the exact matching protocol with two database owners [639], the first database owner encodes the quasi-identifying attribute values of all its records into a regular Bloom filter, while the second database owner encodes the quasi-identifying attribute values of all its records into a garbled Bloom filter. The two database owners then participate in an oblivious transfer protocol where the Bloom filter of the first database owner is used as the selection string to identify the matching records of the second database owner that are encoded in the garbled Bloom filter. In the approximate protocol, each database owner first converts its quasi-identifying attribute values into q-grams and then uses the MinHash locality sensitive hashing technique we discussed in Section 6.2.3 to generate a hash table. The elements in this hash table are then encoded using garbled Bloom filters to calculate the Jaccard similarity between records based on their encoded quasi-identifying attribute values. Experimental results on large synthetic data sets showed an almost linear runtime of this approach while also achieving high linkage quality.

7.9 Choosing Suitable Encoding Techniques

In this chapter we have provided brief descriptions of a variety of techniques to encode and link sensitive values that have been developed since the mid 1990s. This overview is not exhaustive in nature, and this was not our aim with this chapter. New techniques are being developed all the time, while existing techniques are being improved or expanded for example to be able to deal with novel types of data, to be more computationally efficient, or to provide improved privacy protection. Our overview was aimed at illustrating the diversity of methods to encode and compare sensitive values in such ways that no reidentification of such values is possible while at the same time accurate and efficient linkage of encoded sensitive databases is possible.

The developed techniques can be roughly grouped into two categories. The first category consists of techniques that have mainly been developed by computer scientists and statisticians, where the focus of these techniques is to provide provable privacy, either according to some privacy evaluation measure, a formal privacy and security proof (such as for secure multiparty computation [394]), or using concepts such as differential privacy [181, 391].

The second category consists of those techniques that have been developed from an application point of view [180, 488, 505, 507, 608, 637], mainly in the health domain where linking sensitive databases is a common requirement [84]. The majority of these techniques use some form of hashing or, more recently, Bloom filter encoding (the topic of the following two chapters). As a result, the developed and, in some cases applied, techniques are generally efficient, scalable to linking large sensitive databases, and they provide adequate linkage quality for the types of (health) databases they were developed for. However, many of these techniques have not been properly assessed with regard to the privacy protection and security they provide, and they may be vulnerable to some of the attack methods we describe in Section 5.4 and Chapter 9.

For a given scenario or application that requires the linkage of sensitive databases, a diverse range of criteria need to be considered when choosing suitable encoding and linkage techniques. Technical criteria range from the available computing platform, storage capabilities, and communication channels between the organisations involved in such a linkage, to the types of data to be linked and their quality. These data related aspects will determine what kinds of encoding and linkage techniques can be applied to link the available sensitive databases.

Non-technical criteria include the regulatory framework within which the linkage is to be conducted, as well as any organisational policies that govern data access, handling, and sharing of data with other organisations. Crucial aspects are the sets of skills and the expertise of the people tasked with the development, installation, and running of systems to link sensitive databases. Having personnel with deep expertise in computer security is important to ensure sensitive databases are stored, processed, and linked securely and that there are no loop-holes in a deployed system that could lead to a data breach. Experts with knowledge in algorithmic aspects of encoding and linkage methods and algorithms, as well as domain experts who understand the databases to be linked, are also crucial in order to obtain best possible linkage outcomes.

Of the encoding and linkage techniques described in this chapter, many have only been evaluated in academic contexts and only few have been deployed in real-world linkage applications. It can therefore be unclear if a certain technique is applicable in real-world linkage scenarios, where many criteria (as discussed above) need to be considered. Proper large-scale studies using a diverse variety of databases with different characteristics (such as different database sizes, different data quality, different data types, and so on) would ideally need to be conducted. Such studies should include as many privacy-preserving record linkage techniques as possible in order to gain a deeper insight into the advantages and weaknesses of different techniques with regard to the different dimensions of linkage quality, scalability to large databases and number of databases to be linked, as well as privacy protection provided by these techniques.

7.10 Summary and Further Reading

In this chapter we have first reviewed a taxonomy of techniques to link sensitive databases as developed by Vatsalan et al. [619]. This taxonomy described five major dimensions and a total of fifteen criteria ranging from privacy to practical aspects. We then provided a brief description of the history of techniques to link sensitive databases in a privacy-preserving way, categorising techniques into four generations of techniques, where the latest (current) generation is aimed at linking new types of data as well as making existing techniques more secure with regard to recently developed privacy attacks. In the second part of this chapter we then described some selected techniques to encode and link sensitive databases that are based on the various building blocks we covered in the previous chapter.

For more detailed overviews of techniques to link sensitive databases we refer the interested reader to the taxonomy and extensive survey by Vatsalan et al. [619] and the more recent book chapter by Vatsalan et al. [620] that is focused on techniques to link Big data sources. Bonomi et al. [73] also provide an overview of techniques that can be used to link sensitive databases in privacy-preserving ways.

As we discussed in the previous section, many of the techniques we have described in this chapter have only been evaluated in academic research settings, but not in practical linkage applications, or at least no published information is available if a certain technique is used in real-world linkage applications. One of the most popular techniques to link sensitive databases is Bloom filter encoding [543], and in the following two chapters we describe this technique and its various extensions and improvements in detail. We will also highlight the weaknesses of this technique with regard to a variety of cryptanalysis attacks, and how these attacks can be overcome through Bloom filter hardening techniques.

Chapter 8
Bloom Filter based Encoding Methods

Co-authored by Anushka Vidanage and Christian Borgs

Abstract Bloom filter encoding is currently the most popular privacy technique employed in different practical applications to link sensitive databases. In this chapter we describe in detail the main techniques used to encode databases into Bloom filters, and how to calculate similarities between encoded Bloom filters. We cover existing hashing and encoding techniques for Bloom filters, and how they can be used to encode textual and numerical values, as well as hierarchical classification codes. We also discuss how to choose suitable Bloom filter encoding techniques and how to appropriately set the parameters of these techniques for their use in real-world linkage applications.

8.1 Bloom Filter Encoding

One widely used perturbation based encoding technique for linking sensitive data is Bloom filter encoding, as first proposed in the context of privacy-preserving record linkage by Schnell et al. in 2009 [543]. A Bloom filter is a space efficient data structure proposed by Bloom [68] in 1970 for checking element membership in a set [88]. A Bloom filter is a bit vector, a list of 0 and 1 values, where elements in a set are hashed or mapped into using a set of independent hash functions, as we discussed in Section 6.2. When an item is queried from a Bloom filter, false positives[1] [109] can occur because of hash collisions. This means a given bit is set to 1 in a Bloom filter by a different element of the input set, and therefore querying the Bloom filter indicates a certain element is in a set while in fact it is not. However, false negatives are never possible with Bloom filters. As more elements are added to a Bloom filter, the probability of false positives generally increases [417], as we discuss in the side box on page 194.

---

[1] Note that a false positive bit set to 1 in the context of Bloom filter encoding is different from a false positive match in the context of record linkage quality evaluation as discussed in Section 3.4.

© Springer Nature Switzerland AG 2020
P. Christen et al., *Linking Sensitive Data*, https://doi.org/10.1007/978-3-030-59706-1_8

Minimising the Bloom filter false positive rate

In Bloom filter encoding, it is important to use an optimal setting of parameter values which balances the aspects of linkage quality, scalability, and
privacy, when linking sensitive databases. Here we describe how to calculate
an optimal number of hash functions that leads to a minimum false positive
rate (minimum number of hash collisions) [79, 417]. We discuss how to choose
suitable Bloom filter parameters, in the context of security against attacks or
to achieve high linkage quality, in Section 8.6.

For a given Bloom filter length, l, and number of elements to be hashed into
a Bloom filter, n, the optimal number of hash functions, k_{opt}, that minimises
the false positive rate, f, is calculated as [417]:

$$k_{opt} = \frac{l}{n} ln(2),   (8.1)$$

leading to a false positive rate of:

$$f = \left(\frac{1}{2^{ln(2)}}\right)^{l/n}.   (8.2)$$

We can estimate n by calculating the numbers of q-grams that are generated
from all values to be encoded into Bloom filters from the database to be
encoded, and taking the average of these numbers.

For a given l, we can then calculate k_{opt} based on n as calculated from
the database. For a given database and n, longer Bloom filters (with a larger
l) will require more hash functions (larger k_{opt}). However, a larger k_{opt} will
require more computation as more hash values need to be calculated and
mapped into a Bloom filter for each record.

While k_{opt} and l determine the computational aspects of Bloom filter
encoding, linkage quality, and privacy will be determined by the false positive
rate f, the likelihood of collisions. A higher value for f means a larger number
of collisions (where several q-grams are hashed to the same bit position) and as
a result potentially more false matches (when a pair of non-matching records is
classified to refer to the same entity), and thus lower linkage quality. A higher
value for f can however also improve privacy, because false positives (collisions
of q-gram hashes) mean an adversary cannot be absolutely sure that a given
Bloom filter encodes a certain attribute value or not [60, 178, 543].

It was shown [417] that a Bloom filter should ideally have half of its bits
set to 1 (i.e. 50% filled) to achieve the lowest collision probability for given
values of n, l and k_{opt}. Equations 8.1 and 8.2 in fact lead to a probability
that a bit in a Bloom filter is set to 1 as $e^{-kn/l} = 0.5$.

Hash collisions are one aspect of how Bloom filters provide privacy protection [60], because for an adversary it will be difficult to identify exactly
which element has generated a certain 1-bit in a given Bloom filter if several
elements of a set are hashed to the same position. However, unlike for cryptographic techniques and secure multiparty computation based methods, as
we discussed in the previous chapter, so far no formal mathematical proofs
have been developed that show the privacy protection guarantees provided by

Fig. 8.1 Example hashing of a set **s** with three elements into a Bloom filter of length $l = 14$ bits using $k = 2$ hash functions, and querying the Bloom filter with elements of the set **q**, where 66 cannot be encoded in the Bloom filter because one of its hashed bit positions is 0. Therefore, 66 cannot be in the set **s**. Furthermore, element 13 is a false positive because both its hash values point to bit positions set to 1 by other elements.

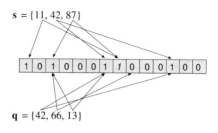

Bloom filter encoding. Rather, as we cover in the following chapter, various attacks on Bloom filter encoding in the context of linking sensitive databases have been developed [120, 367, 371, 415, 438, 629]. These attacks mainly analyse frequent patterns of bits set to 1 in a database of Bloom filters and how they can be aligned to similar patterns (character q-grams, as we discuss next) in a given database of plaintext values.

To encode elements into a Bloom filter **b** of length l bits, where all bits are initialised to 0, a set of k independent hash functions, $h_1, \ldots, h_k$, each with range $[0, \ldots, l - 1]$, is used. Each element s of a set **s** is hashed into the Bloom filter by using these hash functions where the bit position returned by each hash function is set to 1: $\mathbf{b}[h_j(s)] = 1$, with $1 \le j \le k$. For a given query element $s_q \in \mathbf{q}$ (with **q** being a query set), if any of the k hashed positions for s_q is 0 (formally: $\exists h_j : \mathbf{b}[h_j(s_q)] = 0, 1 \le j \le k$), then s_q cannot be in the set **s**. Figure 8.1 shows an example hashing and querying of a Bloom filter.

When linking sensitive data, generally the (string) attribute values of records in the databases to be used for linkage are first converted into a set $\mathbf{s} = \{s_1, s_2, \cdots, s_n\}$ of substrings of length q, known as q-grams [109]. A string is converted into its list of q-grams using a sliding window approach, where overlapping substrings of length q characters are extracted. For example, as shown in Figure 8.2, and assuming $q = 2$ (known as bigrams), 'johnny' is converted into the list of q-grams [jo, oh, hn, nn, ny]. If $q = 3$ (known as trigrams) is used, then the list would become [joh, ohn, hnn, nny].

Because sets are hashed into Bloom filters rather than lists, if a certain q-gram occurs more than once in a string it will be hashed only once. Lists are therefore converted into sets, where each unique q-gram only occurs once. For example, 'berber' has the bigram list [be, er, rb, be, er], resulting in the bigram set {be, er, rb}. Then using a set of hash functions these sets of q-grams are encoded into Bloom filters, as shown in Figure 8.2, as we describe in detail in the following section.

Next, a set-based similarity function, such as the Jaccard or Dice coefficient [109] (as discussed in Section 6.8.1), can be used to calculate the similarity between two Bloom filters, where the Dice coefficient is commonly used because it is insensitive to matching zero bits in long Bloom filters [543]. As shown in Figure 8.2, for two Bloom filters, $\mathbf{b}_1$ and $\mathbf{b}_2$, the Dice coefficient

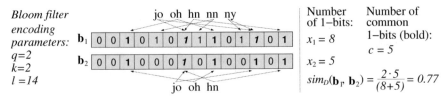

Fig. 8.2 The Dice coefficient similarity calculation between the names 'johnny' and 'john', converted into bigrams and encoded into two Bloom filters $\mathbf{b}_1$ and $\mathbf{b}_2$. The 1-bits shown in italics correspond to hash collisions, for example because 'jo' and 'hn' are both hashed to the seventh bit position. © Springer International Publishing AG, part of Springer Nature 2018, reprinted with permission.

similarity is calculated as:

$$sim_D(\mathbf{b}_1, \mathbf{b}_2) = \frac{2 \cdot c}{x_1 + x_2}, \tag{8.3}$$

where c is the number of bit positions that are set to 1 in both Bloom filters (the common 1-bits), and x_1 and x_2 are the number of 1-bits in $\mathbf{b}_1$ and $\mathbf{b}_2$, respectively. The number of 1-bits in a bit vector such as a Bloom filter is also known as its Hamming weight.

In a linkage protocol where two or more sensitive databases need to be linked, as we discussed in Section 4.3, the database owners will generate Bloom filters for each of their records using appropriate hashing and encoding methods. Depending upon the protocol used, these Bloom filters are either sent to a linkage unit for comparison, or they are directly compared across the database owners [178, 543, 613]. The compared pairs are then classified as matches or non-matches based on their calculated similarities.

In the following section we describe different techniques for the actual hashing of elements into a Bloom filter, while in Sections 8.3 and 8.4 we show how textual and numerical values can be encoded into Bloom filters.

8.2 Hashing Techniques for Bloom Filters

As described in the previous section, in the Bloom filter encoding process a set of k hash functions along with a hashing method is used to map a set of elements (such as q-grams extracted from one or several string attribute values of a record) into a Bloom filter. According to the hashing method used, there are different ways of combining the actual numerical values calculated by hash functions into index numbers (bit positions) in a Bloom filter, which determines which bits in a Bloom filter are set to 1.

In this section we describe four different hashing methods that can be used to encode elements into a Bloom filter as used in privacy-preserving record linkage protocols. We assume a Bloom filter is of length l bit positions, where we index (number) these bit positions from 0 to $l - 1$.

8.2.1 Double Hashing

The use of a double hashing (DH) scheme for Bloom filters was first proposed by Dillinger and Manolios [157] in 2004 to overcome the performance overhead of applying multiple ($k > 1$) hash functions to map an element of a set into a Bloom filter k times. Later, in 2006, Kirsch and Mitzenmacher [352] showed that only two independent hash functions are necessary to implement a Bloom filter encoding with k hash functions without any increase in the asymptotic false positive probability (no increase in the resulting number of collisions). Schnell et al. [543] were the first to use this DH based Bloom filter encoding method for linking sensitive databases.

The idea behind the DH scheme is to use two hash functions to simulate multiple hash functions by using an index value i. For a given element x to be hashed, the DH scheme computes the k bit positions $g_i(x)$, with $1 \leq i \leq k$, to be set to 1 in a Bloom filter as follows:

$$g_i(x) = (h_1(x) + i \cdot h_2(x)) \bmod l, \qquad (8.4)$$

where l is the length of the Bloom filter, and $h_1()$ and $h_2()$ are two independent hash functions [543]. The addition of two hash functions is performed modulo the number of bit positions in the Bloom filter, l, to ensure that this sum is also a valid index (Bloom filter bit position) in the range [0, $l-1$]. The modulo operation, mod, calculates the remainder after dividing one number by another. For example, $7 \bmod 3 = 1$ (because $2 \cdot 3 = 6$ leaving a remainder of 1), while $12 \bmod 4 = 0$ (because $3 \cdot 4 = 12$ leaving a remainder of 0). Figure 8.3 illustrates an example of adding a set of three q-grams into a Bloom filter of length $l = 10$ using $k = 2$ hash functions using DH.

Recent research has shown that DH has a weakness in that it generates a much reduced number of 1-bit patterns in Bloom filters [367, 438], as we describe in Sections 8.2.3 and 9.2. As we discuss in more detail in Chapter 9, the 1-bit patterns generated by DH can be exploited by cryptanalysis attacks [367, 438] which can potentially lead to the reidentification of the q-grams (and thus sensitive attribute values) encoded in a Bloom filter.

8.2.2 Triple Hashing

The triple hashing (TH) scheme was first proposed and empirically analysed by Dillinger et al. [156, 157] as an extension to double hashing (DH) to achieve

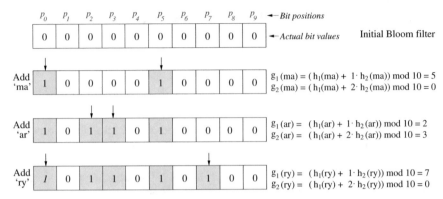

Fig. 8.3 An example illustration of adding the bigrams ($q = 2$) 'ma', 'ar', and 'ry' (extracted from the name 'mary') into a Bloom filter where $k = 2$ and $l = 10$, using double hashing as described in Section 8.2.1. A collision (multiple bigrams hashed to the same bit position, highlighted in italics) occurs at position p_0 when 'ry' is hashed into the Bloom filter.

a lower probability of collision and therefore gain more hashing accuracy. The concept behind TH is to employ a third hash function when generating a hash value for an element being hashed. Given an element x to be hashed and three independent hash functions $h_1()$, $h_2()$, and $h_3()$, the set of k Bloom filter bit positions $g_i(x)$, with $1 \leq i \leq k$, to be set to 1 is calculated as follows:

$$g_i(x) = \left(h_1(x) + i \cdot h_2(x) + \frac{i(i-1)}{2} \cdot h_3(x) \right) \ mod \ l, \qquad (8.5)$$

where l is the length of the Bloom filter. Similar to DH the modulo operation will be used to ensure all indices are mapped into the Bloom filter range $[0, \ l-1]$. Dillinger et al. [157] argued that the TH scheme provides better hashing accuracy than DH by preventing multiple collisions due to utilising an extra hash function. However the computational cost associated with TH will be higher than DH due to the additional hash function employed.

So far no experimental evaluation has been conducted which compares the privacy and linkage quality characteristics of TH when employed for linking sensitive databases.

8.2.3 Enhanced Double Hashing

In double hashing (DH), for an element x, if the second hash function $h_2(x)$ used in Equation 8.4 results in a value of 0 then all k calculated indices (bit positions) will be the same. Furthermore, if the value of $h_2(x)$ is a divisor of the Bloom filter length l, then the unique number of indices that can be obtained is the minimum of $min(l/h_2(x), k)$. According to Dillinger et al. [156], this number could get as small as 2, which again increases the collision probability. The triple hashing (TH) scheme discussed above could be used to overcome these drawbacks of DH. However, as Dillinger et al. [156] discussed, using TH will increase the computational cost by 50% because of the extra third hash function $h_3()$ required.

As the name suggests, enhanced double hashing (EDH) is an improved version of DH proposed to overcome the drawbacks associated with both DH and TH as discussed above. EDH was first proposed and empirically analysed by Dillinger et al. [156] as an enhanced version of DH but with similar computational cost.

Similar to DH, EDH uses two hash functions to simulate $k \geq 1$ hash functions. For a given element x, the k Bloom filter bit positions $g_i(x)$, with $1 \leq i \leq k$, to be set to 1 can be calculated as follows:

$$g_i(x) = \left(h_1(x) + i \cdot h_2(x) + \frac{i^3 - i}{6} \right) \ mod \ l, \tag{8.6}$$

where l is the length of the Bloom filter, and $h_1()$ and $h_2()$ are two independent hash functions. A modulo operation is again applied in order to ensure a valid bit position in the range $0 \leq g_i(x) \leq l - 1$.

8.2.4 Random Hashing

The random hashing (RH) scheme for Bloom filter encoding was proposed and used by Schnell and Borgs [546] to replace the double hashing (DH) scheme and to prevent pattern-based attacks on Bloom filters [367, 438] (which we describe in Section 9.2). The idea behind the RH scheme is to use a specific random seed which is based on the element being hashed to generate a sequence of k random numbers using a pseudo-random number generator (PRNG). These k random numbers are then used to generate the indices (or bit positions) that are to be set to 1 in a Bloom filter. A PRNG, if initialised to a certain seed value x, will always generate the same sequence of pseudo-random numbers, as the example in the side box on page 124 show. We described PRNGs and the use of seeds to generate sequences of random numbers in Section 6.1.

Therefore, if we seed a PRNG with the actual element to be encoded, such as a q-gram, then for the same element the same sequence of random values will be generated by the PRNG. For a given element x to be hashed, the k Bloom filter bit positions $g_i(x)$ to be set to 1 can therefore be calculated as follows:

$$seed(x),$$
$$g_i(x) = randint(0, l-1), \text{ with } 1 \le i \le k, \tag{8.7}$$

where we assume the function $seed(x)$ initialises the PRNG using the seed value x, and the function $randint(start, end)$ returns an integer value in the interval $[start, end]$ with uniform probability generated by the PRNG. For the RH scheme this interval is from $start = 0$ to $end = l - 1$ covering the full Bloom filter length. Therefore, if the element x is hashed into two Bloom filters then the RH scheme will create 1-bits at the same positions in both these Bloom filters.

Unlike the DH approach, the RH scheme will not generate any repeatable patterns because RH is not based on the linear combination and addition of two integer hash values. This makes Bloom filters generated using RH more resilient to certain types of attacks, as we discuss further in Section 9.2.

8.3 Encoding Techniques for Textual Data

Since Bloom filter encoding was first proposed in the context of linking sensitive data [543], several techniques have been developed for either a single or several textual attribute value(s) to be encoded into Bloom filters. All of these approaches assume that the text (string) values are converted into sets of q-grams, as illustrated in Figure 8.2, and then one of the hashing techniques described in the previous section is used to encode these q-gram sets. In the following we present four different encoding techniques that can be used to encode textual attribute values into Bloom filters.

8.3.1 Attribute Level Bloom Filter Encoding

Attribute level Bloom filter (ABF) encoding, also known as field level Bloom filter encoding, was initially proposed by Schnell et al. [543], where it was shown that ABFs can provide accurate linkage results with a reasonable runtime.

In ABF encoding, each quasi-identifying attribute value is treated as a string and converted into a set of q-grams which is then hashed into one Bloom filter using one of the hashing techniques described in Section 8.2.

To emphasise the first and last character in an attribute value, the string can be padded with special characters at each end [109], as we discussed in Section 6.8.1. For q-grams of length q characters a string value will need to be padded with $q - 1$ special characters at both ends. These special characters must be different from any character that can occur in any attribute value to be encoded in any record from the sensitive databases to be linked [109]. For example, if the set of q-grams (with each q-gram of length $q = 2$) extracted from the string value 'smith' is padded with '_' at the beginning and end, then the q-gram set $\mathbf{s} = \{\_s, sm, mi, it, th, h\_\}$ will be generated. The decision to pad or not to pad attribute values before they are encoded depends upon if emphasis needs to be given to the beginning and end of the attribute values to be compared in the linkage process.

Once the set of q-grams is generated for an attribute value, one Bloom filter is generated for this value by hashing each q-gram in the set into the Bloom filter using one of the hashing methods discussed in the previous section and using a suitable value for the Bloom filter length, l, and number of hash functions, k. As a result, for each record in a database to be encoded, a set of Bloom filters is generated (one ABF for each quasi-identifying attribute), and these Bloom filters will be used in the comparison step of the linkage process.

Recent research [367, 371, 372, 438] has shown that basic ABFs can be vulnerable to frequency-based cryptanalysis attacks because a frequent attribute value that occurs many times in the encoded database, such as the name of a large town or city, or a common surname like 'smith', will result in a large number of Bloom filters that have the same 1-bit pattern. We discuss such attacks in detail in Section 9.2.

8.3.2 Cryptographic Long-term Key

The Cryptographic Long-term Key (CLK) encoding mechanism for Bloom filters was introduced by Schnell et al. [545]. CLK was initially proposed as a method that allows error tolerant linkage of sensitive values by encoding multiple quasi-identifying attribute values into one Bloom filter. However, compared to the ABF encoding technique discussed before, CLK also provides improved privacy for sensitive values that are being encoded.

The basic idea behind CLK is to encode multiple attribute values from a single record into one Bloom filter, where it is possible that different hashing methods (as discussed in the previous section) and even different types and different numbers of hash functions, k, can be used for different attributes (we discuss this in more detail in Section 8.3.4). For example, as illustrated in Figure 8.4, if we have a record that contains the three quasi-identifying attributes FIRSTNAME (FN), SURNAME (SN), and CITY (C), with values 'john', 'smith', and 'sydney', we first generate the three individual q-gram sets for 'john', 'smith', and 'sydney', and then hash these three sets into one Bloom filter. Again, attribute values can be padded or not before they are converted into q-gram sets.

In the original proposal of CLK, the same hashing method (as described in Section 8.2) and the same number of hash functions, k, was used to hash all q-gram sets generated from the different quasi-identifying attributes to

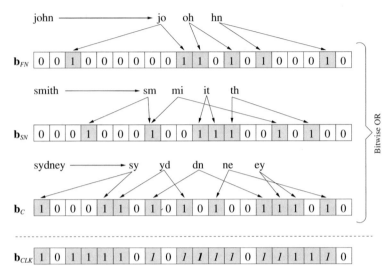

Fig. 8.4 An example illustration of the cryptographic long-term key (CLK) Bloom filter encoding method using three attribute values from FIRSTNAME (john), SURNAME (smith), and CITY (sydney), where $q = 2$ (bigrams), $k = 2$ and $l = 20$ are used. Multiple collisions are illustrated in italics in $\mathbf{b}_{CLK}$, for example both 'oh' (from FIRSTNAME) and 'it' (from SURNAME) are hashed to the eleventh bit position (highligthed in bold).

be encoded. Conceptually, this process can be viewed as first generating one Bloom filter per attribute where only the q-gram set of this attribute is hashed into, followed by the conjunction (bitwise OR operation[2]) of these individual attribute Bloom filters. To improve performance of the encoding process and reduce memory requirements, it is more efficient to hash the q-gram sets from all attribute values from a given record into one Bloom filter one after the other.

Encoding several attribute values into one Bloom filter (and thus representing a record by a single Bloom filter) will only allow the calculation of one similarity value between two records, as described in Section 8.1. Unlike with attribute level Bloom filters, where one similarity can be calculated between the individual values of each quasi-identifying attribute, CLK will potentially result in reduced linkage quality. On the other hand, CLK can provide increased privacy protection because less frequency information is available in a set of CLK Bloom filters compared to the frequency information in a set of ABFs, where each ABF corresponds to an individual quasi-identifying attribute value. There are, for example, generally a much smaller number of 'John Smith' living in 'Sydney' than there are 'John' in a database.

In an experimental evaluation, Schnell et al. [545] have shown that by employing CLK they were able to achieve almost similar linkage quality com-

---

[2] See Notation on page xxii for details on this operation.

pared to when using plaintext attribute values for similarity calculations, while also achieving effective linkage performance.

CLK is generally resilient with regard to several frequency-based cryptanalysis attack methods. However, a recent frequent pattern mining based attack [123, 629], which we discuss in detail in Section 9.2, has shown that even if CLK encoding is employed and all Bloom filters in a database are unique, can certain frequent q-grams in that encoded database be reidentified with high accuracy.

8.3.3 Record Level Bloom Filters

An alternative method to CLK to encode values from several attributes into one Bloom filter per record was proposed by Durham et al. [176, 178]. Similar to CLK, this record level Bloom filter (RBF) encoding method can provide improved protection against cryptanalysis attacks.

The difference between CLK and RBF is that in CLK all attribute values are hashed into the same Bloom filter (in the original approach using the same number and type of hash function), while in RBF initially one Bloom filter is generated per quasi-identifying attribute. The length of each such attribute level Bloom filter (ABF) depends upon the expected length in characters (and therefore the length of the extracted q-gram sets) of the values in a quasi-identifying attribute. A postcode attribute in Australia, for example, contains values consisting of four digits, resulting in a maximum of three (if not padded) q-grams with $q = 2$. On the other hand, Australian city names are on average much longer. It therefore makes sense to represent encoded city name values in longer Bloom filters compared to the Bloom filters that encode postcodes in order to obtain a similar percentage of 1-bits in these different attribute level Bloom filters.

In order to generate one record level Bloom filter, and to improve privacy, Durham [178] proposed to randomly sample certain bit positions from the generated ABFs, and to then combine the sampled bit positions into one Bloom filter per record. Before starting to encode their databases, the database owners need to agree upon (using some form of secure communication) the hash functions to be used for encoding each quasi-identifying attribute (these can be the same hash functions for all or different hash functions per attribute), as well as the selection of bit positions, attribute weights, and the permutation of bit positions in the final step of the encoding method. Overall, the generation of RBFs consists of the following four steps:

1. **ABF generation**: For each attribute a separate ABF is generated using k hash functions and a user defined hashing method as described in Section 8.2. As Durham [178] notes, the length of these ABFs can either be static or dynamic. The lengths of dynamic ABFs are calculated based

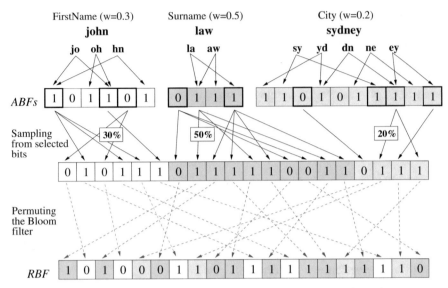

Fig. 8.5 An example illustration of record level Bloom filter (RBF) generation (adapted from [176]). First, the values in the three attributes FIRSTNAME, SURNAME, and CITY are encoded into separate attribute level Bloom filters (ABFs) with lengths $l_{FN} = 6$, $l_{SN} = 4$, and $l_C = 10$, and using the same number of hash functions $k = 2$. Then certain bit positions (identified in bold outline) are selected, and 30%, 50%, and 20% bits from the selected bit positions are sampled using the respective weights $w_{FN} = 0.3$, $w_{SN} = 0.5$, and $w_C = 0.2$ for the three attributes. These sampled bit positions are then concatenated into one Bloom filter for the record. Finally, the concatenated Bloom filter is permuted to obtain the final RBF of length 20 bits.

on the probability that a bit remains unset given a certain number of q-grams occur in an attribute value [176].

2. **Eligible bit identification:** In this step, certain bit positions from each ABF are selected to be sampled in the fourth step below. This bit selection is conducted based on a frequency analysis of attribute values and 1-bits in the corresponding ABFs for a given database. Only bits are selected that cannot be clearly identified as referring to certain rare q-grams based on the number of ABFs that have a 1 in these bit positions [176]. For example, if a certain bit position is set to 1 in only two from 100 ABFs and only the q-gram 'zy' occurs in two quasi-identifying attribute values, then including this bit position into the final RBF would allow easy reidentification of the q-gram 'zy'. Note that for a certain attribute the same bit positions are always selected to ensure the same type of information is added into the final record level Bloom filter.

3. **Attribute weighting:** Based on the discriminatory power of each attribute, a user can weight those attributes accordingly. Based on these weights a certain number of bit positions (from those positions selected in the previous step) will then be randomly sampled from the ABF of

a given attribute in the next step. In the case where no knowledge of the discriminatory power is available, Durham [178] proposed to use the Fellegi and Sunter probabilistic weighting approach [204], as discussed in Section 3.2, which is used in traditional record linkage to calculate weights for each attribute that is used for a linkage [203, 274, 642].

4. **RBF generation:** In the final step, from the bit positions selected in the second step, and based on the weights assigned to each attribute, bits from a certain number of positions are sampled from each ABF, and these bits are concatenated into a single record level Bloom filter. Finally, to improve privacy, the bits in this Bloom filter are permuted to obtain the final record level Bloom filter (RBF), where the same permutation is applied to the RBFs of all records in a database.

Figure 8.5 illustrates a simple example generation of a RBF following the above discussed steps.

8.3.4 CLK-RBF

Schnell et al. [545] first proposed to use different numbers of hash functions k for the different attributes to be encoded into one Bloom filter in the CLK approach. Vatsalan et al. [615] refined this idea which they referred to as CLK-RBF. Using different numbers of hash functions for different attributes can be seen as the weights assigned to different attributes as described in the sidebox on page 54. If a first name attribute, for example, is seen to be more important than a city attribute for the calculation of similarities between records, then when values from the first name attribute are encoded more hash functions should be used to encode each q-gram from first name values compared to the q-grams from city values. For example, we can use $k_{FN} = 20$ hash functions for each q-gram from first name values and $k_C = 10$ hash functions for q-grams from city values.

As with the original CLK approach described in Section 8.3.2 above, all q-grams from the different attribute values are hashed into the same Bloom filter of length l bits. The use of different numbers of hash functions for different attributes can improve the linkage quality, while mapping all attribute values of a record into the same Bloom filter can improve privacy due to collisions between different q-grams and a reduction in frequency information that can be used in attacks [610], as we discuss further in Section 9.2.

8.4 Encoding Numerical Data

The encoding of numerical values into Bloom filters has not been investigated as extensively as the encoding of textual (string) values. While the similarity between strings can be preserved and measured by encoding the q-gram sets generated from strings, the same cannot be achieved with numerical values. Different approaches need to be explored for encoding numerical values. While 1999 and 2000, for example, are very similar numerical values, if they would be represented as strings and converted into q-gram sets ({19,99} and {20,00}, respectively) they would have a set-based similarity of 0. In this section we discuss two such proposed approaches to encode different types of numerical data into Bloom filters.

8.4.1 Absolute Difference Similarity Encoding

Vatsalan and Christen [614] proposed an encoding technique for numerical data using an absolute difference similarity. As we described in Section 6.8.3, the absolute difference similarity of two numerical values, n_1 and n_2, can be calculated as [109] (see also Equation 6.8):

$$sim(n_1, n_2) = \begin{cases} 1.0 - \frac{|n_1 - n_2|}{d_{max}} & \text{if } |n_1 - n_2| < d_{max}, \\ 0.0 & \text{otherwise}, \end{cases} \quad (8.8)$$

where d_{max} is the maximum tolerable absolute difference between two numerical values. To facilitate the privacy-preserving calculation of similarities between numerical values, Vatsalan and Christen proposed to create a list of numbers to represent each numerical value to be encoded, similar to how a set of q-grams represents a string. These lists of numbers are then hashed into Bloom filters using k hash functions similar to q-gram hashing. The idea behind this numerical encoding is as follows.

Each numerical value n to be encoded and compared is used to generate a list, $\mathbf{l}$, of numbers within the range $[n - (d_{max}/2), n + (d_{max}/2)]$ where d_{max} is the maximum tolerable absolute difference used in Equation 8.8. The list $\mathbf{l}$ will contain $2b+1$ numbers, l_i, that includes n, with $2b$ intervals and with the width of each interval being $d_{intv} = d_{max}/(2b)$. The value of b is a user defined parameter which influences the accuracy of the similarity calculations [614]. For a given numerical value n, its list $\mathbf{l} = [l_0, \ldots, l_i, \ldots, l_{2b}]$, with $0 \le i \le 2b$, of numbers is generated as follows:

$$l_i = \begin{cases} n - (b - i) \cdot d_{intv} & \text{if } i < b, \\ n & \text{if } i = b, \\ n + (i - b) \cdot d_{intv} & \text{if } i > b, \end{cases} \quad (8.9)$$

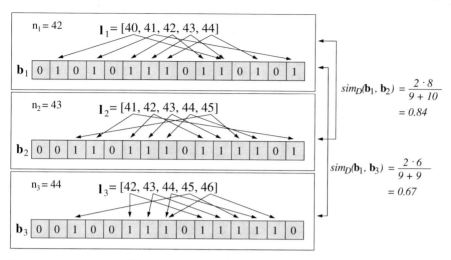

Fig. 8.6 An example illustration of encoding three integer values into Bloom filters using the absolute difference similarity method (adapted from [614]). The values $n_1 = 42$, $n_2 = 43$, and $n_3 = 44$ are first used to generate the lists l_1, l_2, and l_3 of numbers, assuming $d_{max} = 4$ and $b = 2$. These lists are then hashed into Bloom filters using $k = 2$ hash functions. The Dice coefficient similarity can then be calculated between pairs of Bloom filters, showing that the pair (n_1, n_2) is more similar than the pair (n_1, n_3).

where d_{intv} is the numerical interval between two adjacent values in l. This general encoding principle can be applied to different types of numerical data as we describe in the following.

8.4.1.1 Integer Data

As described above, a list l of numbers is generated first for the integer value n based on the user defined values for the maximum tolerable absolute difference, d_{max}, and the value for b, where $b \geq 1$. The list l is then hashed into a Bloom filter using k hash functions similar to how q-gram sets are hashed into Bloom filters. An example of encoding three integer values is shown in Figure 8.6. As with encoded q-gram sets, the Dice coefficient, shown in Equation 8.3, can be used to calculate the similarities between numerical values in a privacy-preserving way.

As can be seen from the examples in Figure 8.6, two numerical values that are more similar to each other will have corresponding lists of numbers that have more elements in common, thus resulting in higher similarities between their corresponding Bloom filters. For a given value of d_{max}, the value of b determines the length of the lists l that encode numerical values and thus the quality of the calculated similarities. However, due to collisions when elements are hashed into Bloom filters, the similarities calculated between the values n_1

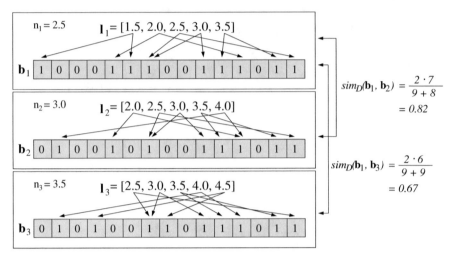

Fig. 8.7 An example illustration of encoding three floating-point values into Bloom filters using the absolute difference similarity method (adapted from [614]). The values $n_1 = 2.5$, $n_2 = 3.0$, and $n_3 = 3.5$ are first used to generate the lists l_1, l_2, and l_3 of numbers assuming $d_{max} = 2$ and $b = 2$. These lists are then hashed into Bloom filters using $k = 2$ hash functions. The Dice coefficient similarity can then be calculated between Bloom filters, showing that the pair (n_1, n_2) is more similar than the pair (n_1, n_3).

and n_2 based on their corresponding Bloom filters will potentially be higher than the absolute difference similarity from Equation 8.8 [614].

8.4.1.2 Floating-point Data

The encoding of floating-point values is similar to the encoding of integer values. For each floating-point value a list l of numbers is generated which is then hashed into a Bloom filter, as illustrated in Figure 8.7. However, the nature of floating-point values requires some specific processing as otherwise potentially no numbers in the two lists that represent two similar floating-point values will occur in common.

For example, assume the two values $n_1 = 2.5$ and $n_2 = 2.8$, with $d_{max} = 2$ and $b = 2$. Following Equation 8.9, the two lists $l_1 = [1.5, 2.0, 2.5, 3.0, 3.5]$ and $l_2 = [1.8, 2.3, 2.8, 3.3, 3.8]$ will be generated. When hashed, the resulting two Bloom filters will unlikely have many common 1-bits and therefore the resulting Dice coefficient similarity will be low.

To overcome this problem, Vatsalan and Christen [614] proposed to first align each numerical value n to a new value n_a, and then use these aligned values to generate the lists of numbers. A new aligned value n_a is calculated as:

$$n_a = \begin{cases} n & \text{if } n \bmod d_{intv} = 0, \\ n - (n \bmod d_{intv}) & \text{if } n \bmod d_{intv} < d_{intv}/2, \quad (8.10) \\ n + (d_{intv} - (n \bmod d_{intv})) & \text{if } n \bmod d_{intv} \geq d_{intv}/2. \end{cases}$$

In the above example, with $b = 2$ and $d_{max} = 2$ we get $d_{intv} = 0.5$. Therefore, n_1 will not be changed by the alignment step (because $2.5 \bmod 0.5 = 0$), while n_2 will be aligned to 3.0 (because $2.8 \bmod 0.5 = 0.3$). This results in the new list $l_2 = [2.0, 2.5, 3.0, 3.5, 4.0]$, which now has four elements in common with list $l_1 = [1.5, 2.0, 2.5, 3.0, 3.5]$.

8.4.1.3 Modulus Data

The absolute similarity distance based approach can also be used to encode various modulus data such as dates, times, and geographic locations. Unlike other numerical data, values for such types of data have a finite range. For example, months have a range of 1 to 12, seconds and minutes have a range of 0 to 59, and longitudes have a range 180 degrees west to 180 degrees east. As a result, the two times 23:58 and 00:07 are closer (more similar) to each other than for example 11:11 and 21:11.

To encode modulo data into Bloom filters, Vatsalan and Christen [614] proposed an additional step to create the list l of numbers for a modulo value n before encoding the list into a Bloom filter. Basically, values outside the given range are wrapped around the boundary of the range using:

$$l_i = \begin{cases} l_i \bmod (max - min + 1) & \text{if } l_i > max, \\ l_i + max + 1 & \text{if } l_i < min, \quad (8.11) \\ l_i & \text{otherwise,} \end{cases}$$

where min and max are the minimum and maximum values in a range, and l_i is a value in the list l.

For example, assume we have two minute values, $n_1 = 1$ and $n_2 = 59$, where their smallest difference would be 2 minutes and not 58 minutes. Assuming $d_{max} = 4$ and $b = 2$, these two values will result in the two lists $l_1 = [-1, 0, 1, 2, 3]$ and $l_2 = [57, 58, 59, 60, 61]$. Using Equation 8.11, and setting $min = 0$ and $max = 59$, the two lists are converted into $l_1 = [59, 0, 1, 2, 3]$ and $l_2 = [57, 58, 59, 0, 1]$, which results in them having three common numbers and therefore several common encoded elements at the same bit positions in their corresponding Bloom filters.

8.4.2 Distance Aware Numerical Encoding

A distance preserving encoding scheme for numerical data was proposed by
Karapiperis et al. [327, 328]. This approach employs bit vectors to anonymise
numerical values, where these vectors can be compared in similar ways as
Bloom filters are compared. While these bit vectors are technically not Bloom
filters, we discuss them in this section because this approach is related to
the absolute difference similarity encoding by Vatsalan and Christen [614]
presented previously.

The main parameters for this encoding approach are a distance threshold,
d_{max}, which is the maximum tolerable Euclidean distance between two numerical values n_1 and n_2, and a list of real numbers $r_i \in \mathbf{r}$, chosen uniformly
and randomly from the interval $[b_{min}, b_{max}]$, where b_{min} and b_{max} are the
minimum and maximum values of the domain of numerical values to be encoded. For example, if human age values (in years) are to be encoded, then
appropriate values might be $b_{min} = 0$ and $b_{max} = 120$. The length of the list
$\mathbf{r}$, denoted as $l = |\mathbf{r}|$, determines the length of the generated bit vector.

A list of l intervals, $\mathbf{I}$, is defined by adding and subtracting d_{max} to/from
each real number $r_i \in \mathbf{r}$, where the interval $\mathbf{I}_i$ for r_i, with $0 \leq i < l$, is defined
as:

$$\mathbf{I}_i = [r_i - d_{max}, r_i + d_{max}]. \tag{8.12}$$

Similar to the hash functions used to encode the elements of a set into
Bloom filters, these intervals are used as the set of hash functions, $h_i()$, with
one function to set each bit in a binary vector of length l to 0 or 1. For a given
numerical value n, the bit value for each interval $0 \leq i < l$ will be calculated
as:

$$h_i(n) = \begin{cases} 1 & \text{if } n \in [r_i - d_{max}, r_i + d_{max}], \\ 0 & \text{otherwise.} \end{cases} \tag{8.13}$$

The probability of setting a bit position to 1 depends on the distance
threshold d_{max}. Furthermore, as the Euclidean distance d_E between two numerical values n_1 and n_2 increases there will be a decrease in the probability
that these two values fall into the same interval. When $d_E > 2d_{max}$ then this
probability becomes 0.

Karapiperis et al. [327, 328] then developed a method to calculate an
optimal length of the list of random numbers $\mathbf{r}$ (and thus the generated bit
vectors), based on a mapping between Hamming and Euclidean distances.
This mapping allows the definition of a Hamming distance threshold between
two bit vectors that can be used to classify the pair as being a match or a non-
match. We refer the reader interested in the mathematical details to [328],
while we illustrate the method in Figure 8.8.

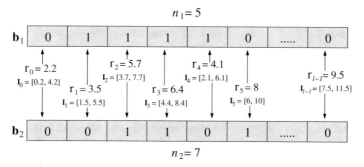

Fig. 8.8 An example illustration of distance aware numerical encoding (adapted from [327, 328]), assuming the value range was specified as $[b_{min}, b_{max}] = [1, 10]$. Given two numerical values, $n_1 = 5$ and $n_2 = 7$, one bit vector, $\mathbf{b}_1$ and $\mathbf{b}_2$, of length l is generated for each of the two values. We can then calculate the Hamming distance between these two bit vectors which will allow the similarity calculation between the two encoded values.

A similar approach to encode numerical values into bit vectors was proposed by Sun et al. [580], where a randomisation approach was employed to improve privacy. The proposed technique embeds numerical values into a Hamming space of bit vectors while preserving the Euclidean distances between numerical values. In order to provide privacy guarantees, random noise is introduced into these bit vectors using a mechanisms that provides differential privacy (a topic we discussed in Section 7.7). To prevent any correlation between records that can potentially be used to identify specific encoded values, such as in time series data, the Pufferfish privacy mechanism [346], a generalised differential privacy framework, is employed. This mechanism adds Laplace noise to numerical values to make values indistinguishable from each other, where each numerical value, with noise added, is embedded into a bit vector. The experimental results show this approach guarantees privacy protection against an adversary with full knowledge of a data distribution [580]. However, the approach does not scale to large databases due to the additional time required on randomising these bit vectors.

8.5 Encoding Hierarchical Classification Codes

Classification codes are used in a variety of scientific domains as well as application areas. Such codes range from classifications of diseases (ICD, International Classification of Diseases)[3] and occupations (ICSO, International Standard Classification of Occupations)[4] all the way to product codes such

---

[3] See: https://www.who.int/classifications/icd/en/

[4] See: http://www.ilo.org/public/english/bureau/stat/isco/index.htm

as book numbers (ISBN, International Standard Book Number)[5]. While not all these codes will be useful for linking sensitive databases, some, such as occupation or disease codes, can be. Because such codes do refer to individuals and potentially contain highly sensitive personal information (such as certain types of illnesses or occupations), they should be appropriately protected and encoded when used in the linkage of sensitive databases.

Different to names and addresses, an important aspect is that codes cannot be meaningfully compared using approximate string comparison functions, such as those generally used for names and addresses. For example, the two ICD-10 codes 'L27.8' and 'A27.8' describe two totally different types of diseases[6].

Furthermore, code systems are often hierarchical, where letters or digits at the beginning of codes indicate commonalities higher up in a code hierarchy. For ISCO occupation codes, for example, all codes starting with digit '1' refer to managers, where codes starting with '11' then correspond to chief executives, senior officials, and legislators, while codes starting with '14' are for hospitality, retail, and other services managers. As a result, codes with the same beginning indicate some form of similarity of concepts, while codes with different beginnings but the same ending do not.

Schnell and Borgs [551] proposed an approach to encode hierarchical classification codes into Bloom filters to enable similarity calculations that give higher weights to the letters or digits at the beginning and lower weights to the letters or digits at the end of such codes. The idea consists of two modifications of the encoding of textual values into Bloom filters. First, the elements to be hashed into Bloom filters are not q-grams but instead consecutively longer substrings generated from the hierarchical codes. The first element to be hashed is the first letter or digit of a code, then the first two, then the first three, and so on. For the example ISCO code '7541' (underwater divers[7]), the elements being hashed are '7', '75', '754' and '7541'.

The second modification is to not use the same number of hash functions, k, for all these elements, but to use more hash functions for the initial shorter elements of a code and less hash functions for the latter, longer elements. The random hashing approach described in Section 8.2.4 is used to encode individual elements, where the number of hash functions to be used to encode a certain element is determined by a weight parameter value set by the user.

In their experimental evaluation [551], Schnell and Borgs showed that this novel encoding approach achieved much improved linkage quality compared to when using a standard q-gram based encoding approach (which simply considers codes to be strings) or even a positional q-gram approach (where each q-gram is concatenated with its position in a code, as we discussed in Section 6.8.1). However, in order to properly evaluate the quality of hier-

---

[5] See: https://www.isbn-international.org/

[6] See: https://icdcodelookup.com/icd-10/codes

[7] See: http://www.ilo.org/public/english/bureau/stat/isco/docs/reso108.pdf

archical codes, modified hierarchical versions of precision and recall (as we described in Section 3.4) were required.

8.6 Choosing Suitable Settings for Bloom Filter Encoding

Since first proposed in 2009 [543], different methods to link sensitive databases using Bloom filter encoding have been developed. A variety of parameter settings, including different Bloom filter lengths, different numbers of hash functions, and different hashing and encoding methods (as we discussed in this chapter) have been used in different linkage applications. Certain Bloom filter encoding methods and parameter settings might be more suitable than others for different types of data, and for data with different characteristics. In the following we discuss how Bloom filter encoding methods and parameters should be selected.

Apart from best practice recommendations by Izakian [297] and Schnell [538], choosing parameters for Bloom filter based encoding methods for linking sensitive databases was first systematically approached by Borgs [77].

8.6.1 Encoding Parameters and Best Practice Suggestions

While the optimal choices for parameters when encoding data into Bloom filters was never formally settled, several best practice suggestions have been provided over time [297, 536]. In Table 8.1 we show an overview of selected works and their respective parameter choices. Some of these are implicit choices used in evaluations, while others are explicit recommendations. Since the length of the Bloom filters, l, varied across different works, for the number of hash functions used, k, we also show a standardised equivalent, $k_{(l=500)}$, for a Bloom filter length of $l = 500$, calculated as $k_{(l=500)} = 500 \cdot (k/l)$. This is based on the assumption that linkage quality will not change as long as the fraction k/l remains constant [77]. Note that this comparison is limited to the encoding of textual attribute values only. No comparative evaluation of the numerical or hierarchical encoding methods described in Sections 8.4 and 8.5 has been published so far.

As Table 8.1 shows, a variety of settings have been used. The most frequently used choice for the q-gram length (character substrings extracted from the textual values to be encoded into Bloom filters) was $q = 2$ (bigrams), while the standardised number of hash functions was most often set to $k_{(l=500)} = 15$.

Table 8.1 Selected publications and their Bloom filter encoding parameters tested or suggested, where l is the length of the Bloom filters used, k is the number of hash functions employed to hash elements into Bloom filters, $k_{(l=500)}$ is the adjusted number of hash functions for a Bloom filter length of $l = 500$, and q is the length of q-grams. (R) indicates works where explicit recommendations have been provided for parameter settings, while for all other publications the shown parameter settings are the ones that have been used in experimental evaluations.

Publication	l	q	k	$k_{(l=500)}$	Comments
Schnell et al. (2009) [543]	1,000	2	30	15	Original publication
Kuzu et al. (2011) [371]	500	2	15	15	First published attack
Durham (2012) [178]	500/1,000	2	15	15	
Randall et al. (2014) [507]	100	2	3	15	Very large database
Schnell et al. (2014) [552]	1,000	2	10	5	
Schnell (2014) [536] (R)	500/1,000	2	10/20	5/10	Only explicit range published
Vatsalan et al. (2014) [615]	1,000	2	30	15	
Schnell (2015) [538]	1,000	2	20	10	
Sehili et al. (2015) [555]	1,000	2	20	10	
Brown et al. (2017) [89]	1,000	2/1	10	5	
Ranbaduge (2018) [494]	1,000	2	30	15	
Izakian (2018) [297] (R)	1,000	1	50	25	Parameter sets for optimal
"	500	1	20	20	approximation of the
"	1,000	2	50	25	cleartext similarity not
"	500	3	50	50	for optimal linkage quality
Lazrig et al. (2018) [383]	1,000	2	15	≈ 8	Actual k (15) only hinted
Pita et al. (2018) [475]	180	2	2	≈ 5	Optimised for memory/speed
Schnell and Borgs (2018) [549]	1,000	2/1	20	10	

As we describe next, two alternatives to best practice settings were discussed by Borgs [77]: (1) The optimal parameter choice aiming to achieve a 50% fill of 1-bits in a Bloom filter [614], and (2) model-based optimal parameter estimation.

8.6.2 Optimal Parameters for Bloom Filter Encoding

In theory, having 50% of bits set to 1 in a Bloom filter should be optimal in terms of minimising the number of collisions of different elements (such as q-grams) being hashed to the same bit positions in a Bloom filter [68, 352]. As we discussed in the sidebox on page 194, this is also known as the false positive rate of a Bloom filter. This false positive rate must, however, not be confused with the false positive rate of linkage quality (false match rate), as we described in Section 3.4. These two false positive rates measure different things, and there is no direct relationship between the two. Minimising the number of collisions when encoding elements into Bloom filters does not necessarily lead to lower rates of false positive matches (higher linkage quality).

The calculation of the optimal number of hash functions, k_{opt}, to have half the bit positions set to 1, requires two parameters: The length of the Bloom filters, l, and the expected number of elements, n, to be hashed into the Bloom filter (see also Equation 8.1) [352]:

$$k_{opt} = \frac{l}{n} ln(2). \tag{8.14}$$

While the length of a Bloom filter is usually constant for all records in the same database that is being encoded, the number of elements to be encoded varies depending upon the actual quasi-identifying attribute values in the records that are encoded into Bloom filters. For example, attributes such as first name, surname, and city name can vary significantly in length. Short two-letter surnames like 'Vo' and 'Li' are common in many Asian cultures, while the longest reported surname[8] is apparently 'Wolfeschlegelsteinhausenberg-erdorff'. Thus, an average has to be calculated for the value of n to be used in the above equation. This is usually the average number of q-grams generated from quasi-identifying attribute values across all records in a database. Such an average, however, might potentially lead to a non-optimal numbers of 1-bits (too many or too few) for many encoded values, depending upon the variance of the lengths of the attribute values to be encoded.

Furthermore, despite having half of the bit positions set to 1 in a Bloom filter, high linkage quality may not be achieved. Avoiding bit positions set to 1 by more than one input element (hash collisions) requires limiting the number of hash functions k to a setting where collisions are avoided as much as possible, assuming that the Bloom filter length, l, is fixed. If we assume that the quasi-identifying attributes used for linking (and to be encoded into Bloom filters) result in unique combinations of identifying values and thus q-gram sets, then it will be unlikely that two different q-gram sets are encoded into the same positions in a Bloom filter. This will therefore lead to a number of false matched record pairs (wrong classifications) close to zero. In such cases the Dice coefficient similarities (see Equation 8.3) calculated between Bloom filters would be high only if the corresponding records contain the same quasi-identifying attribute values (and thus the same q-gram sets).

In this case, the false positive rate for Bloom filter collisions (Equation 8.14) and the false positive rate in terms of linkage quality (as we discussed in Section 3.4) will both be low. Limiting the false positive rate by choosing k will therefore implicitly keep the precision of the final linkage close to 1, because this would mean making next to no false match classifications. In the original application of Bloom filters [68], checking for set membership, this makes sense: falsely classifying an element as belonging to the set should be avoided. In the context of linking sensitive databases, however, the goal is to prevent false matches and to allow for some error tolerance. By limiting k to a setting where false matches are avoided as much as possible, recall (the proportion of true matches correctly classified as matches [260]) will likely become lower, potentially leading to suboptimal linkage quality.

---

[8] See:
https://en.wikipedia.org/wiki/Wolfeschlegelsteinhausenbergerdorff

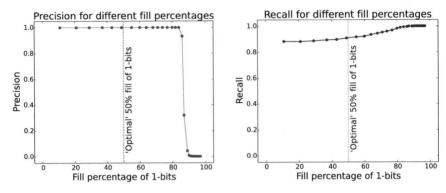

Fig. 8.9 Precision and recall of linkage quality based on simulated data being encoded into Bloom filters with increasing number of hash functions, k, from 1 to 30, and assuming the Bloom filter length $l = 256$. The vertical line at 50% shows the 'optimal' fill percentage as used in the literature [614]. Reproduced from Borgs [77]. © C. Borgs 2019, reprinted with permission.

Using synthetic data, Borgs [77] recently showed that when increasing the number of hash functions, k, while keeping the length of the Bloom filter l constant, then the precision of classified candidate record pairs remains stable. Recall also increases up to a certain point where the number of collisions produces a significant increase in the number of falsely matched records, as is shown in Figure 8.9. The highest combined precision and recall is obtained when the fill percentage of 1-bits in the Bloom filters reaches around 80%, after which it drops sharply to nearly 0 because of too many false matches.

This hypothesis of controlling collisions when hashing elements into Bloom filters in order to obtain optimal privacy protection and optimal linkage quality seems to be a topic not covered in the literature so far. As the only example the authors are aware of, Smith in 2017 wrote [564]: "(experiments) showed that values designed to minimise the false positive rate (...) tended to be very poor for Jaccard score estimation", without however giving further details on neither the experiments nor the cause for this discrepancy.

It therefore seems that choosing the number of hash functions, k, in a way that leads to half the bit positions in Bloom filters to be set to 1 can result in suboptimal linkage quality. This is why a different approach is needed to decide the optimal parameter setting for Bloom filter encoding that can guarantee a high linkage quality while also providing privacy protection. Borgs [77] recently explored model-based parameter settings using supervised machine learning methods which resulted in between 1% to 3% overall improvements of precision and recall compared to the 50% 1-bit fill method described above. On the other hand, Borgs also found that for many of the data sets explored in his work, the 50% fill method obtained better results than the parameter settings found in the literature (such as those in Table 8.1).

Furthermore, the choice of the Bloom filter length, l, is a factor which mainly affects computational efforts as well as memory requirements. If the ratio k/l is held constant and l stays in a reasonable range, linkage quality should not be affected by l. A Bloom filter of length l can have 2^l different patterns of 0- and 1-bits. Therefore, 2^l should not be smaller than the number of unique combinations of elements (unique sets of elements) that possibly can be generated from the quasi-identifying attribute values to be encoded into Bloom filters. Otherwise different sets of elements will be hashed to the same bit positions.

For example, assume we have an attribute POSTCODE where values are four digits long and range from '1000' to '7900', and we hash them as q-grams with $q = 2$ (bigrams). There will be 100 different unique q-grams (from '00' to '99'), resulting in less than 7,000 possible q-gram sets (of length three q-grams) if we follow the q-gram generation process we described in Section 6.8.1. For this example scenario, the first q-gram generated from a postcode cannot start with a '0', '8', or '9' digit, leaving 70 possible first q-grams. The second q-gram then depends upon the second digit of the first q-gram (because q-grams are formed overlapping), leaving only ten possible second q-grams for each first q-gram. Similarly, the third q-gram depends upon the second digit of the second q-gram, again allowing for only ten possible third q-grams for a given second q-gram. This means there will be a maximum $70 \cdot 10 \cdot 10 = 7,000$ possible sequences of q-grams (actually less because we only consider postcodes up to '7900'), where some of these contain the same q-gram more than once. Postcode '2000', for example, will result in the q-gram set $\{00, 20\}$ (remember, a set contains each unique element only once) while postcode '2222' gives the set $\{22\}$. In total, for this attribute with postcode values ranging from '1000' to '7999', there will be only 6,593 unique q-gram sets. Any Bloom filter where $2^l > 6,593$ (any $l \geq 13$ is suitable because $2^{13} = 8,192$) will therefore be able to encode such postcode values without two or more different q-gram sets having to be represented by the same bit pattern.

On the other hand, for an attribute that, for example, contains street addresses a much larger number of unique q-grams and therefore unique q-gram sets can be expected. The number of unique bigrams for letters from an alphabet 'a' to 'z' is 676 ('aa' to 'zz'), for digits '0' to '9' it is 100 ('00' to '99'), and there will be various combinations of letters and digits plus all kinds of punctuation characters. Furthermore, the length of street address strings can vary from short to very long multiword addresses, and therefore the number of unique q-gram sets will likely be very large. However, there is always an upper bound on the number of unique q-gram sets, which is the number of unique attribute values in the database to be encoded. This number is also at most the number of records in that database.

To summarise this topic, several implications for choosing optimal parameters for Bloom filter based methods are of importance. First, the choice of l is mostly a question of computational time and available memory for a given linkage application. Smaller Bloom filter lengths do not change the linkage quality as long as the ratio k/l stays constant and l stays in a reasonable range for the quasi-identifying attribute values to be encoded, as we discussed above.

Second, model-based optimal parameter choice works better than the 50% fill rule [77], which in turn works better than most current parameter suggestions routinely used in the literature. Such a model-based approach however requires extensive experimental evaluation, and is also data dependent.

Finally, using as many high quality stable quasi-identifying attributes as possible (as are available in the databases to be encoded and linked) is highly recommended to improve linkage quality. These include date and place of birth, and gender, as well as first name (which is less likely to change over time compared to surname or address details for a given individual).

8.7 Summary and Further Reading

In this chapter we have presented in detail how Bloom filter encoding can be used to encode textual and numerical data, as well as hierarchical classification codes, in such ways that the resulting encoded bit vectors can be compared to calculate approximate similarities. There are different techniques of how individual elements of a set can be hashed into a Bloom filter, and different methods of how single or multiple attribute values can be encoded into a Bloom filter.

While textual, numerical, and hierarchical codes constitute the majority of data used for comparing records when sensitive databases are being linked, novel types of data that could be used for linking are increasingly becoming available. One specific type of useful data are geographical locations, generally made of pairs of longitude and latitude values. The process of geocoding can help to assign such location information to address records [106, 114, 351]. However, location data can be sensitive private information, and when used in the context of linking sensitive databases then new encoding techniques are required to allow the calculation of geographical distances without revealing the actual locations being compared. Initial work has been proposed by Farrow [200, 202], where locations are first perturbed and then encoded into Bloom filters. However, more work on encoding novel types of data is required.

Another type of data that can be useful are self-generated identification codes [544], as we discussed in Section 1.6.4. Such codes are used, for example, in longitudinal panel studies where sensitive information about individuals is being collected over time [31]. Only limited initial work by Pöge [476] has explored how Bloom filter encoding can facilitate privacy-preserving record linkage of such self-generated identification codes. However, this is an area where more research and development could lead to improved confidence in the used methodology and thus participation of study participants if they know no collected sensitive information about them can be attributed to them.

As we will discuss in the following chapter, some of the encoding methods described in this chapter are potentially vulnerable to certain cryptanalysis attacks that exploit either the occurrences of frequent Bloom filters, or the bit patterns and their frequencies and co-occurrences in a set of Bloom filters. As we also discuss in the next chapter, hardening techniques have been developed that aim to overcome such attacks.

Besides their popular use in the context of linking sensitive databases, Bloom filters have been used in a variety of domains ranging from networking applications to spell checkers and text analysis systems [70], and even to check models in the formal verification of multithreaded software systems [157]. There is a large body of work analysing the characteristics of Bloom filters with regard to the false positive rates caused by collisions, and we encourage the interested reader to consult the relevant literature [70, 88, 417]. However, as we discussed in the previous section, only recent work by Borgs [77] has investigated parameter settings for Bloom filter encodings specifically in the context of linking sensitive databases.

Within the context of linking sensitive databases, since the initial proposal by Schnell et al. [543] to use Bloom filters for efficient and accurate linking of sensitive textual values, many publications have investigated various aspects of Bloom filter encoding, including their use in two-party protocols or how Bloom filter encoded databases can be efficiently blocked. We refer the interested reader to the surveys by Vatsalan et al. [619, 620] and the references provided in them.

Chapter 9
Attacking and Hardening Bloom Filter Encoding

Co-authored by Anushka Vidanage and Sirintra Vaiwsri

Abstract While the Bloom filter hashing and encoding techniques described in the previous chapter have shown to enable the efficient and accurate linkage of large sensitive databases, including the approximate matching of textual and numerical values, as well as hierarchical classification codes, recent research has shown that these techniques can be vulnerable to certain attack methods that are aimed at reidentifying the sensitive information encoded in Bloom filters. In this chapter we discuss the principal ideas of these attacks and describe in more detail several successful attack methods. We then describe a series of hardening techniques that aim to make Bloom filter encoding less vulnerable to such attacks.

9.1 Overview of Attack Methods

Bloom filter encoding, as described in the previous chapter, has received much attention in recent years and this technique is now being used in a variety of real-world applications where sensitive databases need to be linked [24, 475, 480, 507]. We describe some of these applications in more detail in Chapter 13. The majority of applications that do aim to link sensitive databases in privacy-preserving ways using Bloom filters are in the health domain, where for example sensitive patient records need to be linked to facilitate studies not possible on individual databases [84].

There are several major reasons why Bloom filter encoding has been the method of choice in these applications:

- Bloom filters are relatively easy to understand compared to other more complex techniques such as those based on secure multiparty computation or on other cryptographic approaches.
- Bloom filter encoding techniques are easy to implement because they rely on simple bit vector data structures which are readily available in many programming languages.

© Springer Nature Switzerland AG 2020
P. Christen et al., *Linking Sensitive Data*, https://doi.org/10.1007/978-3-030-59706-1_9

- The computations on bit vectors that represent Bloom filters are highly efficient and therefore they are scalable to the encoding and linking of very large databases.
- Finally, as discussed in the previous chapter, both textual and numerical values, as well as hierarchical classification codes, can be encoded into Bloom filters, and approximate similarities can be calculated between Bloom filters that are close to the similarities that are calculated between unencoded values, as was shown in studies on real-world databases [507].

Given these advantages, the use of Bloom filter encoding as the method of choice for privacy-preserving record linkage is no surprise. Initially, Bloom filter encoding was seen as a secure technique ideally suited for linking sensitive databases. However, as we discuss in this chapter, because of the way Bloom filters are generated, by encoding the elements of sets that represent textual or numerical values, there potentially will be patterns in the bit vectors in Bloom filter databases that can be exploited via attack methods that are commonly known as cryptanalysis attacks. The majority of the developed attacks, as we describe in the next three sections, are based on the analysis of frequent bit patterns in large encoded Bloom filter databases.

For example, assume a large population database containing the names and addresses of taxpayers is being encoded into Bloom filters. In English speaking countries, the surnames 'Smith' or 'Miller' will likely be among the most common surnames in such a database, while if the database is from a German speaking country then 'Müller' and 'Schmidt' might be the most frequent surnames. As a result, when these common names are encoded into attribute level Bloom filters (as we discussed in Section 8.3.1), their resulting Bloom filters will also be common. This means there will be certain Bloom filters with the same pattern of 0- and 1-bits that are frequent. Therefore, the frequency distribution of bit patterns in a Bloom filter database can be analysed and compared to the frequency distribution of values in a database of plaintext values, as we discussed in Section 5.4.3.

In Table 9.1 we provide an overview of existing published attacks on Bloom filter encoding for privacy-preserving record linkage. As can be seen in this table, the different attack methods assume an adversary has some knowledge about certain parameters and settings used when the Bloom filters were generated. All attacks so far assume textual values have been encoded into Bloom filters, where an adversary can guess the used length of q-grams, q, and the attributes that have been encoded into Bloom filters based on a frequency analysis of the 1-bit patterns in a Bloom filter database [546]. Other knowledge required by certain attacks includes k, the number of hash functions used; $\mathbf{H}$, the actual set of hash functions; or HM the hashing mechanism used (such as double or random hashing as we described in Section 8.2). The abbreviation fBF-fPT used in the table means both frequently occurring Bloom filters and plaintext values are required. Most attacks have been applied on publicly available voter databases from the US, most commonly a North Carolina Voter Registration (NCVR) database [111], but more recently

Table 9.1 Summary of existing attacks on Bloom filter encoding for privacy-preserving record linkage, as described in Section 9.1. The attributes encoded were FIRSTNAME (FN), SURNAME (SN), CITY (C), and STREETADDRESS (SA).

Attack method	Assumed adversary knowledge	Databases / Attributes Number of Bloom filters	Reidentification Runtime
Kuzu et al. (2011) [371]	k, *fBF-fPT*	NCVR / FN 3,500	400 > 20 min
Kuzu et al. (2013) [372]	k, *fBF-fPT*	Patient names 239,747	4 out of 20 few sec
Niedermeyer et al. (2014) [438]	k, *HM (DH)*, *fBF-fPT*	German / SN 10,000	934 > days
Kroll and Steinmetzer (2015) [367]	k, *HM (DH)*, *fBF-fPT*	German / FN, SN, SA 100,000	44,000 > days
Christen et al. (2017) [120]	*fBF-fPT*	NCVR / FN, SN 222,251	6 to 10 < 2 sec
Mitchell et al. (2017) [415]	k, **H**, *HM*	NCVR / FN, SN 474,319	364,450 395 min
Christen et al. (2018) [119]	*fBF-fPT*	NCVR and MVR / FN, SN 222,251	41 to 27,665 < 22 min
Christen et al. (2018) [123]	Only attributes and q	NCVR / FN, SN, C, SA 222,251	10 to 5,000 < 150 min
Vidanage et al. (2019) [629]	Only attributes and q	NCVR / FN, SN, C, SA 222,251	163 to 36,796 > 1 day

also a Michigan Voter Registration (MVR) database. These databases each contain several million records with details of registered voters, such as their names and addresses, and thus provide the frequency information required by these cryptanalysis attacks.

As can be seen in Table 9.1, the success rates (the number of successful reidentifications) of these attacks are mixed, as are the required runtimes. Therefore, many of these existing attack methods would not be practical in real-world scenarios, also because they require an adversary to have knowledge about a variety of parameter settings used during the encoding. Only recently have more advanced attacks been developed that are both more efficient and also required less knowledge by an adversary [123, 629].

These attacks highlight that Bloom filter encoding can be vulnerable in certain situations and therefore care should be taken when this encoding technique is used in practical applications to encode sensitive data, as we discuss further in Section 9.6. It is also important to properly investigate the limitations and constraints associated with Bloom filter encoding as a privacy-preserving technique.

In the following sections we discuss in more detail the attacks presented in Table 9.1. In Section 9.5 we then describe a variety of so called hardening techniques that have been developed to make Bloom filters more resilient to cryptanalysis attacks. Finally, in Section 9.6, we provide some recommendations on the use of Bloom filter encoding and hardening techniques when used in the context of linking sensitive databases.

9.2 Frequency-based Cryptanalysis Attacks

The first proposed attack methods on Bloom filter encoding in the context of privacy-preserving record linkage were based on the fact that a plaintext value that occurs frequently in the database to be encoded will generate a Bloom filter (that has a specific bit pattern) with the same frequency as the plaintext value. In the following we describe three types of attacks that exploit this weakness of Bloom filters.

9.2.1 Constrain Satisfaction based Attack

The first attack on Bloom filter encoding in the context of linking sensitive databases was proposed by Kuzu et al. [372] in 2011. This cryptanalysis attack was based on a frequency aware constraint satisfaction problem (CSP) solver. A CSP can be seen as a mathematical question that is defined as a set of objects whose state must satisfy a number of limitations or constraints. In the context of reidentifying sensitive values encoded in Bloom filters, two basic types of constraints can be considered. First, assume a plaintext value that occurs in a public database with a certain frequency, for example 10% of all surnames are 'smith'. Then, in a Bloom filter database that encodes surnames from the same or a similar domain (such as a patient database from the same country as a public voter database) the Bloom filter which encodes 'smith' should also have a similar frequency of around 10% of all Bloom filters.

Secondly, if the adversary knows the number of hash functions, k, that were used to encode q-grams into Bloom filters (an assumption made by this attack), then he can calculate the maximum number of 1-bits a Bloom filter (that can encode a certain plaintext value) can contain. For example, assuming $k = 10$ and $q = 2$ (bigrams) were used to encode surnames, then a Bloom filter that can encode 'smith' cannot contain more than 40 1-bits because 'smith' contains four q-grams where each is hashed ten times. Collisions might result in less than 40 1-bits, but no Bloom filter with more than 40 1-bits can possibly encode the value 'smith'.

Based on these two types of constraints, the attack groups plaintext values and records, and aligns those groups that satisfy the defined constrains. The CSP solver is then applied iteratively where in each iteration some information about certain bit positions and corresponding q-grams that could have been hashed into these positions is learned.

This attack is based on three main assumptions: (1) the sensitive database which was used to generate the Bloom filter database is a subset of the public database available to an adversary such that the frequency distributions of values across these two databases are similar; (2) an adversary has access to that public database and also knows the number of hash functions that were used when generating the Bloom filters; and (3) individual Bloom filter bit patterns (of 1s and 0s) must occur multiple times.

According to the experimental evaluation conducted by Kuzu et al. [371] using a North Carolina Voter Registration (NCVR) database, the attack was able to correctly reidentify 400 first names from 3,500 Bloom filters. In a later set of experiments, Kuzu et al. [372] carried out another evaluation of their attack using a real patient database. The attack was successful in reidentifying only 4 out of 20 frequent patient names correctly when a smaller voter database from Tennessee (which had a somewhat different name frequency distribution) was used as the plaintext database. This evaluation highlighted the need for an adversary to have access to highly similar databases as otherwise the attack would unlikely be successful.

9.2.2 Bloom Filter Atoms based Attack

A second type of attack on Bloom filter encoding was proposed by Niedermeyer et al. [438] for Bloom filters that encode a single quasi-identifying attribute, and then extended by Kroll and Steinmetzer [367] to Bloom filters that encode several attributes. The attack is based on Bloom filter atoms, where an atom is defined as a Bloom filter that encodes a single element (such as a q-gram), from a given set. For q-grams of length $q = 2$ (bigrams), for example, and assuming an alphabet containing only the lowercase letters 'a' to 'z', then $26^2 = 676$ possible Bloom filter atoms exist, from 'aa' to 'zz' (note that not all of these possible Bloom filter atoms might actually occur in a value in a database). In Figure 9.1 we provide an example of how Bloom filter atoms for three q-grams are combined using the bitwise OR operation (see the OR Table on page xxii for details) into one Bloom filter that encodes the q-gram set {ma, ar, ry} generated from the first name 'mary'.

While the first version of this attack method was conducted manually [438], the improved version was fully automatic [367]. Both versions of this attack exploit a weakness in the double hashing approach we described in Section 8.2.1. In double hashing, using Equation 8.4 on page 197, two independent hash functions are linearly combined to generate k hash values (bit positions), $g_i(x)$, with $1 \leq i \leq k$, into which an element x (typically a q-gram) of a set is hashed, and with l being the length of the Bloom filter used. Using modulo arithmetic, Equation 8.4 [352]:

$$g_i(x) = (h_1(x) + i \cdot h_2(x)) \; mod \; l$$

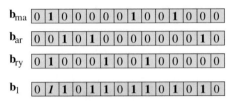

Fig. 9.1 Example of Bloom filter atoms for the three bigrams ($q = 2$) 'ma', 'ar', and 'ry', and how they are combined using the bitwise OR operation into one Bloom filter $\mathbf{b}_1$ that encodes the q-gram set for 'mary', {ma, ar, ry}. As can be seen, each q-gram is hashed using $k = 3$ hash functions, and there is a collision in the second bit position (shown in bold italics in $\mathbf{b}_1$) because both 'ma' and 'ry' are hashed to this position.

can be rewritten as:

$$g_i(x) = [(h_1(x) \bmod l) + (i \cdot h_2(x) \bmod l)] \bmod l. \tag{9.1}$$

If we set $a = h_1(x) \bmod l$ and $b = i \cdot h_2(x) \bmod l$, then it holds that both $0 \le a < l$ and $0 \le b < l$. As a result, for a given Bloom filter length, l, there will be l^2 possible value pairs of (a, b). For $l = 1,000$, for example, these are from $(0, 0)$ to $(999, 999)$. This means that individual elements of the set hashed into Bloom filters are represented by a quite small (in computational and cryptographic terms) number of possible patterns. This is the weakness of double hashing that is exploited in the attacks by Niedermeyer et al. [438] and Kroll and Steinmetzer [367].

The manual attack by Niedermeyer et al. [438] consists of five steps and it was applied on a data set of frequent German surnames. First, 10,000 Bloom filters of lengths $l = 1,000$ were generated from a list of 10,000 surnames that contained 7,580 unique values, with the number of hash functions set to $k = 15$. Then, all those Bloom filters that occurred only once were removed (to ensure rare q-grams are removed), leaving a set of 934 Bloom filters that occurred at least twice in the data set. In the second step, all possible atoms (Bloom filters that are assumed to contain a single q-gram) were generated according to Equation 9.1 for each possible value for a and b, resulting in 1,000,000 candidate atoms (given the Bloom filter length was $l = 1,000$).

In the third step, so called phantom atoms (that could not actually encode a q-gram) were identified and removed from the candidate atoms in two ways:

- In the set of 934 Bloom filters that encoded a surname, some bit positions were 0 for all the 934 Bloom filters. Therefore, any atom which had a 1-bit in at least one bit position where all 934 Bloom filters had a 0 could not have encoded an actual q-gram from these surnames. Applying this method led to 3,952 possible atoms being removed.
- Any atom which had a Hamming weight (number of 1-bits) below 15, the number of hash functions, k, used to encode values into Bloom filters, was

removed because such atoms with high probability were not encoding an actual q-gram. This method led to 3,147 possible atoms being removed.

This left 805 atoms after this third step of the attack. In the fourth step, the attack determined the number of Bloom filters that contain each atom. The atoms were then sorted according to their frequencies. In the final step, using different lists of publicly available German surnames, the q-grams that occurred most frequently in German surnames were identified and assigned to the most frequent atoms. From this assignment of frequent atoms to frequent q-grams, possible German surnames were derived.

From the 7,580 unique German surnames encoded into the 10,000 Bloom filters, the authors were able to correctly reidentify the 934 most frequent surnames in their manual evaluation of the attack [438].

Kroll and Steinmetzer [367] extended this manual attack by Niedermeyer et al. [438] into a fully automated cryptanalysis of multiple encoded quasi-identifying attributes. This attack was also conducted on German surnames. The attack did analyse the relationships between q-grams in a plaintext database and atoms (as described above) in a Bloom filter database to align them using their frequencies. However, the authors realised that results gained from analysing relationships between single q-grams and single atoms are not enough for an automatic reidentification because, except for a few q-gram and atom combinations, frequencies were too similar to allow such kind of assignments with high accuracy.

Therefore, the attack analysed the co-occurrences between q-grams themselves and the co-occurrences between atoms themselves. The attack generated two matrices, $\mathbf{E}$ and $\mathbf{D}$, using those co-occurrences between q-grams and between atoms, respectively. These matrices contained the probabilities that two q-grams or two atoms appear with each other with respect to the total number of records in each database. The matrices $\mathbf{E}$ and $\mathbf{D}$ were then used in an optimisation algorithm, derived from a cryptanalysis attack on substitution ciphers [299], that iteratively swaps the elements in the matrix $\mathbf{D}$ in a predefined manner until an objective function reaches its minimum value. This objective function is defined to measure the difference between the two matrices, $\mathbf{E}$ and $\mathbf{D}$, and the optimisation algorithm is defined to minimise that difference in a way that the atoms in matrix $\mathbf{D}$ have the best possible co-relation with the q-grams in matrix $\mathbf{E}$.

In the evaluation of the attack the authors were able to successfully recover 44% of surnames encoded into 100,000 Bloom filters. However, the limitation of this attack is that it only works when the double hashing approach described in Section 8.2.1 is used for encoding. Furthermore, on 100,000 Bloom filters the attack took 402 minutes to complete.

| **Public database** | | | **Bloom filter database** | | | **(1a) Position candidate sets** |

Public database

FirstName	Freq
karen	242
mary	182
kate	115
mareo	43
...	...

Bloom filter database

	Bloom filter	Freq
b_1	1 0 1 1 0 1	231
b_2	1 1 0 0 1 0	171
b_3	0 0 1 0 1 1	109
b_4	0 1 0 1 1 1	42
		...

$$p_0 \ p_1 \quad p_2 \ \cdots \ p_5$$

(1a) Position candidate sets

$$\mathbf{c}^+[p_0] = \{ka, ar, re, en, ma, ry\}$$
$$\mathbf{c}^-[p_0] = \{ka, at, te, ma, ar, re, eo\}$$

$$\mathbf{c}^+[p_1] = \{ma, ar, ry, re, eo\}$$
$$\mathbf{c}^-[p_1] = \{ka, ar, re, en, at, te\}$$

$$\mathbf{c}^+[p_2] = \{ka, ar, re, en, at, te\}$$
$$\mathbf{c}^-[p_2] = \{ma, ar, ry, re, eo\}$$
$$\cdots \qquad \cdots$$

(1b) Position q–gram sets

$$\mathbf{c}[p_0] = \mathbf{c}^+[p_0] \setminus \mathbf{c}^-[p_0] = \{en, ry\}$$
$$\mathbf{c}[p_1] = \mathbf{c}^+[p_1] \setminus \mathbf{c}^-[p_1] = \{ma, ry, eo\}$$
$$\mathbf{c}[p_2] = \mathbf{c}^+[p_2] \setminus \mathbf{c}^-[p_2] = \{ka, en, at, te\}$$
$$\cdots \qquad \cdots \qquad \cdots$$

(2) Reidentify attribute values (b_1)

$$\mathbf{G} = \{karen, kate, mareo, mary\}$$
$$\mathbf{g}_{p_0} = \mathbf{G} \cap \mathbf{c}[p_0] = \{karen, mary\}$$
$$\mathbf{g}_{p_2} = \mathbf{g}_{p_0} \cap \mathbf{c}[p_2] = \{\mathbf{karen}\}$$

Fig. 9.2 Outline of the frequency alignment based cryptanalysis attack on Bloom filter encodings [120]. Bloom filters and plaintext values are both sorted according to their frequencies and then frequency aligned, as can be seen in the top left hand side. In the first step, (1a) and (1b), the attack exploits the 0 and 1 bit patterns in Bloom filters to identify the sets of q-grams that are possible, $\mathbf{c}^+[p]$, or not possible, $\mathbf{c}^-[p]$, respectively, for each bit position p (note that $\setminus$ denotes the set difference operation). In step (2), the reidentification of sensitive plaintext values, $\mathbf{G}$, is conducted by intersecting (illustrated using $\cap$) the q-gram sets of values in $\mathbf{G}$ with the sets $\mathbf{c}$. For example, for Bloom filter b_1, from the q-gram set $\mathbf{c}[p_0]$ at position p_0 the adversary can learn that only the two q-grams 'en' or 'ry' can be encoded in this position, and therefore only 'karen' and 'mary' could have been encoded into b_1. From $\mathbf{c}[p_2]$ at position p_2 she then learns that one of the q-grams 'ka', 'en', 'at', or 'te' needs to occur in a plaintext value encoded in this Bloom filter, which leaves 'karen' as the only possible plaintext value that could have been encoded into Bloom filter b_1. © Springer International Publishing AG 2017, reprinted with permission.

9.2.3 Bloom Filter Construction Principle based Attack

Christen et al. [120] recently proposed a novel cryptanalysis attack method on Bloom filters which does not require any prior knowledge of the settings and parameters used when Bloom filters were encoded. As with the previously described attack methods, this attack however still requires both frequent Bloom filters and frequent plaintext values that are supposed to come from the same domain and also have similar frequency distributions.

This attack is one of the more practical and efficient attack methods developed so far. It exploits the fundamental way of the Bloom filter construction principle of hashing sets of elements into bit positions, and uses this principle to identify the possible plaintext values encoded into Bloom filters, as is illustrated in Figure 9.2. In the following we describe this attack in more detail, and also discuss its limitations.

- **Preliminaries and Assumptions:** Unlike the previously proposed attacks, this attack method is independent of the encoding function and its parameters used. The attack assumes that the adversary has access to a database of Bloom filters, **B**, and their frequencies, but does not know anything about the parameters used in the encoding process besides being able to guess what quasi-identifying attribute was encoded in the Bloom filter set being attacked, and what value of q was used for the encoding [546]. It is also assumed that the adversary has access to a plaintext database, **V**, which can be a publicly available population database such as a telephone directory or voter list, and the frequencies of the plaintext values in this database. It is also assumed that the adversary can guess the type of attribute value(s) encoded into Bloom filters by analysing the distribution of Hamming weights (number of 1-bits) of Bloom filters in **B**, because different attributes or attribute combinations encoded in a Bloom filter database likely have unique and distinctive distributions of 1-bits [546]. For example, the encoding of a postcode or zipcode attribute (assumed all to be of the same length, like four or five digits), will result in Bloom filters all having a highly similar number of 1-bits compared to Bloom filters that encode name or address values that can have a large variability in their lengths.

- **Attack Methodology:** The attack consists of two main steps, as shown in Figure 9.2. In the first step, the attack first aligns frequent Bloom filters to frequent attribute values from the plaintext database by comparing the frequency values of both, i.e. the most frequent Bloom filter is paired with to the most frequent plaintext value, the second most frequent Bloom filter with the second most frequent plaintext value, and so on. At the end of this step the adversary will have a set of Bloom filter / plaintext value pairs ranked by their frequencies. Next, for each bit position p in the Bloom filters, for all Bloom filter / plaintext value pairs, if a Bloom filter has this particular bit position set to 1 then all the q-grams from the paired plaintext value are added to the set $\mathbf{c}^+[p]$ of possible q-grams that could have been hashed to this position p.

  On the other hand, if the bit position is set to 0 then all the q-grams from the paired plaintext value are added to $\mathbf{c}^-[p]$, the set of not possible q-grams for the bit position p. The attack thus uses the Bloom filter construction principle which states that if a bit position is set to 1 in a Bloom filter then at least one of the q-grams from a q-gram set must have been hashed to that position. Similarly, when a bit position is set to 0 then no q-gram from a given q-gram set could have been hashed to that Bloom filter position.

  After obtaining a set of possible and a set of not possible q-grams for each Bloom filter bit position, the attack generates, for each bit position p, a set of possible q-grams, $\mathbf{c}[p] = \mathbf{c}^+[p] \setminus \mathbf{c}^-[p]$, that could have been hashed into that bit position, and where $\setminus$ denotes the set difference operation. For example, as illustrated in Figure 9.2, Bloom filter bit position p_0 has the potential q-gram set $\mathbf{c}[p_0] = \{$en, ry$\}$, generated by applying the set minus operation, $\mathbf{c}^+[p_0] \backslash \mathbf{c}^-[p_0]$. At the end of the first step, the adversary thus obtains a list of potential q-gram sets, $\mathbf{C} = [\mathbf{c}[p_0], \mathbf{c}[p_1], \ldots, \mathbf{c}[p_{l-1}]]$, one set for each Bloom filter bit position, where l is the length of the given Bloom filters.

In the second step, the attack then tries to reidentify what plaintext values could have been encoded into each Bloom filter $\mathbf{b} \in \mathbf{B}$. For each Bloom filter, based on the bit value in each position (either 0 or 1), the attack removes not possible candidate plaintext values from the set of publicly available plaintext values, $\mathbf{G}$, using the possible and not possible q-gram sets that were generated in the first step of the attack.

For example, as shown in the lower right part of Figure 9.2, for Bloom filter $\mathbf{b}_1$, the values 'kate' and 'mareo' are not possible because in order to set the bit position p_0 to 1 the value encoded in $\mathbf{b}_1$ must either contain the q-gram 'en' or 'ry' in $\mathbf{c}[p_0]$. Similarly, based on position p_2, the value 'mary' is also not possible because in order to set this bit to 1 the value must contain one of the q-grams from the set $\mathbf{c}[p_2] = \{$ka, en, at, te$\}$. Using the same approach, the attack can reidentify the frequent values encoded into each frequent Bloom filter in $\mathbf{B}$.

Several refinement and expansion steps were proposed to improve the accuracy of this attack [119]. The first idea was to base the reidentification of plaintext values in the second step not on the possible q-grams encoded in bit positions but rather on the not possible q-grams. Furthermore, as illustrated in Figure 9.3, in certain cases it is possible to assign with certainty a q-gram to a bit position because it is the only possible q-gram that could have been encoded to that position for a certain frequent plaintext value. The possible and not possible q-gram sets can also be refined by analysing plaintext values that are either shorter or longer variations of a frequent plaintext value, where the corresponding q-gram sets are either subsets or supersets of the q-gram set of the frequent value. These sub- and supersets allow Bloom filters to be identified that must encode a longer or shorter value, as the right side of Figure 9.3 shows.

- **Limitations:** According to an experimental evaluation [120], this attack works even when the Bloom filter hardening techniques Balancing or XOR-folding (which we both describe in Section 9.5) have been applied. As a result, this attack method has shown that it is possible to reidentify some sensitive values encoded into Bloom filters if there are frequent Bloom filters as well as frequent plaintext values that can be accurately aligned such that the frequent Bloom filters do correctly encode their aligned plaintext values.

  The limitation of this attack, as well as all other attack methods described earlier in this chapter, is that both such frequent Bloom filters and frequent plaintext values are required. This will likely only happen when Bloom filters encode individual attribute values (as we discussed in Section 8.3.1), because the combination of several attributes is likely to

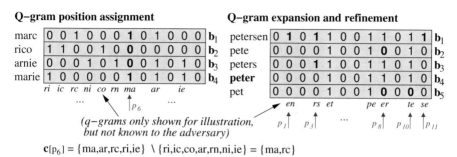

Q-gram position assignment

marc	0 0 1 0 0 0 1 0 1 0 0 0	b_1
rico	1 1 0 0 1 0 0 0 0 0 0 0	b_2
arnie	0 0 0 1 0 1 0 0 1 0 1 0	b_3
marie	1 0 0 0 0 1 0 1 0 1 0	b_4

ri ic rc ni co rn ma   ar   ie

... $\uparrow p_6$ ...

Q-gram expansion and refinement

petersen	0 1 0 1 1 0 0 1 1 0 1 1	b_1
pete	0 0 0 0 1 0 0 1 0 0 1 0	b_2
peters	0 0 0 1 1 0 0 1 1 0 1 0	b_3
peter	0 0 0 0 1 0 0 1 1 0 1 0	b_4
pet	0 0 0 0 1 0 0 1 0 0 0 0	b_5

en   rs et   pe er   te se

$p_1\uparrow$ $p_3\uparrow$ ... $p_8\uparrow$ $p_{10}\uparrow$ $\uparrow p_{11}$

(q-grams only shown for illustration, but not known to the adversary)

$\mathbf{c}[p_6] = \{$ma,ar,rc,ri,ie$\} \setminus \{$ri,ic,co,ar,rn,ni,ie$\} = \{$ma,rc$\}$

Fig. 9.3 The left side shows an example q-gram position assignment, where based on the given set of possible q-grams at position p_6, $\mathbf{c}[p_6]$ ={ma, rc}, for Bloom filter b_4 with its frequency aligned plaintext value 'marie', 'ma' is the only possible q-gram that could have set this 1-bit at position p_6. The adversary therefore can assign 'ma' to position p_6 with certainty. The right side (adapted from [119]) shows the q-gram refinement and expansion process for the frequent plaintext value 'peter' and four not frequent shorter and longer values. For the shorter values, from the bit patterns in the Bloom filters b_2 and b_5, it becomes clear that position p_8 must encode the q-gram 'er' because both $b_2[p_8]$ and $b_5[p_8]$ are 0 and only 'pet' and 'pete' do not contain 'er'. Similarly, p_{10} must encode 'te' because only b_5 with value 'pet' does not contain 'te'. For the longer values, p_1 and p_{10} can only encode the q-grams 'se' or 'en' because only b_1 with value 'petersen' (containing both 'se' and 'en') has a 1-bit in these two bit positions, while p_3 can also encode 'rs' because it occurs in both 'peters' and 'petersen' (b_1 and b_3).

make every combination of attribute values less common and thus results in less frequency information that can be exploited by an attack. This attack, as all previously discussed ones, will not work if each Bloom filter in an encoded database is unique. We discuss this issue in more detail in Section 9.6.

9.3 Pattern Mining based Cryptanalysis Attacks

This attack [123, 629] is, at the time of writing, one of the most practical and most advanced attack methods proposed in the context of Bloom filter encoding for linking sensitive databases. As can be seen from Table 9.1, this attack does require the least amount of knowledge from the adversary, and it is computationally efficient and can thus be applied on large encoded databases such as those that likely occur in practical applications where sensitive databases need to be linked.

The most important advantage of this attack method over all previous attacks is however that it neither requires frequent Bloom filters nor frequent plaintext values. Instead of exploiting the frequent bit patterns resulting from frequent plaintext values, the attack uses the frequencies of individual q-grams as they occur across many values in the quasi-identifying attributes

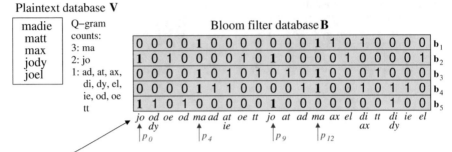

(q−grams only shown for illustration, but not known to the adversary)

Fig. 9.4 Outline of the pattern mining based cryptanalysis attack on Bloom filter encodings (adapted from [123, 629]). Given the list of plaintext values on the left, the extracted corresponding q-grams and their frequencies (as the number of plaintext values that contain the q-gram), and the set of Bloom filters on the right, the attack first identifies that bit positions p_4 and p_{12} have co-occurring 1-bits in the same three Bloom filters b_1, b_3, and b_4. Therefore, these two positions must encode 'ma' which is the only q-gram that occurs in three plaintext values. Next, the attack finds that positions p_0 and p_9 must encode 'jo' because they have co-occurring 1-bits in the same two Bloom filters b_2 and b_5, and 'jo' is the only q-gram that occurs in two plaintext values. Based on these two frequent q-grams and their identified bit positions, an adversary has now learnt that Bloom filters b_2 and b_5 can only encode 'jody' or 'joel', while b_1, b_3, and b_4 can encode 'madie', 'matt', or 'max'.

encoded into Bloom filters. As a result, this attack can be successful even when each Bloom filter in an encoded database is unique and no two Bloom filters have the same 0- and 1-bit pattern. No previous attack method would work in such a situation.

The attack employs frequent pattern mining techniques [8, 98] to identify the maximal co-occurring frequent bit positions with the same pattern in a Bloom filter database that must correspond to a q-gram that occurs frequently in a plaintext database. Frequent pattern mining is a data mining technique commonly used for market basket analysis to, for example, identify which shopping items are commonly purchased together by customers. This is used by supermarkets for marketing purposes such as loyalty cards, or to locate items that are frequently purchased together as far away as possible from each other in their shops to encourage shoppers to walk past a large number of other products (which they do not really need) in hope to increase their sales.

As illustrated in Figure 9.4, in the context of attacking Bloom filters, the items to be mined correspond to bit positions, and each Bloom filter becomes a set of items (its 1-bit positions). Given that Bloom filter encoding in general is based on hashing each element in a set k times, with $k > 1$, there should be k bit positions that have 1-bits in all the Bloom filters that encode a certain q-gram. If a q-gram occurs in many attribute values encoded into Bloom filters, then the same 1-bit pattern for this q-gram must occur in all the Bloom filters that encode the q-gram. This is true even if each Bloom filter in a database has a unique bit pattern (as in the example in Figure 9.4). In the following we describe this attack in more detail, and then discuss its limitations.

- **Preliminaries and Assumptions:** While this attack is independent of the encoding function and its parameters used, as with most other attacks, the attack assumes that the adversary has access to a database of encoded Bloom filters, $\mathbf{B}$, and a plaintext database, $\mathbf{V}$, which can be a publicly available population database such as a telephone directory or a voter database. The attack also assumes that the adversary can guess the type of attribute(s) encoded into Bloom filters by analysing the Hamming weight (number of 1-bits) distribution of Bloom filters in $\mathbf{B}$ because the quasi-identifying attribute(s) encoded in a Bloom filter database provide a distinctive distributions of their 1-bits [548]. Unlike previous attack methods which exploit the bit patterns in and between Bloom filters that occur frequently in $\mathbf{B}$, this attack explores the co-occurrence of 1-bits between Bloom filter bit positions without requiring frequent Bloom filters.

- **Attack Methodology:** The attack consists of two main steps.

  1. Frequently co-occurring bit position patterns in a Bloom filter database, $\mathbf{B}$, are identified and aligned with frequent q-grams using a pattern mining algorithm.

     The attack first calculates the frequencies of all q-grams in the plaintext database as the number of records where their attribute values(s) contain that certain q-gram. Then, the two most frequent q-grams, q_1 and q_2, and their respective frequencies, f_1 and f_2, are identified. The frequency difference, f_d, between q_1 and q_2 is calculated as:

     $$f_d = \frac{2(f_1 - f_2)}{f_1 + f_2} \cdot 100. \tag{9.2}$$

     If this frequency difference is higher than a user provided threshold, d, then this indicates that the Bloom filters that can encode q_1 must occur more often than the Bloom filters that can encode q_2. Therefore, if $f_d \geq d$, the attack applies pattern mining to the Bloom filter database, $\mathbf{B}$, to identify frequently co-occurring bit position patterns. The attack employs the Max-Miner algorithm [46], which is specialised in efficiently identifying the longest frequent patterns. In the case of this attack, the longest pattern will likely be of length k, the number of hash functions used to hash q-grams into Bloom filters. Due to collisions (where multiple hash functions map a q-gram to the same bit position), however, potentially less than k bit positions will encode a certain q-gram [123, 629].

     From the identified frequently co-occurring bit positions, the maximal frequent bit pattern, $\mathbf{b}_{max}$, is selected based on the frequencies and lengths of those patterns, where $\mathbf{b}_{max}$ consists of a set of bit positions, p_i, where $0 \leq i < l$ (and l is the length of the Bloom filters). $\mathbf{b}_{max}$ is then assigned to the most frequent q-gram, q_1, identified before.

For example, as illustrated in Figure 9.4, the attack identifies that bit positions p_4 and p_{12} must encode 'ma', because three Bloom filters have 1-bits in these two bit positions and the only q-gram that occurs in three plaintext values is 'ma'.

To identify the next frequent q-gram, the attack repeats the above process, where all previously identified and assigned sets of bit positions and q-grams are masked so they are not included in the next iteration. This process is repeated as long as the differences f_d between the frequencies of q-grams are above the threshold d and the number of Bloom filters available (not masked) is large enough. At the end of the first step of this attack, the adversary has obtained a set of q-grams where each has a set of bit positions assigned to it. Experiments conducted on large real-world databases showed that the accuracy of the identified bit positions for these q-grams is very high [629].

2. In the second step, the attack initially determines, for each Bloom filter, a set of possible q-grams, $\mathbf{q}^+$, and a set of not possible q-grams, $\mathbf{q}^-$, by referring to the identified q-grams and their assigned bit positions from the first step. The q-grams in $\mathbf{q}^-$ are identified based on having at least one 0 bit in one of those bit positions where frequent q-grams were assigned to in the first step. Then, for each unique possible q-gram set, $\mathbf{q}^+$, the attack obtains a set of plaintext values that contain all the q-grams in $\mathbf{q}^+$. After that, Bloom filters and sets of plaintext values are aligned using the possible q-gram sets assigned to them, such that every Bloom filter, $\mathbf{b} \in \mathbf{B}$, will have a set of plaintext values, $\mathbf{v} \subseteq \mathbf{V}$, that possibly have been encoded in this Bloom filter. Using the not possible q-gram sets, $\mathbf{q}^-$, assigned to each Bloom filter before, the attack then removes those plaintext values from $\mathbf{v}$ which contain any of the q-grams in $\mathbf{q}^-$. At the end of this process each Bloom filter in $\mathbf{B}$ will have a set of plaintext values assigned to it.

- **Limitations:** According to the experimental evaluation presented [123, 629], overall the proposed attack achieved high precision (the bit positions identified for q-grams are mostly correct) and recall (most true bit positions of q-grams are correctly identified) results of over 0.85 in the first step for encodings where up to four quasi-identifying attributes being hashed into Bloom filters. For the second step, depending upon parameter settings, the attack was able to exactly or partially reidentify between around 50% to over 90% of attribute values encoded into Bloom filters. When compared to the earlier attack by Christen et al. [119, 120] described in Section 9.2.3, this pattern mining based attack works even when multiple quasi-identifying attributes have been encoded into a single Bloom filter, and when every Bloom filter in a database has a unique bit pattern. In such a situation all earlier proposed attacks would fail. However, this pattern mining based attack fails when some of the hardening techniques which we describe in Section 9.5 are applied on Bloom filters.

9.4 Graph based Cryptanalysis Attacks

While the attack methods described in the previous two sections exploit the fact that frequent attribute values or frequent q-grams result in frequent bit patterns in an encoded Bloom filter database, we next describe two different types of attacks that either build a graph of the possible q-grams encoded into one single Bloom filter, or a graph with the similarities calculated between Bloom filters. Both these approaches lead to interesting novel attack methods.

9.4.1 Q-gram Graph based Attack

A novel attack on Bloom filters based on a graph traversal mechanism was proposed by Michell et al. [415]. In order for this attack to be possible, it assumes that the adversary has access to the complete Bloom filter encoding information. This includes knowledge of any preprocessing steps applied on the values to be encoded, and of all Bloom filter parameter settings used (the number of hash functions k, the actual hash functions, the q-gram length q, the hashing and encoding technique employed, and the shared secret key used, as we discussed in Sections 8.2 and 8.3). Furthermore, in order to achieve high reidentification accuracy the attack assumes that padded q-grams are being used, as we described in Section 6.8.1, because otherwise the generated q-gram graphs will likely become too ambiguous, as we discuss below.

Using a brute force method the attack first identifies all possible q-grams that could have been mapped into a certain Bloom filter by analysing the 1-bit pattern of the Bloom filter. Similar to the atoms based attack method [367, 438] described in Section 9.2.2, the attack first hashes each unique q-gram extracted from a large database that contains the same values as those that are encoded in the Bloom filter database. For each q-gram x its corresponding atomic Bloom filter, $\mathbf{b}_x$ is generated. This means only the q-gram x is hashed into the Bloom filter $\mathbf{b}_x$, as we described in Section 9.2.2.

Then, for a given Bloom filter, $\mathbf{b}$, where it is unknown what value was hashed into it, the atomic Bloom filters of all unique q-grams are compared using the bitwise AND operation, as shown in the AND Table on page xxii.

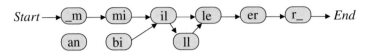

Fig. 9.5 Example q-gram graph for the q-gram set $\{\_m, an, bi, er, il, le, ll, mi, r\_\}$, where the underscore symbol ($\_$) indicates a padded q-gram extracted from the beginning or end of a string value. Based on this q-gram graph, both 'miller' and 'miler' are possible values encoded in the corresponding Bloom filter, however not 'biler' or 'biller' because there is no corresponding padded starting q-gram. Furthermore, while 'an' could have been encoded into the corresponding Bloom filter based on its 1-bit positions, it is not connected to any other q-gram and thus it is unlikely encoded in the Bloom filter from which this q-gram set was generated.

If all 1-bits in the atomic Bloom filter $\mathbf{b}_x$ for q-gram x are also set to 1 in $\mathbf{b}$ (formally: $\mathbf{b} \wedge \mathbf{b}_x = \mathbf{b}_x$), then $\mathbf{b}$ can encode the q-gram x. As a result, for a given Bloom filter, the set of all possible q-grams that could have been encoded in this Bloom filter can be identified.

Using this set of possible q-grams encoded into a Bloom filter, the second step of the attack then aims to find the actual possible plaintext values (strings) that could have been encoded in this Bloom filter. A directed graph is therefore generated from this q-gram set, as illustrated in Figure 9.5. As can be seen, a directed edge is included in this graph for every possible consecutive q-gram pair.

From such a q-gram graph, all possible plaintext values (or words) from a plaintext database that can be generated can now be identified as all possible paths from start to end. In a final step, using a filtering approach the attack obtains the potential plaintext values that could have been encoded into each Bloom filter.

The evaluation of this attack on real-world data sets showed a 76.8% accuracy of correct one-to-one reidentifications. However, despite being efficient and accurate, this cryptanalysis attack has severe limitations, including the assumptions it makes about the prior knowledge of the adversary. The practical applicability of this attack is therefore limited to those situations where an adversary has access to all parameters and settings used to encode values into Bloom filters. One possible such situation is a two-party protocol (as discussed in Section 4.3) where both parties (database owners) have knowledge of all encoding parameters but they do not know each other's full encoded Bloom filter databases. This attack shows that exchanging a Bloom filter database across parties will possibly allow successful reidentification of the majority of encoded sensitive values if the parties know the encoding parameters that were used to generate the Bloom filter databases.

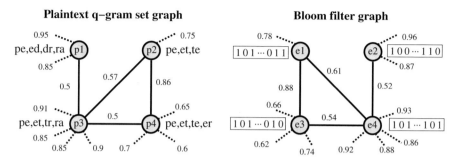

Fig. 9.6 Example of the similarity graph attack idea. The left side shows a subgraph of four q-gram sets and the similarities between them, while the right side shows a corresponding subgraph of four Bloom filters and the similarities between them, where we assume the Dice coefficient similarity was used to compare both q-gram sets and Bloom filters. As can be seen, and as expected, the Bloom filter similarities are higher than the q-gram set similarities because of collisions of 1-bits. However, the neighbourhood structures of these two subgraphs, such as the number of edges to other nodes and their similarities, reveal that node e1 must very likely correspond to node p2, node e2 to node p1, node e3 to node p4, and node e4 to node p3.

9.4.2 Similarity Graph based Attack

A very different type of attack that is independent of the actual encoding technique employed to link sensitive databases has been discussed by Culnane et al. [141] in the context of a pseudonymisation approach proposed by the UK's Office of National Statistics (ONS). The basic idea of the attack is that the organisation that is conducting the linkage of encoded sensitive databases can store all similarity calculations between encoded records (such as between Bloom filters), and then generate a similarity graph where encoded records are nodes and the similarities between them are weights of the edges of the graph. This is illustrated on the right side of Figure 9.6. Any encoding of records that allows approximate similarities to be calculated between encodings, as we discussed in Chapter 7, can potentially be attacked by this method.

As with all other attack methods, if one assumes the adversary has access to a plaintext database that contains values from the same quasi-identifying attribute(s), then the adversary can also calculate the similarities between these plaintext values, for example by converting them into q-grams and calculating the Dice coefficient similarities between q-gram sets, as shown on the left side of Figure 9.6.

Assuming two such graphs have been created, one from a plaintext database and one from an encoded database, respectively, then the attack becomes a graph matching problem where similar nodes are to be matched (or aligned) across the two graphs based on the similarity of their local graph structure. This can be accomplished using features such as the number of neighbours or the similarities to their neighbours. A large number of graph matching and graph alignment algorithms have been developed in research domains ranging from bioinformatics to multimedia information retrieval [189]. Many of these algorithms can be directly applied to identify nodes that have highly similar graph neighbourhoods.

Culnane et al. [141] applied such a graph matching attack on a publicly available list of nearly 400,000 surnames. This attack was able to match over 90% of nodes between the encoded and the plaintext graphs when the HMAC based encoding method (as discussed in Section 6.2.2) and similarity calculations proposed by the UK's ONS was employed to encode and compare these names.

Similar to the attack by Culnane et al. [141], Vidanage et al. [627] proposed an attack that can be applied on any privacy-preserving record linkage technique that calculates approximate similarities between records, and from where a similarity graph can be generated as shown in Figure 9.6. To overcome differences between the similarities calculated on plaintext values versus those calculated on encoded values, the authors applied a similarity alignment between these two similarity graphs. The attack generates various graph features that characterise the local neighbourhood of each node in a similarity graph, and employs locality sensitive hashing as a blocking step to make the graph alignment process more scalable to large data sets. The experimental evaluation showed that the attack can be successfully applied on similarity graphs generated by Bloom filer encoding, tabulation hashing as proposed by Smith [564], and two step-hashing as developed by Ranbaduge et al. [497] (we described both these hashing-based linkage techniques in Section 7.4).

9.5 Hardening Techniques for Bloom Filter Encoding

Bloom filter encoding in the context of linking sensitive databases was shown to be a promising approach, and this technique has now been used in several real-world privacy-preserving record linkage applications [84, 475, 480, 507]. However, privacy concerns still remain because of the vulnerabilities of Bloom filter encoding with regard to the different cryptanaysis attacks described in the previous sections. These vulnerabilities have been addressed in recent research through the development of several types of techniques that aim to harden Bloom filters in order to make them more resilient to these attacks.

The general idea of most hardening techniques is to somehow modify the bit patterns in Bloom filters to reduce the frequency information required by attacks while still allowing accurate approximate similarity calculations. It needs to be noted, however, that any hardening technique applied on Bloom filters can potentially lead to a reduction in linkage quality, as we empirically illustrate in Chapter 12. In the following we describe a set of recently proposed hardening techniques that have shown in empirical studies to reduce the

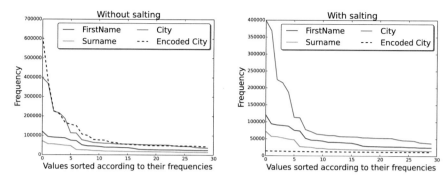

Fig. 9.7 The frequency distributions of plaintext values for the FIRSTNAME, SUR-NAME and CITY attributes, and hash encoded values of the CITY attribute, from a North Carolina Voter Registration database [111], where the plaintext database was from April 2014 and the encoded database was from April 2019. Frequencies for only the thirty most common values are shown (note the different scales on the vertical axis). The left side shows unsalted frequency distributions while the right side shows distributions where the year of birth value of a record was used as the salt concatenated with a corresponding CITY value when this attribute was hash encoded using HMAC (as we discussed in Section 6.2.2). As can be seen, salting significantly reduces the amount of frequency information that would be available to an adversary.

vulnerabilities of Bloom filter encoding. Novel hardening techniques based on new ideas will likely be developed in the future.

We start with salting, which is not a Bloom filter specific technique but can be applied on other encoding techniques as well. Then we describe hardening techniques that modify the 0- and 1-bit pattern in a Bloom filter irrespective of its actual content (balancing, XOR-folding, and Rule 90), followed by hardening techniques that modify a Bloom filter based on its 0- and 1-bit pattern (adding random noise, Bloom and flip, rehashing, and Markov chaining).

9.5.1 Salting

Salting is a hardening technique proposed by Niedermeyer et al. [438] to avoid reidentification attacks on Bloom filters by adding an extra string value to each q-gram before it is hashed, where these string values are very specific for an individual entity and do not change over time. Examples of salting values can be the year of birth, the full date of birth, or the birth place of an individual. Instead of hashing individual q-grams into Bloom filters as described in Sections 8.2 and 8.3, salted q-grams are hashed. As a result, frequent values such as common first name or surnames will not all result in the same Bloom filter bit pattern, but rather differently salted q-gram sets will lead to different bit patterns.

This means, for example, that for two individuals with first name 'john', while their corresponding q-gram sets will be the same (for example with $q = 2$ they will be {jo, oh, hn}), their salted q-gram values will be different if they were born in different years and year of birth is used as the salting attribute. For example, the q-gram 'jo' will become 'jo1968' and 'jo1971' if the birth years of two different John's are 1968 and 1971, respectively. Therefore, these salted q-grams are highly likely hashed to different bit positions during the Bloom filter encoding process.

As we discussed in Section 9.2, exploiting frequency information is the main approach for many cryptanalysis attacks on Bloom filter encoding. With salting, most q-grams that are frequent if unsalted, will occur much less frequent once concatenated with a salting value. This should increase the resilience of Bloom filters hardened with salting to cryptanalysis attacks because there is less frequency information that can be exploited.

Salting can be applied to many forms of encoding, not just Bloom filters. For example, adding a record specific salt value to individual attribute values will significantly reduce the frequency of common attribute values. Figure 9.7 shows both the unsalted and salted frequency distributions of three attributes from a large public voter database [111] (the left side plot of this figure is the same as shown in Figure 5.2).

9.5.2 Balancing

Some known cryptanalysis attacks use the Hamming weight (the number of 1-bits) of a Bloom filter to identify possible bit patterns that can be aligned with frequencies of q-grams in plaintext attribute values [371, 438]. However, a set of Bloom filters, where each Bloom filter has the same constant Hamming weight (number of 1-bits), will potentially make the identification of certain frequent bit patterns more difficult. Therefore, attacks on such balanced Bloom filters will be more difficult than attacks on basic, not hardened Bloom filters [546].

As shown by Berger [56], the Hamming weight distribution of a set of binary strings can be made uniform by joining each binary string with its negated copy. Such bit patterns with constant Hamming weights are known as constant-weight or balanced codes [357]. Schnell and Borgs [546] proposed a hardening approach that uses such balancing of Bloom filters. In this approach a Bloom filter of length l bits is concatenated with its negated copy (all bits flipped, so a 0 becomes a 1 and a 1 becomes a 0), resulting in a new Bloom filter of length $2l$. To improve privacy, this balancing operation is followed by a random permutation (bits are reordered across positions) of the $2l$ bits, where all balanced Bloom filters in a set are permuted in the same way. As a result of this operation, all Bloom filters generated from a sensitive database will have exactly half of their bits set to 0 and half to 1 (have a uniform Hamming weight of l) and therefore less frequency information will be available that could be exploited.

For example, assuming a Bloom filter $\mathbf{b}$ of length $l = 5$ bits: $[1, 0, 0, 1, 1]$. To balance $\mathbf{b}$ we concatenate it with its negated copy, $[0, 1, 1, 0, 0]$, which results in a new balanced Bloom filter $\mathbf{b}_B = [1, 0, 0, 1, 1, 0, 1, 1, 0, 0]$. Then this balanced Bloom filter $\mathbf{b}_B$ is randomly permuted such that the final Bloom filter for example can become $\mathbf{b}_B = [0, 1, 1, 0, 1, 1, 0, 0, 1, 0]$. However, it should be noted that the increased length of balanced Bloom filters increases both computing time and memory requirements.

Compared to its original, a balanced Bloom filter will contain a larger number of 1-bits, some of them corresponding to the 0-bits in the original unbalanced Bloom filter. When the similarity between two balanced Bloom filters is calculated using the Dice coefficient similarity from Equation 8.3, different results might be obtained compared to the similarity between the corresponding original pair of Bloom filters. How exactly these similarities will differ depends on the ratio of 0- and 1-bits in the original Bloom filters. While no analysis of this effect has been formally published, some initial work has found the differences between the similarities of unbalanced and balanced Bloom filters to be very small[1].

It is easily possible to identify if a database of Bloom filters has been balanced by checking if all of their Hamming weights are $l/2$ when the length of these Bloom filters is l. Furthermore, it is also easy to identify the pairs of original and negated bit positions. First, the Bloom filter database is converted from one Bloom filter (bit vector) per row (record) to one bit vector per column (bit position), resulting in l new bit vectors if l is the total length of the Bloom filters. Now, pairs of bit positions can be identified that have complementary numbers of 1-bits (Hamming weights), and when the bitwise AND (as described under Notations on page xxii) is applied on such pairs of bit positions, then pairs that correspond to an original and its negated position will result in a bit vector that only contains 0 (has Hamming weight 0) because due to the balancing operation no Bloom filter can have either 0 or 1 in both an original and negated bit position. It is however not straightforward to then identify which of a pair of complementing bit positions is the original and which is the balanced one.

It has also been shown that some of the recently proposed cryptanalysis attacks, as discussed in the previous section, are able to successfully reidentify q-grams even after a set of Bloom filters has been balanced [119, 123].

---

[1]   See: https://medium.com/@wilko.henecka/similarity-metrics-of-balanced-bloom-filters-42b8f2f4f580

9.5.3 XOR-folding

The folding of a vector was initially proposed in health informatics to efficiently query fingerprints from large chemical databases [99]. Schnell and Borgs [547] proposed a Bloom filter hardening technique that uses vector folding combined with a bitwise XOR (exclusive OR) operation to improve the privacy of attribute values encoded in Bloom filters. The outcomes of a bitwise XOR operation are provided under Notations on page xxii.

As proposed by Schnell and Borgs [547], a Bloom filter $\mathbf{b}$ of length l is first divided into two halves, $\mathbf{b}_1$ and $\mathbf{b}_2$, each of length $l/2$, where $\mathbf{b}_1[i] = \mathbf{b}[i]$ and $\mathbf{b}_2[i] = \mathbf{b}[i + l/2]$, with $0 \leq i < l/2$. Then, the two Bloom filters $\mathbf{b}_1$ and $\mathbf{b}_2$ are combined into a new Bloom filter $\mathbf{b}_F$ of length $l/2$ by applying the bitwise XOR operation $\oplus$ on each bit $0 \leq i < l/2$:

$$\mathbf{b}_F[i] = \mathbf{b}_1[i] \oplus \mathbf{b}_2[i], \tag{9.3}$$

where for one bit the XOR operation has the outcomes shown in the XOR table on page xxii:

$$
\begin{array}{ll}
0 \oplus 0 = 0, & 1 \oplus 0 = 1, \\
0 \oplus 1 = 1, & 1 \oplus 1 = 0.
\end{array}
\tag{9.4}
$$

As can be seen from these outcomes, after an XOR operation has been applied on a bit position it is not possible to recover the original two input bit values. This will provide more resilience of a set of such hardened Bloom filters with regard to the cryptanalysis attacks described in the previous section. However, XOR-folding will likely also lead to a reduction of linkage quality because information about two bit positions (that each likely encode multiple q-grams) is combined and shorter Bloom filters are being generated. The reduction of linkage quality can be overcome by initially generating basic Bloom filters double as long, of length $2l$, to be folded into hardened Bloom filters of length l.

For example, assuming a Bloom filter $\mathbf{b}$ of length $l = 10$ bits: $[1, 0, 0, 1, 0, 1, 0, 1, 0, 1]$. We divide $\mathbf{b}$ into its two halves which are $\mathbf{b}_1 = [1, 0, 0, 1, 0]$ and $\mathbf{b}_2 = [1, 0, 1, 0, 1]$. Then $\mathbf{b}_1$ and $\mathbf{b}_2$ are combined using the bitwise XOR operation resulting in the folded Bloom filter $\mathbf{b}_F = [0, 0, 1, 1, 1]$.

Applying the XOR operation on bits ensures that it is not possible to recover the bit values in the original Bloom filters. Ranbaduge and Schnell [500] further investigated how the XOR operation applied on bits can be used to harden Bloom filters while ensuring there is no reduction in linkage quality. In their work they proposed two approaches where the XOR operation is applied on neighbouring bits in a Bloom filter to generate new bit values. The first approach uses two sliding windows of a certain length that are iteratively moved along the original Bloom filter. In each iteration the bit patterns that are extracted from each window are combined using the XOR

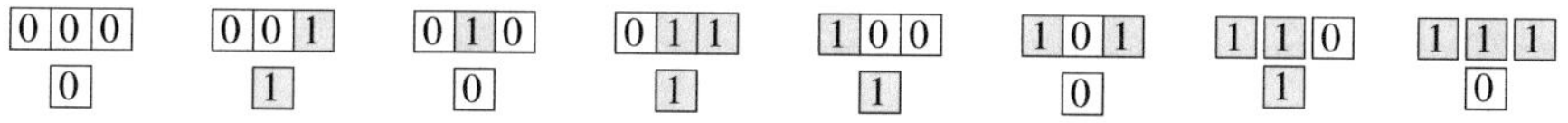

0 0 0	0 0 1	0 1 0	0 1 1	1 0 0	1 0 1	1 1 0	1 1 1
0	1	0	1	1	0	1	0

Fig. 9.8 The transformation rules for the Rule 90 Bloom filter hardening technique, as described in Section 9.5.4 (adapted from [548]). The top row corresponds to all possible 3-bit input patterns from a Bloom filter and the bottom row are the modified (hardened) centre bits, where dark cells refer to 1-bits and white cells to 0-bits.

operation, resulting in new bit values that are used to set the positions in the hardened Bloom filter. The second approach uses an iterative random sampling process with replacement to select bits upon which the XOR operation is then applied. In each iteration two bit positions in the original Bloom filter are selected and their bit values are combined using XOR to generate a bit value which is used to set a position in the hardened Bloom filter. This sampling process is performed l times to generate a hardened Bloom filter of length l. An empirical evaluation using several real data sets has shown that the proposed two approaches can provide strong privacy against frequency attacks [119, 120] while not resulting in a reduction of linkage quality.

9.5.4 Rule 90

Wolfram's Rule 90 is a rule used for cellular automata [648] that is based on the bitwise exclusive OR (XOR) function (see Equation 9.4 for the possible outcomes of the XOR bit operation) of two bits in a bit vector used to generate a new bit vector, as illustrated in Figure 9.8. Schnell and Borgs [548] proposed to use Rule 90 as a hardening technique for Bloom filter encoding in the context of linking sensitive databases because, like XOR-folding, it is a non-reversible process.

Each bit position p, with $0 \leq p < l$, in a Bloom filter of length l is modified by assessing the bits at positions $(p-1)\ mod\ l$ and $(p+1)\ mod\ l$, where the modulo (mod) function is used to 'wrap around' the input bits of the first and last positions in a Bloom filter. The two input bits for the new bit at position $p = 0$ are $p = l - 1$ and $p = 1$, while the two input bits for the new bit at position $p = l - 1$ are $p = l - 2$ and $p = 0$. The new value of bit position p, with $0 \leq p < l$, for the hardened Bloom filter $\mathbf{b}_H$ is calculated as (assuming $\mathbf{b}$ is the basic input Bloom filter):

$$\mathbf{b}_H[p] = \mathbf{b}[(p-1)\ mod\ l] \ \oplus \ \mathbf{b}[(p+1)\ mod\ l]. \tag{9.5}$$

For example, assume a Bloom filter $\mathbf{b}$ of length $l = 5$ bits $[1, 0, 0, 1, 0]$. To transform $\mathbf{b}$ according to Rule 90, the first and last bits are treated as adjacent bits which results in an extended Bloom filter of length $l = 7$: $\mathbf{b}_E = [0, 1, 0, 0, 1, 0, 1]$. Then this extended Bloom filter is transformed based on Rule 90 such that the resulting hardened Bloom filter becomes $\mathbf{b}_H = [0, 1, 1, 0, 0]$.

9.5.5 Adding Random Noise

One can think of a most basic hardening technique which is to add random noise to a Bloom filter [538]. Adding random noise to encode information has been proposed as an alternative to encryption in the context of computer security. Known as chaffing [518], the idea is to hide a secret message by randomly adding pieces of information to a message. Confidentiality is achieved because it will be difficult for an adversary to distinguish the actual information from the randomly added information.

In the context of hardening Bloom filters, the most simple way to add random noise is to flip certain bit positions (from 0 to 1 or from 1 to 0) in each Bloom filter at random after the Bloom filter has been generated. Alternatively, when encoding textual data, one could randomly add or remove q-grams into a q-gram set before the set is being encoded into a Bloom filter. More advanced approaches can take the frequency of q-grams into account and remove or add only rare q-grams, similar to how certain bits are being removed in the record level Bloom filter encoding approach [178] described in Section 8.3.3.

The introduction of random noise, either by flipping bits or adding or removing q-grams prior to their hashing, will influence the similarity calculations between Bloom filters and thus the quality of the obtained links between encoded records. A set of experiments conducted on 10,000 Bloom filters indicated that random modifications of up to 5% of bits in Bloom filters result in only minor degradation of linkage quality [538]. A potentially more important question is how much more privacy, for example with regard to the attack methods described earlier in this chapter, does the addition of random noise provide, and if there is a way to clearly quantify any additional privacy based on the amount of noise added to Bloom filters.

We next discuss a more principled way to add random noise using a differential privacy mechanism.

9.5.6 Bloom and Flip

Similar to randomly adding noise to Bloom filters as described in Section 9.5.5, BLoom and flIP (known as BLIP) [12, 13] is a hardening technique which flips bit values at certain positions in a Bloom filter according to a differential privacy mechanism [181], as we discussed in Section 6.3.3.

Table 9.2 Number of 1-bits in a Bloom filter of length $l = 1,000$ bits after hardening with the two BLIP approaches described in Section 9.5.6 for different fill percentages (number of 1-bits) in the original Bloom filter and different flip probabilities, p_f.

Fill percentage (%)	25 (250 1-bits)			50 (500 1-bits)			75 (750 1-bits)		
Flip probability, p_f	0.05	0.1	0.2	0.05	0.1	0.2	0.05	0.1	0.2
Equation 9.6 [13]	275	300	350	500	500	500	725	700	650
Equation 9.7 [190]	262.5	275	300	500	500	500	737.5	725	700

This approach is similar to the RAPPOR method [190] which is being used for example in Web browsers to anonymously collect user browsing statistics.

The BLIP approach was originally developed as a non-interactive differentially private [181] method to randomise Bloom filters in the context of privacy-preserving comparisons of user profiles in social networks [13]. The idea is to randomly flip bits at certain positions in a Bloom filter based on a user defined flip probability. We refer the interested reader to Alaggan et al. [13] for a theoretical analysis and proof showing that BLIP fulfills non-interactive differential privacy. Schnell and Borgs [546] were the first to explore BLIP in the context of linking sensitive databases.

For a given bit flipping probability, p_f, following Alaggan et al. [13], a bit $\mathbf{b}[p]$ in a Bloom filter $\mathbf{b}$ at position p is flipped according to:

$$\mathbf{b}_H[p] = \begin{cases} 1 & \text{if } \mathbf{b}[p] = 0 \text{ with probability } p_f, \\ 0 & \text{if } \mathbf{b}[p] = 1 \text{ with probability } p_f, \\ \mathbf{b}[p] & \text{with probability } 1 - p_f. \end{cases} \quad (9.6)$$

Applying Equation 9.6 on all bit positions of a Bloom filter results in a new hardened Bloom filter $\mathbf{b}_H$.

Rather than using Alaggan's approach, Schnell and Borgs [546] applied the BLIP method proposed by Erlingsson et al. [190]. Assuming again a flip probability p_f, the new bit $\mathbf{b}_H[p]$ at position p in the new hardened Bloom filter $\mathbf{b}_H$ is flipped from $\mathbf{b}[p]$ according to:

$$\mathbf{b}_H[p] = \begin{cases} 1 & \text{with probability } \frac{1}{2}p_f, \\ 0 & \text{with probability } \frac{1}{2}p_f, \\ \mathbf{b}[p] & \text{with probability } 1 - p_f. \end{cases} \quad (9.7)$$

For example, if the flip probability is set to $p_f = 0.05$ for a Bloom filter of length $l = 1,000$ bits, then around 50 bits will be randomly selected and flipped using the first approach from Equation 9.6, while the rest are unchanged. On the other hand, with the approach used by Schnell and Borgs [546] in Equation 9.7, bits are not flipped according to their original state in the Bloom filter $\mathbf{b}$, rather the bits at around 50 randomly selected positions are either set to 0 or 1 with equal probability. As a result, depending

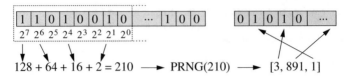

Fig. 9.9 Example of the rehashing hardening technique, where a window of size $w = 8$ bits (left side) is used to generate an integer value (210), which is then used as the seed for a pseudo-random number generator (PRNG) for the generation of a sequence of $k_{re} = 3$ random numbers in the range of the Bloom filter length, and the corresponding bits in a new Bloom filter are set to 1 (right side).

upon which BLIP approach is used to harden Bloom filters, the numbers of 1-bits in a hardened Bloom filter will likely differ, as can be seen in Table 9.2.

Furthermore, if a Bloom filter has less than 50% 1-bits then applying Equation 9.6 will mean the resulting hardened Bloom filter will have more 1-bits compared to when applying Equation 9.7, because the bit flipping of the latter equation is independent of the percentage of 1-bits in the original Bloom filter. This effect is reversed if a Bloom filter has more than 50% of its bits set to 1. Therefore, depending upon the percentages of 1-bits in Bloom filters, applying either of the two different BLIP methods can result in an increase or decrease of the similarities calculated between Bloom filters that were randomised using the BLIP hardening technique.

Recent work by Vaiwsri et al. [607] has investigated the linkage quality that can be obtained from Bloom filter databases hardened with both BLIP methods described above. This work found that BLIP hardening can lower linkage quality especially as the flip probability p_f is increased. With some settings of p_f, recall (the percentage of true matching records identified) dropped significantly, leading to almost no true matches being found. As a way to overcome this drawback of BLIP hardening, the improvement by Vaiwsri et al. [607] was based on reference values (as we discussed in Section 7.5). Their approach randomises highly similar values encoded in Bloom filters using the same reference values as the seeds for the randomisation process. A pseudo-random number generator (PRNG) was employed to randomly generate the sequence of bit positions to randomise. We have discussed the process of generating sequences of random numbers using PRNG in Section 6.1. This approach was able to increase linkage quality for most BLIP parameter settings [607].

9.5.7 Rehashing

Instead of hardening Bloom filters by randomly flipping bits, the rehashing hardening technique uses several bits from a Bloom filter to generate a new set of bits. Proposed by Schnell [538], the idea is to slide a window of width w bits (with proposed values in the range $8 \leq w \leq 16$) over a Bloom filter,

Fig. 9.10 An example of the transition graph for q-gram 'jo' in the centre, as used for Markov chain Bloom filter hardening.

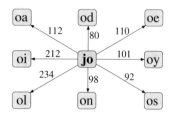

where the window is moved s (the step size) bits forward in each step. The bits in a window are used to calculate an integer value, as is illustrated in Figure 9.9, where this value is then used as the seed for a PRNG.

A sequence of k_{re} random numbers $[p_1, p_2, \ldots, p_{k_{re}}]$, each in the range $0 \leq p_i < l$, where l is the length of the hardened Bloom filter, is then generated by the PRNG. These numbers p_i will be used as the bit positions to set to 1 in the new hardened Bloom filter[2].

Experimental results suggested that the quality of linked records based on Bloom filters generated by the rehashing technique is highly dependent on the choice of the window size, w, step size, s, and the number of positions generated in each step, k_{re} [538]. Optimising these three parameters will depend upon the values and parameter settings that were used to generate the original Bloom filters. However, given that the resulting hardened Bloom filters will have no bit patterns where 1-bits directly correlate to individual input elements (q-grams), they will be very difficult to attack with current cryptanalysis attack methods.

9.5.8 Markov Chaining

Markov Chaining based hardening for Bloom filter encoding was proposed by Schnell et al. [553] to avoid frequency-based attacks on q-grams encoded into Bloom filters. The idea of this technique is to encode additional q-grams into a Bloom filter randomly based on their frequent co-occurrences with the q-grams of the quasi-identifying attribute value(s) that are encoded into that Bloom filter. A probabilistic language model [401] of q-grams is built from a large list of attribute values, which are assumed to be the values to be encoded into Bloom filters, or values from a large plaintext database from the same domain. Important is that all database owners that encode and harden their Bloom filters use the same list of such values to ensure they all have the same language model. Alternatively, the language model is being built by one party of a linkage protocol and then distributed to all other parties to be used in Markov chain hardening.

---

[2] Technically, the hardened bit vector is not a Bloom filter because its 1 bits do not correspond to individual elements (q-grams) of the hashed input set.

The probabilistic language model conceptually builds one star graph for each unique q-gram, extracted from all values in the plaintext database, as illustrated in Figure 9.10, where the q-gram is the centre node in its graph. For each unique q-gram, a list of other q-grams is generated where these other q-grams are those that occur frequently directly after the given q-gram in plaintext values. For example, for the value 'john' with its bigram list ($q = 2$) [jo, oh, hn], for the q-gram 'jo' the subsequent q-gram is 'oh', while for 'oh' its subsequent q-gram is 'hn'. The number of times a certain q-gram is followed by another q-gram in all plaintext values is counted, and the total number of these occurrences become the edge weights of these star graphs, as can be seen in Figure 9.10. For example, the q-gram 'ol' occurred after 'jo' in 234 plaintext values, while 'oi' occurred 212 times, and so on.

During the Markov chain hardening step, for each unique q-gram in a set of q-grams to be encoded into a Bloom filter, we then randomly select c other q-grams based on their probability to occur after this q-gram, where c is the chain length parameter that is used in the Markov chain hardening technique. When applying Markov chain hardening, for each original q-gram extracted from a quasi-identifying attribute value to be encoded, we find $c \geq 1$ such other q-grams and we then encode these extra q-grams into the same Bloom filter as the original q-grams. Values of $1 \leq c \leq 4$ were proposed by Schnell et al. [553], where larger values of c will result in more distorted frequency distributions and thus improved resilience with regard to frequency-based cryptanalysis attacks.

For example, assuming again the value 'john' is being encoded into a Bloom filter, setting $c = 2$, and assuming we have the following other q-grams and their counts for 'jo' from Figure 9.10: 'ol' (234), 'oi' (212), 'oa' (112), 'oe' (110), 'oy' (101), 'on' (98), 'os' (92), and 'od' (80). Then, for the original q-gram 'jo', the q-gram 'ol' is more than twice as likely to be randomly selected than 'oa' (and nearly three times as likely as 'od') to be added to the selected q-grams of the q-gram set that will be encoded into the Bloom filter that will represent 'john'.

As a result of this Markov chain hardening approach, for a certain q-gram that is common in two q-gram sets (that are to be encoded into two Bloom filters which will then be compared), the additional extra q-grams added will likely be similar because based on the language model those q-grams that occur more likely after a certain q-gram have a higher chance to be randomly selected for encoding. Therefore, the Markov chain hardening technique should not significantly change the number of common q-grams for similar attribute values to be encoded. On the other hand, for different original q-gram sets different additional q-grams will likely be added. Overall, the added extra q-grams will distort the frequency distribution of q-grams and therefore make any frequency-based cryptanalysis attack on such hardened Bloom filters more difficult.

9.6 Recommended Best Practice for Bloom Filter Hardening

As we have discussed in this chapter, the general method of encoding sensitive data using Bloom filters to allow their linking across databases, while being efficient and allowing approximate matching, has various weaknesses. In recent times these have been exploited by researchers who have developed a variety of cryptanalysis attacks that are aimed at reidentifying sensitive values encoded into Bloom filters. While the majority of these attacks requires significant knowledge of the encoding process by an adversary, or they have other limitations (as summarised in Table 9.1), this is an active area of research where novel attacks are being developed.

The aim of these attacks is to illustrate the limits of encodings methods, such as Bloom filter encoding, and prevent insecure methods being implemented in practical linkage applications where real damage could be done if actual sensitive values about individuals or organisations could be reidentified from encoded databases.

While a variety of hardening techniques have been proposed to make Bloom filter encoding more resilient to the so far developed attack methods, at the time of writing none of these hardening technique has shown to provide provable security with regard to any current attack method. We however note that provable security might not be required for certain privacy legislation. Furthermore, as empirical evaluations have shown, some combinations of hardening techniques can result in encoded sensitive databases where up to now no cryptanalysis attack has been successful in reidentifying any sensitive values.

It is therefore difficult to provide definite recommendations about how to make Bloom filter encoding secure and resilient to both current and any potential future attack methods that might be developed. Because the 0- and 1-bit patterns in Bloom filters directly reflect the characteristics of the input sets that were hashed into Bloom filters (most commonly sets of q-grams extracted from strings), these patterns can be aligned with the frequencies of common values as well as common elements (q-grams), and the correlations between such elements as they occur in the encodings that represent sensitive plaintext values.

The main aim of hardening techniques is therefore to break down the frequencies of and the correlations between bit patterns. By doing so, many of these techniques however also distort the patterns used to calculate similarities between Bloom filters. Therefore, there is a trade-off between linkage quality and resilience with regard to cryptanalysis attacks when hardened Bloom filters are used to link sensitive data [500].

In combination with the recommendations provided in Section 8.6 for basic Bloom filter encoding, given the current state of hardening techniques as well as cryptanalysis attack methods, we provide the following recommendations:

- If a suitable attribute is available in the databases to be linked, then salting as described in Section 9.5.1 should be applied. Salting does not introduce randomness into the bit patterns in Bloom filters, rather it generates different bit patterns for different subsets of encoded values that have the same value in a salting attribute (for example the same year of birth). The requirement of the values in a salting attribute to be accurate, stable, and complete, might however make this hardening technique difficult to apply. Attributes with a small number of possible values, such as gender, are also not suitable because they do not allow a large enough number of different patterns to be generated.

- In the absence of a suitable attribute for salting, a careful investigation of different other hardening techniques is required. Ideally, such an investigation involves both the evaluation of linkage quality (which would require a ground truth data set of true matched and true non-matched record pairs) and resilience to cryptanalysis attacks (by running all relevant existing attack methods on the encoded and hardened databases). Combined, this will provide information about which hardening technique with which parameter settings leads to still acceptable linkage quality as well as strong enough privacy protection.

At the time of writing, we do not believe that we are in a position to recommend any of the presented hardening techniques to be the one of choice for any situation where sensitive databases are to be linked. The choice depends upon the characteristics and sensitivity of the data to be linked, and the requirements of the linkage application. We encourage the interested reader to follow research on this topic, both about newly developed cryptanalysis attack methods and improved hardening techniques, and even novel encoding methods for linking sensitive databases.

9.7 Summary and Further Reading

In the first half of this chapter we have presented various cryptanalysis attack methods that have been developed with the aim to reidentify sensitive values encoded in Bloom filter databases. These attacks have highlighted shortcomings in the privacy protection provided by some of the basic Bloom filter encoding techniques covered in Chapter 8. To overcome such attacks, a diverse range of hardening techniques have been proposed as we discussed in the second part of this chapter.

Research on both attack methods as well as hardening techniques has only been conducted in recent years, and novel attack ideas and hardening techniques are likely to be proposed in the future. Besides the actual scientific papers which proposed, described, and evaluated individual attack methods or hardening techniques, so far no survey paper has been published that covers these topics. Furthermore, experimental evaluations have been isolated with only few publications comparatively evaluating more than one attack method on the same or at least comparable databases [119, 500, 629]. We are also not aware of any commercially or freely available software products that implement the described cryptanalysis attacks. More research and development is required to ensure the advantages and limitations of both attack methods and hardening techniques are better understood.

Chapter 10
Computational Efficiency

Abstract As the sensitive databases held by many organisations are getting larger, linking them can become computationally more challenging. Techniques known as blocking, indexing, and filtering have been developed and are being used to make linkage techniques more scalable. In this chapter we describe a variety of such techniques, as well as methods for linking large sensitive databases on modern parallel computing platforms and distributed environments. We also discuss scalability aspects when multiple (more than two) databases are to be linked, and the challenges involved when many, possibly hundreds or even thousands, of databases need to be linked.

10.1 Blocking and Indexing Techniques

As we described in Section 3.2, blocking or indexing techniques are generally employed to facilitate the linkage of large databases that potentially can contain many millions of records [461]. We note that the terminology for this step of the record linkage process can be ambiguous across different disciplines, and we refer the reader to Section 3.2 on page 51 for a discussion, and to the glossary for a more detailed description of the terms blocking and indexing.

If two databases are to be linked, then without blocking or indexing, every possible pair of records (with one record from each database) will need to be compared [110]. This would make the computational complexity of the linkage process quadratic in the number of records in the databases to be linked ($O(n^2)$ following the Big-O notation we described on page 68). For example, if two databases both double in the number of records they contain, then without blocking four times as many record pair comparisons would be required [110].

However, the majority of these record pair comparisons would be between non-matching records [109], and the detailed comparison of their quasi-

© Springer Nature Switzerland AG 2020
P. Christen et al., *Linking Sensitive Data*, https://doi.org/10.1007/978-3-030-59706-1_10

identifying attribute values using computationally expensive string comparison functions [109] would be a waste. The aim of blocking and indexing techniques is therefore to identify candidate record pairs that likely refer to true matches in a computationally efficient and fast way. Only these candidate record pairs are then compared in detail, as we discussed in Section 3.2.

The issue of scaling up the linkage of databases has been a topic of research and development right from the early days when computer based linkage techniques have been employed [204]. A variety of blocking and indexing approaches have been developed in the past two decades for reducing the number of candidate record pairs that need to be compared in detail. The surveys by Christen [110] and Papadakis et al. [463] provide comprehensive reviews about existing blocking and indexing techniques and their comparative performance. Generally, blocking and indexing techniques can be categorised according to if they generate distinct or overlapping blocks. In the former category each record in a database is inserted into only one block, while in the latter category a record can be inserted into multiple blocks. Only those records that are in the same block are then compared with each other in more detail [109].

Standard blocking is a common technique used for linking databases. It uses the actual values in selected quasi-identifying attributes, known as blocking keys [110], to group the records in a database into non-overlapping blocks. In general, blocking keys are generated using the value of a single attribute or the concatenation of values from several attributes. An example blocking key could be the first three letters of first name concatenated with the first three letters of surname. In this example, 'Lemira Behrndt' will be represented by the blocking key value 'LemBeh'.

One crucial aspect of standard blocking is that the generated blocks will likely vary in sizes depending upon the frequency distribution of the quasi-identifying attribute values used for blocking. For example, if a surname attribute is used as blocking key, then in most English speaking countries the block generated for 'Smith' will likely be much larger than the block generated for 'Dijkstra' [109]. The number of record pairs to be compared based on standard blocking can therefore be highly dependent upon the sizes of the largest blocks that were generated [110]. A block for 'Smith' containing 2,500 records in both databases to be linked will result in $2,500 \cdot 2,500 = 6,250,000$ record pair comparisons. This issue of how the largest blocks affect the number of generated candidate record pairs needs to be considered with any blocking or indexing technique that does not allow an explicit restriction of the maximum sizes of blocks [212].

While with standard blocking each record in a database is only inserted into one block, blocking techniques such as canopy clustering [132, 407] generate overlapping blocks where a record can be inserted into multiple blocks. Sorted neighbourhood indexing [171, 272] is a completely different approach, where the databases to be linked are first sorted according to a sorting key (generated through the concatenation of one or several quasi-identifying attribute values), and then a sliding window is moved over the sorted databases and only those records within a certain window are compared with each other.

Blocking or indexing techniques are often applied in an iterative manner with different blocking or sorting keys used in each iteration. This can be important because the values in the quasi-identifying attributes used as blocking or sorting keys might change over time for the same person, or they might contain errors and variations [109]. As a result, for a given blocking key, true matching record pairs might not be inserted into the same block and therefore they are not compared. A multipass blocking or indexing approach can improve the quality of blocking by reducing the number of missed true matching record pairs at the cost of an increased number of additional record pairs that need to be compared [109]. For example, if only quasi-identifying attributes containing address details would be used as blocking keys then any person who has changed her or his address would be inserted into different blocks if the two databases to be linked were recorded some time apart.

We next discuss specific requirements that blocking and indexing techniques that are aimed at linking sensitive databases need to fulfil. In the remainder of this section we then present different blocking and indexing techniques that have been proposed in the context of linking sensitive databases.

10.1.1 Requirements of Privacy-Preserving Blocking

In the context of linking sensitive databases, blocking and indexing become challenging because of privacy concerns [494]. As Figure 3.6 (on page 74) shows, this step of the linkage process needs to be conducted in such a way that no party involved in a linkage can learn anything about the sensitive values of another party, and no external adversary is able to reidentify any sensitive values in the blocks of records generated from the sensitive databases. Such privacy concerns therefore introduce a trade-off into the blocking or indexing step not only between quality and efficiency of the generated blocks, but additionally also privacy protection [615]. The following requirements need to be considered when blocking or indexing techniques are employed in a privacy-preserving record linkage protocol.

- **Blocks should be of uniform sizes**: In blocking and indexing approaches that do not consider privacy, as we discussed above, the only criterion that needs to be considered with regard to block sizes is that the largest generated blocks will result in the largest numbers of candidate record pairs that need to be compared. When considering privacy aspects, however, then both large and small blocks, and more generally the size distribution of blocks, can reveal information that potentially allow an adversary to learn what quasi-identifying attributes have been used to generate these blocks. Therefore, the generated blocks should not be too small and not be too large, and ideally not follow any frequency distribution that is similar to the distribution of a quasi-identifying attribute, as we illustrated in Figure 5.2 in the context of a frequency attack.

Furthermore, in the comparison step of encoded records, small blocks and the resulting distributions of similarities of the compared record pairs in a block can potentially also reveal some information about the encoded quasi-identifying attribute values in the records in a block, as we discussed in Section 9.4. A small number of records in a block can potentially increase the probability of suspicion, as we discussed in Section 5.2.2.

- **The number of blocks should not reveal information**: Similar to the distribution of block sizes, the number of blocks generated by a privacy-preserving blocking or indexing technique can potentially also reveal some information which an adversary can use to further investigate the encoded values in these blocks. For example, if the number of blocks generated from a sensitive database roughly corresponds to the number of values in a certain quasi-identifying attribute in a database (or in an external data set) the adversary has access to, then this will tell the adversary how blocking was conducted. For example, assume a linkage unit in a certain country receives an encoded database split into 4,200 blocks. Based on publicly available information, a curious employee of the linkage unit learns that there are 4,250 unique postcodes in this country. Given these two values are very similar, it is much more likely that the blocking approach was based on postcode values and not on any name attributes (first name or surname), or on a combination of attributes.

- **Blocks should contain records of similar but different entities**: To ensure k-anonymous privacy, a suitable blocking technique should ensure each block contains records that correspond to at least k different entities. This follows the generalisation idea of k-anonymity we discussed in Section 6.3.2. Following this requirement improves the privacy of individual entities because an adversary cannot directly identify to which entity a given record belongs to in a block, even if the adversary is able to reidentify some sensitive information (such as certain quasi-identifying attribute values) from that block.

- **Use of third parties to conduct the blocking**: In general, as we discuss later in this chapter, blocking can be conducted either collaboratively by the database owners, or by using a third party such as a linkage unit based on the encoded records sent to it by the database owners. If the database owners perform blocking collaboratively, it will be more difficult to hide sensitive information because all database owners must know the encoding algorithm and its settings, as well as how blocking is being conducted. On the other hand, if a linkage unit is used to conduct the linkage, then blocking is generally easier. More simple encoding approaches of sensitive quasi-identifying attribute values can be employed by the database owners because they do not need to directly share their blocks with each other. Rather, each database owner generates their own blocks, encodes the records in these blocks using a suitable encoding approach, and then sends the encoded blocks to the linkage unit.

- **Use of efficient privacy techniques**: The aim of blocking and indexing is to efficiently and (computationally) cheaply remove record pairs from the comparison space that likely cannot be matches. Any encoding or encryption method used in a privacy-preserving blocking or indexing technique therefore needs to have low computation and low communication requirements when grouping records into blocks, while at the same time preserving the privacy of the individuals in the sensitive databases being blocked.

- **Avoiding collusion between parties**: As we discussed in Section 5.4.5, collusion happens when a subset of parties involved in a protocol work together with the aim to learn about the sensitive data provided by another, not colluding party involved in the protocol. In privacy-preserving blocking and indexing, the participating database owners need to use the same encoding or encryption algorithm and parameter settings to allow the comparison of encoded or encrypted quasi-identifying values. This however opens weaknesses for many privacy-preserving blocking and indexing techniques, especially if a linkage unit is involved in a protocol. If a certain database owner colludes with the linkage unit and shares the secret details of how blocking was conducted (or how sensitive quasi-identifying values were encoded), then the linkage unit can likely mount a dictionary attack, as we discussed in Section 5.4.2, with the aim to re-identify the encoded sensitive values of the non-colluding database owner. Therefore, database owners might need to resort to individually applied hardening techniques, as we discussed in the previous chapter, to prevent such reidentification of their encoded sensitive values by other parties who have access to their encoded data in a given linkage protocol.

10.1.2 Phonetic Blocking

Phonetic encoding based blocking is a widely used technique for linking sensitive databases [320]. As we described in Section 6.6, the idea behind phonetic blocking is to encode the values from selected quasi-identifying attributes using a phonetic encoding function such as Soundex [524] or Double-Metaphone [472], as shown in the examples in Table 6.1. These generated phonetic encodings are then used as the blocking keys [109], and records with the same phonetic encodings, such as values with the same or similar pronunciation, are grouped together into the same block to be compared in detail. Figure 10.1 illustrates an example of using Soundex encoding for blocking.

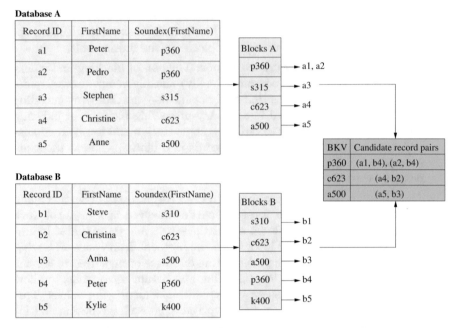

Fig. 10.1 Example phonetic blocking of two databases, **A** and **B**, where blocking key values (BKVs) are generated using the Soundex phonetic encoding algorithm [524] on FIRSTNAME attribute values. Blocks are then generated using a standard blocking approach where records with the same Soundex encoding (same BKV) are grouped into the same block, and candidate record pairs are formed from all records in the same block.

Karakasidis and Verykios [322] proposed a complete framework for the linkage of two sensitive databases. The authors enhanced edit distance based methods used for conventional approximate comparison of string values with privacy-preserving characteristics, and increased the scalability of linkage by incorporating a secure blocking component. In this approach, the Soundex and Metaphone phonetic encoding algorithms [109] were used to encode quasi-identifying attribute values. These phonetic encodings were then encoded a second time using a one-way hash algorithm, as we discussed in Section 6.2. In order for the generated hash values to exhibit a uniform distribution, faked records with appropriate values were added to the sensitive databases before phonetic encoding was applied. Achieving blocks of uniform sizes is important in the context of linking sensitive databases, because both small and large blocks can potentially reveal sensitive information to an adversary about the distribution of the quasi-identifying values used to generate blocks [212, 494]. All records that generated the same hashed phonetic code were then grouped into the same block to be compared in detail using a privacy-preserving comparison function [322].

As part of an empirical evaluation of techniques that are aimed at enabling privacy-preserving blocking, Etienne et al. [193] evaluated the use of phonetic encoding and showed that on synthetic data different types of corrupted values have different impact upon the quality of the generated blocks with regard to the resulting final linkage quality (measured using precision and recall, as we discussed in Section 3.4).

10.1.3 Reference Values based Blocking

In the context of sensitive databases, several approaches have used reference values from public databases (or values made-up randomly) to calculate the distances between quasi-identifying attribute values and reference values [320, 612, 618], as we discussed in Section 7.5. Such reference values can also be used to group records from a sensitive database into blocks, where records that have quasi-identifying attribute values that are the same or similar to one or more reference values are grouped together.

Karakasidis and Verykios [323] introduced a three-party blocking approach for linking sensitive databases that uses nearest neighbour clustering to form initial clusters using a set of reference values that is available to both database owners. To ensure both database owners generate the same set of clusters, they need to agree upon how to generate these clusters. Specifically, they need to agree on the minimum cluster size, k, which is the number of reference values per initial cluster, to ensure k-anonymous privacy (see the side box on page 140 for an example of k-anonymity). The actual blocks are then generated by each database owner by assigning each record in their sensitive database to the most similar cluster based on the similarity between the record's quasi-identifying attribute values and the reference values in all clusters. The same authors then proposed an improved reference values based blocking approach [324] based on sorted neighbourhood clustering [272], where the values in clusters are sorted and only records in those clusters (blocks) that have common values in a sliding window are compared.

Following the same concept of using public reference values, Vatsalan et al. [618] proposed an efficient two-party technique to block sensitive databases also based on sorted nearest neighbourhood clustering. Similar to the three-party approach by Karakasidis and Verykios [324], clusters are first generated by the two database owners using a selected set of reference values. Quasi-identifying attribute values from records in a sensitive database are then added into these clusters such that each cluster will contain at least k quasi-identifying attribute values. This provides k-anonymous privacy characteristics (as we discussed in Section 6.3.2), because each record in a sensitive database can be seen to be similar to at least $k - 1$ other records in that database. Once these k-anonymous clusters are generated, reference values corresponding to each cluster are exchanged between the two database owners. Using a sorted nearest neighbourhood approach [272] of sliding a window over the reference values, similar clusters are identified and record pairs are generated from all records in the corresponding clusters that are in the same window. An experimental evaluation showed that both linkage quality and privacy characteristics of the approach mainly depend on the selected reference values [618].

The use of reference values for blocking of sensitive databases has been extended by Karakasidis et al. [320]. The proposed approach uses multiple reference set samples which assign a record into multiple blocks to provide redundancy in the blocking process. The first step of this approach is for the database owners to agree upon how they generate the common set of reference values. From these common reference values subsets of values are sampled using the Durstenfeld shuffle algorithm [179] (a method to efficiently produce an unbiased permutation of a sequence). Each database owner then independently assigns the records in their sensitive database to blocks based on the edit distance between reference values and values in the quasi-identifying attributes used for blocking. To improve the redundancy of blocking, several blocking keys are used to generate blocks, and the transitive closure is considered over these blocks. An evaluation on real-world databases showed that this approach can achieve high linkage quality even for databases that contain records with errors and variations in quasi-identifying attribute values. This is because of the redundancy in the blocking process, where multiple reference sets are sampled and each record is inserted into multiple blocks [320].

10.1.4 Hashing-based Blocking

The first approach to conduct blocking without revealing any values in the sensitive databases being linked was proposed by Al-Lawati et al. [11], who developed three methods to conduct standard blocking in a privacy-preserving way assuming a three-party protocol. The approach calculates similarities between quasi-identifying attribute values based on term frequency and inverse document frequency (TF-IDF) [647] weight calculations, and distance functions based on hash signatures. Blocking is based on hash encoded tokens, which can be words in or q-grams extracted from the quasi-identifying attributes used for the linkage, as is illustrated in Figure 10.2. This blocking approach basically only compares records that have at least one token in common.

In the first blocking method proposed by Al-Lawati et al. [11], each unique hash value in the hash signatures generated from the quasi-identifying attribute values becomes the key of a block, and each record is inserted into several blocks, potentially leading to a large number of candidate record pairs. The second method proposed improves this approach by adding the record identifiers into the calculation of hash signatures to maintain the uniqueness

DO$_1$

ID	Value
r1	{al, li}
r2	{si}

DO$_2$

ID	Value
r3	{li}
r4	{al, li}

	f[0]	**f[1]**	**f[2]**	**f[3]**
HS(r1)	TF–IDF(r1, li)	0	0	TF–IDF(r1, al)
HS(r2)	0	0	TF–IDF(r2, si)	0
HS(r3)	TF–IDF(r3, li)	0	0	0
HS(r4)	TF–IDF(r4, li)	0	0	TF–IDF(r4, al)

Fig. 10.2 An example of the hash signature based blocking approach proposed by Al-Lawati et al. [11] (adapted from [619]), as we describe in Section 10.1.4. Each row is a hash signature (HS) for a record, where a list **f** of floating-point numbers that contain TF-IDF weights represents each encoded record.

of each record pair. In the third proposed blocking method, the database owners first identify which blocks they have in common by conducting a secure set intersection protocol on their sets of hash values. They then only send the records from these common blocks to a linkage unit, thereby significantly reducing the amount of communication and computation required. An experimental evaluation showed that this third blocking method can reduce the total runtime required by up to two thirds [11].

As we discussed in Section 6.2.3, locality sensitive hashing (LSH) is a popular technique used to find nearest neighbours in high dimensional spaces [291]. LSH uses a set of hash functions to map objects into partitions in such a way that similar objects are mapped to the same partition (bucket) with high probability, while guaranteeing that dissimilar objects are not mapped into the same bucket with high probability [227]. Given these properties, LSH has been used as a blocking technique in several protocols developed to link large sensitive databases.

Durham investigated the use of the Hamming distance based LSH method for blocking sensitive databases that have been encoded into Bloom filters (as we covered in Chapter 8) [178]. This proposed blocking technique can however be applied on any binary vector, not just Bloom filters. The idea is to group together Bloom filters that have similar bit patterns in common, and to only compare the full Bloom filters that are in the same group (or block).

Similar to MinHash (see page 133), in the Hamming LSH approach, in order to achieve the LSH properties [291, 385], multiple hash values need to be generated and combined into a LSH signature for each Bloom filter. To generate a single hash value in such a signature, λ bit positions are randomly sampled from a Bloom filter of length l, with $1 \leq \lambda < l$. The larger the value of λ is the more similar the Bloom filters in the same block will be. This will lead to blocks of higher precision but lower recall. As with MinHash, a number of such blocks are generated from each Bloom filter, by applying the random bit sampling $\mu > 1$ times [178]. In each iteration a different set of λ bit positions is sampled from the l positions of a Bloom filter.

To illustrate Hamming LSH based blocking, let us consider two Bloom filters $\mathbf{b}_1 = [1,1,0,0,1,0,1,0,1,1]$ and $\mathbf{b}_2 = [1,1,1,0,1,0,1,0,0,1]$, and two ($\mu = 2$) sets of randomly sampled bit positions, $\mathbf{p}_1 = \{0,2,4,6\}$ and $\mathbf{p}_2 = \{0,1,5,7\}$, of length $\lambda = 4$. The first sampling results in the hash values (bit pattern) '1011' for $\mathbf{b}_1$ and '1111' for $\mathbf{b}_2$, and therefore the two Bloom filters will be inserted into different blocks. The second sampling gives '1100' for both $\mathbf{b}_1$ and $\mathbf{b}_2$, and therefore these two Bloom filters are inserted into the same block and compared.

The number of blocks into which each Bloom filter (and thus record) of an encoded database is inserted is determined by the value of μ. Increasing the value of λ leads to a larger number of smaller blocks, while decreasing λ results in a smaller number of larger blocks. To obtain high precision and recall linkage results one can increase the values of both λ and μ. However, this can result in high runtime due to a potentially large number of record pairs to be compared [218]. Furthermore, storing intermediate results (compared candidate record pairs) might also mean significant memory requirements. Karapiperis and Verykios [334] theoretically analysed how to set optimal parameter setting for both λ and μ to efficiently achieve high precision and recall linkage results assuming an expected actual similarity (or distance) threshold between matching quasi-identifying attribute values is known.

The concept of using LSH functions for blocking in the context of linking sensitive databases has been extended by Karapiperis and Verykios [333], who presented a Λ-fold redundant blocking framework that employs LSH for identifying candidate record pairs that need to be compared. In their approach, Λ denotes the degree of redundancy, or into how many independent blocking groups a record will be inserted. The proposed approach can be employed with three families of hash functions, the Hamming family (as used by Durham [178]), the MinHash family [291], and the ρ-stable distributions based family [145]. Before records are grouped into blocks, each database owner encodes their records by using either Bloom filters [543] or an embedding method in the Euclidean space [533]. The approach then employs a linkage unit which generates the required set of hash functions based upon the agreed LSH family. This set of hash functions is sent to the database owners to hash their encoded records and populate blocks accordingly. The experimental results indicated that such LSH based blocking approaches can significantly reduce the number of candidate pairs that need to be compared [333].

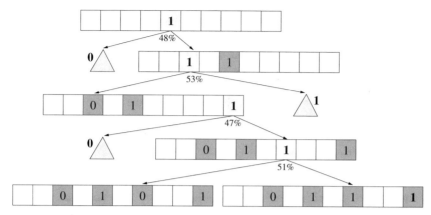

Fig. 10.3 An example of a single bit tree (adapted from [366]), where light shaded squares (with bold numbers) represent the match bit positions chosen for splitting at the given node, while the dark shaded squares mark all match bit positions that were selected at a parent node. The triangles represent subtrees of bit vectors that are not shown. The percentage values under each match bit position used for splitting show the number of bit vectors that are assumed to contain a 1 in the selected bit position out of all the bit vectors assigned to that node.

10.1.5 Multibit Tree based Blocking

The multibit tree data structure was originally proposed by Kristensen et al. [366] to efficiently find similar chemical fingerprints (represented as bit vectors) in a database with a user defined similarity threshold value.

A multibit tree is a binary tree data structure that iteratively assigns bit vectors such as Bloom filters to tree nodes based on selected bit positions called match bits. The construction of a tree starts from the root node, where initially all bit vectors of a database are assigned to this node. At each node in the tree, a set of one or several match bits in the bit vectors is chosen to best split the bit vectors assigned to this node into two parts of ideally equal size, which in turn will keep the tree as balanced as possible. All bit vectors with a certain bit pattern in those match bit positions are stored in a subtree. If a single bit is selected, then all vectors with a 0 in this match bit position are stored in the left subtree, while all bit vectors with a 1 in the match bit position are stored in the right subtree. This division is continued recursively until all bit vectors in a given node are the same, or all bit positions have been used during the tree construction. This process is illustrated in the example in Figure 10.3, where a single bit is used for splitting.

The selection of the best splitting bit position(s) as match bit(s) requires information about all the bit vectors at a given node. One or more bit position(s) which contain 0 in (close to) half of the bit vectors and 1 in the other half are then selected. This recursive division is based on the bit vectors assigned to a given node and the bit positions that have been selected in all its parent nodes (a given bit position is only selected as a match bit once).

The concept of multibit trees was investigated by Bachteler et al. [38] as a new blocking method for privacy-preserving record linkage. In this approach, the string values in the quasi-identifying attributes used for linking are first converted into sets of q-grams, which are then mapped into one Bloom filter per record as we discussed in Section 8.3. The generated Bloom filters of all records in a sensitive database are then partitioned into separate bins according to their number of 1-bits (their Hamming weight). All Bloom filters in a bin are stored in a multibit tree data structure (one per bin). A given Bloom filter from a second database can then be queried against all Bloom filters that are stored in these multibit trees, and at each node the similarity between the node Bloom filter and the query Bloom filter is calculated to find matching Bloom filters.

Similar to the approach by Bachteler et al. [38], Schnell [536] suggested a protocol for linking sensitive databases where the records in one database are first encoded into Bloom filters using the cryptographic long-term key [545] approach we discussed in Section 8.3.2. The generated Bloom filters are stored in a multibit tree data structure, where the use of multibit trees is formally described as a blocking technique for linking sensitive databases. These multibit trees are then queried by the Bloom filters of the other database to be linked in order to generate candidate record pairs. According to experiments, the proposed approach has a linear computational complexity with an increasing number of records in a database, and the approach was found to be more effective than other blocking approaches such as canopy clustering or sorted neighbourhood indexing [90]. Ranbaduge et al. [498] extended this approach to the blocking of multiple encoded sensitive databases, as we discuss in Section 10.4.

10.2 Meta-Blocking Techniques

While the blocking or indexing techniques discussed in the previous section are mainly based on corresponding non privacy-preserving techniques that execute blocking or indexing as a specific step in the overall record linkage process, several block processing techniques have been proposed for both general record linkage as well as privacy-preserving record linkage to further reduce the space of record pair comparisons. These techniques, known as meta-blocking techniques, are employed in-between the blocking and comparison steps of the linkage process. They iteratively apply blocking followed by the comparison and classification of record pairs into matches and non-matches, where the outcomes of this classification are then fed back into the next iteration of the blocking step. Alternatively, these meta-blocking techniques select and refine the blocks generated in the blocking step.

Whang et al. [641] were the first to introduce an interactive block processing technique to reduce the record pair comparison space when deduplicating a database. In their approach, each individual block is repeatedly examined to detect duplicates. The result of record pair comparisons from a processed block is propagated to inform decisions in subsequent blocks. Two records in a block are merged if they are identified as a match and the resulting new merged record is propagated to other blocks based on the values in its quasi-identifying attributes. This approach was able to reduce the number of pairwise comparisons in subsequent blocks because repeated comparisons are avoided. The same concept was extended further by Kim and Lee [349] who used locality sensitive hashing (LSH), as we discussed in Section 6.2.3, for the cleaning and linking of databases.

Papadakis et al. [460] suggested two categories of block processing methods to improve the performance of the linkage of two databases. Assuming overlapping blocks have been generated by a blocking technique, block refining methods, such as block purging (discard non-matching record pair comparisons by removing blocks that contain more records than a given upper block size limit) and block scheduling (sort the set of blocks for comparison to reduce the number of duplicate record pair comparisons), operate at the coarse level of processing individual blocks. The second category of comparison-refinement methods include comparison propagation (order the record pair comparisons in a block to avoid any repetitive comparisons), duplicate propagation (remove record pairs in blocks if they have already been identified as duplicates), comparison pruning (remove any record pair comparisons that are unlikely to be a match), and comparison scheduling (order the record pair comparisons in a given block such that record pairs that are more likely to be a match are compared first). These methods consider a finer level of block processing at the level of individual record pair comparisons within blocks. The experimental results on databases containing more than 100 million records showed that such refinement methods improve the efficiency of the overall deduplication process by significantly reducing the number of required record pair comparisons without much loss of the resulting linkage quality [460].

Papadakis et al. [463] introduced the concept of meta-blocking for record linkage scenarios where two databases need to be linked. The aim of meta-blocking is to restructure a collection of blocks to reduce the overall number of record pairs within blocks. The suggested approach takes a block collection as input and uses a supervised classification technique based on block-feature vectors to identify promising blocks (that likely contain true matches) to be compared. However, this approach requires the selection of suitable features and training data to achieve accurate pruning of candidate comparisons. Efthymiou et al. [184] later extended this approach by incorporating parallelisation based on MapReduce [148] to improve its performance when aiming to block very large databases.

Meta-blocking in the context of linking sensitive databases in a privacy-preserving way has been investigated by Karakasidis et al. [320]. In this approach, sorted neighbourhood blocking [272] based on reference values is used as a meta-blocking technique to reduce the space of record pair comparisons by considering the transitive closure of record pairs across blocks. Ranbaduge et al. [501] proposed a meta-blocking approach for linking multiple databases that is based on a graph structure to schedule the comparison of blocks. The aim of this scheduling is to minimise the number of repeated and superfluous comparisons between records, where repeated record comparisons are defined as the comparison of duplicate record pairs, while the comparison of record pairs that cannot be matches (in the context of linking several databases) are considered as superfluous comparisons. The experimental results of this approach showed that up to five orders of magnitude reduction in the number of record comparisons can be achieved compared to existing approaches [501].

10.3 Filtering Techniques

Apart from blocking and indexing, filtering techniques are additional methods that can be employed to reduce the number of record pair comparisons by efficiently removing those record pairs that have a similarity below a given similarity threshold value. Filtering thereby prevents the detailed and often time consuming comparisons of quasi-identifying attribute values between records that cannot have a high similarity according to some condition. In the context of linking sensitive databases, we assume that these filtering approaches are applied in a three-party protocol by the linkage unit on the encoded sensitive databases it has received from the database owners.

10.3.1 Length Filtering

Length filtering is an efficient similarity based filtering technique that utilises the characteristics of the considered similarity measure and a prespecified similarity threshold to speed up the linkage process [611]. Based on the length of the set of tokens in each record, such as words in or q-grams extracted from quasi-identifying attribute values, or the number of 1-bits in Bloom filters [218], candidate record pairs do not need to be compared if the lengths of the corresponding token sets of a record pair differ by a certain value.

For example, assuming we are interested in record pairs that have a q-gram based Jaccard coefficient similarity of at least $sim_J = 0.8$ (following Equation 6.4). Two records with first name and surname values 'tim ho' and 'maximillian kalotihos' will not be able to have that similarity of 0.8 based on their numbers of q-grams, even though they share the three q-grams 'ti', 'im', and 'ho', and therefore were maybe inserted into the same block. The reason for this is that the first name contains only three q-grams (assuming bigrams with $q = 2$) while the second name contains eighteen q-grams, and therefore their Jaccard coefficient similarity is $sim_J = 3/(3 + 18 - 3) = 3/18 = 0.167$.

A minimum length difference can be calculated based on the similarity threshold, s_t, that each record pair needs to satisfy in order to be considered as a match, such that this minimum similarity can only be achieved if the lengths of the token sets of two records do not differ by too much. To illustrate such a length filtering calculation, let us assume two records, r_1 and r_2, have been converted into their corresponding sets of q-grams, $\mathbf{q}_1$ and $\mathbf{q}_2$, and we want to calculate their similarities using the Jaccard coefficient as defined in Section 6.8.1. If we denote the sizes of the two individual q-gram sets with $l_1 = |\mathbf{q}_1|$ and $l_2 = |\mathbf{q}_2|$, and assume $l_1 \leq l_2$, then to consider the record pair (r_1, r_2) for comparison with a minimum required Jaccard similarity, sim_J, of at least $sim_J \geq s_t$, then the following must hold:

$$sim_J(r_1, r_2) \geq s_t \implies l_1 \geq \lceil s_t \cdot l_2 \rceil,$$

where $\lceil \ldots \rceil$ denotes the ceiling function (rounding to the next larger integer value). For example, if two records differ in the lengths of their q-gram sets by more than 20% then they cannot satisfy a Jaccard similarity threshold $s_t = 0.8$. Therefore, if a record has ten q-grams then this record does not need to be compared with any other record that has less than eight or more than twelve q-grams.

Vatsalan and Christen [611] adapted length filtering for the Dice coefficient similarity on Bloom filters in a two-party protocol to link sensitive databases. This approach classifies record pairs into matches, non-matches, and possible matches in an iterative way to reduce the number of record pairs with unknown match status in each iteration without compromising the privacy of sensitive values. In each iteration the minimum similarity based on the revealed bit positions is calculated using the Dice coefficient similarity in such a way that any Bloom filter pair that has less 1-bits than are required to achieve the similarity threshold s_t is removed from the comparison step. As a result, candidate Bloom filter pairs that cannot be matches are classified efficiently without having to be compared.

10.3.2 Prefix and Position Filtering

Besides length filtering, other filtering techniques that make use of the token sets in records have been developed. PPJoin [652] is a signature-based similarity join algorithm that applies several filtering techniques to reduce the number of comparisons required, in particular a length filter (as discussed previously), a prefix filter, and a position filter. A prefix filter allows to re-

Prefix and position filtering

Prefix filtering exploits the overlap between tokens (words or q-grams from quasi-identifying attribute values). Depending upon the similarity threshold, s_t, required and the sizes of the token sets in two records, a certain number of tokens must occur in both records. If the token sets from two records are ordered in the same way, either alphabetically or based on the frequency of occurrence of tokens [652], then in a prefix (the beginning) of these two token sequences a certain number of tokens must occur in both prefixes because otherwise the two records will not have a high enough similarity to be considered as a match.

To illustrate how prefix filtering works, let us assume two records, r_1 and r_2, have been converted into their corresponding sets of q-grams, $\mathbf{q}_1$ and $\mathbf{q}_2$. We require them to have a Jaccard similarity sim_J of at least s_t. We get the sizes of the two q-gram sets as $l_1 = |\mathbf{q}_1|$ and $l_2 = |\mathbf{q}_2|$, and we define the overlap between r_1 and r_2 as $overlap(r_1, r_2) = |\mathbf{q}_1 \cap \mathbf{q}_2|$. We then calculate the minimum overlap α between the two sets of q-grams, $\mathbf{q}_1$ and $\mathbf{q}_2$, in order to meet the similarity threshold s_t as:

$$sim_J(r_1, r_2) \geq s_t \implies overlap(r_1, r_2) \geq \left\lceil \frac{s_t}{1 + s_t} \cdot (l_1 + l_2) \right\rceil = \alpha.$$

As a result, a pair of records with an overlap less than α cannot meet the similarity threshold s_t and therefore does not need to be compared. Based on this observation, we can now consider what the prefix sizes of the token sets need to be for q-gram sets of a certain size to be able to achieve the minimum required overlap for meeting the minimal similarity, s_t. We can calculate this minimum prefix length for records r_1 and r_2 as $l_1 - \alpha + 1$ and $l_2 - \alpha + 1$, respectively [652]. At least one q-gram must occur in both prefixes for r_1 and r_2 to meet the minimal similarity s_t. For example, two records each with ten q-grams can only meet a minimal Jaccard similarity of 0.8 if they have an overlap of at least nine q-grams. This requires their prefixes to be of length two. If they have no q-gram in common in their prefixes they cannot have a total similarity of 0.8.

Position filtering allows us to approximate the maximal possible overlap between two records when applying the prefix filter. Based on the last common prefix token between two records, each record can be separated into a left part, LP, representing the tokens already seen, and a right part, RP, of unseen tokens. Following the above example, we can define the maximal overlap between two records r_1 and r_2 as:

$$maxoverlap(r_1, r_2) = |LP(\mathbf{q}_1) \cap LP(\mathbf{q}_2)| + min(|RP(\mathbf{q}_1)|, |RP(\mathbf{q}_2)|).$$

Based on this calculation, a record pair does not need to be compared if its maximum overlap is smaller than the minimum overlap α [652].

move records pairs that have an insufficient overlap in their corresponding token sets, while a position filter considers the position overlaps between tokens that are common between the records that are being compared. We describe how prefix and position filters can be used to reduce the number of record pair comparisons in detail in the above side box.

Sehili et al. [555] proposed a filtering technique based on the PPJoin technique, named P4Join, for the privacy-preserving linking of sensitive databases. In this approach the records in the two databases to be linked are first encoded into Bloom filters. The length filter then removes those Bloom filter pairs that differ by more than a certain number of 1-bits based on the predefined similarity threshold value, as we discussed above. The prefix filter is based on the fact that similar Bloom filters need a high degree of overlap in their 1-bit positions in order to satisfy a certain similarity threshold. To achieve this a prefix bit vector is generated for each Bloom filter based on the frequencies of how often a certain bit position is set to 1 in all Bloom filters in an encoded database. Pairs of records can then be excluded from comparison if they have an insufficient overlap (common 1-bits) in their prefixes. Finally, the position filter can remove pairs of Bloom filters even if their prefixes overlap depending on the positions where the overlap occurs.

However, as an experimental evaluation of the proposed P4Join method showed, the use of such filtering techniques can incur significant computational costs due to the required preprocessing of all Bloom filters in an encoded database, and the tests that need to be applied for these filters. This is in contrast to the very efficient simple bitwise AND operation on full Bloom filters (that is required to calculate the Dice coefficient similarity between Bloom filters) when none of these filtering techniques is applied. Furthermore, if the Bloom filters are constructed such that around 50% of their bits are set to 1 (to make them less susceptible to privacy attacks, as we discussed in Section 8.6.2), then all three filtering techniques will be less effective because of the large number of 1-bits in Bloom filters [555].

10.3.3 Metric Space Filtering

A metric space based filtering approach can be used in a record linkage context to embed records into multidimensional data objects where their similarities can be calculated based on the distances between these data objects. The distance function $d()$ for a metric space needs to satisfy the triangular inequality [136, 660], which has been used to reduce the search space for similarity search and record linkage [44, 74]. We discussed the requirements of a metric distance, including the triangular inequality, in the side box on page 158. Figure 10.4 illustrates how the triangular inequality can be used to filter pairs of data objects that are too far away from each other and thus do not need to be compared (because their corresponding records cannot have a high enough similarity to be classified as a match).

Sehili and Rahm [556] proposed a metric space based filtering approach which showed improved efficiency and linkage quality compared to previous approaches to link sensitive databases [543, 555]. In this approach, the records in two databases are first encoded into Bloom filters. The Bloom filters of

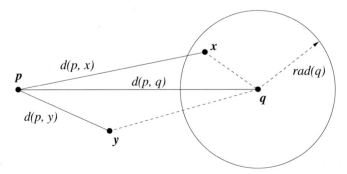

Fig. 10.4 Example of using the triangular inequality to filter data objects from being compared [556]. In this example, data object y does not need to be compared with query object q because y cannot lie within the search radius $rad(q)$ since the distance $d(y, q) > d(p, q) - d(p, y)$, and $d(p, q) - d(p, y) > rad(q)$. © Springer Nature 2016, reprinted with permission.

the first database are then inserted into a metric space using a pivot based technique that selects a certain number of Bloom filters from a sample of this database as pivots. These pivots are iteratively determined from the sample set such that the Bloom filter with the greatest distance to all previously determined pivots becomes the next pivot. Next, all Bloom filters of the first database are assigned to their closest pivot by computing the Hamming distances between the pivots and the Bloom filters (pivots can therefore be seen as the centroids of clusters). Next, the Bloom filters of the second database are queried in the metric space by searching for the pivots within a given minimum Hamming distance. As illustrated in Figure 10.4, the triangular inequality is used together with the selected pivots to only select those Bloom filters that are close to a query Bloom filter for detailed comparison.

10.4 Blocking and Indexing for Multiple Parties

In the previous sections we have discussed blocking, indexing and filtering techniques aimed at reducing the number of record pairs that need to be compared, and how these techniques have been adapted to facilitate the linking of encoded sensitive databases. The majority of the techniques described have been developed for applications where only two (sensitive) databases need to be linked.

As we discuss in this section, some of these techniques can be extended to applications where multiple (more than two) databases are to be linked, while other techniques that are specifically aimed at the blocking or indexing of multiple sensitive databases in a privacy-preserving context have also been

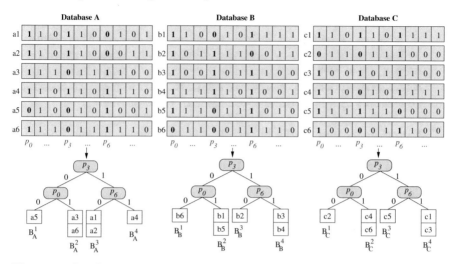

Fig. 10.5 An illustrative example of three multibit trees as generated for three databases **A**, **B**, and **C** held by three database owners. In this example the bit positions p_3, p_0, and p_6 are selected collaboratively by the three database owners to split the databases into blocks, and the corresponding blocks in the leaf nodes are used to generate candidate record pairs to be compared between the databases. Adapted from [498].

developed. In Section 10.5 we then describe techniques that are specifically aimed at linking sensitive databases from many sources.

When linking multiple databases, potentially each record from one database needs to be compared with all records in the other databases in order to determine if a pair or a set of records corresponds to the same entity or not. As was shown by Sadinle and Fienberg [525], separate pairwise linking of databases does not guarantee the transitivity of the linkage decisions and thus requires resolving discrepancies between the linkage results of individual pairs of databases.

The number of naïve pairwise record comparisons of multiple databases grows quadratically as the sizes (number of records) of the databases to be linked get larger, and exponentially with the number of databases to be linked. For two databases with 1,000 records each, without blocking or indexing 1,000,000 record pairs can be generated. For three databases with 1,000 records each, this number would increase by a thousand to 1,000,000,000 pairs. Therefore, in such situations, blocking, indexing, and filtering techniques are crucial to reduce the number of record pair comparisons that are required. In the following we describe several blocking techniques proposed specifically in the context of linking multiple sensitive databases.

- **Multibit tree based techniques**: Ranbaduge et al. [498] proposed a blocking approach for the privacy-preserving linkage of multiple sensitive databases which is based on the multibit tree blocking approach we discussed in Section 10.1.5, as originally proposed by Kristensen et al. [366] and adapted for the context of linking two sensitive databases by Bachteler et al. [38] and Schnell [536]. The multidatabase approach by Ranbaduge et al. allows several database owners to block their databases collaboratively without the use of a linkage unit. Figure 10.5 illustrates an example of this blocking approach with three databases.

In this approach, each database owner iteratively arranges its own Bloom filters into blocks in such a way that similar Bloom filters are placed into the same tree leaf node while dissimilar Bloom filters are placed into different leaf nodes. In each iteration, the set of Bloom filters in a tree node is recursively split based on a selected bit position. This bit position is agreed upon in each iteration by the database owners who exchange those bit positions which result in the best balanced splitting of the set of Bloom filters in the currently processed tree node. Experimental results on large databases showed that the approach is scalable with the sizes of the databases as well as the number of databases to be linked, while leading to high linkage quality. However, the blocks generated using this approach might miss some true matches due to the recursive splitting of the Bloom filter sets of the encoded databases.

- **Clustering based techniques**: A multidatabase blocking technique based on canopy clustering [132, 407] was proposed by Ranbaduge et al. [499]. Canopy clustering is a technique for clustering large high dimensional databases where it groups similar records by efficiently calculating the similarities between their blocking key values. In the proposed approach, the databases are first encoded into Bloom filters, and then the generated Bloom filters are grouped into small miniblocks using a multibit based splitting method. These miniblocks are then merged based on their similarity using a canopy clustering technique. All database owners are collaboratively generating and merging these miniblocks, resulting in a final set of large blocks. Bloom filters are inserted into one or more overlapping clusters based on their similarity to the centroids of these clusters. Each cluster then becomes a block from which candidate record pairs are generated.

  An empirical study conducted using large databases has shown that this approach is scalable with both the size and the number of the databases that are being linked, while providing better privacy protection when linking sensitive databases compared to earlier multidatabase techniques such as standard blocking and the multibit tree approach described before. However, the collaborative way of generating and merging miniblocks requires all database owners to communicate frequently, and therefore this approach lacks in flexibility of the block generation process because all database owners need to agree on the same parameter settings used in the blocking process.

- **Hashing-based techniques**: Karapiperis and Verykios proposed a multidatabase approach to link sensitive databases based on locality sensitive hashing (LSH) [333]. The approach uses a set of hash tables named blocking groups. Each blocking group consists of pairs made of a key and a list, where keys represent the blocking key values and the lists hold similar Bloom filters that need to be compared. The approach uses a linkage unit which generates the sets of hash functions for all blocking groups. These hash functions are sent to all database owners, allowing them to generate their blocking groups individually before sending them back to the linkage unit which can then compare the Bloom filters in the lists that have the same blocking key value.

This approach was recently extended into a new protocol named the frequent pairs scheme [334]. This approach uses a Hamming distance based LSH technique to assign records into independent blocking groups, where the sensitive databases to be linked are hashed into a set of hash tables. If a record pair exhibits a number of LSH collisions above a given threshold (the pair has a certain number of hash values in common), then it is identified as a candidate record pair that needs to be compared. Empirical results showed a significant reduction of the number of candidate record pairs to be compared while maintaining a high level of recall when compared with several baseline blocking approaches, including embedding, hierarchical, and phonetic encoding based blocking [334]. However, while the proposed approach can be used for multidatabase blocking, most experiments were conducted on two databases only, and only three databases were used for multidatabase experiments to evaluate runtime and pairs completeness. In these experiments the proposed approach outperformed several baseline approaches on both measures.

Ranbaduge et al. [503] proposed a communication efficient blocking approach for linking multiple databases using MinHash locality sensitive hashing, as is illustrated in Figure 10.6. The proposed approach uses a linkage unit to identify the candidate blocks that need to be compared. The database owners first generate blocks locally using a suitable private blocking technique, as we discussed in Section 10.1. For each generated block, a block representative in the form of a MinHash signature is calculated (for details on MinHash see the side box on page 133). These block representatives are then sent to a linkage unit, which applies locality sensitive hashing on these block representatives to identify those candidate blocks from where record pairs need to be compared. The local blocking step provides the database owners with more flexibility and control over their own blocks and also eliminates any communications among them. This makes this approach more applicable to real-world multidatabase linkage scenarios where direct and/or frequent communication between the database owners might not be possible.

- **Secure multiparty based techniques**: Han et al. [255] proposed a dynamic k-anonymous blocking approach for multiple databases using the Pallier homomorphic cryptosystem [456]. The approach can only be applied on numerical attributes, where numerical values are used as ref-

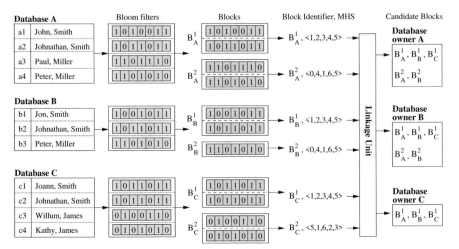

Fig. 10.6 An example of MinHash based candidate blocks generation for three database owners [503]. In this example, the databases **A**, **B**, and **C** are first encoded into Bloom filters by their respective owners. Then, each database owner blocks its own encoded database independently, and sends a set of MinHash signatures (MHS) as block representatives along with their block identifiers to a linkage unit. The linkage unit applies locality sensitive hashing on these MinHash signatures to generate candidate blocks. Record pairs are then compared across these candidate blocks. © Springer International Publishing Switzerland 2016, reprinted with permission.

erence values to generate blocks. Each database owner encrypts the reference values of its blocks by using a public key distributed by a linkage unit. All database owners then participate in a ring communication to perform a homomorphic addition of the encrypted reference values for each block. Once the homomorphic addition is completed, the first database owner sends the summed encrypted reference values of each set of blocks to the linkage unit to decide whether to compare the records from multiple blocks based on their similarity. This approach requires expensive computation and communication steps in measuring the similarities between blocks based on homomorphically encrypted values, which makes the approach less scalable to multiple and large databases.

10.5 Many-Party Linkage Methods

Various application domains require information from multiple sources to be integrated and combined in order to improve data quality and to facilitate further analysis of the linked records [494]. The majority of record linkage techniques proposed so far have focused on linking records from only two databases (two database owners), and only some techniques have been proposed in the context of linking multiple databases. While in the previous sections we have discussed blocking, indexing, and filtering techniques (first for two and then for multiple sensitive databases), in this section we describe techniques to conduct the actual linkage of many, potentially a large number of, sensitive databases. These proposed techniques mostly consider exact matching of quasi-identifying attribute values, or the linkage can only be performed on categorical data [620].

- **Secure multiparty computation based techniques**: O'Keefe et al. [453] proposed a secure multiparty computation (SMC) based exact matching approach for the linking of multiple sensitive databases in a privacy-preserving way. This approach also allowed the privacy-preserving extraction of a cohort of records from a database without revealing to the database owners which records were retrieved. The proposed approach is however computationally expensive due to the use of a SMC based oblivious transfer protocol (see Section 6.5.3) and not capable of linking records that contain errors and variations in their quasi-identifying attribute values.

  Kantarcioglu et al. [319] proposed a multidatabase linkage approach based on the k-anonymity [6] generalisation technique (see Section 6.3.2 for a discussion of k-anonymity) for person specific biomedical data. The database owners first perform a generalisation using k-anonymity on the set of quasi-identifying attributes they have in common. The encrypted generalised quasi-identifying values are then sent to a linkage unit. Before the linkage unit performs an efficient secure join operation using these encrypted identifiers, blocks are constructed that correspond to combinations of k-anonymous values. The secure join operation matches records that have the same encrypted identifiers [318]. The number of secure joins required by the protocol is drastically reduced when a k-anonymous join is applied compared to the full comparison of all pairs of records. However, the suggested approach still has a quadratic complexity for applying generalisation to each database, and it requires significant amounts of communication between the database owners.

- **Bloom filter based techniques**: A multidatabase classification approach proposed by Lai et al. [374] uses Bloom filters to securely compare records between multiple sensitive databases using a private set intersection method. The quasi-identifying attribute values from all records in a database are encoded into a single Bloom filter, as illustrated in Figure 10.7. This encoding is based on the actual words (or more generally tokens) in quasi-identifying attributes and not based on q-gram sets as used by most other Bloom filter based encoding techniques for linking sensitive databases. As a result, this approach can only identify exact matching values across databases (identify which values occur in all databases), but not in which records these values occur. The approach will

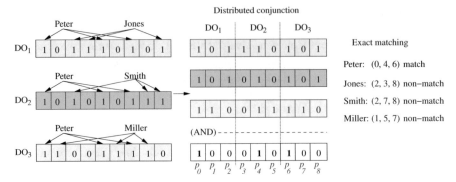

Fig. 10.7 An illustration of the privacy-preserving Bloom filter based exact matching technique proposed by Lai et al. [374] for three databases (adapted from [613]). In this approach each database owner (DO$_1$, DO$_2$, and DO$_3$) distributes segments of its own Bloom filter and performs bitwise AND on all segments it receives. If all bit positions of a certain value are set to 1 by all database owners (such as the bit positions p_0, p_4, and p_6 for 'Peter') then the value is a match.

also produce false positive matches (indicate certain values occur in all databases while they actually do not), as we discussed in Section 8.1.

The single Bloom filter generated by each database owner that encodes all its quasi-identifying attribute values is segmented according to the total number of databases involved in the protocol. Each database owner gets a segment of l/n bits, where l is the Bloom filter length and n is the number of databases being matched. These segments are then shared among the database owners, where each receives corresponding segments of the Bloom filters from all the other database owners, as shown in the middle of Figure 10.7. The database owners then perform a bitwise conjunction (AND) on the segments they received. The conjuncted segments are shared across all database owners and combined into a final conjuncted Bloom filter. Each database owner can now compare its own full Bloom filter with the conjuncted Bloom filter to identify matches from its own sensitive database. An experimental evaluation of this approach showed that the rate of false matches increases with the number of unique quasi-identifying attribute values across all databases being linked. As a result, the correct identification of the attribute values that occur in common in all databases might not be possible.

Karapiperis et al. [331] proposed a multidatabase approach to match sensitive categorical values using a Count-Min sketch data structure [139]. A Count-Min sketch is a probabilistic data structure that can capture frequencies of events, similar to a counting Bloom filter [199]. Karapiperis et al. [331] use Count-Min sketches to summarise the local set of elements which are then intersected to provide a global synopsis. This approach can for example be used to identify which medications have been purchased in a certain number of pharmacies across a whole country, potentially involving thousands of sensitive databases of pharmacy purchase transactions. First, each database owner independently summarises the records in its own database into a local synopsis, which is implemented using a Count-Min sketch. Then these local synopses are intersected in order to create the global synopsis. This global synopsis provides collective count estimates for the common elements across all databases, while hiding the contribution of each individual database for these estimates. Two protocols for generating the global synopsis were proposed, where the first protocol uses homomorphic operations [3] that provide improved privacy and accuracy but at high communication costs, while the second protocol uses a secure summation protocol [502] which exhibits improved efficiency.

Following the work by Lai et al. [374] as discussed before, Vatsalan and Christen [613] proposed a multidatabase approximate classification approach that encodes quasi-identifying attribute values into Bloom filters. The protocol combines Bloom filters with a secure summation protocol (as we discussed in Section 6.5.1) with the aim to identify all quasi-identifying attribute values that occur in the individual sensitive databases that have a Dice coefficient similarity above a certain threshold. The protocol has a communication complexity that is linear in the number and the sizes of the databases to be linked. However, the protocol requires an exponential number of record pair comparisons which makes it not scalable to applications where records from a large number of databases need to be linked.

Vatsalan et al. [616] improved upon this approach by using counting Bloom filters [199]. A counting Bloom filter is a vector (list) of integer counters instead of simple bits, and therefore it can hold the number of times an element was hashed to a certain position. Counting Bloom filters also allow the removal of elements by decreasing the count in a position. The proposed approach allows approximate matching of quasi-identifying attribute values that are encoded into Bloom filters (one per record) by each database owner. To enable more secure approximate matching, counting Bloom filters are then used to count the number of 1-bits in a given bit position across all the databases being linked. To sum the number of 1s in each bit position the approach uses a secure summation protocol which is initiated by the linkage unit. However, because one secure summation (which requires communication) needs to be performed for each set of records that are being compared, the overall communication requirements of this protocol are expensive, making the protocol not scalable for the linkage of very large sensitive databases.

- **Clustering based techniques**: To improve upon the expensive communication costs of previous multiparty linkage approaches for sensitive databases, Vatsalan et al. [617] proposed an incremental clustering protocol for the efficient linking of records from two or more databases held by different parties. The approach uses a linkage unit, where the aim of clustering is to group records from different databases incrementally into clusters such that the final output of the protocol is a set of clusters, and where each cluster contains records that are similar according to some similarity measure such as the Dice coefficient similarity [109].

Two variations of incremental clustering were proposed, both combined with a graph based linkage [617]. In the first variation, named early mapping, records in each database that is to be linked are added into the corresponding clusters in the graph by identifying one-to-one mappings between records and clusters. In contrast to early mapping, the second variation, named late mapping, uses splitting of clusters in the graph at the end of the process, where each record in a sensitive database is grouped with all its highly similar records from the other databases to obtain the one-to-one links between records of highest quality. Due to the incremental record clustering process, this approach has a quadratic computation complexity in the number of records and databases being linked, which is significantly lower compared to the other multidatabase linkage approaches that have exponential complexities in the number of databases and/or database sizes.

10.6 Parallel and Distributed Computing Techniques

Record linkage between multiple (sensitive) databases typically involves the comparisons of millions of pairs of records that represent hundreds of thousands or even more individuals. As we have covered in this chapter, there exist various algorithms and techniques for blocking, indexing, and filtering that aim to reduce the number of record pair comparisons required. However, as the databases to be linked get larger, the time required to link them increases. Furthermore, linking multiple databases still has high computational requirements, as we discussed in the previous section. As a result, the linking of very large databases can still be a challenging and time consuming endeavour. As we move into the era of Big data, the topic of Big data integration [168] has gained increasing interest. Besides blocking, indexing, and filtering, a complementary approach to make the linkage of large databases more efficient is to use parallel and distributed computing techniques. The general idea behind parallelisation is to split a problem into a group of subproblems, process these subproblems in parallel on several computers, and then collect the subresults and combine them to obtain the final overall results.

In the parallel record linkage literature, the approaches developed can be grouped into two different categories. In the first category (these are mostly earlier proposed approaches) the parallelisation is achieved by sharing data over computer networks, which requires complex programs for partitioning, distributing, and gathering data between computing nodes. The approaches under this category do not use any software frameworks for achieving parallel functionalities. In the second category (mainly approaches proposed more recently), new approaches are being developed by using some existing software environments that provide functionalities for parallel and distributed computing. These software environments provide stable frameworks for a developer to use and develop parallel programs to work with large databases. In this section we describe selected approaches developed in both categories, and then we discuss the issue of communication protocols which become important when multiple or even many databases have to be linked.

10.6.1 Non-framework based Parallel Approaches

A first parallel approach to indexing in the context of linking databases was proposed by Hernandez and Stolfo [272], who presented a parallel version of the sorted neighbourhood indexing approach (which we discussed in Section 10.1). The approach is based on a master-worker approach where the master processor distributes the records of the databases to be linked to worker processors. These workers then sort their records using the agreed sorting key, and the master processor joins the sorted list of records it receives back from the workers. Experiments with up to six processors showed a sublinear speedup of this approach because of the requirement of the master processor to read, distribute, collect, and then merge the individual lists of records it receives from the worker processors.

Christen et al. [113] described a parallel record linkage system that was based on the Message Passing Interface (MPI) library [240] for communication between processors in a distributed environment. The assumption of the MPI programming model is that each processor only has access to its own local memory and disk space. While the core steps of the linkage process were parallelised (blocking, comparison, and classification), experiments showed that it is challenging to obtain scalable speedups for the blocking step due to load balancing issues. However, the time consuming comparison of record pairs and the pairwise classification of pairs can be conducted with almost no communication and therefore it can achieve nearly optimal speedups. Overall, a nearly linear speedup was reported because between 94% and 98% of the time was spent in the comparison and classification steps [113].

A family of parallel linkage algorithms based on the Swoosh algorithm [53] was developed by Benjelloun et al. [52]. Swoosh is an iterative linkage approach that combines the linking of records with merging of pairs of records that were classified as matches to improve the overall linkage quality. The distributed version of Swoosh uses a generic 'scoop' function to determine how records are mapped onto processors, and a 'resp' function to determine which processor is responsible for a certain record. The matched and merged sets of records for a certain entity are then distributed to all other processors that hold records that are affected by a merge. Experiments showed that with certain parameter settings this distributed Swoosh algorithm, named D-Swoosh, was able to achieve near linear speedup on a parallel platform consisting of sixteen processors when linking a real-world comparison shopping data set [52]. A variation of D-Swoosh using a master-worker approach, named P-Swoosh [339], investigated different distributions of records to processors, as well as different load balancing techniques. Comparable speedup results were achieved with P-Swoosh as with D-Swoosh on the same experimental data set.

Similar to the Swoosh based approaches, Kim and Lee [348] investigated parallel approaches to link and merge records from two databases. The assumptions of these approaches were that the databases to be linked are either clean (contain only one record per entity, and thus no duplicates) or dirty (there can be several records representing the same entity). The idea of their approaches is to replicate the smaller of the two databases to be linked on all available processors, while the larger database is split into equally large partitions and distributed onto the processors. Each processor then performs a sequential linkage on the records it has received, and the individual linkage results are merged back to get the overall linkage results. Experiments on synthetic bibliographic data showed that the approach can achieve speedups of up to 7.5 on eight processors, and that it is between 11% and 18% more efficient than the P-Swoosh method [339] described above.

Different strategies of how to distribute databases to generate independent linkage tasks that can be executed on different processors were investigated by Kirsten et al. [353]. Such data parallelism approaches aim to determine the number of partitions and their sizes in an optimal way with regard to both communication and memory requirements. A master-worker approach was employed, where the master processor calculates the number and sizes of partitions of the databases to be linked, where these partitions are then distributed to the workers to conduct the linkage. An indexing approach is assumed, which requires load balancing because the sizes of the generated blocks depend on values of the quasi-identifying attributes in the records being linked. A load balancing approach is therefore employed that splits large blocks into smaller ones and merges small blocks into larger ones in order to obtain a balanced amount of work on all processors used. Experiments on a parallel platform with sixteen processors using consumer product databases from a comparison shopping Web site showed that this approach can achieve scalable speedup results.

Guisado-Gámez et al. [246] suggested a mechanism for performing record pair comparisons in parallel using a master-worker approach. For the given databases to be linked, the comparison process is run for different blocking keys. First the master processor sends a copy of the entire databases to be linked to all worker processors. In order to perform the comparisons, each worker processor needs to know which subset of records to compare. Based on a selected blocking key, the master processor divides the databases into a set of blocks and distributes this blocking information to the worker processors. Each worker then performs a sequential comparison over its allocated subsets of records, where it maintains a list of the similarities calculated between the compared record pairs. To prevent redundant record pair comparisons across these iterations, the lists of already compared record pairs are sent back to the master processor after each iteration, merged, and then redistributed to all workers. This process is performed multiple times for different blocking key criteria. The experiments conducted using synthetic data with up to eight million records showed that this approach can achieve nearly linear speedups when using up to sixteen processors.

While the parallel record linkage techniques discussed so far have not considered the sensitive nature of many databases that contain personal information, Sehili et al. [555] investigated the applicability of parallelisation on the PPJoin [652] approach we discussed in Section 10.3. To improve performance, the proposed privacy-preserving version of PPJoin, named P4Join [555], was adapted for use on highly parallel graphical processing units (GPUs). Modern GPUs provide thousands of processors that allow for a massively parallel application of the same instruction set to disjoint data partitions. The evaluation of this approach showed the suitability of modern parallel architectures such as GPUs especially for the efficient processing of binary encodings such as Bloom filters, because bit vectors are simple data structures that can be efficiently distributed and allow extremely fast operations that can facilitate significant speedup results when large sensitive databases have to be linked.

10.6.2 Framework based Parallel Approaches

Compared to the parallel approaches discussed above, more recently distributed software environments have been used to develop parallel record linkage approaches [334]. One such framework is MapReduce [148], a framework for distributed computing best suited for large-scale data processing. MapReduce offers a convenient model for scaling record linkage tasks to very large databases. A detailed argument why MapReduce is suitable for record linkage applications was given in a case study by Lin [393]. According to this case study, there are two main challenges related to distributed architectures for large-scale data processing. The first is the lack of a suitable programming model for managing concurrency, and the second is the difficulty of obtaining accessibility to required distributed hardware resources. These two issues can be resolved when using MapReduce because it provides a large class of algorithms in different programming languages, and the resulting code can be used across commodity clusters of off-the-shelf networked computers.

In MapReduce [148], the databases to be linked are initially stored in a distributed file system (HDFS) as chunks. The map tasks read the input data in parallel and apply a blocking key to assign each record into a block. These records are then dynamically redistributed during the reduce tasks such that all records with the same blocking key are sent to the same reduce task. Comparisons between records are then performed block-wise and in parallel by the reduce tasks, and the results are collected by a map task.

Vernica et al. [623] were the first to study the performance of parallel pairwise comparisons of records using the MapReduce framework. Their approach takes as input a set of records and outputs a set of joined records based on a set-similarity condition. The authors showed how to partition the input databases across nodes in order to balance the workload and to minimise the need for replication.

The Apache Hadoop[1] environment is an open-source software system that uses the MapReduce programming framework. Kolb et al. [358] proposed a parallel solution for database deduplication known as Dedoop. This system supports a browser based specification of complex linkage workflows, including the blocking and comparison steps, as well as the optional use of machine learning algorithms for the automatic generation of linkage classifiers. The specified workflows are then automatically translated into MapReduce programs for parallel execution on a cluster of networked computers. To achieve high performance, Dedoop adopts several advanced load balancing strategies which are not available in the basic MapReduce framework [358].

For linking sensitive databases, Karapiperis and Verykios [332] presented a framework which relies on the MapReduce paradigm in order to uniformly distribute the computations required for the linkage of databases assuming commodity hardware resources, without imposing extra overhead on existing infrastructure. In their approach, records are first encoded into Bloom filters in order to protect the privacy of the underlying sensitive data. These Bloom filters are then sent to a linkage unit that splits and distributes sets of Bloom filters to the underlying parallel file system (HDFS) [78], where replication capabilities are used to improve scalability. The MinHash locality sensitive hashing technique described in Section 6.2.3 is applied on each Bloom filter to arrange Bloom filters into blocks, and to facilitate parallel comparisons of sets of Bloom filters. Figure 10.8 illustrates how MapReduce can be applied on Bloom filters using this approach proposed by Karapiperis and Verykios [332].

10.6.3 Communication Protocols

As we discussed in Section 4.3, protocols that involve the linkage of multiple databases can be categorised as protocols that do not or that do involve a third party, such as a linkage unit, to conduct the linkage.

Protocols in the first category mostly assume an all-to-all communication network, where each database owner can directly communicate with all

---

[1] See: https://hadoop.apache.org/

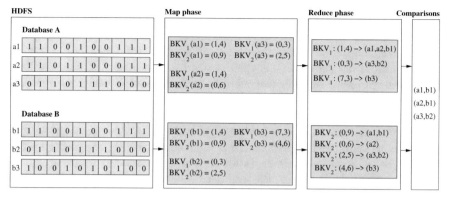

Fig. 10.8 Example of the MinHash based parallel blocking approach proposed by Karapiperis and Verykios [332], where MapReduce is used to achieve scalable parallel record linkage of quasi-identifying attribute values encoded into Bloom filters. The values a1 to a3 and b1 to b3 correspond to record identifiers. The Bloom filters of both databases are first stored in the distributed file system HDFS. In the map phase, records are read and for each Bloom filter several blocking key values (BKVs) are generated. In the reduce phase, records are redistributed, where those records with the same BKV are sent to the same reduce task for comparison.

others [498, 499, 613]. Other protocols assume a ring-based communication, where communication can only happen between consecutive database owners following a ring pattern [616]. This means database owner DO_3 is communicating with database owners DO_2 and DO_4, but not others. For protocols in the second category (the linkage of databases is conducted with the use of a linkage unit), most protocols use an all-to-one communication pattern, where all database owners can communicate directly with a linkage unit by exchanging their encoded databases or intermediate linkage results [503].

However, in scenarios where multiple databases are to be linked across several database owners, as we discussed in Section 10.4, the participating parties often need to communicate in several steps, or iteratively in many rounds, in a protocol. Such complex communication patterns can make a protocol less applicable to realistic linkage scenarios because delays in communication can reduce the overall performance of a record linkage protocol [620].

Vatsalan et al. [616] have investigated how suitable communication patterns between the database owners that participate in multidatabase protocol can improve the overall performance when linking several sensitive databases. In this work, two communication patterns were proposed for reducing the number of required record pair comparisons using counting Bloom filters [199]. Database owners were first arranged into smaller groups. Once all database owners have encoded their sensitive databases into Bloom filters, a secure summation protocol (as we discussed in Section 6.5.1) was used to construct one counting Bloom filter for each set of candidate record pairs using a column-wise summing of the individual Bloom filters of the database owners that were arranged in one group. The Dice coefficient similarity [109] was calculated on each counting Bloom filter to identify the records that match in a group using ring-based communication (as illustrated in Figure 6.5). A second secure summation protocol was then applied on the matched Bloom filters from each group to identify the matching Bloom filters, and thus records, across all sensitive databases.

Due to the arrangement of database owners into smaller groups, the proposed communication patterns were able to reduce the exponential growth of comparisons required between multiple databases, making the linkage more scalable to a larger number of database owners compared to other multi-database protocols. However, the number of database owners to include into a group needs to be chosen carefully, because the size of these groups introduces a trade-off between privacy and scalability of the linkage. An increase in the number of database owners in a group can improve privacy because the resulting counting Bloom filters are less susceptible to privacy attacks. On the other hand, larger groups result in an exponential increase of the number of record pair comparisons to be conducted, depending upon the number of database owners included in a group.

10.7 Summary and Further Reading

Many organisations, including businesses, government agencies, and research organisations, are collecting unprecedented amounts of data, which are generally stored, processed, and analysed in order to identify interesting patterns and knowledge that support efficient and quality decision making [254]. These databases often contain many thousands or even millions of records about individuals, which makes linking such large databases computationally challenging.

In this chapter we have first discussed the blocking and indexing techniques that can be used to scale-up the linkage of sensitive databases in terms of their numbers of records, as well as the number of databases that can be linked. We described different blocking and indexing approaches for linking two or more sensitive databases, where different techniques are used to group records into blocks. These techniques include hashing, secure multiparty computation, and efficient data structures. The surveys by Christen [110] and Papadakis et al. [463] provide comprehensive reviews about existing general (non privacy-preserving) blocking and indexing techniques and their comparative performance.

We further discussed different block processing and filtering techniques that can be applied in-between the blocking and comparison steps of the linkage process to further reduce the number of record pairs that need to be compared in detail. We refer readers who are interested in such block processing techniques to the survey by Papadakis et al. [462].

We finally discussed how modern parallel computing platforms and distributed software frameworks have been used to make the linkage of very large databases even more scalable, and how different communication patterns can influence the performance of linking large databases from multiple database owners. The majority of parallel and distributed record linkage techniques developed so far do not consider the privacy and confidentiality of the content of sensitive databases, and therefore these techniques might not be applicable when sensitive databases need to be linked.

This chapter concludes the second part of this book where we presented many different technical aspects that are of relevance to linking sensitive databases. In the third part of the book we cover various aspects that are of a more practical nature, starting in the following chapter with a discussion of practical considerations and challenges.

Part III
Practical Aspects, Evaluation, and Applications

In this third part of the book we cover practical aspects when linking sensitive data. In Chapter 11 we first discuss practical considerations such as how to deal with noisy and dirty data, as well as incomplete and missing data that commonly occur in real-world databases in many application areas. We also look at temporal and dynamic data which are becoming more widespread in today's connected and always online world. Furthermore we discuss aspects such as ease of implementation, the setting and tuning of parameters for algorithms and techniques, and computational requirements which will be of importance to practical implementations and use of techniques that allow the linkage of sensitive data.

In Chapter 12 we then provide an empirical evaluation of some of the techniques described in the second part of the book using real-world public databases. Our aim in doing so is to provide the reader with information about the suitability of available techniques, as well as their comparative performance on the same data set, as well as the trade-offs between privacy, scalability and linkage quality of different techniques.

Finally, in Chapter 13 we describe several existing application examples from different countries where privacy-preserving techniques are being employed to link real sensitive databases.

Chapter 11
Practical Considerations

Abstract When planning to link real-world sensitive databases, an organisation is likely faced with a variety of practical data related issues that can include, but are not limited to, noisy and dirty data, missing values in the attributes used for linkage, data recorded in different formats and structures, as well as data collected at different points in time. In this chapter we discuss how these issues can affect the linkage of sensitive databases, and how to consider these issues by employing appropriate data cleaning, preprocessing, and standardisation approaches, as well as linkage strategies that can deal with missing data. In the later sections of this chapter we then cover technical as well as institutional aspects that need to be considered when (sensitive) databases are being linked, such as the availability or lack of software, the difficulty of implementation of certain techniques, the setting and tuning of parameters required by different techniques, the requirement and management of computational resources, and the skills and expertise required to link sensitive databases. We conclude the chapter with a discussion of guidelines that have been developed to help practitioners improve their record linkage processes. Our aim with this chapter is to provide the reader with the breadth of issues they need to consider when linking (sensitive) databases.

11.1 Introduction

The process of linking (sensitive) databases across different organisations has over the past two decades gained increasing attention from researchers and practitioners from a variety of domains, ranging from health analytics and national census to crime and fraud detection [109]. The growing interest in linking databases is mainly due to an increase in awareness by organisations that the large volumes of data they collect can contain highly valuable and novel information that is not available in individual databases but only once records about the same entities are linked across diverse databases. In-

P. Christen et al., *Linking Sensitive Data*, https://doi.org/10.1007/978-3-030-59706-1_11

creasingly, organisations are now aiming to link not just their own databases internally, but also with external databases from other organisations, or even with data scraped from the Web or collected otherwise from public sources such as social networking sites. As a result, as we have discussed throughout this book, privacy and confidentiality are of concern when databases are being linked across organisations and when these databases contain sensitive information about entities such as persons or businesses.

Besides the core challenges of linkage quality, scalability to link very large databases, and privacy and confidentiality, there are various other aspects of practical nature that need to be considered when a system to link sensitive databases is being developed and ultimately deployed in a real-world setting. In this chapter we have categorised these into data related, technical, and institutional considerations. As technical we categorise all aspects related to implementing and running a linkage system, while institutional considerations are those non-technical aspects that organisations that aim to link (sensitive) databases can be faced with. We discuss each of these three categories in detail in the following three sections.

11.2 Data Related Considerations

In Section 3.3 we have already discussed the importance of data quality in the general record linkage process, and how data of low quality can and likely will influence the final outcomes of a linkage project (also known as the "garbage-in garbage-out" principle). Besides data quality, there are other aspects, such as the temporal nature of data, that in some applications need to be considered. In this section we revisit this topic and specifically discuss how different data related aspects can influence the process of linking sensitive databases.

Data quality is a point of major concern in any information system, including record linkage. Similar to data mining, challenging and often time consuming steps in any record linkage project are the tasks of understanding, preprocessing (standardising), and cleaning the databases to be linked. In data preprocessing, various data related problems must be dealt with, including missing or erroneous data, and potentially also duplicate records (that refer to the same entity) within the databases to be linked [109, 274, 509].

As a result, the effectiveness of any linkage project can be highly dependent on the quality of the databases to be linked, even more so than on the tools or algorithms used in the linkage process. It is important to select quasi-identifying attributes for linking records that ideally have no errors and are complete (have no missing values). However, when linking different databases, some errors, variations, and missing values might have to be tolerated. For example, a gender wrongly recorded as 'm' (male) instead of 'f' (female) for an individual record may have little effect on the linkage if a low importance (match weight) has been allocated to gender in the similarity calculation between records, and if the other quasi-identifying attributes of this record contain correct values for that individual.

While modern linkage techniques and algorithms can deal with variations in attribute values (for example, recognising 'Ann Miller' as 'Anne Miller'), each difference in a quasi-identifying attribute between two records being compared can result in a lower match similarity thereby reducing the likelihood of a correct match. Data quality aspects therefore require careful consideration when quasi-identifying attributes are selected for the comparison of records, where different data quality aspects require specific methods and techniques in order to achieve high linkage quality.

11.2.1 Dealing with Dirty Data

Dirty data can be defined as any data that are not following what is expected in the context of a certain domain or application. This can include attribute values that contain characters that are not valid for a given attribute, such as letters for date values that are assumed to be in the 'YYYYMMDD' format, or digits in personal name values. Other forms of dirty data are values outside of the expected and valid range, such as a date of birth of 13 Jan 2091, or a numerical human age value of 177 years. More subtle forms of dirty data include variations and mispellings of personal names for the same individual. While 'gayle' and 'gail' are both valid female first names, a single individual will only have one of these as her actual correct first name. Identifying abnormal values, especially in domains such as addresses where a large variety of values are possible, is not a trivial undertaking [117].

As we discussed in Section 3.3, data preprocessing, cleaning, and standardisation are important steps in any project that aims to link databases. The objective of this step of the record linkage process is to make the quasi-identifying attribute values in the databases that are used in the linkage process, either for blocking and indexing or for the detailed comparison of record pairs, as consistent with each other as possible. This means some form of name standardisation might be applied, including phonetic encoding as we covered in Section 6.6. Addresses are often parsed into well-defined fields to allow more accurate and fine-grained comparisons [126].

In the context of linking sensitive databases across organisations, where potentially more than two or even many databases need to be linked, as we discussed in Section 10.5, this task of data cleaning and standardisation needs to be coordinated between all database owners involved in such a multiparty linkage project. Here we assume that the databases are sensitive and cannot be sent to one single organisation, such as a linkage unit, to be cleaned and standardised centrally. Detailed agreements need to be made between all database owners how the values in the quasi-identifying attributes used for linkage are to be cleaned and standardised. Ideally, full automatic data cleaning and standardisaiton processes are employed that do not require manual tuning or setting of parameters, because otherwise there can be editing effects across the databases to be linked that might lead to lower linkage quality.

Potentially a privacy-preserving schema matching approach, such as the secure hashing based method by Scannapieco et al. [533] which we described in Section 7.6, needs to be employed to first map the individual local attribute schema of each database owner into one common global schema to be used for the linkage, without the individual database owners having to reveal their actual database schema because this might reveal sensitive private information.

Ideally, once the databases to be linked are cleaned and standardised, metadata about their quality is being provided by the database owners to the party which will use the linked data set further (known as the data consumer), for example to conduct research studies using the linked data set. Such metadata contain details about the quality of the input data and what types of data cleaning and standardisation have been conducted, and how many missing data values have for example been imputed in certain attributes or how many values have been modified based on some name or address standardisation algorithm [126].

In a record linkage context, consistency of the formats and values across the quasi-identifying attributes is important. An attribute can be characterised in terms of its domain which can include its data type, length (number of digits or characters), and the range of values that it can contain. For some attribute its domain can be difficult to ascertain (think of street addresses), while for others their characteristics can change over time. For example, linkage attributes such as socioeconomic status, or race and ethnicity can be problematic if their definitions or values change over time, especially if these are self-reported by individuals.

It is widely agreed that careful standardisation and data cleaning is a necessary step in any linkage process [226, 644]. It has to be noted, however, that any data cleaning, standardisation, and preprocessing conducted can introduce errors and bias. Randall et al. [509] investigated how data cleaning does affect linkage quality. Using both synthetic (with errors and variations introduced) as well as real data, Randall et al. found that overall data cleaning had little effect on linkage quality as evaluated using the F-measure. Interestingly their analysis showed that while some data cleaning techniques resulted in small improvements of linkage quality, others actually led to significant decrease of F-measure results. This was especially the case with name standardisation (including replacing nicknames with a standardised full name), as this substantially increased the number of false matches [509]. However, these results may be due to the already high quality of the data used before the cleaning started. In any case, this study showed that it is important to ensure that any data cleaning and standardisation does not lead to a reduction of linkage quality, and also not introduce any bias into the linked data set, as we discuss in more detail in Section 11.2.4 below.

11.2.2 Dealing with Missing Values

Missing values are a common data quality problem in many real-world databases. There are various reasons for missing values to occur, where missing data can be categorised into different types as we discuss below. The reasons why attribute values can be missing are highly diverse and include:

- Equipment malfunction, resulting in a set of records having a missing value in one or several attributes. For example, assume the electronic payment machines in a supermarket are not working due to a network error. This means all transactions during that time period of malfunction will only have cash payment details but no credit or debit card numbers that would allow linking these transactions to certain customers.

- Not entered due to misunderstanding or time constraints, which can occur in manual data entry processes when personnel are given unclear or wrong instructions, or they are under time pressure and therefore only the minimum required details are being entered. This can for example occur in a busy hospital emergency department.

- Not considered important during data entry is a similar reason, but here a decision was made not to enter the information from certain attributes, resulting in all (or at least a set of) records in a given database not containing any values for these attributes. For example, email addresses might not have been considered important in a hospital database to contact patients and therefore they were not recorded and entered.

- Deleted due to inconsistency with other values, which might occur in cases when there are input rules and constraints that need to be fulfilled before a record can be entered. Data entry personnel who might be under time pressure (or are being paid by the number of records they are entering in a given time period) will likely find a way to overcome such input rules by simply deleting any values that violate these rules.

- Refusal to provide an answer in a survey questionnaire by the respondent, who might think answering a certain question will potentially lead to embarrassment or shame, or simply decides not to provide an answer because it is of a personal sensitive matter for them. Alternatively, if a value is required somebody might enter a random or faked value such as a telephone number '04 1234 5678' (this will not result in a missing value but will affect data quality in other ways).

- Value not applicable for a certain record depending upon who this record is representing. For example, for children any employment or education details might not be applicable (no job details for children under a certain age) or still be in progress (highest education outcomes).

Based on these diverse reasons of why missing values can occur, there are different types of how missing data can be categorised:

- **Missing completely at random (MCAR)**: This category assumes that missing values occur without any patterns or correlations at all with any other attribute values in the same record or database. Given a set of records that contain MCAR values, it is not possible to predict the fact that a value is missing. However, predicting the actual value might be possible. Therefore, MCAR can be seen as a mechanism that generates a random sample of values. If data are plausible, then MCAR can be evaluated by a test suggested by Little [395] which compares the mean values of different attributes depending on a missingness indicator variable.

  In many real-world databases, MCAR does rarely occur. Rather, missing values occur due to some other mechanism described in the following. One example of MCAR values would be a bank of 30 university exam questions, and where each student is randomly assigned 20 out of these questions. As a result, 10 of 30 questions will have no answer for each student in a MCAR fashion.

- **Missing at random (MAR)**: Unlike MCAR, this category assumes that the missingness of an attribute value can be predicted by other data in the same record and/or database. Therefore, although the missing value is caused by a systematic process, the actual value can still be predicted. For example, assume a database of individuals with their yearly salaries and their profession. Assume the average salary of people with profession 'CEO' is 2M US Dollar and the median is 4.2M US Dollar. For any record where the profession is given as 'CEO' it is therefore possible to impute either the average or median value for CEOs as calculated from this database. While the actual salary value for a given CEO might be missing, an estimate can be imputed based on the records of other CEOs in this database.

  If data are MCAR or MAR, imputation and editing methods [274] can be used to impute the most likely value for a missing value based on other similar records in the same database. Data editing and imputation has a long history in various domains, including national statistics, survey methodology, and more recently in statistical machine learning and data mining [631].

- **Missing not at random (MNAR)** Such patterns of missing data occur if there are specific reasons why there are missing values in certain attributes. For example, if some patients in a medical study suffer strokes and therefore will not return to re-examinations, statistics based on the examined patients will be biased due to an MNAR data generation mechanism. As a result, there can be subsets of records in a database that have missing values not at random but rather due to some underlying mechanism. Data not missing at random should not be ignored in any study conducted on such data because it potentially will introduce bias [396].

Imputing missing values for MNAR data is not possible in the same way as MCAR or MAR values can be imputed based on other values in the data. Since missing data under MNAR cannot be predicted with data available in a given data set, either external data or strong assumptions on the missing data generating process are needed for imputation. Statistical models for MNAR are rare in practice, where substantial subject matter knowledge on the data generating process is required for developing such models.

- **Structurally missing**: These are values that are missing because they should not exist and missing is their correct value. For example, young children should not have any information about employment such as a job title. The best way to deal with such records is to exclude them from any relevant analysis, by for example removing all records with an age value below 18 years if one is interested in analysing the employment characteristics of a population.

  Note that structurally missing data are different to missing not at random data. For the former there exist no correct actual values (the correct value is an empty value), while for the second category there does exist a correct value but for certain reasons it was not included in a given record in a database.

Hand [259], in the more general context of dark data (the different types of how data can be missing without us knowing they are missing) describes three types of how data can be missing: unseen data dependent, seen data dependent, and not data dependent. He provides illustrative examples of how these different types of missing data can occur.

In the context of linking databases, only limited work has investigated how missing values can affect the outcomes of a linkage project, and proposed improved linkage methods that take missing values into account.

Ong et al. [455] proposed three methods to improve the quality of linked data when missing values occur in the databases being linked. The first method distributes the weights assigned to attributes, such as the match weights calculated in the probabilistic record linkage approach proposed by Fellegi and Sunter [204] as we described in the side box on page 54. The weights of the attributes that have a missing value are distributed to other attributes that do have a value (are not missing), and then the weights of the attributes that have a missing value are set to zero. The second method uses imputation rules to calculate the distance between attributes in a record pair if one attribute value is missing, rather than trying to impute an actual missing value. The third method uses alternative quasi-identifying attributes besides those that are used to compare record pairs that do not have missing values. To achieve this, the set of available quasi-identifying attributes is split into a primary and a secondary group, where attributes in the secondary are used for a record pair if one or more of the pair's attributes in the primary group are missing. An experimental evaluation of these three methods showed that all can improve linkage quality compared to not considering missing values. Each of the three methods performed differently based on the characteristics of the missing values patterns in the databases that were linked.

Goldstein and Harron [232] considered the problem of missing values from the perspective of an analyst who requires non-missing values in a set of variables (attributes) in a primary data set that is to be analysed. Some values in these variables might need to be sourced from one or more secondary data sets via linkage. Record linkage can therefore be seen as the tool used to facilitate the analysis, where the aim is to transfer information across data sets rather than linking individual records. It is assumed the probabilistic record linkage approach by Fellegi and Sunter is used for the linkage, as we discussed in Section 3.2 and illustrated in the side box on page 54. A technique based on multiple imputation is then employed where the match weights calculated in the probabilistic linkage step are used to decide how to impute a missing value. Experiments on both real health data as well as synthetic data showed that this approach provided less bias in the final analysis compared to using the data sets linked with probabilistic record linkage [232].

An alternative approach to deal with missing values when linking databases was developed by Ferguson et al. [205], who used the Expectation-Maximisation (EM) algorithm [151], an iterative method to calculate a maximum likelihood estimate for parameters of a given objective function. In the method proposed by Ferguson et al., the EM algorithm is adapted and used in two stages by considering both the imputation of missing values as well as incorporating correlations between values. This adapted EM algorithm is then used to calculate match and non-match weights following the Fellegi and Sunter probabilistic record linkage approach [204]. The proposed approach was evaluated on real health databases with records of nearly 800,000 patients, achieving improved linkage quality compared to not considering missing values.

In the context of linking sensitive databases in a privacy-preserving way, Chi et al. [103] proposed a method to impute missing values in quasi-identifying attributes in a record based on other similar records using a k nearest neighbour approach. The databases to be linked are first blocked, and for a record with a missing value in a certain block its most similar other records in the same block are identified based on the Fellegi and Sunter match weight calculation [204] (only records that have a match weight above a given threshold are considered as nearest neighbours). Quasi-identifying attribute values are encoded into Bloom filters, and for records that have a missing value in a certain quasi-identifying attribute the comparisons are conducted with its k nearest neighbouring records that do not have a missing value in that attribute.

While this approach can improve linkage quality when the databases to be linked contain missing values, the approach is sensitive with regard to the blocking technique employed as well as the choice of the number k of nearest neighbours used. Depending upon the characteristics of the databases and the blocking technique applied, it can be possible that the k nearest neighbours are not very similar to the record which has a missing value. For example, assume blocking was based on first name values concatenated with postcode values (for example 'john2200'). For a record with a missing surname in this block, its most similar records (nearest neighbours) will unlikely have the same or similar surnames to the surname that is missing, and therefore the resulting similarity calculations can be inaccurate.

Given the current state of research, we would not recommend imputing quasi-identifying attribute values for record linkage (with the nearly trivial exception of guessing gender by first name). However, adjusting the decision rule or matching weights according to the available set of quasi-identifying attributes is an option. In practice, often different combinations of quasi-identifying attributes are used in successive blocking and comparison iterations. It should be kept in mind that this strategy might introduce violations of the requirement of transitive closure, as we discussed in the side box on page 56. In general, it is useful to compare subject matter results between linkages of the same databases using different missing data strategies.

11.2.3 Temporal and Dynamic Data

Most traditional record linkage techniques assume that the databases to be linked are static. Furthermore, temporal aspects of data, especially personal data, are generally not considered. However, most of the quasi-identifying attributes, such as names or addresses, that are used to link sensitive databases are subject to possible changes over time as people move and change their address, or get married and change their names. Even gender nowadays can be changed. Addresses can also change over time, such as postcode boundaries that are adjusted due to population changes, or streets and even towns being renamed for a variety of reasons. The only quasi-identifying attribute values that are fixed over time, assuming they are recorded correctly, are date and place of birth[1]. This is the reason why these attributes are suitable as salt values to make encoding more secure, as we discussed in Section 9.5.1.

If two or more databases to be linked have been collected over time (as for example is the case with hospital admission records or birth, death, and marriage certificates), or records in databases collected or extracted at different

---

[1] We acknowledge that the renaming of place names in rare cases will result in changed place of birth values.

points in time (such as national censuses), then it is likely that for some entities their quasi-identifying attribute values will have changed. In Australia, for example, according to the 2007 Survey of Income and Housing on Australian housing mobility, over 40% of household reference persons (head of households) had moved in the five years prior to being interviewed, with on average an estimated 250,000 people changing their address each month [33].

The aspect of such changes over time of quasi-identifying attribute values by the same entity has been addressed by work on temporal record linkage [104, 287, 392]. The basic idea of these techniques is to modify the weights assigned to the similarities of quasi-identifying attributes that are known to change over time. For example, if address details change more often over time than first name values, then two records with timestamps three years apart (the dates when they were collected or last updated) that have a different address might still refer to the same person if their names are the same or highly similar. Therefore, a low address similarity should not penalise the overall similarity for such a record pair.

Thus far, only one approach has been proposed to incorporate such temporal adjustments into the similarity calculations for Bloom filter based privacy-preserving record linkage [496]. The basic idea is for the database owners to first generate attribute level Bloom filters (as we discussed in Section 8.3.1) as well as the temporal similarity adjustments for the different attributes and different time intervals (as the time differences between records increase more individuals will change their address). This process is conducted in such a way that no database owner learns any sensitive information about temporal changes from any other database. The similarity adjustments for the different quasi-identifying attributes are then used to mask (set to 0) certain bit positions in these attribute level Bloom filters, where more masked bits means less weights are given to a certain attribute. Experiments on real-world databases showed that such temporal linkage techniques can lead to a significant increase in the precision of linkage quality while recall only drops sightly. This drop is mainly due to a loss of blocking quality because a change of an attribute value means records are inserted into different blocks and therefore not compared correctly. Privacy protection of this technique was comparable to a corresponding non-temporal Bloom filter based encoding approach [496].

Furthermore, besides temporal aspects that increasingly occur in many sensitive databases that contain personally identifiable information, there is a growing trend that rather than linking static databases, dynamic databases in operational settings are linked in an ongoing fashion. In dynamic databases records of new entities (such as new patients or customers) can be added and records of existing entities be updated and modified (for example with address or name changes) on an ongoing basis [116, 493]. This means that instead of a snapshot being extracted from an operational database, such as a hospital patient database, to be linked in a batch-oriented linkage, individual query records are being linked with a database that contains records about known entities. Such query record can for example be records for patients, where a linkage is required to identify if the patient is already in the database of the health care provider where they are admitted to, or the record is for a new patient. An additional requirement of such dynamic linkage techniques is that they often need to be performed in (near) real time [115, 137, 493] because based on the linkage outcomes a decision needs to be made (for example if a new patient record needs to be created or the medical file of an existing patient is to be retrieved).

Another example domain where such dynamic data occur is law enforcement and national security, as we discussed in Section 1.6.2. The aim of a linkage in this domain is often to identify potential suspects in a variety of databases to build up patterns of their behaviour. Such applications require the privacy-preserving querying and extraction of a set of records that refer to such suspects, a process known as secure cohort extraction [453]. The aim of this process is to link query records with records from a database such that the owner of that database does not learn which records were linked and extracted. The owners of these databases can for example be financial institutions, telecommunication companies, or airlines. Again, real-time linkage of a query record is crucial in such applications.

Some limited work on linking dynamic database has been conducted [115, 116, 137, 492, 493] where a main focus was to develop dynamic indexing or blocking techniques that allow efficient insertion of new or modification of existing records, and improving the speed of similarity calculations. However, none of these techniques have so far been adapted for the linkage of sensitive databases where encoded values need to be blocked or compared as we discussed in previous chapters.

One approach to facilitate fast (near) real-time linkage of sensitive databases encoded into Bloom filters, as we discussed in Chapter 8, has been proposed by Karapiperis et al. [330]. The approach is based on summarising Bloom filters as well as blocks into short encodings to allow both fast blocking and fast comparisons, where these short encodings are generated by sampling certain bit positions from Bloom filters. The proposed approach was evaluated on large databases showing it is highly scalable and requires much less memory compared to other related encoding techniques.

11.2.4 Dealing with Bias in Linked Data

Bias in the context of linking (sensitive) databases can occur due to various reasons, and be introduced at different steps of the record linkage process. In the broader area of data science (and especially machine learning based classification), bias can be defined as obtaining results of a classification task that are systematically prejudiced for certain subsets of records due to some artefacts of the learning algorithm or training data set used to build a classification model. For example, as we discussed in Section 1.7, machine learning models trained on job advertisements where gender information is included have been shown to recommend job offerings with higher income to males than to females because in the training data set men had more lucrative jobs than women [146]. This is known as algorithmic bias.

When linking databases, bias can include that certain subpopulations, for example migrants, students, or indigenous or homeless people, might have lower linkage rates (higher rates of missed matches) compared to the overall population because their names have more variations (such as immigrants from countries with names in different languages or of different structures), they change address more often (young students), or they might have no fixed addresses at all (homeless people). These issues make such subpopulations more difficult to link, and potentially result in higher false match or false non-match rates for certain subpopulations. Any analysis on a linked data set, especially if it is aimed at such a subpopulation, needs to carefully consider such potential bias in a linked data set.

Considering the different steps of the record linkage process, any data cleaning and data preprocessing conducted on the databases to be linked can potentially introduce other types of bias that also need to be accounted for when a linked data set is being processed or analysed further. Name and address standardisation generally reduces the variety of name and address values, and this might lead to an increase in both true as well as false matches (leading to linkage results with higher recall but lower precision) [509]. In the blocking step, the selection of a certain blocking technique, blocking key (blocking criteria), as well as the parameter setting of a blocking algorithm, can lead to either larger and therefore more inclusive blocks, or to smaller and therefore more selective blocks. For the example of not linking younger students who are changing their address, if address attributes are part of a blocking key then it is likely that a higher number of links of older people (who are more settled and thus have a stable address) will be identified compared to younger more mobile individuals. It has, for example, been reported repeatedly that preterm and low birth weight children are harder to link (for a review see Bohensky et al. [71]). In many cases, this seems to be due to missing or incomplete quasi-identifying attribute values [265].

In the classification step of the record linkage process, bias can be introduced if a supervised learning technique is employed that is trained on a ground truth data set that was created using a certain methodology. As we discuss in more detail in Section 11.2.5, ground truth data can be obtained or generated on a variety of methods ranging from the previous linkage of an earlier version of the same databases that are being linked to the generation of synthetic data. It is however common that not every record pair in a ground truth data set is actually a true match. Using ground truth data with different characteristics will likely lead to different classification models being trained and thus result in different linkage outcomes.

In recent times, the topic of bias and fairness in data science has received interest due to the increasingly widespread use of automated machine learning based systems in many aspects of modern life [250]. A discussion of a variety of issues that can influence classification accuracy, ranging from training set selection to algorithmic aspects, were discussed by Hand [256]. He for example cautions to employ advanced classification methods that have shown to have superior performance in academic settings over more simple methods because such improved performance might not generalise into real-world settings.

Once databases have been linked, the resulting linked data set can be used in a variety of applications, ranging from health and social science research studies to crime and national security investigations. Depending upon how databases were linked, as we have discussed, a linked data set will likely contain some false matches and not contain some true matches, and it is possible that there are different types of biases that occur in different subpopulations in the linked data set. In many organisations or applications where databases are being linked, the linkage is conducted by a different group of people (the data linkers) in an organisation compared to the people who conduct any following analysis or processing (the data analysts). For many applications of linked data it is likely that the analysis or further processing of a linked data set is even conducted by a different organisation (such as health or social science researchers at a university who obtain a linked data set from a health linkage centre or a national statistical agency) [84].

Data analysts often are not given any details of how a linked data set has been generated, what data cleaning and standardisation has been conducted on the input databases, how the linkage was performed, and what linkage error rates and bias might occur in the data set. As a result, data analysts commonly assume a linked data set is perfect in that all linked records are correct, and that the data set contains all the correct links for the population under consideration (the assumption is that the linkage is complete and no true links have been missed, and no false links have been included). However, this is unlikely the case for most linked data sets.

Thus far, the aspect of how bias and errors in linked data sets can influence and distort any follow-up use of linked data sets has only received limited attention, most in the statistical and health research communities [81, 661]. Harron et al. [267] investigated linkage error and resulting bias in real as well as synthetic health data sets that were linked using two different classification methods. In the first method links were selected based on their highest match scores, while the second method was based on probabilistic match scores and an imputation method where attribute values from the original databases were used rather than values from the linked records [233]. The experimental results of this study showed large differences in bias in the linked data sets, especially when linkage rates were low or the amount of errors and variations introduced into the quasi-identifying attributes used for linkage was high. This study highlighted the importance of assessing any potential bias that can be introduced into linked data sets, especially if the databases to be linked are known to contain errors and variations.

In follow-up work, Harron et al. [268] then provided guidance of how to evaluate linkage quality. Given linkage errors can be a source of bias for any studies that are using linked data, their work highlights the need of carefully assessing linkage quality. Using the example application of linking hospital records of mothers and babies across two different databases, they illustrated three methods to evaluate linkage quality. The first assumes a gold standard set of known true matches is available for a subset of the linked records. The second method compares the characteristics of linked as well as non-linked records to identify subpopulations that have higher or lower match rates which will indicate potential bias in the linked data set. The third method is based on a sensitivity analysis where settings of the linkage algorithm (such as a classification threshold) are varied and the resulting changed linked record pairs are analysed. All three approaches can help better understand the characteristics of linkage errors and how they might result in bias in a linked data set.

More recently, Doidge and Harron [159] discussed in detail the types of bias that can be introduced in linked data sets for different linkage applications in the health domain. They described eleven linkage structures (when two databases are being linked) of how a linked data set can be generated. These linkage structures range from the intersection (only consider individuals whose records occur in both data sets, such as car accident victims who were admitted to hospital), union (consider all individuals whose records occur in either of the two databases being linked, such as all patients who have been admitted to hospitals A or B), to set differences (individuals whose records occur only in the database of hospital A but not also in the database of hospital B). For each of the eleven linkage structures described, different types of bias can be introduced that need to be considered by a data analyst who will be working with a corresponding linked data set.

Besides bias based on false match and false non-match errors, this work [159] also considered if splitting or merging of records that represent individuals is possible. Splitting is the case where several records about the same individual from one database are linked to records of different individuals in the second database, while merging is the case where records of more than one individual are merged and represented as one linked entity. For some of the eleven linkage structures discussed, such merging and splitting can happen while for others these types of linkage errors are not possible. Important is that a data analyst working with a linked data set should be aware of what types of errors and bias might have been introduced during the linkage.

These studies about how linkage error and bias can affect the quality of any data analysis that is based on linked data sets have raised awareness and concerns especially in the health domain where linked data sets are increasingly being used in research studies. As a result, guidelines and best practice recommendations for record linkage projects and research based on linked data sets have been proposed [225, 264], as we discuss in more detail in Section 11.5.

11.2.5 Availability or Lack of Ground Truth Data

As we have discussed in Chapter 3 and throughout this chapter, the availability of ground truth data for a linkage project is crucial for evaluating the outcomes of the project, and potentially also for training a supervised machine learning classifier [109]. However, in many real-world applications where (sensitive) databases are to be linked, ground truth data are not readily available, or they need to be manually prepared (a potentially expensive and time consuming process). We now discuss various aspects that need to be considered when obtaining ground truth data in the general context of linking databases.

Assuming the databases to be linked contain personal details in the quasi-identifying attributes used for the linkage, then these attributes can have a possibly very large variety of values, including variations of names as well as errors and value changes over time (as we discussed in Section 3.3). Ground truth data should ideally include many examples of this large variety of values in order to allow proper evaluation of how different errors, variations, missing values, and value changes over time, do affect linkage quality. This means a ground truth data set needs to contain a large number of record pairs that correspond to true matches, where these record pairs contain all kinds of data quality issues. In other words, ground truth data need to contain all data quality issues that are expected to occur in the databases being linked. Obtaining a large enough number of record pairs with varying data quality aspects can be very challenging. Note that true non-matches can generally be generated from the set of known true matches, in that any record pair that is not a true match can be labelled as a true non-match (care must however be taken if a linkage between databases does allow many-to-many links and it is known that the ground truth is not complete).

A further challenge is that, even if it is possible to obtain record pairs with various degrees of data quality characteristics, it might be very difficult to ascertain if these pairs really correspond to the same entity (are true matches). Without having access to extra information (such as contacting individuals in selected record pairs and asking them for the correctness of their personal details) it might not be possible to have high confidence in the accuracy of these selected record pairs. This will be especially a problem for large databases that cover large portions of a population, as is the case in many administrative or health databases.

Ground truth data can be acquired or generated in a variety of ways:

- **Use Results of a Previous Linkage Project**: One approach is to use the results of a previous linkage project on databases from the same domain. Ideally, these should be earlier versions of the same databases that are to be linked. If similar databases have been linked previously using the same linkage method, and they have then been manually evaluated with regard to the quality of the linked record pairs, then domain experts will hopefully have identified both false matches and false non-matches in the previously linked databases, and these manual assessed record pairs can be used as ground truth data.

However, different linkage methods might have been used to link previous versions of the current databases, resulting in a linked data set that has a lower quality and is not complete (has more missed true matches). Furthermore, as data changes over time, the data quality characteristics of the current version of the databases to be linked might be quite different from the quality of previous versions of the same databases (potentially due to changes in data entry or capture methods). Additionally, the manual assessment of classified record pairs, especially those classified to be ambiguous (potential matches [109]), is often not one hundred percent correct, as studies have shown [563]. Therefore, a manually prepared ground truth data set will potentially contain errors (false matches) and also not be complete in that some true matching record pairs are likely missing from such a ground truth data set.

- **Sample Record Pairs for Manual Classification**: In applications where no results of a previous linkage of similar databases are available, a related approach to the one described before is to sample records from the databases to be linked, and to manually assess if they correspond to a true match or not. This approach has two difficulties.

  The first is similar to the drawbacks described above when previously linked databases are used as a source for ground truth data, in that the manual classification of record pairs is unlikely always correct [563]. Manual classification will likely introduce mistakes, where these mistakes are not made on the record pairs that are easy to classify, such as two records that differ in all their quasi-identifying attribute values (these are highly likely true non-matches) or pairs where all their quasi-identifying attribute values are the same (these are highly likely true matches). Rather, the challenge lies in correctly classifying the difficult to classify record pairs, those that have some quasi-identifying attributes with the same or highly similar values, while different values in other attributes.

  The second challenge is how to sample a representative set of record pairs across the two databases to be linked, where this set needs to contain pairs that are both easy and difficult to classify. Importantly, as we discussed above, these pairs should cover all (or at least the most common) data quality issues that occur in the databases to be linked. Using simple random sampling of records from the databases and then forming pairs will not result in a representative ground truth data set, because most record pairs (even after blocking or indexing has been applied) will correspond to true non-matches and will likely have mostly different values in the quasi-identifying attributes. This is because of the quadratic comparison space when record pairs are compared, as we discussed in Section 10.1. Some form of stratified sampling needs to be employed, where record pairs are sampled for manual assessment of their match status based on their calculated similarities (such as the example shown in Figure 3.3). Ideally, pairs with a large variety of similarities need to be selected. This can be achieved, for example, by binning the comparison vectors of the compared record pairs according to their summed similarities, and then sampling the same number of pairs from each bin.

- **Use Public Benchmark Databases**: A third approach to obtain ground truth data is to use one of the small number of publicly available test databases, as we discuss in more detail in Section A.2. While a variety of such test databases have been made available by researchers to allow the comparative evaluation of their algorithms [361], the majority of these databases are in the domains of bibliographic records or consumer products, but not in the domain of personal data. This is understandable given the often highly sensitive nature of personal identifying information. Using a ground truth data set from a different domain is however not a suitable approach to evaluate a linkage project, or even to train a supervised classification method. Even using data from the same domain (like personal information such as names and addresses) from a different country is not recommended given the likely different characteristics, values, distributions, and structures of names and addresses between countries.

- **Generate Synthetic Ground Truth Data**: An alternative approach (to the previous three ways of acquiring or generating ground truth data based on real data) is to generate artificial or synthetic data that have similar characteristics as the actual databases that are being linked [118, 121, 598]. The advantages of synthetic data are that their content (the quasi-identifying attributes to be used for the linkage), size (number of records), and data quality aspects (errors and variations) can be controlled by the data generation software, and the match status of every generated record pair is known. The challenges when generating synthetic data are to be able to create data that follow the characteristics of real data close enough to obtain meaningful ground truth data. We discuss this topic of synthetic data generation in more detail in Section A.3.

When sensitive databases are to be linked across different organisations in a privacy-preserving context, then the issue of obtaining ground truth data becomes even more challenging. Given the databases to be linked contain sensitive personal information, it is likely not possible to disclose quasi-identifying attribute values of records across these databases to facilitate human inspection of these values to make manual match or non-match decisions. The use of public benchmark databases or synthetic data might be the only options available to obtain some form of ground truth data for a given project that aims to link sensitive databases across organisations.

11.2.6 Costs of False Matches and False Non-Matches

While only indirectly related to data, the issue of the costs that are associated with any false matches (the record pairs classified as a match that however refer to different entities) as well as false non-matches (missed true matches, the record pairs classified as non-matches that however refer to the same entity) is an important and often neglected aspect of any practical application that is linking (sensitive) databases.

As we discussed in Section 3.4.1, the costs of the four outcomes of a linkage (true matches, false matches, true non-matches, and false non-matches, as illustrated in Figure 3.5 on page 61) are generally not considered by most classification techniques and evaluation measures used in linking sensitive databases. Linkage quality measures such as precision and recall, as we discussed in Section 3.4.1, assume a false match and a false non-match have the same costs assigned to them. Only limited work has explored how to achieve optimal linkage results when the four outcomes of a linkage have different costs associated with them [625].

The costs of a false match and a false non-match can however be different from application to application. In the side box on page 307 we provide a specific example highlighting this issue. As another example, in the context of national security, a missed match could mean a terrorist is not identified and an attack not prevented, while a false match means an innocent individual will be investigated and potentially even arrested under suspicion of planning a terrorist attack [309]. As Fienberg describes [208], there are various other aspects that make the use of record linkage in this context controversial.

While in both the above and the 'Robo-debt' examples there are direct costs (financial or otherwise) involved in both false matches and false non-matches, indirect costs can also occur for these two different types of wrong linkage outcomes. In the health domain, when a linked data set is used for medical research, both including a wrongly linked patient into a study, or missing a patient that should be involved in a study, will potentially lead to bias and errors in the outcomes of that study [159]. As a result, wrong conclusions are being made, such as inappropriate treatment plans which can jeopardise the lives of many patients. Therefore, while the two types of wrong outcomes of a linkage (false matches and false non-matches) might not have directly measurable costs associated with them, whatever decisions are being made based on a linked data set can result in potentially costly errors.

For any practical linkage application, it is therefore important to consider the costs associated with both record pairs wrongly classified as matches, as well as missed true matching record pairs. It is also important to understand that there is always a trade-off between the number (or ratio) of false matches and the number (or ratio) of false non-matches that are being obtained from a linkage project, as we discussed in Section 3.4.1. Finding an optimal outcome for a linkage does depend upon the relative importance and costs one is associating with these two types of errors. This is a subject matter decision

> ### Robo-debt
>
> An example of a very specific linkage project is the 'Robo-debt'[a] program by the Australian government, where databases from Australia's social security department were linked to taxation data with the aim to identify who owns money to the government. Given the sizes of the involved databases, this linkage was conducted largely automatic, with letters being sent to welfare recipients who according to the linkage outcomes had a debt with the government.
>
> Several hundred thousand such letters were sent out, a large number to individuals who did not have a debt at all (these correspond to false matches), or who only had a small debt. Investigations identified various deficiencies in this automatic linkage process. An example was reported by the Australian Broadcasting Corporation (ABC) in February 2020[b]:
>
> > Tracey Donaldson says her problems began when a bill arrived in the mail last month.
> >
> > It was a Centrelink debt for $45,500.
> >
> > The letter was intended for another woman with the same name, who lived in a suburb with the same name in a different state, said Ms Donaldson, whose name has been changed for legal reasons.
> >
> > The woman was also born on the same day of the same month as Ms Donaldson but in a different year.
>
> Clearly, a false match in this context can have significant negative outcomes for the individuals involved. A false non-match, on the other hand, means the government would not have been able to collect outstanding money by an individual who was possibly cheating the welfare system.
>
> ---
>
> [a]   See: https://en.wikipedia.org/wiki/Centrelink#Debt_recovery_controversy_(aka_'robo-debt')
>
> [b]   See: https://www.abc.net.au/news/2020-02-17/centrelink-bill-sent-to-sydney-woman-by-mistake/11964000

and therefore should be made by subject matter specialists, not by the people or units conducting the linkage. It is also nearly impossible to reduce the number of one type of error (such as having no false matches) because this will likely mean the number of errors of the other type will be rather high. Decision rules or classification settings based on exclusion of one type of error (for example, no false matches at any cost), are rarely appropriate. Requiring no errors at all would prevent linkage at all.

11.3 Technical Considerations

Data related issues will influence how sensitive databases can be linked to ideally obtain an unbiased linked data set of high quality that can be used for further processing or analysis. A crucial aspect will be what linkage techniques are best suitable to link two or more databases, and what privacy-preserving techniques need to be employed. In this section we discuss the technical aspects that need to be considered when sensitive databases are to be linked in practical applications.

11.3.1 Suitability of Linkage Protocols

In many record linkage projects, a group of organisations that wish to link their sensitive databases needs to select an actual linkage protocol that is appropriate and suitable to the linkage and follow-up analysis work. If sensitive data are used in the linkage process, as we have described in Section 4.3, the best practice approach is to separate personal quasi-identifying attributes (such as names, addresses, and dates of birth) from the attributes of interest for an analysis (the microdata, also known as content or payload attributes) [340]. With such a separation, personnel conducting the linkage will not have access to sensitive microdata, while those involved in any analysis will not see any quasi-identifying sensitive data. Such an approach will lower the risk of accidental breach of confidentiality. Appropriate technical infrastructure, such as databases and software systems that support such a separation, are required that allow the efficient and secure separation of quasi-identifiers from microdata, and appropriate encryption, storage, and communication of the resulting separated pieces of data [340].

Furthermore, it is important to understand the use of third parties in the linkage process (such as a linkage unit) if sensitive databases are to be linked. The role of third parties ensures that no database owner (or data provider) obtains access to any sensitive data from any other database owner. Furthermore, following the separation principle discussed above, a third party generally only obtains quasi-identifying information to conduct a linkage, or microdata as well as randomised link identifiers to generate the linked data set, but not both [340]. No third party should be able to reidentify any individual during the linkage process nor from the linked microdata. For example, as we have shown in the side box on page 84, if the database owners use a third party (such as a linkage unit) to link records in their databases, this party is only provided with identifying information of the records in these databases, while the sensitive microdata of records that are part of a linked record pair are given to the data consumer based on the linkage results.

In linkage protocols where several third parties are involved that potentially can collude [125], or an adversary would get access to sensitive data held by multiple third parties, the proper use of appropriate encoding and encryption techniques (as we discussed in Chapters 6 to 9) should prevent that any reidentification of individuals or even sensitive attributes in the databases held by these third parties is possible. For example, if the set of sensitive quasi-identifying attributes used for a linkage are split into several subsets and each subset will be linked by a different linkage unit (in the extreme case one linkage unit per quasi-identifying attribute, as proposed by Churches and Christen [125]), then the database owners can use different secret keys during the encoding of the values in each subset, and also use different randomly generated record identifiers for the different subsets. Such an approach will prevent the linkage units from meaningfully combine the encoded or encrypted data they receive from the database owners.

In some domains such as health, it is common to use one or more trusted third parties in the linkage process, either as linkage units, or as global facilitators or global authorities. These are dedicated organisations, likely from the public sector, that offer such third-party linkage services [84]. However, if the databases to be linked are deemed too sensitive then any third party that participates in the linkage process should be considered untrusted. More secure linkage methods based on privacy-preserving techniques that provide stronger privacy guarantees will then need to be used to ensure the privacy of the sensitive data is preserved before it is being used for any linkage and sent to a third party [253, 619].

While determining a suitable linkage protocol also includes organisational aspects, the crucial technical aspects include:

- The IT capabilities of the participating organisations with regard to computational capacities and their capabilities to be able to deploy appropriate software to clean and standardise and then encode and encrypt their sensitive databases. If the data cleaning and encryption are done locally by each database owner, it should be done by software without the need for manual tuning or setting of parameters. Otherwise, there will be editing effects across the different databases to be linked which potentially will result in lower linkage quality. While data quality will increase when a centralised cleaning and standardisation process is employed, this might not be possible for many applications where sensitive databases are to be linked across organisations.

- The IT capabilities of the participating organisations with regard to computational capacities and their capabilities to be able to deploy appropriate software to clean and standardise and then encode and encrypt their sensitive databases.

- The possible communication channels that can be used to transmit sensitive databases across organisations. These can range from secure direct Internet communication between the participating organisations, to manual transport of these databases either by courier or mail (as DVDs, USB flash drives, or hard drives).

- The frequency of how communication can be used to transmit sensitive databases, where in the extreme case it is only possible to access, encode, and encrypt a database once at an organisation before it is transmitted to the organisation undertaking the linkage. More convenient is the situation where it is possible to have multiple interactions between the different organisations where updated databases can be communicated more frequently.

From a practical perspective, deciding upon a suitable protocol is crucial as it will likely determine (and potentially limit) the type of actual linkage techniques that can be employed, as we discuss next.

11.3.2 Suitability of Linkage Techniques

Once a protocol has been decided upon for either a single one-off linkage of sensitive databases, or more commonly for an ongoing collaboration between organisations to link their databases on a regular basis, the next step would be to decide what actual techniques (methods and algorithms) to employ to achieve the desired linkages. In Chapters 7 to 9 we have discussed a wide variety of techniques that facilitate the linkage of sensitive databases. All of these techniques have to balance the trade-off between linkage quality, scalability to large databases, and privacy protection.

Depending upon the regulatory framework within which a certain linkage is being implemented and deployed, only a limited set of privacy-preserving record linkage techniques might be allowed based on the privacy protection they provide, while other techniques might not fulfil regulatory requirements (such as pass an accreditation by a governmental computer security agency).

The expected quality of the databases to be linked does determine what kind of linkage algorithms can be employed to obtain high linkage quality. Techniques that allow for approximate similarity calculations are most commonly required, unless the databases to be linked contain reliable entity identifiers, or they are known to contain quasi-identifying attribute values that are all of high quality. The types of quasi-identifying attributes to be used in a linkage also determine what types of comparisons are required (only for string values, or also for dates, numerical, or other types of values).

The sizes of the database to be linked will influence if some form of blocking or indexing needs to be applied, especially if there are operational requirements such as timeframes or deadlines by when a linkage needs to be completed.

The availability or lack of ground truth data, as we discussed in Section 11.2.5, determines what type of classification techniques can be used to classify the compared record pairs into matches or non-matches. Furthermore, the type of linkage (either one-to-one links are required, or one-to-many, many-to-one, or many-to-many links are possible) will potentially require further post-processing steps to be conducted, such as addressing the transitive closure [109] which we discussed in the side box on page 56.

The process of manual clerical reviewing of potential matches, as for example required when the traditional probabilistic record linkage approach by Fellegi and Sunter is being employed [204], is only feasible if access to plaintext values from the sensitive databases that are being linked is permitted. In many situations where sensitive databases are being linked across organisations this will unlikely be the case. Therefore, linkage techniques that classify the compared record pairs into only the two classes of matches and non-matches are required.

Different privacy-preserving record linkage techniques can be combined depending upon the goals of a record linkage project, such as the requirements on the linked data set and how it will be analysed or used further [520]. For example, if a population parameter is being estimated for a statistical study, an approach based on approximate matching and the probabilistic record linkage approach by Fellegi and Sunter [204] might be most efficient even though wrong individual links might be generated. On the other hand, for applications where the purpose is to make inferences about specific individuals based upon their data contained in two or more databases, the need for a high precision (high positive predictive value) linked data set would favour a deterministic method or a probabilistic method with careful clerical review (which might be impossible when sensitive databases are linked across organisations).

The choice for a suitable linkage technique also depends upon the availability and quality of the quasi-identifying attributes used for a linkage. As discussed by Gu et al. [244], if high quality quasi-identifiers are available in the databases to be linked, then an exact matching approach is often preferred over approximate matching methods. When lower data quality is assumed, an approximate matching technique will likely be required to obtain linked data of acceptable quality [271]. It is also possible to apply a series of different linkage steps (or iterations), where different techniques are being employed in each step, starting with an exact matching approach to capture clear and unambiguous links with high quality, followed by more and more relaxed linkage steps to identify record pairs that are only partially matching based on their quasi-identifying attribute values. However, it should be kept in mind that this strategy might result in inconsistent linkage results (violations of the transitive closure) as we discussed in Section 3.2 and illustrated in the side box on page 56.

Overall, depending upon the operational requirements, available computing resources and communication channels, as well as regulatory frameworks that determine the required levels of privacy and security protection, a decision will need to be made on what techniques will be suitable for a given linkage situation. The next step is then to identify available implementations of such techniques, or alternative ways of how a linkage system can be realised.

11.3.3 Availability of Software

As we have covered in Chapters 7 to 9, over the past two decades different methods and techniques have been proposed to link sensitive databases while preserving the privacy and confidentiality of the records in these databases [619, 620]. However, many of these techniques consist of complex algorithms and require fine-tuning of a number of parameters to achieve an acceptable linkage quality for a certain linkage project. For a novice linkage practitioner or user without much computer science background, the implementation of such an algorithm might seem impossible because of the dependency on different programming languages, as well as complex techniques and methods that require significant amounts of software design and programming skills. Therefore, the involvement of both linkage as well as software development experts in a project is likely required.

Furthermore, at the time of writing, there are only few software packages available that facilitate the privacy-preserving linkage of sensitive databases, as we discuss in more detail in Appendix A. Most of the techniques we discussed in Chapters 6 to 9 have been developed, implemented, and evaluated in an academic context. Many of these are proof-of-concept prototypes (some even only described conceptually) which cannot be used directly in production linkage projects in real-world applications. For other linkage techniques not enough details have been published to allow implementation of the technique [619].

In general, the in-house implementation of a record linkage technique into a production software system will require not just the necessary skills and expertise in the areas of software development, but also funding and resources to maintain and improve such systems once developed and deployed. We discuss these aspects from an institutional point of view in Section 11.4.

Because the task of linking databases has been a requirement for many organisations in a variety of domains for over half a century, a variety of commercial as well as freely available, open-source, software tools do exist to link databases (in non privacy-preserving ways). Many large vendors of business and statistical software packages do provide modules or implementations of some functionalities that allow the linking of records within (known as deduplication) or across databases. However, many of these are either very expensive or they do not provide the full functionality required by an organisation. As a result, even today many organisations are still implementing their own linkage software tailored to their domain and specific application requirements. Many of these implemented linkage software systems are rather ad-hoc and implement either some form of rule based approach, or they follow the probabilistic record linkage model proposed by Fellegi and Sunter in 1969 [204]. Experimental approaches as implemented in some open-source prototypes rarely scale to population covering databases. Some commercial software packages have started to implement machine learning based linkage techniques, however details of these approaches are commonly not made public for commercial reasons.

This lack of transparency of many commercial record linkage systems means it is not clear what exact linkage algorithm or technique, either a variation of a published algorithm or a proprietary approach, has been implemented. Extensive unbiased and independent evaluations between several commercial systems have not, to the best of the authors knowledge, been published. Without knowing the actual details of a linkage algorithm implemented in a commercial software package it might be difficult to customise and adapt such software to a given linkage application.

On the other hand, freely available open-source software is often the result of an academic research project, either by a single PhD student or a larger research group. While the availability of the source code (open-source software) will likely allow detailed inspection of the functionality implemented in a software package, the quality of that software will likely not be at the same level as what one would expect from commercial software [108]. Furthermore, such software might have very limited, if existing at all, support structure compared to commercial software systems. In many cases, once a research project is completed or a student has graduated, such projects are not continued.

For an organisation tasked with linking databases it might therefore be difficult to select software suitable for their operational requirement. There is potentially no software available that fulfils all required specifications, or the available commercial software that does fulfil requirements is not affordable by an organisation. In-house development and implementation in some cases might be the only suitable option.

While the discussion so far has been about general record linkage software, the situation becomes even more challenging when software is required that facilitates the privacy-preserving linkage of sensitive databases between organisations. To the best of the authors knowledge, there are no commercial software systems available that implement state-of-the-art privacy-preserving linkage techniques. Freely available software tools are also limited. While there are several prototype systems available, as we discuss in Appendix A, many only implement a limited number of algorithms, and most do not incorporate the required additional functionalities we discussed in Section 4.5. For example, secret key exchange and user authentication are two core functionalities that a system that is of practical use for real-world linkage applications needs to provide. Furthermore, thorough testing and security assessment, for example by an accredited governmental computer security agency, has not been conducted on most available prototype systems to link sensitive databases. This is however a must to provide organisations that are tasked with linking sensitive databases in practical applications with assurance about the security and reliability of the linkage systems they plan to deploy.

There is clearly a need to develop software, open-source or commercial, to link sensitive databases while at the same time preserving the privacy of individuals in these databases. However, implementing state-of-the-art algorithms and methods, as well as the required infrastructure to facilitate such linkages of sensitive databases, is a complex undertaking that will require significant efforts and investment, either commercially or through community efforts.

11.3.4 Customisation and Parameter Tuning

An often overlooked technical aspect of complex software systems such as privacy-preserving record linkage techniques are the questions of how to adapt these systems and fine tune their parameters for certain linkage scenarios to obtain the best possible linkage outcomes. This is often overlooked because many software systems come with certain default choices of algorithms and parameter settings, and users commonly simply employ these given choices and settings. This can however lead to suboptimal linkage outcomes.

Most steps of the linkage process, as we discussed in Section 3.2, allow a user to select a variety of different alternative algorithms or techniques to achieve a certain objective (for example, different blocking and indexing techniques all aim to reduce the number of record pairs that need to be compared). Furthermore, most of these algorithms and techniques have multiple parameters that need to be set to certain values. Each of these parameters will in some way or another influence the outcomes of an algorithm, and therefore either the algorithms or techniques in the following steps of the linkage process, as well as the final linkage outcomes (with regard to scalability, privacy, or linkage quality).

The big question therefore is how to best customise (if possible) and tune the different used algorithms and modules to obtain high quality final linkage results. Any customisation and setting of parameters will be data dependent, and therefore might need to be conducted individually for each linkage project. To achieve this, deep knowledge is required of all algorithms and techniques (as well as their implementations in a software system), of the databases to be linked (their quality and other characteristics), and of the desired linkage outcomes (which types of errors to minimise and what type of bias to prevent [159]).

11.3.5 Computational Requirements

The final technical aspect is the computational requirement of linkage techniques, including the electronic communication needed when databases are linked across organisations. This aspect is becoming more important as the databases to be linked are getting larger and more complex in many application areas.

While our society is moving into the era of Big data, in the context of linking sensitive databases, it is likely that the sizes of these databases are in some way or another limited by the sizes of the populations one is considering. Compared to other types and sources of data, such as sensor or multimedia data, the number of records about identifiable individuals is only growing slowly in many countries. Furthermore, the quasi-identifying attributes required for linking are generally not expanding significantly in their sizes either. While new forms of quasi-identifying attributes might become available, such as an individual's group of friends and her or his interest from a commercial social network site, or biometric data in the form of fingerprints or iris scans, most databases used for record linkage are owned by organisations that do not have access to or make use of such external data sources. Health, census, or other administrative data will likely continue to only contain names, addresses, other contact details (and sometimes identification numbers) besides the microdata about the individuals stored in such a database.

As a result, while the databases to be linked might contain tens or even hundreds of millions of records, advances in computing power and storage capabilities mean such databases can nowadays be stored and processed on modern high-end desktop computers or even small compute servers. Furthermore, modern blocking and indexing techniques [110, 461, 462], combined with high performance and parallel computing platforms, make the linkage of even large population databases feasible in reasonable timeframes on the computing environments available to many organisations.

However, if one is interested in using state-of-the-art privacy-preserving record linkage techniques that employ sophisticated encryption and encoding algorithms, as we discussed in Chapters 7 to 9, then more powerful computing platforms as well as high-speed network connectivity between organisations might be required. The reason for this is that many existing encryption and encoding techniques have high computation requirements. Some techniques, especially those based on secure multiparty computation (as we discussed in Section 6.5) also have high communication needs as large numbers of messages will need to be exchanged between the parties that participate in such computations.

11.4 Institutional Considerations

Besides the data related and technical considerations discussed so far, any practical application where sensitive databases need to be linked will be embedded within one or several organisations, and therefore covered by the regulations, policies, and guidelines under which these organisations are re-

quired to operate. In the following we discuss some key institutional aspects
that organisations that link sensitive databases might be faced with.

11.4.1 Required Domain and Technical Expertise

Linkage projects often inherit and face challenges that are related to the
correct understanding and interpretation of data, the selection of appropriate linkage technique, as well as the interpretation of the obtained linkage
results. As more sophisticated techniques are being developed and increasingly employed in practical linkage applications to improve the effectiveness
of record linkage, linkage projects rely upon the support not only of domain
experts who do understand the characteristics and quality of the databases
to be linked, but also experts in advanced record linkage techniques and
algorithms.

Both types of experts are required. A lack of domain and data expertise
can result in an unsuitable choice of data preprocessing and potentially a
wrong selection of a linkage technique being employed. On the other hand
a lack of technical expertise in modern linkage algorithms and methods will
likely result in the use of traditional record linkage approaches which might
lead to lower quality linked data as compared to when more advanced linkage
techniques would have been used.

Based on expertise by the authors, the amount of work needed for all
steps of the record linkage process (from data cleaning and standardisation
to manual clerical review of the obtained linkage results) is often substantially
underestimated. Organisations underestimate the time and efforts required
for data cleaning, overestimate software performance, and sometimes have
little knowledge about what resources and skills are required to develop software. Furthermore, there is commonly a lack of awareness that software needs
to be maintained. Staff also need to be trained in record linkage methodologies and techniques, and succession planning is required. It is unfortunately
common that significant technical knowledge is lost when a record linkage
expert retires from an organisation or changes job to another organisation.

One aspect that is relevant to both domain as well as technical expertise
is ground truth data. While ground truth data are commonly obtained or
generated by domain experts, these data are then used by linkage experts
who are familiar with the required techniques of how to properly evaluate
linkage outcomes, and potentially even use ground truth data in the context
of machine learning based classification techniques (for example to train supervised classifiers and evaluate classification models). As such, ground truth
data can be seen as an aspect that connects the two types of complementing
sets of expertise and skill (domain and linkage techniques), and allows personnel from these two areas to interact and learn from each other. In order

to be successful, repeated interaction and exchange of the complementary expertise and skills are likely needed.

Domain expertise is usually required in most of the steps of the linkage process. A data expert knows where suitable databases can be sourced from, how to evaluate data quality and best apply data cleaning and standardisation processes, and how to best link databases from different sources. Linkage expertise is required to generate the linking rules, weights, or select other suitable parameter settings, that determine the likelihood of a candidate record pair to become a match, or to generate suitable ground truth data for machine learning based linkage algorithms and to evaluate the quality of a linkage project. Linkage experts will also be required for the interpretation of linkage results, that is the translation of results into the language of the domain experts and data analysts who will be working on a linked data set.

Such expertise often requires a deep understanding about the domain and the characteristics of the databases to be linked, where continuous changes to both might occur over the lifetime of a linkage project. This means a continuous maintenance and use of domain expertise throughout a project, potentially resulting in linkage projects becoming more expensive and labour intensive and thus less affordable to an organisation.

With the increasing use of privacy-preserving record linkage techniques to link sensitive databases across organisations, it is paramount for the organisations involved in such linkage projects to have the necessary personnel with technical skills not just in linkage techniques and algorithms, but also in the crucial domains of computer security and cryptography. Given the sensitivity of personal data in many databases being linked, it is important to have experts involved in such projects that do understand the potential weaknesses of computer systems as well as of privacy-preserving record linkage techniques, and how these could be attacked by an adversary. Otherwise there is the potential of such techniques being configured or deployed in an inappropriate way leaving open possible loop-holes that could be exploited through one of the attacks we discussed in Section 5.4 or, as we described in Section 5.3, even via unintentional mishaps that also could lead to data breaches that can significantly damage the reputation of an organisation and hamper future linkage projects involving sensitive databases.

11.4.2 Legal and Ethical Concerns

In record linkage projects where sensitive personal data are used, it is important for the management and employees of an organisation to be aware of all relevant legislation concerning data privacy and confidentiality. Though on most occasions the legal framework for conducting a linkage project is clearly defined, linkage projects usually require the approval of multiple jurisdictions due to the distributed nature of the databases to be linked. This is especially the case when sensitive databases held by different organisations are to be linked. As we discussed in Chapter 2, each organisation, if in the public sector, will likely also be bound by an ethics committee or institutional review board which assesses the risks and benefits of a proposed record linkage project.

Regulations and ethics approval can in some cases result in additional difficulties and delays in carrying out a record linkage project (especially if databases are to be linked across organisations) because different legal systems can have different interpretations on how sensitive data can be accessed and processed in a linkage project. On the other hand, ethical concerns are mostly connected to the use of data while balancing competing subjective claims, specifically the rights of the individuals represented by the records in a database against the rights of society that will benefit from the linked data, for example through health research studies.

Whatever techniques are being used, organisations involved in the linkage of sensitive databases must realise that the linking and combination of data sources entails additional ethical obligations beyond the use of each source alone. This requires the personnel involved in the linkage process to ensure all sensitive data are only used according to their approved purpose and within the agreed legal boundaries.

Hand [258] covered the broader topic of data ethics in our rapidly changing world, where data are increasingly a core aspect of many activities of businesses, governments, as well as research organisations. In line with other domains that have checklists for ethical issues, he provided a list of topics that need to be considered when dealing with potentially sensitive data [258]:

- identify which ethics body has oversight of the work;
- be aware of institutional policies and procedures;
- be aware of national regulations and laws (e.g., regarding privacy, consent, discrimination, and requirement to explain analysis);
- keep record of how data are modified and manipulated;
- understand the origin of the data (provenance);
- treat the metadata as rigorously as the data;
- have an explicit data management plan;
- store data securely;
- determine for how long the data must be kept;
- specify who has access to the data;
- ensure that appropriate statistical, machine learning, data mining, and so on tools are being used;
- have systems in place that allow data to be corrected (and deleted if necessary); and
- be clear about the benefits of the analysis, and who derives the benefits.

11.5 Guidelines for Practical Linkage Projects

To help practitioners with their record linkage processes, it is useful for organisations to have policies, regulations, and guidelines about how to best conduct a linkage project. These will need to take into account any data issues, methodological aspects, technical capabilities, as well as all required privacy regulations and policies.

Guidelines have also been developed by research communities to encourage organisations and researchers who conduct linkage projects to follow these guidelines to improve transparency in how linked data sets are being generated. Such guidelines will ultimately lead to better research studies.

One example of such guidelines is GUILD, the GUidance for Information about Linking Data sets [225]. Developed by UK researchers mainly from the health and social sciences who are involved in linking health as well as administrative data, GUILD follows a four step linkage process, where detailed guidance is provided in each of these four steps. The aim is for such GUILD guidance information to be shared between all organisations and personnel involved in a linkage project (from the database owners to the data consumer). The four mains steps of GUILD are:

1. Data provision: This includes information and descriptions about the population(s) included in the databases to be linked, and the linkability of these databases (including how these databases were collected and what types of identifying details they contain).

2. Record Linkage: This includes description of how the linkage was conducted (including any data cleaning and standardisation performed, and what linkage algorithms were employed). Furthermore, the reported outcomes of the linkage should include both record level as well as aggregated information about linkage quality and linkage bias. Details of any statistical disclosure control methods applied to reduce identifiability of linked records should also be reported.

3. Data analyses: The data consumer of a linked data set (the data analyst) needs to report on the quality of the linked data they used in any of their studies. This includes describing how they accounted for any linkage errors and bias that was reported in the previous step.

4. Reporting study findings: Any reports on the findings of a research study based on linked data should include relevant items from the previous three steps.

If relevant, the final, fourth, step of the GUILD guidelines should also include reporting of other information following another set of guidelines, the REporting of studies Conducted using Observational Routinely-collected health Data (RECORD) guidelines [50].

Jones and Ford [311] proposed a list of high level questions under the acronym 'LINKAGE' that address the options available for linking sensitive databases:

L Legislative position – Which are the key legislative instruments and lawful provisions for data processing, and what are the due diligence processes to be followed?

I Information systems – What is the status and readiness of data provider IT systems to supply data, and what additional demands are required to engage in data linkage?

N Nature of datasets – How do the datasets measure up in terms of data quality, completeness and update frequency?

K Knowledge-base – What level of expertise is held by data custodians and what would be the demand upon them to engage in data linkage?

A Aims and purposes – Allowing for flexibility, what are the main anticipated purposes for the linked data?

G Ground truth – Is there a gold standard reference dataset, or is possible to access ground truth via clerical review, for identity verification and matching?

E Environment – Which data management and access models are permissible and feasible considering the range of relevant factors?

Addressing these questions should help a practitioner to obtain a suitable overall approach to link their sensitive databases, taking into account both practical aspects as well as the regulatory framework within which a linkage is to be conducted.

11.6 Summary and Further Reading

In this chapter we have discussed a variety of topics that we believe need to be considered when (sensitive) databases are being linked in practical applications. The discussed practical considerations include aspects about data (ranging from data quality and missing data to how one can obtain ground truth data, and how to take misclassification costs into account), technical aspects (such as the suitability of linkage protocols and techniques for a given linkage project, availability of software and how to tune algorithm parameters, and the computational requirements needed to link potentially very large databases), and finally organisational aspects (considering the required expertise and skills, as well as ethical and legal concerns).

We also discussed guidelines, such as GUILD [225], that have been developed to help record linkage practitioners improve their practises, and we encourage any readers who are tasked with linking databases in practical settings to familiarise themselves with any such guidelines that are relevant to their work and the regulatory framework within they are working.

We refer readers who are interested in general data quality aspects to the books by Lee et al. [384] as well as Pyle [484], while Christen [109] discussed data quality specifically in the context of linking databases. Missing data are covered in detail by the book by Little and Rubin [396], while Hand [259] in his recent book covers the topic of dark data in great detail and provides extensive examples of why data can be missing. Limited work has been conducted on cost-based record linkage classification, and we refer the interested reader to the work by Verykios et al. [625]. The edited book by Zhang and Chambers [661] covers various topics related to the analysis of integrated data.

The topics covered under technical and institutional considerations are based on the authors expertise, having worked in the area of record linkage for two decades. As such, they are likely incomplete and various other aspects are of relevance to readers who are tasked with linking sensitive databases in practical settings.

Chapter 12
Empirical Evaluation

Co-authored by Anushka Vidanage and Sirintra Vaiwsri

Abstract In this chapter we describe an empirical evaluation of selected Bloom filter based encoding and hardening techniques we have described in Chapters 8 and 9 with regard to their linkage quality, scalability, and privacy. We describe the data sets and software used for this evaluation, the experimental platform employed, as well as the evaluation measures we used. The aim of this chapter is to provide the reader with an example of how sensitive databases can be linked using privacy-preserving linkage techniques, and how such a linkage exercise can be evaluated. We further describe how to use the software employed for this evaluation in Appendix B.

12.1 Evaluation Framework and Setup

Over the past few decades the linking of databases has seen increasing interest in various application domains. Often organisations are tasked with linking sensitive or confidential databases. As we have described in Chapter 8, one popular and widely used privacy technique for linking sensitive databases is Bloom filter encoding [543]. Bloom filter encoding is a perturbation based technique that allows both efficient and approximate matching of quasi-identifying attribute values that are encoded into Bloom filters. As we will describe in the following chapter, Bloom filter encoding is now being employed in real-world linkage projects across the world [84, 475, 480, 507, 534]. However, as we have discussed in Chapter 9, recent research has shown that Bloom filter encoding as used for linking sensitive databases can be vulnerable to cryptanalysis attacks that are able to reidentify values encoded into sets of Bloom filters.

In this chapter we provide an experimental evaluation of Bloom filter hashing, encoding, and hardening techniques within the context of linking two real-world databases. In this evaluation, we simulate a three-party protocol (as we discussed in Section 4.3), where two database owners are participating

© Springer Nature Switzerland AG 2020
P. Christen et al., *Linking Sensitive Data*, https://doi.org/10.1007/978-3-030-59706-1_12

in the linkage process [619]. We assume a linkage unit is used in this proto-col where both database owners first encode the quasi-identifying attribute values in their sensitive databases, and then send their encoded databases to the linkage unit to conduct the comparison of Bloom filters.

In our implementation (described in more detail in Appendix B), to sim-plify execution we do not implement any communication between the different parties involved in the linkage (two database owners and one linkage unit). Rather we simulate communication by writing and reading text files into dif-ferent folders (directories) on the same computer. This allows the interested reader to inspect the contents of these files, which correspond to commu-nicated messages. We note that this implementation is not aimed for the real-world linkage of sensitive databases, but only as an educational tool to allow interested readers to become more familiar with Bloom filter encoding techniques and their use in the context of linking sensitive databases.

We conduct the evaluation considering three dimensions: the linkage qual-ity obtainable with different Bloom filter hashing, encoding, and hardening techniques using a variety of parameter settings; the scalability of Bloom fil-ter encoding with different database sizes; and the privacy vulnerability of these hashing, encoding, and hardening techniques with regard to the two cryptanalysis attacks [119, 629] we discussed in Sections 9.2.3 and 9.3. We next provide details about the databases used in the experimental evaluation, and then discuss the settings of parameters we employed.

12.1.1 Databases used in Evaluation

For our experiments we used data sets based on the North Carolina Voter Registration database (NCVR)[1]. To simulate the linkage between two data-bases, we extracted records from two snapshots of the NCVR database, one downloaded in April 2018 and the second in October 2019. A unique voter identifier number (the attribute NCID) allows us to identify true matching records that refer to the same voter across these two snapshots. Because some voters will have changed their addresses and/or names between April 2018 and October 2019, we expect their corresponding true matching records (with the same NCID value) to contain changed quasi-identifying attribute values.

In our evaluation we used the quasi-identifying attributes (fields) FIRST-NAME, MIDDLENAME, SURNAME, BIRTHYEAR, GENDER, STREET, CITY, and ZIPCODE as the linkage attributes, because these are commonly used for record linkage projects [109, 504, 619, 620].

From the two NCVR snapshots we generated three different variations of pairs of data sets as summarised in Table 12.1. CLN-500K and CLN-100K are 'clean' data sets that have between zero and two quasi-identifying attribute

---

[1] We refer the interested reader to Karapiperis et al. [330], footnote 25 on page 28, for the exact URL at the time of writing from where to obtain these data sets.

Table 12.1 The average number of unique values in the different quasi-identifying attributes in the NCVR data sets used in the evaluation.

Data set name	FIRST NAME	MIDDLE NAME	SURNAME	BIRTH YEAR	GENDER	STREET	CITY	ZIP CODE
CLN-500K	40,405	51,791	77,160	101	3	469,139	756	838
CLN-100K	14,699	18,708	26,544	88	3	97,193	706	792
DRT-100K	14,870	18,930	26,796	87	3	96,289	699	784

values that are different for a given voter across the two NCVR snapshots, where the CLN-100K data sets each contain 100,000 records and the CLN-500K data sets each contain 500,000 records. The DRT-100K (dirty) data sets contain 100,000 records each, where for each pair of records of the same voter between one and three (out of the eight available) quasi-identifying attribute values are different between the two NCVR snapshots. We used both the clean and dirty data sets for linkage quality experiments, while only the clean data sets were used for the scalability and privacy experiments. For the privacy attack experiments described in Section 12.4, attacks on dirty data (with more changed quasi-identifying attribute values) will be more difficult than on clean data because more changes mean larger differences in frequency distributions.

Table 12.1 shows the average numbers of unique values in the different quasi-identifying attributes in these data sets. As can also be seen from this table, there are other data quality issues, for example three gender values ('f', 'm', and 'u'), and up to 100 age values (which is somewhat unexpected given the minimum voter age in North Carolina is 17).

12.1.2 Experimental Setup

In all experiments conducted we set the Bloom filter length to $l = 1,000$ bits since this is a commonly used length when sensitive databases are being linked [89, 178, 543], as can also be seen in Table 8.1 on page 214. We set the number of hash functions, k, used to encode each q-gram, to different values. This allowed us to evaluate the effect of having more or less bits set to 1 in the Bloom filters that are being compared. We also set an 'optimal' number of hash functions following the discussion in the side box on page 194. To encode quasi-identifying attribute values (which for simplicity we assume to all be textual values), we convert them into q-gram sets (with $q = 2$, bigrams) which we then hash using the double hashing and random hashing methods we described in Section 8.2. We used these two hashing methods because (compared to triple or enhanced double hashing) they have been used in most experimental evaluations of Bloom filter encoding [546]. We used attribute level Bloom filter (ABF) encoding for single quasi-identifying attributes, while to encode values from multiple quasi-identifying attributes we employed the cryptographic long-term key (CLK) method introduced by Schnell et al. [545], as well as the record level Bloom filter (RBF) encoding method proposed by Durham et al. [176, 178]. The ABF, CLK, and RBF methods were described in detail in Section 8.3. For CLK, we used attribute specific hash functions such that the same q-gram occurring in different quasi-identifying attributes is not hashed to the same bit positions [538]. This will prevent that hash collisions led to increased Dice coefficient similarities and thus more false matched records. For RBF we set the relative weights for the four quasi-identifying attributes to be encoded as 0.2 for FIRSTNAME, 0.3 for SURNAME, 0.4 for STREET, and 0.1 for CITY, based on the average number of q-grams in these attributes across all records in a data set. This means that for a length $l = 1,000$ of all attribute Bloom filters, 200 bits will be randomly selected for the FIRSTNAME attribute from its attribute Bloom filter, 300 for SURNAME, and so on. These are then concatenated into a final RBF which is again 1,000 bits long [176].

To allow a comparison with a non privacy-preserving record linkage technique, we also evaluated a simple q-gram based linkage approach where the selected quasi-identifying attribute values in records are converted into q-grams (as we discussed in Section 6.8.1) where we again used bigrams ($q = 2$). As a result, this non privacy-preserving linkage approach compared record pairs in the same way as the encoded Bloom filters were compared. This allowed us to evaluate how much the various Bloom filter hashing, encoding, and hardening techniques affect the final linkage quality. We used the Dice coefficient similarity for comparison, more specifically using Equation 6.5 for q-gram sets and Equation 8.3 for Bloom filters.

We implemented a blocking approach using MinHash based locality sensitive hashing [291], where we first generated a MinHash signature of length $\lambda \cdot \mu$ hash values for each record. These signatures were then divided into λ bands each with μ MinHash values [385]. For an example of MinHash we refer the reader to the side box on page 133. All records that had the same MinHash value in a given band were inserted into the same block. In our blocking we set $\lambda = 50$ and $\mu = 3$, respectively. Each record was therefore inserted into 50 blocks. We limited the size of blocks to 100 records in order to prevent very large blocks from being generated, because large blocks would have resulted in much longer runtimes. We then compared the same record pairs for q-gram based non privacy-preserving linkage as well as for Bloom filter based linkage.

For implementation we used Python (version 2.7). All experiments were run on a server with 64-bit Intel Xeon (2.4 GHz) CPUs, 128 GBytes of memory, and running Ubuntu 14.04. The programs are freely available on the companion Web site of this book at: https://dmm.anu.edu.au/lsdbook2020.

12.2 Evaluating Linkage Quality

We evaluated linkage quality when using Bloom filter encoding of sensitive quasi-identifying attribute values with different encoding and hardening techniques. We present results using the two NCVR data set pairs that contain 100,000 records, CLN-100K and DRT-100K, where record pairs that correspond to the same voter had either up to two (CLN), or between one and three (DRT) different quasi-identifying attribute values. This allowed us to evaluate linkage quality when data sets contain less or more variations and changes in the attributes used to compare records, and how different Bloom filter encoding methods are able to deal with data of different quality.

We only provide results for different encoding and hardening techniques because based on the experiments we conducted we noted that the selection of a hashing method (random or double hashing, as we described in Section 8.2) in the Bloom filter encoding process did not affect the calculated similarities between record pairs. The reason for this is that the q-grams in similar records are mapped into Bloom filters in a similar manner due to the assumed independence of the hash functions used in all hashing methods. The type of hashing method used should therefore not affect the linkage quality in the context of Bloom filter based linkage of sensitive databases. However, as we discussed in Section 9.2.2, the double hashing method is vulnerable to certain cryptanalysis attacks [367, 438], and therefore random hashing should be used when sensitive databases are being linked.

We show results as precision-recall curves for a Dice coefficient similarity classification threshold being increased from 0.45 to 1.0 with a step size of 0.05. As we discussed in Section 3.4, the compared pairs of records are classified as true matches (true positives, TP), false matches (false positives, FP), or false non-matches (false negatives, FN) based upon if their Dice coefficient similarity was at least a given similarity classification threshold, and their true match status [109]. As we covered in Section 3.4.1, we calculated precision as $P = \frac{TP}{TP+FP}$ and recall as $R = \frac{TP}{TP+FN}$. We do not present F-measure results because recent research has identified some problematic aspects when this measure is used in the context of evaluating record linkage classifiers [260], as we also discussed in Section 3.4.1.

As can be seen from Figure 12.1, CLK encoding results in very similar linkage quality compared to when unencoded q-grams as being used, with a small decrease in linkage quality as the number of hash functions increases. With more hash functions the number of collisions increases, leading to reduced linkage quality. When the 'optimal' number of hash functions is used then linkage quality does not really improve. As we discussed in Section 8.6.2, this setting clearly does not lead the best possible linkage quality, instead from all four experiments with different numbers of hash functions, for CLK the best linkage quality is achieved with the smallest number of hash functions (that leads to the smallest number of collisions).

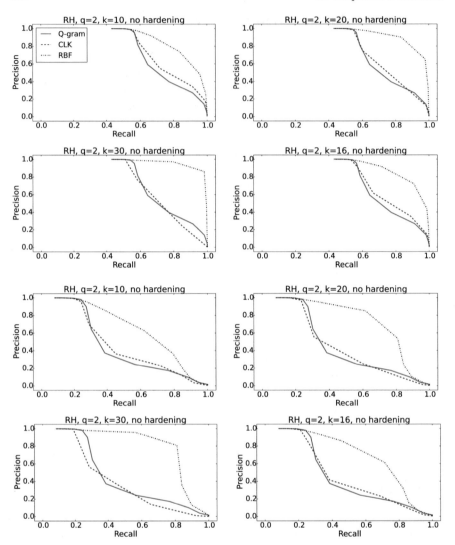

Fig. 12.1 Plaintext q-gram and Bloom filter encoding based linkage results with the CLN-100K (top two rows) and DRT-100K (bottom two rows) data sets for Dice coefficient similarity thresholds varying from 0.45 to 1.0, with different numbers of hash functions, $k = [10, 20, 30, 16 \ (optimal)]$, using the CLK and RBF encoding methods with Bloom filters of length $l = 1,000$ bits. The quasi-identifying attributes FIRSTNAME, SURNAME, STREET, and CITY were used for these linkage experiments.

Figure 12.1 also shows that RBF encoding outperforms CLK encoding for the different numbers of hash functions, k, where the largest number of hash functions used ($k = 30$) achieves the best linkage results on both the clean and dirty data sets. The reason for this is that RBF samples bits according to the weights assigned to the individual quasi-identifying attributes. On the other hand, for CLK the q-grams from all attributes are encoded using the same number of hash functions.

From the bottom two rows in Figure 12.1 it can be seen that both the linkage based on plaintext q-grams as well as Bloom filters generated using the CLK or RBF encoding methods resulted in much reduced linkage quality when dirty data sets with more changed attribute values are being linked. As with the clean data sets, an increase in the number of hash functions used resulted in a small reduction of linkage quality for CLK, while the RBF encoding method, which gives different weights to the different quasi-identifying attributes encoded, can lead to much better overall linkage quality. These experiments highlight that careful weighting of attributes (instead of using the same number of hash functions for all attributes being encoded) can help to obtain substantially higher linkage quality even with databases that contain low quality data.

The linkage results when the different hardening techniques described in Section 9.5 have been applied on encoded Bloom filters are shown in Figures 12.2 and 12.3 for the CLN-100K and DRT-100K data sets, respectively. As can be seen, as with basic non hardended Bloom filters, the RBF encoding method generally outperforms CLK encoding. Of the hardening techniques applied, XOR folding and Rule 90 performed best, even leading to increased linkage quality when CLK encoded Bloom filters were used (for both the clean and dirty data sets). Salting (using the BIRTHYEAR attribute) and balancing did not result in substantially changed linkage results for both CLK and RBF encoding compared to when no hardening was applied (for comparison see the plots in rows two and four in the right hand side of Figure 12.1). BLIP (using Equation 9.7 with the flip probability set to $p_f = 0.05$ as used by Schnell and Borgs [546]) for CLK did not lead to much changed linkage quality compared to no hardening, but resulted in a reduction of linkage quality for RBF encoding. The hardening technique resulting in the lowest linkage quality, especially for RBF encoding, was Markov chaining [553] (with one extra q-gram added per original q-gram, as we discussed in Section 9.5.8). The extra q-grams added introduced too many extra 1-bits compared to unhardened Bloom filters, resulting in more false matches and therefore a drop in precision.

We like to emphasise that these are just example evaluations of different Bloom filter encoding and hardening techniques on data sets with specific data quality characteristics. No general conclusions should be drawn from these limited experiments about the suitability of certain techniques over others. Rather, the reader interested in employing Bloom filter techniques in any practical application to link sensitive data is encouraged to conduct similar experiments on their own databases before deciding upon a set of techniques and corresponding parameter settings to be used for production linkage projects.

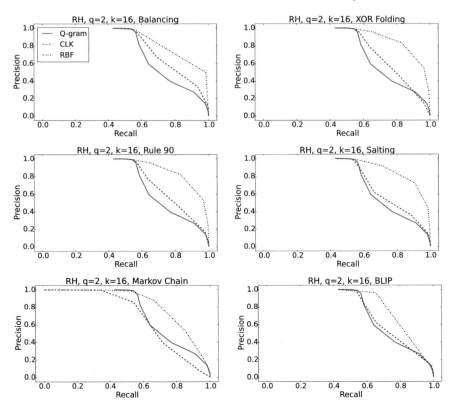

Fig. 12.2 Plaintext q-gram and Bloom filter encoding based linkage results with the CLN-100K data sets for different Dice coefficient similarity thresholds varying from 0.45 to 1.0, using the CLK and RBF encoding methods, with Bloom filters of length $l = 1,000$ bits, the number of hash functions set to $k = 16$ (optimal), and with different hardening techniques applied. The quasi-identifying attributes FIRSTNAME, SURNAME, STREET, and CITY were used for these linkage experiments.

12.3 Evaluating Scalability

As we described in Chapter 8, perturbation based techniques such as Bloom filter encoding are generally more efficient and provide better scalability to linking large databases compared to secure multiparty computation based techniques [619]. In this section we evaluate the scalability of Bloom filter encoding with different numbers of hash functions, k, and different encoding and hardening techniques, where we fixed the Bloom filter length at $l = 1,000$ bits. We present runtime results for encoding records using the clean data set pairs CLN-100K and CLN-500K with 100,000 and 500,000 records, respectively.

Figure 12.4 shows the runtimes for Bloom filter encoding of values from one, two, and four quasi-identifying attributes, with different numbers of

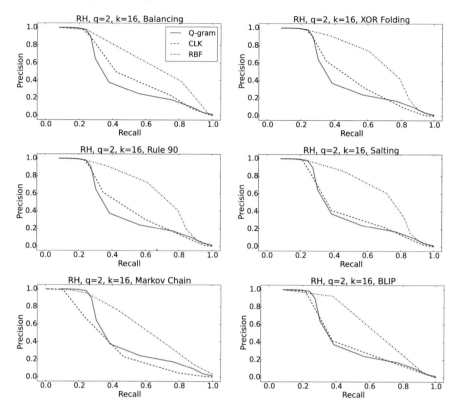

Fig. 12.3 Plaintext q-gram and Bloom filter encoding based linkage results with the DRT-100K data sets for different Dice coefficient similarity thresholds varying from 0.45 to 1.0, using the CLK and RBF encoding methods, with Bloom filters of length $l = 1,000$ bits, the number of hash functions set to $k = 16$ (optimal), and with different hardening techniques applied. The quasi-identifying attributes FIRSTNAME, SURNAME, STREET, and CITY were used for these linkage experiments.

hash functions, k, and for the different encoding methods (ABF, CLK, and RBF). As can be seen, as values from more attributes are encoded into Bloom filters longer runtimes were required because more q-grams need to be hashed. Figure 12.4 also shows how runtimes were affected when we used different numbers of hash functions, k, and different Bloom filter encoding techniques to encode q-gram sets into Bloom filters. As expected, runtimes did increase as the number of hash functions used increased because more hash operations were applied on each q-gram. The encoding of q-grams using the optimal number of hash functions, calculated using Equation 8.1 (see page 194), for one and two attributes resulted in the highest runtimes. This indicates that for these selected quasi-identifying attributes and data sets the fixed values for k used (10, 20, and 30) resulted in Bloom filters that had less than half of their bits set to 1.

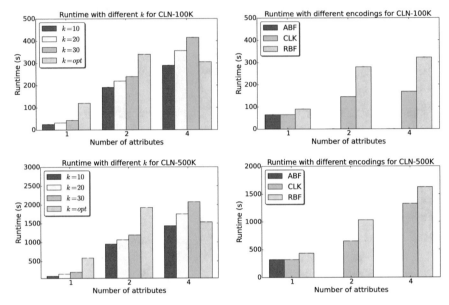

Fig. 12.4 Runtimes (in seconds) for different numbers of hash functions, k, and different Bloom filter encodings (ABF, CLK, and RBF) with different numbers of attributes for the CLN-100K (top row) and CLN-500K (bottom row) data sets. Random hashing with the Bloom filter length set to $l = 1,000$ bits was used in the encoding process, where the optimal number ($k = opt$) of hash functions were set to 136 for one attribute, 55 for two attributes, and 16 for four attributes. The runtimes shown on the left hand side are averaged across the different encoding techniques, while the right hand side plots show runtimes for $k = opt$.

As can also be seen from Figure 12.4, the record level Bloom filter (RBF) encoding method required substantially longer runtimes compared to attribute level Bloom filter (ABF) and the cryptographic long-term key (CLK) encoding technique. This is especially the case when values from several quasi-identifying attributes were encoded. As we described in Section 8.3.3, the reason for these longer runtimes is because RBF first generates one individual ABF per quasi-identifying attribute, then applies random sampling of certain bit positions from these ABFs, and finally combines the sampled bit positions into one Bloom filter per record which is then permuted.

Table 12.2 shows runtime results for Bloom filter encoding with the different hardening techniques we discussed in Section 9.5 applied. As can be seen, for the hardening techniques that work on the actual Bloom filters (balancing, XOR-folding, Rule 90, and BLIP), the relative overhead becomes less as more attributes, and therefore more q-grams, are being hashed because these techniques are independent of the number of q-grams that are hashed.

On the other hand, the hardening techniques that operate on the actual q-gram sets being encoded (salting and Markov chaining), have runtimes that depend upon the number of q-grams that are to be encoded. Encoding

Table 12.2 Runtimes for different hardening techniques with different numbers of attributes encoded using the CLN-500K data sets. Random hashing and cryptographic long-term key (CLK) encoding, with $k = 30$ hash functions, was used in the Bloom filter encoding process. We show total encoding plus hardening runtimes in seconds, and the overhead of hardening techniques in percentages compared to no hardening.

Hardening technique	Runtime (sec)		
	One attribute	Two attributes	Four attributes
No hardening	121	341	832
Salting	125 (3.3%)	593 (73.9%)	984 (18.3%)
Balancing	384 (217%)	812 (138%)	1,325 (59.2%)
XOR-folding	134 (10.7%)	353 (3.5%)	844 (1.4%)
Rule 90	392 (224%)	878 (157%)	1,475 (77.2%)
Markov chain	782 (546%)	1,595 (368%)	3,527 (324%)
BLIP	263 (117%)	593 (73.9%)	984 (18.3%)

more q-grams means longer runtimes, where the overhead of these hardening techniques can be estimated by the expected number of q-grams that occur in the quasi-identifying attribute values being encoded. Markov chaining requires significantly longer runtimes because the total number of q-grams that are being encoded is increased through the selection of extra q-grams (1 in all our experiments), as we described in Section 9.5.8.

12.4 Evaluating Privacy

As we discussed in Sections 5.1 and 5.2, there are currently no accepted standard measures for evaluating the privacy protection that privacy-preserving record linkage techniques provide. To compare the privacy provided by different Bloom filter hashing, encoding, and hardening techniques we therefore first look at the frequency distributions of 1-bits in the generated Bloom filters because these distributions are the basis for the majority of the attack methods on Bloom filter encoding we discussed in Chapter 9. The more uniform the frequency distributions of 1-bits in a set of Bloom filters are the more challenging frequency-based attacks will be. We then apply the two attack methods described in Sections 9.2.3 [119, 120] and 9.3 [123, 629] to compare the vulnerability of different hashing, encoding, and hardening techniques with regard to these attacks.

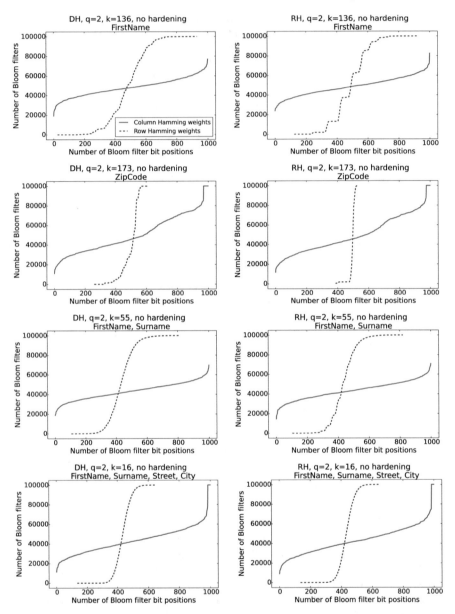

Fig. 12.5 Row- and column-wise distributions of 1-bits (Hamming weights) for the double hashing (DH, left hand side) and random hashing (RH, right hand side) methods with cryptographic long-term key (CLK) encoding, with Bloom filters of length $l = 1,000$ bits, and where we set the number of hash functions to an optimal value using Equation 8.1. The quasi-identifying attributes FIRSTNAME, SURNAME, STREET, CITY, and ZIPCODE for the CLN-100K data set were used for these experiments.

12.4.1 Frequency Distributions of 1-bits in Bloom Filters

Given existing attacks exploit the frequency distributions of 1-bit patterns in a set of Bloom filters that encode sensitive values, one proxy measure of privacy preservation is to visualise these distributions as generated from a set of Bloom filters. In Figure 12.5 we show the row- and column-wise distributions of the number of 1-bits (known as the Hamming weights) in the set of 100,000 Bloom filters generated from the CLN-100K NCVR data set. A larger variance in the number of 1-bits across a set of Bloom filters can provide more information that potentially can be exploited by an attack method. On the other hand, if all rows and/or columns in a set of Bloom filters have the same, or almost the same, number of 1-bits (achievable on rows when using the balancing hardening method we described in Section 9.5.2), an attack method has less frequency information that can be exploited.

As can be seen from Figure 12.5, for both rows and columns in a set of Bloom filters, for most quasi-identifying attributes encoded there are clear distributions of 1-bits that potentially can be exploited by an attack method. The column Hamming weights (number of 1-bits in each Bloom filter bit position) are closest to a uniform distribution when only FIRSTNAME values are encoded, which indicates that many q-grams in first names do occur in roughly a similar number of records. Once attributes like STREET and CITY are also encoded, the column distributions end up much less uniform because these attributes seem to contain certain q-grams that occur much more frequently, such as those in large cities (for example 'ch' from 'charlotte', the largest city in North Carolina). For the ZIPCODE attribute it seems some bit positions have a 1-bit in every Bloom filter. This is not surprising given the encoded data set is from North Carolina, where all zipcodes start with either 27 or 28. Analysing the encoding process, it turns out that the two q-grams '27' and '28' were mapped by some of the k hash functions to the same bit positions (hash collisions), resulting in every Bloom filter generated from this data set to have a 1-bit in some of the $l = 1,000$ bit positions.

Looking at the row Hamming weights (the distribution of the number of 1-bits in individual Bloom filters), one can clearly see that most ZIPCODE values contain, as expected, the same number of unique q-grams, namely four. Some contain less, for example zipcode '27027' only contains three unique bi-grams ($q = 2$): '27', '70', and '02'. When name and address attribute values are encoded then the row Hamming weights become much more spread, because these attributes can contain some very short and some very long values that generate Bloom filters with a very small or a very large number of 1-bits. As the plots in Figure 12.5 show, both the row and column frequency distributions can therefore provide an adversary with information about what type of quasi-identifying attribute(s) have been encoded in a set of Bloom filters, and thus allow further attacks as we discuss below.

As can also be seen from Figure 12.5, the random hashing method shown in the plots on the right side column, have somewhat different row Hamming weights compared to double hashing. This is clearly visible when first names are encoded, where the steps that can be seen show an approximation of the length distribution of first name values. Double hashing, shown in left side column plots, on the other hand shows less clear steps for first names. These different distributions are because of the different ways of how random and double hashing map q-grams into Bloom filters, as we discussed in Sections 8.2.1 and 8.2.4. The patterns generated by double hashing (its weakness, as exploited by the cryptanalysis attacks we discussed in Section 9.2) seem to result in higher rates of collisions of different q-grams into the same bit positions compared to random hashing which seems to generate more distinct bit patterns for different q-grams.

For random hashing, the rate of collisions seems to depend mostly on the number of q-grams (and thus 1-bits) encoded into a Bloom filter. As is clearly visible in the top right plot in Figure 12.5, shorter first names encoded exhibit less collisions (showing a clearer stepwise increase in the Hamming weight of Bloom filters) than longer first name (where more collisions lead to a less clearer stepwise increase in Hamming weights). Therefore, while double hashing is known to have a weakness in the limited number of bit patterns it is able to generate (as exploited by the cryptanalysis attacks described in Section 9.2.2), random hashing seems to have a weakness where an adversary potentially can identify the distribution of the lengths of the q-gram sets that were hashed into a set of Bloom filters.

12.4.2 Attack Evaluation

In this section we evaluate the privacy of Bloom filter encoding when applying the two cryptanalysis attacks based on frequency analysis [119, 120] and pattern mining [123, 629], as we described in Sections 9.2.3 and 9.3, respectively. In this evaluation, we have generated Bloom filters using random hashing, and different encoding and hardening techniques. We evaluated both these attack methods on the pair of CLN-100K NCVR data sets containing 100,000 records, as we described in Section 12.1.1. We used one of the data sets as the encoded Bloom filter data set, and other as the plaintext data set we assume the adversary has access to. As a reminder, each matching record pair in these two data sets has between zero and two quasi-identifying attribute values that are different. This makes the attack challenging because the frequency distributions of quasi-identifying attribute values will be different between the two data sets. In the following subsections we first discuss the frequency-based and then the pattern mining based attack method.

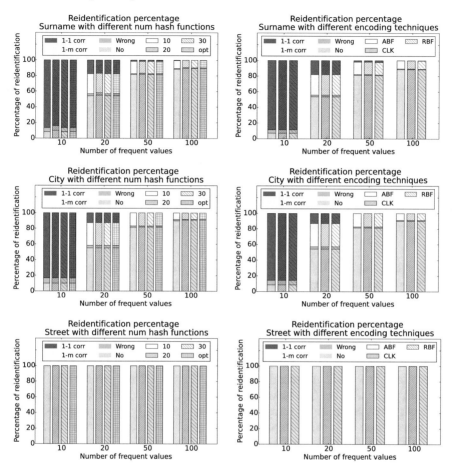

Fig. 12.6 Reidentification results of the frequency-based cryptanalysis attack [119, 120] on the CLN-100K data set with 100,000 records for the attributes SURNAME (top row), CITY (middle row), and STREET (bottom row), for different numbers of hash functions (left) and different Bloom filter encoding techniques (right).

12.4.2.1 Frequency-based Cryptanalysis Attack

As we described in Section 9.2.3, the frequency-based cryptanalysis attack method proposed by Christen et al. [119, 120] exploits the fundamental Bloom filter construction principle (of hashing sets of elements into bit positions) by trying to identify frequent Bloom filters that correspond to frequent encoded quasi-identifying attribute values through their frequent bit patterns.

We evaluate the reidentification accuracy [120] of the attack by calculating (1) the percentage of correctly reidentified attribute values encoded into Bloom filters as one-to-one matches (one Bloom filter is correctly assigned to the sensitive plaintext value that was encoded into it); (2) the percentage

Table 12.3 The ten most frequent SURNAME values and their counts of occurrences in the two CLN-100K data sets with 100,000 records, as used for the frequency-based cryptanalysis attacks.

Plaintext NCVR data set		Encoded NCVR data set	
SURNAME	Count	SURNAME	Count
Smith	1,265	Smith	1,269
Williams	959	Williams	960
Johnson	886	Johnson	880
Jones	831	Jones	845
Brown	741	Brown	752
Davis	630	Davis	641
Moore	484	Moore	476
Miller	465	Miller	464
Wilson	433	Wilson	431
Harris	391	Harris	397

of correct guesses with one-to-many matches (a Bloom filter matches several plaintext values and one of these values was the one encoded in the Bloom filter); (3) the percentage of wrong guesses (a Bloom filter did not encode the plaintext value(s) assigned to it); and (4) the percentage of no guesses (the attack was not able to assign any plaintext values to a Bloom filter). These four percentages sum to 100. In the result plots these four categories are labelled as 1-1 corr, 1-m corr, Wrong, and No, respectively. We conducted the attack for different encoding and hardening techniques for the quasi-identifying attributes SURNAME, STREET, and CITY with different numbers of hash functions and different Bloom filter encoding techniques employed. We considered the reidentification accuracy of the attack on the 10, 20, 50, and 100 most frequent attribute values from the plaintext data set, respectively.

Figure 12.6 shows that this attack can correctly reidentify many of the most frequent SURNAME values encoded into Bloom filters when different numbers of hash functions and different encoding techniques have been used. As Table 12.3 shows, the most frequent surnames are the same in both the plaintext and the encoded data sets, as Table 12.3 shows. However, some of them share certain q-grams (such as 'johnson' and 'jones' share the two bigrams 'jo' and 'on', while 'Williams' and 'Miller' share 'il' and 'll'), and this can lead to the wrong assignment of frequent Bloom filters to frequent surnames. Similar results can be seen for the attribute CITY where most frequent values that are encoded in Bloom filters with different numbers of hash functions and different encoding techniques have also been correctly reidentified.

However, as can also be seen from Figure 12.6, for the attribute STREET the attack was not able to correctly reidentify any values encoded in Bloom filters. This is because no frequent Bloom filters were generated that have the same bit pattern from the CLN-100K NCVR data set we used in these experiments. Because the value for the STREET attribute was different for

Table 12.4 Reidentification percentages of one-to-one correct (1-1 corr), one-to-many correct (1-m corr), Wrong, and No guesses of plaintext values over different Bloom filter hardening techniques with attributes SURNAME and CITY for the CLN-100K data set.

Hardening technique	SURNAME				CITY			
	1-1 corr	1-m corr	Wrong	No	1-1 corr	1-m corr	Wrong	No
No hardening	2	8	4	86	1	10	4	85
Salting	0	2	4	94	0	0	4	96
Balancing	0	12	2	86	0	10	3	87
XOR-folding	0	1	10	89	0	10	1	89
Rule 90	0	8	0	92	0	2	6	92
Markov chain	0	12	2	86	0	12	2	86
BLIP	0	12	2	86	0	2	6	92

every record in this data set, every Bloom filter had a unique bit pattern. With a larger data set, however, this frequency-based attack would likely be more successful since it will be more likely that certain address values, such as apartment blocks or student accommodation, as well as the names of long streets, would appear more frequently and thus result in certain Bloom filters that occur multiple times that the attack can exploit [119, 120].

Table 12.4 shows the reidentification accuracy of plaintext values from the SURNAME and CITY attributes when different hardening techniques are applied during the Bloom filter encoding process. As can be seen, the frequency-based attack was neither able to identify any correct one-to-one matching SURNAME nor CITY values when a hardening technique was applied. Some one-to-many reidentifications occurred for all hardening techniques for the SURNAME attribute, and for most hardening techniques for the CITY attribute. For the majority of Bloom filters, however, no reidentification was possible at all.

As this experimental evaluation has shown, the frequency-based cryptanalysis attack by Christen et al. [119, 120] works only when a database of Bloom filters does contain at least some Bloom filters that occur frequently. If each Bloom filter in a given database is unique then this attack will not be successful. Common Bloom filters can occur when attribute level Bloom filters (ABF) are generated on quasi-identifying attributes that do contain certain values that occur frequently, such as first names and surnames, post- or zipcodes, or city and suburb names. On the other hand, when values from multiple quasi-identifying attributes are encoded into one Bloom filter (using the record level Bloom filter or cryptographic long-term key encodings we discussed in Section 8.3), then the accuracy of this attack will likely be significantly reduced because it is less likely that a certain Bloom filter (with a certain bit pattern) occurs frequently in an encoded database. Only if a certain combination of quasi-identifying attribute values occurs frequently would the corresponding Bloom filter that encodes this combination of val-

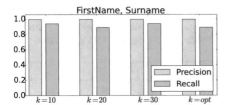
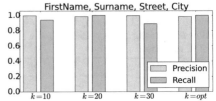

Fig. 12.7 Pattern mining based cryptanalysis attack [123] results on the CLN-100K data set with attribute combinations FIRSTNAME and SURNAME (left side), and FIRST-NAME, SURNAME, STREET, and CITY (right side) for different numbers of hash functions, k. The CLK encoding method with attribute specific hashing functions was used for these experiments.

ues also be common. The pattern mining based attack we describe next aims to overcome this weakness of frequency-based cryptanalysis attacks.

12.4.2.2 Pattern Mining based Cryptanalysis Attack

As we described in Section 9.3, the pattern mining based cryptanalysis attack proposed by Christen et al. [123] makes use of the frequencies of individual q-grams as they occur in many values in the attributes encoded into Bloom filters. The attack employs frequent pattern mining techniques [8, 98] to identify the maximal co-occurring frequent bit positions with the same pattern in a set of Bloom filters that must correspond to a q-gram that occurs frequently in a plaintext database.

We evaluated this attack using the concatenations of two and four of the quasi-identifying attributes FIRSTNAME, SURNAME, STREET, and CITY. Note that except for the experiments on different numbers of hash functions, all experiments were conducted using the optimal number of hash functions, calculated as we described in Section 8.6.2, where for two attributes the optimal number was $k = 55$ while for four attributes it was $k = 16$, respectively. In Figure 12.7 and Table 12.5 we show precision and recall results of the identified bit positions for a given frequent q-gram. Precision measures how many identified bit positions for an identified frequent q-gram are correct, while recall measures from all correct bit positions of a frequent q-gram how many the attack was able to identify correctly. In Table 12.5 we show the average precision and recall values calculated on the identified bit positions of each frequent q-gram identified by the attack, where for one attribute the attack was able to identify seventeen q-grams correctly, for pairs of attributes thirteen q-grams correctly, and for four attributes nine q-grams were correctly identified.

Figure 12.7 shows results for the identified q-grams when different numbers of hash functions were used. As can be seen, both precision and recall have a high value (more than 0.9) with all combinations of attributes. Precision

Table 12.5 Pattern mining based cryptanalysis attack [123] precision and recall results of the identified bit positions for frequent q-grams on the CLN-100K data set with attribute combinations for different Bloom filter encoding techniques.

Encoding technique	One attribute		Two attributes		Four attributes	
	Precision	Recall	Precision	Recall	Precision	Recall
ABF	1.0	0.940				
CLK	1.0	0.940	0.996	0.940	0.995	0.898
RBF	0.139	0.079	0.039	0.033	0.030	0.019

stayed consistently high, which means the bit positions identified for frequent q-grams were mostly correct. Recall, on the other hand, had some variation, which means not all bit positions were identified for these frequent q-grams. For the second step of the attack, to reidentify quasi-identifying attribute values based on the identified q-grams, high precision is more important than high recall, because lower precision will likely mean wrong attribute values will be reidentified.

As Table 12.5 shows, with the attribute level Bloom filter (ABF) and cryptographic long-term key (CLK) encoding techniques both precision and recall of the identified bit positions for frequent q-grams were higher than 0.89. However, with record level Bloom filter (RBF) encoding, as can be seen, both precision and recall of the identified bit positions were much lower. This is because the process of sampling and permutation of bits when RBFs are constructed changes the bit patterns of individual q-grams, thereby making the identification of frequent q-grams very difficult. We also observed that this attack was unable to identify even a single frequent bit pattern in some experiments when the values of four attributes were encoded using the RBF encoding technique.

Table 12.6 shows the attribute value reidentification results for the second step of the pattern mining based attack. In this second step, candidate attribute values are assigned to each Bloom filter based on the frequent q-grams identified in the first step. We then selected Bloom filters which had at most ten values assigned to them and disregard all other Bloom filters that had more candidate values assigned to them. As this table shows, we measured the accuracy of attribute values assigned to Bloom filters in terms of correct one-to-one (1-1 corr) and one-to-many (1-m corr) matches (with up to ten matching Bloom filters). For each one-to-one or one-to-many match we calculated the percentages of exact (E), partial (P), and wrong (W) matches. In this table we set the exact, partial, and wrong percentage values to 0 when all Bloom filters have ten or more candidate values assigned to them.

As can be seen from Table 12.6, for two and three encoded attributes, with different numbers of hash functions, k, the attack always obtained more than 80% exact one-to-one and one-to-many matches except with the optimal number of hash functions used ($k = opt$), where the attack was only able to

Table 12.6 Reidentification percentages of exact (E), partial (P), and wrong (W) matches (either 1-to-1 or 1-to-many correct) of plaintext values over different Bloom filter encoding parameters and different numbers of encoded attributes. A '−' means the corresponding experiment either did not identify any frequent q-grams, or it used more than 100 GBytes of memory and had to be terminated.

		One attribute			Two attributes			Four attributes		
		E	P	W	E	P	W	E	P	W
$k = 10$	1-1 corr	89.7	0.0	10.3	83.2	4.4	12.4	0.0	0.0	0.0
	1-m corr	95.9	0.4	3.7	86.3	5.5	8.2	0.0	0.0	100.0
$k = 20$	1-1 corr	87.6	0.9	11.5	80.6	4.6	14.8	0.0	0.0	0.0
	1-m corr	96.2	0.4	3.4	84.0	6.2	9.8	0.0	0.0	100.0
$k = 30$	1-1 corr	88.8	0.3	10.9	80.6	4.6	14.8	0.0	0.0	0.0
	1-m corr	92.5	0.2	7.3	84.0	6.2	9.8	0.0	0.0	100.0
$k = opt$	1-1 corr	20.3	0.4	78.3	27.7	1.4	70.9	0.0	0.0	0.0
	1-m corr	26.4	1.5	72.1	28.8	1.9	69.4	0.0	0.0	100.0
ABF	1-1 corr	89.4	0.0	10.6						
	1-m corr	90.7	0.0	9.3						
CLK	1-1 corr	89.4	0.0	10.6	68.0	3.8	28.2	0.0	0.0	0.0
	1-m corr	90.7	0.0	9.3	70.8	4.9	24.3	0.0	0.0	100.0
RBF	1-1 corr	0.0	0.0	0.0	0.0	0.0	100.0	0.0	0.0	0.0
	1-m corr	21.6	1.4	77.0	0.0	0.0	100.0	0.0	0.0	100.0
Salting	1-1 corr	0.0	0.0	0.0	0.0	0.0	0.0	0.0	0.0	0.0
	1-m corr	0.0	0.0	0.0	0.0	0.0	0.0	0.0	0.0	0.0
Balancing	1-1 corr	−	−	−	−	−	−	−	−	−
	1-m corr	−	−	−	−	−	−	−	−	−
XOR-folding	1-1 corr	0.0	0.0	0.0	0.0	0.0	0.0	0.0	0.0	0.0
	1-m corr	0.0	0.0	0.0	0.0	0.0	0.0	0.0	0.0	0.0
Rule 90	1-1 corr	0.0	0.0	100.0	0.0	0.0	0.0	−	−	−
	1-m corr	0.0	0.0	100.0	0.0	0.0	0.0	−	−	−
MC-1	1-1 corr	0.1	0.0	99.9	0.0	0.0	0.0	0.0	0.0	0.0
	1-m corr	0.3	0.0	99.7	0.0	0.0	0.0	0.0	0.0	0.0
BLIP	1-1 corr	0.0	0.0	0.0	0.0	0.0	0.0	0.0	0.0	0.0
	1-m corr	0.2	0.0	99.8	0.1	0.0	99.9	0.0	0.0	0.0

obtain a much smaller percentage of Bloom filters with less than ten candidate values assigned to them. This was because with the optimal number of hash functions used the attack was only able to identify a smaller number of frequent q-grams in the first step of the attack. With four attributes encoded, the attack did not obtain any one-to-one matches while it led to 100% wrong one-to-many matches for many parameter settings. The reason behind not getting any exact matches at all was that as more attributes are hashed into the same Bloom filter the attack was less successful in identifying frequent q-grams due to collisions.

The attack achieved lower reidentification results as more quasi-identifying attributes were encoded. We believe this occurs because a smaller number of frequent q-grams were identified in the first step of the attack when more q-grams were hashed into Bloom filters. Compared to CLK encoding, RBF encoding is significantly less vulnerable to this pattern mining based attack because, as can also be seen from Table 12.5, the random sampling of bits from individual attribute level Bloom filters and the permutation of bits in the final constructed RBF make the identification of frequent q-grams very difficult.

Unlike the earlier frequency analysis based attack proposed by Christen et al. [119, 120], this pattern mining based attack [123, 629] did not perform well when any of the hardening technique we discussed in Section 9.5 were applied with the CLK encoding method with the optimal number of hash functions used. We were unable to run some of these attack experiments with salting and balancing due to high memory consumption, which was because of the generation of a very large number of unique bit patterns which led to the attack having to process a very large number of patterns to identify a potential given frequent q-gram. These results with hardening techniques are not unexpected, given hardening techniques modify the bit patterns in Bloom filters, some completely at random, and therefore modify or even destroy any frequent bit patterns that can be assigned to frequent q-grams.

Based on the results of these experiments, it can be seen that the reidentification accuracy of the pattern mining based attack method [123, 629] is highest when only one or two quasi-identifying attributes are encoded into Bloom filters, while with more encoded attributes the accuracy of the reidentification of attribute values decreases substantially.

12.5 Summary and Further Reading

At the time of writing, Bloom filter encoding is the most popular technique used in practical applications to link sensitive databases in privacy-preserving ways. The reasons for its popularity is its efficiency, simplicity to implement, and its ability to facilitate accurate and approximate similarity calculations for string values as well as other types of data, as we discussed in Chapter 8. In this chapter we have conducted an evaluation of Bloom filter encoding using real-world voter databases with specific data quality characteristics. We evaluated the linkage quality, scalability, and privacy protection of different hashing, encoding, and hardening techniques, as presented in Chapters 8 and 9.

As the evaluation results have shown, for the given data sets and blocking approach used, non-hardened Bloom filters generated using the record level Bloom filter (RBF) encoding method [176] are able to achieve high linkage quality because this method prevents any collisions of the same q-gram occurring in different quasi-identifying attributes. Such collisions seem to lead to a reduction of linkage quality for the cryptographic long-term key (CLK) encoding method [545], even when attribute specific hash functions are used. Careful parameter selection is however required. For example, using too many hash functions can potentially lead to an increase in the number of collisions and result in high similarities between Bloom filters even if their q-gram sets do not have a high similarity at all. Furthermore, the applied maximum block size limit of 100 records per block also seems to have helped to achieve high linkage quality on these data sets that contain 100,000 or 500,000 records, respectively.

The modifications and randomness introduced by certain hardening techniques can lead to significantly reduced linkage quality as our experimental results showed, while for other hardening techniques linkage quality did not suffer. All hardening techniques were however able to make Bloom filter encoding more resilient to cryptanalysis attacks. Further research is required to analyse the characteristics of hardening techniques to better understand which ones can provide high linkage quality while at the same time making Bloom filter encoding less vulnerable to attacks.

Our privacy evaluation has confirmed that non-hardened Bloom filters can be vulnerable to existing cryptanalysis attack methods, as was also shown in earlier work [119, 120, 123, 367, 371, 415, 438, 629]. While some hardening techniques proposed make such attacks more difficult or even impossible, there are currently no conceptual or theoretical proofs available that show that Bloom filter encoding and hardening techniques are resilient to all attacks. Further research, both to develop improved hashing, encoding, and hardening techniques, as well as novel cryptanalysis attacks to investigate their vulnerabilities, is required.

It is important to understand that there is currently no single Bloom filter hashing, encoding, and hardening technique available that can provide high linkage quality and provable privacy protection at the same time. Record level Bloom filter (RBF) encoding seems to provide the best compromise between high linkage quality and privacy protection, especially if combined with a suitable hardening technique such as salting. However, the implementation of RBF, especially the dynamic setting of the Bloom filter lengths [178], is more complicated than that of basic Bloom filters or even CLK, resulting in increased encoding runtimes as well as an overhead in the actual implementation and testing of RBF based Bloom filter encoding.

While our evaluation has led to very different overall linkage results for the different encoding and hardening techniques employed, we like to emphasise that these results are based on the linkage of one pair of data sets only, and necessarily these results cannot and should not be generalised. Further extensive evaluation is needed, ideally on many different data sets with various data quality characteristics, to obtain a better overall understanding of the performance of different Bloom filter encoding and hardening techniques with regard to the linkage quality they provide.

Chapter 13
Real-world Applications

Abstract In this chapter we describe several existing real-world applications where sensitive databases are being linked in a practical setting using privacy-preserving techniques. These examples come from different countries, where different privacy frameworks and legislation exist that either make the use of such approaches necessary, or where organisations are using privacy-preserving linkage approaches to make their linkages more secure.

13.1 Australia

Australia has been at the forefront of the development of record linkage methods as well as of applications and linkage centres. The Western Australian Data Linkage System (WADLS)[1] emerged from a collaboration between the University of Western Australia's School of Population Health and the Western Australia Department of Health [280]. WADLS employs an in-house developed probabilistic record linkage system to create, store, update, and retrieve links between over forty population-based administrative and research health data collections in Western Australia. From 1995 until 2014, it reported more than 800 projects resulting in over 2,350 publications [282].

An important contribution pioneered by the WADLS is the separation principle (of quasi-identifying values and sensitive microdata) as we discussed in Section 4.2. Other Australian states followed with their own health linkage centres, such as the Centre for Health Record Linkage (CHeReL)[2] [381] which was established in 2006 in New South Wales (NSW), or SA-NT DataLink[3], established in 2009 in South Australia.

---

[1] See: https://www.datalinkage-wa.org.au/

[2] See: https://www.cherel.org.au/

[3] See: https://www.santdatalink.org.au/

© Springer Nature Switzerland AG 2020
P. Christen et al., *Linking Sensitive Data*, https://doi.org/10.1007/978-3-030-59706-1_13

In 2006 the Australian Federal Government funded the Population Health Research Network (PHRN)[4], which had as its aims the establishment of record linkage centres in all Australian states, as well as the formation of national cross-jurisdictional centre for record linkage, the development of secure remote access laboratories for researchers, as well as data delivery system for the secure electronic transfer of sensitive data between PHRN participants and relevant stakeholders. The overall goal of this initiative was to provide researchers in Australia with the capability to link data from a diverse and rich range of health data sources across jurisdictions and sectors, to carry out population level research with the aim to improve the health and well-being of the population and enhance the effectiveness and efficiency of health services [82, 658].

An example application of such a linkage across various sources and involving two linkage centres, the WADLS and the Centre for Data Linkage (CDL)[5] [83], is the Social Investment Data Resources (SIDR) project. This project aims to link data across a large variety of sources about young offenders in Western Australia, who are provided targeted interventions by the government with the aim to reduce offending. Records about these young offenders will be linked to assess and evaluate the long-term effects of this intervention. While some of these linkages will be conducted using the existing linkage approaches by the WADLS and CDL, for those data where quasi-identifying values cannot be released (such as names and other personal data from the Children's court), Bloom filter based linkage techniques are being employed [83].

A second project that involves the use of Bloom filter based encoding of quasi-identifying values for the linking of sensitive health databases is the Linking Up and Mapping Of Systems (LUMOS) project in New South Wales (NSW)[6]. LUMOS aims to link data from general practices (GPs), hospitals, mortality, as well as other relevant government health databases on a large scale. LUMOS is based on a four year pilot project which linked records of around 1 million patients from over 100 GPs in NSW with other health databases. This pilot project showed for example the contribution of GPs in reducing readmissions of patients, and it provided overviews of how patients move across the healthcare system.

In LUMOS, all quasi-identifying attributes used for linkage are encoded into Bloom filters, which are then encrypted and sent using secure file transfers from the GPs to the CHeReL for linkage. GPs who participate in this project are verified to ensure no adversary is able to provide inappropriate data. The separation principle [340] is also upheld in that encoded Bloom filters and the corresponding sensitive medical microdata of a patient are given

---

[4] See: https://www.phrn.org.au/

[5] See: http://www2.curtin.edu.au/research/cphr/centre-for-data-linkage.cfm

[6] See: https://www.cesphn.org.au/documents/ehealth-1/lumos/2807-lumos-gp-info-pack-final-20190906/file

individual automatically generated identifiers, and different encryption keys are applied. Furthermore, informed consent is required once from a patient before her or his data can be used in LUMOS, while the overall project has been approved by ethical review boards. Linked data are securely stored in a system managed by the New South Wales Ministry of Health.

Besides conducting practical linkages of sensitive databases in the health domain, these Australian linkage centres have also developed various novel methods to link sensitive databases with privacy protection in mind. The CDL has developed Bloom filter encoding based methods that incorporate homomorphic encryption to improve the security of encoded Bloom filters by preventing frequency attacks [506], as well as software that implements these techniques[7] [83]. The SA-NT DataLink has developed a unique linkage approach using graph structures and graph databases, where individual source data sets are represented as layers in a graph. These layers can be included or excluded for linkages based on the sensitivity of these data sets and the permissions the user of a linked data set has [201]. At the same time, this graph based approach provides a repository of links that can be improved over time as new records about people become available.

13.2 Brazil

Interest in record linkage in Brazil has seen a substantial increase in the second decade of the 21st Century, especially in the domain of health and administrative data as collected by hospitals and government programmes. Individual health databases have however been collected for much longer, as surveyed by Ali et al. [15], with some cancer registries containing records all the way back to 1967. A common aspect of all these databases is that they do not contain unique entity identifiers, and therefore any linkage needs to be conducted using quasi-identifying attributes such as names, addresses, and dates of birth. There are, however, significant data quality issues especially with Brazilian names, where an individual can have up to five names (not all are being reported in all databases), and where names can come from any of the many ethnic groups that live in Brazil [15].

The various record linkage projects conducted in Brazil by different research groups and government agencies use a diverse set of linkage methodologies and software tools, ranging from open-source tools to systems developed in-house. The scale of many Brazilian databases (with the country having a population of over 200 million in early 2020[8]) makes the use of most linkage software very challenging. Specific large-scale linkage tools have therefore been developed by several linkage centres in Brazil [15, 26].

---

[7] Named LinXmart, see: https://linxmart.com.au/

[8] See: https://data.worldbank.org/indicator/SP.POP.TOTL?locations=BR

A specific application of large-scale linkage of sensitive databases across organisations is the '100 Million Cohort' project [475]. This project used data collected from a variety of health databases that were linked, using specialised high performance linkage software (which we describe in Appendix A.1), to a large cohort of records of 114 million individuals who received payments from a government cash welfare program. The used software employs a rule based blocking step where records are inserted into the same block if two records had the same values according to the following conditions: (FIRSTNAME *AND* MOTHERFIRSTNAME *AND* MUNICIPALITYCODE) *OR* (LASTNAME *AND* MOTHERLASTNAME *AND* YEAROFBIRTH) [475].

The sensitive nature of the health databases linked required the use of privacy-preserving record linkage techniques. Bloom filter encoding using bigrams ($q = 2$) and attribute level Bloom filters (as we described in Section 8.3.1) was employed, where the number of hash functions was set to $k = 2$. For reason of performance and memory usage of the very large number of records to be encoded and compared, the quasi-identifying attributes FIRSTNAME and MOTHERFIRSTNAME were encoded into Bloom filters of lengths 50 bits each, DATEOFBIRTH into 40 bits, and MUNICIPALITYCODE and GENDER into 20 bits each, resulting in a total length of 180 bits per Bloom filter that represents one record. The Dice coefficient similarity, calculated using Equation 8.3, was then used to categorise compared record pairs as being exact (Dice coefficient similarity is 1.0), strong (Dice coefficient similarity is at least 0.9), weak (Dice similarity is at least 0.8), or unpaired (Dice coefficient similarity is below 0.8) links. Using generated ground truth data showed that this method was able to obtain very high linkage quality [475].

Research studies are now being conducted using this very large linked cohort of individuals. The nationwide coverage of this cohort allows health researchers to investigate, for example, the impacts of cash welfare and housing programs for Brazil's poorer population with regard to their health outcomes, including child and maternal health, tuberculosis, leprosis, cardiovascular diseases, and suicides and homicides [26]. One specific program aims to look at the long-term effects of the Zika virus infection on Brazilian children, and how these effects relate to the health, social, and educational aspects of a child's life circumstances.

13.3 Canada

Similar to Australia, Canada is a federation, where individual states have set up organisations to conduct the linkage of health and related databases to support research in a variety of application domains. Like Australia, Canada also has a long history in the area of record linkage, with pioneering work conducted by Newcombe and Kennedy in the late 1950s [435, 436], who were some of the first to use electronic computers to link databases to facilitate research in the health and social sciences. Canadian organisations also contributed to the development of sophisticated linkage software, such as the Generalized Record Linkage System (GRLS) [198].

As one example of an application where sensitive databases are being linked, the Manitoba Centre for Health Policy (MCHP) is a long-running data linkage centre that has its roots in the 1970s [338]. Formally established in 1991, the MCHP today has access to over ninety data sets sourced from a variety of government agencies, as well as medical laboratories, clinical programs, indigenous governance bodies, as well as community and social outreach organisations. Applying the separation principle [340] we described in Section 4.2, the quasi-identifier attributes required for linking are split from sensitive microdata by the data owners before any linkage is performed. The actual linkage of databases is conducted by Manitoba Health, a trusted third party, which first applies a deterministic followed by a probabilistic linkage approach. Each record is assigned an encrypted person health identification number (PHIN), which can then be used by the MCHP to link sensitive microdata for individual research projects based on the needs of researchers. Privacy is incorporated into the overall running of the centre following the Five Safes principles we outlined in Section 2.7.1.

A wide range of outcomes have been achieved using sensitive databases linked by the MCHP, ranging from improving the academic performance of students from low-income families, predicting future use of care beds for elderly people in need, to establishing the benefits of support for pregnant women [338].

13.4 Germany

As we discussed in Section 2.3.2, the federated political structure of Germany, having sixteen constituent states each having their own data protection agencies, makes the linking of sensitive databases across states a legally very challenging undertaking. As a result, not many applications of linking sensitive databases (in privacy-preserving ways) have so far been developed in Germany.

One example application, the health of newborns, is widely considered as an important indicator of the quality of a medical system. Many countries therefore have observational systems for monitoring the health of newborns. In Germany, this is a task of the G-BA[9], the highest decision making institution of the self-government of health care providers and health insurance companies in Germany. The G-BA is obligated to ensure the quality of medical procedures across all providers. About 700 hospitals provide obstetrical care for an average of 785,000 births per year.

---

[9] Gemeinsamer Bundesausschuss (Federal Joint Committee), see: https://www.g-ba.de/english/

Germany has two different kinds of health insurances. By law, only data of individuals who are covered by the statutory health insurance (roughly 90% of the population) can be used for linkage of newborns. Under current legislation, record linkage of newborns has to be based on hospital identifiers, timestamps, and other procedural information. Names or unique identification numbers are usually not available. G-BA commissioned a comparative empirical evaluation study of alternative linkage procedures [550]. For this study, the data collection in all hospitals providing care for newborns was modified [410]. Communicating the need for the study, obtaining the required permissions and implementing the modifications in 700 hospitals has taken nearly a decade. The study should clarify if linkage could be improved by the additional inclusion of names. The names were encoded by two different methods. The first method is based on the standard procedure in Germany for cancer registries (Kontrollnummernverfahren) [574] which in the later passes of an iterative linkage approach matches records based on a German phonetic encoding technique known as the Kölner Phonetik [479]. The generated phonetic codes were linked using deterministic matching rules. The second method used attribute level Bloom filters (as we discussed in Section 8.3.1) with a length of 1,000 bits and using ten hash functions on quasi-identifying attribute values converted into bigrams. The linkage was made scalable using the multibit tree approach for blocking, a technique we discussed in Section 10.1.5.

The baseline for comparisons was the number of matches found by procedural information alone. Since no gold standard was available for comparisons, an evaluation has to be limited to potential matches found by a single method and the intersections given by all three methods (procedural, cancer registry method, Bloom filters). More than 96% of all matches were found by all three methods. Bloom filters yielded the highest number of potential matches. A combination of Bloom filters with procedural information seems to be most promising. However, since no validation was possible under the given legal constraints, the main message of the study is the urgent need to increase the completeness of available quasi-identifying attributes in this data set. Missing data on procedural information as well as incomplete encoded quasi-identifiers are the main problems for linking neonatal data.

13.5 Switzerland

Switzerland has been an early adopter of Bloom filter based techniques to link sensitive databases in the health domain. Due to the (previous) lack of a unique personal identifier, or privacy protection regulation which prohibits the use of quasi-identifiers to link databases across organisations, linkage based on encoded quasi-identifying attributes is required in many applications in Switzerland [534].

An approach named P3RL (privacy-preserving probabilistic record linkage) was developed as part of the Swiss National Cohort project[10] [571]. The approach combines probabilistic record linkage on Bloom filter encoded personal identifying information such as names, dates of birth, and addresses, combined with a deterministic matching of plaintext values for gender, marital status, and nationality. The separation principle [340] is applied, where a linkage unit is an independent partner in this project setup with privacy and security safeguards and following strict ethical guidelines.

To identify the quasi-identifying attributes across the databases to be linked a masking approach is used where for example all digits are replaced with a '9', all lowercase characters with a 'z', and so on. Based on such masked data each database owner then also generates local data preprocessing templates, which are sent to the linkage unit to be combined into global templates that are then sent back to all database owners. These preprocessing templates are then applied on all databases to be linked to make their structure and the format of quasi-identifying attribute values to conform to each other as much as possible before they are being encoded into attribute level Bloom filters of length 1,000 bits each. The actual probabilistic linkage is then performed by a linkage unit using an enhanced version of the Generalized Record Linkage System (GRLS) as developed by Statistics Canada [198].

Within the context of the Swiss National Cohort project, a variety of studies have been enabled using this privacy-preserving linkage method, ranging from the investigation into deaths due to avalanches [57] to the analysis of dietary questionnaires linked to census data to identify which dietary patterns are associated with mortality based on cancer or cardiovascular diseases [365]. Many of these studies would not have been possible without the use of privacy-preserving record linkage techniques that allowed the linking of sensitive health and administrative databases between organisations.

In another application domain, a German-Swiss research group[11] has obtained the permissions for a population covering project aiming to link economic data on the subset of individuals in Germany and Switzerland which either have a social security insurance as employees in both countries, or are living in one country and working in the other. The research topics to be investigated in this project are labour market problems. The linking will be conducted using a privacy-preserving method where the names, dates of birth, and gender of individuals will be encoded into Bloom filters using the cryptographic long-term key approach we discussed in Section 8.3.2. The Swiss data will be encoded by the Swiss National Statistical Institute (BFS) and the German data by the Institute for Employment Research (IAB). The linkage will be conducted in the secure environment of the Research Data Centre of the German Federal Employment Agency.

---

[10] See: https://www.swissnationalcohort.ch

[11] Personal communication, Manfred Antoni and Rainer Schnell, March 2020.

13.6 United Kingdom

The United Kingdom has a long history of applications of record linkage in a variety of domains. The Oxford Record Linkage Study (ORLS) started in 1962 [4] using the ideas and methods developed by Newcombe et al. in Canada [435, 436]. The ORLS was tasked with investigating the feasibility and costs of collecting and linking health related data, developing computer software for linking such health data, and investigating how linked health data sets can be used for research [226].

Concurrently, in Scotland, since 1968 a record linkage system was developed that aimed to link all birth and death records nationwide, as well as records from hospitals and cancer registries [341]. Today, record linkage projects in Scotland in the health sector and within government are supported through a network of organisations, including National Records of Scotland which is the trusted linkage centre, the University of Edinburgh which provides high performance computing infrastructure, and the Edinburgh BioQuarter which provides safe access to sensitive linked data in secure computing environments [633]. Successful linkage projects in the health sector include the linkage of ambulance data with other medical data sets to investigate out of hospital cardiac arrests, how inequalities and access to dental services affect the health of children, and the effects of homelessness on health outcomes [633].

A large initiative to make administrative and health data collections more accessible to researchers as well as government agencies across the whole of the UK was the government funded Administrative Data Research Network (ADRN), which was later replaced by the Administrative Data Research UK[12]. There are other current linkage projects in the UK that have very specific goals. For example, the Digitising Scotland[13] project aims to link large historical data collections with the objective to reconstruct the full population of Scotland from around 1855 until 1974. While achieving this requires the development of various novel record linkage techniques [10, 425, 426], the potential for novel studies about changes of a society at a large scale and over more than a hundred years are numerous, spanning from historical, demographic, geographical, all the way to health research.

In 2007, the Secure Anonymised Information Linkage (SAIL) database[14] was established in Wales as a repository of linkable anonymised data sets from both the health and non-health domains [215]. SAIL follows the separation principle [340] where a trusted third party, the National Health Services (NHS) Wales Information Services, is used to link the quasi-identifying information sent to it by the different data providers. A succession of exact matching (using a patient's NHS number if available), followed by deter-

---

[12] See: https://www.adruk.org
[13] See: https://digitisingscotland.ac.uk/
[14] See: https://saildatabank.com/

ministic (using phonetic encoding as we described in Section 6.6) and then probabilistic record linkage methods are applied. Linked records are then assigned an anonymised linkage field (named ALF), which is sent back to SAIL to facilitate linkage. To improve security, the ALFs are encrypted a second time before being used in SAIL, preventing that anybody working at SAIL can learn anything about the identity behind a given ALF identifier [311]. For approved researchers, access to linked data sets in SAIL can be done via the SAIL Gateway [312] that applies methods of statistical disclosure control (as we discussed in Section 5.5) to ensure any view of the data a researcher can see does not allow reidentification. Between 2007 and 2017 over 250 research projects have been conducted using data from SAIL[15].

The Clinical Practice Research Datalink (CPRD)[16] is a research service that supports both prospective and retrospective clinical and public health research studies. CPRD is jointly funded by the Medicines and Healthcare products Regulatory Agency and the National Institute for Health Research, as part of the UK's Department of Health and Social Care. CPRD collects deidentified patient data from a network of general practices across the UK, where primary care data are linked to a range of other health related databases to provide a longitudinal data set that is considered as a random sample of the UK population. Following the separation principle [340], participating general practices send patient information (a CPRD pseudonym, the NHS number, date of birth, postcode, and gender) to NHS Digital[17] which then matches records across databases to create a linkage file that does not contain any patient identifiers. These linkage files are sent to CPRD which can then link the health and medical data sets they receive from general practices. All requests from researchers to access linked data need to be approved by an independent scientific advisory committee. As of early 2020, this data set contains information for around 45 million patients, including about 13 million patients that were currently registered, and over 2,400 peer-reviewed publications have been produced based on data from CPRD ranging from the investigation of the effectiveness of drugs and health policies to risk factors for certain diseases[18].

Around 2010, the UK's Office of National Statistics (ONS), conducted a programme named 'Beyond 2011' (after the 2011 UK census). This programme investigated options of how the traditional costly census could be adapted or even replaced for example by using administrative data that are linked in order to create the same information, such as small area socio-demographic statistics, that are traditionally collected from census surveys. One aspect was how to link such potentially sensitive administrative data-

---

[15] See: https://saildatabank.com/wp-content/uploads/SAIL_10_year_anniversary_brochure.pdf

[16] See: https://www.cprd.com/

[17] See: https://digital.nhs.uk/

[18] For an extensive bibliography we refer the interested reader to: https://www.cprd.com/bibliography

bases and keep the collected and linked data safe while still allowing a variety of uses [446, 447]. Data anonymisation was explored by the 'Beyond 2011' programme, with the idea of a one-way hashing approach based on the keyed hashing method HMAC (described in Section 6.2.2) to be applied on quasi-identifying attributes such as names, addresses, and dates of birth [446]. Furthermore, to support approximate matching for example between name variations, the ONS was planning to generate similarity tables between plaintext values and to then anonymise these plaintext values to obtain a similarity table of hash encoded values [446]. The application of these anonymisation techniques and any linkages based on these anoymised data were planned to be employed within the secure computing environments of the ONS, with none of these anonymised data to be published.

However, a group of researchers analysed the descriptions of these anonymisation techniques with regard to their conceptual cryptographic security [141]. While they acknowledged that the use of a secure computing environment provides significant protection to these data, some of the security statements in the reports published by the ONS raised alarm with these researchers. They described several flaws in the proposed anonymisation approach that could be exploited within the secure computing environments of the ONS for example by a curious employee, as we discussed in Section 5.4. Specifically, the use of HMAC did not take into account that frequent values (such as frequent names) will lead to frequent hash codes, potentially allowing a frequency attack to be mounted, as we covered in Section 5.4.3. The similarity tables to be generated allow for a graph matching based attack, as we described in Section 9.4.

In line with the researchers who highlighted the weaknesses of the anonymisation approach proposed by the ONS [141], we do not provide this example to highlight its failure. Rather, we like to emphasise the importance of the ONS having published enough details of their proposed anonymisation approach to allow security experts to detect its flaws. As Culnane et al. write [141]:

> It is commendable that the ONS has published its methodology, and we hope that our analysis is exactly the sort of constructive participation that should happen between academia and government. It is a good thing when weaknesses are identified, because then they can be corrected, and the methodology improved before it is used in an inappropriate way. This process bears witness to openness and transparency being drivers for better security and privacy.

To re-emphasise, the ONS only planned to use these anonymisation methods inside their secure computing environments, and therefore only insider attacks would have been successful. To the best of our knowledge, after the discovery of its weaknesses, this proposed method was never implemented and used by the ONS, and novel approaches to anonymisation and record linkage have been explored [311].

We like to encourage other organisations that are developing and implementing techniques to anonymise and/or link sensitive databases to be similarly open and engage with academia, rather than being secretive and not providing any details of the kinds of techniques and methodologies they are implementing and employing. This will allow weaknesses to be identified resulting in overall more secure systems to link sensitive databases.

13.7 United States

In the United States, the US Census Bureau has been one of the organisations that has pioneered the use of advanced techniques to link very large databases, such as those being collected in nationwide censuses [644, 645]. However, because such linkage projects are conducted within the secure environment of the Bureau, there has been no need to employ privacy-preserving linkage techniques. The US Census Bureau in recent years has however started to investigate the use of advanced techniques, such as differential privacy [181], to publish sensitive data in anonymised ways such that no reidentification is possible [2].

In the health domain, a large number of public as well as private organisations operate in the US, both providing clinical care as well as managing administrative aspects of the health system such as running hospitals and clinics or providing private health insurance. As a result, the collection and analysis of health data is highly fragmented, making access to individual health databases difficult. Due to this fragmentation, as well as different rules and regulations in individual US states, the linking of health databases can be more challenging in the US than in other countries. As we described in Section 2.4, the Health Insurance Portability and Accountability Act (HIPAA) of 1996 is the regulatory framework that governs how sensitive private health data can be processed and linked. Employing privacy-preserving linkage techniques based on encrypted and anonymised data is an allowable deidentification method under HIPAA, and as a result a variety of applications to link sensitive health databases have been developed. We now describe two examples where details of the employed linkage techniques have been scientifically published.

A distributed application to facilitate the secure linking of health databases has been described by Kho et al. [345], who used this system to link and deduplicate seven million electronic health records from six organisations in the Chicago area. Using a HIPAA compliant SHA algorithm (that generated hash codes of length 512 bits), and using a secret key not known to the individuals undertaking the linkage, seventeen hash values were generated for each record using different sets of quasi-identifying attributes as well as social security numbers (SSN)[19]. From those seventeen hash codes, four resulted in

---

[19] It should be noted that SSNs in the United States do not include a checksum and therefore they can be invalid (see: https://secure.ssa.gov/poms.nsf/lnx/0110201035). There is also evidence that SSNs are shared, for example within a family [239].

high linkage quality based on a manually prepared ground truth data set. These four hash codes encoded concatenations of (1) first name, surname, and date of birth; (2) date of birth and SSN; (3) surname and SSN; and (4) three letters of first name, three letters of surname, Soundex [524] encoded first name, Soundex encoded surname, date of birth, and SSN. If a pair of records had the same hash value in at least one of these generated four hash codes then the two records of the pair were classified as a match. The use of a secret key unknown to the individuals undertaking the linkage means a dictionary attack using known quasi-identifying attribute values will be highly challenging.

Based on ground truth data that consist of 11,292 true matches, a recall (sensitivity, as we discussed in Section 3.4.1) of 96% and a specificity (true negative rate [663]) of 100% were achieved. Analyses of the resulting linked data sets using three selected disease examples showed that this privacy-preserving linkage method was able to reduce the number of duplicate records across the six organisations by up to 28%, thereby leading to much improved outcomes of health studies based on these linked data sets. This application of a privacy-preserving linkage technique has been used by commercial companies providing health services.

A related approach to linking sensitive health databases in a privacy-preserving way was described by Bian et al. [59], who were not able to directly use the approach proposed by Kho et al. [345] described above due to different privacy risk regulations. Their system also employed a hashing approach based on SHA, where however different quasi-identifiers were hashed. Developed and employed in Florida, the system is aimed at linking large sensitive health databases held by different health care organisations. To identify which set of hash encoded quasi-identifying attributes can obtain the best linkage quality, the authors used two snapshots (one year apart) of a publicly available Florida voter registration database that contained the same quasi-identifying attributes as their health databases. These voter databases also included voter identification numbers which provided true matches that allowed linkage quality to be evaluated. The obtained two best sets of quasi-identifying attributes (named 'linkage rules') were (1) first name, surname, date of birth, and gender; and (2) first name, surname, date of birth, and race. As with the approach proposed by Kho et al. [345], concatenated strings of these values were encoded using a SHA algorithm with a secret key included to prevent dictionary attacks.

On a small set of 1,000 true matches from two real health databases, a precision of 99.3% and a recall of 75.5% were reported. When applied on a set of seven large health databases containing a total of over 16 million patient records, over 10% duplicate patient records were identified. Around 1.5 million patients were identified in two, and over 1.7 million patients in more than two databases. The developed software, known as OneFL Deduper, is freely available as we describe in more details in Appendix A.1.

13.8 Summary and Further Reading

In this chapter we have described some example applications from various countries where different systems, setups, and techniques are used to link sensitive databases. A common approach is to combine several different privacy methods and techniques, for example by using the separation principle [340] as well as privacy-preserving techniques that encode sensitive quasi-identifying attribute values before they are being used for linkage. The most commonly used such encoding methods are secure one-way hashing and Bloom filter encoding, even though in their basic forms they are both known to have weaknesses, as we for example have discussed in Chapter 9. Within the (often secure) computing environments used by many organisations, these weaknesses might be acceptable.

We believe an important aspect for any organisation that aims to link sensitive databases using privacy-preserving techniques should be transparency with regard to what techniques they are planning to employ and how. Even inviting external experts, such as security researchers, to conduct independent assessments of how these techniques will be used, can help identify the weaknesses such implementations might have [141].

For readers who are interested in real-world outcomes of linkage systems in the health domain we recommend the overview by Holman et al. [282] which covers the history, structure, and example outcomes from a decade of work at the Western Australian Data Linkage System (WADLS). Similarly, Young and Flack [658] summarise outcomes produced from the Australian Population Health Research Network.

Ali et al. [15] describe the databases available to health research in Brazil, and how they have been linked by a variety of organisations using different linkage methodologies. The probabilistic privacy-preserving linkage approach used in Switzerland within the Swiss National Cohort project is described in detail by Schmidlin et al. [534], while Jones and Ford provide an overview of privacy, confidentiality, as well as practical aspects of linking databases [311]. They also briefly discuss various practical linkage applications from Australia, Canada, and the UK.

A special issue of the International Journal of Population Data Science (IJPDS) in late 2019 also focused on profiles of data centres, many of them conducting linkages of large sensitive population databases. We refer the interested reader to the IJPDS Web site: https://ijpds.org/issue/view/13 where these articles are available.

Part IV
Outlook

In this fourth part of the book we provide an outlook to future challenges and research directions in Chapter 14, covering both conceptual research questions as well as practical challenges. We also discuss the challenges that Big data, and biometric and genetic data, pose to linking sensitive databases, as well as what opportunities such new types of data can provide.

Chapter 14
Future Research Challenges and Directions

Abstract The linking of sensitive databases across organisations is an active area of research in several domains. In this chapter we discuss some of the major open research questions that require further investigations. These include the development of frameworks that allow comparative empirical evaluations, the preparation of benchmark data collections, how to link sensitive databases in a cloud data service, how to properly assess the quality and completeness of linked databases in those situations when only encoded or encrypted records are available, improved theoretically grounded privacy measures, how to best deal with missing values, and novel adversary models. We also discuss how the linking of sensitive databases is challenged in the era of Big data, and the challenges and opportunities that novel types of data, such as biometric and genetic data, can provide.

14.1 Conceptual Research Questions

Conceptually, techniques to link sensitive databases can be evaluated across three main dimensions: linkage quality, scalability to link large or multiple databases, and the privacy protection provided by a linkage technique. Each of these dimensions poses its own specific challenges, as we have discussed throughout this book. Every algorithm, technique, method, or protocol, that aims to provide a solution to link sensitive databases in a privacy-preserving way will be having some form of trade-off across these three dimensions. Different applications will potentially put more emphasis and importance on one (or two) of these three dimensions over the other(s).

In the following list we describe other conceptual challenges and corresponding open research questions that need to be addressed to provide solutions to link sensitive databases that are fully applicable to a variety of practical linkage applications and scenarios. We also refer the interested reader to the challenges described by Christen [109] and Vatsalan et al. [620].

© Springer Nature Switzerland AG 2020
P. Christen et al., *Linking Sensitive Data*, https://doi.org/10.1007/978-3-030-59706-1_14

- **New types of data**: As we will discuss in more detail in Sections 14.3 and 14.4, more and more data of novel types are being collected by many organisations as well as individuals. These include multimedia data such as images, audio and video, free-format text data, mobility and location data from portable devices and GPS sensors [662], and even biometric and genetic data about individuals. Some of these data can potentially be useful when linking databases, as the examples described below show. Using such novel types of data, however, will require new methods to process, encode (if the data are seen to be sensitive personally identifying information, such as biometric and genetic data, as we discuss in Section 14.4), and to compare such data.

  An example of using new types of data is an application that aims to estimate the transported shipment weight of trucks by correcting survey responses with capture-recapture methods by matching number plates photographed at automatic highway weight sensors. This is conducted using a database of commercial vehicle numbers to link the measured weights with survey data reported by the owners of the truck [354]. Another example is to link location data from diverse sources (mobile devices, taxis, and so on) to identify patterns of movements of people [368], an application that has the potential to uncover highly sensitive information about individuals. A third example is the use of record linkage techniques to match topographical measurements of cartridge cases as extracted from images with the aim to identify guns that have been used in multiple shootings [585].

- **Techniques that can handle missing values**: Only limited work has investigated how to deal with missing values when sensitive databases are to be linked in privacy-preserving ways [103]. Missing data are, however, a fundamental aspect of many real-world databases, and how best to deal with the different types of missing data (as we discussed in Section 11.2.2) requires further investigation, because the different types of missing data will require different linkage approaches. Trying to estimate a similarity for a missing value based on a nearest neighbour method, the approach proposed by Chi et al. [103], might not be the most suitable approach for missing completely at random (MCAR) or for missing not at random (MNAR) data in the context of linking sensitive databases in a privacy-preserving way.

- **Formalise different types of adversaries**: As we discussed in Section 4.4, the currently used models of an adversary are mainly the honest-but-curious and the malicious models, as used in cryptography and secure multiparty computation [394]. These models however generally do not reflect the risks to data and systems in practical linkage applications, where for example the Five Safes framework we discussed in Section 2.7.1 is followed by an organisation. A conceptual analysis of different attack methods (also called 'attack vectors') is needed, where the motivation, capabilities, accessibility to data, risks, and benefits, of potential types of adversaries are being evaluated. Such an analysis would lead to a much better understanding of the privacy risks that sensitive databases might be exposed to in a certain linkage scenario.

- **Secure encoding techniques**: Many of the privacy-preserving encoding techniques used to link sensitive databases, especially the perturbation based methods we discussed in Chapters 7 and 8, currently lack formal proofs that verify that these techniques cannot be attacked by an adversary. On the other hand, those techniques based on secure multiparty computation approaches, while provably secure, are currently less scalable to linking large databases. In addition, most secure multiparty computations require online computations that involve many communication steps, which might be impossible in secure environments.

  As we have discussed in Chapter 9, unlike with standard cryptographic techniques that rely on a specific algorithm to encrypt a plaintext value into ciphertext, perturbation based encoding techniques have vulnerabilities that occur due to the distribution of quasi-identifying attribute values (and q-grams within them) in the databases that are being encoded, as we covered in Chapter 9. Overcoming such data dependent vulnerabilities will require the development of novel encoding techniques that, while being more secure than current approaches, are still efficient and allow the approximate matching of encoded sensitive quasi-identifying attribute values to make the linking of large sensitive databases practical. While provably secure techniques are desirable, they are commonly not required by law.

  While secure encoding techniques are at the core of any project or application to link sensitive databases, the overall system within which a linkage is conducted also needs to be carefully assessed with regard to the security it provides and if there are any potential weaknesses. This includes the organisations involved in a linkage and their personnel working on linkage projects, as well as the information technology (both computing and communication systems) used by these organisations [188].

- **Scalable blocking, indexing, and filtering techniques**: While blocking, indexing, and filtering techniques as we discussed in Chapter 10 exist for current encoding methods, such as Bloom filters, to facilitate the efficient matching of large databases across multiple organisations [494], these techniques might not be applicable for new and more secure encoding techniques as discussed in the previous paragraph. Existing blocking, indexing, and filtering techniques assume a certain type of encoding is used (as we discussed in Chapter 7), such as binary vectors, and they would not be applicable on other types of encoded data. Novel techniques will therefore be required that facilitate blocking, indexing, or filtering of encoded or encrypted databases. Ideally, such techniques should be independent from the actual encoding or encryption method used, while also being provably secure, scalable, and efficient.

- **Assessing linkage quality without ground truth**: In applications where sensitive databases are being linked across organisations using privacy-preserving methods, it is generally not possible to inspect the actual quasi-identifying attribute values of linked record pairs (nor of unlinked pairs) because these values are often personal identifying information. Similarly, it is unlikely that ground truth data are available in such linkage situations. Therefore, how to assess the outcome of a linkage project with regard to linkage quality (and completeness), as we discussed in Section 3.4.1, is a challenging and not yet solved question. Related to this challenge is the topic of how to deal with bias in linked data sets, as we discussed in Section 11.2.4.

  Some initial work [370, 490] has explored how manual clerical review can be conducted on partially masked (hidden) plaintext values. Such an approach will however be too expensive and time consuming when applied on very large databases. The manual decisions made on partially hidden attribute values might also be less accurate than if the clerical review would have been conducted on fully visible quasi-identifying attribute values. Methods based on synthetic data, as we discuss in Appendix A.3, might be able to provide some form of valuable assessment of linkage quality when encoded or encrypted sensitive databases are being linked.

- **Techniques for linking real-time or dynamic data**: As we discuss in Section 14.3 below, many organisations increasingly require real-time processing, linking, and analysis of data streams, rather than the batch-oriented linking of static databases. This paradigm shift requires novel techniques to deal with dynamic and temporal data, such as adaptive techniques that can link records, ideally in (near) real time, from an incoming stream (such as query records) to a database containing records of known entities. While work on this topic has been conducted on non-sensitive databases [115, 118, 493] (as we discussed in Section 11.2.3), how to link dynamic sensitive databases in privacy-preserving ways (and in near real-time) is an open research problem where only limited work has so far been conducted [330, 495, 496].

- **Adequate privacy measures**: As we discussed in Section 5.2, there are currently no commonly accepted privacy measures available that allow the objective evaluation of privacy-preserving record linkage techniques. The challenges of developing such measures are that they ideally need to be applicable on different techniques to link sensitive databases and they should provide not just a single average privacy measure for an encoded database, but also a measure for the privacy protection provided for the most vulnerable encoded record (a kind of worst-case measure) [615].

  In the context of linking sensitive databases, privacy can be affected by various aspects, including the sizes of the databases being linked, the distributions of the sensitive identifying values within them, the values of the actual content data (microdata) in these databases, as well as the overall linkage environment. Furthermore, privacy measures should be interpretable and easy to understand to allow non-experts to evaluate different encoding techniques, and even allow the public to gain an understanding of how secure their private sensitive data are when encoded using a certain privacy technique. Developing a privacy measure that fits all these requirements will be a challenging undertaking.

- **Evaluation frameworks**: In order to allow the comparative evaluation of different techniques to link sensitive databases, it is imperative to develop frameworks and methods that allow different techniques to be compared. Such comparisons need to be conducted with regard to the main conceptual dimensions of linkage quality, scalability to linking large and/or multiple databases, and the privacy protection these techniques provide. Such frameworks need to facilitate that different algorithms and techniques (for the different steps of the linkage process) can easily be integrated into the framework, and that different measures are available to evaluate the compared techniques along all three dimensions (linkage quality, scalability, and privacy) discussed above.

  Furthermore, from a more practical perspective, such frameworks should be freely available to encourage researchers and practitioners to use the framework. Such frameworks should also include a wide variety of test and benchmark data sets to allow evaluations that are meaningful for a wide variety of practical applications where sensitive databases need to be linked.

Unless progress is made along these conceptual challenges, it will be difficult to develop practical approaches to link large sensitive databases across organisations. This is because either there will be gaps in certain required techniques, or no clear criteria about which the best techniques are to be used in certain real-world linkage applications.

14.2 Practical Challenges

Besides the conceptual open research questions for linking sensitive databases across organisations, there are various practical challenges that potentially might hinder or even prevent such linkages. While we already discussed practical considerations (related to data, techniques, as well as institutional aspects) in Chapter 11, here we briefly describe a few additional challenges that might require careful consideration in certain practical applications where sensitive databases are being linked.

- **Methods for realistic assessments of privacy threats:** One of the main aims of linking sensitive databases is to enrich data from diverse sources such that a final linked data set can be used for different analytical processes such as research studies [232]. As we described in Section 4.2, once a linkage is performed, a data consumer will generally be provided with anonymised (deidentified) microdata (also known as payload data) that are specific to the requirements of their analysis work. However, it is increasingly important to consider what possible privacy threats could arise from such released microdata. Given such data represent records that belong to (possibly large) groups of individuals, any unique combination of attribute values in such microdata can potentially lead to the reidentification of a single person or a small group of individuals [583].

Anonymisation is a common technique used when microdata are released to reduce the likelihood of reidentification. Anonymisation aims to balance privacy risk and data utility. The privacy evaluation of such techniques are generally conducted from a data-centric perspective by applying statistical disclosure control measures, as we discussed in Section 2.6. A common assumption is a worst-case scenario, where an adversary has access to enough resources and external data to perform reidentification on released microdata. As a result of such risk adverse methods to data anonymisation, data are often substantially modified before being released. This can lead to released data that are not very useful for many analysis tasks because too many details are either masked or perturbed.

However, as discussed by Hafner et al. [248], there is an argument to introduce a more user centric approach to assessing privacy risks when microdata are being released. The argument put forward was that the assumptions of worst-case attack scenarios in privacy evaluations are not applicable in most practical scenarios where microdata are being used, for example by researchers who have signed confidentiality agreements. The common assumption, of an adversary having access to external data which are the same or very similar to the encoded microdata, will unlikely hold in most practical situations. Hafner et al. [248] suggest that rather than focusing on the problems of data protection, more focus should be given to the use of microdata from an user perspective considering what information is actually needed, and what likely scenarios of misuse there could be (this includes both intentional as well as unintentional misuse). It would be more sensible to model the worst-case scenario according to realistic situations of data use and evaluate the privacy risks for those situations, rather than assuming an academic worst-case scenario that highly unlikely will happen in real-world usages of released microdata.

While this work by Hafner et al. [248] was conducted in the context of the release and use of microdata for research, similar arguments hold in the context of linking sensitive databases. Specifically, assessing the likelihood of the different types of mishaps and attacks we described in Sections 5.3 and 5.4, as well as the costs, risks, and potentially benefits for the adversary (as we discussed in Section 5.4.7), might result in more sensitive databases being made available for record linkage projects. Developing new methods that can adequately assess such risk from a user perspective could be highly beneficial for any application that aims to assess the risks posed when sensitive databases are being linked.

- **Linkage across jurisdictions**: Organisations in various domains increasingly work across countries. Examples include law enforcement agencies (such as Interpol, the International Criminal Police Organization) or statistical agencies (like Eurostat, the European Statistical Office). Such cross-jurisdictional collaborations require co-operation both at the regulatory as well as at the technical level. Regulations and policies about how sensitive databases can be linked are required, specifying for example what quasi-identifying attributes can be used in a linkage, what kind of encoding and linkage techniques are to be used, and how linked records are to be handled.

- **Compiling dictionaries for research applications**: Many linkage techniques will benefit from dictionaries (lookup tables) with frequency distributions of names (first names and surnames) and addresses, as well as dictionaries of commonly occurring misspellings and phonetic variations. For linkages across countries ideally such lookup tables are being created and shared across the jurisdictions involved in such linkages. Given the changing nature of addresses over time, databases that map historical addresses (such as old street names renamed to modern names) will be highly useful to improve not just the quality of linkages but also for any spatial data analysis that involves historical data [351].

- **Linking multilingual or multicultural databases**: Related to the challenge of linking databases across jurisdictions is the question of how to link databases where the quasi-identifying attribute values are recorded in different languages (such as encoded into different Unicode codecs[1]), or from individuals that have different cultural backgrounds. Besides potentially different character sets being used, names can be translated ('Peter' becomes 'Pierre' or 'Pedro'), there can be a variety of transliterations of names across languages, and even different name structures that potentially change over the lifetime of an individual [467]. As increasingly more people move around the world for work, study, or leisure, it is becoming more common to have databases that contain records about individuals from a variety of cultures and countries. When linking such databases the possible language variations need to be considered in order to achieve high linkage quality.

- **Certification authorities for linkage**: In the domain of computer security, certification agencies are tasked with ensuring that critical systems, such as communication, utilities, finance, transport, and so on, are properly assessed with the aim to identify any potential weaknesses or errors in such systems that could be exploited by an adversary. Certification agencies are sometimes also providing public key authorisation, as we discussed in the side box on page 95.

  Some specific computer security aspects can for example be accredited by the International Organization for Standardization (ISO). A small

---

[1] See: https://home.unicode.org/

number of organisations [83] undertaking the linkage of sensitive databases have successfully obtained such an ISO 27001:2013 accreditation[2].
This accreditation certifies only the security of the information technology
systems used by an organisation that undertakes the linkage of sensitive
databases. That might be required in some jurisdictions but not in others.
However, currently, there are no established procedures for the certification of the security of a privacy-preserving record linkage technique being
employed. Establishing procedures for the certification of the techniques
and algorithms used for linking sensitive databases in privacy-preserving
ways is therefore a necessary step to move some responsibility from data
protection officers to the certification organisation.

- **Linking sensitive databases using cloud computing**: With the increasing availability of large and powerful data centres where organisations can hire processing time and storage, the question arises how such
cloud based systems can be employed to conduct the linkage of sensitive
databases, especially when data sourced from several organisations need
to be linked. While some governments have their own data centres that
provide highly secured computing capabilities, it is more likely that an
organisation needs to rely upon commercially available cloud computing
resources, as provided by various large multinational companies as well
as smaller localised businesses. Given such cloud based services are generally shared between users, when any sensitive data are being transferred
to and stored by such a service it is prudent to assume the cloud service is an untrusted organisation. Therefore, only encoded sensitive data
should ever be transferred to a cloud based system. Any linkage would
then have to be based on a privacy-preserving linkage technique, such as
one of those we discussed in this book.

  The advantages of using cloud based computing resources are that
they can provide large enough storage for large data collections, as well
as powerful computing resources which might not be affordable by an
organisation that otherwise does not have high computing requirements,
and that does not regularly conduct linkages of large databases. Using
cloud based computing resources might be much more cost efficient than
investing in an in-house computing infrastructure powerful enough to link
large sensitive databases using privacy-preserving techniques. The disad-
vantages of using cloud based resources can include that there might be a
lack of control of where the data are physically stored (in which country
or jurisdiction), a lack of trust by data owners and the public that their
data are not stored in a local secure environment, and regulations and
policies that prohibit the use of cloud based systems for any processing
of sensitive data.

- **Automated data cleaning and standardisation**: In the areas of Big
data and data analytics and mining, it is generally accepted that in many

---

[2] See: https://www.iso.org/isoiec-27001-information-security.html

projects up to 80% of time and effort need to be spent on data exploration, data profiling, data cleaning, and data preprocessing [398]. Much of this effort is because human involvement in these tasks is crucial, and only some aspects of these processes can be automated. Furthermore, domain expertise as well as knowledge about techniques and tools are crucial to obtain clean data suitable for a given analysis project.

Similarly, as we have discussed in Section 3.3, data cleaning is crucial when (sensitive) databases are being linked in order to make the input databases to conform as much as possible in their format, structure, and content. When sensitive databases are being linked across organisations, as we discussed in Section 11.2, any manual data exploration, data preprocessing, and data cleaning needs to be done on the individual databases, and sharing of any identified data quality issues might not be possible because sensitive information would have to be revealed. It can be very challenging to obtain databases that are adequate for linking if no or only limited exchange is possible between the indivduals that undertake these data exploration and processing tasks in different organisations.

Therefore, it would be highly beneficial to incorporate automatic data exploration, cleaning, and standardisation techniques into the linkage process, that can be employed without much (or any) manual intervention in order to end up with cleaned and standardised databases that follow the same format, structure, and content across organisations. Such techniques would help to improve the quality of many projects where sensitive databases are to be linked across organisations.

14.3 Linking in the Era of Big Data

While it can be seen as a marketing buzzword, technically Big data is the topic concerned with data that have specific characteristics that distinguish them from traditional data as collected, processed, managed, and analysed by many organisations [665]. Big data are generally characterised using four V's: volume, variety, velocity, and veracity [100].

The **volume** of Big data means that, compared to traditional data that can be stored in an organisation's database or data warehousing system for later processing and analysis, such Big data are considered to be too large to allow storage for later processing and analysis. Rather, any processing and analysis need to be conducted as the data arrive.

The **variety** of Big data considers that many different types and formats of data can occur, including structured (like database records), semi-structured (such as HTML or XML documents), or unstructured data (for example free-format text documents that can include images, graphs, and tables). Being able to manage, process, and analyse such potentially complex data can add significant extra requirements on any data management, processing, and analysis system.

The **velocity** of Big data means that data are being produced and arrive on a constant basis, and they need to be processed, and analysed in (near) real time because the volume characteristics discussed before prohibits storage and later offline analysis. Big data are commonly seen as streams of records, where examples include online financial or shopping transactions, telecommunication records, or data from the multitude of increasingly online sensors, commonly known as the Internet of Things [29, 662]. Such sensors range from traditional temperature and rain sensors, to traffic flow sensors as well mobile phone location data and even video streams of security cameras. An important aspect of many of these data streams is that they have unpredictable arrival rates, in that over time the number of records, transactions, or sensor measurements is fluctuating potentially in unpredictable ways.

The fourth V of Big data is **veracity**, which characterises the quality of data, including anomalies, outliers, noise, missingness, and so on. As Big data are being created through diverse mechanisms and collected from potentially many different sources, such data quality aspects need to be considered and handled in appropriate ways. Sensors, for example, can be malfunctioning producing wrong measurements or no data at all. Any data produced by humans will likely have variations and errors, both unintentional as well as on purpose. In the context of data being produced in an ongoing fashion requiring (near) real-time processing and analysis, dealing with such data quality issues, that likely change over time, can be a challenging task.

Although **value** is sometimes seen as a fifth V of Big data, is not a technical characteristic. It considers that any efforts conducted on Big data should ultimately lead to value for an organisation. No data should be collected, processed, and analysed, if they do not help an organisation to achieve its goals.

In the context of linking sensitive databases, each of the first four V's can provide a challenge if larger and more complex databases are to be linked. Volume means the databases to be linked are becoming larger, and multiple databases from several sources need to be linked, known as multidatabase linkage [494]. Novel blocking and indexing techniques, as we discussed in Chapter 10, are required to allow the linkage of very large databases from potentially many sources.

Variety means that the databases to be linked, potentially held by various organisations, have different structures and content, as well as data of different quality. As we discussed in Section 11.2, appropriate data cleaning and standardisation techniques are crucial to make all databases to be linked follow the same structure and to ensure the values in the quasi-identifying attributes to be compared are in the same format. While traditional linkage approaches, including blocking and indexing techniques, have assumed the databases to be linked follow a specific structure with a set of well-defined attributes, more recently developed techniques do not have such assumptions but they can work on data that do not follow any specified schema [459].

The velocity aspect of Big data means that rather than linking static databases, a linkage application requires one or more streams of query records to be linked to a database that contains records about known entities. Such linkages often need to be done in (near) real-time, requiring novel blocking and indexing techniques that allow the fast retrieval of a set candidate records that are then compared to a query record [115, 492]. The databases containing entity records are commonly also dynamic, where records about new entities (such as new patients or new customers) are constantly added, and the quasi-identifying attribute values of existing entities are updated (for example after name or address changes). Such dynamic databases require novel techniques that are able to link records in such dynamic environments [493].

Similarly, databases that contain temporal information, such as a time-stamp for each record of when it was created or modified last, require the adjustment of the similarity calculations and corresponding classification. These can be based on the likelihood that two records with different timestamps can refer to the same person assuming people do change their details over time, for example as they move or get married. While several approaches have been developed to link temporal data [104, 287, 392], only two approaches so far have considered privacy-preserving record linkage of sensitive temporal databases using a Bloom filter based technique [495, 496], as we discussed in Section 11.2.3.

The aspect of veracity, similar to variety, means more efforts might be required to appropriately clean and standardise the databases to be linked because their structures, formats, characteristics, and quality might change over time. The dynamic nature of Big data also means that data cleaning and standardisation procedures that worked in the past might not be adequate for the future, and changing data characteristics and quality require ongoing monitoring of the different data quality dimensions (as we discussed in Section 3.3) to identify any changes of the databases to be linked that might affect the quality of a linkage.

14.4 Linking Biometric and Genetic Data

Traditionally the databases collected by many organisations contained limited information about the entities in these databases. For example, hospital databases generally contain the names, addresses, and other personal details of patients, as well as their electronic health records. With the easy capturing and availability of other types of data, including multimedia data such as images, audio and video, increasingly organisations include such novel types of data into the databases they are capturing and storing. For example, departments of homeland security or immigration in many countries now capture biometric details such as fingerprint scans and photos of faces of travellers entering and leaving a country, while many police databases now contain digitised DNA information of suspects.

The worldwide use of social media sites by a significant proportion of the population in many countries furthermore allows the crawling and creation of huge databases from publicly available information. Harvesting such data is generally not conducted based on consent by the individuals whose data is being collected, and concerns are being raised that the use of such data can potentially lead to harm to individuals [586]. An example is the start-up company Clearview AI[3], which has built a database of billions of images scraped from online social media sites, and which uses intelligent facial recognition software to match these images to a query image provided by a user. This system has reportedly been employed by various law enforcement agencies [275]. However, there is controversy about this technology and any safeguards (or lack thereof) that prevents its misuse.

Clearview AI is an example of how modern information technology, cheap storage of massive amounts of data, powerful processing capabilities, and increasingly intelligent software systems, when combined, can create applications that provide capabilities that only some years ago seemed impossible. While the privacy and ethical implications of such new technologies are being debated, the reality is that traditional data confidentiality (as implemented by and adhered to by most public service and many private sector organisations), is faced with an unprecedented shift in how it can be accomplished in today's data rich and highly interconnected world.

While such biometric data, collected legally within regulatory frameworks or potentially outside such frameworks, does only effect the individuals whose biometric information has been recorded, the collection of genetic information from individuals opens up a multitude of new questions about sensitive data, privacy and confidentiality, and who is or potentially can be affected by such data.

Collecting and sequencing DNA is becoming increasingly cheaper and thus more popular. Companies such as Ancestry[4], MyHeritage[5], or 23andMe[6] are providing commercial services for individuals to have their DNA sequenced to help them learn more about their genetic ancestry. Genetic data can already be used to identify the increased risks of a person to get certain types of cancer or other serious illnesses. With the rapid advances in medical research, it is likely that in the not too far future it will be possible to use DNA to predict not just the physical aspects of a human being from an analysis of their genomes before she or he is being born, such as their eye or hair colour, or their susceptibility to certain diseases, but also mental, psycholog-

---

[3] See: https://clearview.ai/

[4] See: https://ancestry.com/dna

[5] See: https://www.myheritage.com/dna

[6] See: https://www.23andme.com

ical and cognitive aspects such as somebody's characteristic traits or even their intelligence [306].

An important characteristic of genetic information is that it not only describes an individual but also the closest relatives of that person, their parents, siblings, and children. Any privacy and confidentiality aspects of traditional personally identifiable data, and corresponding approaches to consent by individuals what can be done with their data or not, therefore become less clear. For example, a person who provides consent for their DNA data to be used in a study that investigates genetic aspects of certain types of cancers, might inadvertently reveal sensitive information about their brother or sister such as they also having an increased risk of getting this cancer, even though that person did not participate in this study. The notion of 'my data versus your data' becomes increasingly blurred in the context of the analysis of genetic data [258].

When genetic information is used instead of (or in combination with) quasi-identifying attributes to link records of individuals across sensitive databases, for example in the health or law enforcement domains, then the genetic similarities might identify relatives unknown to an individual. Parental DNA testing is a related application where the aim is to verify who the biological father of a baby or even unborn is. Research by Gymrek et al. [247] has even shown that it is feasible to identify possible surnames from genetic data by matching publicly available anonymised genetic genealogy databases with databases where the surname of the owner of a genome sequence is known. Furthermore, when using Internet searches to obtain additional publicly available information, the authors of this study were able to obtain the full identities for the owners of certain genome sequences in these anonymised genealogy databases [247].

Given the sensitive nature of genetic information, and the need to identify matching genome sequences across different genetic databases, the topic of how to link genome sequences in privacy-preserving ways has attracted increasing interest by researchers in the biomedical community. Compared to the types of values (such as names, addresses, dates, and so on) that occur in the quasi-identifying attributes used to link traditional sensitive databases, genomic databases commonly contain very long sequences of characters from a much smaller alphabet (for example A, T, C, and G for DNA data). Furthermore, while the techniques used for similarity calculations, such as the set or Bloom filter encoding based techniques we discussed in Section 6.8.1 and Chapter 8, do not consider the order of where similar elements (such as q-grams) occur in strings, when trying to identify matching genome sequences the task is often to identify the longest common subsequences (or substrings) that occur in two genome sequences. The comparison functions used to compare genome sequences are therefore related to the edit distance based string comparison functions we discussed in Section 6.8.2.

Techniques to match genomic sequences, such as the Smith-Waterman algorithm [566], make use of the smaller alphabet of genome sequences and also allow for gaps that occur in one of the sequences being compared. Similar to the calculation of edit distance, as illustrated in the side box on page 161, dynamic programming algorithms are commonly used for such sequence comparison algorithms [308].

The privacy-preserving comparison of genome sequences across databases is increasingly required in bioinformatics not just because such data are generally sensitive and considered private identifying information, but also because such databases can contain commercially valuable information for example for genetics based vaccines. The work by Asadova [28] provides a nice introduction to the topic and an overview of selected techniques. Commonly the longest common matching subsequence, or only its length, between two genome sequences needs to be identified without revealing any other information about the compared sequences [560], where these sequences are stored in databases held by different organisations. A related application is to identify such a longest matching subsequence for a given query sequence in a large genome database [636]. Similar to the privacy-preserving record linkage techniques for quasi-identifying attribute values we discussed in this book, building blocks for such privacy-preserving sequence matching techniques include a variety of secure multiparty computation techniques as well as suitable data structures such as suffix trees [408]. The techniques developed in this somewhat different application domain will likely be of use also for the linking of sensitive databases that contain personal identifying information.

14.5 Summary and Further Reading

In this final chapter of this book, we have discussed both conceptual open research questions, as well as practical challenges that need to be investigated in order to make the linkage of large sensitive databases across organisations possible in a large variety of scenarios, ranging from real-time linking of sensitive streams of data to the linking of multilingual databases across jurisdictions. We also described the challenges that Big data pose for linking sensitive databases, and we gave some insight into the particular challenges that biometric and genetic data pose with regard to privacy, while at the same time also providing new opportunities for research studies in the health and social sciences.

These lists of discussed conceptual open research questions and practical challenges is likely incomplete, and novel questions and challenges will be found as the linking of sensitive databases in privacy-preserving ways becomes a more mainstream undertaking.

Open questions and research directions for the general topic of linking databases are covered by Christen [109, 112] and Harron et al. [264], while those specific to the privacy-preserving linking of sensitive databases are discussed by Bonomi et al. [73] and Vatsalan et al. [619, 620]. Zheng et al. [662]

describe various privacy aspects for the use of record linkage in the context of the Internet of Things, where novel types of data are to be linked. The GUILD guidelines [225] presented in Section 11.5 also discuss various issues that are of importance for practical record linkage projects.

While this chapter concludes the main content of this book, in the following Appendix A we discuss several aspects that are of high importance to the practical linkage of sensitive databases: software prototypes that allow the linkage of databases using privacy-preserving techniques, the availability of test and benchmark data sets, and generators and corruptors that can be used to create synthetic data for testing and evaluation of linkage software in situations where no real data are available.

Appendices

In Appendix A we describe currently available software tools as well as public data sets and data generators that will allow the interested reader to get started in further exploring the area of linking sensitive databases. We cover this topic in an appendix because this material will likely be outdated fast as new software is being developed and new data sets are becoming available.

In Appendix B we then provide more details about how the experimental evaluation presented in Chapter 12 was conducted, including an overview of the modules provided and the requirements for the installation of the evaluation software, as well as examples of how to run the evaluation on example data sets.

Appendix A
Software and Data Sets

Abstract The availability of major (commercial or open-source) linkage software systems that provide all the functionalities required to link large sensitive databases across organisations, while preserving the privacy of the content of these databases, is currently very limited. In this appendix, we describe freely available software prototypes as mainly implemented by researchers who are developing novel privacy-preserving record linkage techniques. We also present publicly available test and benchmark data sets that might be of use when testing or evaluating record linkage systems. We then cover the topic of synthetic data that can be used as alternatives to benchmark data for testing and evaluation of techniques, systems, and software aimed at linking sensitive databases.

A.1 Software Prototypes

The topic of linking databases has been an active area of research and development for over fifty years, and a variety of techniques and methods have been developed and are used in diverse application domains. While various commercial as well as freely available record linkage software systems are available, there have only been a few studies that comparatively evaluated such systems [96, 206, 360], where the focus of these comparison studies was on freely available prototype and research systems.

Commercial systems are mainly aimed at the deduplication or linkage of business related databases, such as customer databases, and often record linkage functionalities are embedded in much larger database, data warehousing, or data cleaning software systems. Commercial systems are mostly a black box with regard to the algorithms and methods implemented, which might be based on published research [228] or on unpublished and proprietary techniques.

© Springer Nature Switzerland AG 2020

P. Christen et al., *Linking Sensitive Data*, https://doi.org/10.1007/978-3-030-59706-1

Freely available, open-source software systems for linking databases have mainly been developed in academia, some of these by individual PhD researchers while others as part of larger research projects. Many of these open-source systems will not have been tested and evaluated at the same level as one could expect from commercial software. It is likely that there will be less, if any at all, support provided for such freely available software. On the other hand, freely available software does not have any upfront costs for purchasing the software nor for maintaining a license. In most cases, the source code of the implemented algorithms is available, which allows inspection and possible detection and fixing of any programming mistakes.

While generally not aimed at production level record linkage projects of large databases, freely available open-source software can be ideal tools for novice users to learn about record linkage algorithms and methods, and allow them to experiment with different algorithms and their parameters settings in order to gain a better understanding of how different algorithms and their parameter settings can influence the final outcomes of a linkage project. Such evaluations can benefit from public test or benchmark data sets, or from synthetic data, as we discuss later in this appendix.

While this discussion holds for record linkage software in general, there is even less software available that can be used to link sensitive databases across organisations in privacy-preserving ways. The increased interest in recent years into algorithms and methods to provide such privacy-preserving record linkage functionalities has led to the development of a variety of new techniques (as we covered in Chapters 7 and 8), but also resulted in other researchers identifying weaknesses in such techniques, as we discussed in Chapter 9.

The following list (sorted alphabetically) describes a few selected projects that have developed freely available software prototypes that are able to link sensitive databases in privacy-preserving ways using a variety of implemented algorithms. We also refer the reader interested in exploring such techniques to the software used for the experimental evaluation provided in Chapter 12, as available on the book companion Web site at: https://dmm.anu.edu.au/lsdbook2020.

- **Anonlink**

  Available at: https://github.com/data61/anonlink

  Anonlink is an efficient implementation of the cryptographic long-term key (CLK) encoding method for Bloom filters as proposed by Schnell et al. [545], and developed by the Confidential Computing team at Data61[1]. Anonlink is written in C++ and provides an interface to Python. The software also implements a hashing method to speed up the comparison of sets of Bloom filters, and it supports secret keys for the secure encoding of sensitive quasi-identifying attribute values. Detailed documentation is available at: http://clkhash.readthedocs.io/.

---

[1] For more details see: https://doi.org/10.25919/5c58af003728d

- **AtyImo**

  Available at: `https://github.com/spiros/atyimo`

  AtyImo is an open-source software tool implemented in Python and developed by the Federal University of Bahia in Brazil[2] and University College London [15]. It is aimed at linking very large databases (as we discussed in Section 13.2, some Brazilian health databases contain more than 100 million records) and achieves high performance through parallelisation on GPUs (graphics processing units) and distributed multicore computing platforms, where for the latter AtyImo uses Apache Spark [474]. The software also allows privacy-preserving linking of sensitive data by providing functionalities for Bloom filter encoding and comparison (for more details see Section 13.2). Both deterministic and probabilistic matching techniques are implemented in AtyImo, as are machine learning based classifiers [474].

- **FEMRL + LSHDB**

  Available at: `https://github.com/dimkar121/LSHDB`

  FEMRL is a framework facilitating the privacy-preserving linking of large databases, such as those containing electronic patient records [329]. It is implemented in Java and built on top of the LSHDB library[3] [326], a parallel data engine based on locality sensitive hashing (LSH) and noSQL systems. FEMRL provides methods for blocking using LSHDB and for the comparison of records encoded into Bloom filters. FEMRL and LSHDB can make use of an underlying parallel MapReduce platform to speed up the linkage process.

- **FRIL + LinkIT**

  Available at: `http://fril.sourceforge.net/`

  The LinkIT open-source tool box, developed by Emory University [75], aims to facilitate privacy-preserving record linkage and data integration. It implements and extends the frequent substring embedding technique developed by Bonomi et al. [74] (which we discussed in Section 7.5). LinkIt is implemented in Java and built on top of the FRIL[4] (Fine-Grained Records Integration and Linkage Tool), a collaborative project between Emory University and the Centers for Disease Control and Prevention (CDC) [314], to provide a complete solution to link sensitive databases.

- **OneFL Deduper**

  Available at: `https://github.com/ufbmi/onefl-deduper`

  The OneFL Deduper tool box, developed at the University of Florida [59], provides a deterministic approach to match hash encoded patient records

---

[2] For more details see: `http://www.atyimolab.ufba.br/tools.html`

[3] See: `https://github.com/dimkar121/LSHDB`

[4] See: `http://fril.sourceforge.net/`

in a privacy-preserving way. Implemented in Python, it assumes input data sets in comma separated values (CSV) format, where it generates two hash codes per input record by concatenating the values in the quasi-identifying attributes first name, surname, date of birth, and either gender or race. To prevent dictionary attacks, a secret key only known to the organisations that encode their patient data is incorporated into the hash encoding process. A one-way hash function such as SHA-256 [535] is used to encode attribute values concatenated with the secret key. Records that have the same hash code are then classified as matches.

- **PRIMAT**

  Software available at: `https://github.com/gen-too/primat`

  The Private Matching Toolbox (PRIMAT) is a software prototype developed by the database group at the University of Leipzig [219]. The aim of PRIMAT is to provide functionalities to cover the entire process of linking sensitive databases in a privacy-preserving way. To accomplish this, PRIMAT allows the definition and execution of linkage workflows. Implemented in Java, it contains modules with functionalities for both database owners as well as linkage units. These modules provide a variety of functions ranging from data cleaning to evaluation of linkage quality. Bloom filter encoding and hardening techniques are implemented, as are Hamming locality sensitive hashing (LSH) and metric space based indexing and filtering techniques.

- **R PPRL Toolbox**

  Available at:
  `https://cran.r-project.org/web/packages/PPRL/`

  This toolbox is a package to be used within the R^5 statistical programming language. Developed at the University of Duisburg-Essen and implemented in C++ and R, this toolbox provides both deterministic and probabilistic linkage functionalities. It combines many functionalities of the earlier Merge ToolBox, also developed by researchers at the University of Duisburg-Essen[6]. The toolbox includes functions to generate and compare several versions of statistical and encrypted linkage keys, as well as Bloom filter based encoding methods including the cryptographic long-term key (CLK) and record level Bloom filters (RBF) methods we discussed in Section 8.3. A basic blocking function is also provided, and several of the Bloom filter hardening techniques we described in Chapter 9 are implemented as well.

---

[5] See: `https://www.r-project.org/`

[6] See: `http://record-linkage.de`

- **SOEMPI**

  Available at:

  `https://hiplab.mc.vanderbilt.edu/projects/soempi/`

  The Secure Open Enterprise Master Patient Index (SOEMPI) tool has been developed by the Health Information Privacy Laboratory at Vanderbilt University [596]. It is based on the OpenEMPI[7] (open enterprise master patient index) system and is implemented in Java. SOEMPI provides a variety of blocking, encoding, and comparison methods, as well as match weight calculations based on the Fellegi and Sunter approach [204]. It implements the record level Bloom filter encoding method we discussed in Section 8.3.3 [176], and also provides key distribution and communication modules.

We acknowledge that this is an incomplete list, and there will be other systems that facilitate the linkage of sensitive databases. Some of these have been described in the literature (such as Health Data Link [345]), while for others no methodological or implementation details are available (such as LinXmart[8]). In this brief overview we decided to include only systems with complete documentation and easily available open-source implementations.

A.2 Public Data Collections and Benchmark Data Sets

Given in many application areas the databases to be linked across organisations contain sensitive data, such as personally identifiable information, it is not surprising that there are almost no real such databases publicly available. This is unlike other areas of computer science and information technology such as machine learning, data mining, database systems, or information retrieval, where large repositories exist that provide a wide variety of data sets. Examples of such repositories include the University of California Irvine (UCI) machine learning repository (see: `http://archive.ics.uci.edu/ml/`), Kaggle (see: `https://www.kaggle.com/datasets`), or the Text Retrieval Conference (TREC) data collection (see: `https://trec.nist.gov/data.html`), to name a few. In the following we describe a few test data sets and data collections that might be useful to test and evaluate techniques, systems, and software aimed at linking sensitive databases.

- **RIDDLE**

  Available at:

  `http://www.cs.utexas.edu/users/ml/riddle/data.html`

---

[7] See: `https://www.openempi.org/`

[8] See: `https://linxmart.com.au/`

The Repository of Information on Duplicate Detection, Record Linkage, and Identity Uncertainty, hosted by the University of Texas at Austin, provides several small public data sets as well as one of the data set generators we discuss in the following section. While the majority of the data sets provided do not contain any (artificial) personal information, the SecondString [131] archive contains a small data set named 'census' that contains names (first name and surname) and suburb names, and a data set named 'ucdPeople' which contains name variations of faculty members who were working in a computer science department at a Californian university over twenty years ago. Both these data sets have ground truth data included, however they both contain less than a few thousand records.

- **Eurostat Artificial Data for Record Linkage Training**
  Available at: `https://ec.europa.eu/eurostat/cros/content/job-training_en` (see the link to 'Simulated data')

  The European statistical agency, Eurostat[9] some years ago held a series of training workshops on record linkage and statistical matching. As part of these courses a data collection with artificial personal identifying information was generated[10]. Four data sets are provided, each containing a subset of quasi-identifying attributes including names, addresses, dates of birth, and gender, of around 25,000 made-up individuals. Some of these individuals occur in more than one of these data sets, with errors, variations and changes introduced for the records of the same individual across these four data sets. Unique person identifiers are also provided that allow the calculation of linkage quality for these data sets.

- **Voter Registration Databases**
  Voter registration databases from several US states are publicly available, and such databases have been used by researchers who are developing novel algorithms and techniques to link sensitive databases [111, 119, 176, 330, 496]. Given the application for which these voter databases are being maintained, these data are generally of high quality and they do not contain duplicates (there is only one record per voter). Some of these databases contain detailed personal information including names, addresses, and ages. While a single such database does not allow a linkage, if snapshots of these databases are collected over longer periods of time then there will be changes in both name and address attributes that reflect how voters are moving, and how they are changing their names due to marriage and potentially divorce. Furthermore, any data entry or recording errors, such as name misspellings, are often corrected over time by the affected voter.

---

[9] See: `https://ec.europa.eu/eurostat`

[10] A ZIP file is available for download from: `https://ec.europa.eu/eurostat/cros/system/files/Transfer%20to%20Istat.zip`

An important aspect is that most of these databases contain entity identifiers in the form of voter registration numbers that are unique per voter and generally do not change over time. Such voter registration numbers therefore allow the identification of true matching record pairs across two or more snapshots collected at different points in time. Our evaluation of Bloom filter encoding and hashing techniques presented in Chapter 12 is based on such voter databases from the US state of North Carolina, with details about how to prepare these data sets provided in Appendix B.

We refer the reader interested in downloading and using such voter databases to the URLs provided in recent research publications [119, 330, 496]. We like to emphasise, however, that it is the responsibility of a user to check any licensing agreements or other limitations of use for these databases, and if privacy regulations in their jurisdiction and organisation do permit the use of such data or not. If in doubt we urge the reader to consult with the appropriate legal expert, or their supervisor, in their organisation.

A.3 Synthetic Data Generation

As we discussed in the previous section, there is very limited availability of test and benchmark data collections especially in the domain of personal data. Both researchers and practitioners who aim to evaluate or compare methods and techniques designed specifically to link (sensitive) databases that contain personal identifying information therefore might have difficulties to source suitable data to conduct such evaluations. An alternative to using real data is to generate synthetic (or artificial) data that ideally follow the characteristics of the real data that one is expecting to use in a practical record linkage application [118, 121, 598].

Using synthetic data can be especially useful when sensitive databases are to be linked across organisations. In such scenarios privacy and confidentiality concerns often prevent that real data can be shared between the organisations that are involved in such a linkage. Therefore, it will not be possible to use real data for testing linkage techniques, for training supervised classification techniques, nor for evaluating the overall performance of linkage techniques. Software implementations cannot be evaluated in such scenarios with regard to the linkage quality, scalability, as well as privacy protection (if relevant) they provide.

When compared to using real data that might be available in an organisation (and therefore are likely sensitive or confidential), or publicly available test or benchmark data sets, creating and using synthetic data to evaluate record linkage techniques and systems has several advantages [118]:

- Given synthetic data are being explicitly generated using a set of functions and algorithms, each generated record can be given a unique entity identifier and it can be assigned to a virtual entity. In order to generate other records that refer to the same virtual entity, it is then possible to modify the quasi-identifying attribute values of that record to generate one or several changed or corrupted versions of the original record of that virtual entity. If the process of corrupting and changing values follows the characteristics of real data, it will lead to errors and variations that can create realistic pairs of records (that refer to the same virtual entity). We discuss the requirements for generating realistic data in more detail below.

  Because each record has a unique entity identifier in the generated synthetic data, the true match status of every record pair is known, and therefore linkage quality measures (as we discussed in Section 3.4.1) can be calculated. This allows a comparative evaluation of different linkage techniques and their parameter settings.

- The characteristics of the generated data sets, with regard to the types of quasi-identifying attribute values being generated, their frequency distributions, as well as any corruptions (errors and variations as well as missing values), can be controlled by the data generator program and its parameters. This allows the generation of data that have very specific error characteristics, such as only phonetic variations or only typing errors [118].

  Being able to generate many synthetic data sets with different characteristics allows the evaluation of how well different record linkage systems and techniques can deal with such data. It furthermore allows evaluation of how different variations affect overall linkage quality if a certain linkage technique is being employed.

- It is generally easy to generate synthetic data sets of any (reasonable) sizes, assuming large enough lookup tables and frequency distributions of real values are available (as we discuss below). Data sets larger than any anticipated in a practical real-world linkage system can therefore be generated, and the scalability of different linkage techniques and software implementations can be evaluated using the linkage complexity measures we discussed in Section 3.4.3.

- Both the generated synthetic data sets as well as the generator software itself can be published. This allows other researchers and practitioners to conduct comparative evaluations using such synthetic data sets and reproduce results from other studies. This improves the repeatability of record linkage research studies and can provide practitioners with more confidence that certain techniques or algorithms are suitable for their practical linkage applications. On the other hand, studies conducted on real, confidential, data that cannot be made publicly available or even shared among researchers will prevent any independent validation of the performance of a novel linkage technique proposed.

Furthermore, the publication of the software used to generate synthetic data will allow researchers and practitioners to generate their own data sets, for example based on their own lookup files (of names and addresses and their frequency distributions) and the data characteristics they expect to be dealing with in their practical linkage projects. Data can be generated specifically tailored to their need, for example specific to a country, language, or culture, based on appropriate lookup and frequency tables and settings of the parameters used for the generation of errors and variations.

Given all these advantages of using synthetic data, one might question the need for using real data for evaluation of record linkage systems at all. A major challenge when generating synthetic data, even when extensive and detailed lookup and frequency tables for example of names and addresses are used, is to replicate the intrinsic characteristics of real-world data such as rare and abnormal cases of relationships, value combinations, or geographical and temporal patterns, that occur especially in data that represent people. For example, in reality errors can be clustered, where bad records have errors, missing values, as well as rare values in their quasi-identifying attributes. As such, synthetic data will never be able to provide a fully realistic view of real data with regard to the messiness of errors and variations that can occur in real data. In the context of evaluating techniques and algorithms to link (sensitive) databases, any data generator should therefore be able to accurately model the errors and variations that might occur in the real data that are to be linked, where such errors and variations need to reflect the data quality characteristics that might occur in real databases.

Figure A.1 [118] illustrates how data can be entered in different ways, and what types of errors can be introduced during data entry as well as during the steps that convert data from one format into their final electronic form. As can be seen, different channels have different types of error characteristics. For example, printed documents that are scanned and then processed using optical character recognition (OCR) techniques will contain character changes due to scanning errors (such as a 'w' scanned as 'vv'). On the other hand, phonetic errors, such as variations like 'gail' and 'gayle', are more likely to occur when data (text) are spoken and then either typed (such as over the telephone), or automatic speech recognition techniques are used to convert spoken text into strings.

As can also be seen from this figure, different types of errors and variations can be introduced through these different channels. Accurately modelling such errors and variations requires extensive lookup tables as well as algorithms that can apply for example phonetic variations similar to the phonetic encoding algorithms we discussed in Section 6.6.

Given the lack of real data available to researchers working on the development of novel techniques to link (sensitive) databases, several data generators

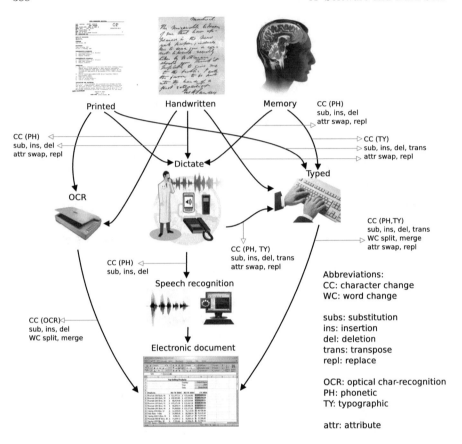

Fig. A.1 Model of data sources and possible types of errors introduced during data entry, with different data entry modes and transition channels, and the types of errors that can be introduced by them (adapted from Christen and Pudjijono [118]). © Springer-Verlag Berlin Heidelberg 2009, reprinted with permission.

have been developed. Some of these are specifically aimed at generating personal quasi-identifying attribute values such as those used to link databases. While many researchers develop their own methods to generate such data, only few of these have been published in scientific publications. In the following we describe a selected few such data generators.

- **UIS database generator**
  Available at:
  `http://www.cs.utexas.edu/users/ml/riddle/data.html`

  A first data generator specifically aimed at creating personal data was developed by Hernandez and Stolfo in the mid 1990 to allow the evaluation of the sorted neighbourhood indexing method to deduplicate large databases [272]. This generator uses simple lists of names, cities, states, and zipcodes, to randomly generate records, and to then create duplicates of these records where errors are introduced into quasi-identifying attribute values. The generator however is not using any frequency information and therefore the distribution of the values in the generated records will unlikely follow the frequency distributions of real-world data (where names and other values often follow a Zipf distribution [217, 261]). The generator can be customised by the user by setting the number of records to be generated, the percentage and distribution of duplicate records to be created, and the types and amount of errors to be introduced.

- **Febrl data generator**
  Available at: `https://sourceforge.net/projects/febrl/`

  The Freely Extensible Biomedical Record Linkage (Febrl) open-source system [108, 113] includes a data set generator that allows a large number of parameters to be set and various lookup and frequency tables to be used [118]. Written in the Python programming language, the types, locations, and the probabilities of how and where modifications are applied to quasi-identifying attribute values when duplicate records are created can be specified. Frequency lookup tables of attribute values, as well as lookup tables for nicknames and spelling mistakes can be loaded and used to generate data that follow real distributions and contain realistic looking errors and variations. Furthermore, the generator allows the modelling of basic dependencies between quasi-identifying attribute values, such as between a gender and a first name attribute.

- **GeCo data generator and corruptor**
  Available at: `https://dmm.anu.edu.au/geco/index.php`

  The data generator and corruptor, GeCo [121, 598], is a system that substantially improves the Febrl data generator described above. Improved and extended functionalities include the ability to generate data in any Unicode character set, as well as the ability to incorporate functions that can generate values for specific types of attributes. Example functions provided with the GeCo system can generate identification numbers, credit card and telephone numbers, as well as blood pressure, weight, or BMI values. Other functions can be developed by the user as Python code and integrated into the GeCo system. Furthermore, complex dependencies between up to three attributes are possible (such as salary values that depend upon a person's age and gender). An online demonstration system is available at the above shown URL, and open-source Python code and an extensive manual can be downloaded. This allows a user to further extend this data generator and corruptor according to their requirements.

- **BART benchmarking algorithms for data repairing and translation**

  Available at: `http://db.unibas.it/projects/bart/`

  While not specifically developed for creating databases to evaluate record linkage algorithms and techniques, the BART system allows the corruption of clean databases with errors in order to benchmark algorithms that aim to repair such errors. Based on the definition of various constraints, and violations of such constraints, the data corruption problem is formalised. An algorithm is then described that allows the generation of errors in very large databases. A Java based implementation is available from the BART project URL shown above.

Besides these data generator and corruption systems, a variety of online data generators are also available, such as Mockaroo[11] or GenerateData[12]. While these tools allow a large variety of types of data to be generated, they are not specifically aimed at personal data to be used for evaluating record linkage algorithms and systems. Some of these online tools also limit the free generation to a small number of records, and require payment for generating larger data sets.

A.4 Summary and Further Reading

As we have discussed in this appendix, there is a significant lack of major software systems that allow privacy-preserving record linkage of sensitive databases across organisations. While a variety of prototype systems exist, they either only provide implementations of some selected blocking, encoding, comparison, and classification techniques, or they do not include functionalities that are crucial for the practical usefulness of such systems in real-world applications, such as the management of secret keys and user access control mechanisms. Similarly, only few public test and benchmark data sets are available that can be used to test and evaluate systems that are aimed at linking sensitive databases such as those containing personal identifying information.

The alternative we discussed is to generate synthetic data. While this approach has various methodological advantages, it also has the drawback that synthetic data will never have the unpredictable data quality characteristics that can occur in personal information. Therefore, prediction of actual linkage results based on simulations with synthetic data might be too optimistic. A recent book by Hoptroff, Mosquera, and El Emam [285] provides a broad overview of topics related to generating synthetic data.

---

[11] See: `https://mockaroo.com/`

[12] See: `https://www.generatedata.com/`

Appendix B
Details of the Empirical Evaluation

Co-authored by Anushka Vidanage and Sirintra Vaiwsri

Abstract In this appendix we provide further details of how to use the programs we employed in the empirical evaluation presented in Chapter 12. The software is written in the Python programming language and freely available on the book companion Web site at: https://dmm.anu.edu.au/lsdbook2020. We first provide an overview of the modules included in the software, then discuss the requirements for installing the software and how to run it, and finally describe the programs we used to generate the data sets we employed in the evaluation.

B.1 Modules Overview

All provided modules are implemented in the Python programming language, with details about installation requirements described in Appendix B.2.

The implemented modules can be categorised into four groups. The first are the core modules implementing the different Bloom filter hashing and encoding techniques described in Chapter 8, and the hardening techniques described in Chapter 9. The second group are the programs we used to run the different evaluations presented in Sections 3.4 and 5.2. The third group are the programs for the two attack methods on Bloom filter encoding we described in Sections 9.2.3 and 9.3. The last group are programs that can be used to generate the input data sets similar to those we described in Section 12.1.1.

In the following we briefly describe the evaluation programs as these are the ones that need to be run by a user, and potentially need to be modified according to their installation. The settings of relevant parameters are either done using command line arguments, or by changing settings within these programs. Each of the programs at the beginning has an extensive comment block (lines starting with '#') that describe in detail the command line argu-

© Springer Nature Switzerland AG 2020
P. Christen et al., *Linking Sensitive Data*, https://doi.org/10.1007/978-3-030-59706-1

ments that are required to run the programs. We assume the programs are run from a terminal / console.

We also briefly describe the programs that we used to run the large number of experiments we conducted for the evaluation in Chapter 12. These programs basically call an evaluation program with a large variety of different parameter settings.

- **evalSimilarity.py**

  This program runs one experiment with a given parameter setup to generate one or two scatter plots comparing the Dice similarities calculated between pairs of q-gram sets versus the Dice similarities calculated between pairs of Bloom filters, based on the pairs of string values loaded from a file as specified on the command line. Optionally, if a hardening technique is provided as a command line argument, then a second scatter plot will be generated that compares the Dice coefficient similarities of basic Bloom filters versus those of hardened Bloom filters.

- **run_evalSimilarity.py**

  This simple program calls the **evalSimilarity.py** program with many different command line arguments to generate several result plots.

- **evalLinkage.py**

  This program runs one experimental record linkage between two data sets given as command line arguments, with a given set of parameters as also provided on the command line, to generate one line plot that shows a precision-recall curve, such as those shown in Section 12.2. Both a q-gram based (using the plaintext string values extracted from the selected quasi-identifying attributes) as well as Bloom filter encoding based linkage are conducted. Note that for larger data sets the implemented Minhash based blocking method (as we discussed in Section 10.1.4) needs to be employed. Without such blocking the linkage will be performed on the full pairwise comparison space and therefore it might take significant amounts of time. To limit the amount of time and memory required the maximum block size can be set to an appropriate value (based on the available computing platform).

- **run_evalLinkage.py**

  This simple program calls the **evalLinkage.py** program with many different command line arguments to generate result plots such as those shown in Section 12.2.

- **evalScalability.py**

  This program runs one experimental evaluation of the runtime and memory usage required by the Bloom filter hashing, encoding, and hardening techniques selected via the command line arguments. All the results are written into a file using the comma separated values (CSV) format.

- **run_evalScalability.py**

  This simple program calls the **evalScalability.py** program with many different command line arguments to conduct experiments such as those described in Section 12.3.

- **evalPrivacy.py**

  This program runs one experimental evaluation of the distributions and frequencies of the 1-bit patterns generated by the Bloom filter hashing, encoding, and hardening techniques selected via the command line arguments. A line plot such as the ones in Section 12.4 is generated.

- **run_evalPrivacy.py**

  This simple program calls the **evalPrivacy.py** program with many different command line arguments to generate several result plots and numerical result files.

- **bfFreqAttack.py** and **bfPatternAttack.py**

  These two programs each run one cryptanalysis attack as described in Sections 9.2.3 and 9.3, respectively, based on the provided parameter settings which specify both Bloom filter hashing, encoding, and possibly hardening, as well as the settings required for the attack method.

- **run_bfFreqAttack.py** and **run_bfPatternAttack.py**

  These two simple programs call the corresponding attack programs with different command line arguments to generate attack result files in the comma separated values (CSV) format, that can then be processed further into corresponding result plots or tables. Note that certain parameter settings might lead to very long run times and/or large memory requirements. This is especially the case for the pattern mining attack run by the **run_bfPatternAttack.py** program.

B.2 Installation Requirements

All programs implementing the described hashing, encoding, hardening, and attack methods have been written using the Python programming language. While we used Python version 2.7.12, any Python version 2.7.X should be able to run these programs.

Python is a freely available, open-source programming language that in recent times has gained popularity in many application areas, and is now seen as one of the most popular programming languages in the area of data science. For more information about Python, and to download implementations that are specific to certain computing platforms, we refer the interested reader to: https://www.python.org.

There are several external (non-standard Python) packages that need to be installed in order to run the programs we used for our evaluation:

- **bitarray**
  Available for download from:
  `https://pypi.org/project/bitarray/`

  This package implements efficient bit vectors and is at the core of all Bloom filter implementations in our modules and programs. The package is highly efficient both with regard to computing speed and memory requirements, because it is fully implemented in the C programming language (a very efficient, low level language commonly used for operating systems functionalities), and because bit vectors are represented by a contiguous block of memory.

  We use version 0.8.1 in our implementation.

- **numpy** Available for download from: `http://www.numpy.org/`

  Numpy is a large general package for scientific computing with Python. It contains many libraries that offer various functionalities such as efficient single- and multidimensional array objects or linear algebra functions, and is implemented in efficient C/C++ or Fortran code.

  We use version 1.8.2 in our implementation.

- **matplotlib**
  Available for download from: `https://matplotlib.org/`

  This package provides a wide range of functionalities to generate high quality figures in a variety of formats. We used this package to generate the experimental result plots included in Chapter 12. The package is not required for the core hashing, encoding, and hardening modules.

  We use version 1.5.1 in our implementation.

Details about how to download and install these extra packages is provided on their respective Web sites.

We implemented and tested, and ran the evaluation programs on a set of desktops, laptops, and servers, running Linux (Ubuntu versions 16.04 and 18.04[1]).

B.3 Examples for Running an Evaluation

We now briefly describe how the programs for an evaluation can be run on two popular operating systems, Ubuntu Linux and Windows. As a prerequisite step, we assume Python and all the required extra modules described before have been installed. Furthermore, we assume all programs and modules from our code have been extracted from their archive and copied into one folder (directory).

---

[1] See: `https://ubuntu.com`

- **Ubuntu Linux**

  Ubuntu is a free and open-source Linux based operating system. In Ubuntu, Python is normally pre-installed, including all its standard modules as well as some third-party packages. However, as we described above, the modules **bitarray**, **numpy**, and **matplotlib**, need to be installed separately in order to run the evaluation software system properly.

  We assume the user is familiar working with a terminal or console, and has opened a terminal window and changed the current directory to where the evaluation programs have been extracted into. After starting Python (using the `python` command in the terminal shell), the prompt shown in the terminal changes to >>>.

  To run the **evalSimilarity.py** program, an example call would be:

  ```
  >>> python evalSimilarity.py
      sim-names-dh-10-2-clk-1000-no_harden.eps
      1000 names_rec_pair.csv 2 False DH 10 1000 None
  ```

  An example call to run of the **evalPrivacy.py** program would be:

  ```
  >>> python evalPrivacy.py
      privacy-encoding-k-dh-opt-clk-city-false.eps
      ncvoter-100000-minmod-0-maxmod-2-a.csv.gz
      [5] 2 False 1000 DH opt CLK None False City
  ```

  Each evaluation program has detailed descriptions of all required parameters (as command line arguments) in the comment block at the beginning of the program file.

- **Windows**

  Microsoft Windows, commonly referred to as Windows, is a group of proprietary graphical operating systems which are developed and sold by Microsoft. In contrast to Ubuntu, Python is not part of a standard Windows distribution and it needs to be installed separately, including the **bitarray**, **numpy**, and **matplotlib** modules we mentioned above to run the evaluation software system within Windows.

  To install Python, a Windows user needs to download the official Python executable installer (MSI package) available from: `https://www.python.org/downloads/`. Next, this installer needs to be run and the user needs to complete the installation steps. Finally, a user can configure the PATH variable to use Python from the command line within the command prompt available in Windows.

  To run the evaluation program, the user needs to use the command prompt, which is a command line interpreter application available in most Windows distributions. Similar to Ubuntu, the user can open a command prompt window and change the current directory to where the evaluation programs have been extracted into. Finally the user can enter the commands as specified above to run the corresponding Python modules within Windows.

B.4 Data Set Generation

As we discussed in Section 12.1.1, the data sets we used for our evaluation are based on a US voter database that is available online for download [330] and that in the past few years has been used in a variety of scientific publications to evaluate newly developed techniques for linking sensitive databases [111]. We refer the interested reader to Karapiperis et al. [330], footnote 25 on page 28, for the exact URL at the time of writing.

The file to be downloaded and used is `ncvoter_Statewide.zip`, as it covers the full state of North Carolina (over seven million voters). Each record in this database contains an NCID attribute, where the values in this attribute are entity identifiers that are unique for individual voters.

To conduct a linkage, two snapshots of this file (or of any of the smaller individual files `ncvoter1.zip` to `ncvoter99.zip`) need to be downloaded. The larger the time difference between two such snapshots is the more voters will have changes in their quasi-identifying attribute values (mainly due to address and name changes).

The program codes provided on the book companion Web site[2] include two Python programs that can be used to analyse and then generate a set of comma separated values (CSV) data sets similar to those we used for our evaluation in Chapter 12.

- **checkDatasetAttrChanges.py**
  This program loads two data sets (`ZIP` files), and analyses the set of quasi-identifying attributes that are specified at the beginning of the program. The program prints details about how many NCID values occur in both data sets (the number of true matching record pairs where each such pair corresponds to one voter), and how many of these pairs contain 0, 1, 2, and so on, number of common (same) values in their quasi-identifying attributes. Pairs with the same value in all their quasi-identifying attributes (no changes or variations) are exact matches.

- **datasetPairGenerator.py**
  This program extends the functionality of the checking program by allowing the user to define a number of record pairs to be selected with a certain number of quasi-identifying attribute values that are not the same. These selected record pairs are then written, together with their NCID values, into two output files (data sets) in the comma separated values (CSV) format, where these files can then be used as the input data sets for the evaluation programs described in Appendix B.1.

---

[2] See: `https://dmm.anu.edu.au/lsdbook2020`

Glossary

The following glossary draws from a glossary on record linkage and data matching by Christen (2012) [109], which itself was based on earlier glossaries covering this topic by Newcombe (1988) [437], Day (1995) [147], Gill (2001) [226], Blakely and Salmond (2002) [65], and Talburt (2011) [587]. The glossary also draws from various online glossaries covering the topic of privacy, specifically the Confidentiality Glossary[3] by the Australian Government, and the Glossary of Privacy Terms[4] by the International Association of Privacy Professionals (IAPP).

The description of terms mostly follows these earlier and related glossaries, however, we have made various modifications to improve the consistency of the terminology used. We have added new terms that are not listed in any of these earlier glossaries, but that are relevant to the topics covered in this book. Any occurrence of a term in this glossary that is also described in the glossary is shown in *italics*.

5 safes   See *five safes*.

Active learning   A type of *classifier* that builds a *classification model* based on the similarity values in *comparison vectors* and optionally the relationships between pairs or groups of *records*. An active learning classifier iteratively improves its *classification model* by asking for manual feedback on the *match status* of selected *candidate record pairs* (that are difficult to classify). This process of manual feedback and building an improved classification model is carried out until a certain stopping criterion has been achieved, or a maximum budget of manual classifications has been reached.

Administrative data   These are data, including *personal data*, collected by an organisation (most commonly a government agency) for the purpose of administering their programs and services, or for developing policies. Administrative data are not *survey data*; however, they can often be useful for

---

[3] https://toolkit.data.gov.au/Confidentiality_-_Glossary.html

[4] https://iapp.org/resources/glossary/

© Springer Nature Switzerland AG 2020
P. Christen et al., *Linking Sensitive Data*, https://doi.org/10.1007/978-3-030-59706-1

statistical analysis purposes. Administrative data are one type of *microdata*. The units in administrative data are most commonly individuals, but they can also be businesses or other types of *entities* as relevant for an organisation.

Adversary   An organisation, group, or individual who aims to attack a system or process concerned with the communication and/or computation of *sensitive* or *confidential data*, in order to learn information about the individual *entities* in such data.

Aggregated data   These data are produced by grouping more detailed data, such as *microdata*, into categories according to some criteria, and aggregating the values of individual *records* (often by summing) in each category. Aggregated data are often stored and provided in the form of *tabular data*.

Agreement weight   See *match weight*.

Algorithm   In computer science and mathematics, an algorithm is a finite sequence of clearly specified steps of instructions that are implementable on a computer. An algorithm typically solves a certain type of problem (such as sorting a list of numbers) on some input data given to it, and produces a prescribed result.

Anonymisation   The process of converting or modifying data that allow *identification* of individual entities, known as *identified data*, into data that no longer can be linked back to the individuals in the original data. The converted data are known as *anonymised* or *deidentified data*.

Anonymised data   These are data that do not allow the *identification* of an individual *entity* represented in such data. Anonymised data are generally created through an *anonymisation* process, where, for example, all identifying information has been removed to prevent both *direct* as well as *indirect identification*. Even when combined with other data the *reidentification* of an entity is not possible with anonymised data.

Approximate match   The status of a *candidate record pair* that has been compared using an *approximate matching* process, and where one or several *attribute values* that have been compared are different between the two *records*.

Approximate matching   The process by which *candidate record pairs* are compared using a set of *comparison functions* that allow for approximate (not exact) similarities.

Area under the curve   An evaluation measure commonly used in statistics, machine learning, and data mining, to assess the performance of a *classifier* in the context of *supervised learning*. This measure can also be used to assess the quality of linked data obtained from a *record linkage* project in situations where *ground truth data* are available.

Attribute   A column in a database table, file, or spreadsheet, that contains a well-defined type of data, such as strings, numbers, dates, and so on. Attributes are also known as fields or variables.

Attribute disclosure   The process where an *adversary* can learn the value of a sensitive *attribute* for an individual or a group of individuals without learning which *record* in an *anonymised* database corresponds to a certain individual. Attribute disclosure for example occurs if the adversary learns that all records in a given group of records correspond to patients who have been treated for a sexually transmitted disease (assuming this is *sensitive personal information*).

Attribute value   A value stored in a specific *attribute* and a specific *record* in a database, data set, file, or spreadsheet.

AUC   See *area under the curve.*

Authentication   In the context of computer systems, the process by which an *entity* (either a person or a computer system) determines whether another entity is who it declares to be.

Authorisation   In the context of computer systems, the process of determining if an *entity* (either a person or a computer system) is allowed to have access to certain resources or data.

Auxiliary data   These are data from an external source that are linked or otherwise integrated to the main data collected in a survey or for a study. Auxiliary data can be used to impute missing values in the main data, or otherwise enrich the main data collected for a survey or study.

Big data   A topic concerned with methods and techniques to process and analyse data that are too large or too complex to be handled by traditional data processing systems. Big data are usually categorised by five Vs: volume (data size), velocity (data are dynamic or streaming), variety (data come from diverse sources), veracity (uncertainty of data and their quality), and value (processing and analysing data should provide benefits).

Biometric data   These are data describing the intrinsic physical or behavioural characteristics of a person. Examples range from genetic material (DNA), fingerprints, retina and iris patterns, to speech, facial features, gait patterns, as well as handwriting and typing characteristics.

Blocking   A type of *indexing* technique that has traditionally been employed in *record linkage* to reduce the number of *record pairs* that need to be compared. Blocking groups the records in the input database(s) into blocks according to a *blocking key*. Only *records* that have the same *blocking key value* are inserted into the same block. *Candidate record pairs* are formed from all records in the same block.

Blocking criteria   See *blocking key.*

Blocking key   Also known as *blocking criteria* or *blocking variable*, a blocking key defines how one or more *attribute values* from *records* in the input database(s) are processed (often using *phonetic encoding algorithms*) and concatenated into *blocking key values* during the *blocking* and *indexing* step of the *record linkage* process. A good blocking key should result in records that are similar with each other to be inserted into the same block, and records that are dissimilar to each other to be inserted into different blocks.

Blocking key value   A value, usually a text string, for an individual *record* in an input database that has been generated using a *blocking key* definition. The blocking key value for a record determines into which block(s) the record is being inserted during the *indexing* step of the *record linkage* process.

Blocking variable   See *blocking key*.

Bloom filter   A space efficient probabilistic data structure based on a bit vector where elements of a set can be mapped into using several *hash functions* to allow for efficient set membership testing. Bloom filters are a popular technique used in the context of *privacy-preserving record linkage* for the *encoding* of *sensitive data*.

Candidate record pair   A *record pair* that is generated from the *records* that have been inserted into the same block (or cluster or window) by a *blocking* or *indexing* technique in the *record linkage* process. All candidate record pairs are then compared in detail in the comparison step of the record linkage process using various *comparison functions*.

Ciphertext   The term used in *cryptography* for *encrypted data*.

Classification model   A model that determines how *candidate record pairs* are classified into *matches*, *non-matches*, and optionally *potential matches* in the classification step of the *record linkage* process. A classification model is generated by a *classifier algorithm*.

Classifier   A type of *algorithm* that builds a *classification model* based on a *supervised*, *unsupervised*, or *active learning* approach.

Cleaning   See *data cleaning*.

Clerical review   The process of manually assessing and classifying as *matches* or *non-matches* the *candidate record pairs* that have been classified as *potential matches* in a *classifier* such as *probabilistic record linkage* or a related approach.

Clustering   A type of *algorithm* that groups similar data objects (*records* in the case of *record linkage*) together according to the similarities calculated between these objects. In record linkage and *deduplication*, the similarities between records are captured in the *comparison vector* of each *candidate record pair*. The objectives of clustering in record linkage and deduplication are to have each generated cluster to correspond to one *entity*, and each entity stored in the database(s) that are linked or deduplicated is assumed to be represented by one cluster only.

Collective entity resolution A type of *algorithm* that aims to solve the *entity resolution* problem in an overall collective fashion by considering the relationships between the *records* stored in the database(s) to be linked or deduplicated as a graph. Based on such a relationship graph, a collective entity resolution approach classifies groups of records into *matches* and *non-matches*. This approach is in contrast to the *pairwise classification* of individual *record pairs*, as for example conducted by the traditional *probabilistic record linkage* approach.

Collusion The process whereby two or more parties that take part in some form of confidential communication and/or computation secretly work together (cooperate) with the aim to learn the *sensitive* or *confidential data* of another party (that is not taking part in the collusion).

Comparison function A function that has as input two *attribute values* (which can be strings, numbers, dates, times, or more complex objects) and that calculates a similarity between these two values. The comparison can either be exact or allow for approximate similarity. An exact comparison function generally returns a similarity value of 0 if the two attribute values are different from each other, or a similarity value of 1 if they are the same. An approximate comparison function generally returns a normalised numerical similarity value between 0 and 1 that indicates the similarity between the two attribute values, with a larger similarity value indicating a higher similarity between the two values. If only exact comparison functions are used when attribute values are compared then this process corresponds to *exact matching*, while when approximate comparison functions are used the process corresponds to *approximate matching*. A popular class of approximate comparison functions are *string comparison functions*. Comparison functions are also known as *similarity functions*.

Comparison vector The vector of similarity values generated for a *candidate record pair* when one or more *attributes* of the pair are compared using *comparison functions* that are appropriate to the content of these attributes. If n comparison functions are used then the resulting comparison vector will contain n similarity values. A comparison vector is also known as a *similarity vector*.

Confidential data These are data that allow the *direct* or *indirect identification* of *entities* such as individuals or organisations. Confidential data are generally *microdata* with one *record* per entity in a population or sample.

Confidentiality The obligation of a *data provider* or *data custodian* to maintain the secrecy of data such as *personal* or otherwise *sensitive data*. Data are confidential if they are protected against unauthorised or unlawful access, processing, and publication.

Consent   The concept of an individual giving permission for the disclosure or use of their *personal data*. Consent needs to be informed, and given freely and unambiguous. Consent can be explicit (*opt in*) where an individual actively agrees with a *data provider* or *data custodian* to allow access and use of their data, or implicit (*opt out*) where a default assumption is that individuals do not opt out from their personal data being accessed and used.

Control of information privacy   The ability of an *entity* to determine by itself how, when, what, and to whom, information about itself is provided to others.

Critical data studies   The academic field dedicated to the study of data science, *Big data*, and data analytics from a societal perspective, investigating aspects such as bias, fairness, trust, and how data based research and applications are influencing society.

Cryptanalysis   A topic in the field of *cryptography*, cryptanalysis is the study of analysing *encoding* and *encryption* systems and *algorithms* with the aim to learn about the hidden aspects of such systems or the data encoded or encrypted with such algorithms.

Cryptography   A topic covering the domains of mathematics, computer science, and statistics, cryptography is the study of developing methods and *algorithms* for *encoding* or *encryption* of information to allow secure communication and computation between parties such that other parties, known as *adversaries*, are not able to learn about the input or output of these communications or computations.

Cryptosystem   A set of methods and *algorithms* required for *encryption* and *decryption* of data that is to be communicated between parties. A cryptosystem consists of an encryption and a decryption algorithm, as well as one or more *secret keys* used to encrypt and decrypt a given message.

Data breach   An unauthorised access to data that is classified to be *confidential data*, where the person or organisation gaining access is doing so in a *malicious* or illegitimate way with the purpose of gaining benefits from the accessed confidential data.

Data centre   A facility that provides dedicated space within a building for computer, storage, and telecommunication systems. A data centre can either provide data management functionalities for a single organisation, or act as a (commercial) third-party provider for managing the data needs of several organisations. Data centres often provide highly secured data access as well as backup storage facilities.

Data cleaning   The process of removing unwanted characters and *tokens* (alphanumerical words) from the *attribute values* in the input database(s) during the *data preprocessing* step of the *record linkage* process.

Data consumer   An organisation or person receiving data from a *database owner*, *data provider*, or *data custodian*.

Data controller   An organisation such as a public authority which, possibly jointly with other organisations, determines the policies and frameworks for the processing of *sensitive* or *confidential data*, such as *personal data*.

Data custodian   An organisation that is responsible for the collection, use, and *disclosure* of data. Data custodians might receive certain types of data from external *data providers* or *database owners*. Data custodians have to ensure that *confidential data* are used for the approved purposes only.

Data lineage   See *data provenance*.

Data linkage   The name used by statisticians, and health and biomedical researchers and practitioners, for the process of *record linkage*.

Data masking   See *encoding*.

Data matching   The name used by many businesses and governments for the process of *record linkage*.

Data owner   See *database owner*.

Data preprocessing   The process of *cleaning, standardising*, and *segmenting*, the *attribute values* stored in the input database(s) to be linked or deduplicated, with the general aim to improve *data quality*, and more specifically, to improve the outcomes of the *record linkage* or *deduplication* process.

Data protection   The process of safeguarding important information from loss, misuse, corruption, and from being compromised.

Data provenance   The process of documenting the sources of where data come from, how they have been produced, and any processes applied on these data. Data provenance provides a *record* of the origins and the history of a given database. Data generated about data provenance is part of the *metadata* of a data set. Data provenance is also known as *data lineage*.

Data provider   An *entity*, group of entities (such as a family or household), or an organisation (such as a business or government agency) that supplies data either for commercial, administrative, or statistical purposes.

Data quality   A set of measures that allow to quantify the quality of a given set of data. The major data quality dimensions include accuracy (data are correct and reflect reality), completeness (there are no *missing data*), consistency (data are consistent across different sources), uniqueness (no *entity* in a database is represented by multiple *records*), validity (all data meet a set of given constraints and rules), and timeliness (all data are up to date and represent the current reality).

Data situation To evaluate *anonymisation*, data has to be seen in its context. The interrelationship of data and its environment has been called the data situation.

Database owner Also known as a *data owner*. An organisation that is generating or collecting data, such as a government agency, research organisation, or a business. Even many individuals are nowadays data owners because much of their daily transactions and interactions with others (individuals and organisations) are generating data.

Decryption The process of converting a *ciphertext* back into its original *plaintext* (unencrypted) form using the decryption *algorithm* and *secret key* of a *cryptosystem*.

Decryption key See *secret key*.

Deduplication The process of *duplicate detection*, followed by a process which for each *entity* in a database either merges the identified *duplicate records* into one combined record, or removes some records from the database until it only contains a single record for each entity. Deduplication is applying *record linkage* on a single data set.

Deidentification See *anonymisation*.

Deidentified data See *anonymised data*.

Deterministic matching A type of *record linkage* where a set of rules (as opposite *probabilistic record linkage*) is used to determine if two *records* are a *match* or a *non-match*. A special case of deterministic matching is a database join where records are matched based on their common value in a specific *attribute* such as a *unique identifier*.

Dictionary attack A type of *cryptanalysis* where an *adversary* aims to learn sensitive or confidential information stored in *encoded* or *encrypted data* using a brute force attack to determine the *secret key* used in the *encryption* process. This is accomplished by trying a very large number, often in the millions, of likely possible *plaintext* values, *encoding* or encryption parameters, and secret keys. Once a certain set of encryption parameters and a secret key are found where the encryption of certain plaintext values matches the encrypted data, the adversary has compromised the security of the *cryptosystem* without initially knowing the *secret key*.

Differential privacy A statistical technique that aims to provide methods to maximise the *utility* of queries on a database that contains *confidential data*, such as *microdata*, while measuring the privacy impact of the query on an individual *entity* whose *record* is stored in that database. Differentially private *algorithms* generally add noise to a database such that it is not possible to ascertain, with a given probability, that a certain entity is represented by a record in the database or not (thus preventing *membership disclosure*).

Differentially private algorithms can be seen as a type of *perturbation* and *obfuscation* approach.

Direct identification   A type of *identification* that occurs when a direct *identifier* is included in data about an individual *entity* that allows unambiguous identification of that entity. An example of an identifier that allows direct identification is a *national identification number* or a patient identification number. Direct identification differs from *indirect identification*.

Disagreement weight   See *non-match weight*.

Disclosure   Disclosure is the process of providing access to *personal* or otherwise *sensitive data* about an *entity*, whereby the person or organisation receiving that data learns something that they did not know about that entity from other data. There are three main types of disclosure: *Membership disclosure*, *attribute disclosure*, and *identity disclosure* (see the corresponding glossary entries for details).

Disclosure control   See *statistical disclosure control*.

Disclosure risk   A measure that defines the risk that confidential information about an *entity* represented in a database can be identified, either via *direct* or *indirect identification*.

Duplicate   The presence in a single database of multiple *records* that refer to the same *entity*.

Duplicate detection   The process of comparing *records* from a single database with the objective to identify pairs or groups of records that refer to the same *entity*. These pairs or groups of records are known as *duplicates*.

Electronic health record   The medical file(s) of an individual stored as one or more computer *records* at one or multiple healthcare providers. Electronic health records can contain a variety of information, including *personal data* such as names, date of birth, gender, addresses, and contact details, as well as health information such as the person's medical history, their medication and allergies, laboratory test results, radiology images, weight, blood pressure, BMI, and so on.

Encoded data   These are data that have been converted from their original format into a different format using an *encoding* method. Note that encoded data can generally not be reversed back into original data.

Encoding   The process of *deidentifying, anonymising*, or otherwise obscuring data such that the discriminatory power of data remains the same but the content does not reveal *sensitive personal information*.

Encrypted data   These are data that have been converted from *plaintext* (unencrypted) data using an *encryption* mechanism. Encrypted data are commonly referred to as *ciphertext*.

Encryption The process of converting *plaintext* (unencrypted) data into *ciphertext* using the encryption *algorithm* and *secret key* of a *cryptosystem*. Encrypted data can be converted back into its *plaintext* using a *decryption* process.

Encryption key See *secret key*.

Entity A real-world subject or object, such as an individual person, business, publication, or consumer product, that has a unique identity and that can be distinguished from any other entity.

Entity identifier A number, code, or text string that uniquely identifies a single *entity* within the database(s) that are linked or deduplicated. See also *unique identifier*.

Entity resolution The process of comparing *records* from one or more databases with the objective to identify pairs or groups of records that refer to the same *entity*, to classify these pairs or groups as *matches* (and pairs or groups of records that do not refer to the same entity as *non-matches*), and to merge (fuse) all records that refer to the same entity into a new combined record. The result of an entity resolution process is a set of combined records that each corresponds to one entity, and each of the entities stored in the database(s) that were linked is represented by a single combined record only. Entity resolution applied on a single database is also known as *deduplication*.

Exact match The status of a *candidate record pair* that has been compared using either an *exact matching* or an *approximate matching* process, and where all *attribute values* that have been compared are the same in both *records* of the pair.

Exact matching The process by which *candidate record pairs* are compared using a set of *comparison functions* that only permit exact similarities.

Factual anonymity The concept of *microdata* being *anonymised* in such a way that only by an unreasonable effort in terms of time, resources, and costs for a *reidentification* process, an *adversary* might be able to reidentify *attribute values* and/or individuals in an anonymised database. To determine factual anonymity both the costs and potential benefits of the reidentification process have to be considered.

False match A *record pair* that is classified as a *match* where, however, the two *records* of the pair refer to two different *entities*. In the context of classification a false match is also known as a false positive.

False non-match A *record pair* that is classified as a *non-match* where, however, both *records* in the pair correspond to the same *entity*. In the context of classification a false non-match is also known as a false negative.

Field See *attribute*.

Filtering   A set of methods that can be employed additionally to *blocking* or *indexing* during the *record linkage* process to further reduce the number of *record pair* comparisons that need to be conducted. Filtering is generally based on efficiently estimating the similarities between record pairs based on their characteristics (such as differences in the length of their *attribute values*), and to remove those pairs that have estimated similarities below a given similarity threshold without comparing them in detail.

Five safes   A framework to assist making decisions about the safe use and publication of *personal, sensitive,* or *confidential data.* It can be used to design methods and systems to allow access to such data for research. The five safes are: (1) safe projects (the use of data for a proposed project is appropriate), (2) safe people (the people who will be using these data can be trusted), (3) safe settings (the data access system prevents unauthorised use), (4) safe data (the data themselves do not allow *disclosure* of confidential information), and (5) safe outputs (the outputs produced from statistical analyses prevent disclosure).

Frequency attack   A type of *cryptanalysis* where an *adversary* aims to learn sensitive or confidential *encoded* or *encrypted* information by comparing the frequency distribution of *plaintext* values the adversary has access to and aligning these with the frequency distribution of *ciphertext* values. If there are clear alignments then the adversary can learn the plaintext value of certain encoded or encrypted values without knowing the *secret key.*

GDPR   See *General Data Protection Regulation.*

General Data Protection Regulation   A set of policies by the European Union (EU) that aim to provide a framework of data protection rules for all EU member states. Each member state has to transform the framework to more detailed laws specific for the given country.

Genetic data   These are types of *personal data* that are related to the inherited or acquired genetic characteristics of an individual. Such data are gathered by analysing biological samples of a person, and they can provide information about the physical and mental state of a person, and also help to uniquely identify a person.

Geocoding   The process of assigning geographic coordinates (latitude and longitude) to non-location data such as addresses, place names, or places of interest. If no exact geocode can be identified then a bounding box can be used which covers a certain geographical area that includes the non-location data item.

Geomasking   A set of techniques to protect privacy of *entities* by *perturbation* of their geographic coordinates while retaining some useful spatial information.

Geotagging   The process of attaching geographical information (such as latitude and longitude) as part of the *metadata* to multimedia data such as images or videos.

Gold standard   See *ground truth data* for a definition. In medical settings, the term *gold standard* is more often used than ground truth. Frequently, the *true match* status is not available and a proxy is used as gold standard instead.

Ground truth data   In the context of *supervised learning*, these are the data used to train a *classifier*. In classification, in the context of *record linkage*, ground truth data consist of *true match* and *true non-match record pairs*.

Hash function   In general, a mathematical function that maps data from an arbitrary input size or range into data of a fixed size or range. In the context of *cryptography*, hash functions are often used as building blocks of *encoding* and *encryption algorithms* as part of a *cryptosystem*.

Hash-based message authentication code   A keyed-cryptographic hashing method used in *cryptography* to simultaneously verify both the data integrity and authentication of a message, by combining a cryptographic *hash function* with a *secret key*. Also known as keyed hashing for message authentication.

HMAC   See *hash-based message authentication code.*

Honest-but-curious   In the context of *cryptography*, this *security* model assumes that all parties that participate in a protocol do follow the agreed protocol steps and provide the input required by the protocol. However, parties are curious in that they aim to learn about the other parties' sensitive input data from any information they obtain throughout the protocol and from the shared final result of the protocol. Note that *collusion* between parties is allowed in the honest-but-curious security model. The honest-but-curious model is in contrast to the *malicious* security model.

Identifiability   The degree to which an individual *entity* can be identified via *direct* or *indirect identification* based on available data. The more unique the characteristics of an entity are the more likely it can be identified.

Identification   The process of identifying an *entity* in a database either via *direct* or *indirect identification.*

Identified data   These are data that include some type of *identifier*, either in the form of a *unique identifier* or a set of *quasi-identifiers*, that allow the *identification* of the *entities* stored in that data.

Identifier   These are data that allow a direct and unambiguous *identification* of *entities* in a database. Also see *unique identifier* and *entity identifier*.

Identity disclosure The process where an *adversary* is able to learn which *record* in an *anonymised* database refers to a certain individual. Identity disclosure corresponds to the *reidentification* of an individual. Identity disclosure generally also results in *attribute disclosure* if the adversary can learn the *sensitive personal information* in an *attribute* of the record identified to refer to a certain individual.

Imputation The process of replacing *missing data* with estimated data. Various imputation techniques exist, ranging from random selection of values to be imputed to statistical and machine learning based imputation techniques.

Indexing The process of splitting a database into smaller blocks or clusters, or sorting a database, with the aim to reduce the number of *record pair* comparisons that need to be conducted in the *record linkage* process. *Records* that have the same *blocking key value* are inserted into the same block or cluster, or they are sorted close to each other if they have the same or a very similar sorting key value. *Candidate record pairs* are formed from all records that are in the same block or cluster. The traditional approach used for indexing has been *blocking*.

Indirect identification A type of *identification* that occurs even when no direct *identifier* is included in data about an individual *entity* through a combination of non-unique *attribute values*, known as *quasi-identifiers*. Their combination needs to be unique for an entity to allow identification. Indirect identification differs from *direct identification*.

Information extraction The process of identifying and extracting instances of particular classes of *entities*, events, or relationships, from unstructured data such as natural text, and their transformation into a structured representation such as a database *record*.

Information privacy See *control of information privacy*.

Information security Methods and processes designed to protect information with the purpose to prevent loss, misuse, and unauthorised access; processes designed to control *confidentiality*, availability, and integrity of data; as well as methods to assess risks and threats to *information systems*.

Information system A set of connected software components that support the collection, storage, processing, analysis, and dissemination of information to support, among other tasks, the decision making processes within an organisation.

Linkability The property of data with regard to how easy or difficult *records* of individual *entities* can be linked to records in another database to allow the *identification* of individual entities.

Linkage unit An organisation that participates in a *record linkage* project and that will conduct the linkage of *records* sent to it by *database owners* or *data providers*. A linkage unit generally does not have their own data, however they often act as *data custodians* of linked databases.

Malicious Generally, the intent by a person or organisation to show malice or be intentionally harmful towards another person or organisation. In the context of *cryptography*, the malicious security model assumes a malicious party that participates in a protocol does not follow the agreed protocol steps, provides arbitrary input, or might abandon the protocol altogether. The malicious model is in contrast to the *honest-but-curious* security model.

Masking See *encoding*.

Match A pair or group of *records* that is classified as referring to the same *entity*.

Match status The outcome of applying a *classification model* on a *candidate record pair*. This outcome can be that the record pair is classified as a *match*, a *non-match*, and (optionally) as a *potential match*. For a *classifier* such as *probabilistic record linkage* or a related approach, the potential matches are those candidate record pairs that are not clear matches or non-matches. These pairs need to be manually assessed and classified in a *clerical review* process.

Match weight In *probabilistic record linkage* and related *classifier* approaches, a match weight is a numerical value that is assigned to a certain *attribute* if the *attribute values* of a *candidate record pair* are the same or similar to each other (assumed to be in agreement). A match weight is also called an *agreement weight*. Match weights are calculated as the likelihood that two attribute values are in agreement assuming that both *records* in a candidate record pair correspond to the same entity, divided by the likelihood that two attribute values are in agreement assuming that the two records in a candidate record pair correspond to different entities.

Matching error The outcomes of a *record linkage* or *deduplication* project where the *classifier* has made a mistake in determining the *match status* of a *record pair*. The two possible match errors are a *false match* (also known as a false positive in the context of classification) and a *false non-match* (also known as a false negative in the context of classification).

Membership disclosure The process where an *adversary* can learn if a *record* about a certain individual is included in an *anonymised data* set or not. While this type of *disclosure* does not necessarily lead to *attribute disclosure* or *identity disclosure*, simply knowing somebody is represented in a database or not might reveal *sensitive personal information* about these individuals, for example if it is known that an anonymised database contains records about patients who have been diagnosed with certain diseases, or records of convicted criminals. Preventing membership disclosure is the purpose of many *statistical disclosure control* methods, for example *Differential privacy*.

Merge/purge   The name used by database and data warehousing researchers and practitioners for the process of *record linkage* and *deduplication*.

Metadata   These are data that describe other data. Metadata include, for example, the names, types, and ranges of *attributes*, descriptions of *data quality* aspects of attributes such as *missing data*, and *data provenance* aspects including the date of data collection or production, the ownership of data, pricing and licensing about data, and so on.

Microdata   These are data that contain information about individual *entities*, where generally each entity in a population (or subpopulation) is represented by one *record*. Microdata are also known as *unit data records* or as payload data.

Missing data   Missing data, also known as missing values, occur when no value is stored in certain *attributes* for a certain *record* in a database. Missing data are a major *data quality* issue that can significantly influence the outcomes of any processing and analysis conducted on a database. *Imputation* is commonly applied with the aim to estimate values for missing data.

National identification number   Many public agencies are using legally specified numeric or alphanumeric strings as a *unique identifier* to process information of the same person. Examples of such national identification numbers are the Social Security Number (SSN) in the US and the National Health Service (NHS) number in the UK.

Non-match   A pair or group of *records* that is classified as referring to different *entities*.

Non-match weight   In *probabilistic record linkage* and related *classifier* approaches, a non-match weight is a numerical value that is assigned to a certain *attribute* where the *attribute values* of a *candidate record pair* are different from each other (not assumed to be in agreement). A non-match weight is also called a *disagreement weight*. Non-match weights are calculated as the likelihood that two attribute values are in disagreement assuming that both *records* in a candidate record pair correspond to the same entity, divided by the likelihood that two attribute values are in disagreement assuming that the two records in a candidate record pair correspond to different entities.

Obfuscation   The process of making something obscure, difficult to understand, unclear, unintelligible, or to hide the true meaning. *Encoding* techniques are commonly used to obfuscate *sensitive* or *confidential data*.

Opt in   The option of choosing to participate in something by making an active affirmative indication of choice. Opt in shows the clear desire by somebody to, for example, allow sharing their *personal data* for a medical research study.

Opt out   The option of choosing not to participate in something by making an active negative indication of choice. Unlike with *opt in*, the lack of action by an individual means that a choice to participate has been made.

Pairwise classification   A type of *classifier algorithm* that classifies individual *candidate record pairs* into *matches*, *non-matches*, and (optionally) into *potential matches*, without taking the *match status* of other candidate record pairs into account. This classification approach is in contrast to *collective entity resolution* techniques that aim to classify all candidate record pairs collectively in an overall optimal fashion.

Parsing   See *segmenting*.

Password   A string or a number used by an *entity* or organisation for *authentication*. The word password is sometimes also used to denote a *secret key* in a *cryptosystem*.

Personal data   These are data that relate to a natural person that can be identified either through *direct* or *indirect identification*. Examples of personal data are people's names and address details, their bank details, their *electronic health records*, and even photos or videos of a person.

Personally identifiable information   Also known as PII, these are any data that potentially can be used to identify a specific individual. Personally identifiable information can either be sensitive or not sensitive. See also *sensitive personal information*, *sensitive data*, and *personal data*.

Perturbation   The process of modifying and changing data in some small way using some function to reduce the risk of *disclosure* while aiming to retain as much as possible the *utility* of the data in the form of their content and structure.

Phonetic encoding   A type of *algorithm* that converts a string (generally assumed to correspond to a name) into a code that represents the pronunciation of that string. Popular phonetic encoding algorithms include Soundex, NYSIIS, and Double-Metaphone.

Plaintext   In the context of *cryptography*, a plaintext is the unencrypted input data, assumed to be sensitive or confidential, which is to be *encoded* or *encrypted* for storage, communication, or for use in a *secure multiparty computation* protocol.

Potential match   A *candidate record pair* that is classified in *probabilistic record linkage* or a related *classifier* approach for *record linkage* as potentially referring to the same *entity*. The final *match status* for these candidate record pairs is often determined through a manual assessment in a *clerical review* process.

Precision   In the context of *supervised learning* when linking databases, a measure used to evaluate the quality of the obtained linked *record pairs* that assesses how many of the record pairs classified as matches are *true matches*. Also see *recall*.

Privacy   The rights of an individual or a group of individuals to have their *personal data* managed by organisations such that these data are being kept confidential, except where either informed *consent* has been given to allow access to their data, or where a legal authority exists that can grant access to their data.

Privacy by design   A framework that states that *privacy* and *data protection* are considered and incorporated throughout the entire life cycle of technology and systems, starting from the design stage to deployment and use, all the way to disposal.

Privacy enhancing technology   These are standards, methods, techniques, and *algorithms* designed for the purpose of improving *privacy* and *data protection* when *sensitive* or *confidential data* are being transmitted, stored, used, or processed.

Privacy paradox   The contradiction between declared privacy concerns and actual behaviour of individuals on the Internet, especially on social networking sites as well as other service providers.

Privacy-preserving record linkage   The process of linking databases from different organisations such that none of the *database owners* has to reveal any of their *sensitive* or *confidential data* to any other party that participates in a linkage protocol, and at the end of the linkage process only limited information, such as the number of *record pairs* that have been classified as *matches*, or only their *record identifiers*, are being revealed to the party that requires the linkage outcomes. Privacy-preserving record linkage generally works on *encoded* or *encrypted data*.

Probabilistic matching   See *probabilistic record linkage*.

Probabilistic record linkage   A statistical *classifier* approach to *record linkage* published by Fellegi and Sunter in 1969. This approach calculates *match weights* and *non-match weights* based on error probabilities and frequency distributions of *attribute values* in the input databases. *Candidate record pairs* are classified based on their *weight vectors* into either *matches*, *non-matches*, or *potential matches*, using a threshold-based and *pairwise classification* approach.

Pseudonymisation   The processing of *personal data* such that the data can no longer be attributed to a specific *entity* stored in the data without the use of additional data, such as a *secret key*, which needs to be stored separately from the *pseudonymised data*. Pseudonymisation can be achieved by replacing identifying *attributes* in a *record* by one or more artificial *iden-*

tifiers or pseudonyms, created for example using *encryption*. A difference between *anonymised* and *pseudonymised data* is that pseudonymisation can be reversed by using the separately held additional data, such as the *secret key* that can be used for *decryption*.

Pseudonymised data   These are data that do not allow the *identification* of individual *entities* stored in such data. Often such data have been processed through *pseudonymisation*. While individual *records* in pseudonymised data cannot be associated with specific entities, either through *direct* or *indirect identification*, multiple records about the same entity can be linked through the artificial *identifiers* or pseudonyms assigned to them in the *pseudonymisation* process.

Public key infrastructure   A set of roles, policies, procedures, and software needed for the creation, management, distribution, usage, storage, and revocation of digital certificates that through the use of *cryptography* verify the authenticity of each party involved in electronic transactions.

Quasi-identifier   A set of *attributes* where the individual *attribute values* are not *unique identifiers* by themselves, but when such quasi-identifiers are combined they create a *unique identifier* value for each *entity* represented in a database. Each individual quasi-identifier is to some degree correlated with an entity. Combined, quasi-identifiers become *sensitive personal information*. An example set of quasi-identifiers can be first name, surname, month and year of birth, gender, and postcode of residence for a person.

Recall   In the context of *supervised learning* when linking databases, a measure used to evaluate the quality of the obtained linked *record pairs* that assesses how many of the *true matches* have been correctly classified as *matches*. Also see *precision*.

Record   A row in a database table, data set, file, or spreadsheet, that contains values in a set of *attributes*. It is assumed that each record represents one *entity*, but that an entity can potentially be represented by more than one record in a database, data set, file, or spreadsheet.

Record identifier   A number, code, or string, that uniquely identifies a single *record* in a database. A record identifier is different from an *entity identifier*.

Record linkage   The process of comparing *records* from two or more databases with the objective to identify pairs or groups of records that refer to the same *entity*. These pairs or groups of records are known as *matches*. Record linkage is also known as *data linkage* or *data matching*.

Record pair   Two *records*, for the process of *record linkage* one record from each of the two input databases that are being linked, while for the *deduplication* of one database both records are sourced from the single input database.

Reidentifiability   The property of *anonymised* or *encoded data* with regard to how easy or difficult the *records* of individual *entities* in such data can be linked to the *personal sensitive information* of these entities using *reidentification* methods.

Reidentification   The process of trying to reassociate *records* about *entities* in *anonymised* or *encoded data* with the *personal sensitive information* of these entities. This process is often based on external, publicly available data about the entities in a population.

Safe harbour   A *privacy* framework developed with the aim to prevent private sector organisations within the European Union or United States that store customer data from accidentally disclosing or losing *sensitive personal information*. The seven safe harbour principles are: (1) notice (organisations must inform individuals that their *personal data* is being collected and how it will be used), (2) choice (individuals must be able to *opt out* from the collection of their data and the sharing of their data with other parties), (3) onward transfer (sharing of personal data with other parties is only allowed if these parties follow adequate *data protection* principles), (4) *security* (reasonable efforts must be made by an organisation to prevent loss of collected information), (5) data integrity (data must be reliable and relevant for the purpose it was collected for), (6) access (individuals must be able to access personal data held about them and be able to ask for correction or deletion of their data), and (7) enforcement (there have to be effective means of enforcing these principles).

Secret key   A value, such as a string or a number, used in a *cryptosystem* for the *encryption* of *plaintext* values into *ciphertext*, and the *decryption* of ciphertext back into plaintext values.

Secure multiparty computation   A topic in *cryptography* that aims to develop methods, *algorithms*, and protocols that allow two or more parties to jointly compute a function on their sensitive private inputs, such that at the end of the computation all parties learn the result of the function but no party learns the private input of any other party.

Security   The concept of safe storage and safe access to data. This includes both physical security as well as IT (computer and networking systems) security. IT security can be achieved using appropriate *authentication* and *authorisation* processes.

Seed   The start value of a pseudo-random number generator (PRNG) is called *seed*. If the same seed is used, a specific PRNG will generate the same specific sequence of pseudo-random numbers.

Segmenting   The process of separating the tokens (*whitespace* separated alphanumeric words) contained in an *attribute value* into well-defined elements during the *data preprocessing* step of the *record linkage* process. Segmenting is commonly based on some type of *information extraction* technique.

Sensitive data   These are data that require protection against unauthorised *disclosure*.

Sensitive personal information   Data about individuals that are, with reasonable expectations, deemed to be private. They include, for example, medical or financial information.

Similarity function   See *comparison function*.

Similarity vector   See *comparison vector*.

Social engineering   In the context of *information security*, social engineering is the term used for how *adversaries* aim to manipulate people to provide *sensitive* or *confidential data*, or *sensitive personal information*, or create some type of security vulnerability.

Spontaneous recognition   An *identification* made without a deliberate attempt. For example, an analyst recognises that the address, gender, and age in a *record* must correspond to somebody they know.

Standardisation   The process of converting the *attribute values* in an input database into a standard format during the *data preprocessing* step of the *record linkage* process. Standardisation includes, for example, converting all letters into lower- or uppercase, by correcting misspellings and replacing nicknames with their proper names, and by expanding abbreviations into full words.

Statistical disclosure control   Methods and techniques designed to protect *sensitive* or *confidential data* from being reidentifiable from the release of *microdata*. The objective of statistical disclosure control methods is to protect the confidentiality of the individuals whose data are being released.

Statistical linkage key   A method to extract selected characters from *quasi-identifier* attribute values (such as first name, surname, gender, and date of birth), and concatenate these characters into one single string for each *record*, where these strings are then used to match records (if they have the same statistical linkage key value).

String comparison function   A type of *comparison function* that takes as input two text strings and that returns an exact similarity value (*exact matching*) or an approximate similarity value (*approximate matching*) calculated for the two input strings.

Supervised learning   A type of *classifier algorithm* that builds a *classification model* based on the similarity values in *comparison vectors* and optionally the relationships between pairs or groups of *records*. A supervised classification model is built based on *ground truth data*, also known as *train-*

ing data, that are in the form of pairs or groups of *records* where their *match status* (*true match* and *true non-match*) is known. Examples for supervised learning models are logistic regression, support vector machines, and decision trees.

Suppression   Suppressing data is the process of not publishing certain pieces of information that are considered too sensitive to be released in order to protect the identities of the *entities* in a database, or their *personal* or otherwise *confidential data*.

Survey data   A type of data that are collected from a (sample of) respondents who answer questions or provide measurements in a survey. Such data often contain detailed information about a certain topic of interest for a target population.

Synthetic data   A type of data that are not obtained from direct measurement or generated by some real-world event. Rather, synthetic data are created using some *algorithm* and computer program such that they have the same or similar characteristics as real data. Synthetic data are often used to test and evaluate novel data processing systems, validate statistical and mathematical models, or novel computer algorithms in situations where it is impossible or difficult to obtain and/or use real-world data.

Tabular data   Data stored in the form of a table, where each row is a *record* that contains information about a single or an aggregated group of *entities*, and each column (also known as a *field* or *attribute*) contains a well-defined type of information about the entity (such as the age of a person) or group of entities (for example the average age of all females with a certain income). Also see *aggregated data*.

Third party   An organisation that is not a *database owner*, *data controller*, *data custodian*, or *data provider*, but that is authorised by these parties to process *personal* or *confidential data*, usually for specific purposes.

Token   A string representing a specific piece of information, for example an academic title in a name field.

Training data   See *ground truth data*.

Transitive closure   The process of deciding the *match status* for all *candidate record pairs* in a group of *records* as *matches*, where some but not all individual pairs of records have been classified as matches, following the transitivity property of the match classification: If the record pair (a, b) is classified as a match (i.e. refer to the same *entity*) and the record pair (a, c) is also classified as a match, then the record pair (b, c) must also be a match.

True match   A *record pair* that is classified as a *match*, where both *records* in the pair correspond to the same *entity*. In the context of classification a true match is also known as a true positive.

True non-match   A *record pair* that is classified as a *non-match*, where the two *records* in the pair correspond to two different *entities*. In the context of classification a true non-match is also known as a true negative.

Trustee   See *third party*.

Unidentified data   See *anonymised data.*

Unique identifier   Also known as an *entity identifier*, a unique value given to each *entity* of a population or subpopulation that directly establishes the identity of the entity. Such unique identifiers can be sequential integer numbers, random integer numbers, or text strings of a specific format. Examples of unique identifiers include social security numbers, patient identifiers, or taxation identifiers.

Unit data record   See *microdata.*

Unsupervised learning   A type of *classifier algorithm* that builds a *classification model* based on the similarity values in *comparison vectors* and optionally the relationships between pairs or groups of *records*. The classification model is built without knowing the true *match status* of these pairs or groups of records, i.e. no *ground truth data* are required. A popular type of unsupervised learning algorithm is *clustering.*

Utility   In the context of data *confidentiality*, utility is the concept of how useful published data are for a certain research analysis. *Microdata* usually have the highest utility as compared to *aggregated data*, because they allow more detailed analysis. Generally, there is a *privacy* versus utility trade-off.

Weight vector   A vector containing numerical values for a *candidate record pair*. Weight vectors are used by *probabilistic record linkage* and related *classifier* approaches to decide the *match status* of candidate record pairs. The values in the weight vector of a candidate record pair are calculated by combining for each compared *attribute* the *match weight* (if *attribute values* are the same or similar) or *non-match weight* (if attribute values are different) for that attribute with the similarity value for that attribute taken from the pair's *comparison vector*.

Whitespace   Characters that represent typographical space such as blanks or tabulators.

References

[1] Aberer, K., Datta, A., Hauswirth, M.: A decentralized public key infrastructure for customer-to-customer e-commerce. International Journal of Business Process Integration and Management **1**, 26–33 (2005)

[2] Abowd, J.: How will statistical agencies operate when all data are private? Journal of Privacy and Confidentiality **7**(3) (2017)

[3] Acar, A., Aksu, H., Uluagac, A.S., Conti, M.: A survey on homomorphic encryption schemes: Theory and implementation. ACM Computing Surveys **51**(4), 79 (2018)

[4] Acheson, E.: Oxford record linkage study: a central file of morbidity and mortality records for a pilot population. British Journal of Preventive and Social Medicine **18**(1), 8 (1964)

[5] Adams, C., Lloyd, S.: Understanding Public-key Infrastructure: Concepts, Standards, and Deployment Considerations. Sams Publishing (1999)

[6] Aggarwal, C.C., Yu, P.S.: Privacy-preserving Data Mining: Models and Algorithms, *Advances in Database Systems*, vol. 34. Springer (2008)

[7] Agrawal, R., Evfimievski, A., Srikant, R.: Information sharing across private databases. In: ACM Conference on Management of Data, pp. 86–97. San Diego (2003)

[8] Agrawal, R., Srikant, R.: Fast algorithms for mining association rules. In: Conference on Very Large Data Bases, pp. 487–499. Santiago de Chile (1994)

[9] Akgün, Ö., Dearle, A., Kirby, G., Christen, P.: Using metric space indexing for complete and efficient record linkage. In: Pacific-Asia Conference on Knowledge Discovery and Data Mining, pp. 89–101. Melbourne (2018)

[10] Akgün, Ö., Dearle, A., Kirby, G., Garrett, E., Dalton, T., Christen, P., Dibben, C., Williamson, L.: Linking Scottish vital event records using family groups. Historical Methods: A Journal of Quantitative and Interdisciplinary History pp. 1–17 (2019)

© Springer Nature Switzerland AG 2020
P. Christen et al., *Linking Sensitive Data*, https://doi.org/10.1007/978-3-030-59706-1

[11] Al-Lawati, A., Lee, D., McDaniel, P.: Blocking-aware private record linkage. In: International Workshop on Information Quality in Information Systems, pp. 59–68. Baltimore (2005)

[12] Alaggan, M., Cunche, M., Gambs, S.: Privacy-preserving Wi-Fi analytics. Privacy Enhancing Technologies **2018**(2), 4–26 (2018)

[13] Alaggan, M., Gambs, S., Kermarrec, A.M.: BLIP: non-interactive differentially-private similarity computation on Bloom filters. In: Symposium on Self-Stabilizing Systems, pp. 202–216. Toronto (2012)

[14] Alhaqbani, B., Fidge, C.: Access control requirements for processing electronic health records. In: BPM, pp. 371–382. Springer, Vienna (2007)

[15] Ali, M.S., Ichihara, M.Y., Lopes, L.C., Barbosa, G.C., Pita, R., Carreiro, R.P., dos Santos, D.B., Ramos, D., Bispo, N., Raynal, F., et al.: Administrative data linkage in Brazil: potentials for health technology assessment. Frontiers in Pharmacology **10** (2019)

[16] Allahbakhsh, M., Ignjatovic, A., Benatallah, B., Bertino, E., Foo, N., et al.: Collusion detection in online rating systems. In: ApWeb, pp. 196–207. Springer, Sydney (2013)

[17] Almquist, Y.B., Grotta, A., Vågerö, D., Stenberg, S.Å., Modin, B.: Cohort profile update: The Stockholm birth cohort study. International Journal of Epidemiology **49**(2), 367–367e (2020)

[18] Alvarez, R., Caballero-Gil, C., Santonja, J., Zamora, A.: Algorithms for lightweight key exchange. Sensors **17**(7), 1517 (2017)

[19] American Academy of Arts & Sciences: Perceptions of science in America. https://www.amacad.org/sites/default/files/publication/downloads/PFoS-Perceptions-Science-America.pdf (2018)

[20] Anderson, K., Durbin, E., Salinger, M.: Identity theft. The Journal of Economic Perspectives **22**(2), 171–192 (2008)

[21] Andreou, A., Goga, O., Loiseau, P.: Identity vs. attribute disclosure risks for users with multiple social profiles. In: IEEE/ACM Conference on Advances in Social Networks Analysis and Mining, pp. 163–170. Calgary (2017)

[22] Angrist, J.D., Krueger, A.B.: Empirical strategies in labor economics. In: O.C. Ashenfelter, D. Card (eds.) Handbook of Labor Economics, vol. 3, pp. 1277–1366. Elsevier, Amsterdam (1999)

[23] Antoni, M.: Record linkage of GDR's 'Data Fund of Societal Work Power' with administrative labour market biography data of the German Federal Employment Agency. German Record-Linkage Center Working paper series, 2018-02, Nürnberg (2018)

[24] Antoni, M., Schnell, R.: The past, present and future of the German Record Linkage Center. Journal of Economics and Statistics (2017)

[25] Arasu, A., Götz, M., Kaushik, R.: On active learning of record matching packages. In: ACM Conference on Management of Data, pp. 783–794. Indianapolis (2010)

[26] de Araujo Almeida, B., Barreto, M.L., Ichihara, M.Y., Barreto, M.E., Cabral, L., Fiaccone, R., Carreiro, R.P., Teles, C., Pita, R., Penna, G., et al.: The center for data and knowledge integration for health (CIDACS). International Journal of Population Data Science **4**(2) (2019)

[27] Arp, D., Quiring, E., Krueger, T., Dragiev, S., Rieck, K.: Privacy-enhanced fraud detection with Bloom filters. In: International Conference on Security and Privacy in Communication Systems, pp. 396–415. Singapore (2018)

[28] Asadova, S.: Privacy-preserving DNA sequence alignment. Ph.D. thesis, Master's thesis, Eindhoven University of Technology (2017)

[29] Ashton, K.: That 'Internet of Things' thing. RFID Journal **22**(7) (2009)

[30] Atallah, M., Kerschbaum, F., Du, W.: Secure and private sequence comparisons. In: Workshop on Privacy in the Electronic Society, pp. 39–44. Washington DC (2003)

[31] Audette, L.M., Hammond, M.S., Rochester, N.K.: Methodological issues with coding participants in anonymous psychological longitudinal studies. Educational and Psychological Measurement (2019)

[32] Aumann, Y., Lindell, Y.: Security against covert adversaries: Efficient protocols for realistic adversaries. In: Theory of Cryptography Conference, pp. 137–156. Amsterdam (2007)

[33] Australian Bureau of Statistics: Housing mobility and conditions, 2007–08 (2009)

[34] Australian National University: Incident Report on the Breach of the Australian National University's Administrative Systems (2019). Canberra, Australia

[35] Averdijk, M., Elffers, H.: The discrepancy between survey-based victim accounts and police reports revisited. International Review of Victimology **18**(2), 91–107 (2012)

[36] Avigad, J., Donnelly, K.: Formalizing O notation in Isabelle/HOL. In: Joint Conference on Automated Reasoning, pp. 357–371. Cork (2004)

[37] Bacher, J., Brand, R., Bender, S.: Re-identifying register data by survey data using cluster analysis: an empirical study. International Journal of Uncertainty, Fuzziness and Knowledge Based Systems **10**(5), 589–607 (2002)

[38] Bachteler, T., Reiher, J., Schnell, R.: Similarity filtering with multibit trees for record linkage. German Record Linkage Center, Nüremberg, Working Paper WP-GRLC-2013-02 (2013)

[39] Bakker, C.: Valuing the census. Technical Report, Statistics New Zealand (2013). URL http://archive.stats.govt.nz/methods/research-papers/topss/valuing-census.aspx

[40] Ballantyne, A.: Adjusting the focus: A public health ethics approach to data research. Bioethics **33**(3), 357–366 (2019)

[41] Ballantyne, A., Schaefer, G.O.: Consent and the ethical duty to participate in health data research. Journal of Medical Ethics **44**(6), 392–396
(2018)

[42] Bar-On, A., Dunkelman, O., Keller, N., Ronen, E., Shamir, A.: Improved key recovery attacks on reduced-round AES with practical data
and memory complexities. In: International Cryptology Conference,
pp. 185–212. Santa Barbara (2018)

[43] Barker, E., Barker, W., Burr, W., Polk, W., Smid, M.: Recommenda-
tion for key management part 1: General (revision 3). NIST Special
Publication **800**(57), 1–147 (2012)

[44] Barros, J.E., French, J.C., Martin, W.N., Kelly, P.M., Cannon, T.M.:
Using the triangle inequality to reduce the number of comparisons re-
quired for similarity-based retrieval. In: Storage and Retrieval for Still
Image and Video Databases IV, vol. 2670, pp. 392–403. La Jolla, San
Diego (1996)

[45] Batini, C., Scannapieco, M.: Data and Information Quality. Data-
Centric Systems and Applications. Springer (2016)

[46] Bayardo, R.: Efficiently mining long patterns from databases. ACM
SIGMOD Record **27**(2), 85–93 (1998)

[47] Bellahsene, Z., Bonifati, A., Rahm, E.: Schema Matching and Mapping.
Data-Centric Systems and Applications. Springer (2011)

[48] Bellare, K., Iyengar, S., Parameswaran, A.G., Rastogi, V.: Active sampling for entity matching. In: ACM Conference on Knowledge Discovery
and Data Mining, pp. 1131–1139. Beijing (2012)

[49] Benaloh, J.C.: Secret sharing homomorphisms: Keeping shares of a secret secret. In: Theory and Application of Cryptographic Techniques,
pp. 251–260. Santa Barbara (1986)

[50] Benchimol, E.I., Smeeth, L., Guttmann, A., Harron, K., Moher, D.,
Petersen, I., Sørensen, H.T., von Elm, E., Langan, S.M., Committee,
R.W., et al.: The REporting of studies Conducted using Observational
Routinely-collected health Data (RECORD) statement. PLOS Med
12(10), e1001,885 (2015)

[51] Benitez, K., Malin, B.: Evaluating re-identification risks with respect to
the HIPAA privacy rule. Journal of the American Medical Informatics
Association **17**(2), 169–177 (2010)

[52] Benjelloun, O., Garcia-Molina, H., Gong, H., Kawai, H., Larson, T.,
Menestrina, D., Thavisomboon, S.: D-Swoosh: A family of algorithms
for generic, distributed entity resolution. In: IEEE ICDCS, pp. 37–37.
Toronto (2007)

[53] Benjelloun, O., Garcia-Molina, H., Menestrina, D., Su, Q., Whang, S.,
Widom, J.: Swoosh: a generic approach to entity resolution. VLDB
Journal **18**(1), 255–276 (2009)

[54] Benschop, T., Machingauta, C., Welch, M.: Statistical disclosure control: A practice guide. https://sdcpractice.readthedocs.io/
en/latest/ (2019)

[55] Berent, M.K., Krosnick, J.A., Lupia, A.: Measuring voter registration and turnout in surveys: Do official government records yield more accurate assessments? Public Opinion Quarterly **80**(3), 597–621 (2016)

[56] Berger, J.M.: A note on error detection codes for asymmetric channels. Information and Control **4**(1), 68–73 (1961)

[57] Berlin, C., Techel, F., Moor, B.K., Zwahlen, M., Hasler, R.M., et al.: Snow avalanche deaths in Switzerland from 1995 to 2014 – Results of a nation-wide linkage study. PLOS One **14**(12) (2019)

[58] Bhattacharya, I., Getoor, L.: Collective entity resolution in relational data. ACM Transactions on Knowledge Discovery from Data **1**(1) (2007)

[59] Bian, J., Loiacono, A., Sura, A., Mendoza Viramontes, T., Lipori, G., Guo, Y., Shenkman, E., Hogan, W.: Implementing a hash-based privacy-preserving record linkage tool in the OneFlorida clinical research network. Journal of the American Medical Informatics Association Open **2**(4), 562–569 (2019)

[60] Bianchi, G., Bracciale, L., Loreti, P.: "Better than nothing" privacy with Bloom filters: To what extent? In: Privacy in Statistical Databases, pp. 348–363. Palermo (2012)

[61] Biemer, P.: Errors and inference. In: I. Foster, R. Ghani, R.S. Jarmin, F. Kreuter, J. Lane (eds.) Big Data and Social Science, chap. 10, pp. 265–297. CRC Press, Boca Raton (2017)

[62] Bilenko, M., Mooney, R.J.: Adaptive duplicate detection using learnable string similarity measures. In: ACM Conference on Knowledge Discovery and Data Mining, pp. 39–48. Washington DC (2003)

[63] Bizer, C., Heath, T., Berners-Lee, T.: Linked data: The story so far. In: Semantic Services, Interoperability and Web Applications: Emerging Concepts, pp. 205–227. IGI Global (2011)

[64] Blair, J., Czaja, R.F., Blair, E.A.: Designing Surveys: A Guide to Decisions and Procedures, 3 edn. Sage, Thousand Oaks (2014)

[65] Blakely, T., Salmond, C.: Probabilistic record linkage and a method to calculate the positive predictive value. International Journal of Epidemiology **31:6**, 1246–1252 (2002)

[66] Blakley, G.R., et al.: Safeguarding cryptographic keys. In: National Computer Conference. New York (1979)

[67] Blondel, B., Cuttini, M., Hindori-Mohangoo, A., Gissler, M., Loghi, M., Prunet, C., Heino, A., Smith, L., van der Pal-de Bruin, K., Macfarlane, A., Zeitlin, J.: How do late terminations of pregnancy affect comparisons of stillbirth rates in Europe? analyses of aggregated routine data from the Euro-Peristat Project. BJOG: An International Journal of Obstetrics and Gynaecology **125**(2), 226–234 (2018)

[68] Bloom, B.: Space/time trade-offs in hash coding with allowable errors. Communications of the ACM **13**(7), 422–426 (1970)

[69] Bloor, M., Leyland, A., Barnard, M., McKeganey, N.: Estimating hidden populations: A new method of calculating the prevalence of drug-

injecting and non-injecting female street prostitution. British Journal of Addiction **86**(11), 1477–1483 (1991)

[70] Blustein, J., El-Maazawi, A.: Bloom filters – a tutorial, analysis, and survey. Tech. rep., Dalhousie University, Halifax (2002)

[71] Bohensky, M.A., Jolley, D., Sundararajan, V., Evans, S., Pilcher, D.V., Scott, I., Brand, C.A.: Data linkage: a powerful research tool with potential problems. BMC Health Services Research **10**(346), 1–7 (2010)

[72] Boneh, D., et al.: Twenty years of attacks on the RSA cryptosystem. Notices of the AMS **46**(2), 203–213 (1999)

[73] Bonomi, L., Fan, L., Xiong, L.: A review of privacy preserving mechanisms for record linkage. In: A. Gkoulalas-Divanis, G. Loukides (eds.) Medical Data Privacy Handbook, pp. 233–265. Springer (2015)

[74] Bonomi, L., Xiong, L., Chen, R., Fung, B.: Frequent grams based embedding for privacy preserving record linkage. In: ACM Conference on Information and Knowledge Management, pp. 1597–1601. Maui, Hawaii (2012)

[75] Bonomi, L., Xiong, L., Lu, J.J.: LinkIT: privacy preserving record linkage and integration via transformations. In: ACM Conference on Management of Data, pp. 1029–1032. New York (2013)

[76] Bopp, M., Spoerri, A., Zwahlen, M., Gutzwiller, F., Paccaud, F., Braun-Fahrlander, C., Rougemont, A., Egger, M.: Cohort profile: The Swiss national cohort – a longitudinal study of 6.8 Million people. International Journal of Epidemiology **38**(2), 379–384 (2009)

[77] Borgs, C.: Optimal parameter choice for Bloom filter-based privacy-preserving record linkage. Ph.D. thesis, University of Duisburg-Essen, Germany (2019)

[78] Borthakur, D., et al.: HDFS architecture guide. Hadoop Apache Project **53**(1-13), 2 (2008)

[79] Bose, P., Guo, H., Kranakis, E., Maheshwari, A., Morin, P., Morrison, J., Smid, M., Tang, Y.: On the false-positive rate of Bloom filters. Information Processing Letters **108**(4), 210–213 (2008)

[80] Bosu, A., Liu, F., Yao, D.D., Wang, G.: Collusive data leak and more: Large-scale threat analysis of inter-app communications. In: ACM Asia Conference on Computer and Communications Security, pp. 71–85. Abu Dhabi (2017)

[81] Boyd, J.H., Ferrante, A.M., Irvine, K., Smith, M., Moore, E., Brown, A., Randall, S.M.: Understanding the origins of record linkage errors and how they affect research outcomes. Australian and New Zealand Journal of Public Health **41**(2), 215–215 (2017)

[82] Boyd, J.H., Ferrante, A.M., O'Keefe, C.M., Bass, A.J., Randall, S.M., Semmens, J.B.: Data linkage infrastructure for cross-jurisdictional health-related research in Australia. BMC Health Services Research **12**, 480 (2012)

[83] Boyd, J.H., Randall, S.M., Brown, A., Max, M., Botes, D., Gillies, M., Ferrante, A.M.: Population data centre profiles: Centre for data linkage. International Journal of Population Data Science **4**(2) (2019)

[84] Boyd, J.H., Randall, S.M., Ferrante, A.M.: Application of privacy-preserving techniques in operational record linkage centres. In: A. Gkoulalas-Divanis, G. Loukides (eds.) Medical Data Privacy Handbook, pp. 267–287. Springer (2015)

[85] Brand, R.: Microdata protection through noise addition. In: Inference Control in Statistical Databases: From Theory to Practice, pp. 97–116. Springer, Berlin, Heidelberg (2002)

[86] Brick, J.M., Williams, D.: Explaining rising nonresponse rates in cross-sectional surveys. The Annals of the American Academy of Political and Social Science **645**(1), 36–59 (2013)

[87] Broder, A.: On the resemblance and containment of documents. In: IEEE Compression and Complexity of Sequences, pp. 21–29. Salerno, Italy (1997)

[88] Broder, A., Mitzenmacher, M., Mitzenmacher, A.: Network applications of Bloom filters: A survey. In: Internet Mathematics (2002)

[89] Brown, A., Borgs, C., Randall, S., Schnell, R.: Evaluating privacy-preserving record linkage using cryptographic long-term keys and multibit trees on large medical datasets. BMC Medical Informatics and Decision Making **17**(83), 1–7 (2017)

[90] Brown, A., Borgs, C., Randall, S., Schnell, R.: High quality linkage using multi-bit trees for privacy-preserving blocking. International Journal of Population Data Science **1**(1) (2017)

[91] Bu-Pasha, S.: Cross-border issues under EU data protection law with regards to personal data protection. Information and Communications Technology Law **26**(3), 213–228 (2017)

[92] Bundesamt für Statistik: Das neue Volkszählungssystem. Evaluationsbericht des Bundesrates. https://www.bfs.admin.ch/bfsstatic/dam/assets/3922064/master, Bern (2017)

[93] Bundesverfassungsgericht: Decision of the first senate, 4. April— 2006. https://www.bundesverfassungsgericht.de/SharedDocs/Entscheidungen/DE/2006/04/rs20060404_1bvr051802.html (2006)

[94] Caldicott, F.: The Information Governance Review. Information: To share or not to share? Department of Health (2013)

[95] Caldicott Committee: Report on the review of patient-identifiable information. Department of Health, 11934 CA Q 1000 1P Dec 97 (1997)

[96] Campbell, K., Deck, D., Krupski, A.: Record linkage software in the public domain: a comparison of Link Plus, The Link King, and a basic deterministic algorithm. Health Informatics Journal **14**(1), 5 (2008)

[97] Carey, P. (ed.): Data Protection: A Practical Guide to UK and EU Law, 5 edn. Oxford University Press, Oxford (2018)

[98] Ceglar, A., Roddick, J.F.: Association mining. ACM Computing Surveys (CSUR) **3**(2), 5 (2006)

[99] Chen, J., Swamidass, S.J., Dou, Y., Bruand, J., Baldi, P.: ChemDB: a public database of small molecules and related chemoinformatics resources. Bioinformatics **21**(22), 4133–4139 (2005)

[100] Chen, M., Mao, S., Liu, Y.: Big data: A survey. Mobile Networks and Applications **19**(2), 171–209 (2014)

[101] Chetty, R.: Time trends in the use of administrative data for empirical research (2012). URL http://www.rajchetty.com/chettyfiles/admin_data_trends.pdf. NBER Summer Institute

[102] Chi, L., Zhu, X.: Hashing techniques: A survey and taxonomy. ACM Computing Surveys **50**(1), 11 (2017)

[103] Chi, Y., Hong, J., Jurek, A., Liu, W., O'Reilly, D.: Privacy preserving record linkage in the presence of missing values. Information Systems **71**, 199–210 (2017)

[104] Chiang, Y.H., Doan, A., Naughton, J.F.: Tracking entities in the dynamic world: A fast algorithm for matching temporal records. VLDB Endowment **7**(6), 469–480 (2014)

[105] Chor, B., Kushilevitz, E.: Secret sharing over infinite domains. Journal of Cryptology **6**(2), 87–95 (1993)

[106] Christen, P.: Privacy-preserving data linkage and geocoding: Current approaches and research directions. In: Privacy Aspects of Data Mining, held at IEEE ICDM. Hong Kong (2006)

[107] Christen, P.: Automatic record linkage using seeded nearest neighbour and support vector machine classification. In: ACM Conference on Knowledge Discovery and Data Mining, pp. 151–159. Las Vegas (2008)

[108] Christen, P.: Development and user experiences of an open source data cleaning, deduplication and record linkage system. ACM SIGKDD Explorations **11**(1), 39–48 (2009)

[109] Christen, P.: Data Matching – Concepts and Techniques for Record Linkage, Entity Resolution, and Duplicate Detection. Data-Centric Systems and Applications. Springer (2012)

[110] Christen, P.: A survey of indexing techniques for scalable record linkage and deduplication. Transactions on Knowledge and Data Engineering **24**(9), 1537–1555 (2012)

[111] Christen, P.: Preparation of a real temporal voter data set for record linkage and duplicate detection research. Australian National University (2014)

[112] Christen, P.: Data linkage: The big picture. Harvard Data Science Review **1**(2) (2019)

[113] Christen, P., Churches, T., Hegland, M.: Febrl – A parallel open source data linkage system. In: Pacific-Asia Conference on Knowledge Discovery and Data Mining, pp. 638–647. Sydney (2004)

[114] Christen, P., Churches, T., Willmore, A.: A probabilistic geocoding system based on a national address file. In: Australasian Data Mining Conference. Cairns (2004)

[115] Christen, P., Gayler, R., Hawking, D.: Similarity-aware indexing for real-time entity resolution. In: ACM Conference on Information and Knowledge Management, pp. 1565–1568. Hong Kong (2009)

[116] Christen, P., Gayler, R.W.: Adaptive temporal entity resolution on dynamic databases. In: Pacific-Asia Conference on Knowledge Discovery and Data Mining, pp. 558–569. Springer, Gold Coast, Australia (2013)

[117] Christen, P., Gayler, R.W., Tran, K.N., Fisher, J., Vatsalan, D.: Automatic discovery of abnormal values in large textual databases. ACM Journal of Data and Information Quality **7**(1-2), 1–31 (2016)

[118] Christen, P., Pudjijono, A.: Accurate synthetic generation of realistic personal information. In: Pacific-Asia Conference on Knowledge Discovery and Data Mining, pp. 507–514. Bangkok (2009)

[119] Christen, P., Ranbaduge, T., Vatsalan, D., Schnell, R.: Precise and fast cryptanalysis for Bloom filter based privacy-preserving record linkage. Transactions on Knowledge and Data Engineering (2018)

[120] Christen, P., Schnell, R., Vatsalan, D., Ranbaduge, T.: Efficient cryptanalysis of Bloom filters for privacy-preserving record linkage. In: Pacific-Asia Conference on Knowledge Discovery and Data Mining, pp. 628–640. Springer, Jeju, Korea (2017)

[121] Christen, P., Vatsalan, D.: Flexible and extensible generation and corruption of personal data. In: ACM Conference on Information and Knowledge Management, pp. 1165–1168. San Francisco (2013)

[122] Christen, P., Vatsalan, D., Wang, Q.: Efficient entity resolution with adaptive and interactive training data selection. In: IEEE International Conference on Data Mining, pp. 727–732. Atlantic City (2015)

[123] Christen, P., Vidanage, A., Ranbaduge, T., Schnell, R.: Pattern-mining based cryptanalysis of Bloom filters for privacy-preserving record linkage. In: Pacific-Asia Conference on Knowledge Discovery and Data Mining, pp. 628–640. Springer, Melbourne (2018)

[124] Christen, V., Christen, P., Rahm, E.: Informativeness-based active learning for entity resolution. In: Workshop on Data Integration and Applications, held at PKDD/ECML. Würzburg (2019)

[125] Churches, T., Christen, P.: Some methods for blindfolded record linkage. BMC Medical Informatics and Decision Making **4**(9) (2004)

[126] Churches, T., Christen, P., Lim, K., Zhu, J.X.: Preparation of name and address data for record linkage using hidden Markov models. BMC Medical Informatics and Decision Making **2**(9) (2002)

[127] Clark, D.E.: Practical introduction to record linkage for injury research. Injury Prevention **10**, 186–191 (2004)

[128] Clarke, N., Vale, G., Reeves, E.P., Kirwan, M., Smith, D., Farrell, M., Hurl, G., McElvaney, N.G.: GDPR: an impediment to research? Irish Journal of Medical Science **188**(4), 1129–1135 (2019)

[129] Clifton, C., Kantarcioglu, M., Doan, A., Schadow, G., Vaidya, J., Elmagarmid, A., Suciu, D.: Privacy-preserving data integration and sharing. In: Workshop on Research issues in Data Mining and Knowledge Discovery, held at ACM SIGKDD, pp. 19–26. Paris (2004)

[130] Cochinwala, M., Kurien, V., Lalk, G., Shasha, D.: Efficient data reconciliation. Information Sciences **137**(1–4), 1–15 (2001)

[131] Cohen, W.W., Ravikumar, P., Fienberg, S.: A comparison of string distance metrics for name-matching tasks. In: Workshop on Information Integration on the Web, held at IJCAI, pp. 73–78. Acapulco (2003)

[132] Cohen, W.W., Richman, J.: Learning to match and cluster large high-dimensional data sets for data integration. In: ACM Conference on Knowledge Discovery and Data Mining, pp. 475–480. Edmonton (2002)

[133] Colquitt, J.A., Rodell, J.B.: Measuring justice and fairness. In: R. Cropanzano, M. Ambrose (eds.) Oxford Handbook of Justice in the Workplace, pp. 187–202. Oxford University Press (2015)

[134] Committee on Professional Ethics of the American Statistical Association: Ethical guidelines for statistical practice. https://www.amstat.org/asa/files/pdfs/EthicalGuidelines.pdf (2018)

[135] Connelly, R., Playford, C.J., Gayle, V., Dibben, C.: The role of administrative data in the big data revolution in social science research. Social Science Research **59**(Supplement C), 1–12 (2016)

[136] Connor, R., Dearle, A.: Querying metric spaces with bit operations. In: International Conference on Similarity Search and Applications, pp. 33–46. Lima, Peru (2018)

[137] Conrad, J.G., Guo, X.S., Schriber, C.P.: Online duplicate detection: Signature reliability in a dynamic retrieval environment. In: ACM Conference on Information and Knowledge Management, pp. 443–452. New Orleans (2003)

[138] Coppersmith, D.: The data encryption standard (DES) and its strength against attacks. IBM Journal of Research and Development **38**(3), 243–250 (1994)

[139] Cormode, G., Muthukrishnan, S.: An improved data stream summary: the count-min sketch and its applications. Journal of Algorithms **55**(1), 58–75 (2005)

[140] Culnane, C., Rubinstein, B.I., Teague, V.: Health data in an open world. arXiv Preprint (2017)

[141] Culnane, C., Rubinstein, B.I., Teague, V.: Vulnerabilities in the use of similarity tables in combination with pseudonymisation to preserve data privacy in the UK Office for National Statistics' privacy-preserving record linkage. arXiv Preprint (2017)

[142] Dalenius, T., Reiss, S.P.: Data-swapping: A technique for disclosure control. Journal of Statistical Planning and Inference **6**(1), 73–85 (1982)

[143] Damerau, F.J.: A technique for computer detection and correction of spelling errors. Communications of the ACM **7**(3), 171–176 (1964)

[144] Das, L.: Role of data in improving care within a health system: A case study of the australian health system. Master's thesis, RAND Corporation (2017)

[145] Datar, M., Immorlica, N., Indyk, P., Mirrokni, V.S.: Locality-sensitive hashing scheme based on p-stable distributions. In: ACM SOCG, pp. 253–262. Brooklyn (2004)

[146] Datta, A., Tschantz, M.C., Datta, A.: Automated experiments on ad privacy settings. In: Privacy Enhancing Technologies, pp. 92–112. Philadelphia (2015)

[147] Day, C.: Record linkage I: Evaluation of commercially available record linkage software for use in NASS. Tech. Rep. STB Research Report STB-95-02, National Agricultural Statistics Service, Washington DC (1995)

[148] Dean, J., Ghemawat, S.: Mapreduce: simplified data processing on large clusters. Communications of the ACM **51**(1), 107–113 (2008)

[149] DeBell, M., Krosnick, J.A., Gera, K., Yeager, D.S., McDonald, M.P.: The turnout gap in surveys: Explanations and solutions. Sociological Methods and Research (2018)

[150] Delnord, M., Szamotulska, K., Hindori-Mohangoo, A., Blondel, B., Macfarlane, A., Dattani, N., Barona, C., Berrut, S., Zile, I., Wood, R., Sakkeus, L., Gissler, M., Zeitlin, J., the Euro-Peristat Scientific Committee: Linking databases on perinatal health: A review of the literature and current practices in Europe. The European Journal of Public Health **26**(3), 422–430 (2016)

[151] Dempster, A.P., Laird, N.M., Rubin, D.B.: Maximum likelihood from incomplete data via the EM algorithm. Journal of the Royal Statistical Society: Series B (Methodological) **39**(1), 1–22 (1977)

[152] Desai, T., Ritchie, F., Welpton, R.: Five safes: Designing data access for research. Tech. rep., Department of Accounting, Economics and Finance, Bristol Business School, University of the West of England (2016)

[153] Deutscher Bundestag: Entwurf eines Gesetzes zur Durchführung des Zensus im Jahr 2021. Tech. Rep. Drucksache 19/8693, Bundestag, Berlin (2019)

[154] DH Informatics: Supplementary guidance: Public interest disclosures. UK Department of Health and Social Care (2010)

[155] Diffie, W., Hellman, M.: New directions in cryptography. Transactions on Information Theory **22**(6), 644–654 (1976)

[156] Dillinger, P.C., Manolios, P.: Bloom filters in probabilistic verification. In: International Conference on Formal Methods in Computer-Aided Design, pp. 367–381. Springer (2004)

[157] Dillinger, P.C., Manolios, P.: Fast and accurate bitstate verification for spin. In: International SPIN Workshop on Model Checking of Software, pp. 57–75. Springer (2004)

[158] Doan, A., Halevy, A., Ives, Z.: Principles of Data Integration. Elsevier (2012)

[159] Doidge, J.C., Harron, K.L.: Reflections on modern methods: linkage error bias. International Journal of Epidemiology **48**(6), 2050–2060 (2019)

[160] Domingo-Ferrer, J., Mateo-Sanz, J.: Practical data-oriented microaggregation for statistical disclosure control. Transactions on Knowledge and Data Engineering **14**(1), 189–201 (2002)

[161] Domingo-Ferrer, J., Ricci, S., Soria-Comas, J.: Disclosure risk assessment via record linkage by a maximum-knowledge attacker. In: IEEE Privacy, Security and Trust, pp. 28–35. Izmir (2015)

[162] Domingo-Ferrer, J., Sánchez, D., Soria-Comas, J.: Database Anonymization: Privacy Models, Data Utility, and Microaggregation-based Inter-model Connections. Synthesis Lectures on Information Security, Privacy, and Trust. Morgan and Claypool Publishers (2016)

[163] Domingo-Ferrer, J., Sebé, F., Castella-Roca, J.: On the security of noise addition for privacy in statistical databases. In: Privacy in Statistical Databases, pp. 149–161. Barcelona (2004)

[164] Domingo-Ferrer, J., Torra, V.: Disclosure risk assessment in statistical microdata protection via advanced record linkage. Statistics and Computing **13**(4), 343–354 (2003)

[165] Dong, B., Liu, R., Wang, W.H.: Prada: Privacy-preserving data-deduplication-as-a-service. In: ACM Conference on Information and Knowledge Management, pp. 1559–1568. Shanghai (2014)

[166] Dong, C., Chen, L., Wen, Z.: When private set intersection meets big data: an efficient and scalable protocol. In: ACM Conference on Computer and Communications Security, pp. 789–800. Berlin (2013)

[167] Dong, X.L., Halevy, A., Madhavan, J.: Reference reconciliation in complex information spaces. In: ACM Conference on Management of Data, pp. 85–96. Baltimore (2005)

[168] Dong, X.L., Srivastava, D.: Big Data Integration. Synthesis Lectures on Data Management. Morgan and Claypool Publishers (2015)

[169] Dove, E.S., Phillips, M.: Privacy law, data sharing policies, and medical data: A comparative perspective. In: A. Gkoulalas-Divanis, G. Loukides (eds.) Medical Data Privacy Handbook, pp. 639–678. Springer (2015)

[170] Draisbach, U., Christen, P., Naumann, F.: Transforming pairwise duplicates to entity clusters for high-quality duplicate detection. Journal of Data and Information Quality **12**(1), 1–30 (2019)

[171] Draisbach, U., Naumann, F., Szott, S., Wonneberg, O.: Adaptive windows for duplicate detection. In: IEEE International Conference on Data Engineering, pp. 1073–1083. Washington, DC (2012)

[172] Du, W., Atallah, M., Kerschbaum, F.: Protocols for secure remote database access with approximate matching. In: ACM Workshop on Security and Privacy in E-Commerce. Athens (2000)

[173] Duncan, G., Elliot, M., Salazar-González, J.J.: Statistical Confidentiality: Principles and Practice. Springer, New York (2011)

[174] Duncan, G., Lambert, D.: The risk of disclosure for microdata. Journal of Business & Economic Statistics **7**(2), 207–217 (1989)

[175] Dunn, H.: Record linkage. American Journal of Public Health **36**(12), 1412 (1946)

[176] Durham, E., Kantarcioglu, M., Xue, Y., Toth, C., Kuzu, M., Malin, B.: Composite Bloom filters for secure record linkage. Transactions on Knowledge and Data Engineering **26**(12), 2956–2968 (2014)

[177] Durham, E., Xue, Y., Kantarcioglu, M., Malin, B.: Quantifying the correctness, computational complexity, and security of privacy-preserving string comparators for record linkage. Information Fusion **13**(4), 245–259 (2012)

[178] Durham, E.A.: A framework for accurate, efficient private record linkage. Ph.D. thesis, Faculty of the Graduate School of Vanderbilt University, Nashville, TN (2012)

[179] Durstenfeld, R.: Algorithm 235: Random permutation. Communications of the ACM **7**(7), 420 (1964)

[180] Dusserre, L., Quantin, C., Bouzelat, H.: A one way public key cryptosystem for the linkage of nominal files in epidemiological studies. Medinfo **8**, 644–647 (1995)

[181] Dwork, C.: Differential privacy. In: International Colloquium on Automata, Languages and Programming, pp. 1–12. Venice (2006)

[182] Dwork, C.: Differential privacy: A survey of results. In: Theory and Applications of Models of Computation, pp. 1–19. Xi'an, China (2008)

[183] Dwork, C., Roth, A., et al.: The algorithmic foundations of differential privacy. Foundations and Trends in Theoretical Computer Science **9**(3–4), 211–407 (2014)

[184] Efthymiou, V., Papadakis, G., Papastefanatos, G., Stefanidis, K., Palpanas, T.: Parallel meta-blocking for scaling entity resolution over big heterogeneous data. Information Systems **65**, 137–157 (2017)

[185] El Emam, K.: Guide to the De-Identification of Personal Health Information. CRC Press (2013)

[186] Elfeky, M.G., Verykios, V.S., Elmagarmid, A.K.: TAILOR: A record linkage toolbox. In: IEEE International Conference on Data Engineering, pp. 17–28. San Jose (2002)

[187] Elliot, M., Mackey, E., O'Hara, K., Tudor, C.: The Anonymisation Decision-making Framework. UKAN Manchester (2016)

[188] Elliot, M., O'Hara, K., Raab, C., O'Keefe, C.M., Mackey, E., Dibben, C., Gowans, H., Purdam, K., McCullagh, K.: Functional anonymisation: Personal data and the data environment. Computer Law and Security Review **34**(2), 204–221 (2018)

[189] Emmert-Streib, F., Dehmer, M., Shi, Y.: Fifty years of graph matching, network alignment and network comparison. Information Sciences **346**, 180–197 (2016)

[190] Erlingsson, Ú., Pihur, V., Korolova, A.: Rappor: Randomized aggregatable privacy-preserving ordinal response. In: ACM SIGSAC, pp. 1054–1067. Scottsdale, Arizona (2014)

[191] Esayas, S.: The role of anonymisation and pseudonymisation under the EU data privacy rules: beyond the 'all or nothing' approach. European Journal of Law and Technology 6(2) (2015)

[192] Etheridge, Y.: PKI (public key infrastructure) – how and why it works. Health Management Technology 22(1), 20 (2001)

[193] Etienne, B., Cheatham, M., Grzebala, P.: An analysis of blocking methods for private record linkage. In: AAAI Fall Symposium Series. Arlington, Virginia (2016)

[194] European Commission: Flash Eurobarometer 443: e-Privacy. doi:10.2759/249540 (2016)

[195] European Parliament: Regulation (EU) 2016/679 of the European Parliament and of the Council of 27 April 2016 on the Protection of Natural Persons with Regard to the Processing of Personal Data and on the Free Movement of such Data, and Repealing Directive 95/46/EC (General Data Protection Regulation). https://eur-lex.europa.eu/eli/reg/2016/679/oj (2016)

[196] European Statistical System Committee: European Statistics Code of Practice. Luxembourg (2018)

[197] European Union Agency for Fundamental Rights: Handbook on European Data Protection Law: 2018 Edition. Publications Office of the European Union, Luxembourg (2018)

[198] Fair, M.: Generalized record linkage system–Statistics Canada's record linkage software. Austrian Journal of Statistics 33(1&2), 37–53 (2004)

[199] Fan, L., Cao, P., Almeida, J., Broder, A.Z.: Summary cache: a scalable wide-area web cache sharing protocol. IEEE/ACM Transactions on Networking 8(3), 281–293 (2000)

[200] Farrow, J.M.: Comparing geospatial distance without revealing location. Presentation given at the International Health Data Linkage Conference, Vancouver (2014)

[201] Farrow, J.M.: Using graph databases to manage linked data. In: K. Harron, H. Goldstein, C. Dibben (eds.) Methodological Developments in Data Linkage, pp. 125–169. John Wiley & Sons (2015)

[202] Farrow, J.M.: Method and system for comparative data analysis (2017). US Patent App. 15/305,335

[203] Fellegi, I.P., Holt, D.: A systematic approach to automatic edit and imputation. Journal of the American Statistical Association 71(353), 17–35 (1976)

[204] Fellegi, I.P., Sunter, A.B.: A theory for record linkage. Journal of the American Statistical Association 64(328), 1183–1210 (1969)

[205] Ferguson, J., Hannigan, A., Stack, A.: A new computationally efficient algorithm for record linkage with field dependency and missing data

imputation. International Journal of Medical Informatics **109**, 70–75 (2018)

[206] Ferrante, A.M., Boyd, J.H.: A transparent and transportable methodology for evaluating data linkage software. Journal of Biomedical Informatics **45**(1), 165–172 (2012)

[207] Fickermann, D., Doll, J.: Potential und Technik der Verknüpfung von Befragungsdaten mit schulstatistischen Individualdaten und Leistungsdaten im Projekt EIBISCH. DDS - Die Deutsche Schule **107**(4), 365–374 (2015)

[208] Fienberg, S.E.: Confidentiality and disclosure limitation. Encyclopedia of Social Measurement **1**, 463–69 (2005)

[209] Fienberg, S.E.: Homeland insecurity: Data mining, privacy, disclosure limitation, and the hunt for terrorists. In: H. Chen, E. Reid, J. Sinai, A. Silke, B. Ganor (eds.) Terrorism Informatics: Knowledge Management and Data Mining for Homeland Security, pp. 197–218. Springer (2008)

[210] Fienberg, S.E., Steele, R.J.: Disclosure limitation using perturbation and related methods for categorical data. Journal of Official Statistics **14**(4), 485 (1998)

[211] Finance, B., Medjdoub, S., Pucheral, P.: Privacy of medical records: From law principles to practice. In: IEEE International Symposium on Computer Based Medical Systems, pp. 220–225. Dublin (2005)

[212] Fisher, J., Christen, P., Wang, Q., Rahm, E.: A clustering-based framework to control block sizes for entity resolution. In: ACM Conference on Knowledge Discovery and Data Mining, pp. 279–288. Sydney (2015)

[213] Flack, F., Adams, C., Allen, J.: Authorising the release of data without consent for health research: The role of data custodians and HRECs in Australia. Journal of Law and Medicine **26**(3), 655–680 (2019)

[214] Flack, F., Kemp-Casey, A., Wray, N.: Using linked administrative data in clinical trials: A guide for clinical trialists and researchers. Australian Clinical Trials Alliance (2019)

[215] Ford, D.V., Jones, K.H., Verplancke, J.P., Lyons, R.A., John, G., Brown, G., Brooks, C.J., Thompson, S., Bodger, O., Couch, T., et al.: The SAIL databank: building a national architecture for e-health research and evaluation. BMC Health Services Research **9**(1), 157 (2009)

[216] Fortini, M., Liseo, B., Nuccitelli, A., Scanu, M.: On Bayesian record linkage. Research in Official Statistics **4**(1), 185–198 (2001)

[217] Fox, W.R., Lasker, G.W.: The distribution of surname frequencies. International Statistical Review pp. 81–87 (1983)

[218] Franke, M., Gladbach, M., Sehili, Z., Rohde, F., Rahm, E.: ScaDS research on scalable privacy-preserving record linkage. Datenbank-Spektrum **19**(1), 31–40 (2019)

[219] Franke, M., Sehili, Z., Rahm, E.: PRIMAT: a toolbox for fast privacy-preserving matching. VLDB Endowment **12**(12), 1826–1829 (2019)

[220] Fu, Z., Zhou, J., Christen, P., Boot, M.: Multiple instance learning for group record linkage. In: Pacific-Asia Conference on Knowledge Discovery and Data Mining, pp. 171–182. Kuala Lumpur (2012)

[221] Fuller, W.: Masking procedures for microdata disclosure. Journal of Official Statistics **9**(2), 383–406 (1993)

[222] Galbraith, S.D.: Mathematics of Public Key Cryptography. Cambridge University Press (2012)

[223] Ganta, S.R., Kasiviswanathan, S.P., Smith, A.: Composition attacks and auxiliary information in data privacy. In: ACM Conference on Knowledge Discovery and Data Mining, pp. 265–273. Las Vegas (2008)

[224] Garfinkel, S.L.: De-identification of personal information. Tech. Rep. NIST IR 8053, National Institute of Standards and Technology (2015)

[225] Gilbert, R., Lafferty, R., Hagger-Johnson, G., Harron, K., Zhang, L.C., Smith, P., Dibben, C., Goldstein, H.: GUILD: Guidance for information about linking data sets. Journal of Public Health **40**(1), 191–198 (2017)

[226] Gill, L.: Methods for automatic record matching and linking and their use in national statistics. Tech. Rep. Methodology Series, no. 25, National Statistics, London (2001)

[227] Gionis, A., Indyk, P., Motwani, R., et al.: Similarity search in high dimensions via hashing. In: Conference on Very Large Data Bases, pp. 518–529. Edinburgh (1999)

[228] Goldberg, A., Borthwick, A.: The Choicemaker 2 record matching system. ChoiceMaker Technologies, Inc. (2004)

[229] Goldreich, O.: Secure multi-party computation. Tech. rep., Department of Computer Science and Applied Mathematics, Weizmann Institute of Science, Israel (2002)

[230] Goldreich, O.: Foundations of Cryptography: Volume 2, Basic Applications. Cambridge University Press (2009)

[231] Goldreich, O., Micali, S., Wigderson, A.: How to play any mental game. In: ACM Symposium on Theory of computing, pp. 218–229 (1987)

[232] Goldstein, H., Harron, K.: Record linkage: a missing data problem. In: K. Harron, H. Goldstein, C. Dibben (eds.) Methodological Developments in Data Linkage, pp. 110–124. John Wiley & Sons (2015)

[233] Goldstein, H., Harron, K., Wade, A.: The analysis of record-linked data using multiple imputation with data value priors. Statistics in Medicine **31**(28), 3481–3493 (2012)

[234] Goldwasser, S., Micali, S.: Probabilistic encryption. Journal of computer and system sciences **28**(2), 270–299 (1984)

[235] Gomatam, S., Larsen, M.D.: Record linkage and counterterrorism. Chance **17**(1), 25–29 (2004)

[236] Gouweleeuw, J.M., Kooiman, P., Willenborg, L.C.R.J., de Wolf, P.P.: Post randomisation for statistical disclosure control: Theory and implementation. Journal of Official Statistics **14**(4), 463–478 (1998)

[237] Goyal, V., Mohassel, P., Smith, A.: Efficient two party and multi party computation against covert adversaries. In: Annual International Con-

ference on the Theory and Applications of Cryptographic Techniques, pp. 289–306. Istanbul (2008)

[238] Grama, J.L.: Legal Issues in Information Security, 2 edn. Jones and Batlett Learning, Burlinton (2015)

[239] Grannis, S.J., Overhage, J.M., McDonald, C.J.: Analysis of identifier performance using a deterministic linkage algorithm. In: AMIA Annual Symposium Proceedings, p. 305. American Medical Informatics Association (2002)

[240] Gropp, W., Thakur, R., Lusk, E.: Using MPI-2: Advanced Features of the Message Passing Interface. MIT press (1999)

[241] Groves, R.M.: Survey Errors and Survey Costs. Wiley Series in Survey Methodology. John Wiley and Sons (2004)

[242] Groves, R.M., Fowler, F.J., Couper, M.P., Lebkowski, J.M., Singer, E., Tourangeau, R.: Survey Methodology, 2 edn. Wiley, Hoboken (2009)

[243] Gu, L., Baxter, R.: Decision models for record linkage. In: Selected Papers from AusDM, pp. 146–160. Springer (2006)

[244] Gu, L., Baxter, R., Vickers, D., Rainsford, C.: Record linkage: Current practice and future directions. CSIRO Mathematical and Information Sciences Technical Report **3**, 83 (2003)

[245] Guesdon, M., Benzenine, E., Gadouche, K., Quantin, C.: Securizing data linkage in French public statistics. BMC Medical Informatics and Decision Making **16**(1), 129 (2016)

[246] Guisado-Gámez, J., Prat-Pérez, A., Nin, J., Muntés-Mulero, V., Larriba-Pey, J.L.: Parallelizing record linkage for disclosure risk assessment. In: Privacy in Statistical Databases, pp. 190–202. Istanbul (2008)

[247] Gymrek, M., McGuire, A.L., Golan, D., Halperin, E., Erlich, Y.: Identifying personal genomes by surname inference. Science **339**(6117), 321–324 (2013)

[248] Hafner, H.P., Lenz, R., Ritchie, F.: User-focused threat identification for anonymised microdata. Statistical Journal of the IAOS **35**(4), 703–713 (2019)

[249] Hagger-Johnson, G., Harron, K., Goldstein, H., Aldridge, R., Gilbert, R.: Probabilistic linkage to enhance deterministic algorithms and reduce data linkage errors in hospital administrative data. Journal of Innovation in Health Informatics **24**(2), 891 (2017)

[250] Hajian, S., Bonchi, F., Castillo, C.: Algorithmic bias: From discrimination discovery to fairness-aware data mining. In: ACM Conference on Knowledge Discovery and Data Mining, pp. 2125–2126. San Francisco (2016)

[251] Hall, M., Frank, E., Holmes, G., Pfahringer, B., Reutemann, P., Witten, I.: The WEKA data mining software: an update. ACM SIGKDD Explorations **11**(1), 10–18 (2009)

[252] Hall, P.A., Dowling, G.R.: Approximate string matching. ACM Computing Surveys **12**(4), 381–402 (1980)

[253] Hall, R., Fienberg, S.: Privacy-preserving record linkage. In: Privacy in Statistical Databases, pp. 269–283. Corfu, Greece (2010)

[254] Han, J., Kamber, M., Pei, J.: Data Mining: Concepts and Techniques, 3 edn. Morgan Kaufmann (2011)

[255] Han, S., Shen, D., Nie, T., Kou, Y., Yu, G.: Private blocking technique for multi-party privacy-preserving record linkage. Data Science and Engineering **2**(2), 187–196 (2017)

[256] Hand, D.J.: Classifier technology and the illusion of progress. Statistical Science **21**(1), 1–14 (2006)

[257] Hand, D.J.: Assessing the performance of classification methods. International Statistical Review **80**(3), 400–414 (2012)

[258] Hand, D.J.: Aspects of data ethics in a changing world: where are we now? Big data **6**(3), 176–190 (2018)

[259] Hand, D.J.: Dark Data: Why What You Don't Know Matters. Princeton University Press (2020)

[260] Hand, D.J., Christen, P.: A note on using the f-measure for evaluating record linkage algorithms. Statistics and Computing **28**(3), 539–547 (2018)

[261] Harada, M., Sato, S., Kazama, K.: Finding authoritative people from the web. In: ACM/IEEE Joint Conference on Digital Libraries, pp. 306–313. Tucson (2004)

[262] Harper, G.: A study of the use of linked routinely collected administrative data at the local level to count and profile populations. Ph.D. thesis, City, University of London (2017)

[263] Harper, G., Mayhew, L.: Using administrative data to count local populations. Applied Spatial Analysis and Policy **5**(2), 97–122 (2012)

[264] Harron, K., Dibben, C., Boyd, J., Hjern, A., Azimaee, M., Barreto, M.L., Goldstein, H.: Challenges in administrative data linkage for research. Big Data and Society **4**(2), 1–12 (2017)

[265] Harron, K., Gilbert, R., Cromwell, D., van der Meulen, J.: Linking data for mothers and babies in de-identified electronic health data. PLOS One **11**(10), 1–18 (2016)

[266] Harron, K., Goldstein, H., Dibben, C.: Methodological Developments in Data Linkage. John Wiley and Sons (2015)

[267] Harron, K., Wade, A., Gilbert, R., Muller-Pebody, B., Goldstein, H.: Evaluating bias due to data linkage error in electronic healthcare records. BMC Medical Research Methodology **14**(1), 36 (2014)

[268] Harron, K.L., Doidge, J.C., Knight, H.E., Gilbert, R.E., Goldstein, H., Cromwell, D.A., van der Meulen, J.H.: A guide to evaluating linkage quality for the analysis of linked data. International Journal of Epidemiology **46**(5), 1699–1710 (2017)

[269] Hassanzadeh, O., Chiang, F., Lee, H.C., Miller, R.J.: Framework for evaluating clustering algorithms in duplicate detection. VLDB Endowment **2**(1), 1282–1293 (2009)

[270] He, X., Machanavajjhala, A., Flynn, C., Srivastava, D.: Composing differential privacy and secure computation: A case study on scaling private record linkage. In: ACM Conference on Computer and Communications Security, pp. 1389–1406. Dallas (2017)

[271] van Herk-Sukel, M.P., Lemmens, V.E., van de Poll-Franse, L.V., Herings, R.M., Coebergh, J.W.W.: Record linkage for pharmacoepidemiological studies in cancer patients. Pharmacoepidemiology and Drug Safety **21**(1), 94–103 (2012)

[272] Hernandez, M.A., Stolfo, S.J.: The merge/purge problem for large databases. In: ACM Conference on Management of Data, pp. 127–138. San Jose (1995)

[273] Hernandez, M.A., Stolfo, S.J.: Real-world data is dirty: Data cleansing and the merge/purge problem. Data Mining and Knowledge Discovery **2**(1), 9–37 (1998)

[274] Herzog, T., Scheuren, F., Winkler, W.: Data Quality and Record Linkage Techniques. Springer Verlag (2007)

[275] Hill, K.: The secretive company that might end privacy as we know it. New York Times (2020)

[276] Hillestad, R., Bigelow, J.H., Chaudhry, B., Dreyer, P., Greenberg, M.D., Meili, R., Ridgely, M.S., Rothenberg, J., Taylor, R.: Identity crisis? An examination of the costs and benefits of a unique patient identifier for the US health care system. RAND Corporation (2008)

[277] Hintze, M., El Emam, K.: Comparing the benefits of pseudonymisation and anonymisation under the GDPR. Journal of Data Protection & Privacy **2**(2), 145–158 (2018)

[278] Hippisley-Cox, J.: Validity and completeness of the NHS Number in primary and secondary care: electronic data in England 1991-2013. Tech. rep., University of Nottingham (2013). URL http://eprints.nottingham.ac.uk/3153

[279] Hochbaum, D.S., Shmoys, D.B.: A best possible heuristic for the k-center problem. Mathematics of Operations Research **10**(2), 180–184 (1985)

[280] Hodges, S., Eitelhuber, T., Merchant, A., Alan, J.: Population data centre profile – the Western Australian Data Linkage Branch. International Journal of Population Data Science **4**(2) (2019)

[281] Hodgins, S., Janson, C.G.: Criminality and Violence among the Mentally Disordered: the Stockholm Metropolitan Project. Cambridge University Press, Cambridge, UK (2002)

[282] Holman, C.D.J., Bass, J.A., Rosman, D.L., Smith, M.B., Semmens, J.B., Glasson, E.J., Brook, E.L., Trutwein, B., Rouse, I.L., Watson, C.R., et al.: A decade of data linkage in Western Australia: strategic design, applications and benefits of the wa data linkage system. Australian Health Review **32**(4), 766–777 (2008)

[283] Holmes, D., McCabe, C.M.: Improving precision and recall for Soundex retrieval. In: IEEE ITCC. Las Vegas (2002)

[284] Honer, M.: BVerfG zu Recht auf Vergessen I und II Teil 2. Legal Tribune Online, https://www.lto.de/persistent/a_id/39109 (2019)

[285] Hoptroff, R., Mosquera, L., El Emam, K.: Practical Synthetic Data Generation. O'Reilly Media (2020)

[286] van den Hout, A., Elamir, E.A.H.: Statistical disclosure control using post randomisation: Variants and measures for disclosure risk. Journal of Official Statistics **22**(4), 711–731 (2006)

[287] Hu, Y., Wang, Q., Vatsalan, D., Christen, P.: Improving temporal record linkage using regression classification. In: Pacific-Asia Conference on Knowledge Discovery and Data Mining, pp. 561–573 (2017)

[288] Hundepool, A., Domingo-Ferrer, J., Franconi, L., Giessing, S., Schulte Nordholt, E., Spicer, K., de Wolf, P.: Statistical Disclosure Control. Wiley, Chichester (2012)

[289] Inan, A., Kantarcioglu, M., Bertino, E., Scannapieco, M.: A hybrid approach to private record linkage. In: IEEE International Conference on Data Engineering, pp. 496–505. Cancun (2008)

[290] Inan, A., Kantarcioglu, M., Ghinita, G., Bertino, E.: Private record matching using differential privacy. In: Conference on Extending Database Technology, pp. 123–134. Lausanne (2010)

[291] Indyk, P., Motwani, R.: Approximate nearest neighbors: towards removing the curse of dimensionality. In: Annual ACM Symposium on Theory of Computing, pp. 604–613. ACM (1998)

[292] Information Commissioner's Office: Data sharing code of practice (2011)

[293] Information Commissioner's Office: Anonymisation: Managing data protection risk code of practice (2012)

[294] Institute for Social and Economic Research: Linked understanding society – national pupil database wave 1 linkage user manual. UK Data Archive Study Number 7642, University of Essex, Colchester (2015)

[295] Institute of Medicine: Health Services Research: Opportunities for an Expanding Field of Inquiry. The National Academies Press, Washington, DC (1994)

[296] International Organization for Standardization: ISO 8601:2004 – Data elements and interchange formats – Information interchange – Representation of dates and times (2019)

[297] Izakian, H.: Privacy preserving record linkage meets record linkage using unencrypted data. International Journal of Population Data Science **3**(4), 61 (2018)

[298] Jacobs, J.A., Boulis, A., Messikomer, C.: The movement of physicians between specialties. Research in Social Stratification and Mobility **18**(1), 63–95 (2001)

[299] Jakobsen, T.: A fast method for cryptanalysis of substitution ciphers. Cryptologia **19**(3), 265–274 (1995)

[300] Japec, L., Kreuter, F., Berg, M., Biemer, P., Decker, P., Lampe, C., Lane, J., O'Neil, C., Usher, A.: Big data in survey research: AAPOR task force report. Public Opinion Quarterly **79**(4), 839–880 (2015)

[301] Jaro, M.A.: Advances in record-linkage methodology a applied to matching the 1985 Census of Tampa, Florida. Journal of the American Statistical Association **84**, 414–420 (1989)

[302] Jentzsch, N.: The Economics and Regulation of Financial Privacy: An International Comparison of Credit Reporting Systems. Physica-Verlag, Heidelberg (2006)

[303] Jiang, W., Clifton, C.: AC-framework for privacy-preserving collaboration. In: SIAM International Conference on Data Mining, pp. 47–56. Minneapolis (2007)

[304] Jiang, W., Clifton, C., Kantarcıoğlu, M.: Transforming semi-honest protocols to ensure accountability. Data and Knowledge Engineering **65**(1), 57–74 (2008)

[305] Jin, L., Li, C., Mehrotra, S.: Efficient record linkage in large data sets. In: Conference on Database Systems for Advanced Applications, pp. 137–146. Tokyo (2003)

[306] Johnson, W.: Understanding the genetics of intelligence: Can height help? Can corn oil? Current Directions in Psychological Science **19**(3), 177–182 (2010)

[307] Johnston, D.: Random Number Generators—Principles and Practices: A Guide for Engineers and Programmers. Walter de Gruyter GmbH & Co KG (2018)

[308] Jokinen, P., Tarhio, J., Ukkonen, E.: A comparison of approximate string matching algorithms. Software – Practice and Experience **26**(12), 1439–1458 (1996)

[309] Jonas, J., Harper, J.: Effective counterterrorism and the limited role of predictive data mining. Policy Analysis (584) (2006)

[310] Jones, K.H., Ford, D.V.: Population data science: advancing the safe use of population data for public benefit. Epidemiology and Health **40** (2018)

[311] Jones, K.H., Ford, D.V.: Privacy, confidentiality and practicalities in data linkage. National Statistician's Quality Review into Privacy and Data Confidentiality Methods, Government Statistical Service (2018)

[312] Jones, K.H., Ford, D.V., Jones, C., Dsilva, R., Thompson, S., Brooks, C.J., Heaven, M.L., Thayer, D.S., McNerney, C.L., Lyons, R.A.: A case study of the secure anonymous information linkage (SAIL) Gateway: a privacy-protecting remote access system for health-related research and evaluation. Journal of Biomedical Informatics **50**, 196–204 (2014)

[313] Jones, K.H., Heys, S., Tingay, K.S., Jackson, P., Dibben, C.: The Good, the Bad, the Clunky. International Journal of Population Data Science **4**(1) (2019)

[314] Jurczyk, P., Lu, J., Xiong, L., Cragan, J., Correa, A.: FRIL: A tool for comparative record linkage. In: AMIA Annual Symposium Proceedings, p. 440. American Medical Informatics Association (2008)

[315] Kalashnikov, D., Mehrotra, S.: Domain-independent data cleaning via analysis of entity-relationship graph. ACM Transactions on Database Systems **31**(2), 716–767 (2006)

[316] Kalkman, S., Mostert, M., Gerlinger, C., van Delden, J.J.M., van Thiel, G.J.M.W.: Responsible data sharing in international health research: a systematic review of principles and norms. BMC Medical Ethics **20** (2019)

[317] Kalton, G.: Designs for surveys over time. In: D. Pfeffermann, C.R. Rao (eds.) Handbook of Statistics: Sample Surveys, vol. 29A, pp. 89–108. Elsevier, Amsterdam (2009)

[318] Kantarcioglu, M., Inan, A., Jiang, W., Malin, B.: Formal anonymity models for efficient privacy-preserving joins. Data and Knowledge Engineering **68**(11), 1206–1223 (2009)

[319] Kantarcioglu, M., Jiang, W., Malin, B.: A privacy-preserving framework for integrating person-specific databases. In: Privacy in Statistical Databases, pp. 298–314. Istanbul (2008)

[320] Karakasidis, A., Koloniari, G., Verykios, V.S.: Scalable blocking for privacy preserving record linkage. In: ACM Conference on Knowledge Discovery and Data Mining, pp. 527–536. Sydney (2015)

[321] Karakasidis, A., Verykios, V.S.: Privacy preserving record linkage using phonetic codes. In: Fourth Balkan Conference in Informatics, pp. 101–106. Thessaloniki (2009)

[322] Karakasidis, A., Verykios, V.S.: Secure blocking + secure matching = secure record linkage. Journal of Computing Science and Engineering **5**(3) (2011)

[323] Karakasidis, A., Verykios, V.S.: Reference table based k-anonymous private blocking. In: ACM Symposium on Applied Computing, pp. 859–864. Trento, Italy (2012)

[324] Karakasidis, A., Verykios, V.S.: A sorted neighborhood approach to multidimensional privacy preserving blocking. In: IEEE ICDM Workshops, pp. 937–944. Brussels (2012)

[325] Karakasidis, A., Verykios, V.S., Christen, P.: Fake injection strategies for private phonetic matching. In: International Workshop on Data Privacy Management. Leuven, Belgium (2011)

[326] Karapiperis, D., Gkoulalas-Divanis, A., Verykios, V.S.: LSHDB: a parallel and distributed engine for record linkage and similarity search. In: IEEE ICDM Workshops, pp. 1–4. Barcelona (2016)

[327] Karapiperis, D., Gkoulalas-Divanis, A., Verykios, V.S.: Distance-aware encoding of numerical values for privacy-preserving record linkage. In: IEEE International Conference on Data Engineering, pp. 135–138. San Diego (2017)

[328] Karapiperis, D., Gkoulalas-Divanis, A., Verykios, V.S.: FEDERAL: A framework for distance-aware privacy-preserving record linkage. Transactions on Knowledge and Data Engineering **30**(2), 292–304 (2017)

[329] Karapiperis, D., Gkoulalas-Divanis, A., Verykios, V.S.: FEMRL: A framework for large-scale privacy-preserving linkage of patients' electronic health records. In: IEEE International Smart Cities Conference, pp. 1–8. Kansas City (2018)

[330] Karapiperis, D., Gkoulalas-Divanis, A., Verykios, V.S.: Summarizing and linking electronic health records. Distributed and Parallel Databases pp. 1–40 (2019)

[331] Karapiperis, D., Vatsalan, D., Verykios, V.S., Christen, P.: Large-scale multi-party counting set intersection using a space efficient global synopsis. In: Conference on Database Systems for Advanced Applications, pp. 329–345. Hanoi (2015)

[332] Karapiperis, D., Verykios, V.S.: A distributed near-optimal LSH-based framework for privacy-preserving record linkage. Computer Science and Information Systems **11**(2), 745–763 (2014)

[333] Karapiperis, D., Verykios, V.S.: An LSH-based blocking approach with a homomorphic matching technique for privacy-preserving record linkage. Transactions on Knowledge and Data Engineering **27**(4), 909 – 921 (2015)

[334] Karapiperis, D., Verykios, V.S.: A fast and efficient Hamming LSH-based scheme for accurate linkage. Knowledge and Information Systems **49**(3), 861–884 (2016)

[335] Karmel, R.: Data linkage protocols using a statistical linkage key. Australian Institute of Health and Welfare (CS1) (2005)

[336] Karnin, E., Greene, J., Hellman, M.: On secret sharing systems. Transactions on Information Theory **29**(1), 35–41 (1983)

[337] Katikireddi, S.V., Whitley, E., Lewsey, J., Gray, L., Leyland, A.H.: Socioeconomic status as an effect modifier of alcohol consumption and harm: analysis of linked cohort data. The Lancet Public Health **2**(6), e267–e276 (2017)

[338] Katz, A., Enns, J., Smith, M., Burchill, C., Turner, K.: Population data centre profiles: Centre for data linkage. Population Data Centre Profile: The Manitoba Centre for Health Policy **4**(2) (2019)

[339] Kawai, H., Garcia-Molina, H., Benjelloun, O., Menestrina, D., Whang, E., Gong, H.: P-Swoosh: Parallel algorithm for generic entity resolution. Tech. Rep. 2006-19, Department of Computer Science, Stanford University (2006)

[340] Kelman, C.W., Bass, J., Holman, D.: Research use of linked health data – A best practice protocol. Aust NZ Journal of Public Health **26**, 251–255 (2002)

[341] Kendrick, S.: The development of record linkage in Scotland: The responsive application of probabilistic matching. In: Record Linkage Techniques, pp. 319–332. Arlington (1997)

[342] Kerckhoffs, A.: Military cryptography. French Journal of Military Science (1883)

[343] Keskustalo, H., Pirkola, A., Visala, K., Leppanen, E., Jarvelin, K.: Nonadjacent digrams improve matching of cross-lingual spelling variants. In: String Processing and Information Retrieval, pp. 252–265. Manaus, Brazil (2003)

[344] Kessler, G.C.: An overview of cryptography. Handbook on Local Area Networks, Auerbach (1998)

[345] Kho, A.N., Cashy, J.P., Jackson, K.L., Pah, A.R., Goel, S., Boehnke, J., Humphries, J.E., Kominers, S.D., Hota, B.N., Sims, S.A., et al.: Design and implementation of a privacy preserving electronic health record linkage tool in Chicago. Journal of the American Medical Informatics Association **22**(5), 1072–1080 (2015)

[346] Kifer, D., Machanavajjhala, A.: Pufferfish: A framework for mathematical privacy definitions. ACM Transactions on Database Systems **39**(1), 1–36 (2014)

[347] Kim, D., Solomon, M.G.: Fundamentals of Information Systems Security, 3 edn. Jones and Bartlett Learning, Burlington (2018)

[348] Kim, H., Lee, D.: Parallel linkage. In: ACM Conference on Information and Knowledge Management, pp. 283–292. Lisboa (2007)

[349] Kim, H., Lee, D.: HARRA: fast iterative hashed record linkage for large-scale data collections. In: Conference on Extending Database Technology, pp. 525–536. Lausanne (2010)

[350] Kim, J.J.: A method for limiting disclosure in microdata based on random noise and transformation. In: Proceedings of the Section on Survey Research Methods, pp. 303–308. American Statistical Association (1986)

[351] Kirielle, N., Christen, P., Ranbaduge, T.: Outlier detection based accurate geocoding of historical addresses. In: Australasian Data Mining Conference, pp. 41–53. Adelaide (2019)

[352] Kirsch, A., Mitzenmacher, M.: Less hashing, same performance: building a better Bloom filter. In: European Symposium on Algorithms, pp. 456–467. Zürich (2006)

[353] Kirsten, T., Kolb, L., Hartung, M., Gross, A., Köpcke, H., Rahm, E.: Data partitioning for parallel entity matching. VLDB Endowment **3**(2) (2010)

[354] Klingwort, J., Buelens, B., Schnell, R.: Capture-recapture techniques for transport survey estimate adjustment using permanently installed highway-sensors. Social Science Computer Review (2019)

[355] Knuth, D.E.: The Art of Computer Programming: Seminumerical Algorithms, vol. 2. Addison Wesley Publishing Company (1969)

[356] Knuth, D.E.: Big omicron and big omega and big theta. ACM SIGACT News **8**(2), 18–24 (1976)

[357] Knuth, D.E.: Efficient balanced codes. Transactions on Information Theory **32**(1), 51–53 (1986)

[358] Kolb, L., Thor, A., Rahm, E.: Dedoop: Efficient deduplication with Hadoop. VLDB Endowment **5**(12), 1878–1881 (2012)

[359] Kong, C., Gao, M., Xu, C., Qian, W., Zhou, A.: Entity matching across multiple heterogeneous data sources. In: Conference on Database Systems for Advanced Applications, pp. 133–146. Dallas (2016)

[360] Köpcke, H., Rahm, E.: Frameworks for entity matching: A comparison. Data and Knowledge Engineering **69**(2), 197–210 (2010)

[361] Köpcke, H., Thor, A., Rahm, E.: Evaluation of entity resolution approaches on real-world match problems. VLDB Endowment **3**(1-2), 484–493 (2010)

[362] Körner, T., Krause, A., Ramsauer, K., Ullmann, P.: Registernutzung in Zensus und Bevölkerungsstatistik in Österreich und der Schweiz. Destatis, Wiesbaden (2017)

[363] Kosa, T.A., El-Khatib, K., Marsh, S.: Measuring privacy. Journal of Internet Services and Information Security **1**(4), 60–73 (2011)

[364] Krawczyk, H., Bellare, M., Canetti, R.: HMAC: Keyed-hashing for message authentication. In: Internet RFCs (1997)

[365] Krieger, J.P., Cabaset, S., Pestoni, G., Rohrmann, S., Faeh, D., Swiss National Cohort Study Group, et al.: Dietary patterns are associated with cardiovascular and cancer mortality among Swiss adults in a census-linked cohort. Nutrients **10**(3), 313 (2018)

[366] Kristensen, T.G., Nielsen, J., Pedersen, C.N.: A tree-based method for the rapid screening of chemical fingerprints. Algorithms for Molecular Biology **5**(1), 9 (2010)

[367] Kroll, M., Steinmetzer, S.: Who is 1011011111...1110110010? Automated cryptanalysis of Bloom filter encryptions of databases with several personal identifiers. In: International Joint Conference on Biomedical Engineering Systems and Technologies, pp. 341–356. Lisbon (2015)

[368] Krumm, J.: A survey of computational location privacy. Personal and Ubiquitous Computing **13**(6), 391–399 (2009)

[369] Kukich, K.: Techniques for automatically correcting words in text. ACM Computing Surveys **24**(4), 377–439 (1992)

[370] Kum, H.C., Krishnamurthy, A., Machanavajjhala, A., Reiter, M.K., Ahalt, S.: Privacy preserving interactive record linkage (PPIRL). Journal of the American Medical Informatics Association **21**(2), 212–220 (2014)

[371] Kuzu, M., Kantarcioglu, M., Durham, E., Malin, B.: A constraint satisfaction cryptanalysis of Bloom filters in private record linkage. In: Privacy Enhancing Technologies Symposium, pp. 226–245. Waterloo, Canada (2011)

[372] Kuzu, M., Kantarcioglu, M., Durham, E., Toth, C., Malin, B.: A practical approach to achieve private medical record linkage in light of public resources. Journal of the American Medical Informatics Association **20**(2), 285–292 (2013)

[373] Kuzu, M., Kantarcioglu, M., Inan, A., Bertino, E., Durham, E., Malin, B.: Efficient privacy-aware record integration. In: Conference on Extending Database Technology. Genoa (2013)

[374] Lai, P., Yiu, S., Chow, K., Chong, C., Hui, L.: An efficient Bloom filter based solution for multiparty private matching. In: Security and Management, p. 7. Las Vegas (2006)

[375] Lait, A., Randell, B.: An assessment of name matching algorithms. Tech. rep., Department of Computer Science, University of Newcastle upon Tyne (1993)

[376] Lambert, D.: Measures of disclosure risk and harm. Journal of Official Statistics **9**, 313–313 (1993)

[377] Larsen, M.D.: Record linkage, nondisclosure, counterterrorism, and statistics. In: Survey Methods Section, Canadian Statistical Society. London (2006)

[378] Lateral Economics: Valuing the Australian census (2019). URL https://www.abs.gov.au/websitedbs/D3310114.nsf/home/Value+of+the+Australian+Census

[379] Laufer, R.S., Wolfe, M.: Privacy as a concept and a social issue: A multidimensional developmental theory. Journal of Social Issues **33**(3), 22–42 (1977)

[380] Lauter, K., Naehrig, M., Vaikuntanathan, V.: Can homomorphic encryption be practical? In: ACM Cloud Computing Security Workshop, pp. 113–124. Chicago (2011)

[381] Lawrence, G., Dinh, I., Taylor, L.: The centre for health record linkage: a new resource for health services research and evaluation. Health Information Management Journal **37**(2), 60–62 (2008)

[382] Lazrig, I., Moataz, T., Ray, I., Ray, I., Ong, T., Kahn, M., Cuppens, F., Cuppens, N.: Privacy preserving record matching using automated semi-trusted broker. In: IFIP Data and Applications Security and Privacy, pp. 103–118. Fairfax, Virginia (2015)

[383] Lazrig, I., Ong, T., Ray, I., Ray, I., Jiang, X., Vaidya, J.: Privacy preserving probabilistic record linkage without trusted third party. In: Privacy, Security and Trust, pp. 1–10. Belfast (2018)

[384] Lee, Y., Pipino, L., Funk, J., Wang, R.: Journey to Data Quality. The MIT Press (2009)

[385] Leskovec, J., Rajaraman, A., Ullman, J.D.: Mining of Massive Datasets. Cambridge University Press (2014)

[386] Levenshtein, V.I.: Binary codes capable of correcting deletions, insertions, and reversals. Soviet Physics Doklady **10**(8), 707–710 (1966)

[387] Leyland, A., Barnard, M., McKeganey, N.: The use of capture-recapture methodology to estimate and describe covert populations: an application to female street-working prostitution in Glasgow. Bulletin de Methodologie Sociologique **38**, 52–73 (1993)

[388] Li, F., Chen, Y., Luo, B., Lee, D., Liu, P.: Privacy preserving group linkage. In: Scientific and Statistical Database Management, pp. 432–450. Portland (2011)

[389] Li, J., Baig, M.M., Sattar, A.S., Ding, X., Liu, J., Vincent, M.W.: A hybrid approach to prevent composition attacks for independent data releases. Information Sciences **367**, 324–336 (2016)

[390] Li, N., Li, T., Venkatasubramanian, S.: t-closeness: Privacy beyond k-anonymity and l-diversity. In: IEEE International Conference on Data Engineering, pp. 106–115. Istanbul (2007)

[391] Li, N., Lyu, M., Su, D., Yang, W.: Differential Privacy: From Theory to Practice. Synthesis Lectures on Information Security, Privacy, and Trust. Morgan and Claypool Publishers (2017)

[392] Li, P., Dong, X., Maurino, A., Srivastava, D.: Linking temporal records. VLDB Endowment **4**(11) (2011)

[393] Lin, J.: Scalable language processing algorithms for the masses: A case study in computing word co-occurrence matrices with mapreduce. In: Empirical Methods in Natural Language Processing, pp. 419–428. Honolulu (2008)

[394] Lindell, Y., Pinkas, B.: Secure multiparty computation for privacy-preserving data mining. Journal of Privacy and Confidentiality **1**(1), 5 (2009)

[395] Little, R.J.: A test of missing completely at random for multivariate data with missing values. Journal of the American Statistical Association **83**(404), 1198–1202 (1988)

[396] Little, R.J.A., Rubin, D.B.: Statistical Analysis with Missing Data, 3 edn. Wiley, Hoboken (2020)

[397] Liu, H., Wang, H., Chen, Y.: Ensuring data storage security against frequency-based attacks in wireless networks. In: Distributed Computing in Sensor Systems, pp. 201–215. Santa Barbara (2010)

[398] Lohr, S.: For big-data scientists,'janitor work' is key hurdle to insights. New York Times **17**, B4 (2014)

[399] Lyons, R.A., Ford, D.V., Moore, L., Rodgers, S.E.: Use of data linkage to measure the population health effect of non-health-care interventions. The Lancet **383**(9927), 1517–1519 (2014)

[400] Machanavajjhala, A., Gehrke, J., Kifer, D.: l-density: Privacy beyond k-anonymity. In: IEEE International Conference on Data Engineering. Atlanta (2006)

[401] Manning, C., Schütze, H.: Foundations of Statistical Natural Language Processing. MIT Press (1999)

[402] Martini, M., Kienle, T., Wagner, D., Weinzierl, Q., Wenzel, M.: Rechtliche Rahmenbedingungen für ein nationales Bildungsregister. Legal Expertise on Behalf of the Federal Ministry of Education and Research (BMBF), Speyer (2019)

[403] Martini, M., Wagner, D., Wenzel, M.: Rechtliche Grenzen einer Personen- bzw. Unternehmenskennziffer in staatlichen Registern. Speyer (2017)

[404] Massey, C.G., Genadek, K.R., Alexander, J.T., Gardner, T.K., O'Hara, A.: Linking the 1940 U.S. Census with modern data. Historical Methods: A Journal of Quantitative and Interdisciplinary History **51**(4), 246–257 (2018)

[405] Matwin, S., Nin, J., Sehatkar, M., Szapiro, T.: A review of attribute disclosure control. In: G. Navarro-Arribas, v. Torra (eds.) Advanced Research in Data Privacy, pp. 41–61. Springer (2015)

[406] Maxfield, M.G., Weiler, B.L., Widom, C.S.: Comparing self-reports and official records of arrests. Journal of Quantitative Criminology **16**(1), 87–110 (2000)

[407] McCallum, A., Nigam, K., Ungar, L.H.: Efficient clustering of high-dimensional data sets with application to reference matching. In: ACM Conference on Knowledge Discovery and Data Mining, pp. 169–178. Boston (2000)

[408] McCreight, E.: A space-economical suffix tree construction algorithm. Journal of the ACM **23**(2) (1976)

[409] McKeganey, N., Barnard, M., Leyland, A., Coote, I., Follet, E.: Female streetworking prostitution and HIV infection in Glasgow. British Medical Journal **305**(6857), 801–804 (1992)

[410] Meier, J., Jakscha, T., Schnell, R., Heller, G.: Verknüpfung der Module Geburtshilfe und Neonatologie des QS-Verfahrens Perinatalmedizin. technical report, IQTIG, Berlin (2017). URL https://iqtig.org/downloads/spezifikation/2018/v01/TechDok_Verknuepfung_Peri_Neo_V03.pdf

[411] Menard, S. (ed.): Handbook of Longitudinal Research: Design, Measurement, and Analysis. Elsevier, Amsterdam (2007)

[412] Mészáros, J., Ho, C.h.: Big data and scientific research: The secondary use of personal data under the research exemption in the GDPR. Hungarian Journal of Legal Studies **59**(4), 403–419 (2018)

[413] Meyer, B.D., Mok, W.K., Sullivan, J.X.: Household surveys in crisis. Journal of Economic Perspectives **29**(4), 199–226 (2015)

[414] Mitchell, R.J., Cameron, C.M., McClure, R.J., Williamson, A.M.: Data linkage capabilities in Australia: Practical issues identified by a Population Health Research Network 'proof of concept project'. Australian and New Zealand Journal of Public Health **39**(4), 319–325 (2015)

[415] Mitchell, W., Dewri, R., Thurimella, R., Roschke, M.: A graph traversal attack on Bloom filter-based medical data aggregation. International Journal of Big Data Intelligence **4**(4), 217–226 (2017)

[416] Mittelstadt, B., Benzler, J., Engelmann, L., Prainsack, B., Vayena, E.: Is there a duty to participate in digital epidemiology? Life Sciences, Society and Policy **14**(1), 9 (2018)

[417] Mitzenmacher, M., Upfal, E.: Probability and Computing: Randomized Algorithms and Probabilistic Analysis. Cambridge University Press, Cambridge (2005)

[418] Mohammed, N., Fung, B.C., Debbabi, M.: Anonymity meets game theory: secure data integration with malicious participants. VLDB Journal **20**(4), 567–588 (2011)

[419] Mondschein, C.F., Monda, C.: The EU's General Data Protection Regulation (GDPR) in a Research Context. In: P. Kubben, M. Dumontier, A. Dekker (eds.) Fundamentals of Clinical Data Science, pp. 55–71. Springer (2019)

[420] Monge, A.E.: Matching algorithms within a duplicate detection system. IEEE Data Engineering Bulletin **23**(4), 14–20 (2000)

[421] Monge, A.E., Elkan, C.P.: The field-matching problem: Algorithm and applications. In: ACM Conference on Knowledge Discovery and Data Mining, pp. 267–270. Portland (1996)

[422] Moore, H.C., Guiver, T., Woollacott, A., de Klerk, N., Gidding, H.F.: Establishing a process for conducting cross-jurisdictional record linkage in Australia. Australian and New Zealand Journal of Public Health **40**(2), 159–164 (2016)

[423] Mulder, T., Tudorica, M.: Privacy policies, cross-border health data and the GDPR. Information and Communications Technology Law **28**(3), 261–274 (2019)

[424] Muralidhar, K., Sarathy, R.: Data shuffling – a new masking approach for numerical data. Management Science **52**(5), 658–670 (2006)

[425] Nanayakkara, C., Christen, P., Ranbaduge, T.: Robust temporal graph clustering for group record linkage. In: Pacific-Asia Conference on Knowledge Discovery and Data Mining, pp. 526–538. Macau (2019)

[426] Nanayakkara, C., Christen, P., Ranbaduge, T., Garrett, E.: Evaluation measure for group-based record linkage. International Journal of Population Data Science **4**(1) (2019)

[427] National Academies of Sciences, Engineering, and Medicine: Reducing Response Burden in the American Community Survey. National Academies Press, Washington, D.C. (2016)

[428] National Academies of Sciences, Engineering, and Medicine: Improving the American Community Survey. Washington, DC (2019)

[429] National Data Guardian: Review of data security, consent and opt-outs. Document 2904918 (2016)

[430] National Health and Medical Research Council: National statement on ethical conduct in human research. www.nhmrc.gov.au/file/9131 (2018)

[431] National Research Council: Protecting Individual Privacy in the Struggle Against Terrorists: a Framework for Program Assessment. National Academy of Sciences, Washington, DC (2008)

[432] Naumann, F., Herschel, M.: An Introduction to Duplicate Detection. Synthesis Lectures on Data Management. Morgan and Claypool Publishers (2010)

[433] Navarro, G.: A guided tour to approximate string matching. ACM Computing Surveys **33**(1), 31–88 (2001)

[434] Neubauer, T., Heurix, J.: A methodology for the pseudonymization of medical data. International Journal of Medical Informatics **80**(3), 190–204 (2011)

[435] Newcombe, H., Kennedy, J.: Record linkage: making maximum use of the discriminating power of identifying information. Communications of the ACM **5**(11), 563–566 (1962)

[436] Newcombe, H., Kennedy, J., Axford, S., James, A.: Automatic linkage of vital records. Science **130**(3381), 954–959 (1959)

[437] Newcombe, H.B.: Handbook of Record Linkage: Methods for Health and Statistical Studies, Administration, and Business. Oxford University Press, Inc., New York (1988)

[438] Niedermeyer, F., Steinmetzer, S., Kroll, M., Schnell, R.: Cryptanalysis of basic Bloom filters used for privacy preserving record linkage. Journal of Privacy and Confidentiality **6**(2), 59–79 (2014)

[439] Nisbet, M.C., Nisbet, E.C.: The Public Face of Science Across the World. American Academy of Arts and Sciences (2019)

[440] Nissenbaum, H.: Privacy in Context: Technology, Policy, and the Integrity of Social Life. Stanford University Press, Stanford (2010)

[441] Nissenbaum, H.: Contextual integrity up and down the data food chain. Theoretical Inquiries in Law **20**(1), 221–256 (2019)

[442] Nissim, K., Steinke, T., Wood, A., Altman, M., Bembenek, A., Bun, M., Gaboardi, M., O'Brien, D.R., Vadhan, S.: Differential privacy: A primer for a non-technical audience. In: Privacy Law Scholars Conference. Berkeley (2017)

[443] Norberg, P.A., Horne, D.R., Horne, D.A.: The privacy paradox: Personal information disclosure intentions versus behaviors. Journal of Consumer Affairs **41**(1), 100–126 (2007)

[444] Obar, J.A., Oeldorf-Hirsch, A.: The biggest lie on the Internet: ignoring the privacy policies and terms of service policies of social networking services. Information, Communication and Society pp. 1–20 (2018)

[445] OECD: Health Data Governance: Privacy, Monitoring and Research. OECD Publishing, Paris (2015)

[446] Office for National Statistics: Beyond 2011 matching anonymous data (2013). Methods and Policies Report M9

[447] Office for National Statistics: Beyond 2011 safeguarding data for research: Our policy (2013). Methods and Policies Report M10

[448] Office for National Statistics: 2011 census England and Wales general report (2015)

[449] Office for National Statistics: 2011 census benefits evaluation report (2019). URL https://www.ons.

```
gov.uk/census/2011census/2011censusbenefits/
2011censusbenefitsevaluationreport
```
[450] O'Hare, W.P.: Differential Undercounts in the U.S. Census: Who is Missed? Springer, Cham (2019)

[451] Ohm, P.: Broken promises of privacy: Responding to the surprising failure of anonymization. UCLA Law Review **57**, 1701 (2009)

[452] Ohm, P.: Sensitive information. Southern California Law Review **88**, 1125–1196 (2014)

[453] O'Keefe, C., Yung, M., Gu, L., Baxter, R.: Privacy-preserving data linkage protocols. In: ACM Workshop on Privacy in the Electronic Society, pp. 94–102. Washington DC (2004)

[454] O'Keefe, C.M., Rubin, D.B.: Individual privacy versus public good: protecting confidentiality in health research. Statistics in Medicine **34**(23), 3081–3103 (2015)

[455] Ong, T.C., Mannino, M.V., Schilling, L.M., Kahn, M.G.: Improving record linkage performance in the presence of missing linkage data. Journal of Biomedical Informatics **52**, 43–54 (2014)

[456] Paillier, P.: Public-key cryptosystems based on composite degree residuosity classes. In: Theory and Application of Cryptographic Techniques, pp. 223–238. Prague (1999)

[457] Panel for the Future of Science and Technology: How the General Data Protection Regulation changes the rules for scientific research. European Parliamentary Research Service (2019)

[458] Pang, C., Gu, L., Hansen, D., Maeder, A.: Privacy-preserving fuzzy matching using a public reference table. In: S. McClean, P. Millard, E. El-Darzi, C. Nugent (eds.) Intelligent Patient Management, pp. 71–89. Springer (2009)

[459] Papadakis, G., Alexiou, G., Papastefanatos, G., Koutrika, G.: Schema-agnostic vs schema-based configurations for blocking methods on homogeneous data. VLDB Endowment **9**(4), 312–323 (2015)

[460] Papadakis, G., Ioannou, E., Palpanas, T., Niederee, C., Nejdl, W.: A blocking framework for entity resolution in highly heterogeneous information spaces. Transactions on Knowledge and Data Engineering **25**(12), 2665–2682 (2012)

[461] Papadakis, G., Palpanas, T.: Blocking for large-scale entity resolution: challenges, algorithms, and practical examples. In: IEEE International Conference on Data Engineering, pp. 1436–1439. Helsinki (2016)

[462] Papadakis, G., Skoutas, D., Thanos, E., Palpanas, T.: Blocking and filtering techniques for entity resolution: A survey. ACM Computing Surveys **53**(2), 1–42 (2020)

[463] Papadakis, G., Svirsky, J., Gal, A., Palpanas, T.: Comparative analysis of approximate blocking techniques for entity resolution. VLDB Endowment **9**(9), 684–695 (2016)

[464] Park, J., Sandhu, R.: Towards usage control models: beyond traditional access control. In: ACM Symposium on Access Control Models and Technologies, pp. 57–64. Monterey (2002)

[465] Parker, M.: Humble Pi – A Comedy of Maths Errors. Penguin Random House (2019)

[466] Paterson, M., McDonagh, M.: Data protection in an era of Big data: The challenges posed by big personal data. Monash University Law Review **44**(1) (2018)

[467] Patman, F., Thompson, P.: Names: A new frontier in text mining. In: Intelligence and Security Informatics, pp. 27–38. Tuscon (2003)

[468] Patrascu, M., Thorup, M.: The power of simple tabulation hashing. In: ACM Symposium on Theory of Computing, pp. 1–10. San Jose (2011)

[469] Paul, C., Noel, H., Charles, A., Jeffrey, W., Daniel, E.: Options for encoding name information for use in record linkage. Tech. Rep. 1351.0.55.162, Australian Bureau of Statistics, Canberra (2018)

[470] Perlman, R.: An overview of PKI trust models. IEEE Network **13**(6), 38–43 (1999)

[471] Petrila, J.: Legal issues in the use of electronic data systems for social science research. In: J. Fantuzzo, D.P. Culhane (eds.) Actionable Intelligence, pp. 39–75. Palgrave Macmillan US, New York (2015)

[472] Philips, L.: The double-metaphone search algorithm. C/C++ User's Journal **18**(6) (2000)

[473] Phua, C., Smith-Miles, K., Lee, V., Gayler, R.: Resilient identity crime detection. IEEE Transactions on Knowledge and Data Engineering **24**(3) (2012)

[474] Pita, R., Mendonça, E., Reis, S., Barreto, M., Denaxas, S.: A machine learning trainable model to assess the accuracy of probabilistic record linkage. In: Big Data Analytics and Knowledge Discovery, pp. 214–227. Lyon (2017)

[475] Pita, R., Pinto, C., Sena, S., Fiaccone, R., Amorim, L., Reis, S., Barreto, M., Denaxas, S., Barreto, M.: On the accuracy and scalability of probabilistic data linkage over the Brazilian 114 million cohort. Journal of Biomedical and Health Informatics **22**(2), 346–353 (2018)

[476] Pöge, A.: Persönliche Codes bei Längsschnittuntersuchungen III. Methoden – Daten – Analysen **5**(1), 109–134 (2011)

[477] Pollock, J.J., Zamora, A.: Automatic spelling correction in scientific and scholarly text. Communications of the ACM **27**(4), 358–368 (1984)

[478] Porter, E.H., Winkler, W.E.: Approximate string comparison and its effect on an advanced record linkage system. Tech. Rep. RR97/02, US Bureau of the Census (1997)

[479] Postel, H.J.: Die Kölner Phonetik: Ein Verfahren zur Identifizierung von Personennamen auf der Grundlage der Gestaltanalyse. IBM-Nachrichten **19**, 925–931 (1969)

[480] Pow, C., Iron, K., Boyd, J., Brown, A., Thompson, S., Chong, N., Ma, C.: Privacy-preserving record linkage: an international collabora-

tion between Canada, Australia and Wales. International Journal for Population Data Science **1**(1) (2017)

[481] Preisendörfer, P., Wolter, F.: Who is telling the truth? a validation study on determinants of response behavior in surveys. Public Opinion Quarterly **78**(1), 126–146 (2014)

[482] Prewitt, K.: Why it matters to distinguish between privacy and confidentiality. Journal of Privacy and Confidentiality **3**(2), 41–47 (2011)

[483] Productivity Commission: Data availability and use. Report No. 82, Canberra (2017)

[484] Pyle, D.: Data Preparation for Data Mining. Morgan Kaufmann (1999)

[485] Quantin, C., Benzenine, E., Allaert, F., Guesdon, M., Gouyon, J., Riandey, B.: Epidemiological and statistical secured matching in France. Statistical Journal of the IAOS **30**(3), 255–261 (2014)

[486] Quantin, C., Bouzelat, H., Allaert, F., Benhamiche, A., Faivre, J., Dusserre, L.: How to ensure data quality of an epidemiological follow-up: Quality assessment of an anonymous record linkage procedure. International Journal of Medical Informatics **49**(1), 117–122 (1998)

[487] Quantin, C., Bouzelat, H., Allaert, F.A., Benhamiche, A.M., Faivre, J., Dusserre, L.: Automatic record hash coding and linkage for epidemiological follow-up data confidentiality. Methods of Information in Medicine **37**(3), 271–277 (1998)

[488] Quantin, C., Bouzelat, H., Dusserre, L.: Irreversible encryption method by generation of polynomials. Medical Informatics and the Internet in Medicine **21**(2), 113–121 (1996)

[489] Rabin, M.O.: How to exchange secrets with oblivious transfer. Tech. Rep. TR-81, Aiken Computation Lab, Harvard University (1981)

[490] Ragan, E.D., Kum, H.C., Ilangovan, G., Wang, H.: Balancing privacy and information disclosure in interactive record linkage with visual masking. In: Human Factors in Computing Systems, pp. 1–12. Montreal (2018)

[491] Rahm, E., Do, H.H.: Data cleaning: Problems and current approaches. IEEE Data Engineering Bulletin **23**(4), 3–13 (2000)

[492] Ramadan, B., Christen, P.: Unsupervised blocking key selection for real-time entity resolution. In: Pacific-Asia Conference on Knowledge Discovery and Data Mining, pp. 574–585. Ho Chi Minh City (2015)

[493] Ramadan, B., Christen, P., Liang, H., Gayler, R.W.: Dynamic sorted neighborhood indexing for real-time entity resolution. ACM Journal of Data and Information Quality **6**(4), 15 (2015)

[494] Ranbaduge, T.: A scalable blocking framework for multidatabase privacy-preserving record linkage. Ph.D. thesis, Research School of Computer Science, The Australian National University (2018)

[495] Ranbaduge, T., Christen, P.: Privacy-preserving temporal record linkage. In: IEEE International Conference on Data Mining, pp. 377–386. Singapore (2018)

[496] Ranbaduge, T., Christen, P.: A scalable privacy-preserving framework for temporal record linkage. Knowledge and Information Systems pp. 1–34 (2018)

[497] Ranbaduge, T., Christen, P., Schnell, R.: Secure and accurate two-step hash encoding for privacy-preserving record linkage. In: Pacific-Asia Conference on Knowledge Discovery and Data Mining. Singapore (2020)

[498] Ranbaduge, T., Christen, P., Vatsalan, D.: Tree based scalable indexing for multi-party privacy-preserving record linkage. In: Australasian Data Mining Conference, vol. 158. Brisbane (2014)

[499] Ranbaduge, T., Christen, P., Vatsalan, D.: Clustering-based scalable indexing for multi-party privacy-preserving record linkage. In: Pacific-Asia Conference on Knowledge Discovery and Data Mining. Hanoi (2015)

[500] Ranbaduge, T., Schnell, R.: Securing Bloom filters for privacy-preserving record linkage. In: ACM Conference on Information and Knowledge Management. Galway (2020)

[501] Ranbaduge, T., Vatsalan, D., Christen, P.: Scalable block scheduling for efficient multi-database record linkage. In: IEEE International Conference on Data Mining, pp. 1161–1166. Barcelona (2016)

[502] Ranbaduge, T., Vatsalan, D., Christen, P.: Secure multi-party summation protocols: Are they secure enough under collusion? Transactions on Data Privacy **13**(1), 25–60 (2020)

[503] Ranbaduge, T., Vatsalan, D., Christen, P., Verykios, V.S.: Hashing-based distributed multi-party blocking for privacy-preserving record linkage. In: Pacific-Asia Conference on Knowledge Discovery and Data Mining, pp. 415–427. Auckland (2016)

[504] Randall, S.M., Boyd, J.H., Ferrante, A.M., Bauer, J.K., Semmens, J.B.: Use of graph theory measures to identify errors in record linkage. Computer Methods and Programs in Biomedicine **115**(2), 55–63 (2014)

[505] Randall, S.M., Brown, A.P., Ferrante, A.M., Boyd, J.H.: Privacy preserving linkage using multiple dynamic match keys. International Journal of Population Data Science **4**(1) (2019)

[506] Randall, S.M., Brown, A.P., Ferrante, A.M., Boyd, J.J., Semmens, J.B.: Privacy preserving record linkage using homomorphic encryption. In: Workshop Population Informatics for Big Data, held at ACM SIGKDD. Sydney (2015)

[507] Randall, S.M., Ferrante, A.M., Boyd, J.H., Bauer, J.K., Semmens, J.B.: Privacy-preserving record linkage on large real world datasets. Journal of Biomedical Informatics **50**, 205–212 (2014)

[508] Randall, S.M., Ferrante, A.M., Boyd, J.H., Brown, A.P., Semmens, J.B.: Limited privacy protection and poor sensitivity: Is it time to move on from the statistical linkage key-581? Health Information Management Journal **45**(2), 71–79 (2016)

[509] Randall, S.M., Ferrante, A.M., Boyd, J.H., Semmens, J.B.: The effect of data cleaning on record linkage quality. BMC Medical Informatics and Decision Making **13**(1), 64 (2013)

[510] Rao, F.Y., Cao, J., Bertino, E., Kantarcioglu, M.: Hybrid private record linkage: Separating differentially private synopses from matching records. ACM Transactions on Privacy and Security **22**(3), 1–36 (2019)

[511] Rastogi, V., Dalvi, N., Garofalakis, M.: Large-scale collective entity matching. VLDB Endowment **4**, 208–218 (2011)

[512] Rastogi, V., Suciu, D., Hong, S.: The boundary between privacy and utility in data publishing. In: Conference on Very Large Data Bases, pp. 531–542. Vienna (2007)

[513] Rat für Sozial- und Wirtschaftsdaten: Handreichung Datenschutz. RatSWD, Berlin (2017)

[514] Reid, A., Davies, R., Garrett, E.: Nineteenth-century Scottish demography from linked censuses and civil registers: A 'sets of related individuals' approach. History and Computing **14**(1–2), 61–86 (2002)

[515] Reiter, M.K., Rubin, A.D.: Crowds: Anonymity for web transactions. ACM Transactions on Information and System Security **1**(1), 66–92 (1998)

[516] Richterich, A.: The Big Data Agenda: Data Ethics and Critical Data Studies. University of Westminster Press, London (2018)

[517] Rivera Drew, J.A., Flood, S., Warren, J.R.: Making full use of the longitudinal design of the current population survey: Methods for linking records across 16 months. Journal of Economic and Social Measurement **39**(3), 121–144 (2014)

[518] Rivest, R.L.: Chaffing and winnowing: Confidentiality without encryption. MIT Lab for Computer Science (1998). Available at:
`http://theory.lcs.mit.edu/~rivest/chaffing.txt`

[519] Rivest, R.L., Shamir, A., Adleman, L.: A method for obtaining digital signatures and public-key cryptosystems. Communications of the ACM **21**(2), 120–126 (1978)

[520] Roos, L.L., Walld, R., Wajda, A., Bond, R., Hartford, K.: Record linkage strategies, outpatient procedures, and administrative data. Medical Care pp. 570–582 (1996)

[521] Royal Society and British Academy: Data governance: Landscape review. `https://royalsociety.org/-/media/policy/projects/data-governance/data-governance-landscape-review.pdf`, London (2017)

[522] Ruggles, S., Fitch, C.A., Roberts, E.: Historical census record linkage. Annual Review of Sociology **44**(1), 19–37 (2018)

[523] Rumbold, J.M.M., Pierscionek, B.: The effect of the general data protection regulation on medical research. Journal of Medical Internet Research **19**(2), e47 (2017)

[524] Russell, R.: The Soundex coding system. US patent 1261167 (1918)

[525] Sadinle, M.: Bayesian estimation of bipartite matchings for record link-age. Journal of the American Statistical Association **112**(518), 600–612 (2017)

[526] Samarati, P., Sweeney, L.: Protecting privacy when disclosing infor-mation: k-anonymity and its enforcement through generalization and suppression (1998)

[527] Samarati, P., de Vimercati, S.C.: Access control: Policies, models, and mechanisms. In: Foundations of Security Analysis and Design, pp. 137–196. Springer (2000)

[528] Sandhu, R.S., Samarati, P.: Access control: principle and practice. IEEE Communications Magazine **32**(9), 40–48 (1994)

[529] Sarathy, R., Muralidhar, K.: Secure and useful data sharing. Decision Support Systems **42**(1), 204–220 (2006)

[530] Sarawagi, S.: Information extraction. Foundations and Trends in Data-bases **1**(3), 261–377 (2008)

[531] Saris, W.E., Gallhofer, I.N.: Design, Evaluation, and Analysis of Ques-tionnaires for Survey Research, 2 edn. Wiley, Hoboken (2014)

[532] Sayers, A., Ben-Shlomo, Y., Blom, A.W., Steele, F.: Probabilistic record linkage. International Journal of Epidemiology **45**(3), 954–964 (2016)

[533] Scannapieco, M., Figotin, I., Bertino, E., Elmagarmid, A.: Privacy pre-serving schema and data matching. In: ACM Conference on Manage-ment of Data, pp. 653–664. Beijing (2007)

[534] Schmidlin, K., Clough-Gorr, K.M., Spoerri, A.: Privacy preserving probabilistic record linkage (P3RL): a novel method for linking existing health-related data and maintaining participant confidentiality. BMC Medical Research Methodology **15**(1), 46 (2015)

[535] Schneier, B.: Applied Cryptography: Protocols, Algorithms, and Source Code in C, 2 edn. John Wiley and Sons, Inc., New York (1996)

[536] Schnell, R.: An efficient privacy-preserving record linkage technique for administrative data and censuses. Journal of the International Associ-ation for Official Statistics **30**(3), 263–270 (2014)

[537] Schnell, R.: Linking surveys and administrative data. In: U. Engel, B. Jann, P. Lynn, A. Scherpenzeel, P. Sturgis (eds.) Improving Survey Methods: Lessons from Recent Research, pp. 273–287. Routledge, New York (2014)

[538] Schnell, R.: Privacy-preserving record linkage. In: K. Harron, H. Gold-stein, C. Dibben (eds.) Methodological Developments in Data Linkage, pp. 201–225. John Wiley & Sons (2015)

[539] Schnell, R.: 'Big Data' aus wissenschaftssoziologischer Sicht: Warum es kaum sozialwissenschaftliche Studien ohne Befragungen gibt. Tech. Rep. WP-GRLC-2018-01, German Record Linkage Center (2018). URL https://papers.ssrn.com/sol3/papers.cfm?abstract_id=3548537

[540] Schnell, R.: 'Big Data' aus wissenschaftssoziologischer Sicht: Warum es kaum sozialwissenschaftliche Studien ohne Befragungen gibt. In:

D. Baron, O. Arránz Becker, D. Lois (eds.) Erklärende Soziologie und soziale Praxis, pp. 101–125. Springer, Wiesbaden (2019)

[541] Schnell, R.: Survey-Interviews: Methoden standardisierter Befragungen, 2 edn. Springer VS, Wiesbaden (2019)

[542] Schnell, R., Bachteler, T., Bender, S.: A toolbox for record linkage. Austrian Journal of Statistics **33**(1 & 2), 125–133 (2004)

[543] Schnell, R., Bachteler, T., Reiher, J.: Privacy-preserving record linkage using Bloom filters. BMC Medical Informatics and Decision Making **9**(1) (2009)

[544] Schnell, R., Bachteler, T., Reiher, J.: Improving the use of self-generated identification codes. Evaluation Review **34**(5), 391–418 (2010)

[545] Schnell, R., Bachteler, T., Reiher, J.: A novel error-tolerant anonymous linking code. German Record Linkage Center (WP-GRLC-2011-02) (2011)

[546] Schnell, R., Borgs, C.: Randomized response and balanced Bloom filters for privacy preserving record linkage. In: Workshop on Data Integration and Applications, held at IEEE ICDM. Barcelona (2016)

[547] Schnell, R., Borgs, C.: XOR-folding for Bloom filter-based encryptions for privacy-preserving record linkage. German Record Linkage Center (WP-GRLC-2016-03) (2016)

[548] Schnell, R., Borgs, C.: Hardening encrypted patient names against cryptographic attacks using cellular automata. In: Workshop on Data Integration and Applications, held at IEEE ICDM. Singapore (2018)

[549] Schnell, R., Borgs, C.: Protecting record linkage identifiers using a language model for patient names. Studies in Health Technology and Informatics **253**, 91–95 (2018)

[550] Schnell, R., Borgs, C.: Abschlussbericht des Record Linkage für die Leistungsbereiche Geburtshilfe und Neonatologie. Tech. rep., IQTIG, Berlin (2019)

[551] Schnell, R., Borgs, C.: Encoding hierarchical classification codes for privacy-preserving record linkage using Bloom filters. In: Workshop on Data Integration and Applications, held at ECML/PKDD, pp. 142–156. Springer, Würzburg (2019)

[552] Schnell, R., Richter, A., Borgs, C.: Performance of different methods for privacy preserving record linkage with large scale medical data sets. In: International Health Data Linkage Conference. Vancouver (2014)

[553] Schnell, R., Rukasz, D., Borgs, C., Brumme, S., et al.: R PPRL toolbox. https://cran.r-project.org/web/packages/PPRL/ (2018)

[554] Schröder, D.: Transcript of the public hearing, health committee, 16.10.2019. Tech. rep., Deutscher Bundestag (2019)

[555] Sehili, Z., Kolb, L., Borgs, C., Schnell, R., Rahm, E.: Privacy preserving record linkage with PPJoin. In: BTW Conference. Hamburg (2015)

[556] Sehili, Z., Rahm, E.: Speeding up privacy preserving record linkage for metric space similarity measures. Datenbank-Spektrum **16**(3), 227–236 (2016)

[557] Settles, B.: Active learning. Synthesis Lectures on AI and ML (2012)

[558] Shamir, A.: How to share a secret. Communications of the ACM **22**(11), 612–613 (1979)

[559] Shannon, C.E.: A mathematical theory of communication. Bell System Technical Journal **27**(3), 379–423 (1948)

[560] Shimizu, K., Nuida, K., Rätsch, G.: Efficient privacy-preserving string search and an application in genomics. Bioinformatics **32**(11) (2016)

[561] Shlomo, N.: Probabilistic record linkage for disclosure risk assessment. In: Privacy in Statistical Databases, pp. 269–282. Ibiza (2014)

[562] Singh, S.: The Code Book: The Secret History of Codes and Code-breaking. Fourth Estate (2000)

[563] Smalheiser, N.R., Torvik, V.I.: Author name disambiguation. Annual Review of Information Science and Technology **43**(1), 1–43 (2009)

[564] Smith, D.: Secure pseudonymisation for privacy-preserving probabilistic record linkage. Journal of Information Security and Applications **34**, 271–279 (2017)

[565] Smith, H.J., Dinev, T., Xu, H.: Information privacy research: An interdisciplinary review. MIS Quarterly **35**(4), 989–1015 (2011)

[566] Smith, T.F., Waterman, M.S.: Identification of common molecular subsequences. Journal of Molecular Biology **147**(1), 195–197 (1981)

[567] Smith, T.T.: Examining data privacy breaches in healthcare. Ph.D. thesis, School of Business Administration, Walden University (2016)

[568] Snae, C.: A comparison and analysis of name matching algorithms. International Journal of Applied Science, Engineering and Technology **4**(1), 252–257 (2007)

[569] Sowey, E.R.: A chronological and classified bibliography on random number generation and testing. International Statistical Review pp. 355–371 (1972)

[570] Spindler, G., Schmechel, P.: Personal data and encryption in the European General Data Protection Regulation. Journal of Intellectual Property, Information Technology and Electronic Commerce Law **7**(2), 163–177 (2016)

[571] Spoerri, A., Zwahlen, M., Egger, M., Bopp, M.: The Swiss National Cohort: a unique database for national and international researchers. International Journal of Public Health **55**(4), 239 (2010)

[572] Stalla-Bourdillon, S., Knight, A.: Anonymous data v. personal data – a false debate: An EU perspective on anonymization, pseudonymization and personal data. Wisconsin International Law Journal **34**(2), 284–322 (2017)

[573] Stallings, W.: Information Privacy Engineering and Privacy by Design: Understanding Privacy Threats, Technology, and Regulations Based on Standards and Best Practices. Pearson (2020)

[574] Stegmaier, C., Hentschel, S., Hofstädter, F., Katalinic, A., Tillack, A., Klinkhammer-Schalke, M.: Das Manual der Krebsregistrierung. Zuckschwerdt, Munich (2018)

[575] Stenberg, S.Å.: Born in 1953: The Story about a Post-war Swedish Cohort, and a Longitudinal Research Project. Stockholm University Press (2018)

[576] Stenberg, S.Å., Vågerö, D., Österman, R., Arvidsson, E., Von Otter, C., Janson, C.G.: Stockholm birth cohort study 1953—2003: A new tool for life-course studies. Scandinavian Journal of Public Health **35**(1), 104–110 (2007)

[577] Stiles, P.G., Boothroyd, R.A.: Ethical use of administrative data for research purposes. In: J. Fantuzzo, D.P. Culhane (eds.) Actionable Intelligence, pp. 125–155. Palgrave Macmillan US, New York (2015)

[578] Stinson, D.R.: Cryptography: Theory and Practice. Chapman and Hall/CRC (2005)

[579] Stocks, P.: The measurement of morbidity. Proceedings of the Royal Society of Medicine **37**(10), 593 (1944)

[580] Sun, L., Zhang, L., Ye, X.: Randomized bit vector: Privacy-preserving encoding mechanism. In: ACM Conference on Information and Knowledge Management, pp. 1263–1272. Turin (2018)

[581] Sušelj, M., Marčun, T., Trček, D., Kandus, G.: Application of PKI in health care—needs, ambitions, prospects. In: Medical Informatics Europe. St Malo, France (2003)

[582] Sweeney, L.: Weaving technology and policy together to maintain confidentiality. The Journal of Law, Medicine & Ethics **25**(2-3), 98–110 (1997)

[583] Sweeney, L.: Computational disclosure control: A primer on data privacy protection. Ph.D. thesis, Massachusetts Institute of Technology, Dept. of Electrical Engineering and Computer Science (2001)

[584] Sweeney, L.: K-anonymity: A model for protecting privacy. International Journal of Uncertainty Fuzziness and Knowledge Based Systems **10**(5), 557–570 (2002)

[585] Tai, X.H., Eddy, W.F.: Automatically matching topographical measurements of cartridge cases using a record linkage framework. arXiv Preprint (2020)

[586] Takhshid, Z.: Retrievable images on social media platforms: A call for a new privacy tort. Buffalo Law Review **68**(1) (2020)

[587] Talburt, J.: Entity Resolution and Information Quality. Morgan Kaufmann (2011)

[588] Taylor, L., Zhou, X.H., Rise, P.: A tutorial in assessing disclosure risk in microdata. Statistics in Medicine **37**(25), 3693–3706 (2018)

[589] Tejada, S., Knoblock, C.A., Minton, S.: Learning domain-independent string transformation weights for high accuracy object identification. In: ACM Conference on Knowledge Discovery and Data Mining, pp. 350–359. Edmonton (2002)

[590] Templ, M.: Statistical Disclosure Control for Microdata: Methods and Applications in R. Springer, Cham (2017)

[591] Templ, M., Meindl, B., Kowarik, A., Chen, S.: Introduction to statistical disclosure control (SDC). Working paper 7, `https://ihsn.org/sites/default/files/resources/ihsn-working-paper-007-Oct27.pdf`, International Household Survey Network (2014)

[592] Thomas, R., Walport, M.: Data sharing review report. Ministry of Justice (2008)

[593] Thompson, S.A., Warzel, C.: Twelve million phones, one dataset, zero privacy. New York Times (2019)

[594] Tinabo, R., Mtenzi, F., O'Shea, B.: Anonymisation vs. pseudonymisation: Which one is most useful for both privacy protection and usefulness of e-healthcare data. In: IEEE Internet Technology and Secured Transactions, pp. 1–6. London (2009)

[595] Torra, V.: Data Privacy: Foundations, new Developments and the Big Data Challenge. Springer, Cham (2017)

[596] Toth, C., Durham, E., Kantarcioglu, M., Xue, Y., Malin, B.: SOEMPI: A secure open enterprise master patient index software toolkit for private record linkage. In: AMIA Annual Symposium Proceedings, vol. 2014, p. 1105. American Medical Informatics Association, Washington DC (2014)

[597] Tourangeau, R., Yan, T.: Sensitive questions in surveys. Psychological Bulletin **133**(5), 859–883 (2007)

[598] Tran, K.N., Vatsalan, D., Christen, P.: GeCo: an online personal data generator and corruptor. In: ACM Conference on Information and Knowledge Management, pp. 2473–2476. San Francisco (2013)

[599] Trepetin, S.: Privacy-preserving string comparisons in record linkage systems: a review. Information Security Journal: A Global Perspective **17**(5), 253–266 (2008)

[600] Trinckes, J.J.: The Definitive Guide to Complying with the HIPAA/HITECH Privacy and Security Rules. CRC Press, Boca Raton (2013)

[601] UNECE: Main results of the UNECE-UNSD survey on the 2010 round of population and housing censuses. Technical Report ECE/CES/GE41/2009/25, United Nations Economic Commission for Europe (2009)

[602] UNECE: Census methodology: Key results the UNECE survey on national census practices, and first proposals about the ces recommendations for the 2020 census round. Technical Report ECE/CES/GE41/2013/3, United Nations Economic Commission for Europe (2013)

[603] United Nations Secretariat: Post enumeration surveys: Operational guidelines. Department Of Economic And Social Affairs, Statistics Division, United Nations, New York (2010)

[604] U.S. Census Bureau: Availability of census records about individuals. `www.census.gov/prod/2000pubs/cff-2.pdf` (2008)

[605] Vaidya, J., Clifton, C.: Secure set intersection cardinality with application to association rule mining. Journal of Computer Security **13**(4), 593–622 (2005)

[606] Vaidya, J., Clifton, C., Zhu, M.: Privacy Preserving Data Mining. Springer (2006)

[607] Vaiwsri, S., Ranbaduge, T., Christen, P.: Reference values based hardening for Bloom filters based privacy-preserving record linkage. In: Australasian Data Mining Conference, pp. 189–202. Bathurst (2018)

[608] Van Eycken, E., Haustermans, K., Buntinx, F., Ceuppens, A., Weyler, J., Wauters, E., Van, O.: Evaluation of the encryption procedure and record linkage in the Belgian National Cancer Registry. Archives of Public Health **58**(6), 281–294 (2000)

[609] Van Oorschot, P.C., Menezes, A.J., Vanstone, S.A.: Handbook of Applied Cryptography. CRC Press (1996)

[610] Vatsalan, D.: Scalable and approximate privacy-preserving record linkage. Ph.D. thesis, Research School of Computer Science, The Australian National University (2014)

[611] Vatsalan, D., Christen, P.: An iterative two-party protocol for scalable privacy-preserving record linkage. In: Australasian Data Mining Conference, vol. 134. Sydney (2012)

[612] Vatsalan, D., Christen, P.: Sorted nearest neighborhood clustering for efficient private blocking. In: Pacific-Asia Conference on Knowledge Discovery and Data Mining, pp. 341–352. Gold Coast, Australia (2013)

[613] Vatsalan, D., Christen, P.: Scalable privacy-preserving record linkage for multiple databases. In: ACM Conference on Information and Knowledge Management. Shanghai (2014)

[614] Vatsalan, D., Christen, P.: Privacy-preserving matching of similar patients. Journal of Biomedical Informatics **59**, 285–298 (2016)

[615] Vatsalan, D., Christen, P., O'Keefe, C.M., Verykios, V.S.: An evaluation framework for privacy-preserving record linkage. Journal of Privacy and Confidentiality **6**(1) (2014)

[616] Vatsalan, D., Christen, P., Rahm, E.: Scalable privacy-preserving linking of multiple databases using counting Bloom filters. In: IEEE ICDM Workshops. Barcelona (2016)

[617] Vatsalan, D., Christen, P., Rahm, E.: Incremental clustering techniques for multi-party privacy-preserving record linkage. Data and Knowledge Engineering (2020)

[618] Vatsalan, D., Christen, P., Verykios, V.S.: Efficient two-party private blocking based on sorted nearest neighborhood clustering. In: ACM Conference on Information and Knowledge Management, pp. 1949–1958. San Francisco (2013)

[619] Vatsalan, D., Christen, P., Verykios, V.S.: A taxonomy of privacy-preserving record linkage techniques. Information Systems **38**(6), 946–969 (2013)

[620] Vatsalan, D., Sehili, Z., Christen, P., Rahm, E.: Privacy-preserving record linkage for Big Data: Current approaches and research challenges. In: A.Y. Zomaya, S. Sakr (eds.) Handbook of Big Data Technologies, pp. 851–895. Springer (2017)

[621] van Veen, E.B.: Observational health research in Europe: understanding the General Data Protection Regulation and underlying debate. European Journal of Cancer **104**, 70–80 (2018)

[622] Verknüpfungsstelle: Verknüpfungsrichtlinen, Version 1.1. Tech. rep., Bundesamt für Statistik BFS, Bern (2017)

[623] Vernica, R., Carey, M.J., Li, C.: Efficient parallel set-similarity joins using mapreduce. In: ACM Conference on Management of Data, pp. 495–506. Indianapolis (2010)

[624] Verykios, V.S., Christen, P.: Privacy-preserving record linkage. Wiley Interdisciplinary Reviews: Data Mining and Knowledge Discovery **3**(5), 321–332 (2013)

[625] Verykios, V.S., George, M.V., Elfeky, M.G.: A Bayesian decision model for cost optimal record matching. VLDB Journal **12**(1), 28–40 (2003)

[626] Verykios, V.S., Karakasidis, A., Mitrogiannis, V.K.: Privacy preserving record linkage approaches. International Journal of Data Mining, Modelling and Management **1**(2), 206–221 (2009)

[627] Vidanage, A., Christen, P., Ranbaduge, T., Schnell, R.: A graph matching attack on privacy-preserving record linkage. In: ACM Conference on Information and Knowledge Management. Galway (2020)

[628] Vidanage, A., Ranbaduge, T., Christen, P., Randall, S.: A privacy attack on multiple dynamic match-key based privacy-preserving record linkage. International Journal of Population Data Science **5**(1) (2020)

[629] Vidanage, A., Ranbaduge, T., Christen, P., Schnell, R.: Efficient pattern mining based cryptanalysis for privacy-preserving record linkage. In: IEEE International Conference on Data Engineering. Macau (2019)

[630] Voigt, P., von dem Bussche, A.: The EU General Data Protection Regulation (GDPR): A Practical Guide. Springer, Cham (2017)

[631] de Waal, T., Pannekoek, J., Scholtus, S.: Handbook of Statistical Data Editing and Imputation. John Wiley & Sons, Hoboken (2011)

[632] Wagner, D., Lane, M.: The person identification validation system (PVS): Applying the center for administrative records research and applications' (CARRA) Record Linkage Software. Working Paper 2014-01, Center for Administrative Records Research and Applications, U.S. Census Bureau, Washington (2014)

[633] Wainwright, C., Fallon, L.: Evidence in policy making – Scottish Government sponsored data linkage projects. Government Statistical Service Conference (2018)

[634] Waldman, A.E.: Privacy as Trust: Information Privacy for an Information Age. Cambridge University Press, Cambridge (2018)

[635] Wan, Z., Vorobeychik, Y., Xia, W., Clayton, E.W., Kantarcioglu, M., Ganta, R., Heatherly, R., Malin, B.A.: A game theoretic framework for analyzing re-identification risk. PLOS One **10**(3), e0120,592 (2015)

[636] Wang, B., Song, W., Lou, W., Hou, Y.T.: Privacy-preserving pattern matching over encrypted genetic data in cloud computing. In: IEEE Computer Communications, pp. 1–9. Atlanta (2017)

[637] Weber, S.C., Lowe, H., Das, A., Ferris, T.: A simple heuristic for blindfolded record linkage. Journal of the American Medical Informatics Association **19**(1), 157–161 (2012)

[638] Weisberg, H.F.: The Total Survey Error Approach: A Guide to the New Science of Survey Research. The University of Chicago Press, Chicago (2005)

[639] Wen, Z., Dong, C.: Efficient protocols for private record linkage. In: ACM Symposium On Applied Computing, pp. 1688–1694. Gyeongju, Korea (2014)

[640] Westphal, C.: Data Mining for Intelligence, Fraud, and Criminal Detection: Advanced Analytics and Information Sharing Technologies. CRC Press, Boca Raton (2009)

[641] Whang, S.E., Menestrina, D., Koutrika, G., Theobald, M., Garcia-Molina, H.: Entity resolution with iterative blocking. In: ACM Conference on Management of Data, pp. 219–232. Providence, Rhode Island (2009)

[642] Winkler, W.E.: Using the EM algorithm for weight computation in the Fellegi-Sunter model of record linkage. Tech. Rep. RR2000/05, US Bureau of the Census, Washington, DC (2000)

[643] Winkler, W.E.: Record linkage. In: D. Pfeffermann, C. Rao (eds.) Handbook of Statistics, vol. 29, pp. 351–380. Elsevier (2009)

[644] Winkler, W.E.: Quality and analysis of sets of national files. In: Proceedings of the Section on Survey Research Methods, pp. 1432–1442. American Statistical Association (2014)

[645] Winkler, W.E., Thibaudeau, Y.: An application of the Fellegi-Sunter model of record linkage to the 1990 U.S. decennial census. Tech. Rep. RR1991/09, US Bureau of the Census, Washington, DC (1991)

[646] Winterleitner, A.D., Spichiger, A.: Personenidentifikatoren: Analyse der gesamtschweizerischen Kosten. In: J. Stember, W. Eixelsberger, A. Spichiger (eds.) Wirkungen von E-Government: Impulse für eine wirkungsgesteuerte und technikinduzierte Verwaltungsreform, pp. 383–424. Springer, Wiesbaden (2018)

[647] Witten, I.H., Moffat, A., Bell, T.C.: Managing Gigabytes, 2 edn. Morgan Kaufmann (1999)

[648] Wolfram, S.: A New Kind of Science. Wolfram Media, Champaign (2002)

[649] Woo, M.J., Reiter, J., Oganian, A., Karr, A.: Global measures of data utility for microdata masked for disclosure limitation. Journal of Privacy and Confidentiality **1**, 111–124 (2009)

[650] World Health Organization: WHO Guidelines on Ethical Issues in Public Health Surveillance. WHO, Geneva (2017)

[651] Xiao, C., Wang, W., Lin, X.: Ed-join: an efficient algorithm for similarity joins with edit distance constraints. VLDB Endowment **1**(1), 933–944 (2008)

[652] Xiao, C., Wang, W., Lin, X., Yu, J.X., Wang, G.: Efficient similarity joins for near-duplicate detection. ACM Transactions on Database Systems **36**(3), 1–41 (2011)

[653] Yakout, M., Atallah, M., Elmagarmid, A.: Efficient private record linkage. In: IEEE International Conference on Data Engineering, pp. 1283–1286. Shanghai (2009)

[654] Yancey, W.E.: Evaluating string comparator performance for record linkage. Tech. Rep. RR2005/05, US Bureau of the Census (2005)

[655] Yancey, W.E., Winkler, W.E., Creecy, R.H.: Disclosure risk assessment in perturbative microdata protection. In: J. Domingo-Ferrer (ed.) Inference Control in Statistical Databases, pp. 135–152. Springer (2002)

[656] Yao, A.C.C.: How to generate and exchange secrets. In: IEEE Symposium on Foundations of Computer Science, pp. 162–167. Toronto (1986)

[657] Yi, X., Paulet, R., Bertino, E.: Homomorphic Encryption and Applications. Springer (2014)

[658] Young, A., Flack, F.: Recent trends in the use of linked data in Australia. Australian Health Review **42**(5), 584–590 (2018)

[659] Yu, V.Y.: Promotion of global perinatal health. In: J. Ehiri (ed.) Maternal and Child Health, pp. 43–51. Springer, Boston (2009)

[660] Zezula, P., Amato, G., Dohnal, V., Batko, M.: Similarity Search: the Metric Space Approach. Springer Science & Business Media (2006)

[661] Zhang, L.C., Chambers, R.L.: Analysis of Integrated Data. CRC Press, Boca Raton (2019)

[662] Zheng, X., Cai, Z., Li, Y.: Data linkage in smart internet of things systems: A consideration from a privacy perspective. Communications Magazine **56**(9), 55–61 (2018)

[663] Zingmond, D., Ye, Z., Ettner, S., H., L.: Linking hospital discharge and death records – accuracy and sources of bias. Journal of Clinical Epidemiology **57**, 21–29 (2004)

[664] Zobel, J., Dart, P.: Phonetic string matching: Lessons from information retrieval. In: ACM Conference on Research and Development in Information Retrieval, pp. 166–172. Zürich (1996)

[665] Zomaya, A.Y., Sakr, S.: Handbook of Big Data Technologies. Springer (2017)

Index

Page numbers shown in bold refer to entries in the glossary.

active learning, 55, **397**
Administrative Data Research
    Network (ADRN), 35, 352
adversarial model, 90, 170, 362
  accountable computing, 92
  covert, 91
  honest-but-curious, 90, 114, **408**
  malicious, 91, **410**
adversary, 39, 101, 102, 106, 109, 127,
    129, 143, 222, 256, 362, **398**
agreement weight, 54
algorithm, 49, 66, 94, 123, 128, 143,
    153, 159, 310, 314, 379, **398**
analysis, 70, 83, 84, 308, 318
Ancestry, 372
anonymisation, 135, 353, 366, **398**
anonymity, 19
  factual, **406**
  functional, 39
artificial intelligence, 49
attack, 120
  collusion, 113, 129, 257
  composition, 112
  costs, 117, 366
  cryptanalysis, 109, 222, 224, 249,
    336, 393, **402**
  dictionary, 112, 127, 129, 174, **404**
  effort, 31
  frequency, 111, 130, 222, 224, 228,
    337, 354, **407**
  gains, 117
  graph matching, 237, 354
  insider, 41, 109, 113, 116, 117, 354

  known scheme, 113
  linkage, 115
  man-in-the-middle, 147
  pattern mining, 231, 340
  skewness, 139
attribute, 7, 36, 49, 52, 54, 57, 115,
    120, 156, 200, 205, 291, **399**
  multivariate, 51
authentication, 95, 147, **399**
authorisation, 96, 367, **399**

bias, 64, 70, 299, 301
  algorithmic, 23, 300
Big data, 6, 23, 50, 69, 369, **399**
big-O, 66, 68, 170, 253
binning, 119, 181
blocking, 51, 52, 67, 69, 166, 182, 253,
    326, 347, 363, 370, 392, **399**
  block size, 113, 256
  hashing-based, 260, 272, 274, 283
  key, 52, 254, 257, 272, 300, **399**
  multibit tree based, 263, 271
  phonetic, 153, 257
  standard, 52, 254
Bloom filter, 177, 188, 193, 215, 221,
    275, 323, 347, 348, 380, 391, **400**
  atom, 225, 235
  attribute level, 200, 326, 341
  balancing, 240
  counting, 173, 277, 283
  cryptographic long-term key, 201,
    205, 326, 331, 341, 380, 382
  false positive rate, 194, 214

Printed in the United States
by Baker & Taylor Publisher Services